Easy Home
FURNITURE PROJECTS

100 INDOOR & OUTDOOR PROJECTS YOU CAN BUILD

COOL
SPRINGS
PRESS

Contents

Inspiring | Educating | Creating | Entertaining

Brimming with creative inspiration, how-to projects, and useful information to enrich your everyday life, Quarto Knows is a favorite destination for those pursuing their interests and passions. Visit our site and dig deeper with our books into your area of interest: Quarto Creates, Quarto Cooks, Quarto Homes, Quarto Lives, Quarto Drives, Quarto Explores, Quarto Gifts, or Quarto Kids.

First published in 2015 by Cool Springs Press, an imprint of The Quarto Group, 401 Second Avenue North, Suite 310, Minneapolis, MN 55401 USA. T (612) 344-8100 F (612) 344-8692 www.QuartoKnows.com

Cool Springs Press titles are also available at discount for retail, wholesale, promotional, and bulk purchase. For details, contact the Special Sales Manager by email at specialsales@quarto.com or by mail at The Quarto Group, Attn: Special Sales Manager, 401 Second Avenue North, Suite 310, Minneapolis, MN 55401 USA.

Cover photo: Rau + Barber   Printed in China

FSC
www.fsc.org
MIX
Paper from responsible sources
FSC® C104723

Introduction

The craft of woodworking is admired around the world—and in many cultures woodworkers continue to be a revered group of artists. The most common woodworking projects to this day are featured in *Easy Home Furniture Projects*—namely furniture, storage, dishware, and decorative items. And you can get started on them right away with common tools and materials available at every homestore.

Some of the featured projects are suitable for beginners, like the bread box, while others will put an experienced woodworker's skills to the test, like the Adirondack chair. Included are both interior projects, like a mission lamp, mitten chest, and bookshelf, and exterior projects, such as a cabin porter, porch swing, and plant boxes.

First you'll find an overview of techniques for interior projects. This is followed by several projects for entryways, living rooms, dining rooms, home offices, bedrooms, and kitchens. Then you'll find projects designed for the outdoors, including ornaments and decorations, benches and seats, tables, children's play projects, bird and pet projects, storage and utility, and garden accessories.

For each of the 100 projects in this book, you will find a complete cutting list, a lumber shopping list, and a detailed construction drawing.

Full-color photographs of major steps and clear, easy-to-follow directions will guide you through each project. And because you want your finished project to look its best, we illustrate the products available for painting, staining, and varnishing, and give you directions for how to achieve the best possible results.

By making the projects in this book, you'll develop a fine-tuned appreciation for the materials, tools, and skill that all contribute to beautifully constructed wood objects. And you'll sense the accomplishment of creating beautiful finished projects with your very own hands.

NOTICE TO READERS

This book provides useful instructions, but we cannot anticipate all of your working conditions or the characteristics of your materials and tools. For safety, you should use caution, care and good judgment when following the procedures described in this book. Consider your own skill level and the instructions and safety precautions associated with the various tools and materials shown. The publisher cannot assume responsibility for any damage to property, injury to persons, or losses incurred as a result of misuse of the information provided.

Woodworking and Finishing Techniques

Here are some basic woodworking techniques and tips to get you started—and to help you finish your project well. You'll find information on choosing wood, types of materials, and how best to achieve a beautiful finish.

Materials

Tools You Will Use

At the start of each project, a set of symbols shows which power tools are used to complete the project as it is shown. In some cases, optional tools, such as a power miter saw or a table router, may be suggested for speedier work. You will also need a set of basic hand tools: hammer, screwdrivers, tape measure, level, combination square, framing square, compass, wood chisels, nail set, putty knife, utility knife, straightedge, C-clamps and pipe or bar clamps. Where required, specialty hand tools are listed for each project.

Circular saw to make straight cuts. For long cuts, use a straightedge guide. Install a carbide-tipped combination blade for most projects.

Drill for drilling holes and driving screws. Accessories help with sanding and grinding tasks. Use a corded or cordless drill with variable speed.

Jig saw for making contoured and internal cuts and for short straight cuts. Use the recommended blade for each type of wood or cutting task.

Power sander to prepare wood for a finish and to smooth sharp edges. Owning several types of power sanders is helpful.

Belt sander for resurfacing rough wood. Can also be used as a sta tionary sander when mounted on its side on a flat worksurface.

Router to cut structural grooves (rabbets) in wood. Also ideal for making a variety of decorative edges and roundover cuts.

Power miter saw for making angled cuts in narrow stock. Miter scales and a guide fence make it easy to set the saw quickly for precise angles.

Organizing Your Worksite

Working safely and comfortably is important to successfully completing your woodworking projects. Taking the time to set up your worksite before you begin will make your progress from step to step much smoother.

You will need a solid work surface, usually at waist level, to help you maintain a comfortable work angle. A portable work bench is sufficient for many of the smaller projects in this book. For larger projects, a sturdy sheet of plywood clamped to sawhorses will work well. In some cases you will need to use the floor for layout or assembly space.

Portable power tools and hand tools offer a level of convenience that is a great advantage over stationary power tools, but using them safely and conveniently requires some basic housekeeping. Whether you are working in a garage, a basement, or outdoors, it is important to establish a flat, dry holding area where you can store tools. Dedicate an area of your worksite for tool storage, and be sure to return tools to that area once you are finished with them.

It is also important that all waste, including lumber scraps and sawdust, be disposed of in a timely fashion. Check with your local waste disposal department before throwing away any large scraps of building materials or finishing material containers.

If you are using corded power tools outdoors, always use grounded extension cords connected to a ground fault interrupter circuit (GFCI) receptacle. Keep cords neat and out of traffic lanes at all times. Remember that most of the materials you will be working with are flammable and should be stored away from furnaces and water heaters.

Materials Used in This Book

Self-adhesive wood veneer edge tape

Oak plywood

Pine plywood

Birch plywood

Wood plugs

Oak

Pine

Cedar

Aspen

Brads

Wire nail

Finish nails

Steel wood screws

Brass wood screws

Deck screws

Sheet goods:

AB PLYWOOD: A smooth, paintable plywood, usually made from pine or fir. The better (A) side is sanded and free from knots and defects.

BIRCH PLYWOOD: A sturdy plywood with birch veneer on both sides. Excellent for painting but attractive enough for stain or clear finish.

OAK PLYWOOD: A plywood with high-quality oak veneers. A workable, stainable product that blends well with solid oak lumber.

PINE PANELS: Edge glued pine boards, cut and sanded. Usually ⅝" or ¾" thick.

LAUAN PLYWOOD: A relatively inexpensive plywood with a smooth mahogany veneer on one side. The natural color varies widely.

MEDIUM-DENSITY FIBERBOARD (MDF): A smooth highly workable product made from compressed wood fibers.

HARDBOARD: A dense fiberboard with one hard, smooth side.

MELAMINE BOARD: Fiberboard or particleboard with a glossy, polymerized surface that is water resistant and easy to clean.

TILEBOARD: Vinyl sheet goods resembling ceramic tile.

SHEET ACRYLIC: Clear plastic product available in thicknesses from ¹⁄₁₆" to 1".

Dimension lumber:

The "nominal" size of lumber is usually larger than the actual size. For example, a 1 × 4 board measures ¾" × 3½".

SELECT PINE: Finish-quality pine that is mostly free of knots and other imperfections.

#2-OR-BETTER PINE: A grade lower than select but more commonly available.

RED OAK: A common, durable hardwood, oak is popular for its color, straight grain and solid appearance.

ASPEN: A soft, workable hardwood. Aspen is good for painting but should be sealed for an even stain.

CEDAR: A lightweight softwood with a natural resistance to moisture. Smooth cedar is best for furniture.

POPLAR: A soft light wood that is easy to cut and good for painting.

Other wood products:

WOOD MOLDINGS: Available in a vast range of styles and sizes. Most types of molding are available in a variety of woods.

VENEER EDGE TAPE: Self-adhesive wood veneer sold in ¾"-wide strips. Applied to plywood edges with a household iron.

WOOD PLUGS: ⅜"-dia. × ¼"-thick disks with a slightly conical shape.

Fasteners and adhesives:

WOOD SCREWS: Steel, zinc-coated steel, brass or brass-coated steel screws with a heavy shank and fine threads. Steel screws are stronger than brass but can stain acidic wood, such as oak, if exposed to moisture. The gauge number refers to shank diameter.

DECK SCREWS: Similar to wallboard screws, these have a light shank and coarse threads, making them ideal for fastening soft woods.

FINISH NAILS AND BRADS: Thin-shank, steel nails with a small, cup-shaped head. They are driven below the surface with a nail set.

WIRE NAILS: Small, steel nails with a flat, round head.

WOOD GLUE: Yellow (or "carpenter's") glue is good for indoor furniture projects. Application and drying time depend on the product.

CERAMIC TILE ADHESIVE: Multipurpose thin-set mortar or latex mastic. Each is applied with a V-notch trowel.

Other materials:

CERAMIC FLOOR TILE: Sturdy tile suitable in situations where durability is required. Available in sizes from 1 × 1" to 12 × 18".

TEMPERED GLASS: Stronger than regular glass. Used for glass shelving.

Lumber: Redwood (A) and cedar (B) are warm-colored softwoods. Because of their attractive color and grain, they usually are left unfinished or coated with a clear finish. Pine (C) is an easy-to-cut softwood often used for projects that will be painted. Framing lumber (D) includes rough grades of softwood pine and fir. It is used for structural framing and utility shelving. Poplar (E), a light-colored hardwood with very straight grain, is an excellent wood for fine painted surfaces. Maple (F) and oak (G) are heavy, strong hardwoods with attractive grain patterns. They usually are finished with tinted oils or stains.

These easy woodworking projects vary considerably in size and style, but they can be constructed with materials available at any home improvement center. If you prefer to use unique woods or unusual moldings, you may need to visit a woodworker's supply store or large wholesale lumber yard to find them.

To save money, construct your projects using finish-grade plywood for the main body (carcass), then trim exposed areas with more costly solid woods and moldings.

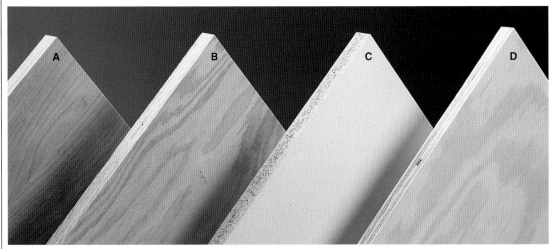

Sheet goods: Finish-grade plywood, including birch plywood (A) and oak plywood (B) are made from several layers of softwood veneer sandwiched between hardwood surface veneers. Finish-grade plywoods are used for exposed areas, and usually are edged with hardwood strips or moldings. Birch plywood frequently is used for surfaces that will be painted, and oak plywood is usually finished with tinted oils or stains. Particleboard (C), coated with a plastic resin called melamine, is used for making contemporary-style projects. Sanded pine plywood (D) is a good material for projects that will be painted or parts in hidden areas. NOTE: Most sheet goods are sold in 4 ft. × 8 ft. sheets, in ¼", ½", or ¾" thicknesses; some types also are sold in 2 ft. × 4 ft. and 4 ft. × 4 ft. sheets.

Trim moldings

Are both decorative and functional. They can be used to cover gaps around the base and sides of cabinets and shelves, to hide the edges of plywood surfaces, or simply to add visual interest to the project. Moldings are available in dozens of styles, but the samples shown here are widely available at home improvement centers.

Baseboard molding (A) is used to trim the bottom edge of a project along the floor line. Choosing molding that matches the baseboard used elsewhere in your home gives your project a custom look.

Hardwood strips (B) are used to construct face frames, and to cover unfinished edges of plywood shelves. Maple, oak and poplar strips are widely available in 1×2, 1×3 and 1×4 sizes.

Crown moldings (C, D) add a decorative accent to a project.

Cove molding (E) is a simple, unobtrusive trim for covering gaps.

Ornamental moldings, including spindle-and-rail (F) and embossed moldings (G, H), give a distinctive decorative look.

Door-edge molding (I), sometimes called cap molding, is used with finish-grade plywood to create panel-style doors and drawer faces.

Shelf-edge molding (J), sometimes called base cap molding, gives a decorative edge to plywood shelves.

Base shoe molding (K) covers gaps around the top, bottom, and sides of a project.

Materials

These outdoor wood projects vary considerably in size and style, but they can be constructed with materials readily available at any home improvement center.

Lumber: Cedar (A, B, C, D, and F) and redwood (E) are warm-colored softwoods that are insect and rot resistant. Both are ideal for outdoor furnishings. Because of their attractive color and grain, they usually are left unfinished or coated with a clear finish. Pine (G) is an easy-to-cut softwood often used for projects that will be painted. Cedar is available as dimensional lumber and timbers with either smooth (C) or rough sawn surfaces (A).

Sheet goods: Plywood siding (A and B) is available in a number of textures and patterns. Exterior plywood (C) is made with exterior grade glue. Plywood products should be stained or painted to increase their longevity. Cedar lattice (D) is available in ¼" or ⅜" thicknesses. NOTE: Most sheet goods are sold in 4 ft. × 8 ft. sheets, in ¼", ½", or ¾" thicknesses; some types also are sold in 2 ft. × 4 ft. and 4 ft. × 4 ft. sheets.

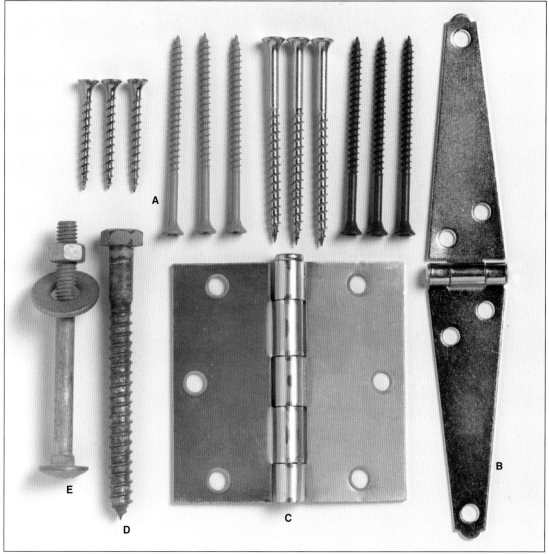

Hardware: Corrosion resistant hardware is necessary for your outdoor wood projects. Deck screws (A) are available as zinc coated, coated, or stainless steel. Zinc coated and galvanized hardware will stain unsealed cedar and redwood. Galvanized strap hinges (B) are readily available in many sizes. Brass butt hinges (C) add a nice touch to any project and are weather resistant as well. Galvanized lag screws (D) are useful for securing larger lumber. Galvanized carriage bolts (E) are used for parts that need to rotate.

TREATED LUMBER

Lumber treated with CCA (green treated), a long-time favorite for building decks, play structures and landscaping features, has been banned due to its arsenic content. Arsenic is a proven poison and a carcinogen and children are highly sensitive to it because they are still developing. Children ingest arsenic from treated lumber when they place their hands in their mouths. Do not use CCA treated lumber for any projects that children will be using. New treatment chemicals do not contain arsenic, but do contain other chemicals that are dangerous if you inhale sawdust or if you burn the wood. Always wear gloves when handling treated lumber and always wear an OSHA approved particle mask when sawing, sanding or routing. Never burn treated lumber scraps or sawdust.

Woodworking Techniques

Cutting

Circular saws and jig saws cut wood as the blade passes up through the material, which can cause splintering or chipping on the top face of the wood. For this reason, always cut with your workpiece facedown.

To ensure a straight cut with a circular saw, clamp a straightedge to your workpiece to guide the foot of the saw as you cut **(photo A).**

To make an internal cutout in your work- piece, drill starter holes near cutting lines and use a jig saw to complete the cut **(photo B).**

A power miter saw is the best tool for making straight or angled cuts on narrow boards and trim pieces **(photo C).** This saw is especially helpful for cutting hardwood. An alternative is to use an inexpensive hand miter box fitted with a backsaw **(photo D).**

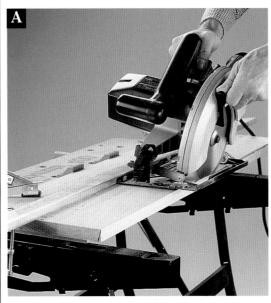

The foot of the circular saw rides along the straightedge to make straight, smooth cuts.

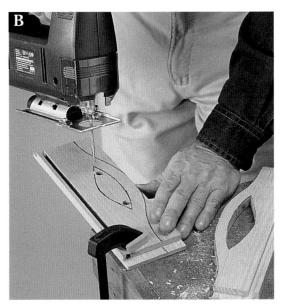

Make contoured cutouts by drilling starter holes and cutting with a jig saw.

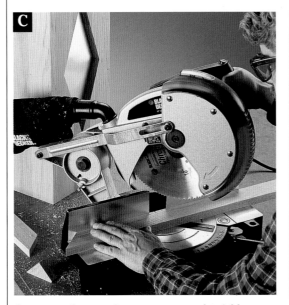

A power miter saw is easy to use and quickly makes clean, accurate angle cuts in any wood.

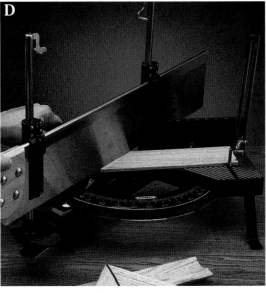

A hand miter box keeps your backsaw in line for making a full range of angle cuts.

Shaping

Create detailed shapes by drawing a grid pattern on your workpiece. Use the grid to mark accurate centers and endpoints for the shapes you will cut. Make smooth roundovers and curves using a standard compass **(photo E).**

You can also create shapes by enlarging a drawing detail, using a photocopier and transferring the pattern to the workpiece.

A belt sander makes short work of sanding tasks and is also a powerful shaping tool. Mounting a belt sander to your workbench allows you to move and shape the workpiece freely—using both hands **(photo F).** Secure the sander by clamping the tool casing in a benchtop vise or with large handscrew or C-clamps. Clamp a scrap board to your bench to use as a platform, keeping the workpiece square and level with the sanding belt.

To ensure that matching pieces have an identical shape, clamp them together before shaping **(photo G).** This technique is known as gang-sanding.

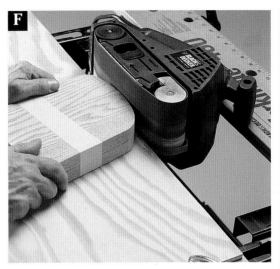

Clamp a belt sander and a scrap board to the workbench to create a stationary shaping tool.

Use a square grid pattern and a compass to draw patterns on your workpiece.

Gang-sanding is an easy method for creating two or more identical parts.

Squaring a Frame

Squaring is an important technique in furniture construction. A frame or assembly that is not square will result in a piece that teeters on two legs or won't stand up straight. Always check an assembly for square before fastening the parts together.

To square a frame, measure diagonally from corner to corner **(photo H).** When the measurements are equal, the frame is square. Adjust the frame by applying inward pressure to diagonally opposite corners. A framing square or a combination square can also be used to see if two pieces form a right angle.

Clamp frame parts together. Then, measure the diagonals to check for square before fastening.

Piloting and Drilling

Pilot holes make it easier to drive screws or nails into a workpiece, and they remove some material and so keep the fastener from splitting the wood. If you find that your screws are still difficult to drive or that the wood splits, switch to a larger piloting bit. If the screws are not holding well or are stripping the pilot holes, use a smaller bit to pilot subsequent holes. When drilling pilot holes for finish nails, use a standard straight bit.

A combination pilot bit drills pilot holes for the threaded and unthreaded sections of the screw shank, as well as a counterbore recess that allows the screw to seat below the surface of the workpiece **(photo A).** The counterbore portion of the bit drills a ⅜"-dia. hole to accept a standard wood plug. A bit stop with a setscrew allows you to adjust the drilling depth.

When drilling a hole through a workpiece, clamp a scrap board to the piece on the side where the drill bit will exit **(photo B).** This "backer board" will prevent the bit from splintering the wood and is especially important when drilling large holes with a spade bit.

To make perfectly straight or uniform holes, mount your drill to a portable drill stand **(photo C).** The stand can be adjusted for drilling to a specific depth and angle.

A combination pilot bit drills pilot holes and counterbores for wood screws in one step.

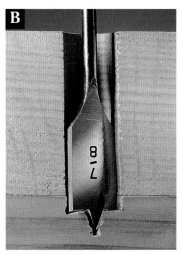
Use a scrap backer board to prevent tearout when drilling through a workpiece.

A portable drill stand helps you drill straight or angled holes.

Gluing

A gluing surface should be smooth and free of dust but not sanded. Glue and fasten boards soon after they are cut—machined surfaces, which dry out over time, bond best when they are freshly cut.

Clean the mating surfaces with a cloth to remove dust.

Spread glue evenly over the entire mating surface of both pieces.

Before gluing, test-fit the pieces to ensure a proper fit. Then, clean the mating edges with a clean, dry cloth to remove dust **(photo D).**

Apply glue to both surfaces and spread it evenly, using a stick or your finger **(photo E).** Use enough glue to cover the area, with a small amount of excess.

Promptly assemble and clamp the pieces with enough clamps to apply even pressure to the joint. Watch the glue oozing from the joint to gauge the distribution of pressure. Excessive "squeeze-out" indicates that the clamps are too tight or that there is too much glue. Wipe away excess glue with a damp—not wet—cloth.

Prepping Wood for Finishing Touches

Most projects require that nail heads be set below the surface of the wood, using a nail set **(photo F).** Choose a nail set with a point slightly smaller than the nail head.

Screws that have been driven well below the surface (about ¼") can be hidden by filling the counterbores with glued wood plugs **(photo G).** Tap the plug into place with a wood mallet or a hammer and scrap block, leaving the plug just above the surface. Then, sand the plug smooth with the surrounding surface.

Fill nail holes and small defects with wood putty **(photo H).** When applying a stain or clear finish to a project, use a tinted putty to match the wood, and avoid smearing it outside the nail holes. Use putty to fill screw holes on painted projects.

A power drill with a sanding drum attachment helps you sand contoured surfaces smooth **(photo I).**

Use a palm sander to finish-sand flat surfaces. To avoid sanding through thin veneers, draw light pencil marks on the surface and sand just until the marks disappear **(photo J).**

To finish-sand your projects, start with medium sandpaper (100- or 120-grit) and switch to increasingly finer papers (150- to 220-grit).

Set finish nails below the surface, using a nail set slightly smaller than the head of the nail.

Apply glue to wood plugs and insert them into screw counterbores to hide the screws.

Fill holes and wood defects with plain or tinted wood putty.

Smooth curves and hard-to-reach surfaces with a drum attachment on your power drill.

Draw pencil marks on veneered surfaces to prevent oversanding.

Selecting a Finish

A good finish both protects and beautifies wood. To achieve both goals, a finish is made up of several layers, each with its own specific purpose. Each element of a finish should be chosen carefully, according to the features of the wood, the function of the project piece, and your tastes. On new wood, apply a seal coat made of sanding sealer to create more even finish absorption and more consistent color. For a fine finish, some woods are best treated with grain filler instead of sealer.

The next layer is the color layer, which is usually created with wood stain or penetrating oil. Color can either enhance or minimize grain pattern and other wood features, and it can beautify plain wood. With fine woods or to create a more

rustic look, the color layer can be omitted. Dampen the wood surface with mineral spirits to see how it will look with a clear finish. To create a specific decorative look or to cover wood defects, apply paint as the color layer.

Finally, a topcoat is applied to seal the wood and protect the finished surface from scratches and wear. Topcoats can be created with traditional finishing products, like tung oil, or more contemporary materials, like polyurethane A layer or two of well-buffed paste wax can be applied over most topcoat materials to create a glossy, protective surface that is easily renewed with fresh wax.

When selecting a new finish, it helps if you know the wood species of your project.

A typical wood finish is composed of three basic layers: the seal coat, the color layer, and the topcoat.

Topcoat layer

Color layer

Seal coat (or grain filler)

Unfinished wood

Softwoods, like pine, should always be treated with sanding sealer or primer, for example. And open-grained hardwoods, like red oak or mahogany, look better when treated with grain filler. The finish samples on pages 20 to 21 show how some common finishes look on different woods. As a general rule, base your finish selection on color. Simply choose a color you like, then select a coloring agent and a compatible topcoat.

Consider use, as well. If the finished piece will be used by children or as a food preparation surface, use nontoxic water-based products to finish the wood. For more information on finishing products, refer to the sections indicated above.

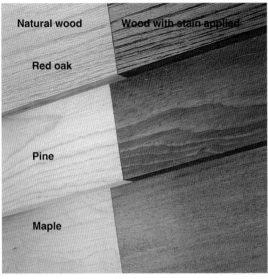

Consider absorption rates. Some wood types absorb more finish materials than others, depending on the porosity of the wood grain. In the photo above, the same stain was applied to three different unsealed woods, resulting in three different levels of darkness. Sealing the wood or filling the grain minimizes this effect.

Highly figured wood, like the walnut shown above, usually is given a clear finish so the grain is not obscured. In some cases, however, tinted penetrating oil can be used to enhance an already striking grain pattern. Experiment with different coloring agents on a piece of similar wood or in an inconspicuous area of the project.

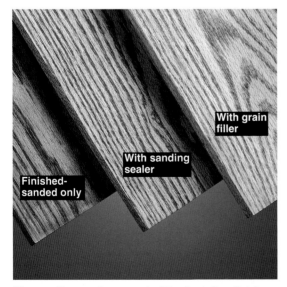

Use sanding sealer or grain filler for a fine finish. Sealing evens out the stain absorption rates, yielding a lighter, more even finish. Filling the grain creates a lighter finish that feels as smooth as it looks.

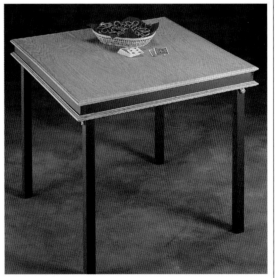

Consider combining colors to create interesting decorative effects. Contrasting stains and paints on the same piece can create a dramatic finish when used with good design sense.

Sample Finishes: Dark

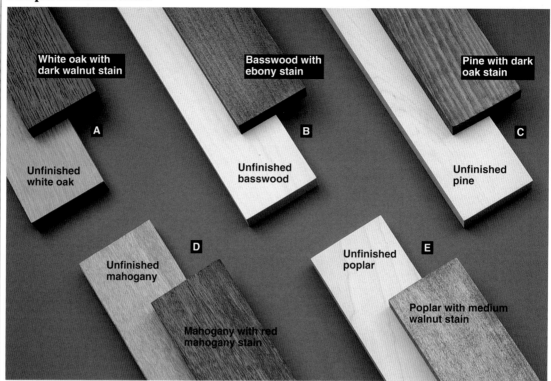

Use dark finishes to: enhance a distinctive grain pattern (A); add interest to plain wood (B); give a rich, formal look to softwoods (C); create a traditional finish (D); simulate the appearance of a finer hardwood on inexpensive wood (E).

Sample Finishes: Light

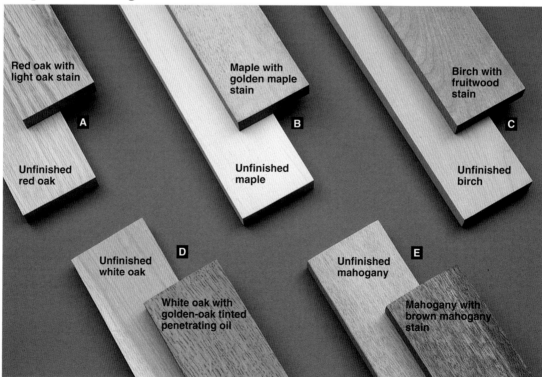

Use light finishes to: highlight subtle grain patterns (A); amplify attractive wood tone (B); modify wood tones to match a particular decor or color scheme (C); add a sense of depth (D); give unfinished wood a seasoned, antique appearance (E).

Sample Finishes: Clear

Clear finishes protect and seal wood while allowing the natural beauty of the wood to speak for itself. Choose clear finishes for exotic woods that are prized for their color or grain pattern, or for more common woods when a natural, rustic look is desired.

Sample Finishes: Painted

Painted finishes mask undesirable qualities, like old finish residue, and create decorative effects. Surface defects, like repairs, stains, knots, and holes should be filled with wood putty to create an even surface when painted. Man-made wood products, like plywood, also benefit from painted finishes.

Making Final Surface Preparation

Use a finishing sander on flat surfaces and specialty sanding blocks on contours.

Examine the workpiece with bright sidelighting during finish sanding to gauge your progress.

Use sanding blocks to handsand the entire workpiece with the finest-grit paper in the sanding sequence.

Finish Sanding

Ensure an even, quality finish for your woodworking project by carefully preparing the wood surface. Finish-sand with progressively finer grits of sandpaper, starting with 150-grit. Generally, hardwood requires finer-grit sandpaper than softwood. For speed and even results, use a power sander for the first stages of finish sanding. Use hand-sanding with the finest grit in the sequence so you do not oversand. Seal wood with sanding sealer to create more even finish absorption.

Finish-sand all surfaces with 150-grit sandpaper, following the direction of the grain. Use a finishing sander on flat surfaces and specialty sanding blocks on contours. When sanding hardwood, switch to 180-grit paper and sand again **(photo A).**

Examine the workpiece with bright sidelighting during finish sanding to gauge your progress. If shadows, scratches, or sanding marks are visible, more sanding is needed **(photo B).**

Your sandpaper will last longer and work better if you clean it regularly. Use a wire brush or rubber cleaning stick to remove sawdust and grit that can clog the sandpaper and cause burnishing of the wood surface.

Whenever you change sandpaper grits, wipe the wood surface clean using a cloth slightly dampened with mineral spirits. This removes dust and grit from coarser sandpaper that cause scratches when you continue sanding.

To decrease the chance of raising the wood grain during finishing, raise the grain during sanding by dampening the surface with a wet rag. Let the wood dry, then skim the surface with a fine abrasive pad, following the grain. The pad will pull out any raised fibers.

Use sanding blocks to handsand the entire workpiece with the finest-grit paper in the sanding sequence **(photo C).** Sand until all sanding marks are gone and the surface is smooth. If using sanding sealer, apply a coat now, then sand lightly with 220-grit when dry.

Applying Grain Filler

Especially when using oak, you will want to apply grain filler to guarantee a deep, smooth finish. Grain filler decreases stain absorption, which will result in a lighter finish. Sand, fill and stain small pieces of scrap wood to determine what your final finish will look like.

After finish sanding, use a rag or putty knife to spread a coat of grain filler onto the wood surface. With a polishing motion, work the filler into the grain **(photo D).** Let the filler dry until it becomes cloudy, usually about five minutes.

Remove excess filler by drawing a plastic putty scraper across the grain of the wood at a 45° angle **(photo E).** Let the grain filler dry overnight.

Lightly hand-sand the surface, following the direction of the grain, with 320-grit sandpaper **(photo F).** Clean thoroughly with a cloth dampened in mineral spirits before applying the finish **(photo G).**

Use a rag or putty knife to spread a coat of grain filler onto the wood surface.

Remove excess filler by drawing a plastic putty scraper across the grain of the wood at a 45° angle.

Lightly hand-sand the surface, following the direction of the grain, with 320-grit sandpaper.

Wipe the wood surface clean, using a cloth slightly dampened with mineral spirits.

A well-chosen, properly applied color layer is the most important component of an attractive wood finish.

Coloring Wood

There are several reasons to color wood. The most common reason is to enhance the appearance of the wood by showing off a fine or distinctive grain pattern or creating a beautiful wood tone. But stain and penetrating oil, the two most basic coloring agents, can accomplish more practical results as well. Using a dark color conceals uneven color in your wood and can blend together two or more different wood types.

When selecting a coloring agent for your project, you will find a vast selection of products to choose from. There are oil-based stains, water-based stains, wipe-on gel stains, penetrating oils, one-step stain-and-sealant products—the options seem endless. To sort through the many products and make the selection that is best for your project, start by finding a color you like. Then check the specific properties of the coloring

agent to determine if it is the best general type for your project. Make sure it has no compatibility problems with the topcoat you plan to use, or with any sanding sealers or grain fillers (see charts, next page).

Whichever coloring agent you select, read the directions very carefully before applying it to the wood. Drying time, application techniques, and cleanup methods vary widely between products—even products that are similar. Also test the product on a wood sample similar to your project. When using a stain, apply enough coats to create the exact color shade you want (stain will become darker with each new coat that is applied). Keep careful records of how many coats you applied so you can refer to them when you finish the actual workpiece.

PENETRATING OIL

Penetrating oil (often called "Danish oil" or "rubbing oil") delivers color deep into the wood for a rich-looking finish that can be buffed to form a protective surface.

ADVANTAGES:
•easy to apply
•creates very even coloration
•does not "paint over" wood grain
•compatible with most topcoats
•penetrates deeper than stain for very rich color
•can be used without a topcoat

DRAWBACKS:
•may fade in direct sunlight
•limited range of colors
•cannot darken color with multiple coats
•toxic fumes; flammable

COMPATIBILITY:
•avoid using with oil-based polyurethane

RECOMMENDED USES:
•wood with attractive grain pattern
•antiques and fine furniture
•decorative items

COMMON BRAND NAMES:
•Watco® Danish Oil Finish, Deft® Danish Oil Finish

WATER-BASED LIQUID STAIN

Water-based liquid stain is wiped or brushed on to create a color layer than can be darkened with additional applications.

ADVANTAGES:
•easy to clean up, safe to use
•wide range of colors available
•can be built up in layers to control final color
•dries quickly

DRAWBACKS:
•can raise wood grain (requires sanding for an even surface)
•can chip or scuff if not properly topcoated.

COMPATIBILITY:
•bonds well with most topcoats

RECOMMENDED USES:
•floors
•woodwork
•previously finished furniture—can be "painted" on to cover color variations
•tabletops, eating surfaces, children's furniture and toys

COMMON BRAND NAMES:
•Carver Trip® Safe & Simple Wood Stain, Behr® Water-based Stain, Varathane Elite Wood Stain®

OIL-BASED LIQUID STAIN

Oil-based liquid traditionally has been the most common type of wood stain, but its availability and popularity are declining due to environmental factors.

ADVANTAGES:
•does not raise wood grain
•slow drying time increases workability
•permanent and colorfast
•can be built up to control color
•conditions and seals wood
•less likely to bleed than water-based stain

DRAWBACKS:
•harmful vapors; flammable; hard to clean
•regulated or restricted in some states
•decreasing availability
•unpleasant odor

COMPATIBILITY:
•can be used with most topcoats

RECOMMENDED USES:
•previously stained wood
•wood finish touch-up

COMMON BRAND NAMES:
•Minwax® Wood Finish, Carver Tripp® Wood Stain, Zar® Wood Stain

GEL STAIN

Gel stains, usually oil-based, provide even surface color that is highly controllable due to the thickness of the product. Gel finishes are growing in popularity.

ADVANTAGES:
•very neat and easy to apply—will not run
•does not raise wood grain
•dries evenly
•can be built up to deepen color
•can be buffed to create a hard surface

DRAWBACKS:
•limited color selection
•more expensive than other stain types
•hard to clean up
•requires buffing between coats

COMPATIBILITY:
•can be used with most topcoats

RECOMMENDED USES:
•woodwork and furniture with vertical surfaces
•furniture with spindles and other rounded parts

COMMON BRAND NAMES:
•Bartley® Gel Stain, Behlen® Master Gel

Applying Liquid Stain

The end grain of wood will absorb more color than the face grain, so seal all end grain and test the stain color before staining.

Oil-based or water-based stain in liquid form can be lightened by scrubbing, and it usually can be darkened by applying additional coats. Prepare for the stain, then stir the stain thoroughly and apply a heavy coat with a brush or cloth. Stir the stain often as you work **(photo A).** Let the stain soak in for about 15 minutes (see manufacturer's directions).

Prepare for the stain, then stir the stain thoroughly and apply a heavy coat with a brush or cloth. Stir the stain often as you work. Let the stain soak in for about 15 minutes (see manufacturer's directions).

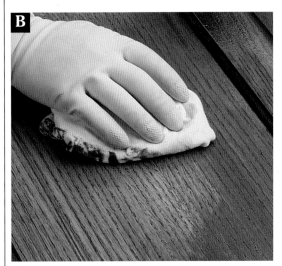

Remove excess stain with a clean, lint-free cloth. Wipe against the grain first, then with the grain. If the color is too dark, try scrubbing with water or mineral spirits. Let the stain dry, then buff with a fine abrasive pad.

Remove excess stain with a clean, lint-free cloth **(photo B).** Wipe against the grain first, then with the grain. If the color is too dark, try scrubbing with water or mineral spirits. Let the stain dry, then buff with a fine abrasive pad.

Apply light coats of stain until the desired color tone is achieved, buffing with an abrasive pad between coats. Buff the final coat of stain before top-coating **(photo C).**

Applying Gel Stain

Creating consistent color is especially easy with gel stain, which clings to awkward surfaces without pooling.

Prepare for the stain. Stir the gel stain, then work it into the surfaces of the workpiece with a staining cloth, using a circular motion **(photo D).** Cover as much of the workpiece as you can reach with the staining cloth, recoating any areas that dry out as you work. Gel stain penetrates better if it is worked into the wood with a brush or rag, rather than simply wiped onto the wood surface.

Use a stiff-bristled brush, like a stenciling brush, to apply gel stain into hard-to-reach areas, where it is difficult to use a staining cloth **(photo E).**

Let the stain soak in (see manufacturer's directions), then wipe off the excess with a clean rag, using a polishing motion. Buff the stained surface with the wood grain, using a soft, clean cloth.

Apply light coats of stain until the desired color tone is achieved, buffing with an abrasive pad between coats. Buff the final coat of stain before top-coating.

Apply additional coats of stain until the workpiece has reached the desired color tone. Gel stain manufacturers usually recommend at least three coats to provide a thick stain layer that helps protect the wood against scratches and other surface flaws. Let the stain dry, then buff with a fine abrasive pad before applying a topcoat.

Applying Penetrating Oil

Prepare for the stain, then apply a heavy coat of penetrating oil to all surfaces, using a staining cloth. Wait 15 to 30 minutes, recoating any areas that begin to dry out. Apply oil to all surfaces, and let it soak into the wood for 30 to 60 minutes **(photo F).**

Wipe the surface dry with a clean cloth, rubbing with the wood grain. Apply another coat of oil with a clean cloth, then let the oil dry overnight. Two coats are sufficient in most cases, since further coats will not darken the finish color. Dab a few drops of penetrating oil onto a fine abrasive pad, then rub the surfaces until smooth **(photo G).** Let the oil dry for at least 72 hours before applying a topcoat. If you do not plan to topcoat the finish, buff with a soft cloth to harden the oil finish.

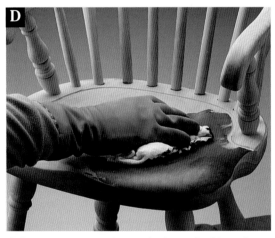

Gel stain penetrates better if it is worked into the wood with a brush or rag, rather than simply wiped onto the wood surface.

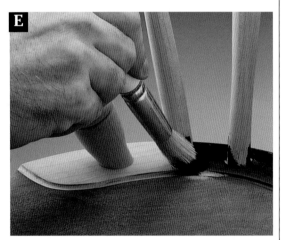

Use a stiff-bristled brush, like this stenciling brush, to apply gel stain into hard-to-reach areas.

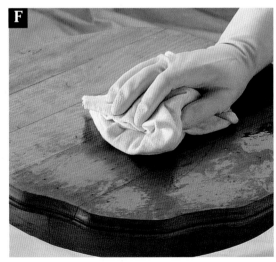

Wipe the surface dry with a clean cloth, rubbing with the wood grain. Apply another coat of oil with a clean cloth, then let the oil dry overnight. Note: Two coats are sufficient in most cases, since further coats will not darken the finish color.

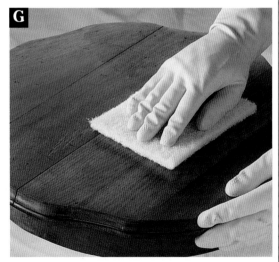

Dab a few drops of penetrating oil onto a fine abrasive pad, then rub the surfaces until smooth. Let the oil dry for at least 72 hours before applying a topcoat. If you do not plan to topcoat the finish, buff with a soft cloth to harden the oil finish.

Painting Wood

Most woodworkers want to showcase the natural wood tones of their projects, so painting is a finishing option that is sometimes overlooked. However, there are many wood projects that are designed to be painted, including a number in this book. Painting surfaces also allows you to use less expensive woods, yet still have impressive results.

Use paint as an alternative to wood stain to give plain wood a splash of color or a decorative touch; or simply use it to hide wear, low-quality materials, or unattractive wood.

Furniture and woodwork generally should be painted with water-based or oil-based enamel paint except when using decorative painting techniques that call for flat wall paint. Enamel paint forms a tough, protective coat that resists moisture, chipping, and scratching. It is available in dozens of premixed colors, and in gloss and semi-gloss versions. Or, you can have special colors custom-mixed at a paint store.

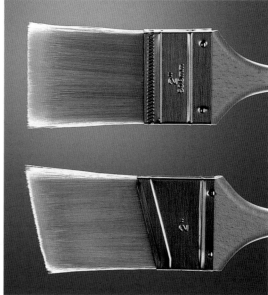

Paint brushes for wood include straight trim brushes for flat areas, and tapered brushes for edges. Use synthetic brushes (nylon or polyester bristles) for both water-based and oil-based paint.

WATER-BASED PAINT

Water-based paint for wood is usually sold as "latex enamel" or "acrylic enamel." Because water-based paint can raise wood grain, use a water-based primer to prepare the wood, then sand the primed surface before applying the paint. The coloring agents in water-based paint settle quickly, so stir the paint often as you work.

ADVANTAGES:
- *safer for the environment*
- *less toxic than oil-based paints*
- *easy cleanup with soap and water*
- *dries quickly*
- *can be thinned with water*

DRAWBACKS:
- *raises wood grain*
- *scratches easily*
- *cleanup is difficult after paint dries*
- *softens with exposure to moisture*
- *cannot be applied in thick coats*

COMPATIBILITY:
- *will not adhere to most topcoats*
- *may be used over other water-based paints*

RECOMMENDED USES:
- *children's toys and furniture*
- *cabinetry*
- *woodwork*

OIL-BASED PAINT

Oil-based paint (also called alkyd paint) dries to a harder finish than water-based paint and offers the best protection for wood that is exposed to wear. It is still the preferred paint type of most professional painters, but this preference is changing as water-based paints become stronger and more versatile. Use oil-based primer with oil-based paint.

ADVANTAGES:
- *hard, scratch-resistant finish*
- *unaffected by moisture*
- *does not raise wood grain*
- *dries to a very smooth finish*

DRAWBACKS:
- *releases toxic vapors*
- *slow drying time*
- *requires mineral spirits for cleanup*
- *use is restricted in some states*

COMPATIBILITY:
- *may be applied over varnish or oil-based polyurethane*
- *may be used over oil- or water-based paints*

RECOMMENDED USES:
- *stairs and railings*
- *floors and doors*
- *woodwork*
- *previously finished wood*

Stir paint with a mixing bit attached to a portable drill for fast, thorough mixing. Keep the mixer bit moving constantly. Repeatedly lower the mixer blade to the bottom of the can, then raise it to the top of the can to mix in settled pigment.

Strain paint to remove lumps, dirt, and other foreign materials. Commercial paint strainers are available, or you can make your own from cheesecloth or nylon stockings.

Applying Paint

Painting wood is very much like painting walls and other common do-it-yourself painting projects. Whenever you paint anything, preparation is critical. For wood, that means sanding the surface until it is flat and smooth, then sealing with primer so the paint absorbs evenly. Open grained hardwoods, like oak, must have the grain filled before painting unless you want to see the texture of the wood grain underneath the paint.

Although it is a different product, primer is applied using the same techniques as paint. In addition to sealing the wood, it keeps resins in the wood from bleeding through the paint layer. If the wood you're painting has highly resinous knots, like pine, you may need to use a special stain killing primer.

Cleanup solvents, thinning agents, drying time, and coverage vary widely from one enamel paint to another. Read the manufacturer's directions carefully. Most paints will be dry to the touch quite quickly, and are ready for a second coat in a short time period. Since you will be sanding in between paint coats, you will get the best results if you allow each coat to dry for 12 to 24 hours.

For best results, designate a clean, dust-free area for painting. Ideally you should sand in one area and paint in another.

Finish-sand the wood (page 20) and apply grain filler if necessary. Vacuum the surfaces or wipe with a tack cloth after you sand to remove

Finish-sand the wood.

Prime the wood with an even coat of primer.

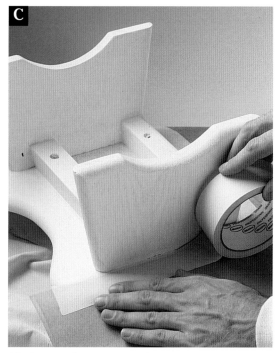

Mask any adjacent areas that will be painted a different color, using masking tape.

all traces of sanding dust from the workpiece **(photo A).**

Prime the wood with an even coat of primer **(photo B).** Use water-based primer with water-based paint, and oil-based primer with oil-based paint. Smooth out brush marks as you work, and sand with 220-grit sandpaper when dry.

Mask any adjacent areas that will be painted a different color, using masking tape. Press the edges of the tape firmly against the wood **(photo C).**

Apply a thin coat of paint, brushing with the grain **(photo D).** Heavy layers of paint will tend to sag and form an uneven surface. Loading your brush with too much paint will also cause drips to form on edges and around joints.

For a smooth surface that's free from lap marks, hold your paint brush at a 45° angle, and apply just enough pressure to flex the bristles slightly **(photo E).**

When dry, sand with 400-grit sandpaper, then wipe with a tack cloth. Apply at least one more heavier coat, sanding and wiping with a tack cloth between additional coats. Darker colors may require more coats than lighter colors. Do not sand the last coat.

Option: Apply clear polyurethane topcoat to surfaces that will get heavy wear. Before applying, wet-sand the paint with 600-grit wet/dry sandpaper, then wipe with a tack cloth. Use water-based polyurethane over latex paint, and oil-based over oil-based paint **(photo F).**

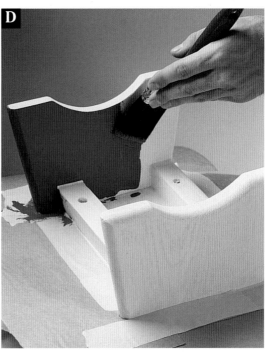

Apply a thin coat of paint, brushing with the grain.

For a smooth surface free from lap marks, hold your paint brush at a 45° angle, and apply just enough pressure to flex the bristles slightly.

Option: Wet sand the last coat of paint and apply clear polyurethane topcoat to surfaces that will get heavy wear.

Decorative Painting

Apply a creative touch to your project with decorative painting techniques. Antique finishes, stencils, and color washes give furniture and decorative items a rustic look. A handful of specialty paint brushes, some quality finishing materials, a few helpful tools, and a little creativity are all you need to create these unique painted finishes on your projects. With all of these techniques, it is best to practice on scraps before applying to your project.

Antique finishes re-create the look of worn paint. Finish sand the piece and apply a base coat of wood stain. If you use water based stain and water based paint, the stain may bleed through the paint. For certain colors this may be a desirable effect. To prevent bleed through, apply a topcoat of satin finish polyurethane. Allow the topcoat to dry and apply a layer of water-based paint. You may want to apply a second coat of paint in a different color, to enhance the illusion of age. Once the paint is dry, sand off randomly chosen areas of paint with 100-grit sandpaper, applying varying degrees of pressure to imitate natural wear **(photo A).** Sand the corners of the workpiece and any detail areas with 220-grit sandpaper, then wipe with a lint-free cloth and denatured alcohol to complete this vintage finish.

Stenciled designs add a bright, decorative touch to varnished or painted wood. Purchase ready-made clear acetate stencils at a craft store, or cut your own. Position the stencil on the wood, and secure it with tape. Stipple the wood by dabbing paint onto the surface through the stencil, using a stenciling brush **(photo B).** Acrylic craft paints are a good choice for stenciling, or you can purchase special stenciling paints. Allow the paint to dry before removing the stencil. If more than one color will be used, realign the stencil and apply each color, one at a time, starting with the lightest color. Allow the stenciled area to dry completely and topcoat with a clear finish for protection.

Color washes produce a thin, semi-transparent coat of paint on bare wood. Dilute water-based paint by mixing one part paint to four parts water (the more diluted the paint mixture, the thinner the paint layer will be). Brush the thinned paint onto the wood, working with the grain. Wipe the surface immediately with a lint-free cloth, removing paint until you achieve the desired color tone **(photo C).** Repeat the process to darken the color, if needed. Soften the look by scuffing the painted surface with a fine abrasive pad when dry.

Sand corners and high spots to create a worn appearance.

Use a special stencil brush to get the best results.

A color wash allows the wood grain to show through.

Applying Sealers and Stains

You can leave your solid cedar and redwood outdoor wood projects unfinished, or seal or stain them. Leaving cedar unfinished allows it to weather and age to a mellow gray. Sealing protects the grain from raising but allows for a slow progression to gray, unless you use a product containing ultra-violet blockers. Staining protects the wood grain and adds color. Plywood, plywood siding and pine boards need to be sealed, stained or painted because they do not have the natural rot resistance of solid cedar and redwood.

New, raw cedar varies in color from a light tan to a deep red. Without a finish, cedar, redwood and teak will weather to a light gray. Semi-transparent stains are available in wood tones and offer a small amount of protection from graying. Solid color stains are the most durable and obscure the natural colors of the wood, but allow the wood's texture to be visible.

A brush is the best applicator for exterior stain. To prevent uneven coverage, brush from dry to wet.

Sealers and stains differ from paint. Paints require primers to bond properly to wood and usually require multiple coats for coverage. Because of the layers of paint, all but the roughest wood textures are obscured or hidden. Paint bonds to the wood surface, but does not penetrate. It also forms a moisture resistant layer. If moisture does penetrate the wood, the paint will blister and peel when the water evaporates. Exterior oil-based polyurethane finishes are similar to paint in this way. Properly applied stain penetrates the wood surface, rather than sitting on top of it and allows water vapor to evaporate from within the wood. Depending on the type, wood sealers may create a waterproof barrier somewhat like paint, or may create a semi-permeable barrier like stain.

Wood sealers partially or totally block the wood's pores, preventing water penetration. When wood absorbs water and dries repeatedly, the grain becomes raised and rough. While most wood sealers do not prevent the wood from graying, some sealers now come with ultra-violet blockers to prevent graying. Because sealers are clear, the wood's grain and color are still visible after treatment. Sealers and waterproofers must be reapplied annually for best results. Exterior staining products are available in a number of water- or oil-based options. The options are based on how much pigment is in the product. Wood-toned stains have only a small amount of pigment. This stain does not provide much protection from ultra-violet rays unless it also contains a UV blocking agent. Semi-transparent stains have more pigment than wood-toned stains, but still allow the grain and texture of the wood to show through. Solid color stain is the most durable of the wood stains. It allows the texture of the wood to show, but obscures the color and most of the grain **(photo A).**

To seal or stain new wood, the wood must be clean and dry. Sanding is not necessary when applying sealers and stains because the products penetrate the wood. Mix the products thoroughly, especially stains. The pigments in stains settle very quickly, so to ensure consistent color it is important to stir frequently. Apply stain in a well-ventilated area or wear a respirator.

Use a natural bristle brush for applying oil based products and a synthetic brush for latex products. Special staining brushes with shorter bristles drip less than a standard paint brush but can be difficult to find. Do not apply sealers or stains in direct sun. Stain absorbs and dries more quickly than paint, and hot surfaces will further speed this process, making it difficult to create a consistent finish. Remember to protect surrounding surfaces with drop cloths (it is difficult or impossible to remove wood stains from cement).

To apply stain using a brush, load the brush and apply the stain in the direction of the wood grain. To prevent lap marks, brush backward from dry to wet for subsequent brush strokes **(photo B).** Always work on one board at a time. For sheet goods, move from left to right, covering an entire top to bottom swath at a time.

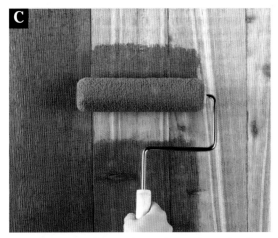

Rough-sawn or textured woods can be stained with a ⅜" nap roller. Cover one section at a time and roll back from dry to wet to prevent uneven color distribution.

Before applying stain or sealer to previously finished wood, test the wood's absorbency by sprinkling it with drops of water. If they are not absorbed after 5 minutes, the wood will need to be stripped before refinishing.

Maintain a wet edge as you go. Do not stop in the middle of a board or panel. Check the manufacturer's instructions concerning application of a second coat.

Stain can be applied with a roller, but it is recommended only for rough surfaces. Use a roller with a ⅜" nap. Stir the stain thoroughly and pour a small amount into a roller tray. Apply the stain to one board at a time in the direction of the grain. For sheet goods, cover top-to-bottom swath at a time. Do not stop in the middle of a board or panel. Roll from dry to wet (backrolling) to prevent lap marks **(photo C).**

To apply sealers and preservatives, stir the product thoroughly. Saturate the surface until the wood absorbs no more sealer and a wet sheen forms. Do not overapply (puddling of the product indicates overapplication) and do not apply a second coat.

Wood sealers may need to be reapplied every year or two years. Stains usually last 3 to 7 years depending on the pigment content and exposure to weather. Before reapplying sealer or stain, it is important to do a "splash test" to determine if the wood is porous enough to absorb a new application of sealer or stain. Drip or spray large water droplets onto the wood surface. If the droplets are not absorbed within 5 minutes, the old finish must be removed **(photo D).** Use an exterior deck stripper and wood cleaners to prepare the surface for refinishing.

Maintain your outdoor wood projects by regularly cleaning or refinishing them. A power washer can make this a quick job **(photo E).** Make sure you follow directions carefully.

In harsh climates, move items to a sheltered area in the winter, or cover with a tarp. This will prevent excess weathering and help your projects last longer.

A pressure washer can be used to clean and brighten unfinished outdoor projects, or to strip and clean finished surfaces for refinishing. Remember that high water pressure can destroy the soft wood fibers of cedar and redwood.

Protect your finish and wood with a topcoat layer, like the wipe-on tung oil being applied to this dresser.

Applying Topcoats

Topcoat finishes seal the wood, protect the finish from scratches and other wear, and increase the visual appeal of the wood. Because they dry clear, topcoats highlight the coloring and natural figure of the wood. For most projects, a topcoat of tung oil finish, polyurethane, or paste wax will give your wood the protection it needs and the finished appearance you desire.

When choosing a topcoat, consider durability, sheen, and compatibility with any coloring layers you use (see opposite page). Other factors, like drying time, ease of application and cleanup, and safeness, should also influence your choice. If possible, check samples at building centers or paint stores to see if a particular topcoat is suitable for your workpiece. Some one-step stain-and-seal products are also available. Test these products on scrap wood before using them.

Make tack cloths by moistening cheesecloth in mineral spirits. Apply a spoonful of varnish (or any other clear topcoat material) to the cheesecloth, and knead the cloth until the varnish is absorbed evenly. Make several tack cloths and store them in a glass jar with a lid.

TUNG OIL FINISH

Tung oil is extracted from the nut of the tung tree. Good for creating a matte or glossy hand-rubbed finish, tung oil products are available in clear and tinted form.

ADVANTAGES:
- easy to apply
- flexible finish that resists cracking
- very natural appearance that makes minimal changes in wood appearance
- penetrates into the wood
- easily renewed and repaired

DRAWBACKS:
- not as durable as other topcoats

COMPATIBILITY:
- not compatible with polyurethane

RECOMMENDED USES:
- uneven surfaces like chairs and other furniture with spindles
- woodwork
- antiques
- wood with highly figured grain

COMMON BRAND NAMES:
- Minwax® Tung Oil Finish, Zar® Tung Oil, Tung Seal by McCloskey®

OIL-BASE POLYURETHANE

Despite the emergence of water-based polyurethanes, many refinishers still prefer oil-based polyurethane.

ADVANTAGES:
- easier to get a smooth finish than with a water-base polyurethane
- forms durable, hard finish
- impervious to water and alcohol

DRAWBACKS:
- slow drying time
- disposal and use closely regulated in some states
- decreasing availability
- difficult cleanup
- toxic
- gives off unpleasant fumes

COMPATIBILITY:
- not compatible with other topcoats

RECOMMENDED USES:
- furniture
- surfaces where a very thick, durable topcoat is desired

COMMON BRAND NAMES:
- Defthane by Deft®, Heirloom Varnish by McCloskey®, Minwax® Polyurethane

WATER-BASED POLYURETHANE

Water-based polyurethane is a popular topcoat because of its fast drying time and easy cleanup.

ADVANTAGES:
- fast drying time
- easy cleanup
- nonflammable
- nontoxic
- impervious to water and alcohol

DRAWBACKS:
- can raise wood grain
- can have an unnatural "plastic" appearance

COMPATIBILITY:
- do not apply over other topcoats, or directly over commercial sanding sealer

RECOMMENDED USES:
- floors
- interior woodwork and furniture
- children's furniture and toys
- tabletops, eating surfaces

COMMON BRAND NAMES:
- EnviroCare®, Varathane® Diamond Finish, Carver Tripp® Safe & Simple, Zar® Polyurethane

PASTE WAX

Paste wax is natural waxes dissolved in mineral spirits or naphtha. It is favored for its handrubbed sheen.

ADVANTAGES:
- easy to renew with fresh coats
- very natural appearance
- can be buffed to desired sheen
- can be applied over most topcoats

DRAWBACKS:
- easily scratched and worn away
- needs to be restored regularly
- water or alcohol spills will damage wax

COMPATIBILITY:
- No restrictions

RECOMMENDED USES:
- antiques
- fine furniture
- floors

COMMON BRAND NAMES:
- Antiquax®, Johnson & Johnson® Paste Wax, Minwax® Paste Finishing Wax

Choosing and Using Topcoats

For safe use and low toxicity, water-based polyurethane is an excellent choice. Use it for children's furniture and toys, as well as for eating surfaces **(photo A).**

Choose the finish gloss that best meets your needs. Product availability has expanded among polyurethane products in recent years to include gloss, semi-gloss, and matte (or satin) sheens. Because of the expanding product lines, polyurethane-based topcoat products have almost completely replaced traditional wood varnish **(photo B).**

Stir topcoat finishes gently with a clean stir stick. Shaking the container or stirring too vigorously can create air bubbles that cause pockmarks in the finish when dry **(photo C).**

Wet-sand with a fine abrasive pad on the final topcoat layer to create a finish with the exact amount of gloss you want **(photo D).**

Transfer leftover topcoat materials to smaller containers to minimize the amount of air that can react with the product. Tung oil and polyurethane are especially susceptible to thickening when exposed to air **(photo E).**

Use water-based polyurethane for children's furniture and toys, as well as for eating surfaces.

Choose the finish gloss that best meets your needs.

To prevent bubbles, stir topcoats gently, and never shake.

Wet-sand to create the exact amount of gloss you want.

Store leftover topcoat materials in smaller containers to minimize thickening due to air exposure.

Applying Tung Oil Finishes

Tung oil is an extremely popular finish both for its easy application and its appearance. Several well-buffed coats applied with a clean cloth will form a suitably hard finish. With added coats and more buffing, you can achieve a glossy finish. Tung-oil-based products are suitable for most furniture, including antiques. Seldom sold in pure form, tung oil is usually blended with tinting agents or other topcoats, and is usually described by manufacturers as "tung oil finish."

Because tung oil forms a relatively thin coat, renew finished surfaces with a fresh coat of tung oil every year or so. Or, you can apply a protective layer of paste wax to guard the finish, and renew the wax topcoat periodically. Use lemon oil to refresh a tung oil finish without recoating.

Finish sand your project and clean the surfaces thoroughly with a cloth and mineral spirits **(photo A)**. Apply a thick coat of tung oil finish with a cloth or brush. Let the tung oil penetrate for 5 to 10 minutes, then rub off the excess with a cloth, using a polishing motion.

Use a paint brush to apply tung oil to very uneven surfaces. Because the excess tung oil is wiped off before it dries, there is no need to worry about drips or lap marks from brushes **(photo B).**

Buff the tung oil with a clean cloth after 24 hours, then apply additional coats as needed to build the desired finish. Three coats is generally considered the minimum for a good finish. Use a clean cloth for each application **(photo C).**

Let the finish dry completely, then buff it lightly with a fine abrasive pad **(photo D).** For a higher gloss, buff with a polishing bonnet and portable drill.

Tung oil is especially susceptible to thickening when exposed to air. Transfer leftover materials to smaller, air-tight containers to minimize the amount of air that can react with the product. Make sure you clearly label containers with the date and product.

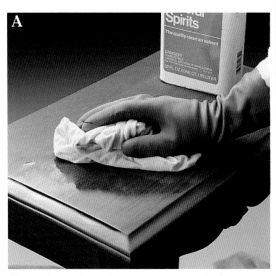

Clean the surfaces thoroughly with a cloth and mineral spirits.

Use a paint brush to apply tung oil to very uneven surfaces.

Buff the tung oil with a clean cloth after 24 hours, then reapply additional coats.

Let the finish dry completely, then buff it lightly with a fine abrasive pad.

Applying Polyurethane

Polyurethane (often called polyurethane varnish or simply varnish) is a hard, durable topcoat material commonly used on floors, countertops, and other heavy-use surfaces. Available in both water-based and oil-based form, polyurethane is a complex mixture of plastic resins, solvents, and drying oils or water, that dries to a clear, nonyellowing finish.

A wide array of finishing products contain some type of polyurethane, which can causes a good deal of confusion. If a label uses the descriptive terms "acrylic" or "polymerized," the product is most likely polyurethane-based. Your safest bet in choosing the best polyurethane product for the job is to refer to the suggestions for use on the product label.

For safe use and low toxicity, water-based polyurethane is an excellent choice. Use it for children's furniture and toys as well as for eating surfaces.

Polyurethane products are available in a range of sheens. Choose the gloss level that best fits your project's intended use.

Hardening agents are available for some brands of water-based polyurethane for outdoor applications or high-traffic areas. Hardening agents lose their effectiveness quickly, so harden only as much product as you plan to apply in one coat.

Seal unstained wood. Check the product label for recommended sealer.

Seal unstained wood with a 1:1 mixture of polyurethane and thinning agent (check product label), applied with a clean cloth or brush **(photo A).** Wipe off excess sealer with a clean cloth. Let the sealer dry. Wood that has been colored with stain or penetrating oil does not need a seal-coat.

Apply a coat of polyurethane, starting at the top of the project and working your way down. Use a good quality brush. When the surface is covered, smooth out the finish by lightly brushing in one direction only, with the grain. Let dry, then sand between coats using 600-grit wet/dry sandpaper **(photo B).**

Apply polyurethane in several thin layers for best results. Applying too much finish at once slows down the drying time, and causes running, wrinkling or sagging **(photo C).**

Brush out lap marks to create a smooth surface before the polyurethane dries. Small brush marks will show, but will blend together as the

Apply a coat of polyurethane, starting at the top of the project and working your way down.

finish dries. Because it dries slowly, oil-based polyurethane gives you more time to brush out lap marks.

Examine the surface after each coat of polyurethane dries, using a bright side light **(photo D).** Wet-sand with a fine abrasive pad to remove dust and other surface problems, like air bubbles. After sanding, wipe the surface clean with a tack cloth.

Apply the second coat. To keep the finish from running, always try to position the workpiece so the surface being topcoated is horizontal **(photo E).**

Applying too much finish at once causes running, wrinkling or sagging.

Examine the surface after each coat of polyurethane dries, using a bright side light.

To keep the finish from running, always try to position the workpiece so the surface being topcoated is horizontal.

Applying Wax

Wax is an easily renewable topcoat that protects and beautifies wood. It is often applied over oil finishes and other topcoats to absorb small scratches and everyday wear and tear. Then, simply by removing the old wax and applying a fresh coat, you can create a new-looking topcoat without refinishing.

Paste wax is the best wax product for wood because it can be buffed to a hard finish. But other types of wax, like liquid wax, can be used for specific purposes.

Apply several coats of paste wax for best results. The hardness of a wax finish is a direct result of the thickness of the wax and the vigor with which it is buffed. Extensive buffing also increases the glossiness of the finish. For the hardest possible finish, choose products with a high ratio of wax to solvent (see label).

Apply a moderate layer of paste wax to the wood using a fine abrasive pad or a cloth. Rub the wax into the wood with a polishing motion **(photo A)**.

Allow the wax to dry until it becomes filmy in spots **(photo B).** Gently wipe off any excess, undried wax, then allow the entire wax surface to dry until filmy (usually within 10 to 20 minutes). NOTE: Do not let the wax dry too long or it will harden and become very difficult to buff. Begin buffing the wax with a soft cloth, using a light, circular motion. Buff the entire surface until the filminess disappears and the wax is clear **(photo C)**.

Continue buffing the wax until the surface is hard and shiny **(photo D).** Apply and buff another coat, then let the wax dry for at least 24 hours before applying additional coats. Apply at least three coats for a fine wax finish.

Buff wax to a hard, glossy finish with a polishing bonnet attached to a portable drill. Keep the drill moving to avoid overheating the wax **(photo E)**.

Use liquid wax on detailed areas, where paste wax is difficult to apply. Apply the wax with a stiff brush, then buff with a soft cloth **(photo F)**.

Apply a moderate layer of paste wax by rubbing the wax into the wood with a polishing motion.

Allow the wax to dry until it becomes filmy in spots.

Begin buffing the wax with a soft cloth, using a light, circular motion. Buff the entire surface until the filminess disappears and the wax is clear.

Continue buffing the wax until the surface is hard and shiny.

Buff wax to a hard, glossy finish with a polishing bonnet attached to a portable drill. Keep the drill moving to avoid overheating the wax.

Use liquid wax on detailed areas, where paste wax is difficult to apply. Apply the wax with a stiff brush, then buff with a soft cloth.

Entryway Projects

Your home's entryway is a busy space. Building any one of these beautiful, hardworking furnishings will make your entryway more appealing and less cluttered. What could be nicer than coming home and being greeted at the door by charming furnishings you made yourself?

Kids' Coat Rack

Kids love using this monkey-topped coat rack, and you'll have fun building it.

CONSTRUCTION MATERIALS

Quantity	Lumber
1	2 × 2" × 4' oak
1	1 × 6" × 2' oak
1	¾" × 2 × 2' birch plywood
1	1 × 3" × 4' oak

This stand is designed to hold eight coats or jackets, but kids will hang almost anything on the shaker pegs, including mittens, scarves, sweaters and pants. The decorative monkey acts as a motivator and reminder that it's more fun to hang your clothes on the stand than throw them on the furniture or floor. The monkey also gives you an opportunity to put your artistic talents to work. This popular stand is easy to construct and takes up little space, so it can fit in an entryway or bedroom with ease.

OVERALL SIZE:
58½" HIGH
16" WIDE
16" DEEP

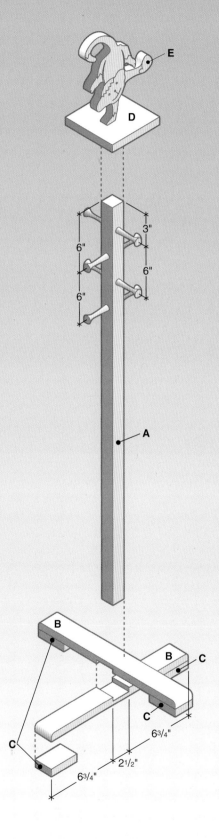

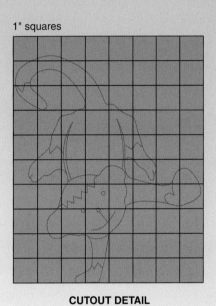

1" squares

CUTOUT DETAIL

Cutting List				
Key	**Part**	**Dimension**	**Pcs.**	**Material**
A	Post	1½ × 1½ × 46¼"	1	Oak
B	Leg	¾ × 2½ × 16"	2	Oak
C	Foot	¾ × 2½ × 3"	4	Oak
D	Platform	¾ × 5½ × 5½"	1	Oak
E	Monkey	¾ × 8 × 10"	1	Birch plywood

Materials: Wood glue, #8 × 1¼" wood screws, 4d
finish nail, birch shaker pegs (8), finishing materials.

Note: Measurements reflect the actual thickness of
dimension lumber.

Clean out the half lap joints with a chisel and a hammer. To ensure a tight fit, keep the edges square.

Mark and drill holes in the post to match the diameter of your shaker pegs.

TIP

To ensure accurate cuts, build a shooting board from a straight piece of 1 × 4" lumber about 24" long, and a smooth piece of ¼"-thick plywood about 6" wide and 24" long. Attach the 1 × 4" board along one edge of the plywood strip, using glue and screws. Then, run your circular saw along the 1 × 4" straightedge, trimming the plywood base to the exact distance between the edge of the saw foot and the blade. To use the shooting board, simply clamp it in place with the edge of the plywood along the cutting line, then run your saw over the plywood with the base of the saw tight against the straightedge.

Directions:
Kids' Coat Rack

CUT THE COAT RACK PARTS.

1. Cut the post (A), legs (B) and feet (C) to length.
2. Align the legs side by side, and clamp together. Mark a 2½"-wide notch on each leg (see *Diagram*).
3. Build a shooting board (see *Tip*), and set the depth of the saw blade at ⅝" (allowing for the ¼"-thick plywood base, this will give you a ⅜"-deep cut).
4. Clamp the shooting board next to one side of the notch and make the first cut, keeping the saw base flat on the plywood and tight against the straightedge. Reposition the shooting board and cut the other side of the notch. Leave the shooting board in place after the second cut, and make additional cuts within the notch to remove the wood between the first two cuts.
5. Carefully clean any waste from the notch with a sharp ¾" chisel **(photo A).**
6. Test-fit the legs. If necessary, adjust the lap joint by chiseling, filing or sanding more stock from the notches.
7. Round off the top edges of the leg ends with a router or belt sander.

ASSEMBLE THE PARTS.

1. Glue and clamp the feet to the legs.
2. Position the post on the leg

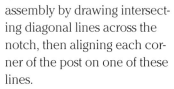

Drill a pilot hole into the base of the monkey so it doesn't split when attaching it to the platform.

Attach the monkey to the platform using glue and a wood screw.

assembly by drawing intersecting diagonal lines across the notch, then aligning each corner of the post on one of these lines.

3. Drill two countersunk pilot holes through the bottom of the leg assembly, then attach the legs to the post with glue and wood screws.

4. Mark two peg holes on each side of the post (see *Diagram*). Carefully drill holes straight into the sides of the post, matching the diameter of the shaker pegs **(photo B).**

MAKE THE MONKEY AND PLATFORM.

1. Lay out the monkey pattern (E) on birch plywood (see *Diagram*), and cut out the pattern with a jig saw.

2. Use wood putty to fill any voids on the edges of the plywood.

3. Cut the platform (D) to size.

4. Drill a countersunk pilot hole into the bottom of the platform at the centerpoint for attaching the monkey. Drill two offset pilot holes in the top of the platform, about ¾" from the center hole. Counterbore one of these holes. Drill a pilot hole into the center of the monkey's paw **(photo C).**

5. Paint the monkey.

ASSEMBLE THE UNIT.

1. Attach the monkey to the platform, using glue and a wood screw **(photo D).**

2. Attach the monkey and platform to the post assembly with

TIP

For better control when painting faces and figurines, use latex paint as a base coat, and outline the pattern details with a permanent-ink marker. To protect your work, seal the monkey with a low-luster water-based polyurethane.

glue, a wood screw and a 4d finish nail.

3. Attach the shaker pegs with glue, and wipe off any excess.

APPLY FINISHING TOUCHES.

Sand the project smooth and apply oil or a clear finish.

Hallway Bookcase

*A stable base that tapers to a low-profile top lets you add storage
and display space in even the tightest quarters.*

CONSTRUCTION MATERIALS

Quantity	Lumber
2	1 × 10" × 8' pine
1	1 × 8" × 6' pine
1	1 × 6" × 6' pine
3	1 × 4" × 8' pine

Hallways are frequently underutilized areas of a home. The reason is simple—large furnishings would cramp the area. When foot traffic is heavy and space is at a premium, this hallway bookcase makes the most of the situation. Fitting flush against the wall, it allows you to store your books and display your knick-knacks without cluttering up the hall or consuming valuable floor space. The bookcase is tapered, so it is thinner at the top than at the bottom. This design reduces the chance of tipping and cuts down on space consumption. This bookcase is a very simple and inexpensive project to build.

OVERALL SIZE:
60" HIGH
36" WIDE
9" DEEP

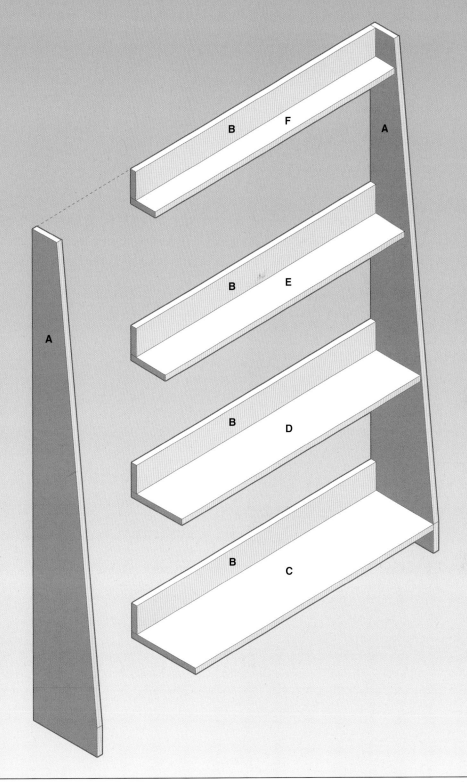

Cutting List

Key	Part	Dimension	Pcs.	Material
A	Standard	¾ × 9¼ × 60"	2	Pine
B	Spreader	¾ × 3½ × 34½"	4	Pine
C	Shelf	¾ × 9¼ × 34½"	1	Pine

Cutting List

Key	Part	Dimension	Pcs.	Material
D	Shelf	¾ × 7¼ × 34½"	1	Pine
E	Shelf	¾ × 5¼ × 34½"	1	Pine
F	Shelf	¾ × 3½ × 34½"	1	Pine

Materials: Wood glue, #8 × 2" wood screws, finishing materials.

Note: Measurements reflect the actual size of dimension lumber.

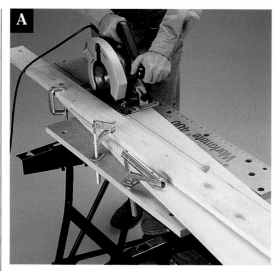

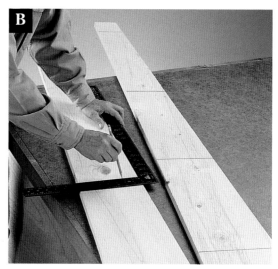

Clamp a straightedge to the standard, and make the taper cut with a circular saw.

Use a framing square to mark reference lines on the standards for shelf placement.

Directions:
Hallway Bookcase

MAKE THE STANDARDS.
The tapered standards are wide at the bottom for stability and narrow at the top to conserve space in a busy hallway.
1. Cut the standards (A) to length from 1 × 10 pine boards.
2. Mark a point on the front edge of each standard, 3½" up from the bottom. Mark another point on the top of each standard, 3½" in from the back edge. Draw a straight line connecting these points to form a tapered cutting line for the standard.
3. Clamp a straightedge to the board, parallel to the cutting line, and cut the taper with a circular saw **(photo A)**.
4. Sand the parts to smooth out any sharp edges or rough surfaces.

CUT THE SHELVES
AND SPREADERS.
The shelves and spreaders are all the same length, but in order to conform with the taper in the standards, the shelves at the top of the hall bookcase are narrower than those at the bottom.
1. Cut the spreaders (B) and shelves (C).
2. Check the lengths again, and sand the parts to smooth out any rough edges.

INSTALL THE SPREADERS.
The spreaders help support the shelves while providing side-to-side strength for the bookcase. The spreaders also keep books and decorative objects from hitting the wall behind the bookcase or falling back behind the shelves and out of reach. Each spreader should fit flush with the back edges of the standards, directly above a shelf reference line.

1. Use a framing square and a pencil to mark reference lines on each standard, 3½", 20¾", 37½" and 56½" up from the bottoms **(photo B).** These reference lines mark the tops of the shelves. Make sure the shelf reference lines are the same distance from the bottom on both standards, or you may end up with sloping shelves.
2. Set the standards on their back edges so their outside faces are 36" apart. Position a spreader just above the bottom shelf reference lines.
3. Drill counterbored pilot holes through the standards and into the ends of the spreader.
4. Attach the bottom spreader with glue and #8 × 2" wood screws.
5. Attach the remaining spreaders in the same way, making sure the top spreader is flush with the top and back edges of the standards **(photo C).**
6. Check the bookcase to make sure it is square after the final spreader has been installed. Measure diagonally from corner to corner. If the measurements are equal, the bookcase is

---

TIP

Special tapered drill bits make drilling counterbores for screws a snap. Simply select a counterbore bit that matches the shank size of the screws you will use (usually #6 or #8), then drill a pilot hole for each screw with a plain twist bit. Counterbore the pilot holes, using the counterbore bit, to the correct depth for the wood plugs that will be inserted into the counterbores.

Fit the spreaders between the bookcase standards. Make sure the bookcase is square as you fasten them in place.

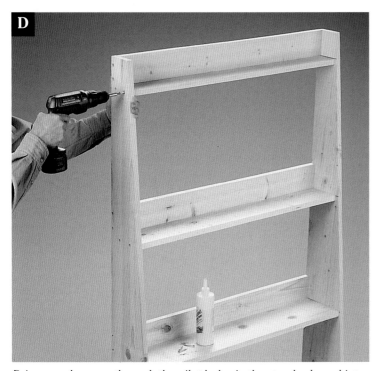

Drive wood screws through the pilot holes in the standards and into the ends of the shelves.

TIP

Anchor smaller furnishings to the wall in heavy traffic areas. In many cases, as with this open-back hallway bookcase, the exposed spreaders can be used as strips for screwing the project to the wall. For best results, drive screws into wall studs through the top spreader and at least one lower spreader. Counterbore the screws, cover the heads with wood plugs, then paint the plugs to match.

shelf will not be visible, you don't need to counterbore and plug them. Countersink them slightly so you can apply wood putty before finishing.)

3. Apply glue to the ends of the shelf and the bottom edge of the spreader, and attach the shelf with #8 × 2" wood screws. Attach the remaining shelves in the same way, working your way up the bookcase **(photo D).**

APPLY FINISHING TOUCHES.

1. Insert glued, ⅜"-dia. wood plugs into all counterbored screw holes. Fill the holes on the bottoms of the shelves with wood putty.

2. Finish-sand the entire project with fine sandpaper.

3. Finish or paint the bookcase. We finished ours with a light, semitransparent wood stain and two light coats of water-based polyurethane to protect and seal the wood.

square. If the project is out of square, apply pressure to one side or the other with your hand or clamps to push it back into square before you fasten the shelves.

INSTALL THE SHELVES.

1. Position the bottom shelf between the standards. Make sure the top edge of the bottom shelf is butted up against the bottom edge of the bottom spreader and is flush with the reference line.

2. Drill counterbored pilot holes through the standards and into the ends of the shelf. Drill pilot holes through the shelf and into the bottom edge of the spreader. (Because the screw holes underneath the

Umbrella Stand

Keep your umbrellas, canes and walking sticks within easy reach with this classic umbrella stand.

CONSTRUCTION MATERIALS

Quantity	Lumber
2	1 × 10" × 6' oak
1	¾ × ¾" × 4' oak cove molding
2	8 × 22" tin

This umbrella stand is the perfect rainy-day project. It easily holds up to six umbrellas, canes or walking sticks, so you'll never again have to search for these items on the way out the door. The umbrella stand is a natural in a hallway, entryway or foyer and a classy alternative to storing umbrellas in your closet.

Built from solid oak for sturdiness and good looks, the umbrella stand has miter-cut top trim and cove molding, and decorative diamond cutouts backed with tin panels. This project can be painted or finished with natural stain. Stain or paint the feet and trim so your umbrella stand blends in nicely with staircases or doors in your entryway.

OVERALL SIZE:
24½" HIGH
13" WIDE
13" DEEP

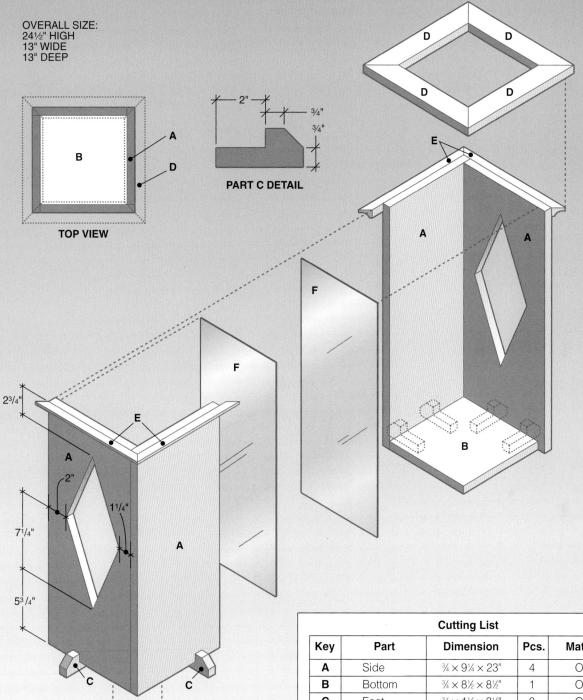

B

A

D

TOP VIEW

2"

¾"

¾"

PART C DETAIL

D   D

D   D

E

A   A

F

F

B

2¾"

E

A

2"

1¼"

7¼"

A

5¾"

C   C

C

		Cutting List		
Key	**Part**	**Dimension**	**Pcs.**	**Material**
A	Side	¾ × 9¼ × 23"	4	Oak
B	Bottom	¾ × 8½ × 8½"	1	Oak
C	Foot	¾ × 1½ × 3½"	8	Oak
D	Top trim	¾ × 2 × 12"	4	Oak
E	Cove	¾ × ¾ × 11½"	4	Molding
F	Panel	8 × 22"	2	Tin

Materials: #6 × 1¼" wood screws, #6 × ½" panhead screws, 2d and 4d finish nails, 16-ga. × 1" brads, wood glue, finishing materials.

Specialty tools: Aviation snips.

Note: Measurements reflect the actual size of dimension lumber.

Drill starter holes. Then, cut out the diamond shapes with a jig saw.

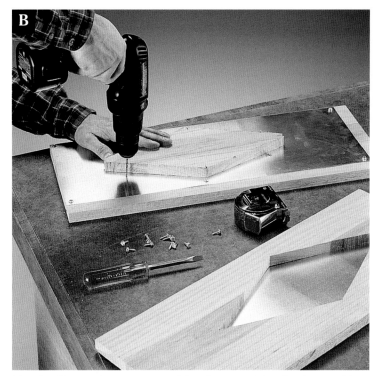

Use the diamond cutout as a guide when attaching the tin panel behind the cutout.

Directions: Umbrella Stand

CUT THE SIDES AND BOTTOM.
1. Cut the sides (A) and bottom (B) to size. Sand the cuts smooth with medium-grit sandpaper.
2. Draw the diamond on two side pieces. First, draw reference lines at 2¾", 10", and 17" down from the top and 5" in from the left side. On the 10" line, mark points 2" in from the left edge and 1¼" in from the right. Use these reference points to complete the diamond shape (see *Diagram*). NOTE: When the box is assembled, the diamonds will be centered side to side.
3. Drill starter holes, using a backer board to prevent splintering. Cut out the diamond shapes with a jig saw **(photo A).** Sand the cutouts smooth.
4. Cut the tin panels (F) to size with aviation snips. Position the

Attach the cove molding to the sides with glue and 1" brads.

tin panels on the inside face of each cutout side, leaving a ¾" space at the bottom and along the right edge for the bottom piece and adjoining side. Drill ³⁄₃₂" pilot holes, and attach the tin panel with ½" panhead screws. Drive screws at the corners and along the edges of the cutout. Use a cutout diamond section as a guide to position the screws **(photo B).**

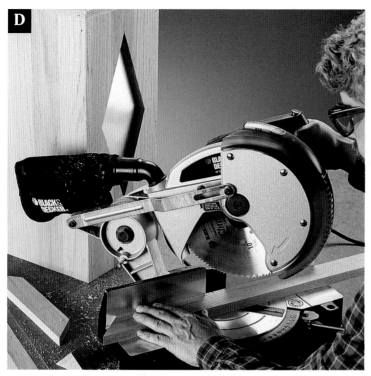

Use a miter saw to cut 45° angles on the top trim.

Attach the feet with 1¼" wood screws.

ASSEMBLE THE BOX.

1. Lay one of the plain sides on your worksurface. Butt a cutout side upright at a 90° angle against the left edge (make sure the tin panel is not covered). Drill pilot holes through the cutout side and into the edge of the plain side. Counterbore the holes ⅛" deep, using a ⅜" counterbore bit. Join the pieces with glue and 1¼" wood screws.

2. Rotate the assembly so the cutout is facedown. Butt the other plain side against the left edge. Drill pilot holes through the plain side and into the edge of the cutout side. Counterbore the holes. Attach the piece with glue and 1¼" wood screws.

3. Position the bottom piece inside the assembly, flush with the bottom edges. Drill pilot holes through the sides and into the bottom. Counterbore the holes. Attach the bottom with glue and 1¼" wood screws.

4. Rotate the assembly, and attach the remaining cutout side.

ATTACH THE COVE MOLDING AND TOP TRIM.

Miter the cove molding on the ends, and lock-nail the joints together to prevent separation (see *Tip*, page 150).

1. Cut the cove molding (E) to length, mitering the ends at 45° angles.

2. Position the molding so the top edges are flush with the tops of the sides. Drill 1⁄16" pilot holes through the molding, and attach the molding with glue and 1" brads **(photo C)**.

3. Cut the top trim (D) to size, mitering the ends at 45° angles **(photo D)**.

4. Position the trim so it overhangs the outer edges of the cove by ¼". Drill 1⁄16" pilot holes through the trim pieces. Attach them with glue and 4d finish nails. Lock-nail the mitered

ends with 2d finish nails. Set all nails with a nail set.

CUT THE FEET.

1. Cut blanks for the feet (C).

2. With a jig saw, trim off the corners, and make the notches (see *Diagram*). Sand the cut edges smooth.

APPLY FINISHING TOUCHES.

1. Fill all nail and screw holes with wood putty. Sand the wood and finish as desired.

2. Mask the cove and trim, cover the tin panel with contact paper and paint the sides. When the paint dries, remove the paper and apply amber shellac to the tin.

3. Apply finish to the cove, trim and feet. Position two feet at the bottom of each side, 2⅛" in from the outside edges. Drill pilot holes and counterbore the holes. Attach the feet with 1¼" wood screws **(photo E)**.

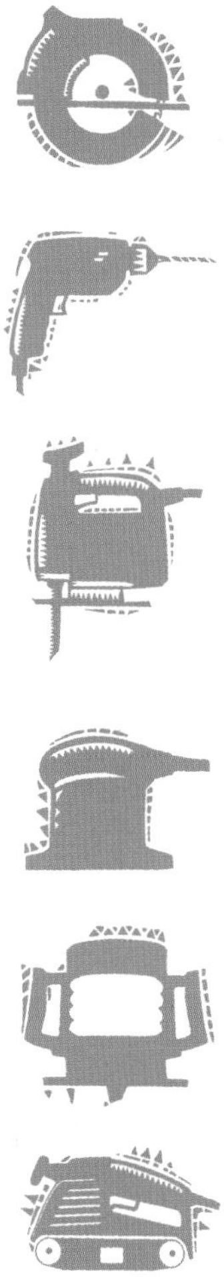

Mirrored Coat Rack

*Nothing welcomes visitors to your home like an elegant,
finely crafted mirrored coat rack.*

CONSTRUCTION MATERIALS

Quantity	Lumber
1	1 × 2" × 3' oak
1	1 × 3" × 4' oak
1	1 × 4" × 6' oak
1	½ × ¾" × 4' molding
1	¼" × 2 × 4' hardboard
1	⅛ × 15¾ × 24¾" mirrored glass

An entryway or foyer can seem naked without a coat rack and a mirror, and this simple oak project gives you both features in one striking package. The egg-and-dart beading at the top and the decorative porcelain and brass coat hooks provide just enough design interest to make the project elegant without overwhelming the essential simplicity of the look.

You can use inexpensive red oak to build your mirrored coat rack. Or, if you are willing to invest a little more money, use quarter-sawn white oak to create an item with the look of a true antique. For a special touch, have the edges of the mirror beveled.

OVERALL SIZE:
22³⁄₄" HIGH
32" WIDE
1¹⁄₂" DEEP

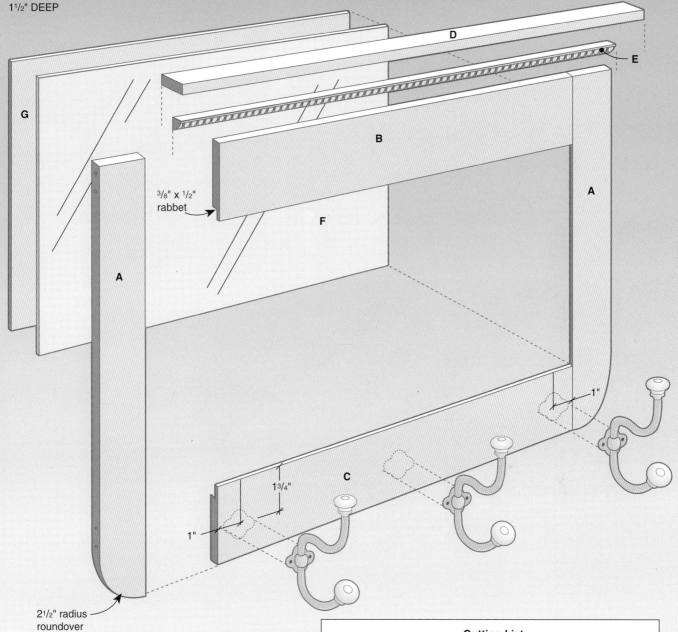

G

D

E

A

B

³⁄₈" x ¹⁄₂"
rabbet

F

A

1"

C

1³⁄₄"

1"

2¹⁄₂" radius
roundover

	Cutting List			
Key	**Part**	**Dimension**	**Pcs.**	**Material**
A	Stile	¾ × 2½ × 22"	2	Oak
B	Top rail	¾ × 3½ × 24"	1	Oak
C	Bottom rail	¾ × 3½ × 24"	1	Oak
D	Cap	¾ × 1½ × 32"	1	Oak
E	Molding	½ × ¾ × 29"	1	Oak
F	Mirror	⅛ × 15¾ × 24¾"	1	Mirror
G	Mirror back	¼ × 15¾ × 24¾"	1	Hardboard

Materials: #6 × 1½" wood screws, 16-ga. × 1" brads, coat hooks with screws (3), ¼ × 36" oak dowel, wood glue, finishing materials.

Note: Measurements reflect the actual size of dimension lumber.

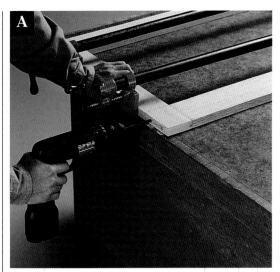

Clamp the frame components together. Then, drill 3½"-deep guide holes for the through-dowel joints.

Drive glued 4"-long oak dowels into the guide holes to make the dowel joints.

Mount a belt sander to your worksurface, and use it to smooth the roundover cuts on the frame.

Directions: Mirrored Coat Rack

MAKE THE MIRROR FRAME. Dowel joints hold the frame together.

1. Cut the stiles (A) to length.

Cut the top rail (B) and bottom rail (C) to length.

2. Lay the rails between the stiles on your worksurface to form a frame. Square the frame and clamp with bar or pipe clamps to hold it together.

3. Drill two evenly spaced ¼"-dia. × 3½"-deep guide holes at each joint, drilling through the stiles and into the rails **(photo A).** Cut eight ¼"-dia. × 4"-long oak dowels. Unclamp the frame assembly, and squirt a little glue into each guide hole. Coat each dowel with a light layer of

glue. Drive a dowel into each guide hole, using a wood mallet so you don't break the dowels **(photo B).**

4. When all joints are made, clamp the frame assembly together. Once the glue has dried, remove the clamps, and trim off the ends of the dowels with a backsaw. Sand them flush with the surface, and scrape off excess glue.

ROUND OVER THE FRAME ENDS.

1. On the bottom end of each stile, draw an arc with a 2½" radius to mark the decorative roundovers. Cut along the arc line, using a jig saw.

2. Smooth the cut with a belt sander mounted to your worksurface **(photo C).**

DRILL MOUNTING HOLES AND CUT THE MIRROR RECESS.

1. Drill ¹¹⁄₆₄" holes through the fronts of the stiles, 6" down from the top, so you can attach the rack to a wall. With a counterbore bit, drill ⅜"-dia. × ¼"-deep counterbores for oak plugs to cover the screw heads after you

TIP

Through-dowel joints are the easiest dowel joints to make—all you need is a good bar or pipe clamp and the ability to drill a reasonably straight guide hole. The visible dowel ends at the joints contribute to the traditional design of the project.

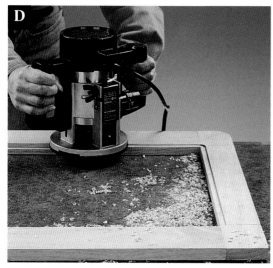

Use a router with a ⅜" rabbeting bit to cut a recess for the mirror in the frame back.

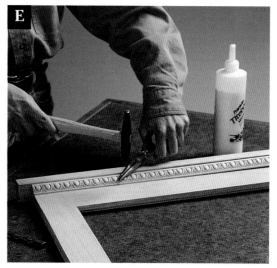

Center egg-and-dart trim molding under the cap, and attach it with glue and brads.

Install the mirror and mirror back. Then, secure them to the frame with brads, using a brad pusher.

hang the coat rack.

2. Cut a rabbet around the back inside edges of the frame to make a recess for the mirror and back. Use a router and a ⅜" rabbeting bit. Set the cutting depth of the router to ⅜", then trim around the back inside edges of the frame **(photo D).** Reset the router depth to ½", and make another pass around the edges to complete the rabbet. Square the grooves at the corners with a wood chisel.

INSTALL THE CAP AND MOLDING.

1. Cut the cap (D) to length.
2. Drill ⁵⁄₃₂" counterbored pilot holes through the cap and into the top rail. Attach the cap flush with the back edge of the rail, using glue and 1½" wood screws. The cap overhangs the stiles 1½" on each end.
3. Cut a piece of egg-and-dart style molding (E) to length. Sand a slight bevel at each end.
4. Attach the molding flush against the underside of the cap, centered side to side, using

glue and 1" brads driven with a tack hammer **(photo E).** Drill ¹⁄₁₆" pilot holes through the molding to prevent splitting. Set the nail heads, using a nail set.

APPLY FINISHING TOUCHES.

1. Fill the screw holes with oak plugs, and sand them flush with the surface.
2. Apply a finish. When it's dry, install the coathooks (see *Diagram*).
3. Set the mirror into the rabbet in the frame. Cut ¼"-thick hardboard to make the mirror back (G), and install it behind the mirror. Secure the mirror and mirror back by driving 1" brads into the edges of the frame with a brad pusher **(photo F).**
4. Hang the coat rack (see *Tip*). Fill the mounting screw holes with oak plugs. Sand them flush with the surface and touch up the area with finish. For a less permanant installation, use decorative brass screws that match the coathooks.

> **TIP**
>
> *Try to hit a wall stud with the mounting screws when hanging heavy objects on a wall. Use toggle bolts to mount where no studs are present.*

Mitten Chest

*This convenient mitten chest keeps your entryway clutter-free
and stores hats and mittens right where you need them.*

CONSTRUCTION MATERIALS

Quantity	Lumber
1	¾" × 4 × 8' plywood
2	½ × 1⅜" × 7' stop molding
1	¼ × ¹⁵⁄₁₆" × 7' corner molding
2	¾ × 1⅜" × 7' cap molding

This roomy mitten chest makes the most of valuable floor space in your entryway. It's large enough to hold all your family's mittens, hats and scarves. Move it to your den or family room, and this chest also makes a fine coffee table.

The mitten chest is a very simple project made from four plywood panels, top and bottom panels and some decorative trim molding.

For a neat, contemporary appearance, paint your mitten chest in soft pastel tones. Or try an antiquing technique to make it look like a family heirloom.

Another finishing option for the mitten chest is to line the interior with aromatic cedar liners to ward off moths and give your hand and head gear a fresh scent. Aromatic cedar liners are sold in 4 × 8 sheets or self-adhesive strips.

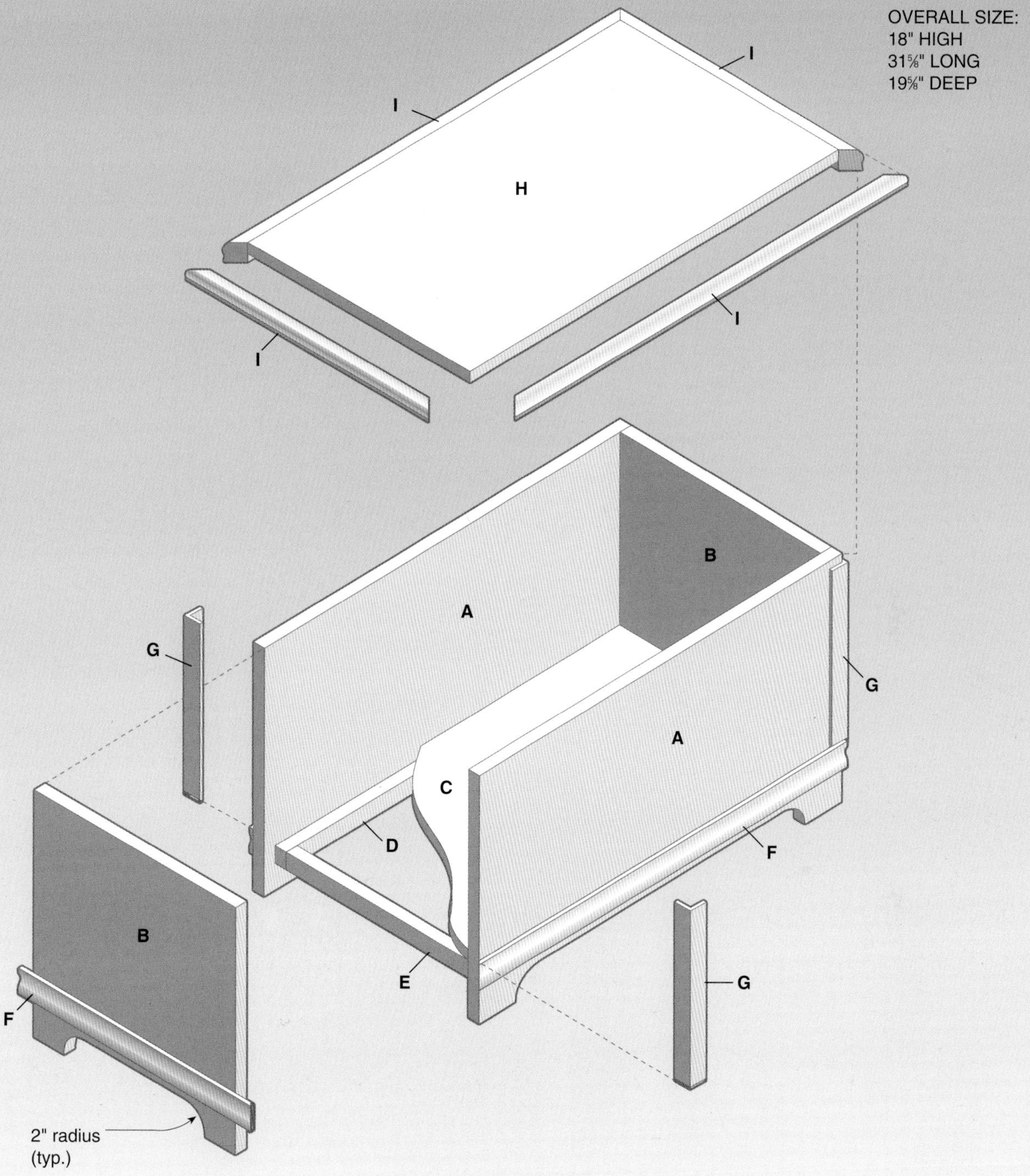
OVERALL SIZE:
18" HIGH
31⅝" LONG
19⅝" DEEP
I
I
H
I
I
B
A
G
G
A
C
D
F
B
E
G
F
2" radius
(typ.)

Cutting List

Key	Part	Dimension	Pcs.	Material
A	Side panel	¾ × 17¼ × 30"	2	Plywood
B	End panel	¾ × 17¼ × 16½"	2	Plywood
C	Bottom panel	¾ × 16½ × 28½"	1	Plywood
D	Side cleat	¾ × 1½ × 28½"	2	Plywood
E	End cleat	¾ × 1½ × 15"	2	Plywood

Cutting List

Key	Part	Dimension	Pcs.	Material
F	Bottom molding	½ × 1⅜" × *	4	Stop molding
G	Corner molding	¼ × 1$\frac{5}{16}$ × 12"	4	Corner molding
H	Lid	¾ × 18⅛ × 30⅛"	1	Plywood
I	Top cap	¾ × 1⅜" × *	4	Cap molding

Materials: #6 × 1¼" and 2" wood screws, 16-ga. × ¾" and 1¼" brads, 2d and 4d finish nails, wood glue, finishing materials.

Note: Measurements reflect the actual size of dimension lumber.

*Cut to fit.

A

Use a jig saw and a straightedge as a guide to make the "kick space" cuts in the end and side panels.

Directions:
Mitten Chest

MAKE THE SIDES AND ENDS.
1. Cut the side panels (A) and end panels (B) to size.
2. Draw cutting lines on the sides, 2" up from one long edge to mark the cutouts on the bottom edges of the sides. Use a compass to draw the curved lines at the ends of each cutout. Set the compass for a 2"-radius, and position the point of the compass as close as possible to the bottom edge, 5" in from the ends of the side panels. Draw the semi-circles. Clamp the sides to your worksurface, and make the cutouts with a jig saw, using a straightedge to guide the long, straight portion of the cut **(photo A)**.

3. Draw the cutting lines 2" up from the bottom of each end panel. Set the compass for a 2"-radius, and position the point of the compass as close as possible to the bottom edge, 4¼" in from the ends of the end panels. Draw the semicircles, and make the cutouts with a jig saw and straightedge. Sand all edges smooth.

ASSEMBLE THE CHEST.
Attach cleats to the inside faces of the side and end panels. The cleats support the bottom panel of the chest, so it is important to attach them so their top edges are aligned and level.
1. Cut the side cleats (D) and end cleats (E) to size.
2. Draw reference lines on the side and end panels, 3½" up from the bottom edges and ¾" in from the side edges. Position the cleats so their top edges are

B

Center the end cleats over the kick spaces, leaving ¾" at each end where the side cleats will fit.

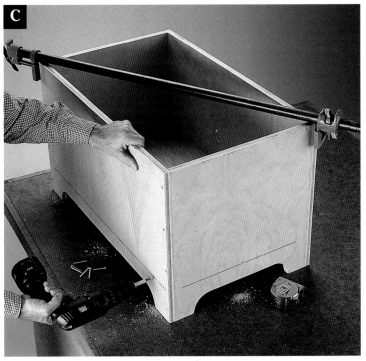

C

Draw opposite chest corners together with a bar or pipe clamp to keep the chest square.

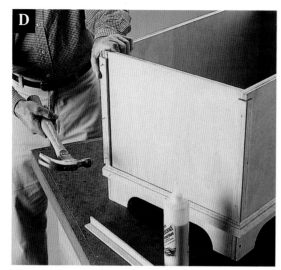

Fasten the corner molding over the corners to conceal the joints and screw heads.

Attach the top cap around the perimeter of the lid. Drive nails in partially before positioning the strips.

flush with the reference lines. Drill ⁵⁄₆₄" pilot holes through the cleats and into the panels. Counterbore the holes ⅛" deep, using a ⅜" counterbore bit. Fasten with glue and 1¼" wood screws **(photo B).**

3. Position the end panels between the side panels with the cleats facing in. Drill counterbored pilot holes through the side panels and into the end panels. Fasten with glue and evenly spaced 2" wood screws. Make sure the top and bottom edges are flush and the outside faces of the ends are flush with the side edges.

4. Cut the bottom panel (C) to size, and sand it smooth. Test-fit the bottom panel by setting it on top of the cleats. Remove the panel. Apply glue to the top edges of the cleats and along the underside edges of the panel, and reposition the panel inside the chest. Clamp diagonal chest corners with a bar or pipe clamp to hold the piece square while you fasten the bottom panel **(photo C).** To make sure you drive the screws directly into the bottom, mark

the screw centerpoints 3⅞" up from the bottoms of the sides and ends. Drill pilot holes through the sides and ends and into the edges of the bottom panel. Counterbore the holes. Attach with 2" wood screws.

ATTACH THE MOLDING.
1. Cut the bottom molding (F) to fit around the chest, mitering the ends at 45°.

2. Position the molding so the top edges are 4⅜" up from the bottom edges of the sides and ends. Fasten it with glue and 4d finish nails, driven through ¹⁄₁₆" pilot holes. Apply glue, and drive 2d nails through the joints where the molding pieces meet to lock-nail the pieces (see *Tip*, page 154).

3. Cut the corner molding (G) to length. Use glue and ¾" brads to fasten the corner molding over the joints between the end and side panels **(photo D).** Make sure the bottom edges of the corner molding butt against the top edges of the bottom molding. Sand the bottom edges of the corner molding to meet the

bottom molding. Sand the top edges of the ends and sides to smooth the edges and corners.

MAKE THE LID.
1. Cut the lid (H) to size, and sand it smooth.

2. Cut four pieces of top cap (I) to fit around the perimeter of the lid.

3. Drill ¹⁄₁₆" pilot holes. Use glue and 4d finish nails to attach the top cap pieces, keeping the top edges flush with the top face of the lid **(photo E).** Glue and lock-nail the mitered corner joints. Set the lid into the top opening—no hinges are used.

APPLY FINISHING TOUCHES.
1. Use a nail set to set all nails and brads on the chest.

2. Fill all visible nail holes with wood putty and sand any rough spots smooth.

3. Finish-sand the entire chest. Finish as desired. We used two coats of glossy enamel because it is easiest to clean.

Mission Window Seat

*Curl up with a good book,
or just enjoy the view from this cozy window seat.*

CONSTRUCTION MATERIALS

Quantity	Lumber
3	1 × 2" × 8' oak
1	1 × 2" × 6' oak
1	1 × 3" × 6' oak
4	1 × 4" × 6' oak
9	½ × 1¾" × 4' oak*
1	½ × 2¾" × 2' oak*
8	½ × 2¾" × 3' oak*
2	½ × 2¾" × 4' oak*
1	½ × 2¾" × 5' oak*
6	½ × 3¾" × 5' oak*
1	¾" × 2 × 6' oak plywood

*Stock sizes commonly available at most wood-
working supply stores.

You'll find this Mission-style window seat to be an excellent place to spend an afternoon. Though it fits nicely under a window, the frame is wide enough so you won't ever feel cramped. The length is perfect for taking a nap, enjoying a sunset or watching children playing in the yard. Or perhaps you'd prefer to sit elsewhere to simply admire your craftsmanship from a distance.

The window seat uses oak for its strength and warm texture, and includes a frame face and nosing trim for a more elegant appearance. The rails are capped to make comfortable armrests, and the back is set lower than the sides so it won't block your window view. Though this project has many parts, it requires few tools and is remarkably easy to build. A few hours of labor will reward you with a delightful place to enjoy many hours of relaxation.

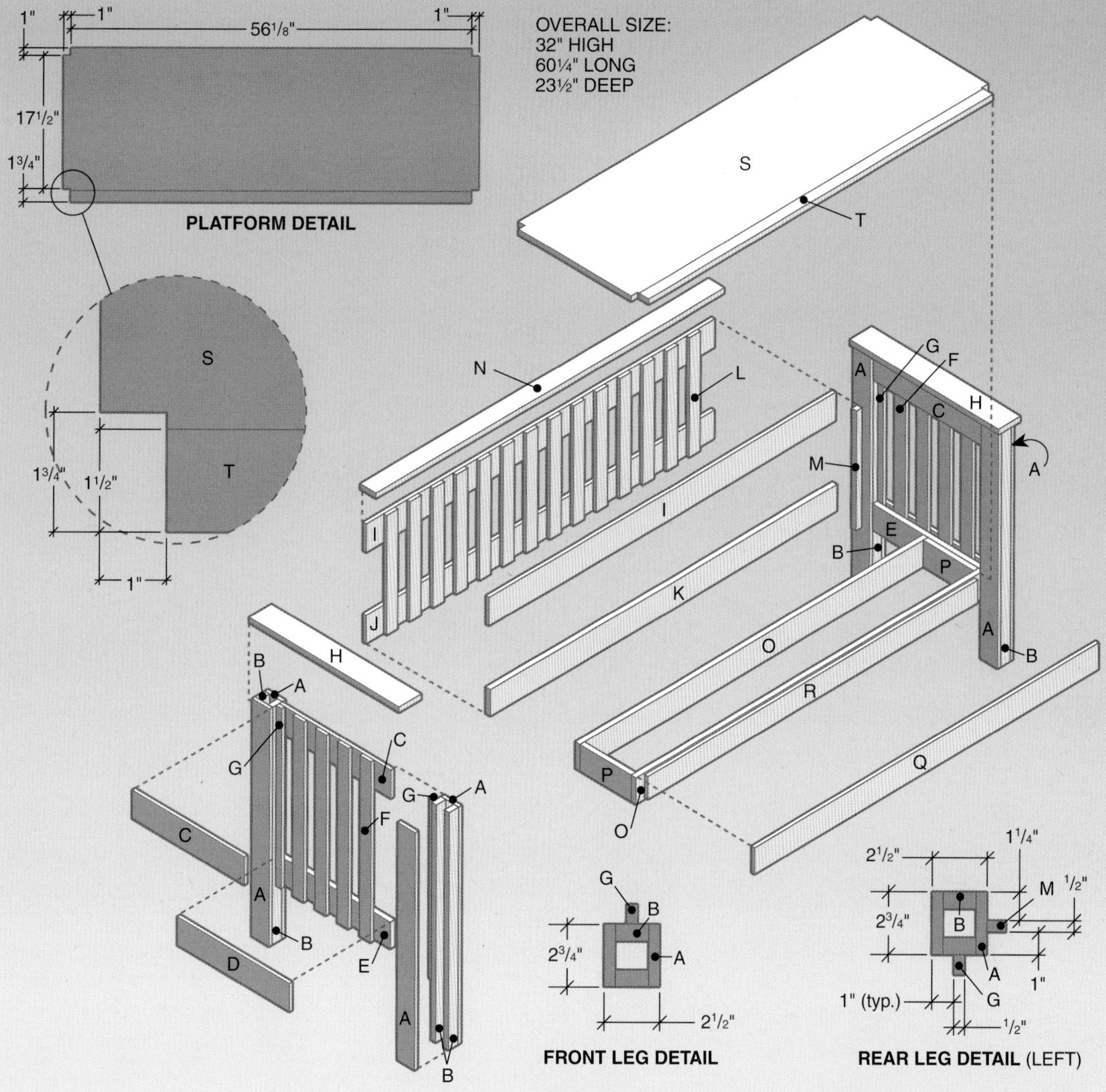
OVERALL SIZE:
32" HIGH
60¼" LONG
23½" DEEP
PLATFORM DETAIL
56⅛"
17½"
1¾"
1"
1½"
FRONT LEG DETAIL
2¾"
2½"
REAR LEG DETAIL (LEFT)
2½"
1¼"
2¾"
½"
1" (typ.)
1"

Key	Part	Dimension	Pcs.	Material
A	Wide leg piece	½ × 2¾ × 31¼"	8	Oak
B	Narrow leg piece	¾ × 1½ × 31¼"	8	Oak
C	End top rail	½ × 3¾ × 17½"	4	Oak
D	Outer bottom rail	½ × 3¾ × 17½"	2	Oak
E	Inner bottom rail	¾ × 3½ × 17½"	2	Oak
F	End slat	½ × 1¾ × 23¾"	8	Oak
G	End half slat	½ × ⅞ × 23¾"	4	Oak
H	End cap	¾ × 3½ × 23½"	2	Oak
I	Back top rail	½ × 3¾ × 54¼"	2	Oak
J	Outer bottom rail	½ × 3¾ × 54¼"	1	Oak

Cutting List

Key	Part	Dimension	Pcs.	Material
K	Inner bottom rail	¾ × 3½ × 54¼"	1	Oak
L	Back slat	½ × 1¾ × 15¾"	14	Oak
M	Back half slat	½ × ⅞ × 15¾"	2	Oak
N	Back cap	¾ × 2½ × 54¼"	1	Oak
O	Support side	¾ × 3½ × 54¾"	2	Oak
P	Support end	¾ × 3½ × 8"	2	Oak
Q	Frame face	½ × 3¾ × 54¼"	1	Oak
R	Spacer	½ × 2¾ × 52"	1	Oak
S	Platform	¾ × 18¾ × 56⅛"	1	Plywood
T	Platform nosing	¾ × 1½ × 54⅛"	1	Oak

Materials: #6 × ⅝", 1¼" and 1½" wood screws, 16-ga. × 1" brads, 3d finish nails, ¾" oak veneer edge tape (8'), ⅜"-dia. oak plugs, wood glue, finishing materials.

Note: Measurements reflect the actual size of dimension lumber.

Assemble the legs with glue and clamps, using wax paper to protect your worksurface.

Attach the end slats to the outer rails with glue and wood screws, using a spacer as a guide.

Directions: Mission Window Seat

For all screws used in this project, drill ³⁄₃₂" pilot holes. Counterbore the holes ¼" deep, using a ⅜" counterbore bit.

ASSEMBLE THE LEGS.
1. Cut the wide leg pieces (A) and narrow leg pieces (B) to length.
2. Lay a narrow leg piece on your worksurface. Butt a wide leg piece against an edge to form an "L." Apply wood glue, and clamp the pieces together **(photo A).**
3. Assemble and glue together another "L" in the same fashion. Glue the two L-assemblies together to form a leg. Repeat to make the other legs.

BUILD THE END ASSEMBLIES.
To ensure that the end rails and slats remain square during the assembly process, build a simple jig by attaching two 2 × 2 boards at a 90° angle along adjacent edges of a 24 × 48" piece of plywood.
1. Cut the end top rails (C), outer bottom rails (D), inner bottom rails (E) and end slats (F) to length. Sand the pieces smooth.
2. Place a top rail and an outer bottom rail in the jig. Position two slats over the rails, 2⅝" in

> **TIP**
>
> *Take care to counterbore for all screw heads when building furniture that will be used as seating.*

from each end. Adjust the pieces so the ends of the slats are flush with the edges of the rails, and keep the entire assembly tight against the jig. Attach with glue, and drive ⅝" wood screws through the slats and into the rails.
3. Using a 1¾"-wide spacer, attach the remaining end slats with glue and ⅝" wood screws **(photo B).** NOTE: Make sure to test-fit all of the slats for uniform spacing before attaching them to the rails.
4. Position an inner bottom rail over the slats, ¼" up from the

Attach the end half slats to the legs with glue and wood screws.

Attach the lower inner rail with glue and screws and the upper inner rail with glue and finish nails.

bottom edges of the slats. Attach it with glue, and drive 1¼" wood screws through the inner bottom rail and the slats.

5. Place a top rail over the slats, and attach it with glue and 1" brads.

6. Repeat the process to build the other end assembly.

BUILD THE BACK ASSEMBLY.
1. Cut the back top rails (I), the outer bottom rail (J), the inner bottom rail (K) and the back slats (L) to length. Sand the pieces smooth.

2. Place a top rail and the inner bottom rail in the jig. Place two back slats on the rails, 2¾" in from each end. Adjust the pieces so the ends of the slats are flush with the edge of the top rail and overhang the edge of the bottom rail by ¼". Attach

the pieces with glue, and drive ⅝" wood screws through the slats and into the rails. Test-fit the remaining slats, spacing them about 1⅞" apart. Attach them with glue and screws.

3. Position the outer bottom rail so the edge is flush with the bottom edges of the slats. Attach the bottom rail with glue and 1" brads.

4. Place the remaining top rail over the slats. Attach it with glue and 1" brads.

JOIN THE LEGS TO THE END ASSEMBLIES.
Half slats attached to the legs serve as cleats for attaching the end assembly.

1. Cut the end half slats (G) to size from ½ × 2¾" × 4' stock.

2. Place each leg on your work-surface with a narrow leg piece

facing up. Center the half slat on the face of the leg (see *Diagram*), with the top ends flush. Attach the half slats to the legs with glue. Drive 1¼" wood screws, locating them so the screw heads will be hidden by the rails when the seat is completed **(photo C).**

3. Position an end assembly between a front and rear leg so the half slats fit between the rails and the top edges are flush. Attach the parts with glue. Drive 1¼" wood screws through the inner bottom rail and into the half slats, taking care to avoid other screws.

4. Attach the top rail to the half slats with glue and 3d finish nails driven through ¹⁄₁₆" pilot holes **(photo D).**

5. Repeat this process for the other end assembly.

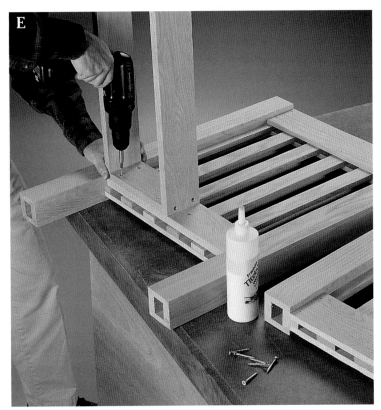

Attach the support frame with glue, and drive screws through the support end and into the inner bottom rail.

Glue the platform nosing to the platform and hold it in place with bar clamps.

MAKE THE SUPPORT FRAME.

The support frame attaches to the inner bottom rails on the end assemblies and supports the seat.

1. Cut the support sides (O) and ends (P) to length.

2. Position the ends between the sides. Join the pieces with glue and 1¼" wood screws.

3. Lay one end assembly on your worksurface. Position the support frame upright so the front corner of the frame is tight against the front leg and the edges of the frame are flush with the edges of the bottom rail. Attach the support frame to the end assembly with glue and 1¼" wood screws **(photo E).**

4. Stand the window seat upright, and clamp the other end in position. Attach it with glue and 1¼" wood screws.

ATTACH THE BACK.

Like the end assemblies, the back assembly attaches to the legs with half slats.

1. Cut the back half slats (M) to size from ½ × 2¾" × 2' stock.

2. Measure 7½" up from the bottom on the inside face of each rear leg, and draw a horizontal line. Measure in 1¼" from the back edge of the leg along this line, and draw a vertical line upward.

3. Position a half slat against the leg so its rear edge is on the vertical line and its bottom edge is on the horizontal line. Attach the half slat to the leg with glue and 1¼" wood screws. Repeat this step with the other rear leg.

4. Slide the back assembly over the half slats so the top edges are flush. Attach with glue, and drive 1¼" wood screws through the inner bottom rail and into

the half slats.

5. Drill ¹⁄₁₆" pilot holes, and join the top rail to the back half slats with glue and 3d finish nails.

ATTACH THE CAPS.

Caps attach to the ends and back of the window seat to create armrests and a backrest.

1. Cut the end caps (H) and back cap (N) to length.

2. Center the end caps over the end assemblies, with the back edges flush. Attach the pieces with glue, and drive 1½" wood screws through the end caps and into the legs.

3. Position the back cap over the back assembly so the front edge is flush with the front edges of the legs. Attach with glue, and drive 1½" wood screws through the back cap and into the top rails.

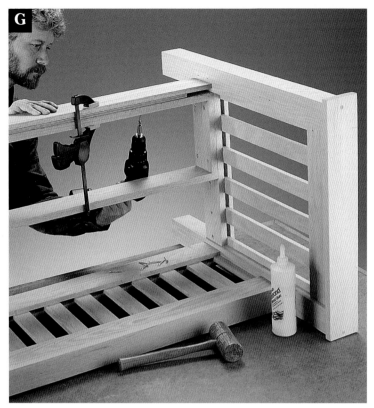

Clamp the spacer and frame face to the support frame. Attach them with glue, and drive screws through the inside of the support frame.

Attach the platform to the rails, frame face and support frame with glue and wood screws.

MAKE THE PLATFORM.

The oak nosing and edge tape create the appearance of solid wood.

1. Cut the platform (S) and platform nosing (T) to size. Sand the top face of the platform smooth.

2. Glue the nosing to the front edge of the platform, leaving 1" exposed on each end. Clamp the nosing in place until the glue dries **(photo F).**

3. Use a jig saw to cut a 1 × 1" notch in each back corner of the platform and a 1 × 1¾" notch in each front corner to accommodate the legs (see *Diagram*). Apply self-adhesive oak veneer edge tape to the side and back edges of the platform. (Don't apply tape to the notches.) Lightly sand the edges of the tape.

ATTACH THE FRAME FACE.

1. Cut the frame face (Q) and spacer (R) to length.

2. Glue the pieces together, centering the spacer on the frame face. Clamp the pieces together until the glue dries.

3. Position the frame face assembly against the front of the support frame so the top edges of the face and support frame are flush. Attach with glue, and drive 1¼" wood screws from inside the support frame **(photo G).**

ATTACH THE PLATFORM.

Attach the platform to the support frame, frame face and bottom rails with glue and 1½" wood screws **(photo H).**

APPLY FINISHING TOUCHES.

1. Fill the screw holes with glued oak plugs. Sand them flush with the surface. Set all nails with a nail set, and fill the nail holes with wood putty. Scrape off any excess glue, and finish-sand the window seat.

2. Apply the stain of your choice and a coat of polyurethane.

3. Add seat cushions that complement the wood tones of the window seat and the decorating scheme of your room.

> **TIP**
>
> *If you find nail holes that were not filled before you applied stain and finish, you can go back and fill the holes with a putty stick that closely matches the color of the wood stain.*

Living Room Projects

H ere are some great projects to customize your living room. You can display your collections on a rotating basis with the versatile collector's table or the space saving corner display stand. Make use of underutilized space by building a behind-the-sofa bookcase or mantel. Always wanted to add some vintage charm, but not willing to pay antique dealer prices? Try the wall-mounted knickknack shelf or the dry sink. From the two-tier bookshelf made without fasteners or glue to the picture frames that require precision cuts and joining—you're sure to find a challenging and rewarding project here.

PROJECT
POWER TOOLS

Two-tier Bookshelf

*Here's a smart looking, easy-to-build project
that requires no glue, screws or nails!*

CONSTRUCTION MATERIALS

Quantity	Lumber
1	¾" × 4 × 8' Baltic birch plywood
1	1" × 2' birch dowel

This two-tier bookshelf provides ample room for encyclopedias, dictionaries and other useful references. Its distinctive profile complements many decorating motifs, and with the right finish, it can become a vibrant accent piece. The bookshelf uses a joinery method, known as *pinned* *mortise-and-tenon*, that requires no glue, screws or nails. Instead, wedges hold the joints together. When moving or storing the unit, you can simply remove the wedges.

With the included plan for a mortising jig, you can easily make several of these bookshelves to give as gifts.

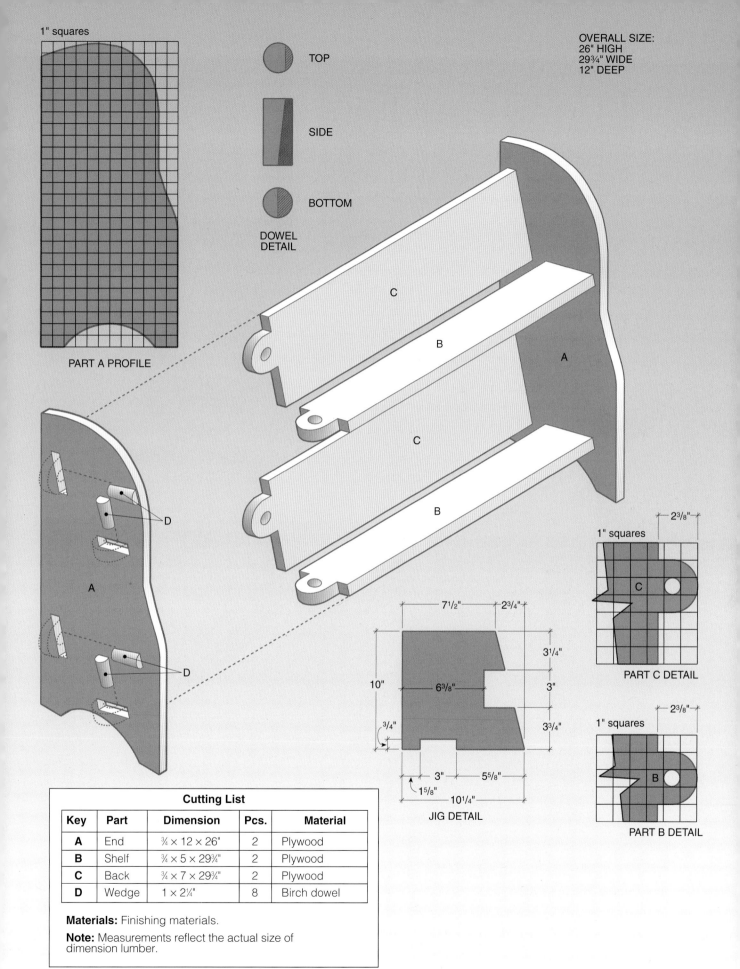

1" squares

PART A PROFILE

TOP

SIDE

BOTTOM

DOWEL
DETAIL

OVERALL SIZE:
26" HIGH
29¾" WIDE
12" DEEP

C

B

A

C

B

A

D

D

2³/₈"

1" squares

C

PART C DETAIL

7¹/₂"   2³/₄"

3¹/₄"

10"   6³/₈"   3"

³/₄"   3³/₄"

3"   5⁵/₈"

1⁵/₈"

10¹/₄"

JIG DETAIL

2³/₈"

1" squares

B

PART B DETAIL

Cutting List

Key	Part	Dimension	Pcs.	Material
A	End	¾ × 12 × 26"	2	Plywood
B	Shelf	¾ × 5 × 29¾"	2	Plywood
C	Back	¾ × 7 × 29¾"	2	Plywood
D	Wedge	1 × 2¼"	8	Birch dowel

Materials: Finishing materials.

Note: Measurements reflect the actual size of
dimension lumber.

Directions:
Two-tier Bookshelf

MAKE THE JIG.
A jig will help you accurately mark the location of mortises.
1. Cut a 10 × 10¼" blank from a scrap of ¼" material.
2. Measure and mark the diagonal line and the locations for the mortise guides (see *Diagram*). Use a jig saw to cut out the jig **(photo A).**

CUT THE ENDS.
1. Cut the ends (A) to size. Transfer the pattern (see *Diagram*), and cut with a jig saw.
2. Lay both ends on your workbench with the back edges together, forming a mirror image. Measure from the bottom back corners and mark reference points at ⅞" and 14¾" **(photo B).**

3. Lay out the mortises by positioning the bottom back corner of the jig at the first reference point, keeping the back edges flush. Outline the two lower mortises. Slide the jig up to the second reference point, and mark the two higher mortises **(photo C).**
4. Remove the jig, and draw lines to close the ¾ × 3" rectangles. Drill starter holes, using a backer board. Cut the mortises with a jig saw **(photo D).**

CUT THE SHELVES
AND BACKS.
1. Cut the shelves (B) and backs (C) to size.
2. Lay out the profile for the tenons (see *Diagram*), and cut them out with a jig saw. Sand the edges smooth.

TIP

To yield an opening large enough to accommodate the tenons, make sure the mortises on your pattern are slightly oversized.

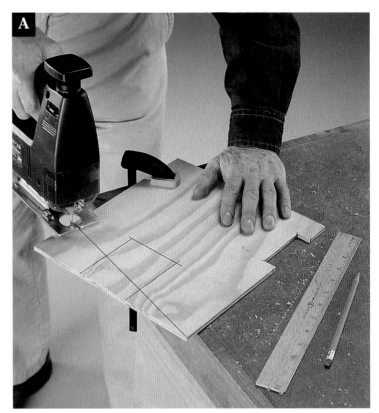

Use a piece of ¼" scrap plywood and your jig saw to create the mortising jig.

Mark reference points at ⅞" and at 14¾" along the backs of both sides as guides for positioning the mortising jig.

3. Drill wedge holes with a 1" spade bit. Use a backer board to prevent tear outs. Test-fit the tenons in the mortises. Adjust them if necessary.

MAKE THE WEDGES.
1. Cut 1"-dia. dowels to 2¼" lengths.
2. Measure from the edge, and mark reference lines across the top of the dowel at ¼" and across the bottom at ½".

Use the jig to mark the locations of both pairs of mortises. Then, flip the jig and mark corresponding mortises on the other end piece.

Drill pilot holes, using a backer board to prevent splintering, and cut the mortises with a jig saw.

TIP

When a project has modern lines, you can create a very interesting accent piece by applying an exotic-colored aniline dye. A rich burgundy or a bright green would create vibrant accents.

Connect the lines. Sand down the dowels to this line, using a belt sander clamped to your worksurface **(photo E).**
3. Assemble the shelves and backs between the ends, and test-fit the wedges. Disassemble the bookshelf for finishing.

APPLY FINISHING TOUCHES. Finish-sand the entire project. Then, paint or finish the bookshelf as desired. When the finish dries, assemble the pieces.

Sand the wedges to the lines, using a belt sander clamped to your worksurface.

Plant Stand

Our plant stand is a great way to display your favorite potted foliage. Build it for a corner in your sunniest room.

This plant stand is a perfect platform on which to set your favorite indoor plants. The simple lines and ceramic tile surfaces help focus the attention on the plants themselves, rather than on the stand. Make no mistake, however—our plant stand has a sleek design that fits nearly any

environment or decor. Once you paint it, you can put it almost anywhere to showcase your plants. It's lightweight, so you can move it easily from place to place. But it's strong enough to support heavy pots easily.

The leg assemblies provide a sturdy base, while ceramic tile inserts on the shelf and top give our plant stand some weight

and stability. It's perfect for a corner nook in a sun room or kitchen, and the tile pieces make cleaning up spills an easy task. What's more, the ceramic tile will not fall apart or rot due to moisture and aging. So, you are sure to enjoy this original and practical plant stand for many years.

CONSTRUCTION MATERIALS

Quantity	Lumber
1	1 × 8" × 4' pine
2	1 × 3" × 10' pine
1	½ × 1" × 8' pine stop molding
1	½" × 2 × 2' plywood

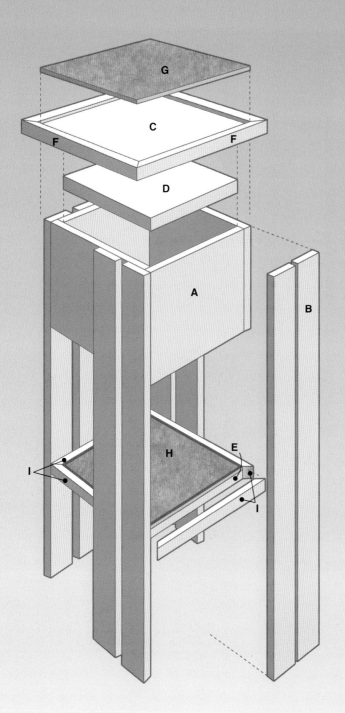

OVERALL SIZE:
30⅜" HIGH
13¼" WIDE
13¼" DEEP

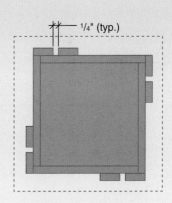

¼" (typ.)

LEG LAYOUT DETAIL

Cutting List				
Key	**Part**	**Dimension**	**Pcs.**	**Material**
A	Box side	¾ × 7¼ × 8"	4	Pine
B	Leg	¾ × 2½ × 29½"	8	Pine
C	Top tile base	½ × 12¼ × 12¼"	1	Plywood
D	Box top	¾ × 7¼ × 7¼"	1	Pine
E	Shelf	½ × 7¾ × 7¾"	1	Plywood

Cutting List				
Key	**Part**	**Dimension**	**Pcs.**	**Material**
F	Top frame	½ × 1 × 13¼"	4	Molding
G	Top tile	12 × 12"	1	Ceramic
H	Shelf tile	7½ × 7½"	1	Ceramic
I	Shelf frame	½ × 1 × 8¾"	4	Molding

Materials: 1", 1¼" and 1½" deck screws, 3d and 4d finish nails, wood glue, finishing materials, ceramic tile, ceramic tile adhesive, tinted grout.

Specialty tools: V-notch adhesive trowel, grout float.

Note: Measurements reflect the actual size of dimension lumber.

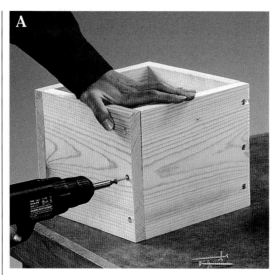

Assemble the box using simple butt joints.

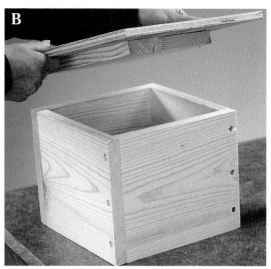

Place the top tile base and box top onto the box, and fasten them with screws.

Attach the leg pairs with glue and screws, obscuring the visible joints on the box.

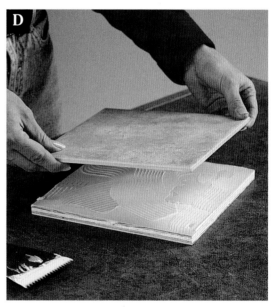

Spread an even layer of adhesive over the shelf, and attach the tile.

Directions: Plant Stand

BUILD THE BOX.
Tile size varies from piece to piece, so measure your tile before cutting the top tile base (C). Allow a ⅛" gap for the

grout joint between the tile and the top frame.
1. Cut the box sides (A), top tile base (C) and box top (D) to size. Sand with 150-grit sandpaper.
2. Fasten the sides with simple butt joints, which will be obscured by the legs. Drill ⁵⁄₆₄" pilot holes. Counterbore the holes ⅛" deep, using a ⅜" counterbore bit. Use glue and 1½" deck screws to attach the sides together, making sure the edges

are flush **(photo A).**
3. Center the box top on the bottom face of the top tile base. Fasten the pieces by driving 1" deck screws through the top tile base and into the box top.
4. Place the top tile base and box top onto the box **(photo B).** Drill counterbored pilot holes through the box sides and into the box top. Attach the box top with 1½" deck screws.

ATTACH THE LEGS.

1. Cut the legs (B) to length.
2. Drill countersunk pilot holes through the legs and into the box sides. Fasten the legs to the sides with glue and 1¼" deck screws. Each outside leg is flush with the side edge and each leg pair has a ¼"-wide space between the pieces **(photo C).**

ATTACH THE SHELF.

1. Cut the shelf (E) to size.
2. Miter-cut the shelf frame (I) pieces to length.
3. Attach the shelf tile (H) to the shelf with tile adhesive **(photo D).** Spread the adhesive on the shelf, using a V-notch trowel. Press the tile into place, centered on the shelf, and allow to dry.
4. Fasten the shelf frame to the shelf with 3d finish nails. Align the top frame edges flush with the top face of the tile.
5. Attach the shelf to the legs by driving 4d finish nails through the legs and into the frame and shelf **(photo E).** The lower edge of the shelf should be 10" from the legs' bottom edges.

ATTACH THE TOP TILE.

1. Miter-cut the top frame (F) pieces to length.
2. Attach the top tile (G) to the top tile base with adhesive. Nail the top frame in place against the top tile base, keeping the top edges flush with the tile face **(photo F).** When driving the nails, be sure they line up with the top tile base, not the tile.

APPLY FINISHING TOUCHES.

1. Set all nails with a nail set, fill nail and screw holes with wood putty, and finish-sand all surfaces.
2. Prime and paint the plant stand. Coat it with two coats of satin-gloss polyurethane finish and allow to dry.
3. Mask the frame pieces with masking tape. Fill the gaps between the tiles and frames with tinted grout. Use a small grout float to pack the grout into the gaps. Smooth the joints with a damp sponge to remove excess grout.

(left) Use pieces of scrap wood as spacers, and attach the shelf with 4d finish nails.
(above) Install the top frame around the top tile base, using a lightweight tack hammer and 3d finish nails.

PROJECT
POWER TOOLS

Tile-top Coffee Table

*The dramatic, contrasting textures of floor tiles and warm red oak
will make you forget that this table is designed to create storage.*

CONSTRUCTION MATERIALS

Quantity	Lumber
1	¾" × 4 × 8' oak plywood
2	1 × 2" × 8' oak
2	1 × 4" × 8' oak
1	⅞ × ⅞" × 8' oak corner molding

Functionally, the trim size and the ample proportions of the storage shelf are the two most important features of this tile-top coffee table. But most people won't notice that. They'll be too busy admiring the striking tile tabletop and the clean oak lines of the table base.

Measuring a convenient 45" long × 20¼" wide, this coffee table will fit nicely even in smaller rooms. The shelf below is ideal for storing books,

magazines, newspapers, photo albums or anything else you want to keep within arm's reach when sitting on your sofa.

We used 6 × 6" ceramic floor tiles for our coffee table, but you can use just about any type or size of floor tile you want—just be sure to use floor tile, not wall tile, which is thinner and fractures more easily.

After you've built this tile-top coffee table, you may like it so much that you'll want to build a tile-top end table to match.

OVERALL SIZE:
16" HIGH
20¼" WIDE
45" LONG

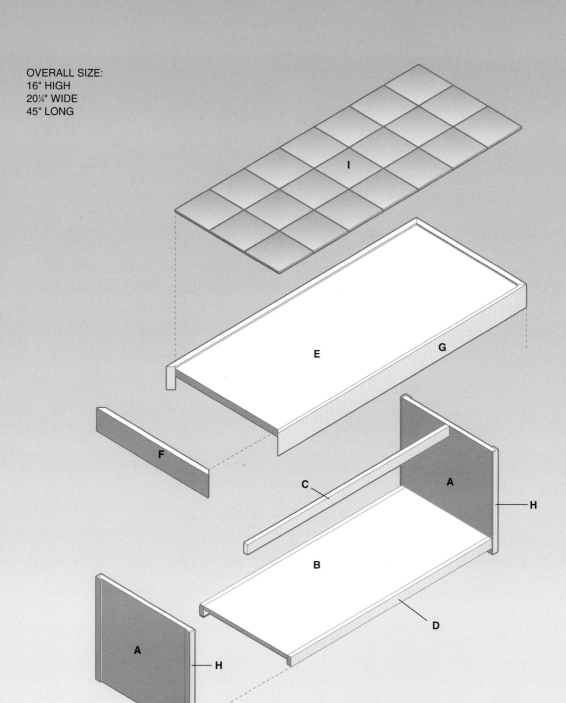

Cutting List

Key	Part	Dimension	Pcs.	Material
A	Side panel	¾ × 16 × 15"	2	Plywood
B	Shelf panel	¾ × 14½ × 35"	1	Plywood
C	Stringer	¾ × 1½ × 35"	1	Oak
D	Shelf edge	¾ × 1½ × 35"	2	Oak
E	Top panel	¾ × 18¾ × 43½"	1	Plywood

Cutting List

Key	Part	Dimension	Pcs.	Material
F	End skirt	¾ × 3½ × 20¼"	2	Oak
G	Side skirt	¾ × 3½ × 45"	2	Oak
H	Corner trim	⅞ × ⅞ × 15"	4	Corner molding
I	Table tiles	¼ × 6 × 6"	21	Ceramic

Materials: #6 × 1½" wood screws, 3d and 6d finish nails, ⅜"-dia. oak plugs, wood glue, finishing materials, ceramic tile adhesive, tinted grout, ³⁄₁₆" plastic tile spacers, silicone grout sealer.

Specialty tools: V-notch adhesive trowel, rubber mallet, grout float.

Note: Measurements reflect the actual size of dimension lumber.

Fasten the shelf edges to the shelf panel with glue and 6d finish nails.

Secure the stringer in place with glue and screws.

Directions:
Tile-top Coffee Table

ASSEMBLE THE TABLE BASE.

1. Cut the side panels (A) and shelf panel (B) to size using a circular saw and a straightedge as a cutting guide. Sand the faces of the plywood smooth with medium-grit sandpaper.

2. Cut the shelf edges (D) to length.

3. Fasten the shelf edges to the shelf panel with glue and 6d finish nails **(photo A).** Be sure to drill ³⁄₃₂" pilot holes through the edge pieces so you don't split them. Keep the top surfaces of the shelf edges and shelf panel flush when fastening.

4. Position the shelf upright, and set the shelf edging on ¾"-thick spacers. Stand a side panel upright on its bottom edge, against the end of the shelf panel. Keep

Miter-cut and attach one skirt board at a time to ensure a proper fit.

the edges of the side panel flush with the outside surfaces of the shelf edging. Drill ⁵⁄₆₄" pilot holes through the side panels and into the edges of the shelf panel. Counterbore the holes ¼" deep, using a ⅜" counterbore bit. Fasten the side panel to the shelf panel with glue and 1½" wood screws. Fasten the other side panel to the shelf panel.

5. Cut the stringer (C) to length.

6. Position the stringer between the side panels, flush with the top edges and centered midway across the side panels. Clamp it in place with a bar or pipe clamp. Drill pilot holes through the side panels and into the stringer. Counterbore the holes.

Remove the clamps and secure the stringer with glue and 1½" wood screws **(photo B).**

MAKE THE TABLETOP FRAME.

The tabletop frame is a plywood panel framed with 1 × 4 oak. The joints in the 1 × 4 frame are mitered—you can use most manual miter boxes to cut a 1 × 4 placed on edge, but a power miter box is ideal for the job.

1. Cut the top panel (E) to size, using a circular saw and a straightedge as a cutting guide.

2. Position the top panel on the side panels. Be sure to leave an equal overhang on the ends

---

TIP

Ceramic tile varies greatly in size and style. This tabletop design is based on using 6 × 6" tiles with ³⁄₁₆" gaps between tiles. If you use tiles of a different size, you may need to resize the plywood table panel to fit your layout. Or, you can have the tiles cut to fit at the tile store.

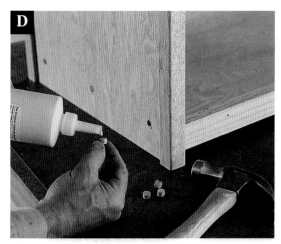

Fill all visible screw holes with oak plugs.

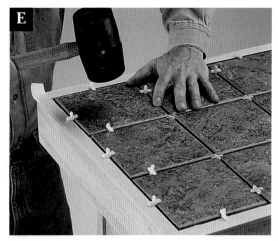

Tap the tiles lightly with a rubber mallet to set them firmly in the adhesive.

and sides. Drill pilot holes through the top panel and into the side panels and stringer. Counterbore the holes. Fasten with glue and 1½" wood screws.

3. Cut the end skirts (F) and side skirts (G) to length. Although the *Cutting List* on page 79 gives exact dimensions for these parts, it's best to cut the first part slightly longer than specified. Then, custom-cut it to fit. Cut all the other skirt boards to length, using the first board as a guide **(photo C).**

4. Using a tile as a gauge, position the skirt pieces to create a lip slightly higher than the top of the tile. Drill pilot holes through the skirt boards, and fasten the boards to the edges of the top panel with glue and 6d finish nails.

FASTEN THE CORNER TRIM.
1. Cut the corner trim (H) pieces to length.
2. Fasten the corner trim to the side panel edges with glue and 3d finish nails—be sure to drill ⅟₁₆" pilot holes through the trim pieces to prevent splitting.

FINISH THE WOOD.
For clean results, perform the finishing steps on the table

before installing the tile.
1. Fill all visible screw holes with oak plugs, and sand them flush with the surface **(photo D).** Finish-sand the entire coffee table, and apply sanding sealer to all exposed surfaces except the top panel. Let the sealer dry thoroughly. Then, lightly sand the sealed surfaces with 180- or 220-grit sandpaper.
2. Apply stain to the sealed oak surfaces, if desired. Then, apply two or three light coats of polyurethane.

INSTALL THE CERAMIC TOP.
1. Once the finish has dried, mask off the top edges of the skirts to protect the finished surfaces.
2. Test-fit the table tiles (I). Apply a layer of tile adhesive over the entire table surface, using a V-notch adhesive trowel. Line the borders of the table surface with plastic spacers. (We used ¾₆" spacers with 6" ceramic floor tile to make a surface that fits inside the tabletop frame.)
3. Begin setting tiles into the adhesive, working in straight lines. Insert plastic spacers between tiles to maintain an even gap. Tap each tile lightly with a rubber mallet to set it into the

adhesive **(photo E).** Once the tiles have been set in place, remove the spacers, and let the adhesive set overnight.
4. Use a grout float to apply a layer of grout to the tile surface so it fills the gaps between tiles **(photo F).** Wipe excess grout from the tile faces with a damp sponge. Let the grout dry for about 30 minutes (check manufacturer's directions). Wipe off the grout film from the tiles with a dry cloth, wiping diagonally across the grout joints. Let the grout set for at least a week. Then, apply silicone grout sealer to the grout joints, following manufacturer's directions.

Use a grout float to apply tile grout in the gaps between tiles in the tabletop.

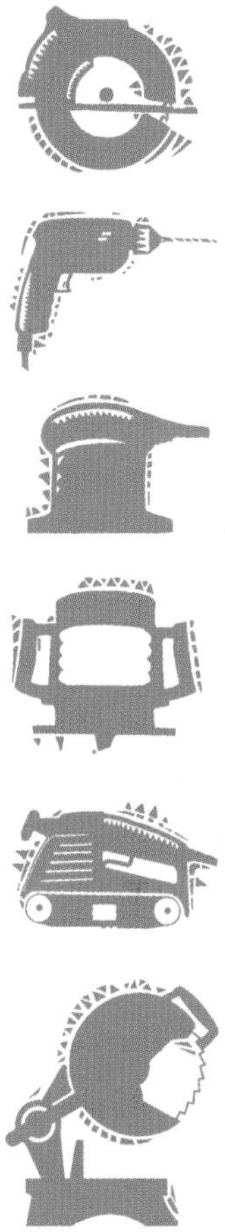

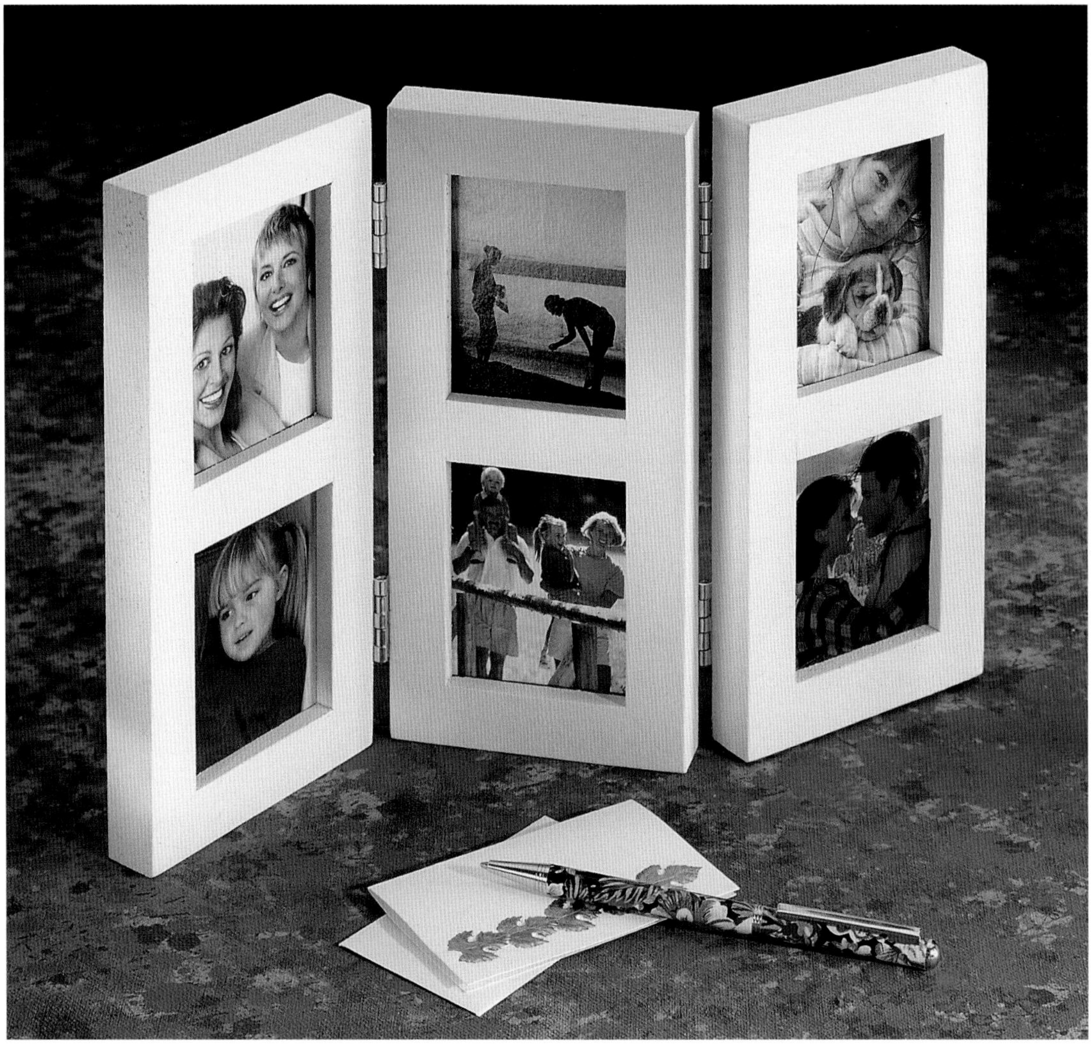

Picture Frame

*Here's a great gift project that displays fond memories
and your fine craftsmanship.*

CONSTRUCTION MATERIALS

Quantity	Lumber
1	¾ × ¾" × 8' birch
1	¼ × 2 × 12" birch
1	⅛ × 8 × 8" hardboard
3	⅛ × 2½ × 6½" glass

This project makes an ideal gift for grandparents, uncles, aunts, friends and neighbors. In fact, once word starts to spread that you're making these attractive tri-fold picture frames, you may become a busier woodworker, trying to keep up with all the requests. These paintable frames are designed to hold six 2¾ × 2¼" photographs, but you can make larger frames by proportionately increasing the dimensions and applying the same construction methods. The end frames have hinges mounted on opposite sides so you can open the picture frames to create a free-standing, S-curved display of your treasured memories.

OVERALL SIZE:
7¾" HIGH
11½" WIDE
¾" DEEP

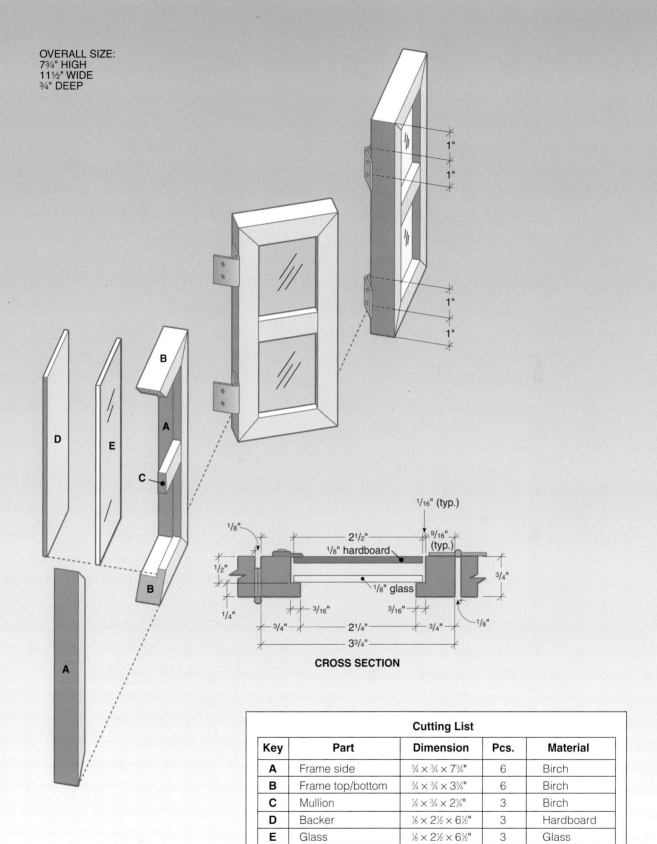

CROSS SECTION

Cutting List				
Key	**Part**	**Dimension**	**Pcs.**	**Material**
A	Frame side	¾ × ¾ × 7¾"	6	Birch
B	Frame top/bottom	¾ × ¾ × 3¾"	6	Birch
C	Mullion	¼ × ¾ × 2¼"	3	Birch
D	Backer	⅛ × 2½ × 6½"	3	Hardboard
E	Glass	⅛ × 2½ × 6½"	3	Glass

Materials: Wood glue, 4 brass hinges (1 × ½"), 12 retaining clips, finishing materials.

Note: Measurements reflect the actual thickness of dimension lumber.

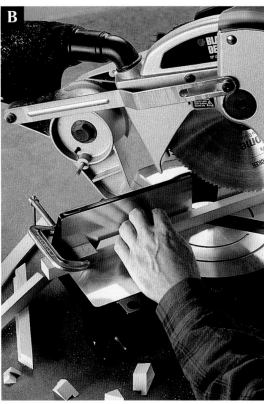

Use a router table and straight bit to cut the rabbets on the frame pieces.

Use a power miter box to miter-cut the frame pieces to length.

Directions: Picture Frame

CUT THE PARTS.
To cut the rabbets on the inside faces of the frame pieces, we recommend using a router table and a straight router bit. Make test cuts on scrap material to ensure accurate rabbets. If you don't have a router table, use bar clamps, a straightedge, and ¾" scrap wood to hold the pieces in place while routing.

1. Set the fence of the router table to ³⁄₁₆". Cut the rabbets on the frame pieces by making multiple passes, gradually extending the depth of the cut until you achieve the ½" depth **(photo A)**. This technique creates a cleaner rabbet and reduces the risk of tearouts.
2. Using a power miter box, carefully cut the frame sides (A) and tops/bottoms (B) to length, mitering the ends at 45° **(photo B).** Clamp a stop block to the fence of the miter saw to ensure that the pieces are cut to the exact same length.

ASSEMBLE THE FRAMES.
1. Glue the frame sides, bottoms and tops together, and secure with band clamps **(photo C).** Make sure the frames are square.
2. Leave excess glue until it

hardens, then gently remove the dried glue with a sharp chisel.
3. Rip-cut ¼" stock to ⅞" width, then cut the mullions (C) to length.
4. Mark a "sand-to" line on each mullion. Clamp a belt sander onto your worksurface in a horizontal position, then grind down the mullions to the marked lines **(photo D).**
5. Test-fit the mullions in the frames. Attach with glue, and clamp until dry.

ALIGN THE HINGES.
1. Measure, mark and drill pilot holes for attaching the hinges. Make sure the hinge barrels face front in one reveal and face back in the other reveal. The hinges with front-facing barrels are attached to the sides of the frames; the other hinges are mounted on the back of

Join the frame pieces with glue and secure them with band clamps until the glue dries.

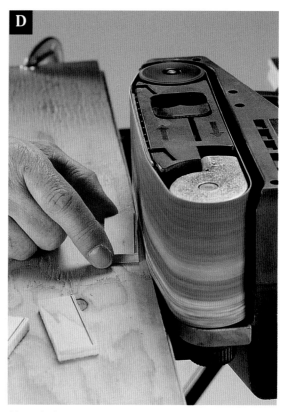

Use a belt sander to grind down the mullions to the "sand-to" lines.

the frames.

2. Install the hinges, then remove them from the frames (they will be reinstalled after the finish is applied).

APPLY FINISHING TOUCHES.

1. Finish-sand the project, then finish as desired. If you want to highlight the wood grain, you can use an aniline dye to stain the wood, provided the joints are tight and clean. Otherwise, paint is always a good option.

2. After the finish dries, reinstall the hinges **(photo E).**

3. Cut the hardboard backers (D) to size.

4. Insert the glass, photographs and backers. Add a layer of cardboard as a spacer, then secure with retaining clips.

One pair of hinges is attached with the barrels facing the front; the other hinges are attached so the barrels face the back.

Behind-the-sofa Bookshelf

This efficient bookshelf fits right behind your sofa or up against a wall to provide display space and a useful table surface.

CONSTRUCTION MATERIALS

Quantity	Lumber
2	1 × 10" × 8' aspen
1	1 × 8" × 8' aspen
3	1 × 4" × 8' aspen
2	1 × 2" × 8' aspen
2	¾ × 2½" × 8' casing molding

The space behind your sofa may not be the first area that comes to mind when you're searching for extra storage, but it does hold many possibilities for a space-challenged home. This clever behind-the-sofa bookcase has display space below and a spacious top that combine to make a useful wood project.

The top is high enough so it can be used as an auxiliary coffee table, if you don't mind reaching up for your beverage or snack.

We used aspen to build this table, then stained it for a natural appearance. If you prefer, you can build it from pine and paint it to match or complement a sofa.

OVERALL SIZE:
34" HIGH
59" LONG
9¼" DEEP

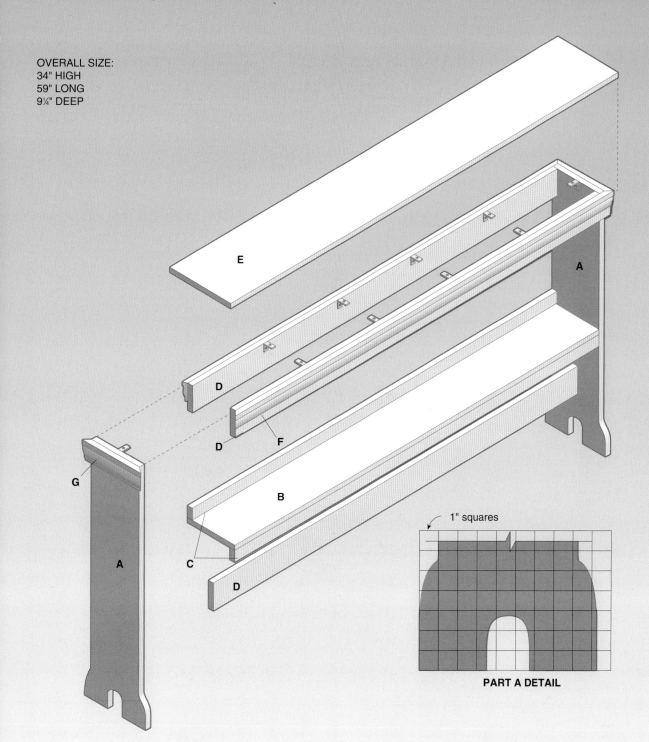

1" squares

PART A DETAIL

Cutting List				
Key	**Part**	**Dimension**	**Pcs.**	**Material**
A	Leg	¾ × 9¼ × 33¼"	2	Aspen
B	Shelf	¾ × 7¼ × 55½"	1	Aspen
C	Shelf rail	¾ × 1½ × 55½"	2	Aspen
D	Stretcher	¾ × 3½ × 55½"	3	Aspen

Cutting List				
Key	**Part**	**Dimension**	**Pcs.**	**Material**
E	Top	¾ × 9¼ × 59"	1	Aspen
F	Face trim	¾ × 2½ × *	2	Molding
G	End trim	¾ × 2½ × *	2	Molding

Materials: #6 × 1¼" and 2" wood screws, #8 × ½" wood screws, 16-ga. × 1¼" brads, 1½" brass corner braces (10), ⅜"-dia. wood plugs, wood glue, finishing materials.

Note: Measurements reflect the actual size of dimension lumber.

*Cut to fit

Directions:
Behind-the-sofa Bookshelf

MAKE THE LEGS.

The decorative cutouts at the bottoms of the legs add style and create feet that add stability.

1. Cut the legs (A) to size.

2. Use the Part A Detail pattern to lay out the cutting lines for the feet at the bottoms of the legs. You may want to draw a 1"-square grid pattern at the bottom of one of the legs first. Lay out the leg shape on one leg, using a straightedge to make sure the 1" relief cuts that run all the way up the edges of the legs are straight.

3. Cut the straight section of one leg with a circular saw and a straightedge guide, and cut the patterned bottom with a jig saw. Sand the edges smooth.

4. Trace the profile onto the second leg and cut the shape to match **(photo A).**

ATTACH THE
SHELF AND RAILS.

The rails attach to the front and back of the shelf to add strength and to create a lip in back so display items don't fall between the bookcase and the sofa. The front rail fits up against the bottom of the shelf, flush with the front edge. The rear rail fits on the top of the shelf, flush with the back edge.

1. Cut the shelf (B) and shelf rails (C) to length.

2. Drill rows of ³⁄₃₂" pilot holes for #6 × 1¼" wood screws, ³⁄₈" in from the front and back edges of the shelf, for attaching the rails. Locate the pilot holes at 8" intervals. Using a counterbore bit, counterbore each hole ¼" deep to accept a ³⁄₈"-dia. wood plug. Make sure to drill the rows of counterbores on

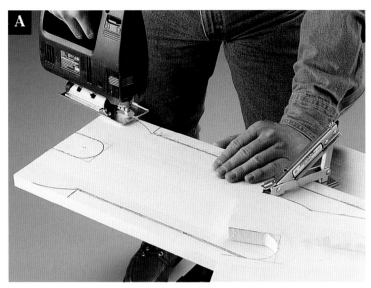

Draw the shapes for the legs onto pieces of 1 × 10, then cut out the legs with a jig saw. Make the long, straight cuts with a circular saw.

Attach the shelf by driving wood screws through counterbored pilot holes in the legs.

opposite faces of the shelf.

3. Apply glue to the top edge of one rail, and clamp it to the shelf, making sure the front of the rail is flush with the edge of the shelf. Drive 1¼" wood screws through the counterbored pilot holes to secure the rail. Then, attach the other rail to the opposite face of the shelf.

4. Attach the shelf and rails to the legs, use a combination square to mark reference lines across one face of each leg, 16"

up from the bottom. Drill pilot holes ³⁄₈" down from the guide-lines and counterbore the holes.

5. Apply glue to the ends of the shelf and rails, and position them between the legs so the top of the shelf is flush with the reference lines. Drive 2" screws through the legs and into the shelf ends **(photo B).**

ATTACH THE STRETCHERS.

Three stretchers fit between the legs at the bottom and top to

Use 1½" corner braces and ½" wood screws to attach the top to the stretchers and the insides of the legs.

add stability. The top stretchers anchor the top.

1. Cut the stretchers (D) to length and sand them smooth.

2. Center one stretcher 6" up from the bottoms of the legs. Drill pilot holes through the legs and into the ends of the stretcher. Counterbore the holes. Attach the stretcher with glue and 2" wood screws.

3. Attach the remaining two stretchers at the tops of the legs, flush with the front, top and back edges.

ATTACH THE TOP.

Attach the top to the leg assembly with 1½" brass corner braces. Once the top is fastened, cut the molding to fit, and attach it to the top stretchers and legs to complete the bookshelf.

1. Cut the top (E) to length. Sand the top with medium-grit sandpaper to smooth out all of the edges.

2. Turn the leg assembly upside down, and position it on the underside of the top. Center the legs to create a 1" overhang on all sides. Clamp the legs to the top. Use #8 × ½" wood screws and corner braces to secure the top to the legs and stretchers **(photo C).** Use four braces per side and one on each end.

INSTALL THE TRIM.

1. Cut a piece of 2½" casing molding to about 64" in length to use for one face trim (F) piece.

2. Place the molding against a top stringer and mark the ends of the bookcase onto the molding. Make 45° miter cuts away from the marks. Tack the piece in place with a 1¼" brad. Mark and cut the other long trim piece the same way, and tack it in place.

3. Use the face trim pieces as references for cutting the end trim (G) pieces to fit.

4. Remove the trim pieces, then refasten them with glue, and drive 1¼" brads at regular intervals **(photo D).**

5. Drive two brads through each joint to lock-nail the mating trim pieces together. Set all nails with a nail set.

APPLY FINISHING TOUCHES.

1. Glue ⅜"-dia. wood plugs into all screw holes, and sand them flush with the surface.

2. Fill all nail holes with wood putty and finish-sand the bookcase with 180- or 220-grit sandpaper.

3. Apply the finish of your choice. We used mahogany-tone stain and two coats of polyurethane.

Wrap the bookcase with trim pieces made from 2½" casing molding.

Mantel

Deceptively simple to build, this elegant mantel mimics the look of hardwood at a fraction of the cost.

CONSTRUCTION MATERIALS

Quantity	Lumber
1	1 × 8" × 6' poplar
1	2 × 4" × 4' poplar
1	2 × 2" × 6' poplar
1	¾ × 3¾" × 5' crown molding
1	½ × ⅝" × 5' dentil molding

This mantel will receive high praise from friends and relatives. With its wide shelf and 4' length, the mantel is a great place to display family photographs or prized possessions. It is also an excellent starting point for holiday or seasonal decorating.

Though the mantel appears to be a solid piece of milled hardwood, its looks are deceiving. Stock moldings, miter cuts and lock-nailing hide a simple support framework, and an antique white paint finish disguises the mantel's use of inexpensive poplar lumber.

Don't skip this project just because you don't have a fireplace—this mantel makes a wonderful display shelf anywhere in your home.

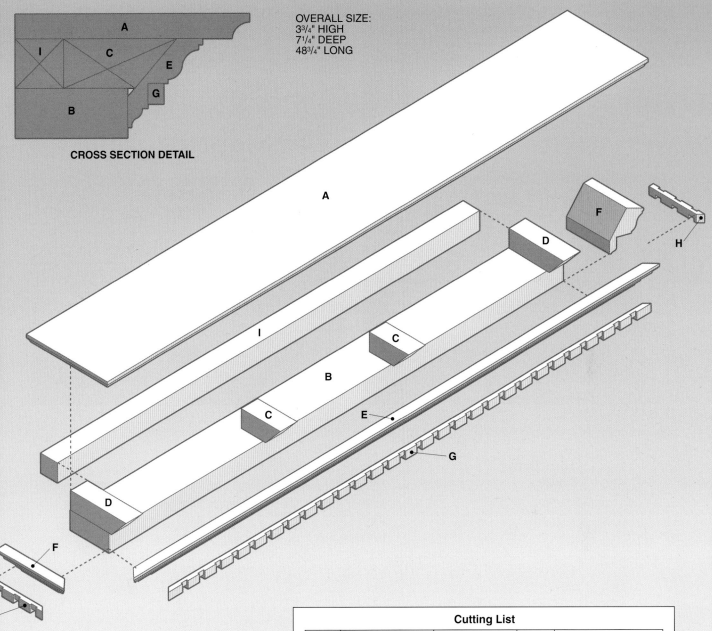

CROSS SECTION DETAIL

OVERALL SIZE:
3¾" HIGH
7¼" DEEP
48¾" LONG

Cutting List				
Key	**Part**	**Dimension**	**Pcs.**	**Material**
A	Top	¾ × 7¼ × 48¾"	1	Poplar
B	Bottom	1½ × 3½ × 41"	1	Poplar
C	Center support	1½ × 1½ × 3½"	2	Poplar
D	End support	1½ × 1½ × 5"	2	Poplar
E	Front crown	¾ × 3¾ × 46¼"	1	Crown molding
F	Side crown	¾ × 3¾ × 6"	2	Crown molding
G	Front dentil	½ × ⅝ × 43½"	1	Dentil molding
H	Side dentil	½ × ⅝ × 4⅝"	2	Dentil molding
I	Ledger	1½ × 1½ × 39"	1	Poplar

Materials: Wood glue, wood screws (#8 × 2¼", #6 × 1½"), 3½" wallboard screws, finish nails (2d, 4d), ⅜" wood plugs, finishing materials.

Note: Measurements reflect the actual thickness of dimension lumber.

Use a combination square to mark the location of the center supports on the ledger, then attach with glue and screws.

Attach the front crown and side crown to the bottom and supports with glue and 4d finish nails.

Directions: Mantel

CUT AND ASSEMBLE THE BOTTOM AND SUPPORTS.
1. Cut the bottom (B), center supports (C) and end supports (D) to size.
2. Miter one end of each support at 45°.
3. Mark 13" and 14½" in from each end on the bottom, and use your combination square to draw a line at each mark. Position the center supports along the reference lines, drill countersunk pilot holes, and fasten with glue and 2¼" screws **(photo A).**
4. Position the end supports (see *Diagram*), drill countersunk pilot holes, and attach with glue and 2¼" wood screws.
5. Cut the ledger (I) to length, and test-fit it between the end supports so the back edges of the ledger and bottom are flush.

ATTACH THE CROWN MOLDING.
1. Cut the front crown (E) and side crown (F) to size. Miter the ends at 45° by positioning the molding upside down in a power miter box, with one flat lip against the base of the saw, and the other lip against the saw fence.
2. Position the front crown so the top edge is flush with the top edge of the supports and the lower edge rests against the edge of the bottom. Drill pilot holes and attach the front crown to the supports and the bottom with wood glue and 4d finish nails **(photo B).**
3. Attach the side crowns in the same way, and lock-nail the crown molding joints with 2d finish nails (see *Tip*, page 150). Set all the nail heads.

ATTACH THE TOP.
1. Cut the top (A) to size and sand smooth with medium-grit sandpaper.
2. Use a router with a ⅜" roundover bit set for a ⅛" shoulder to shape the ends and front edge (first test the cut on a piece of scrap wood).
3. Place the top facedown on

TIP

We chose inexpensive poplar for our primary building material. If a more natural look is desired, you can also build the mantel from oak and finish it with stain.

For placement of drill holes, measure and mark the location of the supports on the top.

Keep the mitered joints tight when attaching the dentil molding.

your worksurface, and mark the positions of the supports on the underside **(photo C).**

4. Drill pilot holes and attach the top to the supports with glue and 4d finish nails. Set all nail heads.

ATTACH THE DENTIL MOLDING.

1. Cut the front dentil (G) and side dentil (H) to size, mitering the mating ends at 45° angles. Be sure to cut through the thicker "tooth" portion of each molding piece to ensure that the repeat pattern will match at the corners.

2. Position the front dentil molding and side dentil molding on the crown molding (see *Diagram*). Drill pilot holes and attach with glue and 4d finish nails, keeping the mitered

joints tight **(photo D).** Lock-nail the joints with 2d finish nails, and set the nail heads.

MOUNT THE MANTEL.

When completed, the mantel is attached to the ledger. Anchor the ledger to the wall and test-hang the mantel before finishing it.

1. Position the ledger on the wall, checking for level. Drill pilot holes and attach the ledger to the wall with 3½" wallboard screws driven into studs.

2. Fit the mantel over the ledger and drill counterbored pilot holes through the top into the ledger.

APPLY FINISHING TOUCHES.

1. Remove the mantel from the wall and apply putty to all nail holes. Scrape off any excess

glue.

2. Finish-sand the mantel, apply the finish, and allow to dry. We chose a glossy antique white paint.

3. Position the mantel over the ledger and mount it with 1½" screws driven into the counterbored holes. Insert glued plugs into the holes, sand, and touch up the finish.

TIP

The mantel can be shortened or lengthened to meet your needs. To resize, simply adjust the sizes of the top, bottom, moldings and ledger accordingly.

Knickknack Shelf

Add some country charm to your home with this rustic pine knickknack shelf.

CONSTRUCTION MATERIALS

Quantity	Lumber
1	1 × 4" × 8' pine
2	1 × 8" × 6' pine
1	1 × 10" × 4' pine
9	¼ × 3½" × 3' beaded pine paneling
1	¾ × ¾" × 6' cove molding

Country-style furniture is becoming increasingly popular throughout the world because of its honest appearance and back-to-basics preference for function over ornate styling. In interior design catalogs, you may find many country shelving projects that are similar to this one in design and function. But our knick-knack shelf can be built for a tiny fraction of the prices charged for its catalog cousins.

From the beaded pine paneling to the matching arcs on the apron and ledger, this knick-knack shelf is well designed throughout. The shelf shown above has a natural wood finish, but it is also suitable for decorative painting techniques, like milkwash or farmhouse finishes.

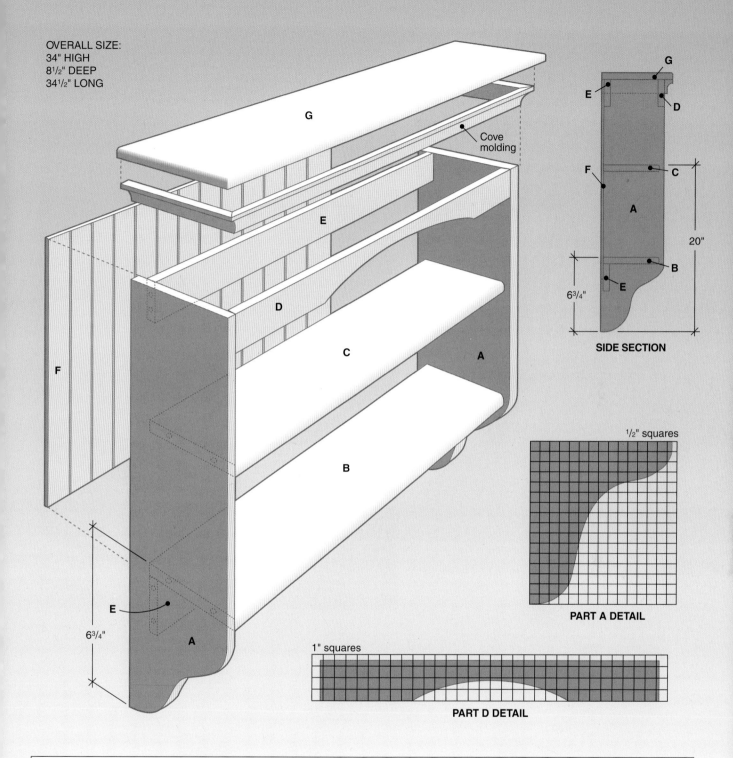

OVERALL SIZE:
34" HIGH
8½" DEEP
34½" LONG

G

Cove molding

E

D

F

C

A

B

E

A

6¾"

SIDE SECTION

G

E

D

F

C

A

20"

B

E

6¾"

½" squares

PART A DETAIL

1" squares

PART D DETAIL

Cutting List				
Key	Part	Dimension	Pcs.	Material
A	Shelf side	¾ × 7¼ × 33¼"	2	Pine
B	Bottom shelf	¾ × 6¾ × 30½"	1	Pine
C	Middle shelf	¾ × 6¾ × 30½"	1	Pine
D	Apron	¾ × 3½ × 30½"	1	Pine

Cutting List				
Key	Part	Dimension	Pcs.	Material
E	Ledger	¾ × 3½ × 30½"	2	Pine
F	Back panel	¼ × 3½ × 28"	9	Pine paneling
G	Cap	¾ × 8½ × 34½"	1	Pine

Materials: Wood glue, #8 × 1½" wood screws, 3d and 6d finish nails, mushroom-style button plugs, finishing materials.

Note: Measurements reflect the actual thickness of dimension lumber.

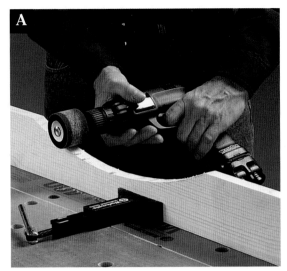

Smooth out the jig saw cuts on the apron and ledger with a drill and drum sander.

Clamp the sides and ledgers in position, then fasten with glue and screws.

Directions:
Knickknack Shelf

MAKE THE FRAME COMPONENTS.

1. Cut the sides (A) to length from 1 × 8 pine.

2. Transfer the side pattern to one side (see *Diagram*). Cut out the shape and smooth the cut with a drum sander attached to your drill. Trace the finished profile onto the other side, and make the cutout.

3. Cut the apron (D) and the ledgers (E) to length from 1 × 4 pine. Transfer the apron pattern to the apron and one of the ledgers and cut with a jig saw. (see *Diagram*).

4. Smooth out any irregularities with a drum sander or belt sander **(photo A)**.

ASSEMBLE THE FRAME.

1. Stand the sides on their back edges and place the upper ledger between them, with the top edges flush.

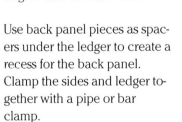
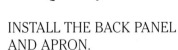

Fasten the tongue-and-groove beaded pine panel pieces to the ledgers with 3d finish nails.

Use back panel pieces as spacers under the ledger to create a recess for the back panel. Clamp the sides and ledger together with a pipe or bar clamp.

2. Insert the lower ledger with its top edge 6" up from the bottoms of the sides, also resting on spacers.

3. Clamp in place, and drill two counterbored pilot holes through the sides into the ends of the ledgers.

4. Attach the sides to the ledgers with glue and wood screws **(photo B)**.

INSTALL THE BACK PANEL AND APRON.

To make the back panel (F), we used tongue-and-groove pieces of pine wainscoting paneling.

1. Attach the back panel to the backs of the ledgers, using 3d finish nails, but no glue **(photo C)**. The top of the back panel should be flush with the tops of the sides.

2. Fasten the apron across the top front of the sides with wood glue and 6d finish nails. Be sure to keep the top edge of the apron flush with the tops of the sides.

BUILD AND INSTALL THE SHELVES.

1. Cut the bottom shelf (B) and middle shelf (C) to size from 1 × 8 pine.

2. Use a router with a ⅜" piloted roundover bit to round over the top and bottom edges on the fronts of the shelves **(photo D).**

3. Clamp the bottom shelf in place on top of the lower ledger, keeping the back edges flush. Drill counterbored pilot holes, and attach the shelf to the sides with glue and wood screws.

4. Install the middle shelf using the same procedure **(photo E).**

ATTACH THE CAP AND COVE.

1. Cut the cap (G) to size from 1 × 10 pine.

2. Use a router with a ⅜" roundover bit to shape the top and bottom edges of the ends and front.

3. Place a bead of glue along the top edges of the sides, apron and ledgers. Position the cap on top of the shelf assembly, overlapping 1¼" on each end and at the front.

4. Drill pilot holes to prevent splitting, and nail the cap in place with 6d finish nails.

5. Cut the pine cove molding to the appropriate lengths with mitered corners, and attach just below the bottom of the cap (see *Diagram*). Fasten in place with glue and 3d finish nails **(photo F).**

APPLY FINISHING TOUCHES.

1. Drill counterbored pilot holes in the upper ledger for mounting screws. If the mounting screws won't be going into wall studs, use hollow wall anchors.

2. Scrape off any excess glue, then finish-sand.

3. Install mushroom-style button plugs in all counterbores.

4. Apply the finish. We chose to finish our knickknack shelf with light oak stain and a satin-gloss polyurethane topcoat. You can stain the button plugs a contrasting color before inserting them into the counterbore holes.

Use a router with a ⅜" piloted roundover bit to shape the front edges of the shelves.

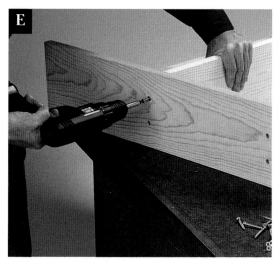

Drill counterbored pilot holes for the shelves, then attach with glue and 1½" wood screws.

Attach the cove molding with glue and 3d finish nails. Hold the nails with needlenose pliers when nailing in hard-to-reach areas.

Folding Table

*Sturdy, spacious and portable, this indoor/outdoor
table folds up to be stored.*

CONSTRUCTION MATERIALS

Quantity	Lumber
5	2 × 4" × 8' pine
6	1 × 6" × 8' pine
3	1 × 4" × 8' pine

Bigger and better than a card table, this efficient folding table can provide additional seating at a moment's notice when company arrives. With more than 15 square feet of table surface, it is roomy enough for six adult diners. When folded up for storage, it shrinks to a diminutive 3 × 3' package that is less than 12" thick—small enough to fit into just about any closet.

If you live in a house or apartment where outdoor security is an issue, this folding table can be opened on your patio or balcony, then taken inside when you are finished. If you plan to use the table outdoors, be sure to use exterior-rated paint.

OVERALL SIZE:
29¼" HIGH
36" DEEP
63¼" LONG

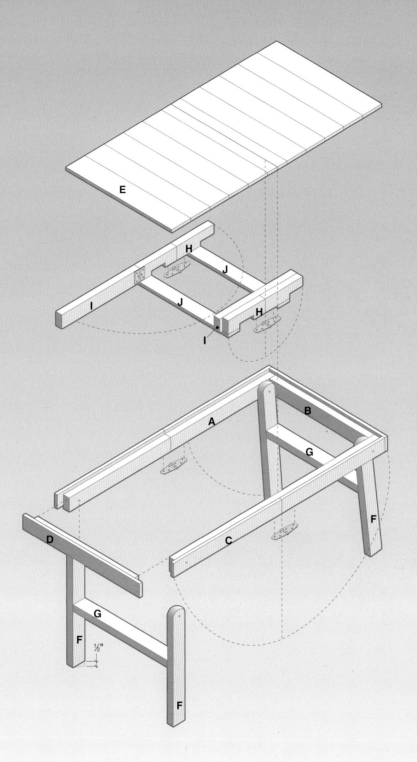

Cutting List				
Key	**Part**	**Dimension**	**Pcs.**	**Material**
A	Side rail	1½ × 3½ × 62"	2	Pine
B	End rail	1½ × 3½ × 31½"	2	Pine
C	Side skirt	¾ × 3½ × 63½"	2	Pine
D	End skirt	¾ × 3½ × 34½"	2	Pine
E	Slats	¾ × 5½ × 34½"	11	Pine

Cutting List				
Key	**Part**	**Dimension**	**Pcs.**	**Material**
F	Legs	1½ × 3½ × 28½"	4	Pine
G	Stretcher	1½ × 3½ × 28⅜"	2	Pine
H	Cleat	1½ × 3½ × 22"	2	Pine
I	Sweep	1½ × 3½ × 23"	2	Pine
J	Guide	¾ × 3½ × 28"	2	Pine

Materials: Wood glue, deck screws (1¼", 2", 2½"), 1½ × 6"-long strap hinges (4), 2 × 2" brass butt hinges (2), ⅜ × 4½" carriage bolts with lock nuts (4), 1"-dia. washers (8), finishing materials.

Note: Measurements reflect the actual size of dimension lumber.

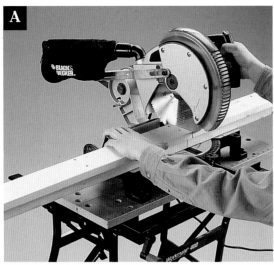

After attaching the side rails and side skirts, cross-cut them in half.

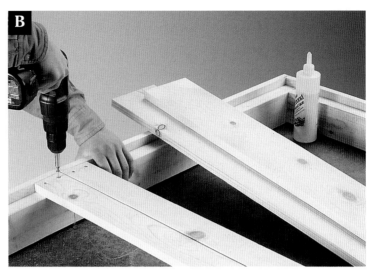

The middle slat is rip-cut in half and attached on each side of the hinged joint between the sides of the tabletop frame.

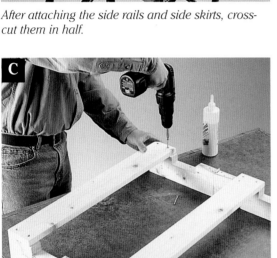

Attach the guides to the cleats, flush with the edges of the notches.

Directions: Folding Table

MAKE THE SIDE SECTIONS.
Countersink all screws when assembling this table.
1. Cut the side rails (A), end rails (B), side skirts (C) and end skirts (D) to size.
2. Position a side skirt against each side rail. Make sure the side skirts overhang the side rails by ¾" on one long edge. This ¾"-wide overhang will face the top on the completed table, creating a lip for the slats (E) to sit on. Center the side skirts on the side rails so ¾" of the side skirts extends beyond the side rails at each end.
3. Clamp the side skirts to the side rails, and attach the parts with 1¼" deck screws. Leave the middles of the side skirts and side rails free of screws so they can be cut in half.
4. Draw reference lines across the center of the side skirts. Cut along the reference lines with a power miter saw, cutting the boards into two equal lengths **(photo A).** Connect the halves with 6" strap hinges, attached to the bottom edges of the side rail halves. Unscrew the parts and hinges before proceeding.

ATTACH THE END SECTIONS.
1. Cut the end rails (B) and end skirts (D) to size.
2. Position the end rails between the side rails, flush with the side rail ends. Apply glue, and drive 2½" deck screws through the side rail faces and into the end rails.
3. Position an end skirt against each end rail. Leave a ¾"-wide gap from the tops of the end skirts to the tops of the end rails to create a lip for the slats to sit on. With the ends of the end skirts flush with the side rails, drive 2½" deck screws through the end skirts and into the side rails and end rails. Reattach the side skirts with glue and wood screws, and reattach the strap hinges in their former positions.

ATTACH THE SLATS.
1. Cut the slats (E) to size.
2. Rip-cut one slat in half, using a circular saw and a straight-edge guide. This divided slat will fit in the middle of the tabletop. Position one half of the ripped slat on each side of the cut at the center of the side rails. Butt the divided slat pieces together at the center so no gap is apparent. Attach each half to the side rails, using glue and 2" deck screws **(photo B).**
3. Position the other slats across the tabletop frame, spaced evenly, and attach them with 2" deck screws.
4. Drill ⅜"-dia. holes for carriage bolts through each end of the side skirts and side rails. Center the holes 4¼" in from

Drive deck screws through the slats and into the cleats below.

Fit the legs into place and attach them with carriage bolts, washers and lock nuts.

the ends of the side skirts and 1¾" up from the bottoms of the side rails. The holes will be used to attach the legs.

MAKE THE LEGS.
1. Cut the legs (F) and stretchers (G) to size.
2. Mark a point along one wide face of each leg, ½" in from the end. Draw a reference line from that point to the opposite corner on each leg. Cut along the reference lines with a circular saw. These slanted ends will be the bottoms of the legs.
3. Use a compass to draw a centered, 1¾"-radius semicircle at the other end of each leg. Mark the center of the semicircle where the point of the compass was in contact with the workpiece. Drill a ⅜"-dia. hole for a carriage bolt through the centerpoint. Use a jig saw to cut the rounded leg tops. Sand the legs smooth.
4. Use a combination square to draw a reference line across one face of each leg, 14" down from the top.
5. Position the legs in pairs on your worksurface. Slide a stretcher between each leg pair

with their top faces on the reference lines. Drill pilot holes, and attach the stretchers between the legs with glue and 2½" deck screws.

MAKE THE CLEATS.
1. Cut the cleats (H) to size. The cleats are notched on one long edge to allow the table to fold in half. Each notch is 1"deep × 3½" wide.
2. Draw reference lines across one edge of each cleat, 3½", 7¼" and 18½" from one end. Use a pencil to shade from the 3½" line to the 7¼" line, and from the 18½" line to the ends of the cleats. These shaded areas mark the notches.
3. Cut the notches with a jig saw, then cut each cleat in half. Attach the cleat halves with strap hinges, positioned across the centerline.

ATTACH THE SWEEPS & GUIDES.
1. Cut the sweeps (I) and guides (J) to size.
2. Position the guides on the cleats, flush with the edges of the notches. Attach the guides to the cleats with glue and 2"

deck screws **(photo C)**.
3. Turn the tabletop upside down, and position the cleats and guides inside the tabletop so their hinged centers align. Center the cleats between the side rails.
4. Trace the cleat outline onto the table slats with a pencil. Remove the cleats, and drill pilot holes through the slats in the tabletop. Reposition the cleats and guides. Fasten them to the bottom of the table with glue and 2" deck screws **(photo D)**.
5. Attach a 3" brass butt hinge to one end of each sweep, then attach the hinge to one end of each cleat. Make sure the sweeps are attached at opposite ends of the cleats (see *Diagram*).

APPLY FINISHING TOUCHES.
1. Fasten the legs inside the tabletop, using carriage bolts, washers and lock nuts **(photo E)**.
2. Remove the hardware and fill all countersunk screw holes with wood putty. Sand the surfaces with medium sandpaper, and apply primer and paint.
3. Reattach the legs.

Corner Display Stand

This light and airy unit brings hardworking display shelving to any corner of your house.

The open back on this corner display stand lets you add a lot of display space to any room, without adding a lot of weight to the decor. Its roomy shelves are perfect for flower vases, fine china, souvenirs, picture frames and other knickknacks and collectibles.

CONSTRUCTION MATERIALS

Quantity	Lumber
7	1 × 4" × 8' pine
1	¾" × 4' × 8' plywood
1	¾ × ¾" × 6' cove molding

Much more than a practical space-saver, the gentle arches on the front and the slatted back design of this corner display stand blend into just about any decorating style. Because it's such a simple design, it doesn't draw attention away from the items on display.

This corner display stand is also very inexpensive to build. A single sheet of plywood is more than enough to make the triangular shelves, and the shelf rails and standards are made from 1 × 4 pine. The decorative trim pieces on the edges of the shelves are cut from ordinary ¾" cove molding. These materials, together with the painted finish, give the display stand a contemporary style. You might want to try a distressed antique finish to give the stand a vintage look, or, if you're looking for furnishings with a more formal appearance, substitute oak boards and plywood, then apply a warm-toned wood stain.

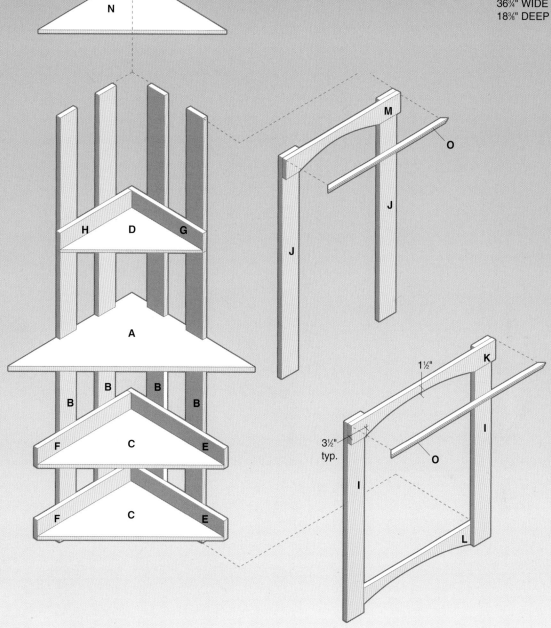

OVERALL SIZE:
76" HIGH
36¾" WIDE
18⅜" DEEP

1½"

3½"
typ.

Cutting List

Key	Part	Dimension	Pcs.	Material
A	Center shelf	¾ × 26 × 26"	1	Plywood
B	Standard	¾ × 3½ × 75¼"	4	Pine
C	Bottom shelf	¾ × 19½ × 19½"	2	Plywood
D	Top shelf	¾ × 15 × 15"	1	Plywood
E	Bottom rail	¾ × 3½ × 20¼"	2	Pine
F	Bottom rail	¾ × 3½ × 19½"	2	Pine
G	Top rail	¾ × 3½ × 15¾"	1	Pine
H	Top rail	¾ × 3½ × 15"	1	Pine

Cutting List

Key	Part	Dimension	Pcs.	Material
I	Lower stile	¾ × 3½ × 35¼"	2	Pine
J	Upper stile	¾ × 3½ × 39¼"	2	Pine
K	Middle front rail	¾ × 3½ × 32"	1	Pine
L	Lower front rail	¾ × 3½ × 30¼"	1	Pine
M	Upper front rail	¾ × 3½ × 25¼"	1	Pine
N	Top	¾ × 21¼ × 21¼"	1	Plywood
O	Trim	¾ × ¾ × *	2	Cove molding

Materials: Wood glue, wood screws (#6 × 1½", #6 × 2"), 1¼" brads, finishing materials.

Note: Measurements reflect the actual size of dimension lumber.   *Cut to fit.

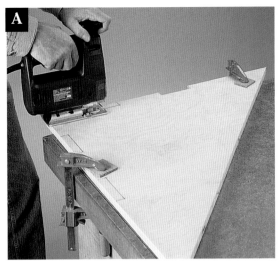

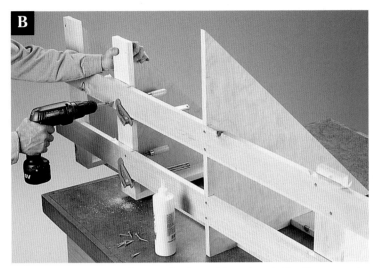

Use a jig saw to cut notches for the standards in the back edges of the center shelf.

Drive screws through the standards and into the shelf rails.

Directions:
Corner Display Stand

MAKE THE SHELVES.
1. Make the center shelf (A), using a circular saw and a straight-edge guide to cut a 26⅛" plywood square in half diagonally.
2. Use a square to lay out ¾ × 3½"-long notches for the standards on the shelf sides, starting 4" and 12¼" in from each 90° corner, on each side. Cut the notches with a jig saw **(photo A).**
3. Cut a 19⅝"-square plywood piece in half diagonally to make the bottom shelves. Cut the top shelf (D) to size.
4. Sand the shelves to remove any rough spots.
5. Cut the bottom rails (E, F) and the top rails (G, H) to length from 1 × 4 pine.
6. Attach one longer rail (E) and one shorter rail (F) to the back edges of each bottom shelf so they make a butt joint and are flush with the ends of the shelf. Use glue and #6 × 2" wood screws. Countersink all the screw pilot holes. Attach a longer top rail (G) and shorter top rail (H) to the back edges

Use a flexible marking guide to draw the arches in the front rails.

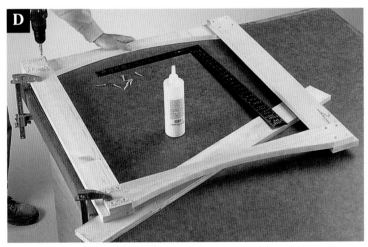

Assemble the arched front rails and the stiles into face frames.

of the top shelf, so the bottoms are flush.

ATTACH THE STANDARDS.
1. Cut the standards (B) to length.

2. Sand the standards, and clamp them together with their tops and bottoms flush. Draw reference lines across the standards 3½", 16", 35¼" and 52" from one end. Draw reference lines on the shelf rails, 3¼" and 11½" on each side of the corner to mark the positions of the inside edges of the standards.

3. Clamp the shelves to the standards so the reference lines are aligned, then attach the standards to the shelves with glue and #6 × 2" wood screws, driven through pilot holes in the backs of the standards and into the shelves **(photo B).** Note that the center shelf should be installed so the notches fit over the standards.

BUILD THE FACE FRAMES.

1. Cut the lower stiles (I), upper stiles (J), lower front rails (K, L) and upper front rail (M) to length.

2. Mark the top and bottom arches using a thin, flexible piece of metal, plastic or wood as a marking guide. Find the center lengthwise of each rail. Mark a point 13" in from the center in both directions. Tack a 1¼" brad at these points, as close to the edge as possible. Tack a brad at the center of each workpiece, 2" up from the same edge. Hook the marking guide over the middle brad, and flex each end of the guide to the marked points. Trace the curve on each rail **(photo C),** and cut the curves with a jig saw.

3. Position the shorter of the two lower front rails (L) across the inside face of the lower stiles, with the arc pointing down. The edge of the rail containing the arc should be flush with the ends of the stiles, and the rail should be ⅞" in from the outside edges of each stile (see *Diagram*). This is the bottom of the face frame. Clamp the rail to the stiles.

4. Clamp the longer of the lower front rails (K) to the outside top face of the stiles, with the straight edge flush with the tops. The ends of the rail should be flush with the edges of the stile. Attach the rails to the lower stiles with four #6 × 1¼" screws driven at each joint **(photo D).**

ATTACH THE FACE FRAMES AND TOP.

1. Turn the stand upright, slip the lower face frame in position. The bottom rail should fit beneath the lowest shelf and the top rail should fit beneath the center shelf. Center the face frame from side to side so the overhang is equal.

2. Clamp the face frame to the stand, then attach it with #6 × 2" wood screws driven through the stiles and into the edges of the shelves, and also driven into the top of each rail through the shelf above it **(photo E).**

3. Position the upper face frame so the bottoms of the stiles rest on the center shelf, and the stiles overhang the ends of the top shelf by equal amounts. Tack the face frame in place by driving one #6 × 2" wood screw through each stile and into the front edge of the top shelf.

4. Drive screws up through the underside of the center shelf and into the bottom ends of the stiles **(photo F).**

APPLY FINISHING TOUCHES.

1. Cut the top (N) to size, and attach it to the tops of the standards and the top rail of the upper face frame with glue and screws. The back sides of the top should be flush with the outside faces of the standards.

2. Cut strips of ¾" cove molding (O) to fit along the front edges of the center shelf and top shelf, with the ends miter-cut to follow the line of each shelf. Attach the trim pieces with 1¼" brads driven into pilot holes.

3. Set all nail heads, then cover the nail and screw heads with wood putty.

4. Sand the entire piece, and paint it with primer and two coats of enamel paint.

Drive screws through the center shelf and into the face frame.

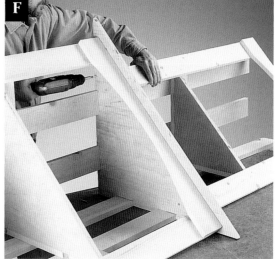

Drive wood screws up through the center shelf to secure the upper stiles.

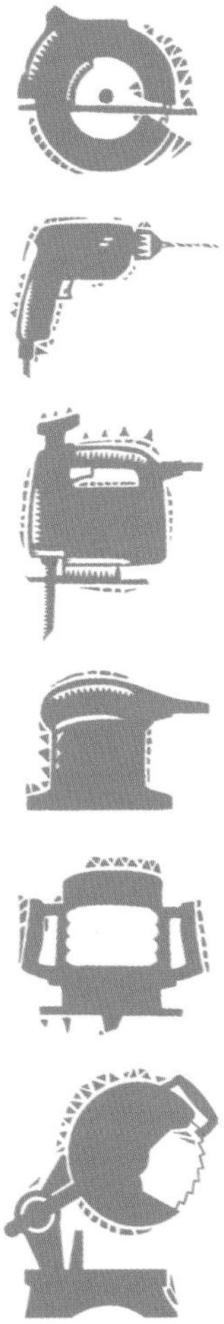

Collector's Table

Store your fine collectibles in this eye-catching conversation piece.

Quantity	Lumber
1	½" × 4 × 4' oak plywood
1	½" × 4 × 8' oak plywood
1	⅜" × 2 × 2' oak plywood
2	1 × 2" × 6' oak
4	1 × 3" × 8' oak
2	1 × 4" × 6' oak
1	2 × 2" × 6' oak
3	½ × ½ × 30" scrap wood
1	¼ × 18¾ × 34¾" tempered glass

This beautiful, glass-topped collector's table is perfect for storing and displaying shells, rocks, fossils, figurines or other collectibles. It has three interchangeable drawers, so you can change the display whenever you choose—simply by rotating a different drawer into the top position under the glass. Built from oak and oak plywood, this table gives you the opportunity to demonstrate your woodworking skills and display your collections.

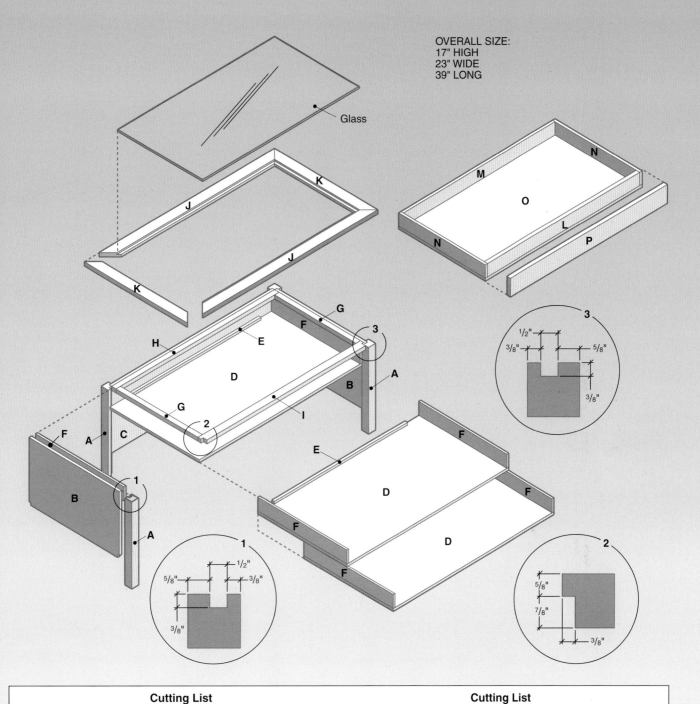

OVERALL SIZE:
17" HIGH
23" WIDE
39" LONG

Glass

Cutting List

Key	Part	Dimension	Pcs.	Material
A	Leg	1½ × 1½ × 16¼"	4	Oak
B	End panel	½ × 20¼ × 12½"	2	Oak ply.
C	Back panel	½ × 36¼ × 12½"	1	Oak ply.
D	Shelf	½ × 19⅞ × 36¼"	3	Oak ply.
E	Drawer stop	½ × ½ × 30"	3	Scrap wood
F	Drawer guide	⅜ × 3⅛ × 19⅞"	6	Oak ply.
G	End cleat	¾ × 1 × 18¼"	2	Oak
H	Back cleat	¾ × 1 × 36¼"	1	Oak

Cutting List

Key	Part	Dimension	Pcs.	Material
I	Top rail	¾ × 1½ × 36¼"	1	Oak
J	Frame, long side	¾ × 2½ × 39"	2	Oak
K	Frame, short side	¾ × 2½ × 23"	2	Oak
L	Drawer box front	¾ × 2½ × 34¼"	3	Oak
M	Drawer box back	½ × 2½ × 34¼"	3	Oak ply.
N	Drawer box side	½ × 2½ × 19½"	6	Oak ply.
O	Drawer bottom	½ × 19½ × 35¼"	3	Plywood
P	Drawer face	¾ × 3½ × 35¼"	3	Oak

Materials: Wood glue, wood screws (1", 1¼"), ⅝" brads, 4d finish nails, finishing materials.

Note: Measurements reflect the actual thickness of dimension lumber.

Directions: Collector's Table

CUT THE LEGS.

It is important to distinguish between the left and right legs when building this table. Each pair of front and back legs has a stopped dado to hold the end panel in place. The back legs also have a second stopped dado to support the back panel (see *Detail*). We recommend that you use a router table to make these cuts.

1. Cut the legs (A) to length.
2. Measure and mark 12"-long dadoes on the legs. On the front legs, cut the dadoes on one face, using a ½" straight bit set to ⅜" depth. On the back legs, cut dadoes on two adjacent faces **(photo A)**.
3. Remove the waste section between the back leg dadoes with a saw, and square off the dado ends, using a ½" chisel.

CUT THE PANELS AND ATTACH THE LEGS.

1. Cut the end panels (B) and back panel (C) to size.
2. Cut a ⅜ × ½" notch (see

waste piece

Cut ½ × ⅜"-deep stopped dadoes in the legs, using a router table. Note the waste pieces on the back legs, which you will need to remove with a handsaw and chisel.

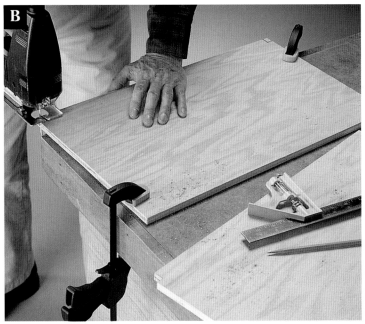

Cut a ⅜ × ½" notch out of the bottom corners of the back and side panels where they will overhang the dadoes in the legs.

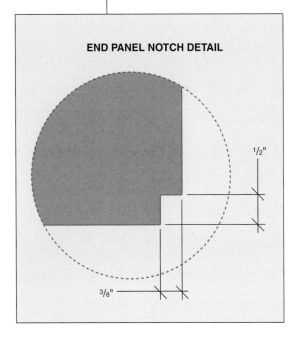

END PANEL NOTCH DETAIL

1/2"

3/8"

Detail) into the bottom corner of each panel, using a jig saw **(photo B).**
3. Attach a pair of legs to each end panel, using glue and brads. Set the back panel aside until later.

CUT THE SHELVES, DRAWER STOPS AND DRAWER GUIDES.

Because the drawer stops are hidden, they can be built from any scrap ½" lumber.
1. Cut shelves (D), drawer

Drill pilot holes and attach the bottom drawer guides to the end panel sides, using wood glue and ⅜" brads.

1. Cut shelves (D), drawer stops (E) and drawer guides (F) to size.

2. Attach the stops to the shelves with glue and brads (see *Diagram*).

ASSEMBLE THE CABINET. Precision is crucial when assembling your collector's table. Sloppy construction will make it difficult to fit the drawers into the cabinet.

1. Attach the lowest drawer guides to the inside of the end panels by measuring up from the bottom edge and marking a line at ¹¹⁄₁₆". Position the bottom edge of the drawer guide on this line and attach with glue and brads **(photo C).**

2. Attach the back to the side assemblies by setting the back panel into the dadoes on the back legs, keeping all top edges flush. Drill pilot holes and secure the back panel with glue and brads.

3. Turn the cabinet upside down, then drill counter-sunk pilot holes and attach the bottom shelf to the edge of the drawer guides with 1" wood screws.

4. Turn the cabinet right-side-up and attach the middle shelf to the top edge of the drawer guide with 1" screws.

5. Rest the center drawer guides on the middle shelf and fasten to the end panels with glue and ¾" screws **(photo D).**

6. Install the top shelf and upper guides in similar fashion.

7. Cut the cleats (G, H) and top rail (I) to size.

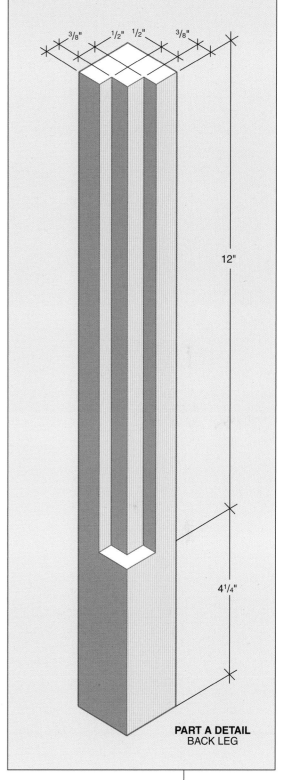

3/8" · 1/2" · 1/2" · 3/8"

12"

4¹/₄"

PART A DETAIL
BACK LEG

TIP

Cutting stopped dadoes is a precision task. It's a good idea to practice these skills on scrap wood before you attempt this project.

D

Drill countersunk pilot holes and attach the center guides to the end panels, using wood screws.

E

Glue the miters of the top frame together, using a band clamp. Check for square by measuring diagonals.

8. Drill counterbored pilot holes and attach cleats flush with the tops of the back and side panels, using wood glue and 1¼" screws (see *Diagram*).

BUILD THE TOP FRAME.
1. Cut the long frame sides (J) and short frame sides (K) to length, mitering the ends at 45°.
2. Cut a rabbet along the inside top edge of the frame pieces, using a router with a ½" straight bit set at ⁵⁄₁₆" depth.
3. Apply glue to the mitered ends and clamp the frame to-

gether, using a band clamp **(photo E).** Allow the glue to dry thoroughly.
4. Center the frame over the

cabinet with a ¼" overhang on all sides, drill pilot holes and attach the frame using wood glue and 4d finish nails.

TIP

For easier access to stored collections, you can attach pull knobs to the face of each drawer.

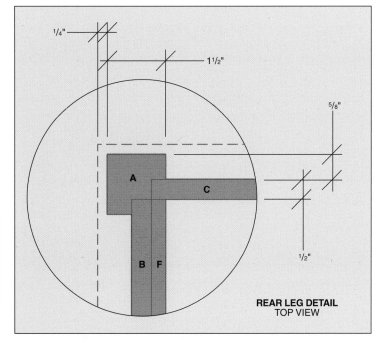

REAR LEG DETAIL
TOP VIEW

Assemble the drawer boxes and attach the bottoms with wood glue and brads. Make sure to check for square as you build each drawer.

Attach drawer faces with glue, and drive wood screws through the inside of the drawer box into the drawer face.

1. Cut the drawer box parts (L, M, N, O) to size.

2. Assemble each drawer box by positioning the front and back between the sides, drilling pilot holes, and attaching the pieces with glue and brads. Make sure drawer assemblies are square.

3. Attach the drawer bottoms, using glue and brads **(photo F).**

4. Cut the drawer faces (P) to size. Position the drawer faces on the front of the drawer boxes, so the ends are flush and there is a ⁵⁄₁₆" overhang at the top edge and a ³⁄₁₆" overhang at the bottom.

5. Drill pilot holes and attach by driving 1¼" wood screws from inside the drawer box fronts into the drawer face **(photo G).**

6. Test-fit the completed drawers in the cabinet, making sure

there is ⅛" spacing between drawer faces.

FINISH THE CABINET.

1. Fill all visible nail holes with stainable putty, then sand all surfaces smooth.

2. Paint the insides and top edges of the drawer boxes (not the drawer faces) with flat black paint to highlight your collectibles. Stain the rest of the wood with a color of your choice. We used a light Danish walnut, and apply several coats of water-based polyurethane finish, sanding lightly between coats.

INSTALL THE GLASS TOP.

Wait until the project is built before ordering the glass for your collector's table. Measure the length and width of the

opening, and reduce each measurement by ⅛". Tempered safety glass is a good choice, especially if you have children. Seat the glass on clear, self-adhesive cushions to quiet any potential rattles.

TIP

If you wish, the inside of the collection drawers can be lined with black velvet to provide an elegant setting for your finest collectibles.

Dry Sink

This classic cabinet brings antique charm to any setting.

CONSTRUCTION MATERIALS

Quantity	Lumber
4	1 × 2" × 6' birch
5	1 × 3" × 8' birch
1	1 × 4" × 8' birch
2	1 × 6" × 6' birch
1	½" × 4 × 4' birch plywood
1	¾" × 4 × 8' birch plywood
3	⅜" × 4' birch dowling

Traditional dry sinks were used to hold a wash-basin in the days before indoor plumbing, but today they can serve a variety of decorative and practical functions around the house. Our classic dry sink is used as a garden potting table. It's the ideal height for mixing soils, planting seeds and watering plants. The top has a handy back shelf to hold plants and accessories, while the curved front and sides are especially designed to contain messy spills. The roomy cabinet has two hinged doors for easy access and enough interior space to store pots, planters, fertilizers, insecticides and an assortment of gardening tools. This project features birch plywood panels with solid birch frames secured with strong "through-dowel" joinery.

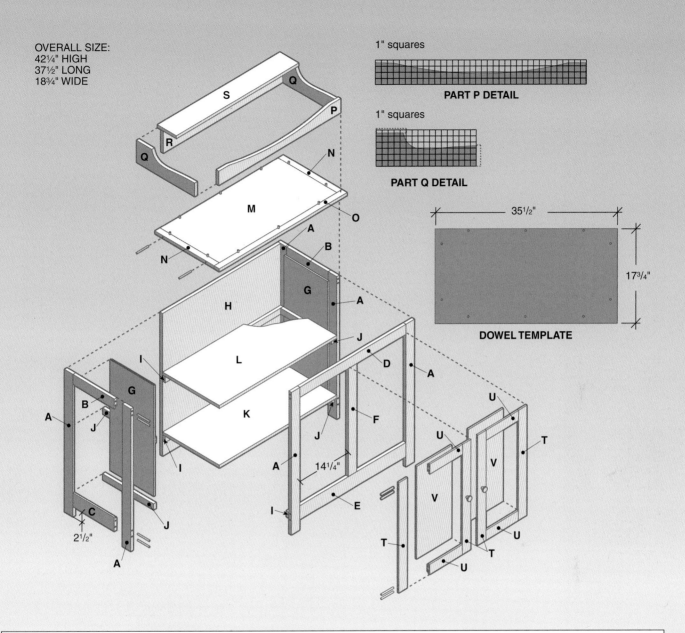

OVERALL SIZE:
42¼" HIGH
37½" LONG
18¾" WIDE

1" squares

PART P DETAIL

1" squares

PART Q DETAIL

35½"

17¾"

DOWEL TEMPLATE

2½"

14¼"

Cutting List

Key	Part	Dimension	Pcs.	Material
A	Stile	¾ × 2½ × 35¼"	6	Birch
B	Side rail, top	¾ × 2½ × 12¼"	2	Birch
C	Side rail, bottom	¾ × 3½ × 12¼"	2	Birch
D	Front rail, top	¾ × 2½ × 31"	1	Birch
E	Front rail, bottom	¾ × 3½ × 31"	1	Birch
F	Mullion	¾ × 2½ × 26¾"	1	Birch
G	Side panel	½ × 12⅞ × 27½"	2	Birch ply.
H	Back panel	¾ × 34½ × 35¼"	1	Birch ply.
I	Back, front cleat	¾ × 1½ × 34½"	3	Birch
J	Side cleat	¾ × 1½ × 15"	4	Birch
K	Bottom	¾ × 16½ × 34⅜"	1	Birch ply.

Cutting List

Key	Part	Dimension	Pcs.	Material
L	Shelf	¾ × 16⅜ × 34⅜"	1	Birch ply.
M	Top	¾ × 17¼ × 34½"	1	Birch ply.
N	Top side edge	¾ × 1½ × 17¼"	2	Birch
O	Top front edge	¾ × 1½ × 37½"	1	Birch
P	Top assem. front	¾ × 3½ × 35¼"	1	Birch
Q	Top assem. side	¾ × 5½ × 17"	2	Birch
R	Top assem. back	¾ × 5½ × 34"	1	Birch
S	Top assem. cap	¾ × 5½ × 35¾"	1	Birch
T	Door stile	¾ × 2½ × 27¼"	4	Birch
U	Door rail	¾ × 2½ × 9¾"	4	Birch
V	Door panel	½ × 10½ × 23"	2	Birch ply.

Materials: Wood glue, birch shelf nosing (⅛ × ¾ × 34½"), 16-ga. brads, #8 wood screws (1¼", 1⅝"), 4d finish nails, ⅜" inset hinges (4), ⅜ × 1" dowels (10), ⅜ × 3" dowels (40), door pulls (2), finishing materials.

Note: Measurements reflect the actual thickness of dimension lumber.

Drill holes and insert the dowels after the frame pieces have been glued together.

Carefully square the corners of the rabbets in the side panels and door panels, using a sharp chisel.

Directions:
Dry Sink

CUT AND ASSEMBLE THE CABINET FRAMES.
The dry sink is built with two side frames, a face frame and two door frames—all made from birch rails and stiles joined with through dowels.

1. Cut the stiles (A) and rails (B, C, D, E) and mullion (F) to length.

2. Build each side frame by gluing a top and bottom side rail between two stiles. The bottom rail should be raised 2½" from the bottoms of the stiles. Clamp in place, check for square and let dry.

3. Drill two ⅜"-dia. × 3"-deep holes through the stiles at each rail location **(photo A).**

4. Cut 3"-long dowels, and score a groove along one side. Apply glue to the dowels, then use a mallet to drive them into the holes.

5. Repeat this process to construct the front frame, using two stiles, the top and bottom front rails, and the mullion. Make sure the mullion is centered between the stiles.

6. Cut the door frame stiles (T) and rails (U) to size with a circular saw, and assemble frame parts in the same way.

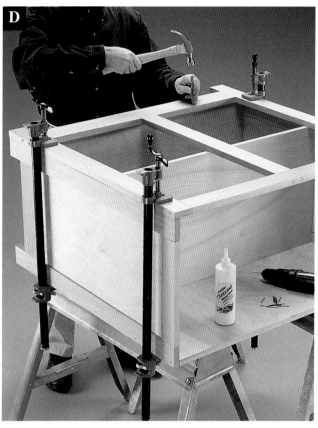

Drill pilot holes, and attach cleats with wood screws to the frame but not into the ½" panel.

Clamp one side of the face frame and check for square, then clamp the other side and check for square again. Attach with finish nails and set the nailheads.

ADD THE PANELS.

The ½" plywood side panels and door panels fit into rabbets cut around the inside of the side frames and door frames.

1. Mount a ⅜" rabbet bit in your router, set to ½" depth. Cut a continuous rabbet around the inside of the side frames.

2. Square off the corners of the rabbet, using a chisel **(photo B).** On the back face of each door frame, cut a rabbet around the inside of the frame in a similar fashion.

3. Change the depth of the router bit to ⅜", and cut another rabbet around the outside edge of the door frame. This creates a lip that will overlap the face frame when the doors are attached.

4. Cut the side panels (G) and the door panels (V) to size.

5. Position each panel inside its frame, then drill pilot holes and attach the panels with 16-ga. brads.

6. Position and attach hinges and knobs on the cabinet doors.

PREPARE THE REMAINING PIECES.

1. Cut the back panel (H), bottom (K) and shelf (L) to size.

2. Cut and attach shelf nosing to the front edge of the shelf, using glue and brads.

3. Cut the front and back cleats (I) and side cleats (J) to size. On the inside faces of the face frame stiles, mark reference lines 5¼" from the bottom. On the inside faces of the back panel and side frame stiles, mark reference lines at 5¼" and 21" from the bottom.

4. Position the cleats with the top edges flush with the reference lines, with the ends of cleats set back ¾" from the front edge and 1½" from the back edge. Drill countersunk pilot holes, and attach the cleats with 1¼" wood screws **(photo C).** NOTE: Take care to screw the side cleats into the frame members only, not into the ½" panels.

5. Attach the back cleats to the back panel, and the front cleat to the inside of the face frame, using the same process.

Cut the top side edges and top front edge, and attach the pieces with wood glue. Clamp in place until the glue dries, then drill and insert dowels to strengthen the joints.

When creating the top assembly, first attach the front piece to the sides, then attach the sides to the back, using wood glue and 4d finish nails.

ASSEMBLE THE CABINET.

1. Position the back panel between the side assemblies. Drill countersunk pilot holes, and attach the sides to the back panel with 1⅝" wood screws.
2. Position the bottom over the cleats. Check to make sure the cabinet is square, then drill pilot holes and attach the bottom by driving 4d finish nails into the cleats. Position and attach the shelf in the same manner.
3. Lay the cabinet on its back and clamp the face frame in position. Check for square, then drill pilot holes and attach the face frame to the cabinet with glue and 4d finish nails driven into the side frames, bottom and shelf **(photo D).** Drive finish nails through the

bottom and into the front cleat. Set all nail heads.
4. Position and mount the doors in their openings, then remove them and detach the hinges and knobs until the wood has been finished.

ASSEMBLE AND ATTACH THE TOP.

1. Cut cabinet top (M), side edges (N) and front edge (O) to size.
2. Attach the edges around the top, using glue. Clamp the pieces in place until the glue dries **(photo E).**
3. Drill holes and reinforce the joints with 3"-long dowels, following the same procedure used to construct the cabinet frames.

4. Position the top on the cabinet, leaving a ¾" overhang on both ends and the front. Drill countersunk pilot holes, and attach the top with glue and 1⅝" wood screws driven into the cabinet frames and back panel.

CREATE THE TOP ASSEMBLY.

1. Cut the top assembly parts (P, Q, R and S) to size.
2. Transfer the patterns to the pieces (see *Diagram*), then cut them out with a jig saw. Sand the cut edges smooth.
3. Position the front piece against the side pieces, so there is a ⅛" overhang on both ends. Drill pilot holes and attach the front piece to the side pieces with glue and 4d finish nails.

Use a template to ensure that the dowel holes in the top assembly will match those drilled in the top of the cabinet.

FINISH THE CABINET.

To give our dry sink a vintage look, we used a unique antiquing method that uses both stain and paint.

1. Finish-sand all surfaces and edges of the cabinet.

2. Stain the entire project and allow to dry. We used medium cherry stain.

3. Apply latex paint to the desired surfaces. We used Glidden® Centurian blue paint, applying it to all surfaces except the top.

4. Use a cloth and denatured alcohol to remove color while the paint is still damp. To mimic the look of a genuine antique, try to remove most of the paint from the corners and edges, where a cabinet typically receives the most wear.

5. Reinstall the hardware and hang the doors after the finish has dried.

4. Position the back piece between the sides, then drill pilot holes and attach the pieces with glue and 4d finish nails **(photo F).**

5. Position the cap piece so it overlaps by ⅛" on each end, then drill pilot holes, and attach with glue and 4d finish nails.

ATTACH THE TOP ASSEMBLY.

The top assembly is attached to the cabinet with dowels, positioned with the benefit of an easy-to-build template.

1. Create the template by tracing the outer outline of the top assembly on a piece of scrap plywood or hardboard. Cut the template to this size.

2. Place the template over the bottom of the top assembly, then drill ⅜"-dia. × ½"-deep dowel holes through the template and into the top assembly.

3. Place the template on the cabinet top, centered side to side with the back edges flush, and tape it in place. Drill corresponding dowel holes into the top **(photo G).**

4. Remove the template and attach the top assembly to the cabinet with glue and 1" dowels. Use weights or clamps to hold the top assembly in place until the glue dries.

Dining Room Projects

Show off your china and your woodworking skills with these projects for your dining room. The china cabinet has a small footprint, but plenty of space to store and display dishes. The vertical display cabinet uses oak and glass to create a formal yet airy showpiece. The wine and stemware cart makes entertaining just a little bit easier. Even the functional trivet and serving tray are handsome projects that you'll be proud to show friends and family.

Serving Tray

Smooth joinery and sturdy construction
make serving food and beverages a snap.

CONSTRUCTION MATERIALS

Quantity	Lumber
1	½ × 3¾" × 2' oak
1	½ × 2¾" × 3' oak
1	¼ × 12" × 2' birch plywood

Our serving tray is just the thing for ferrying food, drinks and dishes from kitchen to patio or dining room with a dash of style. The solid oak and warm birch tones of the tray always highlight whatever you're carrying, whether an outdoor snack of fruit and cheese or an indoor treat of coffee and cookies. The sculpted carrying handles ensure a good grip while carrying food to your guests. The serving tray is also an introduction to some advanced joinery techniques. Rabbet joints connect the frame to provide a more professional-looking appearance. The bottom panel fits into dadoes cut along the inside of each piece, and stays in place without glue. This is a great project for practicing router skills, or for showing them off if you're an accomplished woodworker.

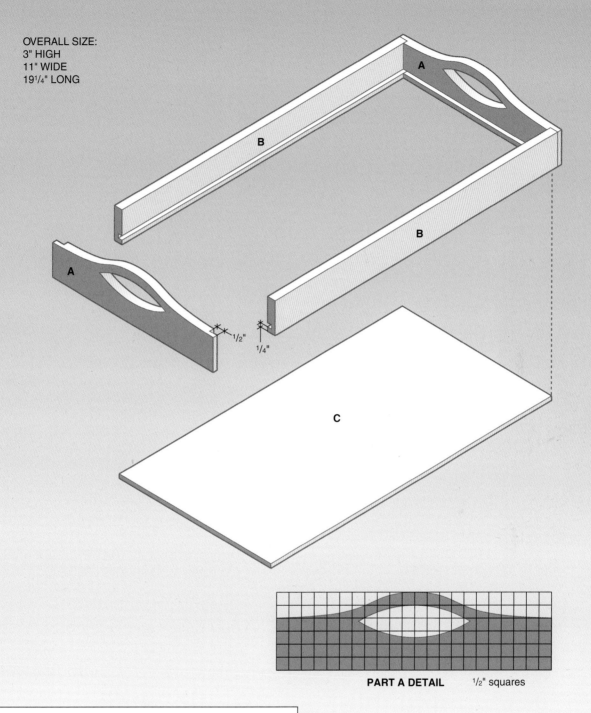

OVERALL SIZE:
3" HIGH
11" WIDE
19¼" LONG

A

B

B

A

½"

¼"

C

PART A DETAIL   ½" squares

Cutting List

Key	Part	Dimension	Pcs.	Material
A	Frame end	½ × 3 × 11"	2	Oak
B	Frame side	½ × 2 × 18¾"	2	Oak
C	Tray bottom	¼ × 10⅜ × 18⅝"	1	Birch

Materials: Wood glue, 4d finish nails, finishing materials.
Optional: ⅜" stop molding (5'), brads (½", ¾").

Note: Measurements reflect the actual thickness of
dimension lumber.

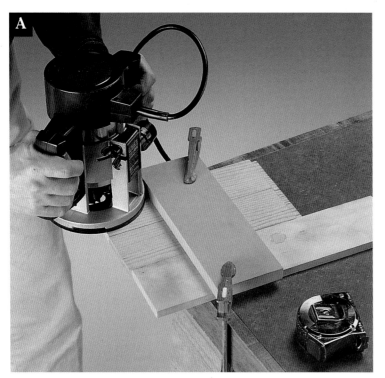

A

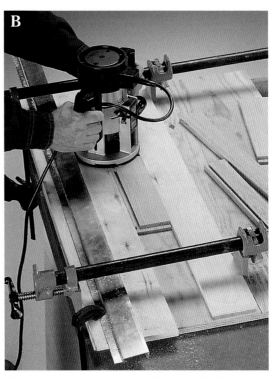

B

Rabbet the frame ends, using a straightedge to guide the cuts.

Use bar clamps and a straightedge to hold pieces in place and ensure uniform dadoes.

Directions:
Serving Tray

MAKE THE RABBETS.
The corners of the tray feature ½" rabbet joints for strength and a unified look.

1. Measure and cut the frame ends (A) to length.

2. Place the frame ends side by side on your worksurface with their ends aligned, and butt them against a scrap piece of ¾"-thick wood placed to the right of them. (Continuing each rabbet cut into the scrap wood helps prevent tearouts.) Place a straight board or straightedge over the frame ends to guide your cut, align the board and

clamp in place. Use a ½" straight-cutting router bit set ¼" deep, and rabbet the two frame ends, completing the cut into the scrap board **(photo A).** Cut rabbets on both ends of the tray ends.

MAKE THE DADOES.
Dadoes in the frame sides and frame ends secure the tray bottom in place. A simple jig is used to help make uniform, straight dadoes.

1. Cut the frame sides (B) to size, and sand smooth.

2. Draw parallel lines ¼" and ½" from the bottom edges of the frame sides and frame ends to mark the dadoes. Create a cutting jig by clamping two pieces of ¾" scrap wood against the long edges of a frame side.

Clamp a straightedge over the board to guide the router base while cutting the long dadoes. Make the dadoes in both frame sides with a ¼" straight-cutting router bit set ¼" deep **(photo B).** Adjust the clamps, and dado the frame ends in the same fashion.

OPTION: If you don't want to cut dadoes, you can support the tray bottom with cleats made from ⅜" stop molding. Cut the cleats to fit inside the tray, and attach them flush to the bottom edge with ¾" brads and a nail set **(photo C).** Place the bottom over the cleats, and secure with ½" brads. When using this method, you'll need to subtract ⅜" from the length and width of the tray bottom when cutting to size.

MAKE THE HANDLES.
1. Transfer the handle pattern onto each end (see *Diagram*).

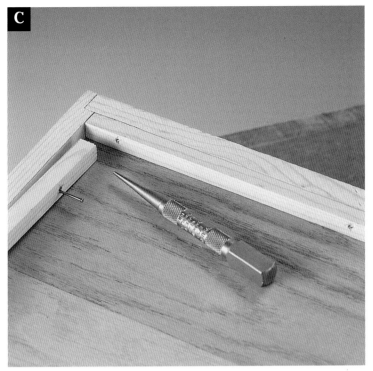

OPTION: Rather than cut dadoes, you can attach ⅜" stop molding nailed to the tray frame to support the bottom.

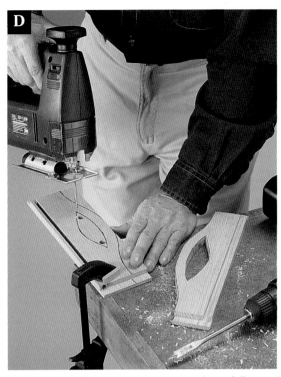

Drill access holes for your jig saw, and carefully cut the handles and curves.

2. Drill access holes in the handle and use a jig saw to complete each cut **(photo D).** Sand the cuts smooth.

ASSEMBLE THE TRAY.

1. Cut the tray bottom (C) to size from birch plywood and sand smooth.

2. Test-fit the tray bottom in the grooves of the frame sides and ends. Do not glue the tray bottom in the grooves. When the tray bottom is properly fitted, apply a thin film of glue to the rabbet joints. Use bar clamps to keep the unit tight from end to end and from side to side **(photo E).** Check for square by measuring diagonally from corner to corner. Realign the bar clamps until the diagonal measurements are the same.

3. Drill pilot holes through the frame ends into the frame sides, and secure the joints with 4d finish nails.

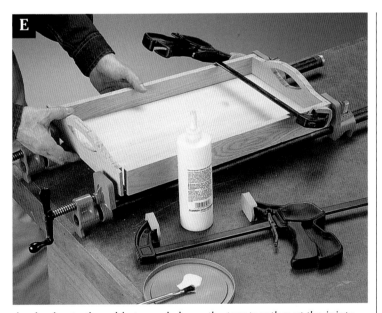

Apply glue to the rabbets, and clamp the tray together at the joints.

APPLY FINISHING TOUCHES.

1. Scrape off any excess glue at the joints. Finish-sand the tray, wipe off any sanding residue and apply a finish.

2. Mask the bottom, apply a stain on the oak sides and ends—we used rustic oak—then apply a water-resistant topcoat to the sides and ends. A natural oil applied to the birch tray bottom brings out the grain and helps resist moisture from spills. Do not wash the tray or allow it to sit on wet surfaces.

PROJECT
POWER TOOLS

Trivet

*Protect your countertops, tables or furniture during teatime
with our oak and ceramic trivet.*

CONSTRUCTION MATERIALS

Quantity	Lumber
1	¾" × 2 × 2' MDF
1	⅝ × 2¼" × 4' oak molding
1	¼ × 12 × 12" tile

MDF = medium-density fiberboard

You'll love this easy-to-construct trivet with arched legs. The heavy tile stabilizes the base, making it ideal for keeping hot pots or cups off your favorite furniture or serving cart. For this project, we selected a standard colonial oak trim pattern to make the arched legs and a neutral-color tile for the base, but you can customize this trivet by using tile that matches your tea set or suits your taste. Our basic design features a single 12 × 12" tile cut down to a finished size of 6 × 9". Using one tile is a simple method that doesn't require grout, but you will find it easy to adapt this design for smaller tiles or mosaic tiles that do require grout. Simply match the size of the substrate to the finished dimensions of the tile-and-grout surface (including a grout border between the tiles and the oak frame), and cut the oak molding pieces accordingly. The construction steps remain the same.

OVERALL SIZE:
2¹⁄₄" HIGH
7⁵⁄₁₆" WIDE
10⁵⁄₁₆" LONG

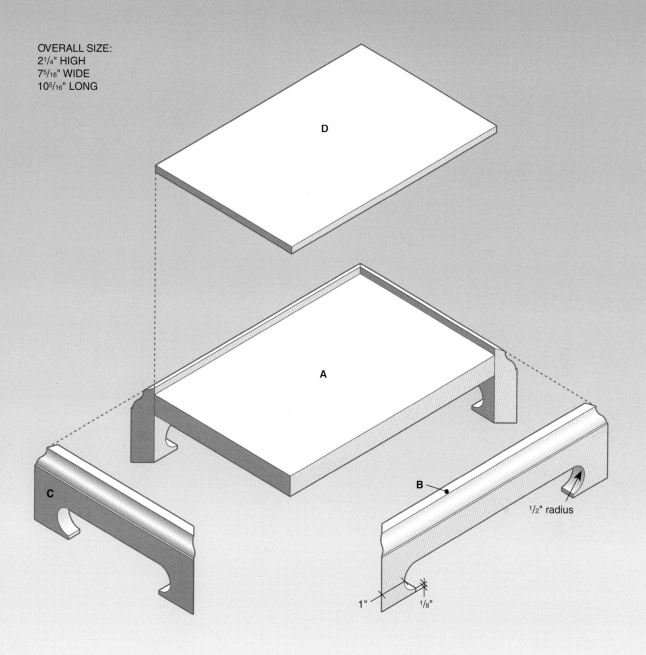

½" radius

1"

¹⁄₈"

Cutting List				
Key	**Part**	**Dimension**	**Pcs.**	**Material**
A	Substrate	¾ × 6 × 9"	1	MDF
B	Side	⅝ × 2¼ × 10⁵⁄₁₆"	2	Oak molding
C	End	⅝ × 2¼ × 5⁵⁄₁₆"	2	Oak molding
D	Tile	¼ × 6 × 9"	1	Ceramic tile

Materials: Waterproof wood glue, tile adhesive, 1" brads, finishing materials. (Optional: grout, clear silicone caulk.)

Note: Measurements reflect the actual thickness of dimension lumber.

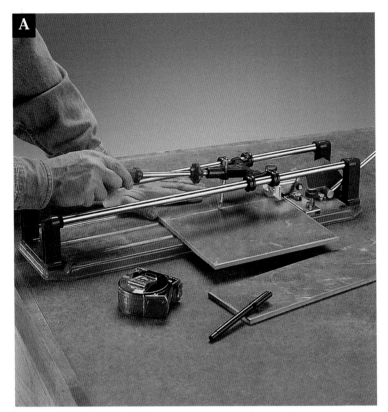

Use a tile cutter to make fast, clean cuts on ceramic tile.

Test-fit the base molding side and end pieces to the substrate and tile before applying glue.

Directions: Trivet

CUT THE TILE, SUBSTRATE, AND MOLDING.

A 12 × 12" tile cut to 6 × 9" is a convenient size for a trivet. It is large enough to hold a good-sized teapot, yet small enough to handle easily.

1. Mark and cut the tile to the correct size with a tile cutter **(photo A).** If you don't have a tile cutter, clamp the tile to your worksurface and cut it using a rod saw (like a coping saw, but with an abrasive blade designed for cutting tile).
2. Measure and cut the MDF substrate (A) to match the finished tile size.
3. Cut the sides (B) and ends (C) to length from the base molding. Make 45° miter cuts at the ends of each piece.

ATTACH THE MOLDING TO THE SUBSTRATE.

1. Place the tile face down on the worksurface and position the substrate, bottom side up, over the tile. Test-fit each side and end against the substrate.
2. Scribe a line along the edge of the substrate to mark where the substrate joins the molding **(photo B).**
3. Apply waterproof glue to the sides and ends, and attach them to the substrate so the reference marks are aligned. With the tile temporarily in place, fasten a band clamp around the perimeter at the line where the substrate edges meet the base molding **(photo C).**
4. Remove the band clamp and the tile after the glue dries.
5. Drill pilot holes through the molding into the substrate.

Secure the molding with 1" brads, and recess the nail heads with a nail set.

CREATE THE LEGS.

Legs are formed by cutting holes in the molding near each corner joint.

1. Measure in 1½" inches from each corner and ⅝" up from the bottom edge. This is the centerpoint for each hole.
2. Construct a small support backer board to fit inside the skirt formed by the base molding. Attach the jig to the bench so it overhangs the edge.
3. Place the trivet on the jig, and drill holes at each centerpoint with a 1" spade bit **(photo D).** Drill only through the sides and ends, and not into the substrate.
4. Draw a connecting line

Use a band clamp to hold base and ends in contact with the substrate while glue dries.

Use scrap plywood to support trivet and prevent tearouts while drilling "leg" holes in the molding.

between the tops of each set of holes, and cut along this line with your jig saw.

5. Complete each cutout by cutting straight up from the bottom edge into the center of each hole **(photo E).**

SAND AND FINISH.

1. Sand the cutout edges, making sure to round the sharp edges on the bottom of the legs. Finish the trivet as desired.

2. Apply an even coat of tile adhesive to the top of the substrate, and set the tile into the base. Depending on the width of the gap between the molding and the tile on the finished piece, you may want to fill it with a clear silicone caulk to prevent moisture or crumbs from collecting. If you selected mosaic tiles for this project,

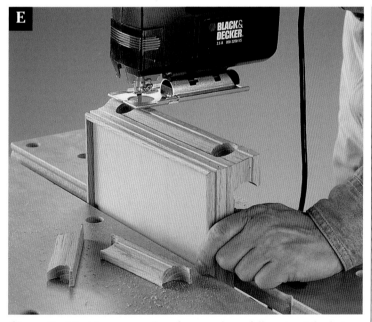

Clamp the trivet to your worksurface, and carefully cut out the legs, using a jig saw.

mask the sides of the base before grouting to protect the molding and apply a silicone

grout sealer when finished to prevent stains from penetrating the grout.

Plate & Spoon Rack

This easy-to-build rack displays your collectibles and shows off your woodworking ability.

Construction Materials

Quantity	Lumber
1	$^{21}\!/_{32} \times 24 \times 47\frac{1}{2}$" ponderosa pine panel

This decorative fixture, made from edge-glued ponderosa pine panels, has features you'll appreciate as your collection continues to grow. The back features three heart cutouts, and scallops along the top edge accentuate your most prized plates. The plate shelf has a groove cut into it to help stabi-

lize up to three full-size plates, while the sides are curved to soften the edges and to better display the plates. The spoon rack sits in front of a curved background that adds interest to the unit, while the rack itself has notches that hold up to seventeen collectible teaspoons.

OVERALL SIZE:
18" HIGH
3⅝" WIDE
27¹³⁄₁₆" LONG

1" squares

12½"

4¼"

SIDE VIEW

PART A DETAIL

1³⁄₈"

3⁄₈"

1⁄₄"

1⅛" ↦ 1¼" (typ.) ↦ 1½" (typ.) ↦ 3⁄₁₆" (typ.)

7⁄₁₆"

PART C DETAIL

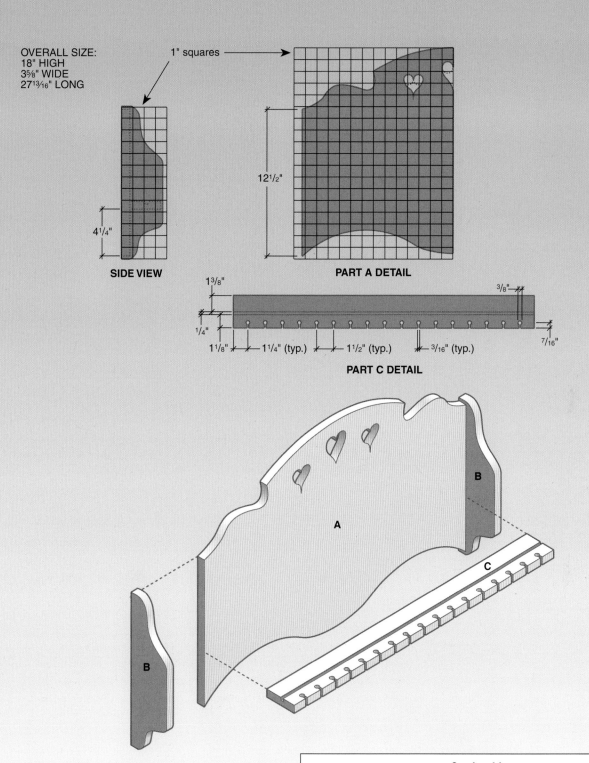

B

A

B

C

Cutting List				
Key	**Part**	**Dimension**	**Pcs.**	**Material**
A	Back	²¹⁄₃₂ × 18 × 26½"	1	Pine panel
B	Side	²¹⁄₃₂ × 3⅝ × 13"	2	Pine panel
C	Shelf	²¹⁄₃₂ × 2¾ × 26½"	1	Pine panel

Materials: #6 × 1½" wood screws, 4d finish nails, 2 steel keyhole hanger plates.

Note: Measurements reflect the actual thickness of dimension lumber.

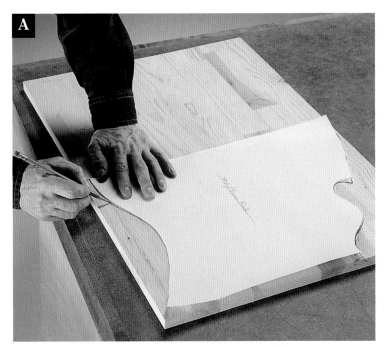

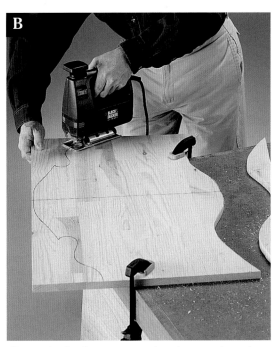

Lay out the pattern on the back piece by tracing half the pattern on one side of the centerline, then flipping the pattern and tracing the other side.

Clamp the back to your worksurface, and cut the pattern, using a jig saw.

Drill out the larger heart using a 1" spade bit. Use a ⅞" spade bit to create the smaller hearts. Complete the cutouts with a jig saw.

Directions:
Plate & Spoon Rack

CUT AND SHAPE THE BACK.

1. Cut the back blank (A) to overall size.

2. Transfer the decorative profile onto cardboard or heavy paper (see *Diagram*). Locate the back piece centerline and work both ways, tracing the pattern on one side of the centerline, then flipping the pattern over at the centerline and tracing the other symmetrical side **(photo A).**

3. Cut the edge shapes with a jig saw, taking care that the ends, which will be attached to the sides, are finished at 12½" **(photo B).**

CUT THE HEART DETAILS.

The back has two different-sized heart cutouts (see *Diagram*).

1. Trace the heart cutouts onto the back piece.

2. Protect your worksurface with a piece of scrap, and drill two horizontally adjacent holes, using a 1" spade bit for the larger heart and a ⅞" bit for the smaller hearts **(photo C)**.

3. Complete the cutouts with a jig saw.

CUT THE SIDES.

1. Cut the side blanks (B) to overall size. Transfer the side profile to cardboard (see *Diagram*) and then trace onto one side.

2. Cut one side with a jig saw, then use it as a pattern to mark and cut the other side.

CUT AND SHAPE THE SHELF.

The shelf has a groove to hold the plates, and notches to hold the spoons.

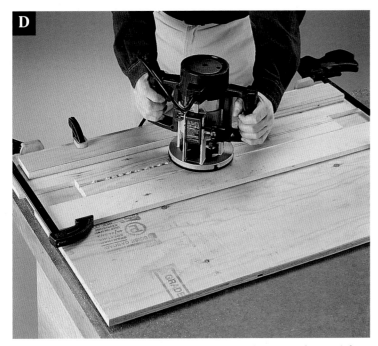

Cut the plate groove into the shelf, using bar clamps and a straightedge to hold the shelf in place and guide the router.

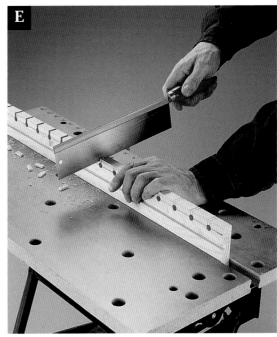

Cut a ³⁄₁₆"-wide notch along the front edge for each of the spoon rack holes, using a backsaw.

1. Cut the shelf (C) to size.

2. Make a simple routing jig by clamping two pieces of ¾" scrap wood against the edges of the shelf. Securely clamp a straightedge over the scrap wood to guide the router base and cut the groove at the desired location (see *Diagram*) with a ¼" straight router bit set ¼" deep **(photo D).**

3. Measure and mark the 17 spoon hole centerpoints (see *Diagram*). Drill the holes, using a ⅜" bit.

4. Complete the spoon hole cutouts, using a backsaw to make two straight cuts into the holes, leaving a ³⁄₁₆" slot **(photo E).**

5. Sand all cut edges before assembling.

ASSEMBLE THE RACK.

1. Drill pilot holes into the sides and attach to the back using glue and 4d finish nails.

2. Position the shelf, then drive 4d finish nails through the sides into the shelf **(photo F).**

3. Drill countersunk pilot holes and drive wood screws through the back into the shelf.

APPLY FINISHING TOUCHES.

1. Drill or chisel out space so the keyhole hanger plates are flush with the back surface of the rack. Drive screws through the hanger plates into the back of the rack.

2. Sand smooth and apply a finish.

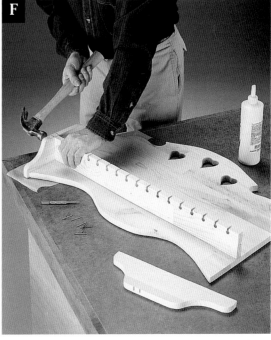

Attach the shelf to the sides with finish nails and to the back with wood screws.

> **TIP**
>
> *Pine wood actually sands better with a vibrating sander than a belt sander because pitch typically builds up faster in the belt and causes burn marks or unevenness.*

China Cabinet

This tall, sleek fixture displays and stores fine china and other housewares without occupying a lot of floor space.

This modern-looking china cabinet features a snappy, efficient design to showcase and store all types of china and dishware with equal elegance. The bottom half of the cabinet is a simple cupboard for storing everyday serving trays, napkins, silverware and miscellaneous houseware.

The upper half is an open rack for displaying your favorite porcelain statues, china, vases and collectibles.

The asymmetrical design allows you to store and display a wider range of items than if the cabinet was equally weighted on the right and left. And the overall slenderness of the cabinet means you can fit it into just about any room, whether it's tucked into a corner or featured prominently along the center of a wall.

Plates and other items that are displayed in the rack area of the cabinet can be accentuated with plateholders. Or, you can do as we did and build a few custom-sized plate holders from scraps of molding. Just cut the molding into strips about the same width as the plates, and inset the strips at ¼" intervals in a plain wood frame.

CONSTRUCTION MATERIALS

Quantity	Lumber
2	¾" × 4 × 8' birch plywood
2	1"-dia. × 3' dowel
1	½ × ½ " × 3' quarter-round molding

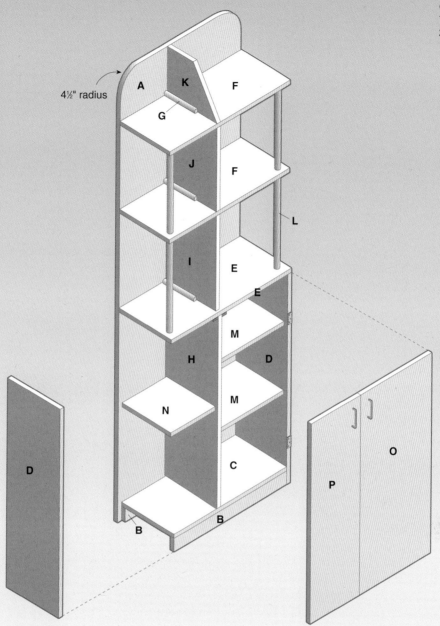

OVERALL SIZE:
75" HIGH
24" WIDE
12" DEEP

4½" radius

Cutting List

Key	Part	Dimension	Pcs.	Material
A	Back	¾ × 24 × 75"	1	Plywood
B	Bottom rail	¾ × 2¼ × 22½"	2	Plywood
C	Cupboard bottom	¾ × 10½ × 22½"	1	Plywood
D	Cupboard side	¾ × 10½ × 35¼"	2	Plywood
E	Cupboard top	¾ × 10½ × 24"	1	Plywood
F	Rack shelf	¾ × 10 × 24"	2	Plywood
G	Cleat	½ × ½ × 6"	6	Toe molding
H	Cupboard divider	¾ × 10½ × 32¼"	1	Plywood

Cutting List

Key	Part	Dimension	Pcs.	Material
I	Rack divider	¾ × 10 × 15⅛"	1	Plywood
J	Rack divider	¾ × 10 × 14¾"	1	Plywood
K	Rack divider	¾ × 10 × 7½"	1	Plywood
L	Column	1 × 30⅝"	2	Dowel
M	Cupboard shelf	¾ × 13¼ × 10"	2	Plywood
N	Cupboard shelf	¾ × 8½ × 10"	1	Plywood
O	Large door	¾ × 14⅜ × 33¾"	1	Plywood
P	Small door	¾ × 9½ × 33¾"	1	Plywood

Materials: Wood glue, wood screws (#6 × 1¼", #6 × 2"), birch veneer edge tape (50'), ⅜"-dia. birch wood plugs, 1¼" brass butt hinges (4), 1¼" brads, magnetic door catches (2), 2½" brass door pulls (2), finishing materials.

Note: Measurements reflect the actual size of dimension lumber.

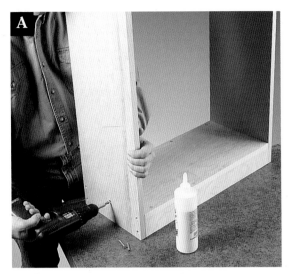

Attach the cupboard bottom by driving screws through the cupboard sides and into the edges.

Carefully sand the wood plugs to level, using a belt sander or power hand sander.

Directions: China Cabinet

MAKE THE BACK PANEL.
The back panel runs the entire height of the china cabinet, anchoring both the rack and cupboard units.
1. Cut the back (A) to size.
2. Use a compass to draw a semicircle roundover with a 4½" radius at each top corner of the back panel. Cut the curves with a jig saw.
3. Use a household iron to apply birch veneer edge tape to the side and top edges of the back. Trim the excess tape with a sharp utility knife, then sand the edges smooth.
4. Mark reference points 51⅞" and 67⅜" up from the bottom edge, and 9¼" in from one side edge.

MAKE THE CUPBOARD.
1. Cut the bottom rails (B) and cupboard bottom (C) to size.
2. Apply edge tape to one long edge of the cupboard bottom.
3. Position the bottom rails beneath the cupboard bottom, flush with the edges. Drill counterbored pilot holes through the cupboard bottom and into

the tops of the rails, then attach the parts with glue and #6 × 2" wood screws.
4. Cut the cupboard sides (D) to size, and apply edge tape to the front edges.
5. Position the cupboard bottom between the cupboard sides. Drill counterbored pilot holes, then apply glue and drive wood screws through the sides and into the edges of the cupboard bottom **(photo A).**
6. Cut the cupboard top (E) to size, and apply edge tape to the front and side edges. Attach it to the tops of the cupboard sides with glue and screws driven down through the cupboard top and into the tops of the sides.

ATTACH CUPBOARD SHELVES AND DIVIDER.
1. Cut the cupboard divider (H) and cupboard shelves (M, N) to size. Apply veneer tape to the front edges of all shelves.

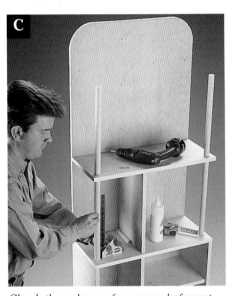

Check the columns for square before attaching them to the cabinet top.

2. Draw reference lines on the cupboard bottom and cupboard top, 9¼" in from the left cupboard side, for positioning the divider between them.
3. Set the divider between the cupboard top and bottom, so the left face is aligned with the reference lines. Attach the divider with glue and wood screws, driven through the top and bottom and into the divider.
4. Draw reference lines on the right side and right face of the

divider, 12" and 24" up from the bottoms, for positioning the larger cupboard shelves (M). Draw reference lines for the smaller cupboard shelf (N) 16" up from the bottoms on the left side and left face of the divider.

5. Apply glue to the side edges of all three shelves and position them between the cupboard sides and the divider, with their bottoms on the reference lines. Make sure the back edges of the shelves are flush with the back edges of the sides. Fasten the shelves with #6 × 2" wood screws, driven through the sides and the divider, and into the edges of the shelves.

6. Glue ⅜"-dia. birch wood plugs into all the exposed counterbores in the cupboard. When the glue has dried, carefully sand down the plugs. **(photo B).**

7. Attach the back panel to the cupboard with glue and #6 × 2" wood screws.

MAKE AND MARK THE RACK PARTS.

1. Cut the rack dividers (I, J, K) to full size. The upper divider (K) is trimmed off at an angle on the front edge by marking a point on one long edge, 5¼" from one end. Draw a straight line from that point to the bottom corner on the opposite end and cut along the line.

2. Cut the two rack shelves (F) to size, sand smooth, then attach veneer edge tape to the front edges of the rack dividers, and to the front and side edges of the rack shelves. With the taped edges facing you, draw reference lines on the shelves, 9¼" in from the left sides.

3. Drill two 1"-dia. holes for the columns (L) all the way through one shelf. The center

of each hole should be 1¾" in from the front edge and 1¼" in from the side edge of the shelf. This shelf will become the lower rack shelf.

4. Cut the columns (L) to length.

INSTALL THE RACK.

1. Use glue and #6 × 2" wood screws, driven through counterbored pilot holes in the back panel, to fasten the lower rack divider (I) in position at the marks on the shelf and back panel. Use a square to make sure the divider is perpendicular to the back panel.

2. Cut cleats from quarter-round molding (G) to size, and use glue and 1¼" brads to attach the cleats on each side of the divider, flush against the back.

3. Apply glue to the top edge of the lower divider, and position the shelf with the 1"-dia. holes on top of the divider, so the holes are in front. Attach the shelf to the divider with wood screws, driven through the back and into the shelf, and through the shelf and into the lower divider.

4. Apply glue to the bottom of each column, and slide them through the holes in the shelf. Use a square to make sure they are straight **(photo C),** then drive a #6 × 1¼" wood screw up through the cabinet top and into the bottom of each column.

5. Position the middle rack divider (J) on the shelf. Fasten it with glue, screws and cleats.

6. Attach the upper shelf to the middle divider and back panel with glue and wood screws.

7. Drive #6 × 1¼" wood screws through the shelf and into the tops of the columns.

8. Apply glue to the back and bottom edges of the upper divider, and attach it with wood screws and cleats.

INSTALL THE DOORS.

1. Cut the doors (O, P) to size. Apply edge tape to all edges of each door.

2. Attach 1¼" brass butt hinges to the doors, 3½" down from the top edges, and ½" up from the bottom edges. Fasten the doors to the cupboard sides, flush with the cabinet top **(photo D).**

3. Install magnetic door catches on the cupboard divider and doors. Attach door pulls to the outside faces of the doors, 1½" down from the top edges of the doors, and 1½" in from the inside edges.

4. Finish-sand, wipe clean with a tack cloth, then apply your finish of choice. We applied two coats of polyurethane over unstained wood.

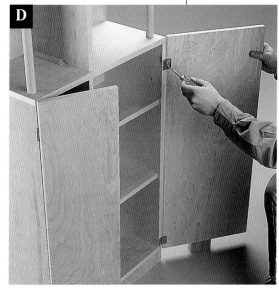

Hang the doors with brass butt hinges.

PROJECT
POWER TOOLS

Sideboard

This elegant sideboard has plenty of room to hold everything from a meal with all the trimmings to stacks of important files.

The sideboard is an attractive, multipurpose fixture that can be used as a food serving counter, file holder—anything that requires shelf or counter space. The sideboard is a traditional home fixture, adding low-profile storage to just about any area of the home. Positioned against a wall or behind a desk, the sideboard is out of the way, yet is perfect for storing games, photo albums and other items you want to keep close at hand.

We made the sideboard out of oak and oak plywood. The construction is simple and sturdy. Two long interior shelves span the length of the project, giving you a surprising amount of storage space for such a small unit. The top shelf is concealed by two plywood doors, while the bottom shelf is left open for easy access to stored items. Cove molding fastened around the edges of the top and the curved profiles of the legs add a touch of style to this simple project.

CONSTRUCTION MATERIALS

Quantity	Lumber
1	¾" × 4 × 8' oak plywood
2	1 × 4" × 8' oak
2	¾ × ¾" × 8' oak cove molding

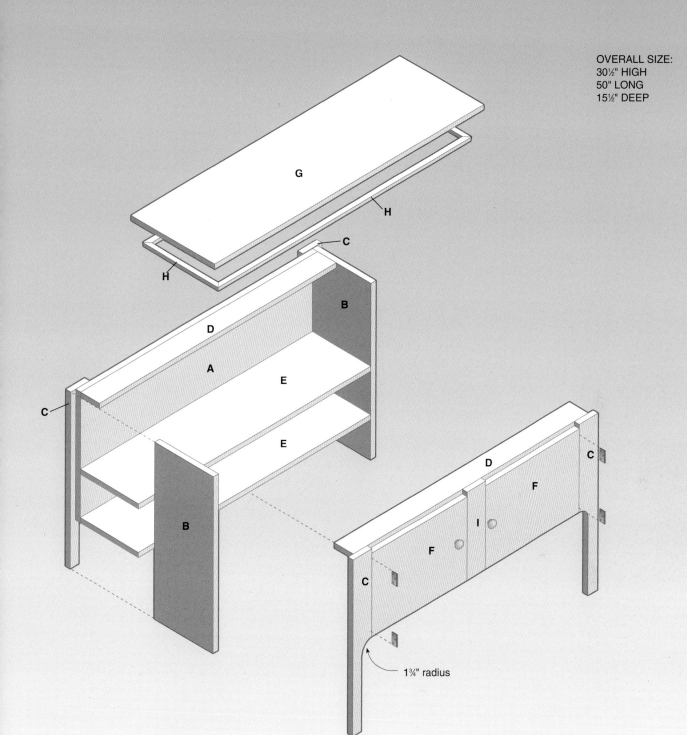

OVERALL SIZE:
30½" HIGH
50" LONG
15½" DEEP

1¾" radius

Cutting List

Key	Part	Dimension	Pcs.	Material
A	Back panel	¾ × 20 × 44"	1	Plywood
B	End panel	¾ × 11 × 29¾"	2	Plywood
C	Leg	¾ × 3½ × 29¾"	4	Oak
D	Cleat	¾ × 2½ × 44"	2	Plywood
E	Shelf	¾ × 10¼ × 44"	2	Plywood

Cutting List

Key	Part	Dimension	Pcs.	Material
F	Door	¾ × 13⅛ × 17⅜"	2	Plywood
G	Top panel	¾ × 15½ × 50"	1	Plywood
H	Top trim	¾ × ¾ × *	4	Cove molding
I	Stile	¾ × 3½ × 14"	1	Oak

Materials: #6 × 1" and 2" wood screws, 16-ga. × 1¼" brads, 1½ × 3" brass butt hinges (4), ⅞"-dia. tack-on furniture glides (4), 1"-dia. brass knobs (2), roller catches (2), ¾" oak veneer edge tape (35'), ⅜"-dia. oak plugs, wood glue, finishing materials.

Note: Measurements reflect the actual size of dimension lumber.
*Cut to fit.

Directions: Sideboard

MAKE THE CARCASE.

For all screws used in this project, drill $\frac{3}{32}$" pilot holes. Counterbore the holes $\frac{1}{4}$" deep, using a $\frac{3}{8}$" counterbore bit.

1. Cut the back panel (A), end panels (B) and shelves (E) to size. Sand the shelf edges.

2. Use a household iron to apply self-adhesive edge tape to one long edge of each shelf. Trim the edges with a utility knife. Sand all parts smooth.

3. Set the back flat on your worksurface. Position one face of an end panel against each short edge of the back panel, making sure the top edges are flush. Attach the panels with glue and drive 2" wood screws through the end panels and into the back. Be sure to keep the outside face of the back panel flush with the back edges of the end panels.

4. Position the bottom shelf between the end panels, making sure the edge with the veneer tape faces away from the back panel. The bottom face of the shelf should be flush with the bottom edge of the back. Attach the bottom shelf with glue and drive 2" wood screws through the end panels and back panels and into the shelf.

5. Set the carcase (or cabinet frame) upright. Position $5\frac{1}{4}$"-wide spacer blocks on the bottom shelf. Set the top shelf on the spacer blocks. Attach the top shelf with glue and 2" wood screws **(photo A)**.

6. Cut the cleats (D) to size, and sand them smooth.

7. Use glue and 2" wood screws to fasten one cleat between the end panels so one long edge is flush with the front edges of the end panels.

8. Attach the remaining cleat to the end and back panels so one long edge is butted against the back panel. Both cleats should be flush with the tops of the carcase.

MAKE THE LEGS.

The sideboard legs have curves that taper them to $1\frac{3}{4}$" in width.

1. Cut the legs (C) to length.

2. Designate a top and bottom of each leg. Draw a centerline from top to bottom on each leg. Then, draw reference lines across the legs, 14" and $15\frac{3}{4}$" up from the bottom. Set a compass to draw a $1\frac{3}{4}$"-radius semicircle. Set the point of the compass on the lower reference line, as close as possible to one long edge. Draw the semicircle to complete the curved portion of the cutting line.

3. Clamp the legs to your worksurface, and use a jig saw to cut them to shape, starting at the bottom and following the centerline and semicircle all the way to the end of the top reference line **(photo B)**. Sand the cutouts smooth.

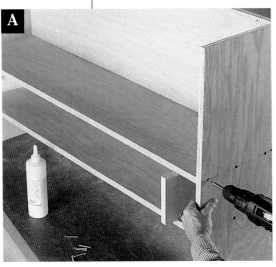

Use $5\frac{1}{4}$" spacer blocks set on the bottom shelf to position the top shelf for fastening.

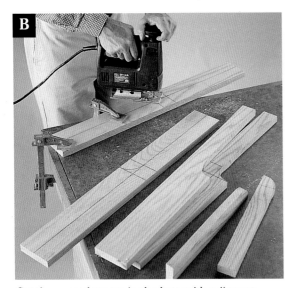

Cut the curved tapers in the legs with a jig saw.

Fasten the legs to the front edges of the end panels. Make sure the outside edges of the legs overhang the end panels by $\frac{1}{4}$".

Measure the front and back overhang to make sure the carcase is centered on the top panel.

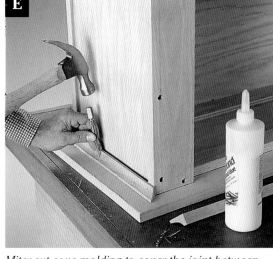

Miter-cut cove molding to cover the joint between the top panel and the carcase.

ATTACH THE LEGS AND STILE.

1. Position two legs against the front edges of the end panels, with the cutout edges facing in. Make sure the legs are flush with the end panels at the top and bottom edges, and that they overhang the outside faces of the end panels by ¼". Attach the legs to the edges of the end panels with glue and 2" wood screws **(photo C).**

2. Cut the stile (I) to length.

3. Center the stile between the legs so it spans the gap between the cleat and top shelf. Make sure the bottom edge of the stile is flush with the bottom of the top shelf. Attach it with glue and 2" wood screws.

4. Turn the project over. Fasten the remaining legs to the back and ends. Maintain the ¼" overhang of the end panels, and keep the top edges flush.

INSTALL THE TOP PANEL.

1. Cut the top panel (G) to size.

2. Apply edge tape to all four edges of the top. Sand the surfaces smooth.

3. Lay the top on your worksurface with its better face down.

Center the carcase over the top. The top should extend 1½" beyond the front and back of the legs, and 2¼" beyond the outside faces of the end panels **(photo D).** Drive 1" wood screws through the cleats and into the top.

4. Cut the top trim (H) to fit around the underside of the top, miter-cutting the ends at 45° angles so they fit together at the corners.

5. Drill ¹⁄₁₆" pilot holes through the trim pieces to prevent splitting. Apply glue and drive 1¼" brads through the top trim and into the top panel. Set the brads with a nail set **(photo E).**

ATTACH THE DOORS.

1. Cut the doors (F) to size.

2. Apply edge tape to all four edges of each door.

3. Attach 1½ × 3" brass butt hinges to one short edge of each door, starting 2" in from the top and bottom. Mount the doors on the carcase by attaching the hinges to the legs **(photo F).** Make sure the bottom edges of the doors are flush with the bottom of the top shelf.

Attach each door to a leg, using 1½ × 3" butt hinges.

APPLY FINISHING TOUCHES.

1. Fill all nail holes with stainable wood putty. Glue oak plugs into all screw holes. Finish-sand all of the surfaces. Remove the door hinges and apply the finish of your choice.

2. Reattach the doors after the finish has dried. Fasten 1"-dia. brass knobs to the door fronts, and mount roller catches on the doors and stile, 5" down from the top of the stile. Tack furniture glides to the bottom ends of the legs.

Wine & Stemware Cart

PROJECT
POWER TOOLS

This solid oak cart with a lift-off tray allows you to transport and serve your wine safely and provides an elegant place to display your vintage selections.

CONSTRUCTION MATERIALS

Quantity	Lumber
2	1 × 12" × 6' oak
1	1 × 4" × 8' oak
1	1 × 4" × 6' oak
1	1 × 3" × 2' oak
1	1 × 2" × 4' oak
1	½ × 2¾" × 2' oak*
1	½ × 3¾" × 4' oak*

*Available at woodworker's supply stores.

With our versatile oak wine and stemware cart, you can display, move and serve wine and other cordials from one convenient station. This cart can store up to 15 bottles of wine, liquor, soda or mix, and it holds the bottles in the correct downward position to prevent wine corks from drying out.

The upper stemware rack holds more than a dozen long-stemmed wine or champagne glasses, and a removable serving tray with easy-to-grip handles works well for cutting cheese and for serving drinks and snacks. Beneath the tray is a handy storage area for napkins, corkscrews and other items. Sturdy swivel casters make this wine rack fully mobile over tile, vinyl or carpeting.

OVERALL SIZE:
40³/₈" HIGH
23¹/₂" WIDE
11¹/₄" DEEP

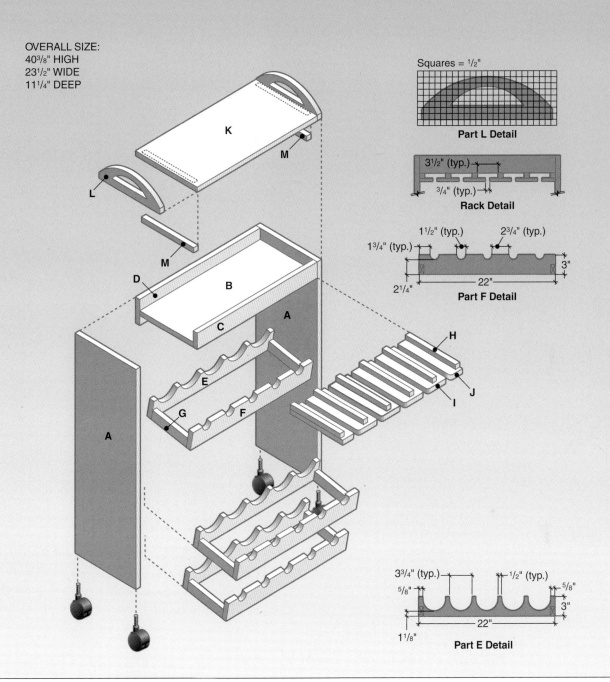

Squares = ¹/₂"

Part L Detail

3¹/₂" (typ.)
³/₄" (typ.)

Rack Detail

1³/₄" (typ.)   1¹/₂" (typ.)   2³/₄" (typ.)
2¹/₄"   22"   3"

Part F Detail

3³/₄" (typ.)   ¹/₂" (typ.)   ⁵/₈"
⁵/₈"   3"
22"
1¹/₈"

Part E Detail

Key	Part	Dimension	Pcs.	Material
A	Side	¾ × 11¼ × 34"	2	Oak
B	Top	¾ × 9¾ × 22"	1	Oak
C	Front stretcher	¾ × 2½ × 22"	1	Oak
D	Back stretcher	¾ × 4 × 22"	1	Oak
E	Wine rack, back	¾ × 3 × 22"	3	Oak
F	Wine rack, front	¾ × 3 × 22"	3	Oak
G	Wine rack, cleat	¾ × 1½ × 6½"	6	Oak

Key	Part	Dimension	Pcs.	Material
H	Stemware slat	¾ × ¾ × 9¼"	6	Oak
I	Stemware plate	½ × 3½ × 9¾"	4	Oak
J	End plate	½ × 2⅛ × 9¾"	2	Oak
K	Tray	¾ × 11¼ × 22"	1	Oak
L	Tray handle	¾ × 3½ × 11¼"	2	Oak
M	Tray feet	¾ × ¾ × 9½"	2	Oak

Table headers: **Cutting List** (both tables)

Materials: #6 × 1", 1¼" and 1½" wood screws, ⅜"-dia. oak plugs, casters (4), wood glue, finishing materials.

Note: Measurements reflect the actual size of dimension lumber.

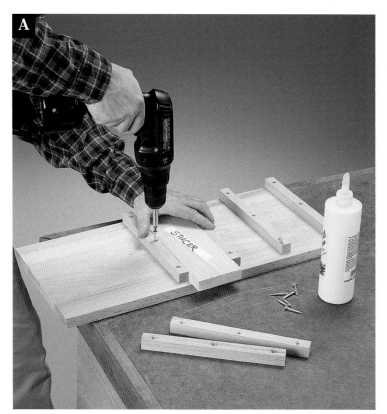

Use a spacer to keep the slats aligned properly, and attach them with glue and screws.

Use a drum sander attached to your portable drill to smooth the jig saw cuts on the wine racks.

Directions:
Wine & Stemware Cart

CONSTRUCT THE SIDES AND STEMWARE RACK.

Before fastening frame parts together, make sure the assembly is square (see *Tip*).

1. Cut the cart sides (A), top (B) and back stretcher (D) from 1 × 12 oak. Cut the front stretcher (C) from 1 × 3 oak and the stemware slats (H) from 1 × 4 oak. Cut the plates (I) and end plates (J) from ½"-thick oak.

2. Clamp a belt sander to your worksurface, and use it as a grinder to round over the front corners of the stemware plates, and one front corner of each end plate.

3. Sand all of the pieces smooth.

4. Place the top flat on your worksurface. Arrange the slats on its bottom face, flush with the back edge. Space the slats 3½" apart, using a piece of scrap wood as a spacer **(photo A).** Keep the outer slats flush with the ends of the top. Drill ³⁄₃₂" pilot holes through the slats, and counterbore the holes ⅛" deep, using a ⅜" counterbore bit. Attach the slats with glue and 1¼" wood screws.

BUILD THE WINE RACKS.

First assemble the wine racks as individual units. Then, attach them to the sides of the cart.

1. Cut the wine rack backs (E)

and fronts (F) from 1 × 4 oak, and cut the cleats (G) from 1 × 2 oak.

2. Measuring from one end, mark points at 2½", 6¾", 11", 15¼" and 19½" on the long edges of the wine rack backs and fronts.

3. Use a compass set at 1⅞" for the rack back. Set the point of the compass on each reference mark, as close as possible to the edge, and draw the five semicircles. Set the compass for ¾" and draw the semicircles for the rack front. Carefully make the cutouts with a jig saw.

4. Position the cleats between the rack fronts and backs, and drill two pilot holes through the faces of the fronts and backs and into the ends of the cleats. Counterbore the holes ¼" deep. Join the pieces with glue and 1½" wood screws.

TIP

To check for square, measure your project from one corner diagonally to its opposite corner. Repeat the procedure for the other two corners. If the two diagonal lines are equal, your assembly is square.

Measure ½" along the front and 2½" along the back of each side, and connect the marks for the bottom rack alignment.

Clamp a 4 × 10" spacer between the bottom and middle racks for proper positioning.

Drive screws through the slats to secure the top to the sides.

5. Fill the counterbores with glued oak plugs. Sand the plugs flush with the surface, and smooth any rough edges. Clamp each completed rack to your worksurface, and sand the cutouts smooth with a drum sander **(photo B).**

ATTACH THE WINE RACKS.

1. Measure up ½" from the bottom on the inside face of each side piece, and make a mark at the front edge. Measure up 2½" from the bottom, and make a mark at the back edge. Draw an angled reference line between the marks **(photo C).**
2. With one of the side pieces lying flat on your worksurface, position a wine rack so the bottom edge is on the reference line and the front edge is set back ¾" from the front edge of the side piece. Drill pilot holes through the rack cleats, and counterbore the holes ⅛" deep. Attach the rack to the side with glue and 1¼" wood screws.
3. Attach the middle and top racks in the same manner, using a 4 × 10" spacer to position them correctly **(photo D).**
4. Use bar or pipe clamps to hold the remaining side piece in position. Make sure the bottom rack is on the reference line, and use the spacer to set the positions of the middle and top racks. Fasten the racks to the side piece.
5. Arrange the stretchers

between the sides so their top and outside edges are flush with the tops and outside edges of the sides. Drill pilot holes through the sides and into the ends of the stretchers. Counterbore the holes ¼" deep. Attach the stretchers with glue and 1½" wood screws.

ATTACH THE TOP ASSEMBLY.

1. Lay the cart on its side, and clamp the top between the side pieces. The bottom face of the top should be flush with the bottom edge of the front stretcher.

2. Measure the distance between the top and the top ends of the sides to make sure the top is level. Drill pilot holes through the outer slats and into the sides, and counterbore the holes ⅛" deep. Apply glue to the edges of the top and to the outside edges of the outer slats. Position the top, and drive 1¼" wood screws through the outer slats and into the sides **(photo E).**

3. Drill three evenly spaced pilot holes, counterbored ¼" deep, through both stretchers and into the edges of the top, and secure the pieces with 1½" wood screws.

COMPLETE THE RACK AND FIT THE CASTERS.

Attach the stemware plates to the slats to complete the stemware rack.

1. Set the cart upside down on your worksurface. Position an end plate onto an outside slat, with its square side flush against the side panel and its square end flush against the back stretcher. Drill two pilot holes down through the end plate, taking care to avoid the

Use a ¾"-thick spacer to guide the placement of the stemware plates.

TIP

Jig saw blades cut on the upward stroke, so the top side of the workpiece may splinter. To protect the finished or exposed side of a piece, make the cut with the piece's face side down. This way, if the edge splinters, it will remain hidden on the unexposed side. Remember to maintain a fast blade speed if you are cutting with a coarse-tooth blade. When cutting curves, use a narrow blade, and move the saw slowly to avoid bending the blade. Some jig saws have a scrolling knob that allows you to turn the blade without turning the saw.

---

screws in the slat beneath. Counterbore the holes ⅛" deep, and fasten the plate with glue and 1" wood screws.

2. Repeat these steps to position and attach the remaining plates. Use a ¾"-thick spacer between the plates to ensure uniform spacing **(photo F).**

3. Drill holes into the bottom edges of the cart sides, and test-

fit the casters **(photo G).** Position the holes so they are centered on the edge from side to side and are no less than 1" from the front and back side edges. For the casters to work properly, the holes must be perpendicular to the bottom edges of the sides.

Drill holes for the casters in the bottom edges of the sides.

Drill a pilot hole, and cut the inside handle profile with a jig saw. Use scrap wood as a backer board to prevent splintering.

MAKE THE TRAY.

The wine cart tray is an oak board with handles and narrow feet.

1. Cut the tray (K) from 1 × 12 oak, and cut the tray handle (L) blanks from 1 × 4 oak. Cut the ¾ × ¾" feet (M) from leftover 1 × 12.

2. Transfer the pattern for the handles onto one of the blanks (see *Diagram*).

3. Drill a starter hole on the inside portion of the handle, using a backer board to prevent splintering. Use a jig saw to cut along the pattern lines **(photo H).**

4. Trace the outline of the shaped handle onto the remaining handle blank. Cut the pattern on the second handle. Clamp the two handles together, and gang-sand them so

their shapes are identical.

5. Position the tray between the handles, and drill three evenly spaced pilot holes through the side of each handle. Counterbore the holes ¼" deep. Attach the handles to the ends of the tray with glue and 1½" wood screws.

6. Position the tray feet on the bottom edge of the tray, ⅛" in from the side edges and ⅞" from the front and back edges. Drill pilot holes through the feet, and counterbore the holes ⅛" deep. Attach the feet with glue and 1" wood screws.

APPLY FINISHING TOUCHES.

1. Glue oak plugs into all visible counterbore holes, and sand flush with the surface. Finish-sand the entire cart.

TIP

Applying a thin coat of sanding sealer before staining helps the wood absorb stain evenly and can eliminate blotchy finishes. Sanding sealer is a clear liquid, usually applied with a brush. Read the package labels of the different products you plan to use to make sure the finishes are compatible.

2. Apply your choice of stain and a polyurethane topcoat and allow the finish to dry. We used a rustic oak stain and two coats of polyurethane.

NOTE: If you will be using the tray as a cutting board, be sure to apply a nontoxic finish.

3. Install the casters on the bottom of the cart. You may want to use at least one locking caster so your cart stays put.

Vertical Display Cabinet

Sturdy but airy, this open display unit combines the warmth of oak with the glimmer of glass.

PROJECT
POWER TOOLS

Construction Materials

Quantity	Lumber
1	1 × 1" × 8' oak
12	1 × 2" × 8' oak
2	1 × 4" × 8' oak
1	1 × 4" × 4' oak
1	1 × 6" × 8' oak
1	¾" × 4 × 4' oak plywood
1	3½" × 8' oak crown
1	8' oak base shoe
3	⅜ × 16¾ × 39¼" tempered glass

Compare the design and price of our vertical display cabinet to those available in stores, and you'll be impressed. Though the materials are not expensive, this project is by no means cheaply constructed. The slender stiles are made from oak for strength.

The oak back braces perform double duty by adding an unusual visual element as well as reinforcing the cabinet. Transparent glass shelves give the cabinet a modern appeal, while oak crown and base trim pieces lend classic elegance.

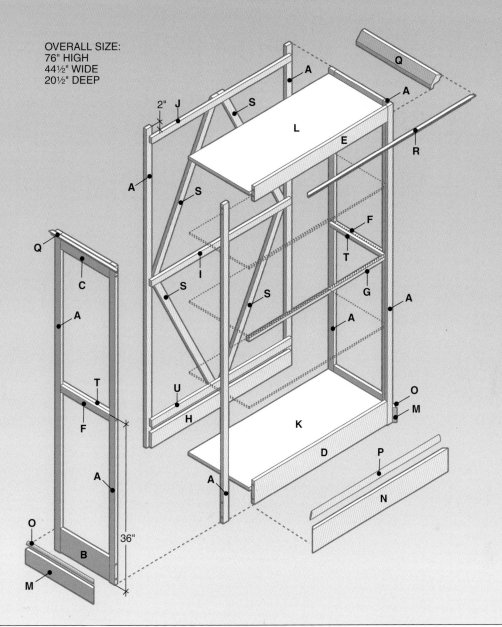

OVERALL SIZE:
76" HIGH
44½" WIDE
20½" DEEP

Cutting List

Key	Part	Dimension	Pcs.	Material
A	Stile	¾ × 1½ × 76"	8	Oak
B	Short bottom rail	¾ × 5½ × 14"	2	Oak
C	Short top rail	¾ × 3½ × 14"	2	Oak
D	Long bottom rail	¾ × 5½ × 38"	1	Oak
E	Long top rail	¾ × 3½ × 38"	1	Oak
F	Center rail	¾ × 1½ × 14"	2	Oak
G	Front shelf rail	¾ × ¾ × 39½"	1	Oak
H	Back bottom cleat	¾ × 3½ × 39½"	1	Oak
I	Back shelf rail	¾ × 1½ × 39½"	1	Oak
J	Back top cleat	¾ × 1½ × 39½"	1	Oak
K	Bottom	¾ × 17 × 39½"	1	Oak ply.

Cutting List

Key	Part	Dimension	Pcs.	Material
L	Top	¾ × 17 × 39½"	1	Oak ply.
M	Side base	¾ × 3½ × 19¼"	2	Oak
N	Front base	¾ × 3½ × 42½"	1	Oak
O	Side base cap	⅜ × ¾ × 19¼"	2	Oak base shoe
P	Front base cap	⅜ × ¾ × 42½"	1	Oak base shoe
Q	Side crown mldg.	¾ × 3½ × 21"	2	Oak crown
R	Front crown mldg.	¾ × 3½ × 44½"	1	Oak crown
S	Back brace	¾ × 1½ × 39¾"	4	Oak
T	Center shelf cleat	¾ × ¾ × 15⅜"	2	Oak
U	Bottom stretcher	¾ × 1½ × 39½"	1	Oak

Materials: Wood glue, #6 wood screws (1¼", 1½"), 4d finish nails, 1" brads, ⅜" × 4' oak doweling (2), ⅜" oak plugs, plastic pin-style shelf supports (12), self-adhesive shelf cushions, finishing materials.

Note: Measurements reflect the actual thickness of dimension lumber.

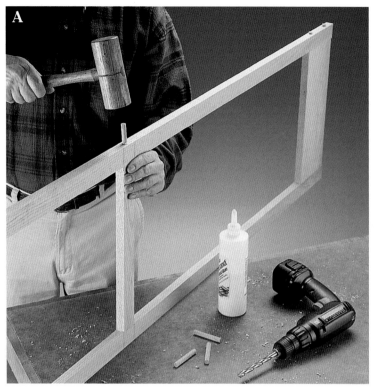

Use a wood mallet to pound ⅜" glued oak dowels into the end frame.

Measure the diagonals to check for square. If the measurements are equal, the frame is square.

**Directions:
Vertical Display Cabinet**

MAKE THE END FRAMES.
Dowel joints make the end frames sturdy and rigid. Through-dowel joints are the easiest dowel joints to make— all you need is a good bar or pipe clamp and the ability to drill a reasonably straight guide hole.

1. Cut the stiles (A), short bottom rails (B), short top rails (C) and center rails (F) to size, and sand smooth.

2. Make a reference mark on each stile 36" down from the top edge. Position a top short rail between two stiles with the top edges flush. Position a bottom rail ¼" up from the bottom of the stiles, and place the center rail so the top edge lies on the 36" mark.

3. Cut 20 lengths of ⅜" dowling, 2½" long. Score the edges of the dowels to make them easier to insert (see *Tip*).

4. Drill ⅜ × 2½"-deep holes through the stiles into the rails (see *Diagram*).

5. Apply glue to the joints and drive dowels into the holes **(photo A).**

6. Check to make sure the end frames are square, then clamp the pieces together until the glue dries.

MAKE THE FRONT FRAME.
You'll want to choose wood with matching or similar grain patterns for the front frame, base and crown molding to further enhance the beauty of your project.

1. Cut the long bottom rail (D) and long top rail (E) to size, and sand smooth.

2. Position the rails between the two stiles (the top rail should be flush, the bottom rail should be ¼" up from the ends of the stiles).

3. Drill holes and attach the

TIP

Custom-cut dowels can be difficult to fit into snug holes. To make insertion easier, score a groove along the length of each dowel. This groove allows air and excess glue to escape when driving the dowels into their holes.

C

Position the back over the end frames at the ¾" space, and join with glue and screws.

rails and stiles with glued ⅜" dowels.

4. Cut the front shelf rail (G) to size, and sand smooth.

5. Lay the front frame face-down, then position the front shelf rail so the top edge is flush with the 36" reference lines on the stiles and the ends are set back ¾" from the edges of the stiles.

6. Drill countersunk pilot holes and fasten the shelf rail with glue and 1¼" screws.

MAKE THE BACK FRAME.

1. Cut the back bottom cleat (H), the back shelf rail (I) and the back top cleat (J) to size, and sand smooth.

2. Lay two stiles on your work-surface, and position the bottom cleat over the stiles so the bottom edges are flush and

the ends of the cleat are set in ¾" from the edges of the stiles.

3. Drill countersunk pilot holes and attach the cleat with glue and 1¼" screws.

4. Position the back top cleat over the stiles so the top edge is 2" down from the top of the stiles and the ends are set in ¾" from the edges. Attach the top cleat with glue and counter-sunk screws.

5. Measure the diagonals of the frame to check for square **(photo B).**

ASSEMBLE THE CABINET.

1. Position the end frames up-right on their back edges, then lay the front frame over them (the stiles on the end frames should fit tightly against the in-set cleats on the front frame).

2. Check for square by measur-

ing diagonals, then drill coun-terbored pilot holes and join the front frame to the end frames with glue and 1½" screws.

3. Turn the assembly over so the front frame faces down, then position and attach the back frame with glue and coun-terbored 1½" screws **(photo C).**

ATTACH THE BOTTOM, TOP AND STRETCHER.

1. Cut the bottom (K) and top (L) to size, and sand the edges smooth.

2. Position the bottom piece in the cabinet so its bottom sur-face is set 3½" up from the lower ends of the stiles (at the rear, the bottom piece will rest on the back cleat).

3. Drill countersunk pilot holes through the bottom rails and into the bottom, then attach with glue and 1½" screws.

4. Fasten the top in similar fash-ion. Position the top piece in the cabinet so the top surface is 1¼" below the top ends of the stiles (at the back, the top piece will rest on the back cleat). Drill countersunk pilot holes and attach the top with glue and 1½" screws.

5. Cut the bottom stretcher (U) to size, and sand smooth. Posi-tion it over the rear edge of the bottom piece, then attach it to the stiles with glue and coun-tersunk 1¼" screws.

ATTACH THE BACK BRACES.

The easiest way to cut the an-gled back braces is to position the 1½" stock for the first brace across the back of the cabinet, mark and cut the proper

Secure the back braces at the centerpoints to create a diamond.

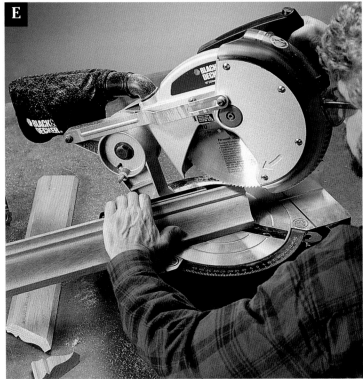

Miter the crown molding by positioning the molding upside down in the miter box. Cut the moldings about ½" too long, then test-fit the pieces and trim as needed for a tight fit at the mitered corners.

angles, then use this piece as a template for cutting the remaining braces.

1. Cut blanks for the back braces (S) to length.

2. Mark the horizontal centerpoints of the back stretcher and back top cleat. On each end of the back shelf rail, mark vertical centerpoints ¾" inch from the bottom edge.

3. Position a back brace diagonally from the back top cleat to

the back shelf rail, with the ends touching the reference marks. Use a T-bevel to mark horizontal cutting lines across the ends of the brace, parallel to the edges of the top cleat and shelf cleat.

4. Cut the angles on the ends of the brace, then use this brace as a template to cut the other three.

5. Drill countersunk pilot holes, and attach the back braces with glue and 1¼" screws **(photo D).**

ATTACH THE TRIM.
Cut the trim pieces slightly longer than needed so you can test fit and trim to the exact length for a precise fit.

1. Cut all base pieces (M, N), cap pieces (O, P) and crowns (Q, R) to length, mitering the appropriate ends at 45° **(photo E).**

2. Position the base pieces around the front and sides of the cabinet, flush with the bottom ends of the stiles, then drill pilot holes and attach with 4d finish nails.

3. Position the caps on the base pieces, drill pilot holes and secure with glue and brads.

4. Position the crown moldings so the bottom edges are 1½" from the bottom of the top rails, drill pilot holes and attach with 4d finish nails. Lock-nail the mitered joints (see *Tip*).

TIP

Lock-nailing is a technique used to reinforce mitered joints. The idea is to drive finish nails through both mating surfaces at the joint. Start by drilling pilot holes all the way through one board (to avoid splitting the wood) and partway into the other mating surface. Drive a small finish nail (2d or 4d) or a brad through each pilot hole to complete the lock-nailing operation.

Attach the center shelf cleats to the center rails with glue, and clamp the pieces together.

Use a pegboard template to align the shelf support holes in the stiles and back braces.

ADD THE SHELF SUPPORTS.

The shelves are spaced for an airy, open feeling, but more shelves could be added if you wish. Simply determine the shelf placement and repeat steps 3 and 4.

1. Cut the center shelf cleats (T) to size, and sand smooth.
2. Apply glue, then position the cleats against the center rails so the top edges are flush, and clamp in place until the glue dries **(photo F).**
3. Cut an 8 × 20" pegboard template to position the shelf support holes. Outline a horizontal row of holes 16" up from the bottom.
4. Rest the template on the top edge of the bottom rails and bottom stretcher, and drill holes in the back braces and stiles **(photo G).**
5. Drill holes for the upper shelf in similar fashion, resting the template on the center rails and back shelf rail.

APPLY FINISHING TOUCHES.

It's a good idea to order the glass shelves after you have completed the project. Measure the length and width for each shelf opening and reduce each measurement by ⅛". Let the glass shop know that you are providing the finish cut dimensions, so the cutter doesn't add an additional reduction.

Order tempered safety glass because it is stronger than ordinary glass and does not form sharp shards if broken.

1. Insert ⅜" glued oak plugs into counterbores, and apply stainable putty to all visible nail holes.
2. Finish-sand, then apply the finish of your choice. We used a walnut stain and a polyurethane finish. Because oak is an open grained wood, you may want to apply grain filler to create a smoother finish.
3. Attach self-adhesive plastic cushions to the shelf supports to prevent rattling, then install the glass shelves.

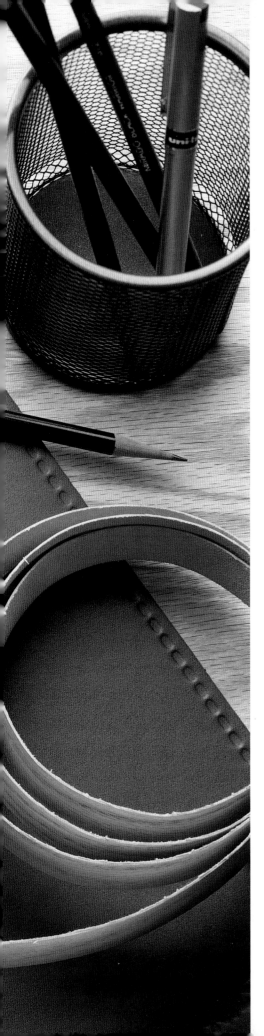

Home Office Projects

Make your home office space work harder with these projects that increase storage options or work surfaces. The library table is a perfect place for the kids to spread out their homework and the card table comes in handy when a bit of extra work space is needed. The secretary topper is sized to fit on the writing desk, but it doesn't need to stay in the office—these useful cubbyholes can be equally helpful in the kitchen or bedroom. You're sure to enjoy getting down to business using furniture you have made yourself.

PROJECT
POWER TOOLS

Secretary Topper

Transform a plain table, desk or cabinet top into a fully equipped secretary with this box-style topper.

I n the furniture world, a secretary is a free-standing, upright cabinet with a drop-down worksurface that conceals numerous storage cubbies when raised. The traditional secretary also has two or three large drawers at the bottom. With this secretary topper, we zeroed in on the cubby-hole feature, creating a simple storage unit that will convert just about any flat surface into a functioning secretary.

The fixed shelves are designed to accommodate papers up to legal size, while the adjustable shelf can be positioned to hold address and reference books. The vertical slats with the cutout dividers are good for storing incoming or outgoing mail, and the handy drawer is an ideal spot to keep small desktop items.

We made this simple wood project from oak and oak plywood. If you are building a secretary topper to complement an existing piece of furniture, try to match the wood type and finish of the piece.

NOTE: This secretary topper is sized to fit on top of the Writing Desk featured on pages 178 through 183.

CONSTRUCTION MATERIALS

Quantity	Lumber
1	¼" × 2 × 3' oak plywood
2	1 × 10" × 8' oak
1	½ × 8" × 6' oak
1	¼ × 2" × 7' oak mull casing

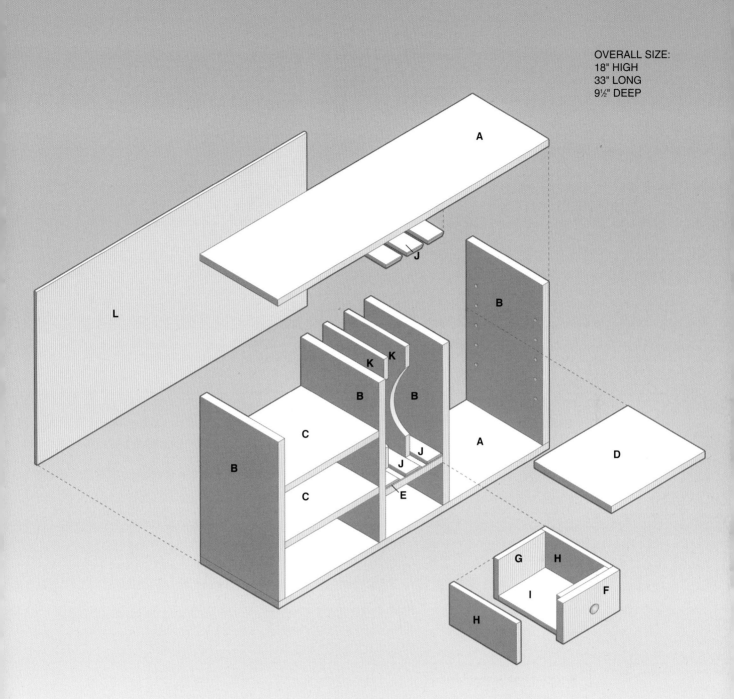

OVERALL SIZE:
18" HIGH
33" LONG
9½" DEEP

Cutting List				
Key	**Part**	**Dimension**	**Pcs.**	**Material**
A	Top/bottom	¾ × 9¼ × 33"	2	Oak
B	Partition	¾ × 9¼ × 16½"	4	Oak
C	Fixed shelf	¾ × 9¼ × 11½"	2	Oak
D	Adjustable shelf	¾ × 9¼ × 11¼"	1	Oak
E	Bin top	¾ × 9¼ × 7"	1	Oak
F	Drawer front	¾ × 4⅛ × 6¾"	1	Oak

Cutting List				
Key	**Part**	**Dimension**	**Pcs.**	**Material**
G	Drawer end	½ × 4⅛ × 5¾"	2	Oak
H	Drawer side	½ × 4⅛ × 8¼"	2	Oak
I	Drawer bottom	½ × 5¾ × 7¼"	1	Oak
J	Bin spacer	¼ × 2 × 9"	6	Mull casing
K	Divider	½ × 7¼ × 11½"	2	Oak
L	Back panel	¼ × 17⅞ × 32¾"	1	Plywood

Materials: #6 × 1⅝" wood screws, 16-ga. × ¾" and 1" brads, ¼"-dia. shelf pins (4), ¾"-dia. brass knob (1), ⅜"-dia. oak plugs, adhesive felt pads (6), wood glue, finishing materials.

Note: Measurements reflect the actual size of dimension lumber.

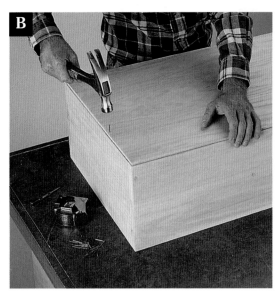

Use pegboard as a drilling template to align the shelf pin holes in the partitions.

Fasten the back panel to the cabinet with brads, keeping the framework square.

Directions:
Secretary Topper

For all screws used in this project, drill ³⁄₃₂" pilot holes. Counterbore the holes ¼" deep, using a ⅜" counterbore bit.

MAKE THE SHELF FRAMEWORK.

1. Cut the partitions (B), fixed shelves (C) and bin top (E) to length. Sand the parts smooth.
2. Draw reference lines across the faces of two partitions, 5" up from the bottom edge and 5¾" down from the top edge. Use glue to fasten the shelves between the two partitions, keeping their bottom edges flush with the reference lines. Drive 1⅝" wood screws through the partitions and into the ends of the shelves.
3. Draw reference lines on the outside face of the left partition, 4¼" up from the bottom edge. Use glue and 1⅝" wood screws to fasten the bin top to the partition, with its bottom edge on the reference line. Make sure the front and rear edges are flush.
4. Fasten an unattached parti-

tion to the free end of the bin top with glue and 1⅝" wood screws, keeping the front and back edges flush.
5. Drill holes in the partitions for the adjustible shelf in the left section. Clamp a piece of pegboard to one face, and use it as a drilling template **(photo A).** Drill ¼"-dia. × ⅜"-deep holes into the partition. Wrap masking tape around your drill bit as a depth marker to keep you from drilling through the pieces. After you drill holes in one partition, use tape to mark the locations of the pegboard holes you used. Repeat the drilling with the opposing partition. Keep the same end up and the same edge in front. Sand the pieces smooth.

COMPLETE THE CABINET.

1. Cut the top/bottom panels (A) to length.
2. Attach a panel to the ends of the partitions at the top and at the bottom of the framework. Apply glue, and drive 1⅝" wood screws through the outside faces of the panels and into the ends of the partitions.

3. Fasten the remaining partition between the top and bottom panels, making sure the outside face is flush with the ends of the panels.
4. Cut the back (L) to size, and sand it smooth.
5. Fasten the back to the cabinet with ¾" brads **(photo B).** Fasten one end of the back and check for square. Adjust it as needed, and fasten the remaining sides. The panel should be centered on the framework, with a slight reveal at all of the edges.

MAKE THE DRAWER.

Cut the drawer parts from ½"-thick × 8"-wide oak stock.
1. Cut the drawer ends (G), drawer sides (H) and drawer bottom (I) to size. Sand the parts smooth.
2. Fasten the drawer ends between the drawer sides with glue, and drive ¾" brads through the drawer sides and into the drawer ends. Make sure the outside faces of the drawer ends are flush with the ends of the drawer sides.
3. Position the drawer bottom

Drill pilot holes and fasten the drawer bottom with ¾" brads.

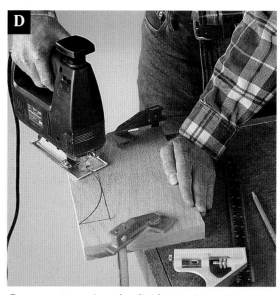

Gang-cut curves into the dividers, using a jig saw.

inside the drawer ends and sides. Drill ¹⁄₁₆" pilot holes through the sides and ends, and fasten the bottom with ¾" brads **(photo C)**. Do not use glue to fasten the bottom.

4. Cut the drawer front (F) to size from 1 × 10 stock, and sand it smooth.

5. Center the drawer front on one drawer end. With the edges flush, attach the drawer front with glue, and drive 1" brads through the end and into the front.

INSTALL THE VERTICAL DIVIDERS.

1. Cut the bin spacers (J) and dividers (K) to length.

2. Draw a curve on the front edge of one divider, starting 2¼" in from the top and bottom edges, and making it 2" deep at the center. Clamp the dividers together with their edges flush. Gang-cut them along the cutting line with a jig saw **(photo D)**. Gang-sand the pieces, using a drum sander attachment on an electric drill.

3. Bevel the front edges of the bin spacers by mounting a belt

sander to your workbench, and clamp a scrap guide to the worksurface to stabilize the parts as you sand the ends of the dividers **(photo E).**

4. Use ¾" brads to fasten two of the bin spacers to the bin top, flush against the partitions and butted against the back panel. Fasten two more bin spacers to the top panel.

5. Insert the dividers. Fasten the last bin spacers between them.

APPLY FINISHING TOUCHES.

1. Cut the adjustable shelf (D) to length.

2. Fill all screw holes with glued oak plugs. Set all nails with a nail set, and fill the holes with wood putty. Remove the dividers, and finish-sand all the parts. Apply a finish.

3. Attach a ¾" brass knob to the drawer front. Insert the shelf pins and adjustable shelf. Attach self-adhesive felt pads to the bottom of the topper.

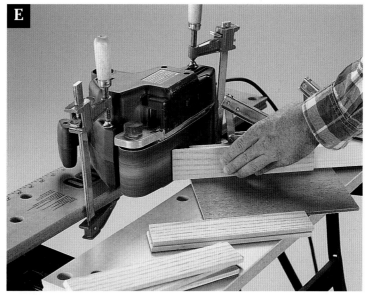

Clamp a belt sander to your workbench to make the divider bevels.

Bookcase

A simple, functional bookcase on which to set your picture frames, books and decorations, this project is as useful as it is attractive.

PROJECT POWER TOOLS

An attractive bookcase adds just the right decorative and functional touch to a family room or den. And you don't need to shell out large amounts of cash for a high-end bookcase or settle for a cheap, throw-together particleboard unit—this sturdy bookcase looks great and will last for many years.

Four roomy shelf areas let you display and store everything from framed pictures to reference manuals. The decorative trim on the outside of the bookcase spices up the overall appearance of the project, while panel molding along the front edges of the shelves softens the corners and adds structural stability. With a few coats of enamel paint, this bookcase takes on a smooth, polished look.

Although the project is constructed mostly of plywood, the molding that fits around the top, bottom and shelves allows the bookcase to fit in almost anywhere in the house. This bookcase is a great-looking, useful addition to just about any room.

CONSTRUCTION MATERIALS

Quantity	Lumber
1	¾" × 4 × 8' birch plywood
1	¼" × 4 × 8' birch plywood
2	¾ × 1⅝" × 8' panel molding
1	¾ × ¾" × 6' cove molding
2	¾ × ¾" × 8' quarter-round molding
1	¾ × 2⅝" × 6' chair-rail molding

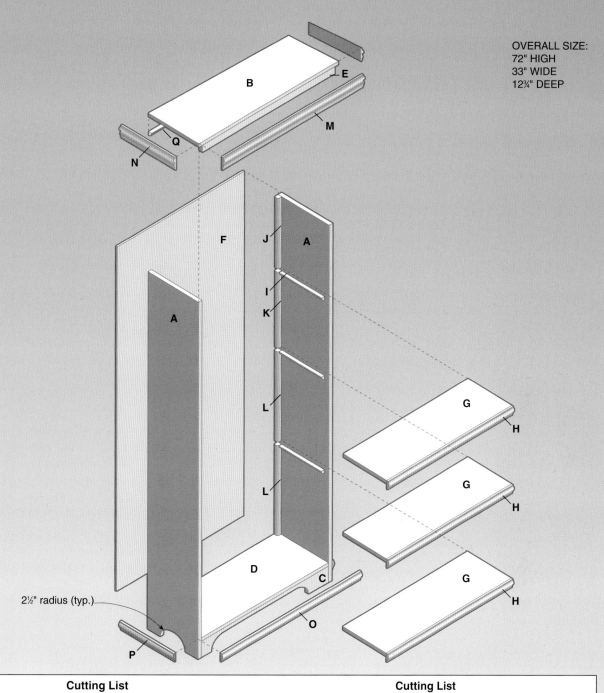

OVERALL SIZE:
72" HIGH
33" WIDE
12¾" DEEP

2½" radius (typ.)

Cutting List

Key	Part	Dimension	Pcs.	Material
A	Side	¾ × 12 × 71¼"	2	Plywood
B	Top	¾ × 11¾ × 31½"	1	Plywood
C	Front rail	¾ × 3¼ × 30"	1	Plywood
D	Bottom	¾ × 11¾ × 30"	1	Plywood
E	Top rail	¾ × 1½ × 30"	1	Plywood
F	Back	¼ × 30 × 68¾"	1	Plywood
G	Shelf	¾ × 10½ × 30"	3	Plywood
H	Shelf nosing	¾ × 1⅝ × 30"	3	Panel molding
I	Shelf cleat	¾ × ¾ × 9¾"	6	Cove molding

Cutting List

Key	Part	Dimension	Pcs.	Material
J	Back brace	¾ × ¾ × 14"	2	Quarter-round
K	Back brace	¾ × ¾ × 15"	2	Quarter-round
L	Back brace	¾ × ¾ × 18"	4	Quarter-round
M	Top facing	¾ × 2⅝ × 33"	1	Chair-rail molding
N	Top side molding	¾ × 2⅝ × 12¾"	2	Chair-rail molding
O	Bottom facing	¾ × 1⅝ × 33"	1	Panel molding
P	Bottom side molding	¾ × 1⅝ × 12¾"	2	Panel molding
Q	Back brace	¾ × ¾ × 28½"	1	Quarter-round

Materials: #6 × 2" wood screws, 4d and 6d finish nails, 16-ga. × 1" and 1¼" brads, 16-ga. × ¾" wire nails, ¾" birch veneer edge tape (25'), wood glue, finishing materials.

Note: Measurements reflect the actual size of dimension lumber.

Directions: Bookcase

MAKE THE SIDES AND FRONT RAIL.

1. Cut the sides (A) and front rail (C) to size from ¾"-thick plywood. Sand the parts smooth and clean the edges thoroughly.

2. Cut two strips of self-adhesive edge tape slightly longer than the long edge of the side piece. Attach the tape to one long edge of each side piece by pressing it onto the wood with a household iron set at a medium-low setting. The heat will activate the adhesive. Trim and sand the edges of the tape.

3. Designate a top and bottom to each side. Draw a cutting line across each side, 2½" up from the bottom edge. Draw marks on the bottom edges of the sides, 5½" in from the front and rear edges. Set a compass to draw a 2½"-radius arc, using the marks on the bottom edges as centerpoints. Set the point of the compass as close as possible to the bottom edges of the sides, and draw the arcs. Use a jig saw to cut the arch.

4. Repeat these steps to make the arch in the front rail, but place the point of the compass 4¾" in from each end of the front rail. Cut the front rail to shape with a jig saw **(photo A).**

BUILD THE CARCASE.

The top, bottom and sides of the bookcase form the basic cabinet—called the carcase.

1. Cut the top (B), bottom (D) and top rail (E) to size. Sand the parts smooth.

2. Draw reference lines across the faces of the sides, 3¼" up from the bottom edges. Set the sides on edge, and position the bottom between them, just above the reference lines. Attach the bottom to the sides with glue and 2" wood screws, keeping the front edges flush. Drill ⁵⁄₆₄" pilot holes for the screws. Counterbore the holes ⅛" deep, using a ⅜" counterbore bit.

3. Set the sides upright, and position the front rail between the sides, flush with the side and bottom edges. Glue the rail edges. Then, clamp it to the bottom board. Drill ¹⁄₁₆" pilot holes, and secure the front rail with 6d finish nails driven through the sides, and 1¼" brads driven through the bottom **(photo B).** Set all nails with a nail set.

4. Use glue and 6d finish nails to attach the top to the top ends of the sides, keeping the side and front edges flush.

5. Fasten the top rail between the sides, flush with the front edges of the sides and top. Use glue and 6d finish nails to secure the top rail in place.

MAKE THE BACK.

1. Cut the back braces (J, K, L, Q) to length.

2. Set the carcase on its side. Starting at the bottom, use glue and 1¼" brads to fasten the back braces to the sides and top, ¼" in from the back edges **(photo C).** Use a ¾"-thick spacer to create gaps

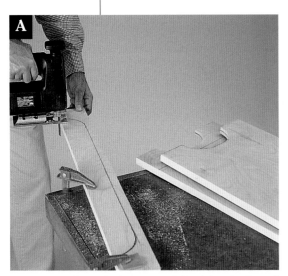

Cut arches along the bottoms of the side panels and front rail to create the bookcase "feet."

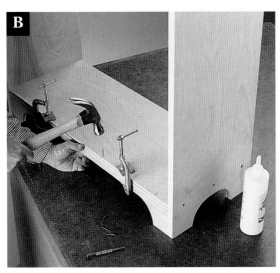

Clamp the front rail to the bottom, and fasten it with glue, finish nails and brads.

Attach the back braces to the sides, creating a ¼" recess for the back panel.

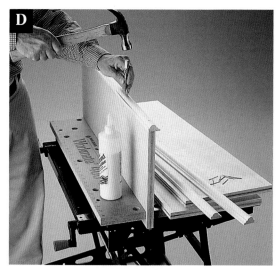

Attach strips of panel molding to the front edges of the shelves.

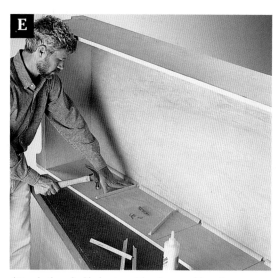

Attach the shelf cleats with glue and brads.

for the shelves between the strips. Install the top back brace (Q) flush with the back edge of the top. Place the carcase on its front edges.

3. Cut the back (F) to size.

4. Set the back in place so it rests on the back braces. Check for square by measuring diagonally from corner to corner across the back. When the measurements are the same, the carcase is square. Drive ¾" wire nails through the back and into the back braces. Do not glue the back in place.

MAKE THE SHELVES.

1. Cut the shelves (G) and shelf nosing (H) to size.

2. Drill ¹⁄₁₆" pilot holes through the nosing pieces. Use glue and 4d finish nails to attach the nosing to the shelves, keeping the top edges flush **(photo D).** Set the nails with a nail set.

3. Cut the shelf cleats (I) to length.

4. Use a combination square to draw reference lines perpendicular to the front edges of each side to help you position the

shelf cleats. Start the lines at the top of the lower back braces (K, L), and extend them to within 1" of the front edges of the sides. Apply glue to the cleats, and position them on the reference lines. Attach the shelf cleats to the inside faces of the sides with 1" brads **(photo E).**

5. Apply glue to the top edges of the shelf cleats. Then, set the shelves onto the cleats. Drive 6d finish nails through the sides and into the ends of the shelves.

6. Drive ¾" wire nails through the back panel and into the rear edges of the shelves.

APPLY FINISHING TOUCHES.

1. Cut the top facing (M), top side molding (N), bottom facing (O) and bottom side molding (P) to length. Miter-cut both ends of the top facing and bottom facing and the front ends of the side moldings at a 45° angle so the molding pieces will fit together at the corners.

2. Fasten the top molding with glue and 4d finish nails, keeping the top edges flush with the top face of the top piece.

3. Attach the bottom facing, keeping the top edges flush with the top face of the bottom.

4. Draw reference lines on the sides to help you align the bottom side molding. The reference lines should be flush with the top of the bottom facing **(photo F).** Attach the bottom side molding.

5. Set all nails with a nail set, and fill the nail holes with wood putty. Finish-sand the project and apply the finish of your choice—we used primer and two coats of enamel paint.

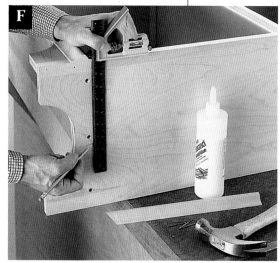

Using a combination square, draw lines on the sides, aligned with the top of the bottom facing.

Library Table

*This oak library table features a clean, sophisticated
appearance that suits any family room or study.*

CONSTRUCTION MATERIALS

Quantity	Lumber
1	¾" × 4 × 8' oak plywood
1	½" × 2 × 4' oak plywood
2	1 × 2" × 8' oak
3	1 × 4" × 8' oak
2	1 × 6" × 6' oak
2	2 × 2" × 8' oak

High-quality, stylish furniture doesn't need to be overly expensive or difficult to make, and this library table is the proof. We used a traditional design for this old favorite. The simple drawer construction, beautiful oak materials and slender framework add up to one great-looking table.

Consider the possibilities for this table in your family room or study. These areas of the home call out for a simple yet elegant table to support a lamp or books, or just to add a decorative accent. We applied a two-tone finish. But no matter how you finish it, this library table serves many needs—and it looks great in the process.

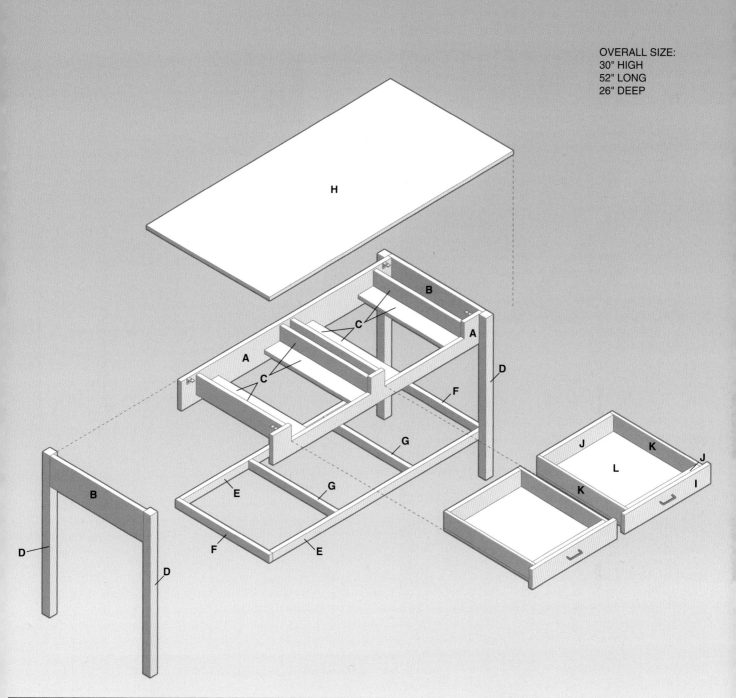

OVERALL SIZE:
30" HIGH
52" LONG
26" DEEP

Cutting List

Key	Part	Dimension	Pcs.	Material
A	Side	¾ × 5½ × 44½"	2	Oak
B	End	¾ × 5½ × 20"	2	Oak
C	Guide	¾ × 3½ × 18½"	8	Oak
D	Leg	1½ × 1½ × 29¼"	4	Oak
E	Side rail	¾ × 1½ × 44½"	2	Oak
F	End rail	¾ × 1½ × 20"	2	Oak

Cutting List

Key	Part	Dimension	Pcs.	Material
G	Cross rail	¾ × 1½ × 18½"	2	Oak
H	Top	¾ × 26 × 52"	1	Plywood
I	Drawer front	¾ × 3½ × 18"	2	Oak
J	Drawer end	¾ × 2⅜ × 15⅞"	4	Oak
K	Drawer side	½ × 2⅜ × 19"	4	Plywood
L	Drawer bottom	½ × 16⅞ × 19"	2	Plywood

Materials: #6 × 1", 1⅝" and 2" wood screws, 4d and 6d finish nails, 2" corner braces with ⅝" screws (4), 4" drawer pulls (2), ⅞"-dia. rubber feet (4), tack-on furniture glides (4), ¾" oak veneer edge tape (15'), ⅜"-dia. oak plugs, wood glue, finishing materials.

Note: Measurements reflect the actual size of dimension lumber.

A

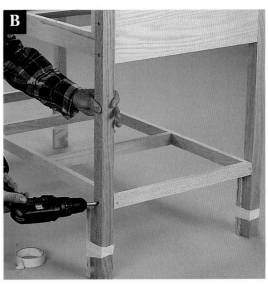

B

Measure the diagonals and adjust the apron frame as needed until it is square.

Tape 8"-long blocks of scrap wood to the legs to hold the rail assembly for installation.

Directions: Library Table

For all screws used in this project, drill ³⁄₃₂" pilot holes. Counterbore the holes ¼" deep, using a ⅜" counterbore bit.

MAKE THE APRON ASSEMBLY.

1. Cut the sides (A) and ends (B) to length and sand the pieces smooth.
2. Draw two 3"-deep × 17"-long rectangular outlines for the drawer cutouts on the front side. The outlines should start 3¾" in from each end of the front. Make cutouts with a jig saw, using a straightedge as a guide.
3. Attach the sides between the ends with glue, and drive 1⅝" wood screws through the ends and into the sides. The outside faces of the sides should be flush with the ends of the end pieces.
4. Cut the guides (C) to length.
5. Fasten the guides together in right-angle pairs by butting one guide's long edge against the face of another guide, while keeping the ends flush. Attach the guides with glue and 1⅝" wood screws.

6. Position the guide pairs between the sides so the inside faces are flush with the bottom and sides of the rectangular cutouts. Make sure the vertical halves of the guides do not extend above the top edges of the sides. (Set the guide pairs on spacers to keep them aligned with the cutouts as you work.) Before fastening the guides, check the apron frame for square by measuring from corner to corner **(photo A).** If the measurements are not the

same, adjust as needed. Drill ¹⁄₁₆" pilot holes and drive 6d finish nails through the sides and into the guides to fasten them in place. Set the nails with a nail set.

MAKE THE RAIL ASSEMBLY.
1. Cut the side rails (E), end rails (F) and cross rails (G) to length.
2. Position the side rails on edge. Attach the side rails between the end rails with glue and 1⅝" wood screws. The

C

Support the drawer with ½"-thick scrap wood. Then, center the drawer front by measuring the overhang on both sides.

resulting frame should sit flat on your worksurface.

3. Attach the cross rails between the side rails, 14" in from the inside faces of the end rails.

4. Fill all screw holes with oak plugs, and sand them flush with the surface. Sand the rail assembly smooth.

ASSEMBLE THE TABLE.

1. Cut the legs (D) to length, and sand them smooth.

2. Use glue and 2" wood screws to fasten the legs to the apron so the top edges and outside end faces are flush. Position the screws so they do not strike the screws joining the apron parts.

3. Stand the table up. Clamp or tape 8"-long scrap blocks to the inside edges of the legs, flush with the bottom leg ends. These blocks hold the rail assembly in place as you attach it. Fasten the rail assembly to the legs with glue and 2" wood screws. Make sure the end rails are flush with the outside edges of the legs **(photo B).**

4. Cut the top (H) to size. Clean the edges thoroughly.

5. Cut strips of self-adhesive edge tape slightly longer than all four edges of the top. Attach the tape by pressing it onto the edges with a household iron set at a medium-low setting. The heat will activate the adhesive. Trim the excess tape and sand the edges smooth.

6. Sand the top. Choose the smoothest, most attractive side to face up. Draw reference lines on the underside of the top, 3¾" in from the long edges. Fasten two 2" corner braces on each line, 5¼" in from the ends, using ⅝" screws. Center the apron assembly on the top and attach it to the braces.

MAKE THE DRAWERS.

1. Cut the drawer ends (J) and drawer sides (K) to size. Sand the pieces smooth.

2. Fasten the drawer ends between the drawer sides, using glue and 4d finish nails. Drill ¹⁄₁₆" pilot holes through the sides to prevent splitting. Make sure the outside faces of the drawer ends are flush with the ends of the drawer sides.

3. Cut the drawer bottoms (L) to size, and sand them smooth.

4. Center the bottoms over the drawer assemblies, and drill pilot holes for 4d finish nails. Attach the bottom to the drawer ends and sides, driving the nails through the bottom and into the edges. Do not use glue to attach the drawer bottoms.

5. Cut the drawer fronts (I) to length.

6. Attach the drawer fronts by first setting the drawers on a ½"-thick piece of scrap wood. This will ensure that the top-to-bottom spacing is correct when you attach the drawer fronts. Position the drawer fronts against the drawer ends, centering them from side to side **(photo C).** Clamp the drawer fronts in place. Drive 1" wood screws through the drawer ends and into the drawer fronts. Test-fit the drawers and adjust the fronts if they are uneven on the front of the apron.

APPLY FINISHING TOUCHES.

1. Set all nails with a nail set, and fill the nail holes with wood putty. Fill all screw holes with oak plugs. Finish-sand the entire project. Apply the finish of your choice and allow to dry.

2. Install the drawer pulls on the drawer fronts. Wax the tops of the guides with paraffin. Insert the drawers, and set the table on its back edges. Attach ⅞"-dia. rubber feet to the bottoms of the drawers to prevent them from being pulled out of the table **(photo D).** Tack furniture glides to the leg bottoms.

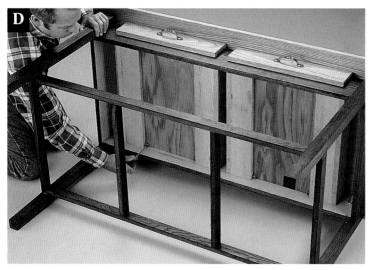

Slide the drawers into place. Then, install rubber feet at the back corners to serve as drawer stops and keep the drawers centered.

Card Table

This stylish table proves that card tables don't always have to be flimsy and unappealing.

CONSTRUCTION MATERIALS

Quantity	Lumber
1	½" × 4 × 4' oak plywood
2	2 × 2" × 8' pine
2	1 × 3" × 8' pine
4	¾ × ¾" × 8' oak edge molding

The card table has always been thought of as over-flow seating for those houseguests who are most lacking in seniority. But the diners assigned to this contemporary wood card table will feel more like they have favored status. The warm tones of the oak tabletop contrast vividly with the painted legs and apron for a lovely effect that will blend into just about any setting—from formal dining to a Friday night poker game.

The fold-up legs on this card table are attached with fasteners designed especially for card tables. You can find these fasteners and the oak apron trim at most hardware and wood-working supply stores.

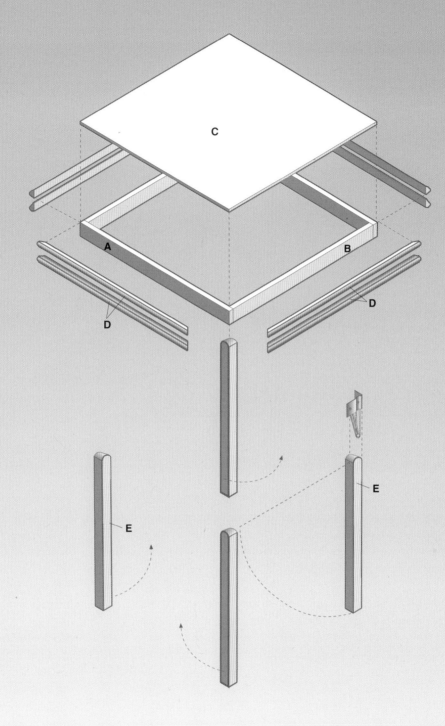

OVERALL SIZE:
29" HIGH
33½" WIDE
33½" DEEP

	Cutting List			
Key	**Part**	**Dimension**	**Pcs.**	**Material**
A	Side apron	¾ × 2½ × 32"	2	Pine
B	End apron	¾ × 2½ × 30½"	2	Pine
C	Tabletop	½ × 32 × 32"	1	Plywood

	Cutting List			
Key	**Part**	**Dimension**	**Pcs.**	**Material**
D	Edge trim	¾ × ¾ × *	8	Edge molding
E	Leg	1½ × 1½ × 28"	4	Pine

Materials: #6 × 1½" wood screws, 3d finish nails, ¼ × 2" machine bolts with locking nuts (4), card-table leg fasteners (4), oak-tinted wood putty, wood glue, finishing materials.

Note: Measurements reflect the actual size of dimension lumber.

* Cut to fit.

Directions: Card Table

BUILD THE TABLETOP.

The tabletop for this card table is a sheet of oak plywood framed with an apron made from 1 × 3 pine. Strips of oak molding attached around the top and bottom of the apron protect the edges of the table when it is being stored.

1. Cut the side aprons (A) and end aprons (B) to length.

2. Fasten the end aprons between the side aprons with glue and 1½" wood screws to form a square **(photo A).** Drill 5⁄64" pilot holes for the screws. Counterbore the holes ⅛", using a ⅜" counterbore bit. Keep the outside edges and faces of the aprons flush.

3. Cut the tabletop (C) to size, using a circular saw and a straightedge as a cutting guide.

4. Position the tabletop on the frame, keeping the edges flush with the outer faces of the aprons. Fasten the tabletop to the top of the frame with glue and 3d finish nails **(photo B).**

SHAPE THE LEGS.

1. Cut the legs (E) to length.

2. Round over one end of each leg so it will pivot smoothly inside the card-table leg fastener: Center the point of a compass ¾" in from the end of the leg, and draw a ¾"-radius curve. Cut the curves with a jig saw.

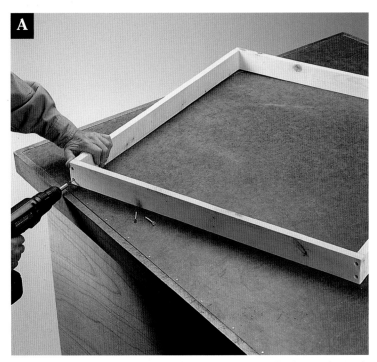

Fasten the end aprons between the side aprons with glue and wood screws to construct the apron frame.

PAINT THE FRAME AND LEGS.

If you plan to apply a combination finish, paint the legs and frame before you assemble the table and attach the edge trim.

1. Finish-sand the pine surfaces and wipe them clean. Apply primer to the aprons and legs.

2. Apply several coats of enamel paint in the color of your choice.

ATTACH THE EDGE TRIM.

When the paint has dried, attach the edge trim to the tabletop edges and the aprons. Use a plain or decorative molding, but be sure to use oak to match the tabletop.

1. Miter-cut the edge trim pieces (D) to length, using a power miter saw or hand miter box. The best method is to cut the 45° miter on one end of the first piece, and position the trim against the apron or tabletop edges. Mark the appropriate length, and miter-cut the other end.

2. Fasten the edge trim to the aprons or the tabletop edge using wood glue and 3d finish nails. To prevent splitting, drill 1⁄16" pilot holes through the trim pieces before driving the nails. Continue this process, keeping the mitered ends tight when marking for length **(photo C).** Be sure to keep the tops of the upper trim pieces flush with the surface of the tabletop. Keep the bottoms of the lower trim pieces flush with the bottoms of the aprons.

FASTEN THE LEGS AND HARDWARE.

The legs attach to the table with locking card-table leg fasteners.

1. Attach a leg fastener to the rounded end of each leg. Fastening methods may vary, so read and follow the manufacturer's directions that come with the hardware.

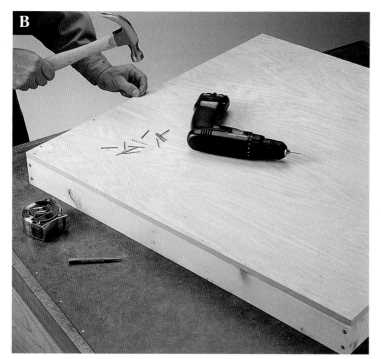

Fasten the oak plywood tabletop to the top of the apron frame with glue and finish nails.

Glue and nail oak trim around the tabletop and apron, making mitered joints at the corners.

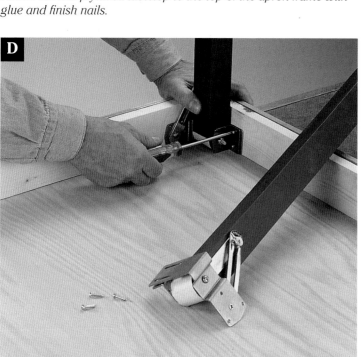

Attach the card-table leg fasteners to the rounded ends of the legs. Then, attach them at the inside corners of the tabletop frame.

2. Lay the tabletop upside down on a flat worksurface. Attach the leg fasteners to the insides of the aprons at each corner of the tabletop frame **(photo D).** Test the legs to make sure they fit properly when folded up and that the fasteners operate smoothly. Also, check to make sure the table is level and stable when resting on a flat surface. Make any needed adjustments to the positioning or length of the legs. Then, fully tighten all hardware screws.

APPLY FINISHING TOUCHES.
1. Set all nails with a nail set, and fill the nail holes with oak-tinted wood putty. Finish-sand the unfinished surfaces and wipe them clean.
2. Apply sanding sealer for an even finish (see *Tip*). If desired, apply a wood stain to color the wood. If you are using medium to dark stain, mask the painted surfaces first. Apply two or three light coats of a protective topcoat to the entire table.

Drafting Stool

Simple and sturdy, this oak beauty keeps your posture perfect as you work at your drafting table or writing desk.

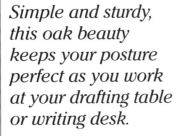

Proper seating is the key to comfort and productivity at a writing desk, drafting table or any workstation. An ultra-soft reclining or swiveling chair can sometimes make you drowsy, resulting in poor seated posture and sore muscles. On the other hand, an unsupportive, rigid chair with a low backrest can make working at your desk uncomfortable and unpleasant. This drafting stool offers firm support without lulling you to sleep.

We designed this solid oak stool for use with the writing desk (page 178). The style and scale of the stool match those of the writing table, but you'll find there are many additional uses for this versatile project. You may want to use it as a bar stool in your den, or place it in the kitchen to provide seating at your breakfast counter.

We used oak lumber, but you can select building materials to match your desk or room decor. For a finished look, we filled the screw holes in our chair with oak plugs, but contrasting plugs would provide an interesting design element. There certainly are many options for building and using this drafting stool. Best of all, this piece is much easier to build than its appearance suggests.

CONSTRUCTION MATERIALS

Quantity	Lumber
3	1 × 2" × 8' oak
2	1 × 4" × 6' oak
2	2 × 2" × 8' oak

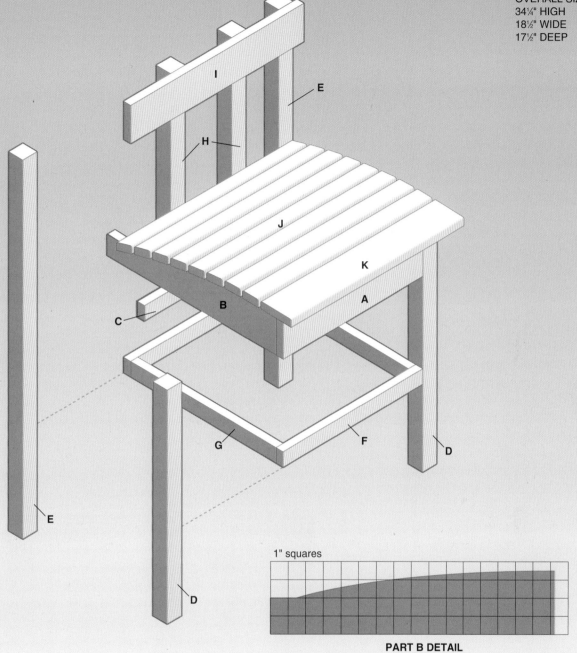

OVERALL SIZE:
34¼" HIGH
18½" WIDE
17½" DEEP

1" squares

PART B DETAIL

Cutting List				
Key	**Part**	**Dimension**	**Pcs.**	**Material**
A	Front	¾ × 3½ × 15"	1	Oak
B	Side	¾ × 3½ × 16¼"	2	Oak
C	Back	¾ × 2 × 13½"	1	Oak
D	Front leg	1½ × 1½ × 21¼"	2	Oak
E	Rear leg	1½ × 1½ × 34¼"	2	Oak
F	End rail	¾ × 1½ × 15"	2	Oak

Cutting List				
Key	**Part**	**Dimension**	**Pcs.**	**Material**
G	Side rail	¾ × 1½ × 15½"	2	Oak
H	Back brace	1½ × 1½ × 16½"	2	Oak
I	Backrest	¾ × 3½ × 18½"	1	Oak
J	Slat	¾ × 1½ × 18½"	8	Oak
K	Front slat	¾ × 3½ × 18½"	1	Oak

Materials: #6 × 1⅝" wood screws, 10d finish nails, ⅜"-dia. oak plugs, wood glue, finishing materials.

Note: Measurements reflect the actual size of dimension lumber.

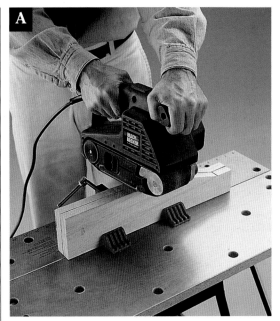

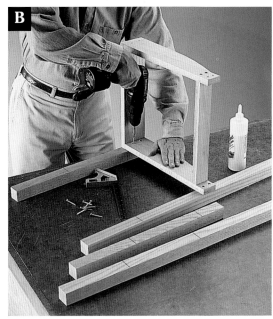

Gang-sand the sides with a belt sander, making sure their profiles are identical.

Align the seat frame on the top reference lines, and fasten it to the legs.

Directions: Drafting Stool

MAKE THE SEAT FRAME.
For all screws used in this project, drill ³⁄₃₂" pilot holes. Counterbore the holes ¼" deep, using a ³⁄₈" counterbore bit. The seat frame is sloped from front to back, forming the seat shape. Make this slope by cutting the side pieces, following the pattern on page 175.
1. Cut the front (A), sides (B) and back (C) to length.
2. Draw a grid with 1" squares onto a face of a side piece (use *Part B Detail*). Cut the side to shape with a jig saw, and sand the cut edges.
3. Trace the outline of the finished side onto the other side piece, and cut it to shape. Clamp the sides together, and gang-sand them with a belt sander to make sure their profiles are identical **(photo A).**
4. Position the front against the front ends of the sides. Fasten the front to the sides with glue, and drive 1⅝" wood screws

through the front piece and into the ends of the sides.
5. Position the back (C) between the sides so the rear face is 1½" in from the ends of the sides. Make sure the bottom edges of the parts are flush. Fasten the back with glue, and

drive 1⅝" wood screws through the sides and into the back.

ATTACH THE LEGS.
Before attaching the frame and legs, draw reference lines to mark the positions for the legs.
1. Cut the front legs (D) and

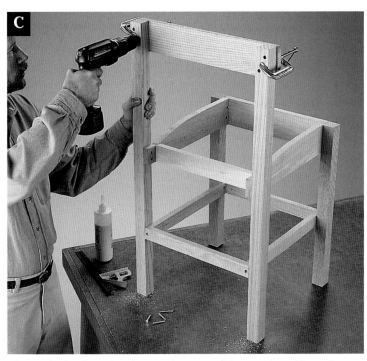

Clamp the backrest in place at the tops of the rear legs. Then, fasten it with glue and wood screws.

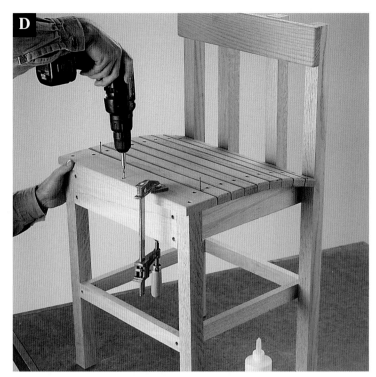

Using 10d nails as spacers, fasten the seat slats to the top of the seat frame, finishing with the front slat.

rear legs (E) to length. Sand the parts smooth. Draw reference lines on the inside face of each leg, 8" and 17¾" up from the bottom end.

2. Position one front leg and one rear leg on your worksurface. Set the seat frame on the legs so the bottom edge is flush with the top reference lines. Apply glue and fasten the seat frame to the rear leg, keeping the ends flush and the frame square to the leg. Drive 1⅝" wood screws through the seat side and into the leg.

3. Fasten the frame to the front leg with glue and 1⅝" wood screws **(photo B).** Make sure the seat frame is flush with the front edge of the front leg and with the top reference line.

4. Turn the assembly over. Attach the remaining front leg and rear leg, using the same methods.

ATTACH THE RAILS.

1. Cut the end rails (F) and side rails (G) to length.

2. Position the side rails between the end rails so their top edges are flush and the outside faces of the side rails are flush with the ends of the end rails. Fasten the pieces with glue and 1⅝" wood screws.

3. Position the rail assembly between the legs so its bottom edges are flush with the bottom reference lines. Attach the assembly with glue, and drive 1⅝" wood screws through the side rails and into the legs. To avoid hitting the screws in the rail assembly, these screws must be slightly off center. The front and rear edges of the rail assembly should be flush with the front and rear leg edges.

ATTACH THE BACK BRACES AND BACKREST.

1. Cut the back braces (H) and backrest (I) to length.

2. Clamp the backrest to the fronts of the rear legs so the top edges are flush. The backrest should extend ¼" past the rear legs on both sides. Check the back legs for square, and drill staggered pilot holes with ⅜"-deep counterbores through the legs. Apply glue and fasten the backrest to the rear legs with 1⅝" wood screws **(photo C).**

3. Drill ⅜"-deep counterbores into the braces. Attach the back braces to the back and backrest with glue and 1⅝" wood screws. Use a piece of 1 × 4 scrap as a spacer to maintain an equal distance between the rear legs and back braces.

ATTACH THE SLATS.

1. Cut the slats (J) and the front slat (K) to length. Sand the slats, slightly rounding over the top edges.

2. Attach the slats with glue and 1⅝" wood screws, starting at the rear of the seat, with the first slat flush against the legs and back braces. Maintain a ⅛"-wide gap between slats—10d finish nails make good spacers. The slats should overhang both sides of the seat frame by ¼".

3. Test-fit the front slat, and trim it, if necessary, so it overhangs the front piece by ½". Clamp the front slat to the seat frame, and attach it with glue and 1⅝" wood screws **(photo D).**

APPLY FINISHING TOUCHES.

1. Insert glued oak plugs into all screw holes, and sand the plugs flush with the surface.

2. Finish-sand all surfaces with 180-grit sandpaper.

3. Apply the finish of your choice. We used three coats of tung oil.

PROJECT
POWER TOOLS

Writing Desk

*Build this practical, attractive writing desk for a fraction of the cost
of manufactured models.*

CONSTRUCTION MATERIALS

Quantity	Lumber
1	¾" × 4 × 8' oak plywood
2	1 × 2" × 6' oak
2	1 × 4" × 6' oak
1	1 × 6" × 8' oak
1	1 × 10" × 6' oak
2	2 × 2" × 8' oak
1	¼" × 2 × 4' acrylic sheet
2	¾ × 1⅝" × 6' oak panel molding
2	⅜ × 1¹⁄₁₆" × 6' oak stop molding

A beautiful piece of furniture, this writing desk is based loosely on popular Shaker styling. With its hinged top, you have access to a storage area for keeping important papers organized and out of the way. We built the writing desk out of red oak, an attractive and durable hardwood, so the project will look great for a long time. Designed to match the drafting stool (page 174) and secretary topper (page 158), the writing desk also works well as a standalone piece. And, it can be built for a fraction of the cost of similar furnishings, even those sold by catalog. The worksurface is covered with a sheet of clear acrylic, giving you a hard, smooth surface for writing. When the acrylic gets scratched or worn, just slip it out of the top frame and turn it over.

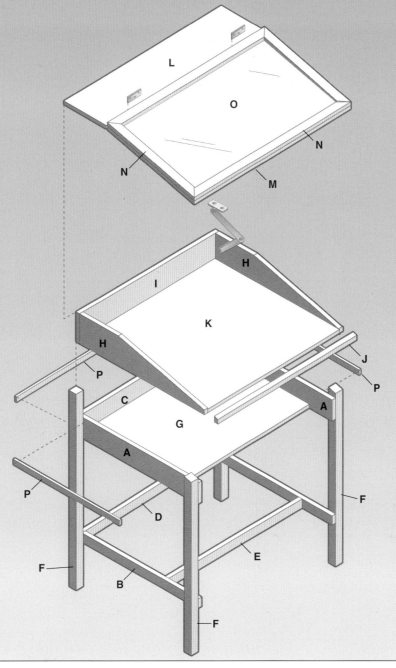

OVERALL SIZE:
37¼" HIGH
34" WIDE
30½" DEEP

Cutting List

Key	Part	Dimension	Pcs.	Material
A	Apron side	¾ × 3½ × 24¾"	2	Oak
B	Side rail	¾ × 1½ × 24¾"	2	Oak
C	Apron back	¾ × 3½ × 30"	1	Oak
D	Back rail	¾ × 1½ × 30"	1	Oak
E	Kick rail	¾ × 1½ × 28½"	1	Oak
F	Leg	1½ × 1½ × 35¾"	4	Oak
G	Shelf	¾ × 20 × 28½"	1	Plywood
H	Desk side	¾ × 5½ × 26½"	2	Oak

Cutting List

Key	Part	Dimension	Pcs.	Material
I	Desk back	¾ × 5½ × 30"	1	Oak
J	Desk front	¾ × 1 × 30"	1	Oak
K	Desk bottom	¾ × 26½ × 28½"	1	Plywood
L	Desk top	¾ × 9¼ × 34"	1	Oak
M	Worksurface	¾ × 21 × 34"	1	Plywood
N	Top molding	¾ × 1⁵⁄₁₆ × *	4	Panel molding
O	Top protector	¼ × 19⅛ × 32⅛"	1	Acrylic
P	Side trim	⅜ × 1¹⁄₁₆ × *	3	Stop molding

Materials: #6 × 1⅝" and 2" wood screws, #6 × 1" brass wood screws, 16-ga. × ¾" and 1" brass brads, 1½ × 3" brass butt hinges, 6" heavy-duty lid-support hardware, ¾" oak veneer edge tape (25'), ⅜"-dia. oak plugs, wood glue, finishing materials.

Specialty tools: Block plane, plastic cutter.

Note: Measurements reflect the actual size of dimension lumber.   * Cut to fit.

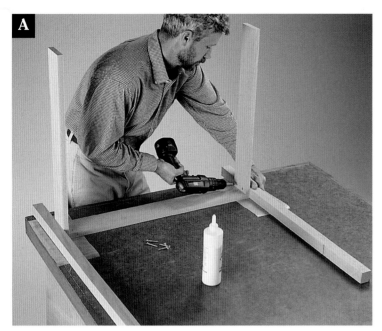

Fasten the apron assembly between the back legs with glue and wood screws.

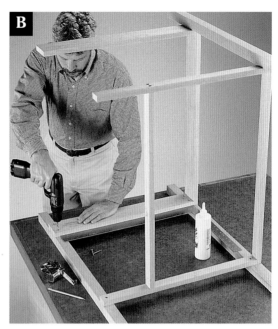

Attach the front legs to the free ends of the apron sides and side rails.

Directions: Writing Desk

JOIN THE LEGS AND THE APRON.

For all screws used in this project, drill ³⁄₃₂" pilot holes. Counterbore the holes ¼" deep, using a ⅜" counterbore bit.

1. Cut the legs (F) to length. Sand the parts smooth.

2. Set the legs together, edge to edge, with their ends flush. Draw reference lines across the legs, 8" and 30¼" up from one end. These lines mark the positions of the apron and rail assemblies.

3. Cut the apron sides (A) and apron back (C) to length.

4. Butt the ends of the apron sides against the face of the apron back. Attach the pieces with glue, and drive 2" wood screws through the apron back and into the sides. Make sure the outside faces of the sides are flush with the ends of the apron back.

5. Set a pair of legs on your worksurface, about 30" apart,

Use a block plane to trim the desk front to match the slanted profiles of the desk sides.

with the reference lines facing each other. Position the apron assembly between the legs so the top edges of the assembly are flush with the top reference lines. The back face of the apron should be flush with the back edges of the legs. Drive 1⅝" wood screws through the

apron sides and into the legs **(photo A).** Position the screws so they do not strike the screws in the apron assembly.

INSTALL THE FRAME RAILS.

1. Cut the side rails (B), back rail (D) and kick rail (E) to length.

2. Attach the side rails to the

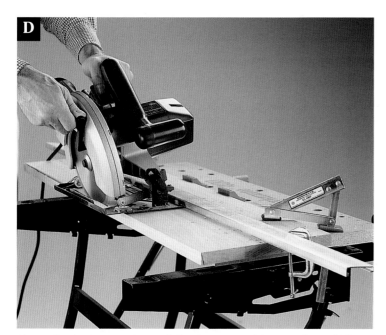

D

Use a circular saw and a straightedge as a guide to make a slight bevel on the front edge of the desk top.

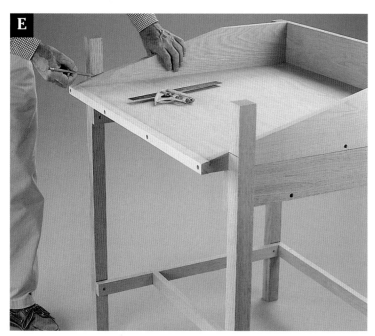

E

Trace the angles of the desk sides onto the front legs. Then, trim the legs to follow the sides.

lines. Keep the back face of the back rail flush with the back edges of the legs, and attach the assembly with glue. Drive 1⅝" wood screws through the side rails and into the legs.

5. Position the front legs on the apron sides and side rails, keeping the edges flush with the reference lines **(photo B).** The front edges of the legs should be flush with the ends of the apron sides and side rails. Make sure the parts are square, and fasten the legs with glue. Drive 1⅝" wood screws through the apron sides and side rails and into the legs.

MAKE THE SHELF.

1. Cut the shelf (G) to size.
2. Apply self-adhesive edge tape to one long edge of the shelf, using a household iron. Trim and sand the taped edges.
3. Position the shelf between the apron sides so it butts against the face of the apron back. The shelf should be flush with the bottom edges of the apron assembly, and the taped edge of the shelf should face forward. Attach the shelf to the apron with glue, and drive 1⅝" wood screws through the apron sides and back and into the edges of the shelf.

BUILD THE DESK BOX.

1. Cut the desk sides (H) to length.
2. Make the slanted cuts on the top edges by marking points on one long edge of each desk side, 8¼" in from one end.

back rail with glue. Drive 2" wood screws through the back rail and into the ends of the side rail. Make sure the outside faces of the side rails are flush with the ends of the back rail.
3. Position the kick rail between the side rails so its front face is 7" in from the front ends of the side rails. Make sure the top and bottom edges are flush. Attach the kick rail with glue, and drive 2" wood screws through the side rails and into the ends of the kick rail.
4. Position the rail assembly between the legs with the bottom edges on the lower reference

Draw reference lines on the opposite end of each side, 1" up from the bottom edge. Draw straight cutting lines connecting the marks. Cut along the lines with a circular saw, using a straightedge as a cutting guide.

3. Cut the desk back (I) and desk bottom (K) to size.

4. Cut the desk front (J), using a circular saw and a straightedge as a cutting guide to rip-cut a 1"-wide strip from a 1 × 4 or 1 × 6.

5. Attach the desk sides to the desk back, flush with the ends of the desk back. Apply glue and drive 2" wood screws through the back and into the edges of the sides.

6. Position the desk bottom between the desk sides, keeping the front and bottom edges flush. Attach the bottom with glue, and drive 1⅝" wood screws through the desk sides and back and into the bottom.

7. Fasten the desk front to the front edge of the desk bottom with glue and 1⅝" wood screws. The ¾"-thick edge should be flush with the bottom face of the desk bottom.

8. Trim the desk front to match the slanted profiles of the desk sides. Draw reference lines on each end of the desk front, extending the slanted profiles of the desk sides. Use a combination square to draw a reference line across the front face of the desk front, connecting the ends of the reference lines. Use a block plane to trim the profile of the desk front to match the angles of the desk sides **(photo C).** To avoid damaging the desk sides, start the trimming with the plane and finish with a sander.

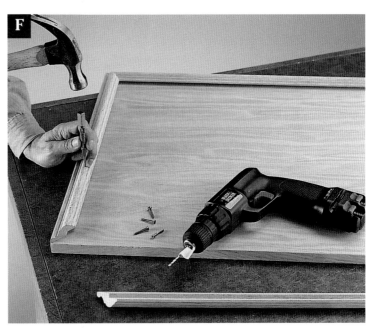

Permanently fasten the top and side pieces of the frame around the worksurface.

MAKE THE DESK TOP.

1. Cut the desk top (L) to length.

2. Bevel the desk top along one long edge where it meets the worksurface (M). To make the cut, adjust the blade angle on a circular saw to cut a ⅛" bevel on the front edge of the desk top. First make test cuts on scrap pieces. Clamp a straightedge guide to the desk top, and make the bevel cut on one long edge of the workpiece **(photo D).**

INSTALL THE DESK BOX.

1. Stand the leg assembly up. Set the desk assembly on top of the side aprons, making sure the back edges are flush.

2. To cut the front legs to match the slanted profiles of the desk sides, first trace the angles of the desk sides onto the front legs **(photo E).** Remove the desk assembly, and use a circular saw to cut the front legs along the cutting lines.

3. Replace the desk, and make sure the front legs are cut at, or slightly below, the desk side

profiles. Fasten the desk assembly with glue, and drive 1⅝" wood screws through the desk sides and into the legs.

4. Position the desk top on the flat section of the desk sides so the back edge of the desk top overhangs the back of the legs by ⅛". The top should overhang the outside faces of the back legs by ½" on each side. Make sure the beveled edge faces forward and slants in from top to bottom. Attach the desk top with glue, and drive 1⅝" wood screws through the top and into the edges of the desk sides and back.

5. Cut the side trim (P) pieces to fit between the legs on the sides and back, covering the joint where the desk assembly meets the aprons. Tack the side trim over the joint, using ¾" brass brads.

MAKE THE WORK-SURFACE.

The molding nailed to the top of the plywood worksurface holds

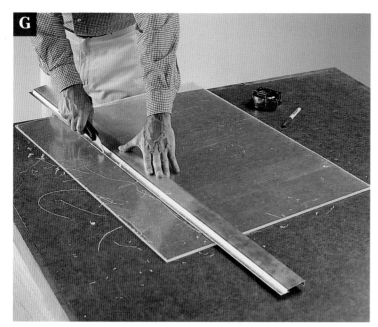

Score the acrylic sheet repeatedly, using a plastic cutter and a straightedge as a guide.

the acrylic protector in place. One piece of the molding is removable, allowing you to replace the acrylic if it gets worn.

1. Cut the worksurface (M) to size. Apply edge tape to all four edges of the board.

2. Cut the top molding (N) to fit around the edges of the worksurface. Miter-cut the corners of the molding pieces to make miter joints.

3. Use glue and ¾" brads to attach the top molding to the sides and top of the worksurface **(photo F).**

4. Drive 1" brads through one molding piece and into the other at each joint, lock-nailing the pieces. To secure the bottom piece of molding, clamp it in place on the worksurface. From underneath the worksurface, drill 1¼"-deep pilot holes, ³⁄₁₆" in from the front edge. Place a piece of tape on your drill bit as a depth guide to avoid drilling through the face of the molding. Counterbore the holes. Drive 1" brass wood

screws through the pilot holes and into the molding.

ADD THE TOP PROTECTOR.
Cut the top protector (O) to size, using a plastic cutter and a straightedge as a cutting guide. Make repeated cuts to score the material deeply **(photo G).**

Then, holding the straightedge next to the score line, bend the sheet to break it at the line.

APPLY FINISHING TOUCHES.
1. Fill all screw holes with oak plugs. Set the nails with a nail set, and fill the nail holes with wood putty. Finish-sand all of the surfaces, and apply a finish to the project. We used three coats of clear tung oil.

2. Attach 1½ × 3" brass butt hinges to the top edge of the worksurface, and fasten it to the desk top **(photo H).** Because the worksurface is fairly heavy, you may need to support it from behind as you fasten the hinges.

3. Install a 6" heavy-duty lid support on one desk side inside the storage compartment. Fasten the arm of the support to the worksurface, near the top edge of the bottom face.

4. Remove the screws holding the removable top molding piece, and insert the top protector into the frame. Attach the molding.

Attach the worksurface to the beveled edge of the desk top with evenly spaced hinges.

PROJECT
POWER TOOLS

Nesting Office

*The basic building blocks of a home office, designed to
fit together in one small space.*

CONSTRUCTION MATERIALS

Quantity	Lumber
3	2 × 2" × 8' oak
4	1 × 4" × 8' oak
2	1 × 2" × 8' oak
4	¾" × 2 × 4' oak plywood
1	⅜ × 1¹⁄₁₆" × 6' oak stop molding
2	¾ × ¾" × 8' oak cove molding

The desk and credenza are the two principal furnishings needed in any home office. This nesting office pair features both components at full size. But because they fit together, they can be stored in about the same amount of space as a standard medium-size desk. Made of oak and oak plywood, both pieces are well constructed and pleasing to the eye. The desk has a large writing surface, and the credenza is a versatile rolling storage cabinet with a hanging file box and shelves for storage of books, paper and other materials. Flip-up tops let you use the credenza as an auxiliary writing or computer surface while storing office supplies below.

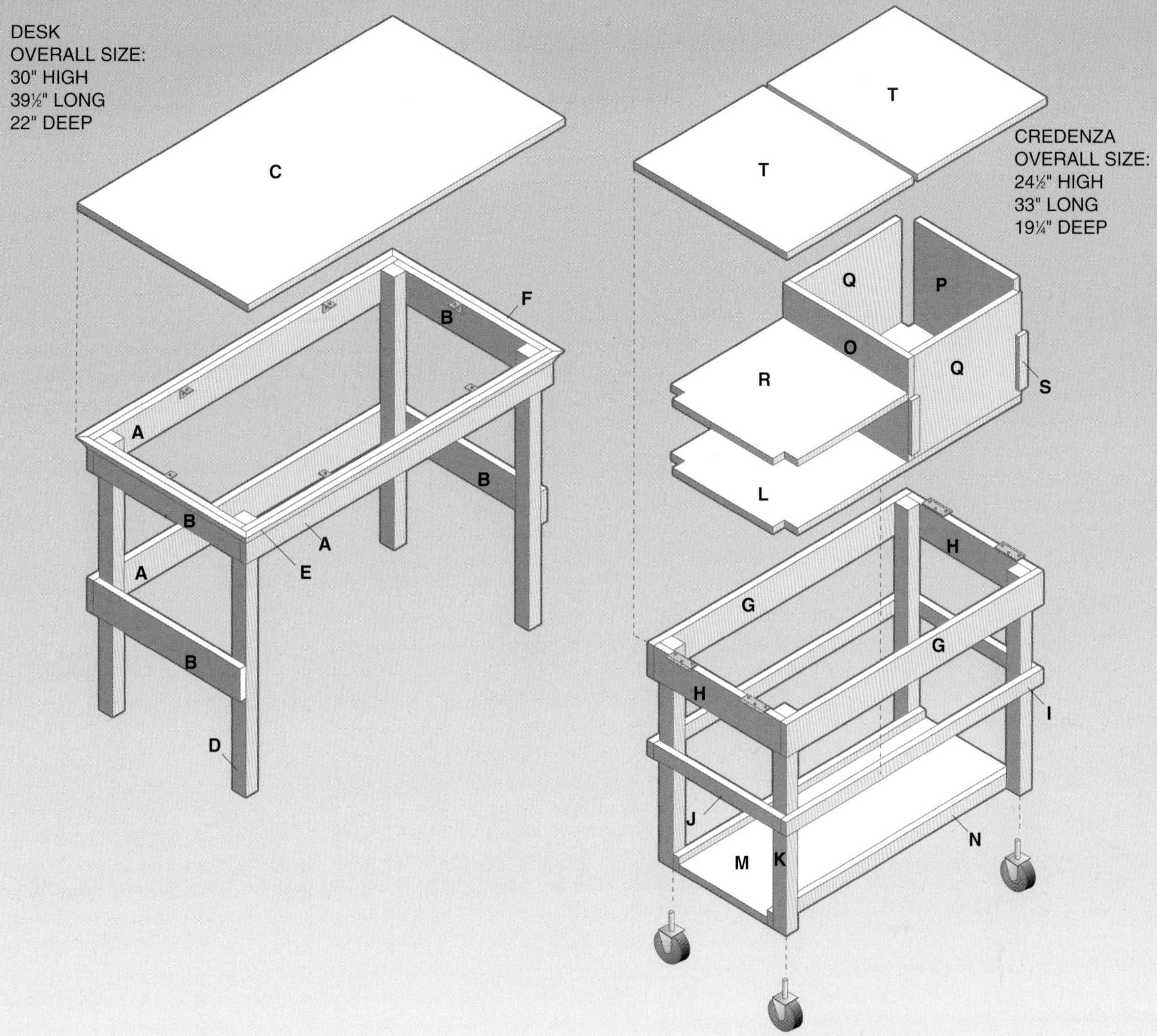
DESK
OVERALL SIZE:
30" HIGH
39½" LONG
22" DEEP
C
F
B
A
B
B
A
E
A
B
D
T
T
CREDENZA
OVERALL SIZE:
24½" HIGH
33" LONG
19¼" DEEP
Q
P
O
Q
S
R
L
H
G
G
H
I
J
N
M
K

Cutting List				
Key	**Part**	**Dimension**	**Pcs.**	**Material**
A	Desk side	¾ × 3½ × 38"	3	Oak
B	Desk end	¾ × 3½ × 19"	4	Oak
C	Desktop	¾ × 22 × 39½"	1	Plywood
D	Desk leg	1½ × 1½ × 29¼"	4	Oak
E	Side molding	¾ × ¾ × *	2	Cove molding
F	End molding	¾ × ¾ × *	2	Cove molding
G	Credenza side	¾ × 3½ × 33"	2	Oak
H	Credenza end	¾ × 3½ × 16"	2	Oak
I	Middle rail	¾ × 1½ × 33"	2	Oak
J	End rail	¾ × 1½ × 16"	2	Oak

Cutting List				
Key	**Part**	**Dimension**	**Pcs.**	**Material**
K	Credenza leg	1½ × 1½ × 21¼"	4	Oak
L	Middle shelf	¾ × 16 × 31½"	1	Plywood
M	Bottom shelf	¾ × 11½ × 31½"	1	Plywood
N	Bottom rail	¾ × 1½ × 31½"	2	Oak
O	Divider	¾ × 11¼ × 16"	1	Plywood
P	End panel	¾ × 11¼ × 13"	1	Plywood
Q	Side panel	¾ × 11¼ × 13⅞"	2	Plywood
R	Bin bottom	¾ × 15⅜ × 16"	1	Plywood
S	Stop	⅜ × 1 1/16 × 7"	6	Stop molding
T	Bin lid	¾ × 16⅜ × 19¼"	2	Plywood

Materials: #6 × 1" and 1⅝" wood screws, 16-ga. × 1" brads, 1½ × 3" brass butt hinges (4), 2½" swivel casters (4), 1¼" brass corner braces with ⅝" brass wood screws (6), brass lid supports (4), ¾" oak veneer edge tape (50'), ⅜"-dia. oak plugs, wood glue, finishing materials.

Note: Measurements reflect the actual size of dimension lumber.

***** Cut to fit.

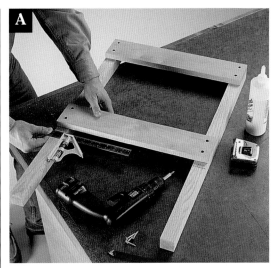

Check with a combination square to make sure the desk legs are square to the ends.

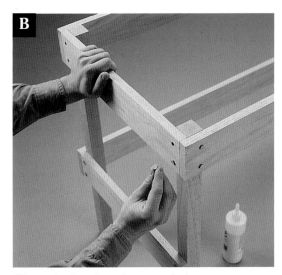

Glue oak plugs into the screw holes to cover the screws.

Directions: Nesting Office

For all screws used in this project, drill ³⁄₃₂" pilot holes. Counterbore the holes ¼" deep, using a ⅜" counterbore bit.

MAKE THE DESK-LEG PAIRS.

1. Cut the desk ends (B) and desk legs (D) to length. Sand the pieces smooth.

2. Lay the legs on a flat surface, arranged in pairs. Lay the desk ends across the legs to form the leg pair assemblies. One desk end in each leg pair should be flush with the tops of the legs, and the bottom of the other desk end should be 10½" up from the bottoms of the legs. Apply glue to the mating surfaces, then clamp the leg pair assemblies together. Check the assemblies with a square to make sure the legs are square to the end boards **(photo A).** Fasten the pieces together by driving 1⅝" wood screws through the desk ends and into the legs.

ASSEMBLE THE DESK BASE.

1. Cut the desk sides (A) to length and sand them smooth.

Fasten the desktop to the desk base with brass corner braces.

2. Drill a pair of pilot holes about 1½" in from each end of each desk side board. Before drilling the pilot holes, check the leg pairs to make sure the pilot holes will not run into the screws joining the end boards and the legs.

3. Apply glue to the mating ends of one side board, and clamp it in place so it spans between the leg pairs, flush with the tops of the legs and the outside faces of the desk ends. Check to make sure the leg pairs are square to the desk side. Drive 1⅝" wood screws

through the pilot holes. Install the other top desk side, using the same method.

4. Use glue and 1⅝" wood screws to attach the lower side board to the legs so the top is flush with the tops of the end boards in the leg pairs. After the glue has set, insert glued oak plugs into all screw holes **(photo B).** Sand the plugs flush with the surface.

5. Sand the entire desk base with medium-grit sandpaper to smooth the surfaces and dull any sharp edges.

Install strips of oak cove molding along the underside of the desktop.

(photo D).

ATTACH THE DESKTOP.

Fasten the plywood desktop to the base with corner braces. These allow the desktop to expand and contract without splitting the wood.

1. Cut the desktop (C) to size.

2. Sand the edges smooth, and wipe them clean.

3. Cut strips of self-adhesive edge tape to fit the edges. Use a household iron set at low to medium heat to press the veneer onto the edges. After the adhesive cools, trim any excess tape with a utility knife. Sand the edges of the tape smooth with fine-grit sandpaper.

4. Place the desktop on your worksurface with the top face-down, and center the desk base on the desktop. The desktop should overhang the base by ¾" on all sides. Clamp the base in place, and arrange 1¼" brass corner braces along the inside edges of the desk side and end boards. Use two braces on each side and one at each end. Drill pilot holes, and drive ⅝" brass wood screws to attach the desktop **(photo C)**.

ATTACH THE DESK MOLDING.

Fit the side and end molding pieces underneath the desktop, and fasten them to the desk sides and ends.

1. Cut the side molding (E) and end molding (F) pieces to fit the desk dimensions, miter-cutting the ends at a 45° angle.

2. Drill 1/16" pilot holes through the molding pieces, and position them against the bottom of the desktop. Apply glue to the

molding, including the mitered ends, and attach the pieces with 1" brads **(photo D).**

MAKE THE CREDENZA BASE.

The credenza base is similar to the desk base. Build the leg pairs first, then join them together with long side boards. Remember to check the frame parts for square before you fasten them.

1. Cut the credenza sides (G), credenza ends (H), middle rails (I), end rails (J) and credenza legs (K) to length.

2. Arrange the legs in pairs with the end rails and credenza ends positioned across them. The credenza

Plain file boxes can be easily converted to hanging file boxes by installing a self-standing metal hanger system. Sold at office supply stores, the thin metal standards and support rods are custom-cut to fit the box, then assembled and set in place. The metal tabs on the hanging folders fit over the metal support rods.

Attach the credenza ends and end rails to the legs with glue and wood screws.

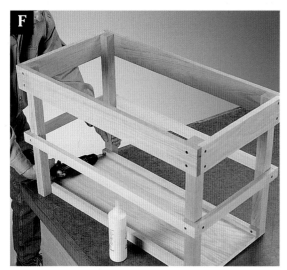

Fasten the bottom shelf by driving wood screws through the bottom rails and into the legs.

Cut notches at each corner of the middle shelf so it will fit between the credenza legs.

ends should be flush with the outside edges and tops of the legs. The end rails should be flush with the outside edges of the legs, with the bottom edges of the rails 12" down from the tops of the legs. Apply glue to the mating surfaces, and clamp the parts together. Make sure the assemblies are square, then drive 1⅝" wood screws through the ends and rails and into the legs **(photo E).**

3. Set the leg pairs on one side edge, spacing them about 30" apart. Position a credenza side so its top edge is flush with the tops of the credenza ends. The ends of the side board should be flush with the outside faces of the credenza ends. Fasten the side piece with glue, and drive 1⅝" wood screws through the side and into the legs.

4. Attach the middle rail, flush with the end rails in the leg assemblies, using the same methods. Attach the other credenza side and middle rail to complete the base.

MAKE THE CREDENZA SHELVES.

1. Cut the middle shelf (L), bot-

Glue the bin bottom between the credenza sides, flush with their bottom edges, and secure it with screws.

tom shelf (M) and bottom rails (N) to size. Apply self-adhesive edge tape to both short edges of the bottom shelf.

2. Position a bottom rail against each long edge of the bottom shelf. Make sure the ends are flush and the bottom edges of the rails are flush with the bot-

tom face of the shelf. Fasten the parts with glue, and drive 1⅝" wood screws through the bottom rails and into the edges of the bottom shelf.

3. Position the bottom shelf between the credenza legs so the bottom edges are flush. Drive 1⅝" wood screws through the

Attach strips of oak stop molding to cover the exposed plywood edges of the bins on the outside of the credenza.

bottom rails and into the credenza legs **(photo F).**

4. Use a jig saw to cut a 1½ × 1½" notch in each corner of the middle shelf so it will fit between the credenza legs **(photo G).**

5. To attach the middle shelf between the middle rails and end rails, apply glue to the inside edges of the rails, and slide the shelf into position. The shelf should be flush with the bottom edges of the rails. Drive 1⅝" wood screws through the middle and end rails and into the middle shelf.

MAKE THE CREDENZA BINS.

The credenza bins include a file box for hanging file folders and a supply storage box. Both bins have a flip-up lid.

1. Cut the divider (O), end panel (P), side panels (Q) and bin bottom (R) to size.

2. Cut 1½ × 1½" notches in both corners at one end of the bin bottom so it will fit between the credenza legs.

3. Position the side panels on top of the middle shelf so their outside edges are flush against

the legs. Apply glue and drive 1" wood screws through the side panels and into the credenza sides and middle rails.

4. Position the end panel between the legs, with its bottom edge flush against the middle shelf. Apply glue and drive 1" wood screws through the end panel and into the credenza end and end rail.

5. Slide the divider into place so it butts against the inside edges of the side panels and is flush with the tops of the side panels. Fasten the divider with glue, and drive 1⅝" wood screws through the divider and into the edges of the side panels.

6. From the outside of the credenza, drill evenly spaced pilot holes for the bin bottom in the credenza sides and end, ⅜" up from the bottom edges of the boards. Apply glue to the edges of the bin bottom and slip it into place, flush with the bottom edges of the credenza sides and ends **(photo H).** Drive 1⅝" wood screws through the sides and ends and into the edges of the bin bottom.

7. Cut the stops (S) to length.

8. Drill ¹⁄₁₆" pilot holes through

the stop pieces. Position the stops to conceal the joints and the edges of the panels that make up the large credenza bin. Use glue and 1" brads to attach the stops **(photo I).**

9. Cut the lids (T) to size from a single plywood panel. Apply edge tape to all of the edges. Do not attach the lids until after the finish has been applied.

APPLY FINISHING TOUCHES.

1. Insert glued oak plugs into all visible screw holes in the desk and credenza. Sand the plugs flush with the surface. Set all nails with a nail set, and fill the nail holes with wood putty.

2. Finish-sand both furnishings with 180- or 220-grit sandpaper. Then, apply the finish of your choice. You may find it easier to finish the desk if you remove the desktop first. It is important that you finish the underside as well as the top. We used only a clear topcoat for a light, contemporary look. You may prefer to use a light or medium wood stain first.

3. When the finish has dried, reattach the desktop. Fasten 1½ × 3" brass butt hinges to the bottom faces of the credenza lids, 2¼" in from the side edges. The backs of the hinge barrels should be flush with the back edges of the lids when closed. Attach the bin lids to the credenza by fastening the hinges to the credenza ends. Attach sliding lid supports to the lids and inside faces of the credenza sides to hold the lids open for access to the bins.

4. Attach a 2½" swivel caster to the bottom end of each credenza leg.

Bedroom Projects

A beautiful mission lamp and a practical night stand to put it on; a spacious armoire and a delightful jewelry box. These projects and more are here for you to create. Sleep tight and dream of creating more attractive and practical projects.

Mission Lamp Base

The beauty and texture of oak combine with a simple style and charm in this traditional table lamp.

PROJECT
POWER TOOLS

CONSTRUCTION MATERIALS

QUANTITY	LUMBER
1	$1 \times 8" \times 2'$ oak
2	$1 \times 2" \times 10'$ oak
1	$1 \times 3 \times 12"$ oak

This decorative lamp base provides just the right accent for a family room tabletop or bedside stand. It's made of red oak, and the design is simple and stylish. The clean, vertical lines of the oak slats are rooted in the popular Mission style.

The oak parts are joined with glue and nails, so the lamp base goes together with a minimum of time and fuss.

Once the base is assembled, just insert the lamp hardware, which you can buy at any hardware store. Lamp hardware kits include all of the components you need—harp, socket, cord and tubing. Make sure to follow manufacturer's directions when installing the hardware.

When you're finished, buy an attractive shade, either contemporary or classic, and set the lamp on a nightstand or table.

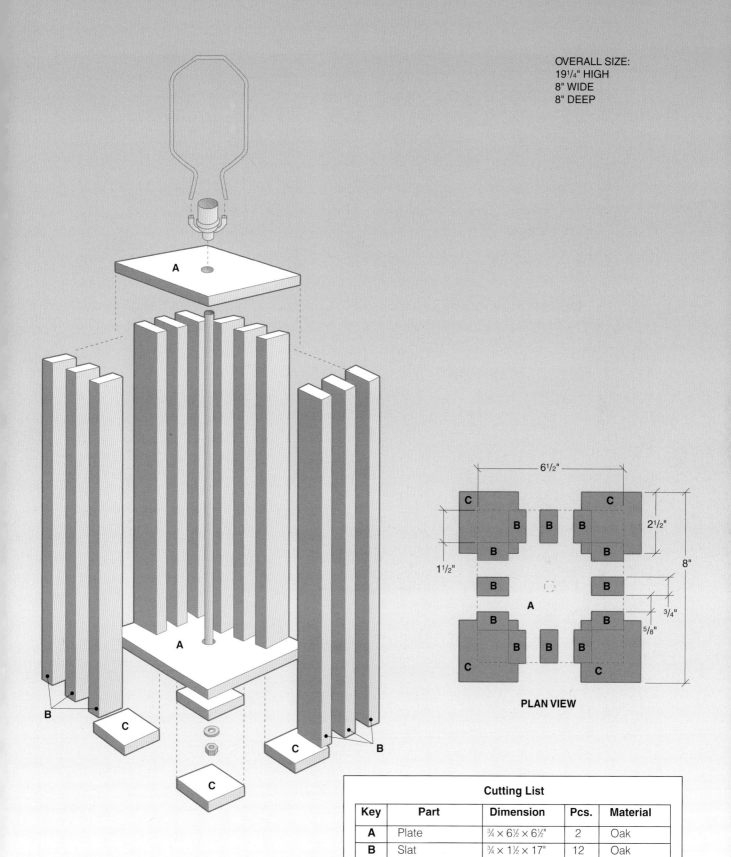

OVERALL SIZE:
19¼" HIGH
8" WIDE
8" DEEP

6½"

2½"

1½"

8"

¾"

5/8"

A

PLAN VIEW

Cutting List				
Key	**Part**	**Dimension**	**Pcs.**	**Material**
A	Plate	¾ × 6½ × 6½"	2	Oak
B	Slat	¾ × 1½ × 17"	12	Oak
C	Foot	¾ × 2½ × 2½"	4	Oak

Materials: 3d and 6d finish nails, lamp hardware kit, felt pads, wood glue, finishing materials.

Note: Measurements reflect the actual size of dimension lumber.

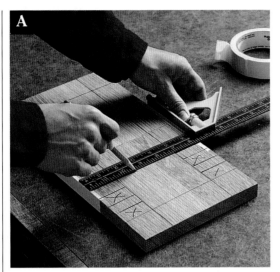

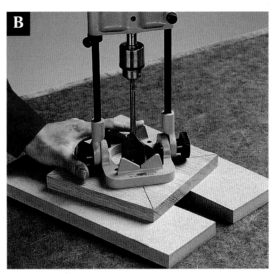

Tape the plates edge to edge, and use a square to lay out the slat positions.

Use a portable drill guide to make accurate center holes in the plates.

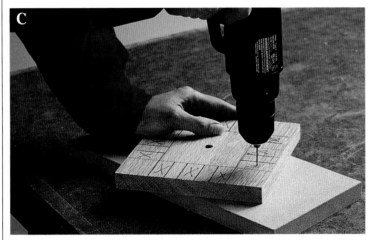

Drill pilot holes through the plates for finish nails.

4. Use the same technique to drill a ⅜"-dia. hole through the center of the counterbore and the center of the other plate for the lamp rod. To prevent splintering when the drill bit exits the other side, use a backer board when drilling holes through your workpiece.
5. Drill ⅟₁₆" pilot holes for finish nails through the plates to secure the slats **(photo C).** Each slat should have two finish nails attaching it to each plate.

Directions:
Mission Lamp Base

PREPARE THE PLATES.
1. Cut the plates (A) to size, and sand the pieces smooth with medium-grit sandpaper.
2. Set the plates flat on your worksurface, edge to edge, with their ends flush, and tape

them together. Following the *Diagram*, lay out the slat placement, using a combination square to ensure the lines are square and identical on both plates **(photo A).**
3. Draw diagonal lines from corner to corner, on the opposite sides of each plate, to locate the centers of the pieces. Drill a 1"-dia. × ¼"-deep counterbore hole on the bottom center of the lower plate, using a spade bit **(photo B).** Use a portable drill stand to hold the drill straight. This hole will receive a washer when you assemble the lamp.

CUT AND ATTACH THE SLATS.
1. Cut the slats (B) to length. Only a portion of each slat will be fully visible on the completed lamp, so choose the best sides and edges of the slats to be exposed.
2. Finish-sand the slats. Be careful not to round the edges.
3. Attach the slats to the top plate, one at a time. First, apply glue to the top end of the slat. Then, drive 6d finish nails through the pilot holes in the top plate and into the end of the slat **(photo D).** For best results, fasten each slat with one nail, and check the positioning.

Then, make any necessary adjustments, and drive the second nail.

4. Fasten the bottom ends of the slats to the lower plate, using glue and 6d finish nails. Make sure the counterbore for the lamp hardware is on the bottom.

CUT AND ATTACH THE FEET.

1. Cut the feet (C) to size from the leftover 1 × 8 stock.

2. Gang-sand the pieces to a uniform shape, and finish-sand them with fine-grit sandpaper.

3. Draw reference lines on each foot to mark its position on the base plate. Measure ¾" from the outside edge of two adjacent sides, and draw lines across the face of the foot, parallel to the side edges. These lines show where the four feet meet the plate corners (see *Diagram*).

4. Drill two ¹⁄₁₆" pilot holes for finish nails through each foot. Apply glue, and follow the reference lines to position the feet on the bottom face of the bottom plate. The two outside edges of the feet should overhang the corner edges of the plate by ¾".

5. Secure the feet by driving 3d finish nails through the feet and into the bottom plate.

APPLY FINISHING TOUCHES.

1. Set all nails in the lamp base with a nail set. Fill the nail holes with tinted wood putty, and sand the putty flush with the surface. Then, finish-sand the entire project.

2. Finish the lamp as desired (see *Tip*). We used a light oak stain and added two coats of wipe-on tung oil for a protec-

Attach the slats to the top plate with glue and 6d finish nails.

Install the threaded lamp rod, and secure it to the bottom plate with a washer and nut.

tive topcoat.

3. When the finish has dried, attach self-adhesive felt pads to the bottom of the feet to prevent scratching on tabletop surfaces.

INSTALL THE HARDWARE.

With the wood parts assembled, install the lamp kit components to complete the project. Always follow manufacturer's instructions when installing hardware.

1. Cut the lamp rod to length so that it extends from plate to plate. Insert the rod through the holes in the plates.

2. Attach the harp to the top plate. Then, secure the tube to the bottom plate with a washer and nut **(photo E).**

3. Thread the cord through the rod, and wire the ends to the socket according to the manufacturer's directions.

PROJECT
POWER TOOLS

Room Divider

*Crafted from cedar boards and lauan plywood, this portable
room divider makes it easy to create a new living space.*

CONSTRUCTION MATERIALS

Quantity	Lumber*
3	1 × 4" × 8' cedar
3	¾ × ¾" × 8' mahogany cove molding
1	¼" × 4 × 4' lauan plywood

*Materials for a single room divider section.

Strips of lauan plywood are woven together and set in rustic cedar frames to make this room divider. Held together with brass hinges, the sections of the divider can be arranged to fit almost any room. Use it as a partition to make a romantic dining nook in a large living area. Or, position the room divider near a sunny window to establish a tranquil garden retreat without adding permanent walls. There are many creative uses for this versatile decorative barrier.

The instructions for building the room divider show you how to make one section. Add as many additional sections as required.

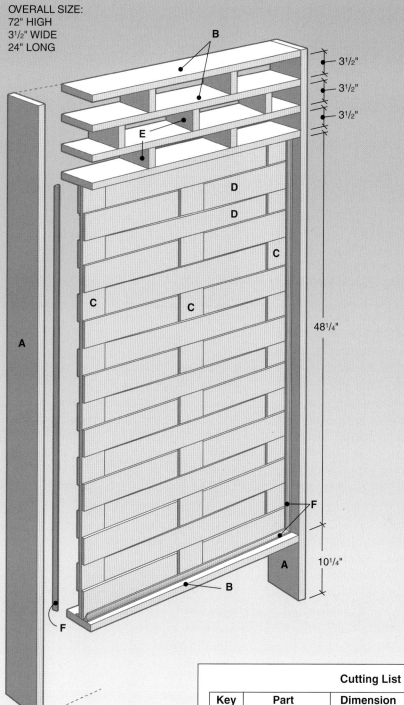

OVERALL SIZE:
72" HIGH
3½" WIDE
24" LONG

B

3½"

3½"

3½"

E

D

D

C

C

C

A

48¼"

F

A

B

F

10¼"

Cutting List

Key	Part	Dimension	Pcs.	Material
A	Leg	¾ × 3½ × 72"	2	Cedar
B	Stretcher	¾ × 3½ × 22½"	5	Cedar
C	Vertical slat	¼ × 3 × 48"	3	Plywood
D	Horizontal slat	¼ × 3 × 22½"	16	Plywood
E	Divider	¾ × 3½ × 3½"	7	Cedar
F	Retaining strip	¾ × ¾" × *	8	Cove molding

Materials: 2" deck screws, 2d finish nails, 2" brass butt
hinges, wood glue, finishing materials.

Note: Measurements reflect the actual size of dimension
lumber.

*Cut to fit.

Directions: Room Divider

MAKE THE FRAME.

The frame consists of two legs and five stretchers. Starting from the bottom, the first and second stretchers form the top and bottom borders of the woven panel.

1. Cut the legs (A) and stretchers (B) to length.

2. Measure and mark the positions for the stretchers on the inside faces of the legs. To make sure the measurements are exactly the same on both legs, tape the pieces together, edge to edge. Make sure the top and bottom edges are flush. Measure and mark a reference line 10¼" from the bottom ends of both legs. These lines mark the top edge of the bottom stretcher. Next, measure and mark lines 48¼" up the legs from the first reference lines **(photo A)**. These lines mark the bottom edge of the second stretcher. The top stretcher should be positioned between the legs, flush with the top ends. Mark the remaining stretcher positions as desired. We arranged them equally between the top and second stretchers, about 3½" apart.

3. Drill two ⁵⁄₃₂" pilot holes through the outside faces of the legs at the center position of each stretcher. Counterbore the holes ⅛" deep, using a ⅜" counterbore bit. Glue the ends of the stretchers and position them between the legs. Clamp the frame together and measure diagonally from corner to corner to make sure the frame is square. Fasten the stretchers to the legs with 2" deck screws.

MAKE THE DIVIDER PANEL.

The divider panel consists of 19

Tape the legs together with their edges flush, and gang-mark the stretcher positions on the inside faces.

Weave the 16 horizontal slats through the three vertical slats to make the divider panel.

strips of ¼"-thick lauan plywood woven together without fasteners or glue. This step is easy to complete if you work on a flat surface.

1. Cut the vertical slats (C) and horizontal slats (D) to size. Sand the edges smooth.

2. Lay the vertical slats on your worksurface. Weave the horizontal slats between the vertical slats in an alternating pattern to form the panel **(photo B)**.

INSTALL THE DIVIDER PANEL.

To hold the divider panel in the frame, fasten retaining strips along the inside faces of the legs and stretchers on both sides of the panel.

1. Use a miter box or a power miter saw to cut the retaining strips (F) to length from ¾"-thick mahogany cove molding. Miter-cut the retaining strips to fit the inside of the frame.

2. Mark reference lines along

Attach the retaining strips with 2d finish nails.

Connect the divider sections with brass butt hinges.

TIP

There is significant color variation in lauan plywood, ranging from soft yellow to deep purple—sometimes within the same panel. Keep this in mind when you are selecting your lumber.

pieces are purely decorative and can be spaced apart in any pattern. Cut them to fit snug between the top stretchers so they won't need fasteners.

1. Measure the distance between the top stretchers, and cut the dividers (E) to length. Sand the dividers smooth.

2. Set the dividers between the stretchers, positioning them in a way that is visually pleasing.

3. Fill all visible screw holes with tinted wood putty, and sand the legs smooth.

4. Join individual dividers with evenly spaced 2" butt hinges **(photo D).** To attach the hinges, clamp the sections together with scrap wood spacers in between. The spacers should have the same thickness as the barrels of the hinges. Use cardboard pads to prevent the clamps from damaging the soft wood of the frames.

5. Cedar lumber, mahogany trim and lauan plywood do not require a protective finish, so we left them unfinished. If you prefer a glossier look, apply a coat of tung oil to the parts before assembly.

the inside faces of the legs, and on the faces of the stretchers at either end of the divider panels, 1⅜" in from one edge. Position the molding on the outside of the reference lines, so one flat face is flush with the line. Attach the retaining strips to the frame with 2d finish nails **(photo C).** Set the nails with a nail set.

3. Place the woven panel against the retaining strip frame, and secure the panel by attaching the other retaining strips so they are snug against the opposite face of the panel.

APPLY FINISHING TOUCHES. Inserting the dividers is the final construction step for the room divider section. These

PROJECT
POWER TOOLS

Jewelry Box

*This piece of fine furniture will
be a worthy home for your family treasures.*

CONSTRUCTION MATERIALS

Quantity	Lumber
1	¾ × 24 × 48" MDF*
1	½ × 12 × 30" birch plywood
1	½ × 24 × 30" birch plywood
1	¼ × 12 × 24" hardboard

*Medium-density fiberboard

Without a suitable home, jewelry has a way of getting jumbled, tangled or misplaced. This elegant and roomy jewelry box solves that problem with pizzazz.

Our classically proportioned chest—like all fine furniture—is as functional as it is beautiful. Three spacious drawers accommodate everything from fun and funky costume jewelry to the finest family heirlooms. A simple system of dadoes and

rabbets achieves the close tolerances and tight joints that characterize true quality woodwork.

The timeless design of this piece allows for many options in materials and finish, providing great flexibility for customizing your box to suit a special person or unique situation.

Building this project as a gift will showcase your thoughtfulness as well as your woodworking skills.

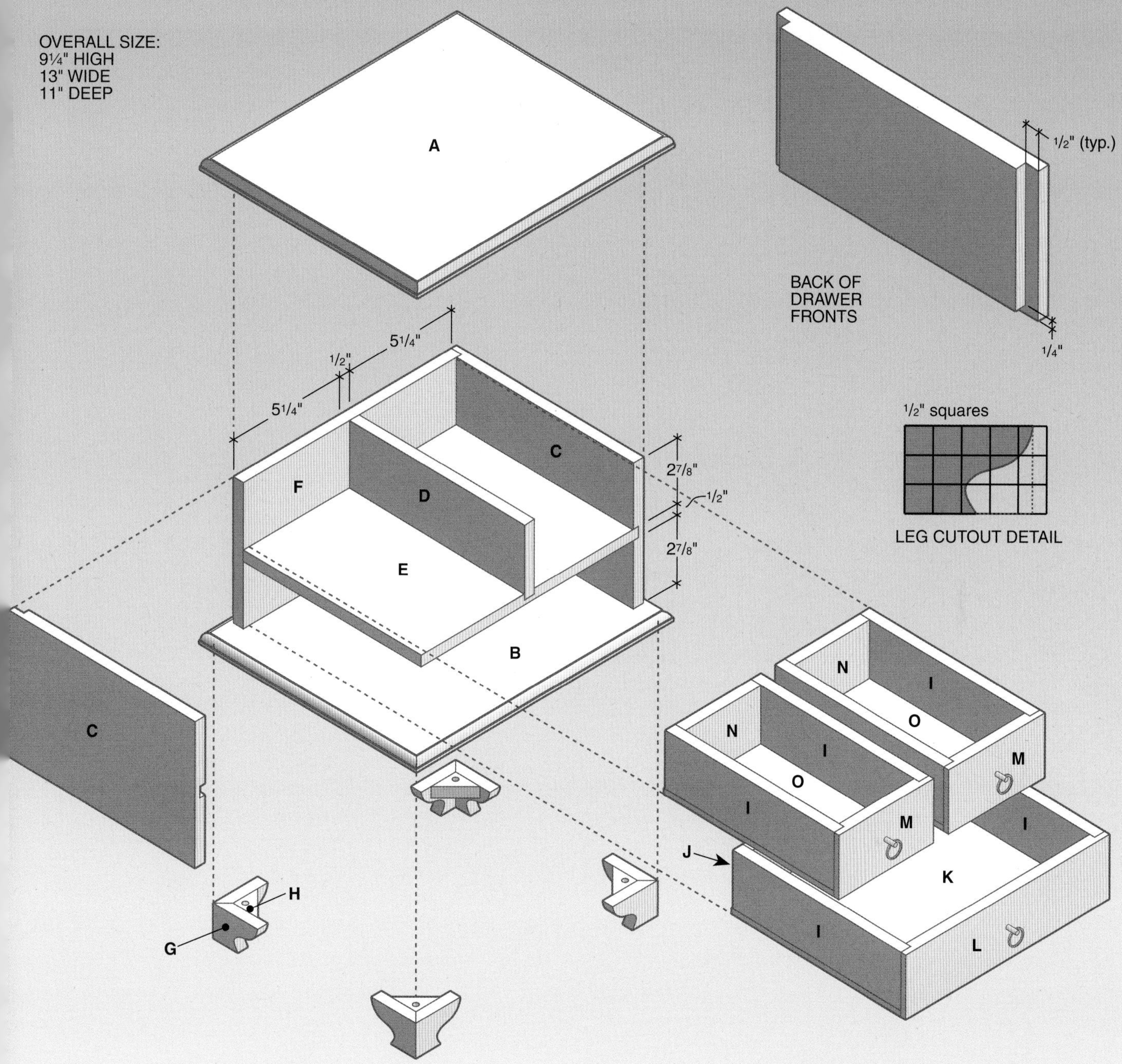
OVERALL SIZE:
9¼" HIGH
13" WIDE
11" DEEP
A
1/2" (typ.)
BACK OF
DRAWER
FRONTS
1/4"
5 1/4"
1/2"
5 1/4"
C
F
D
E
B
2 7/8"
1/2"
2 7/8"
1/2" squares
LEG CUTOUT DETAIL
C
N
I
O
N
I
O
M
M
I
I
J
K
I
L
H
G

Cutting List

Key	Part	Dimension	Pcs.	Material
A	Top	¾ × 11 × 13"	1	MDF
B	Bottom	¾ × 11 × 13"	1	MDF
C	Side	½ × 6¼ × 9½"	2	Birch ply.
D	Divider	½ × 3⅛ × 9"	1	Birch ply.
E	Shelf	½ × 9 × 11"	1	Birch ply.
F	Back	½ × 6¼ × 11"	1	Birch ply.
G	Leg	½ × 1½ × 2¼"	8	Birch ply.
H	Glueblock	½ × 1¼ × 1¼"	4	Birch ply.

Cutting List

Key	Part	Dimension	Pcs.	Material
I	Drawer side	½ × 2½ × 8 11/16"	6	Birch ply.
J	Long drwr. back	½ × 2½ × 9⅜"	1	Birch ply.
K	Long drwr. bottom	¼ × 8¾ × 10⅜"	1	Hardboard
L	Long drwr. front	½ × 2¾ × 10⅜"	1	Birch ply.
M	Short drwr. front	½ × 2¾ × 4⅞"	2	Birch ply.
N	Short drwr. back	½ × 2½ × 3⅞"	2	Birch ply.
O	Short drwr. bottom	¼ × 4⅞ × 8¾"	2	Hardboard

Materials: Wood glue, brads, 4d finish nails, #6 × 1" screws, drawer pulls (3), finishing materials.

Note: Measurements reflect the actual thickness of dimension lumber.

To cut the shelf dadoes, rout both sides in one pass, using a clamped straightedge as a guide for the router base.

Apply glue to the shelf, the divider and the shoulders of the rabbets before attaching the back.

Directions:
Jewelry Box

CUT AND SHAPE THE CABINET PARTS.

1. Cut the top (A) and bottom (B) from ¾" MDF.

2. Rout the top edges of both pieces using a ⅜" roundover bit set for a ⅛" shoulder.

3. Measure and cut the sides (C), divider (D), shelf (E) and back (F).

4. Mark the sides and the shelf for location of dadoes (see *Diagram*), and mark the back edges of the sides for rabbets.

5. Cut the dadoes. Clamp the side blanks with back edges butted. Clamp a straightedge in place to guide the router base **(photo A),** and use a ½" straight router bit set ¼" deep.

6. Cut the divider dado in the shelf and the back rabbets in the sides.

7. Drill pilot holes in the dadoes and rabbets.

ASSEMBLE THE CABINET.

1. Attach the divider to the shelf with glue and brads. Stand the shelf/divider assembly on end and attach one side with glue and brads; flip the assembly and attach the other side.

2. Stand the partially assembled cabinet on its front and attach the back with glue and brads **(photo B).**

3. Center the top on the assembly, drill pilot holes, and fasten with glue and 4d finish nails.

4. Flip the cabinet over and attach the bottom the same way.

MAKE AND ATTACH THE LEGS.

1. Cut four blanks, 6" or longer, from ½ × 1½" stock.

2. Transfer the leg profile (see *Diagram*) to the ends of the blanks and cut the profiles with a jig saw.

3. Clamp the blanks together and gang-sand the cut edges with a drum sander mounted in your drill.

4. Cut four pairs of legs (G) to length, mitering the ends at 45° **(photo C).** Cut four *pairs* rather than eight identical pieces. Cut the glueblocks (H) to size from ½" scrap.

5. Assemble the legs by gluing them in pairs to the glueblocks. Use masking tape to hold the pieces together. Allow the glue to dry.

6. Position the legs on the cabinet bottom, drill pilot holes and attach with glue and 1" screws **(photo D).**

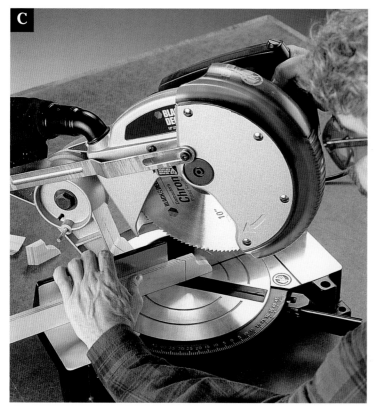

After the leg blanks have been profiled and sanded, cut the leg pieces to length with a power miter box.

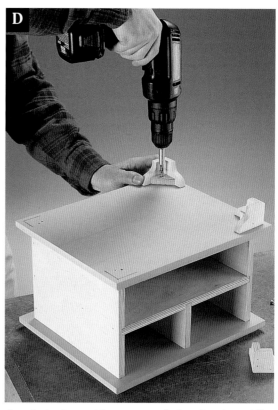

Attach the legs with screws and glue, leaving a ⅜" overhang along both sides.

BUILD THE DRAWERS.

1. Cut the drawer faces (L, M) to size.

2. Rabbet the drawer faces to accept the ½" drawer sides and ¼" bottoms (see *Diagram*).

3. Cut the drawer sides (I) and drawer backs (J, N) to size.

4. Drill pilot holes and assemble the drawer boxes with glue and brads.

5. Cut the drawer bottoms (K) and (O) to size from ¼" hardboard and fasten with glue and brads (**photo E**).

6. Measure and drill holes for the drawer pulls.

APPLY FINISHING TOUCHES.

Set all nail heads, and fill voids with putty. Finish-sand the project, finish as desired and install drawer pulls.

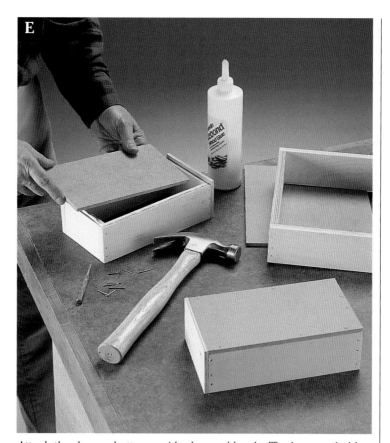

Attach the drawer bottoms with glue and brads. The bottoms hold the drawers square so they fit within their compartments.

Nightstand

A back rail adds style to our nightstand and keeps you from knocking bedside items to the floor. Put our night-stand at your bedside for a classic touch of bedroom beauty.

PROJECT
POWER TOOLS

The nightstand is a classic piece of furniture that will never go out of fashion. Our nightstand has a simple design with a solid, tra-ditional look. The arched back rail and base pieces add style and grace to the nightstand,

while the handy drawer gives you a great place to store bed-side items.

Assembling this little beauty is easy. The box frame is made by attaching the sides, back and shelves. It is topped with a decorative back rail and wings. These pieces do more than dress up the nightstand—they reduce the risk of knocking over that insistent alarm clock when you lurch to shut it off in the morning.

Once the top sections are complete, you can make and attach the arched base. The drawer comes next. We avoided expensive metal track glides and instead used friction-reducing plastic bumpers and tack-on glides for easy installa-tion and convenience.

Our nightstand is built from edge-glued pine panels that you can purchase at most building centers.

CONSTRUCTION MATERIALS

Quantity	Lumber
2	1 × 16" × 8' edge-glued pine
1	1 × 4" × 4' pine

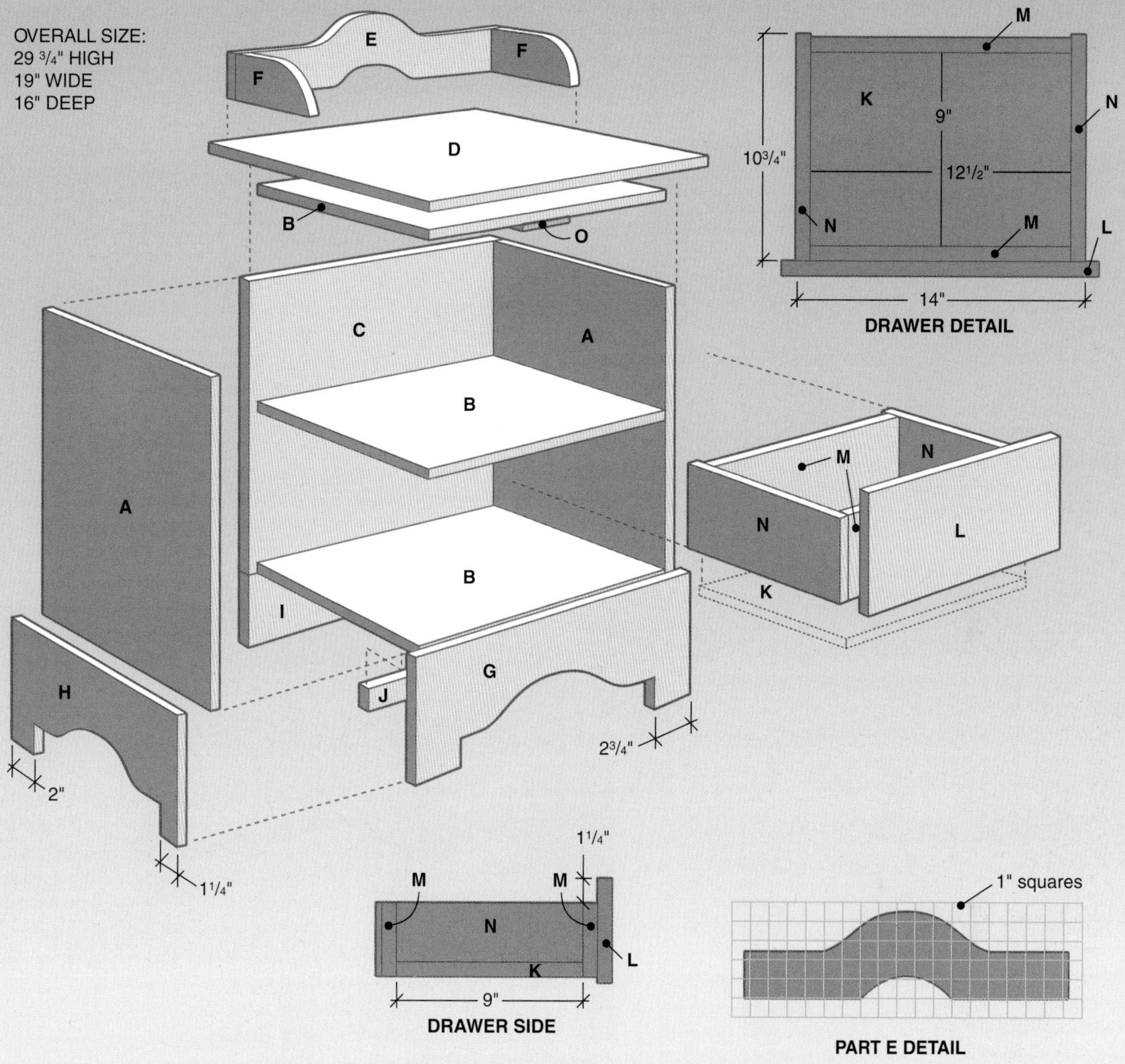

OVERALL SIZE:
29 3/4" HIGH
19" WIDE
16" DEEP
A
B
C
D
E
F
G
H
I
J
K
L
M
N
O
2"
1 1/4"
2 3/4"
10 3/4"
9"
12 1/2"
14"
DRAWER DETAIL
1 1/4"
9"
DRAWER SIDE
1" squares
PART E DETAIL

Cutting List

Key	Part	Dimension	Pcs.	Material
A	Side	¾ × 13¼ × 17"	2	Pine
B	Shelf	¾ × 13¼ × 14½"	3	Pine
C	Back	¾ × 16 × 17"	1	Pine
D	Top	¾ × 16 × 19"	1	Pine
E	Back rail	¾ × 4½ × 17½"	1	Pine
F	Wing	¾ × 2½ × 5½"	2	Pine
G	Base front	¾ × 8 × 17½"	1	Pine
H	Base side	¾ × 8 × 14"	2	Pine

Cutting List

Key	Part	Dimension	Pcs.	Material
I	Base back	¾ × 4 × 16"	1	Pine
J	Base cleat	¾ × 2 × 16"	1	Pine
K	Drawer bottom	¾ × 9 × 12½"	1	Pine
L	Drawer front	¾ × 5 × 15¾"	1	Pine
M	Drawer end	¾ × 3½ × 12½"	2	Pine
N	Drawer side	¾ × 3½ × 10¾"	2	Pine
O	Stop cleat	¾ × 1½ × 3"	1	Pine

Materials: 1¼", 1½", and 2" deck screws, 6d finish nails, wooden knobs (2), plastic drawer stop, tack-on drawer glides, stem bumpers, wood glue, finishing materials.

Note: Measurements reflect the actual size of dimension lumber.

Attach the back to one side. Then, check for square.

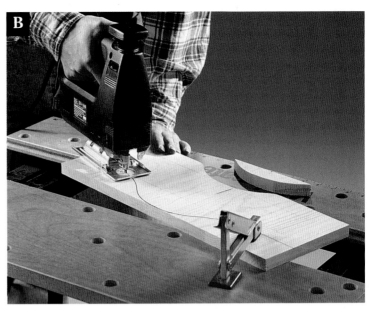

Trace the back rail pattern and cut the piece to shape with a jig saw.

Directions: Nightstand

For all screws used in this project, drill ³⁄₃₂" pilot holes. Counterbore the holes ⅛" deep, using a ⅜" counterbore bit.

BUILD THE BOX FRAME.
1. Cut the sides (A) and shelves (B) to size, and finish-sand the pieces.
2. Use glue and 2" deck screws to fasten the top and bottom shelves between the sides. Attach one shelf flush with the top ends of the sides and the other shelf flush with the bottom ends. Make sure the screws are centered and the front and back shelf edges are flush with the side edges.
3. Cut the back (C) to size, and sand it smooth. Attach it along the back edge of one side with

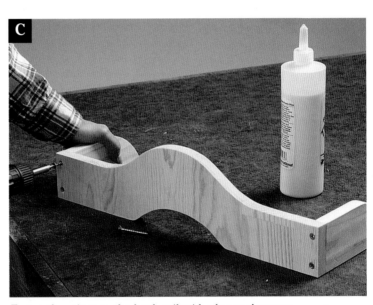

Fasten the wings to the back rail with glue and screws.

glue and 2" deck screws **(photo A).**
4. Use a framing square to check the outside of the box to be sure the sides are square with the shelves. If they are not, apply pressure to one side to draw the pieces square. This can be done by hand or by attaching a bar or pipe clamp diagonally from one side to the other. When the pieces are

square, clamp them in place, and finish attaching the back to the remaining sides and shelves.
MAKE THE BACK RAIL AND WINGS.
1. Cut the back rail (E) and wings (F) to size.
2. Transfer the pattern (see *Part E Detail*) for the back rail (see *Tip*). Cut the piece to the finished shape, using a jig saw

TIP

When transferring a grid diagram, you can enlarge the diagram on a photocopier and trace it onto a piece of cardboard to form a tracing template.

Draw reference lines on the top. Then, drill pilot holes and attach the back rail and wings.

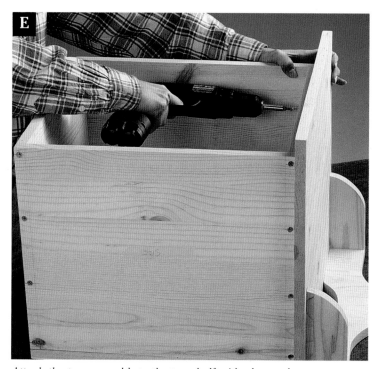

Attach the top assembly to the top shelf with glue and screws.

(photo B). Sand the back rail smooth.

3. Shape the wings by using a compass to draw a 2½" radius arc. Place the compass point as close as possible to the bottom edge, 2½" back from the front and trace the arc. Cut the curve

with a jig saw. Cut the second wing, and gang-sand the wings smooth.

4. Drill pilot holes in the back rail ⅜" in from the ends. Fasten the wings to the back rail with glue and 1½" deck screws **(photo C).**

COMPLETE THE TOP SECTION.

1. Cut the top (D) to size, and sand it smooth.

2. Center the back rail and wings onto the top with the back rail flush with the top's back edge. Draw a 5½"-long line marking the outside edge of each wing. The lines should be ¾" in from the side edges of the top.

3. Drill pilot holes through the top, ⅜" inside each line for attaching the wings **(photo D).** Attach the back rail and wings to the top with glue, and drive 1½" deck screws through the bottom face of the top and into the back rail and wings.

4. Center the top assembly over the top shelf, with the back edges flush. Attach the top assembly by driving 1¼" deck screws through the top shelf and into the top **(photo E).**

ATTACH THE MIDDLE SHELF.

1. Draw reference lines across the inside faces of the sides, 5½" down from the top edges of the sides.

2. Position the top of the middle shelf below the reference lines with its front edge flush with the front edges of the sides. Fasten the shelf with glue, and drive 2" deck screws through the sides and into the edges of the shelf. This shelf supports the drawer, so make sure it is square to the sides.

MAKE THE BASE CUTOUTS.

1. Cut the base front (G), base sides (H), base back (I) and base cleat (J) to size.

2. Make the decorative cutout on the base front, by draw verti-

Use a combination square to mark the finish nail position on the base front and sides.

cal lines 2¾" in from each end. Using the template you made for the back rail, center the top of the arc 3" down from the top edge of the base front. Trace the curved line along the top of the template until it intersects the two vertical lines (see *Diagram*). Cut out the detail with a jig saw, and sand the piece smooth.

3. Make the cutout on one of the base sides, using the template. Draw a vertical line on the base side piece, 1¼" in from the front end and 2" in from the rear end. Center the arc of the template 3" from the top of the base side, and trace the curve to meet the vertical lines. Cut the piece with a jig saw and sand it smooth.

4. Use the finished base side to trace an identical pattern onto the other base side. Make the cutout with a jig saw, and sand the piece smooth.

ASSEMBLE THE BASE.

1. Butt the front ends of the base sides against the base front so the top edges are flush and the outside faces of the base sides are flush with the ends of the base front. Drill ¹⁄₁₆" pilot holes through the base front and into the sides. Attach the pieces with glue and 6d finish nails.

2. Position the base back between the base sides so that its top edge is ½" below the top edges of the base sides and the back edges are flush. Attach the base back with glue, and drive 6d finish nails through the

sides and into the ends of the base back.

3. Attach the base cleat to the inside face of the base front with glue, and drive 1¼" deck screws through the cleat and into the base front. Leave a ½" space between the top edge of the cleat and the top edge of the base front.

ATTACH THE FRAME.

1. Draw a reference line for finish nails, ¼" below the top edge of the base front and sides **(photo F).**

2. Set the nightstand box frame into the base so it rests on the base back and base cleat.

3. Drill evenly spaced ¹⁄₁₆" pilot holes along the reference lines. Fasten the base by driving 6d finish nails through the base front and sides and into the sides and bottom shelf.

BUILD THE DRAWER.

1. Cut the drawer bottom (K), drawer front (L), drawer ends (M) and drawer sides (N) to size. Sand the parts smooth.

2. Position the drawer bottom between the drawer ends, keeping the bottom edges and the ends flush. Attach the pieces with glue, and drive 1½" deck screws through the drawer ends and into the drawer bottom.

3. Align the drawer sides so their front edges are flush with the front face of the front drawer end. Fasten the sides to the bottom and ends with glue and 1½" deck screws **(photo G).** The rear ends of the drawer sides should overhang the rear end of the drawer by ¼".

4. Draw a reference line along the inside face of the drawer front ¼" above the bottom edge. Lay the drawer front flat on your worksurface. Center the drawer from side to side on the drawer front with its bottom edge on the reference line. Apply glue, and drive 1¼" deck screws through the drawer end and into the drawer front **(photo H).**

INSTALL THE STOP CLEAT AND DRAWER KNOBS.

Used in conjunction with a purchased drawer stop, the stop cleat prevents the drawer from pulling completely out of the nightstand. A drawer stop is a small plastic bracket with an adjustable stem that catches the stop cleat when the drawer is opened.

1. Cut the stop cleat (O) to size.
2. Center the cleat on the bottom face of the top shelf so its front edge is ¾" in from the front edge of the top shelf. The length of the cleat should run parallel to the front edge of the shelf, and its 1½" face should contact the shelf face.
3. Attach the stop cleat with glue, and drive 1¼" deck screws through the cleat and into the top shelf.
4. Fasten the drawer knobs to the drawer front. Be sure to space the knobs evenly, and center them from top to bottom on the drawer front.

APPLY FINISHING TOUCHES.

1. Set all nails with a nail set, and fill the nail and screw holes with wood putty. Finish-sand the entire project.
2. Paint the nightstand inside and out, including the drawer. Apply a polyurethane topcoat to protect the painted finish.

INSTALL THE HARDWARE.

You have a number of glide op-

Fasten the drawer sides to the drawer ends and drawer bottom with glue and screws.

tions for the drawer. We used inexpensive plastic glides and stem bumpers. You can buy these glides and bumpers at any building center. Always follow manufacturer's directions when installing hardware.

1. Align the glides along the path of the drawer, and tack them in place.The glides we used have metal points, and they are installed like thumbtacks.
2. Drill holes for the stem bumpers into the drawer bottom. Apply glue to the bumpers, and insert them into the holes.
3. Install the drawer stop by drilling a ³⁄₁₆"-dia. hole on the rear drawer end, ½" below the top edge. Apply glue to the drawer stop and attach it to the drawer end.
4. Insert the drawer. With the drawer open slightly, reach in and rotate the drawer stop until it is in position to catch the stop cleat.

Align the drawer front, and attach the pieces by driving screws through the drawer end.

Cedar Chest

*This compact cedar chest has the potential to become
a cherished family heirloom.*

CONSTRUCTION MATERIALS

Quantity	Lumber
3	1 × 2" × 8' cedar
1	1 × 3" × 10' cedar
1	1 × 6" × 8' cedar
3	1 × 8" × 8' cedar
1	2 × 2" × 8' cedar
1	¾" × 2 × 4' plywood

The cedar chest has a long history as a much-appreciated graduation gift. The appreciation will be even greater for a cedar chest you have built yourself. And short of a packing crate, you won't find a simpler chest to build anywhere.

Despite its simplicity, this cedar chest has all the features of a commercially produced chest costing hundreds of dollars. The framed lid is hinged in back and can be locked open with an optional locking lid support. A removable tray fits inside the chest for storing delicate items. The main compartment is fitted with aromatic cedar panels to keep sweaters or your favorite linen treasures safe from moth damage and musty odors.

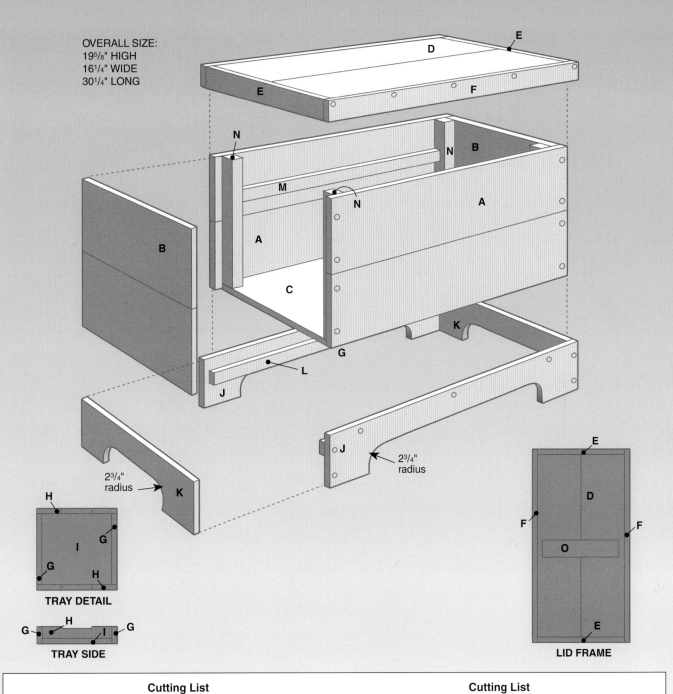

OVERALL SIZE:
19⅝" HIGH
16¼" WIDE
30¼" LONG

2¾" radius

2¾" radius

TRAY DETAIL

TRAY SIDE

LID FRAME

Cutting List

Key	Part	Dimension	Pcs.	Material
A	Side	⅞ × 7¼ × 28"	4	Cedar
B	End	⅞ × 7¼ × 12½"	4	Cedar
C	Bottom	¾ × 12½ × 26¼"	1	Plywood
D	Top	⅞ × 7¼ × 28½"	2	Cedar
E	End lip	⅞ × 1½ × 14½"	2	Cedar
F	Side lip	⅞ × 1½ × 30¼"	2	Cedar
G	Tray side	⅞ × 2½ × 12¾"	2	Cedar
H	Tray end	⅞ × 2½ × 11¾"	2	Cedar

Cutting List

Key	Part	Dimension	Pcs.	Material
I	Tray bottom	⅞ × 2½ × 12¾"	4	Cedar
J	Side plate	⅞ × 5½ × 29¾"	2	Cedar
K	End plate	⅞ × 5½ × 14¼"	2	Cedar
L	Base cleat	⅞ × 1½ × 28"	2	Cedar
M	Chest cleat	⅞ × 1½ × 23¼"	2	Cedar
N	Corner post	1½ × 1½ × 13¾"	4	Cedar
O	Top cleat	⅞ × 2½ × 12"	1	Cedar

Materials: 1¼" and 2" deck screws, 2d finish nails, 1½ × 2" brass butt hinges (2), lid support, optional hardware accessories, aromatic cedar panels, panel adhesive, ⅜"-dia. cedar plugs, wood glue, finishing materials.

Note: Measurements reflect the actual size of dimension lumber.

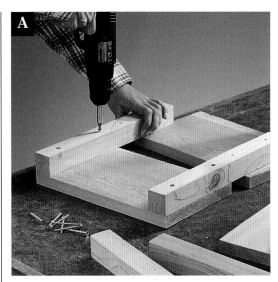

Drive screws through the posts and into the ends.

Install the bottom onto the corner posts and fasten it to the sides and ends of the chest.

Directions: Cedar Chest

For all screws used in this project, drill ³⁄₃₂" pilot holes. Counterbore the holes ¼" deep, using a ⅜" counterbore bit.

BUILD THE BOX FRAME.

1. Cut the chest sides (A), chest ends (B) and corner posts (N) to length. Sand the pieces smooth with medium-grit sandpaper.

2. Use glue and 2" deck screws to fasten two chest ends to each pair of corner posts, with their tops and side edges flush **(photo A).** When using cedar that is rough on one side, be sure that exposed surfaces are consistent in texture. For this project, make sure all rough surfaces are facing inside.

Attach the top cleat to the undersides of the tops, making sure it is centered between the ends and the sides.

3. Apply glue to the outside edges of the corner posts, and fasten the chest sides to the chest ends by driving 2" deck screws through the chest sides and into the edges of the chest ends. Make sure the top and side edges are flush. If the box frame is assembled correctly, there will be a ¾"-wide space between the bottom of the corner posts and the bottom edges of the box frame.

4. Cut the bottom (C) to size.

5. Turn the box frame upside down. Fasten the bottom to the corner posts, ends and sides with glue and 2" deck screws **(photo B).**

6. Seal the inside surfaces with an oil finish or sealer to prevent warping and splitting.

BUILD THE TOP ASSEMBLY.

1. Cut the top pieces (D) and the top cleat (O) to length. Cut the end lips (E) and side lips (F) to length. Sand the pieces smooth.

2. Use bar or pipe clamps to

TIP

Cedar is a good wood type for the beginner because it is very forgiving of mistakes. It is also a traditional wood for building chests and trunks. But if you want to create a more elegant chest that is better able to take a fine finish, substitute clear redwood.

Smooth the jig saw cuts on the radius cutouts using a drum sander attachment and drill.

Set the box frame into the base, and fasten it with evenly spaced screws.

hold the tops together, edge to edge, with their ends flush. Use a combination square to measure and mark the top cleat position on the inside faces of the tops. Make sure the top cleat is centered, with its side edges 13" from the ends of the tops and with its ends centered between the side edges of the tops. Attach the cleat to the tops with glue and 1¼" deck screws **(photo C).**

3. Attach the side lips and end lips to the edges of the tops with glue and 2" deck screws. Make sure the top edges of the lips and tops are flush.

BUILD THE BASE.

1. Cut the side plates (J) and end plates (K) to length.
2. Use a compass and a straight-edge to draw the curved cutouts on the side and end plates. Make marks along the bottom edge of the side plates, 6¾" in from each end. Set a compass to draw a 2¾" radius curve. Hold the compass point

on the mark, as close as possible to the bottom edge, and draw the curve onto the face of the side plate. Then, using a straightedge, draw a straight line 2¾" from the bottom edge of the side plate, intersecting the tops of the curves. Repeat these steps to draw the cutouts on the end plates, but hold the compass point 5⅞" from the ends. Make the cutouts with a jig saw.

3. Use a drill and a drum sander attachment to smooth the curves of the cutouts **(photo D).** Finish-sand the side plates and end plates.
4. Fasten the end plates between the side plates with glue. Drive 2" deck screws through the faces of the side plates and into the ends of the end plates.
5. Cut the two base cleats (L) to length.
6. Use glue to fasten the base cleats to the inside faces of the side plates, 2¾" from the bottom edges, flush with the top of the cutouts. Drive 1¼" deck screws through the cleats and into the side plates.

ATTACH THE BOX FRAME AND BASE.

1. Test-fit the box frame in the base, making sure it sits squarely on top of the cleats.
2. Apply glue to the mating surfaces, and attach the base by driving evenly spaced 1¼" deck screws through the end plates and side plates and into the box frame **(photo E).**

TIP

When constructing pieces that fit inside other pieces (as the chest fits inside the base), build the inside piece first. The outer parts can always be cut larger or smaller to fit the inner ones.

Tape the tray ends together. Then, draw a slot across the joint to mark identical handle cutouts.

Attach the tray bottoms to the tray ends and sides with glue and screws.

MAKE THE TRAY.

1. Cut the tray sides (G), tray ends (H) and tray bottom (I) pieces to length.

2. Lay out the tray handles by placing the tray ends side by side, with the ends flush. Tape the pieces together. Mark a 1½"-wide × 5"-long slot with ¾"-radius curves centered on each end of the slot where the two pieces meet **(photo F).** Make the cuts with a jig saw. Use a drum sander attachment on a drill to smooth out the radius cuts.

3. Attach the tray sides between the tray ends with glue and 2" deck screws.

4. Fasten the tray bottoms between the tray sides and ends with glue and 2" deck screws **(photo G).** Finish-sand the entire tray, and smooth out any sharp edges.

INSTALL AROMATIC CEDAR PANELS.

1. Cut aromatic cedar liner panels to fit the inside of the chest. Use panels that are no thicker than ¼".

2. Attach the liner panels to the sides, ends and bottom with panel adhesive and 2d finish nails **(photo H).** Set the nails with a nail set.

> ### TIP
>
> *Aromatic cedar paneling, often described as "closet liner," has a strong cedar scent that keeps away insects that can damage stored items. The paneling is sold in board packages (usually covering 14 square feet) or in thin sheets that resemble particleboard.*

MAKE AND INSTALL THE CHEST CLEATS.

1. Cut the chest cleats (M) to length. Finish-sand the cleats.

2. Install the chest cleats so their top edges are 3½" from the tops of the chest sides. They should fit snugly between the corner posts. Attach the cleats with glue, and drive 1¼" deck screws through the cleats and into the sides.

INSTALL THE TOP ASSEMBLY.

1. Place the top assembly over the chest box, and use masking tape to mark where the lower edge of the lip contacts the back side. Install two 1½ × 2" brass butt hinges on the back of the chest box, 6" in from each end. Mount the hinges so the leaves are above the contact line and the barrels are below the contact line.

2. Place the chest and top assembly on a flat worksurface. Prop the chest box against the top so the unfastened leaves of the hinges rest on the inside of the lip of the top assembly. Insert spacers equal to the thickness of the hinge barrel between the chest and lip. (Ordinary wood shims work well for this.) Fasten the hinges to the lip using the screws provided with the hinge hardware **(photo I).** Test the lid assembly and hinges for proper operation and fit.

3. Install a locking lid support between the lid assembly and

Install aromatic cedar panels to the sides, ends and bottom, using panel adhesive and 2d finish nails.

TIP

Use the right tools and techniques when applying stencils. A special brush is recommended for stencils (they resemble old-style shaving brushes). Use special stenciling paint, which is very dry so it does not leak under the stencil. Attach the stencil securely, and dab the dry paint onto the surface with the brush. Do not remove the stencil until the paint has dried.

the chest box to hold the lid in an open position during use. For just a little more money, you can purchase hardware accessories called soft-down supports, which let the lid close gently instead of slamming down.

4. Install chest handles and brass corner protectors, if desired.

APPLY FINISHING TOUCHES.
1. Fill all exposed counterbore holes with cedar plugs. Apply glue to the edges of the plugs and tap them in place with a hammer. Sand the plugs flush with the surrounding surface. Finish-sand all of the outside surfaces of the chest.
2. Set the tray on the chest cleats and slide it back and forth to test the fit. Adjust the fit, if necessary, using a belt or palm sander and medium-grit sandpaper. Finish-sand the tray to remove any sanding scratches and roughness.
3. Finish the chest and tray as desired. We chose a traditional

clear finish to provide a rustic, natural appearance. To apply this type of finish, first brush on a coat of sanding sealer to ensure even absorption (a good idea with soft wood like cedar). Then, apply two light coats of tung-oil finish, and buff the surface to a medium gloss with a buffing pad. Apply finish to the chest cleat pieces but leave the cedar panels bare. After the finish is applied, dried and buffed, you may want to stencil a design or monograms

onto the chest. If you choose to monogram the chest, look for plain stencils that are 1" to 2" tall, to keep in scale with the size of the chest. Very ornate typestyles are hard to stencil, and generally are not in tune with the rustic look of a cedar chest (see *Tip,* above). If you are interested in stenciling a design or emblem onto the chest, consider a simple pattern. Almost any nature motif (like pinecones) is a good choice.

Install brass butt hinges on the chest box and lid assembly. Use wood shims as spacers to help align the hinges.

PROJECT
POWER TOOLS

Armoire

*With a simple, rustic appearance, this movable closet
can blend into almost any bedroom.*

CONSTRUCTION MATERIALS

Quantity	Lumber
3	¾" × 4 × 8' birch plywood
1	¼" × 4 × 8' birch plywood
1	1 × 2" × 8' pine
6	1 × 3" × 8' pine
1	1 × 6" × 8' pine
1	1½"-dia. × 2' fir dowel

Long before massive walk-in closets became the norm in residential building design, homeowners and apartment-dwellers compensated for cramped bedroom closets by making or buying armoires. The trim armoire design shown here reflects the basic styling developed during the heyday of the armoire, but at a scale that makes it usable in just about any living situation. At 60" high and only 36" in width, this compact armoire still boasts plenty of interior space. Five shelves on the left side are sized to store folded sweaters and shirts. And you can hang several suit jackets or dresses in the closet section to the right.

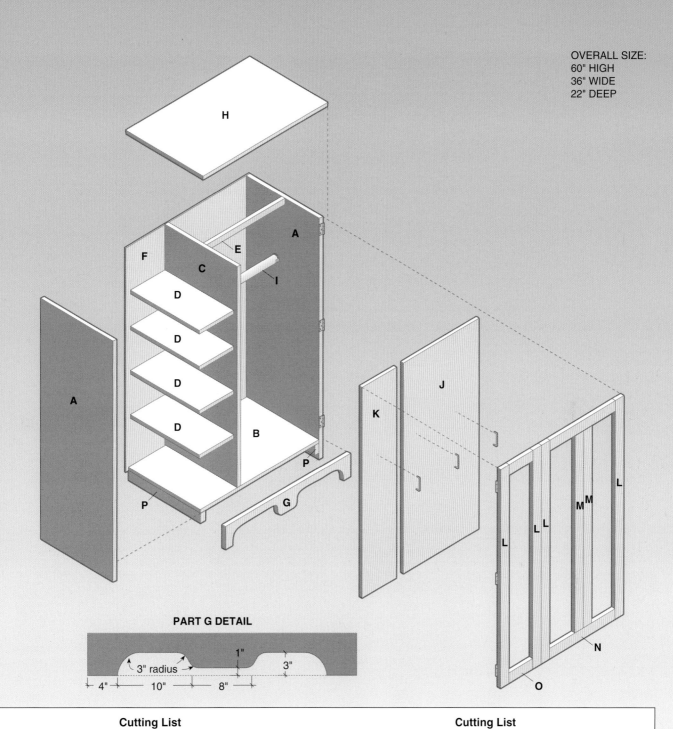

OVERALL SIZE:
60" HIGH
36" WIDE
22" DEEP

PART G DETAIL

3" radius
1"
3"
4"
10"
8"

Cutting List

Key	Part	Dimension	Pcs.	Material
A	Side panel	¾ × 21 × 59¼"	2	Plywood
B	Bottom panel	¾ × 21 × 34½"	1	Plywood
C	Center panel	¾ × 21 × 53¾"	1	Plywood
D	Shelf	¾ × 10⅞ × 20¼"	4	Plywood
E	Stringer	¾ × 1½ × 22⅞"	1	Pine
F	Back	¼ × 36 × 54½"	1	Plywood
G	Front skirt	¾ × 5½ × 36"	1	Pine
H	Top panel	¾ × 22 × 36"	1	Plywood

Cutting List

Key	Part	Dimension	Pcs.	Material
I	Closet rod	1½ × 22⅞"	1	Fir
J	Closet door panel	¾ × 22⁷⁄₁₆ × 52⅛"	1	Plywood
K	Shelf door panel	¾ × 10⁷⁄₁₆ × 52⅛"	1	Plywood
L	Door stile	¾ × 2½ × 53⅝"	4	Pine
M	False stile	¾ × 2½ × 48⅝"	2	Pine
N	Closet door rail	¾ × 2½ × 18¹⁵⁄₁₆"	2	Pine
O	Shelf door rail	¾ × 2½ × 6¹⁵⁄₁₆"	2	Pine
P	Cleat	¾ × 1½ × 21"	2	Pine

Materials: #6 × 1¼" wood screws, 3d and 6d finish nails, closet rod hangers (2), wrought-iron hinges and pulls, magnetic door catches, ¾" birch veneer edge tape (50'), wood glue, finishing materials.
Note: Measurements reflect the actual size of dimension lumber.

Apply veneer edge tape to the exposed plywood edges. Trim off excess tape with a sharp utility knife.

Directions: Armoire

PREPARE THE PLYWOOD PANELS.

Careful preparation of the plywood panels that become the sides, bottom, top and shelves is key to creating an armoire with a clean, professional look. Take the time to make sure all the parts are perfectly square.

Then, apply self-adhesive veneer edge tape to all plywood edges that will be visible. If you plan to paint the armoire, you can simply fill the edges with wood putty and sand them smooth before you apply the paint.

1. Cut the side panels (A), bottom panel (B), center panel (C) and shelves (D) to size, using a

circular saw and a straightedge as a cutting guide. We used birch plywood because it is easy to work with and takes wood stain well. Smooth the surfaces of the panels with medium-grit sandpaper.

2. Apply self-adhesive veneer edge tape to the front edges of the center panel, side panels and shelves. Cut the strips of edge tape to length and position them over the plywood edges. Then, press the strips with a household iron set on a low-to-medium heat setting. The heat from the iron activates the adhesive.

3. Trim the excess tape with a sharp utility knife **(photo A).** Sand the trimmed edges and surfaces of the edge tape with medium-grit sandpaper.

ASSEMBLE THE CARCASE.

The *carcase* for the armoire (or any type of cabinet) is the main cabinet box. For this project, the carcase includes the

Clamp the bottom panel between the sides and fasten it to the cleats with glue and finish nails.

Fasten the shelves between the side panel and center panel with glue and finish nails.

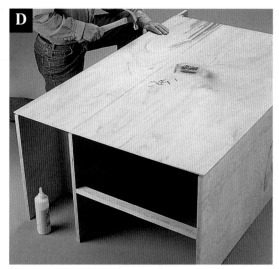

Nail the ¼"-thick back panel to the back edges of the carcase to help keep it square.

Lay out the decorative cutout at the bottom of the front skirt board, using a compass to make the curves. Then, cut with a jig saw.

side, bottom and center panels. Fasten the panels together with wood glue and finish nails. Make sure all of the joints are square and the edges are flush.
1. Lay out the cleat positions on the lower sections of the side panels. Measure up 4¾" from the bottom edges of the side panels, and draw a reference line across the inside face of each side panel.
2. Cut the cleats (P) to length.
3. Position the cleats just below the reference lines. Secure them with glue, and drive 3d finish nails through the cleats and into the side panels.
4. Stand the side panels upright on their bottom edges. Apply a bead of wood glue to the top of each cleat. Place the bottom panel between the side panels on top of the cleats, and clamp it in place. Make sure the taped front edges of the side panels and bottom panel are flush. Drive 6d finish nails through the bottom panel and into each cleat. Then, drive nails through the side panels and into the edges of the bottom panel **(photo B).**

5. Lay the assembly on its back edges. Use a pair of shelves as spacers to set the correct distance between the center panel and the left side panel (as seen from the front of the carcase). Make sure the taped panel edges are at the front of the carcase. Fasten the center panel to the bottom panel with glue, and drive 6d finish nails through the bottom panel and into the edge of the center panel.

INSTALL THE SHELVES.
1. Draw reference lines for the shelves on the inside face of the left side panel and on the left face of the center panel. Measure up from the top of the bottom panel, and draw lines at 13", 23⅜", 33¾" and 44⅛". Use a framing square to make sure the lines are perpendicular to the front and back edges of the panels.
2. Arrange the shelves so the tops are just below the reference lines, flush with the back edges of the carcase (creating a ¾" recess in front of each shelf). Attach the shelves with glue, and drive 6d finish nails

through the side panel and center panel, and into the edges of the shelves **(photo C).** Brace each panel from behind as you drive the nails.

ATTACH THE STRINGER AND BACK PANEL.
1. Cut the stringer (E) to length.
2. Fasten the stringer between the center panel and side panel with glue and 6d finish nails. The stringer should be centered between the fronts and backs of the panels and flush with the tops.
3. Cut the back panel (F) to size from ¼"-thick plywood.
4. Measure the distances between opposite corners of the carcase to make sure it is square (the distances between corners should be equal). Adjust the carcase as needed. Then, position the back panel over the back edges of the carcase so the edges of the back panel are flush with the outside faces and top edges of the side panels. Fasten the back panel by driving 3d finish nails through the back and into the edges of the side, center and bottom panels **(photo D).**

Mount the top panel so it covers the top edge of the back panel and overhangs the front edges of the side panels by ¾".

Attach strips of 1 × 3 to the fronts of the door panels to create a frame.

MAKE AND ATTACH THE FRONT SKIRT.

1. Cut the front skirt (G) to length.

2. Lay out the curves that form the ends of the decorative cutouts on the skirt board (see *Diagram*), by making a mark 7" in from each end. Use a compass to draw a 3"-radius curve to make the outside end of each cutout, holding the point of the compass on the 7" mark, as close as possible to the bottom edge of the board. Then, make a mark 11¾" in from each end of the skirt board. Holding the compass point at the bottom edge, draw a 3"-radius curve to mark the top, inside end of each cutout. Measure 16⅜" in from each end of the skirt board, and mark points that are 1¾" down from the top edge of the board. Set the point of your compass at each of these points and draw 3"-radius curves that mark the bottom, inside ends of the cutouts. Then, at the middle of the bottom edge of the board,

measure up 1" and draw a line parallel to the bottom edge, intersecting the inside ends of the cutout lines. Finally, draw lines parallel to the bottom edge of the board, 3" up, to create the top of each cutout. Make the cutout on the skirt board with a jig saw **(photo E).** Sand the saw cuts smooth with medium-grit sandpaper.

3. Position the skirt board against the front of the armoire carcase to make sure the ends of the skirt are flush with the outside faces of the side panels and the top of the skirt is flush with the top of the bottom panel. Fasten the front skirt to the front edges of the side panels and bottom panel with glue and 6d finish nails.

MAKE AND ATTACH THE TOP PANEL.

1. Stand the armoire upright, and measure the distance between the outside faces of the side panels—it should be 36".
2. Cut the top panel (H) to size.
3. Test-fit the top panel to make

sure the edges are flush with the outside faces of the side panels. The back edge should be flush with the outside face of the back panel, and the front edge of the top should overhang the front of the carcase panels by ¾". Apply veneer edge tape to all four edges of the top panel.

4. Fasten the top panel to the center panel, side panels and stringer with glue and 6d finish nails, making sure it is in the same position as it was when you test-fit the piece **(photo F).**

BUILD THE DOORS.

1. Cut the closet door panel (J) and shelf door panel (K) to size. Sand the edges and surfaces of the door panels to smooth out the saw blade marks and any rough spots. Apply edge tape to the edges of each door panel. Trim off the excess tape, and sand the edges smooth.
2. Cut the door stiles (L), false stiles (M), closet door rails (N) and shelf door rails (O) to

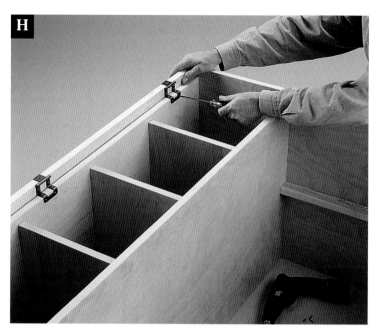

Hang the armoire doors with pairs of hinges attached to the door stiles and the front edges of the side panels.

length. *(Rails* are the horizontal frame pieces; *stiles* are the vertical frame pieces.)

3. Position the rails and stiles on the front faces of the door panels so they overhang all edges of the panels by ¾". Make sure the rails and stiles meet at right angles to make perfectly square frames. Attach the rails and stiles to both door panels with glue, and drive 3d finish nails through the frame pieces and into the panels.

4. Turn the door panels over on your worksurface. To reinforce the joints between the stiles and rails and the door panels, drill ⁵⁄₆₄" pilot holes through the panels and into the stiles and rails. Counterbore the holes ⅛" deep, using a ⅜" counterbore bit. Fasten the pieces together with 1¼" wood screws **(photo G).**

5. Mark points along the outside edge of each outer door stile, 8" down from the top and 8" up from the bottom. Mount door hinges to the edges of the stiles at these points. Then, po-

sition the doors in place, and fasten the hinges to the side panels **(photo H).** Be sure to adjust the hinges to allow for a ⅛"-wide gap between the doors. Also leave a slight gap between the top end of the doors and the top panel and between the bottom of the doors and the front skirt.

APPLY THE FINISH.
It is easiest to finish the parts of the armoire before you attach the rest of the hardware.

1. Set all nails with a nail set. Fill all nail and screw holes with wood putty, and sand the dried putty flush with the surface. Sand all of the wood surfaces with medium (150-grit) sandpaper. Finish-sand the surfaces with fine sandpaper (180-or 220-grit).

2. Wipe the wood clean. Then, brush on a coat of sanding sealer so the wood will accept the wood stain evenly. Be sure to read the manufacturer's directions before applying any finishing products. Apply a

wood stain and let it dry completely. Apply several coats of topcoating product. We used two thin coats of water-based, satin polyurethane. If you prefer, you can leave the wood unstained and simply apply a protective topcoat.

INSTALL THE HARDWARE.
1. Install door pulls on the door panels, 25" up from each bottom rail and centered between the stiles. We used hammered wrought-iron pulls for a rustic appearance.

2. Mount closet rod hangers to the sides of the closet compartment, 11" down from the top panel. Cut the closet rod (I) to length, and set it into the closet rod hangers. Applying finishing materials to the closet rod is optional.

3. To keep the doors closed tight when not in use, install magnetic door catches and catch plates on the upper inside corners of the doors and at the corresponding locations on the bottom of the top panel. For extra holding power, also install catches at the bottoms of the doors.

DYSPEPSIA B

(from page 97, Ladie
Companion)

1 cup warm wate
2 teaspoons sug
2 cups warm m
¼ cup plus 2 t
   margarine,
¼ cup molas
1 tablespoo
7 cups who

Kitchen Projects

There's something for everyone in this chapter. You can add storage space or organize it more efficiently with a pantry cabinet or a pine pantry. Roll out more work space with the utility cart or create a permanent addition with the kitchen island. Simplify outdoor dining with a silverware caddy and display your favorite colorful mugs with the mug rack. Any project you choose will make your kitchen more efficient and user-friendly.

Cookbook Easel

*The acrylic shield on this easel protects your cookbooks
and lets you concentrate on the cooking.*

CONSTRUCTION MATERIALS

Quantity	Lumber
1	¾" × 2' × 2' basswood panel
1	¼" × 1' × 2' acrylic

Cookbooks are hard to read when they're covered with flour, batter or tomato sauce. And they tend to take up precious counterspace when open. Our cookbook easel has a removable acrylic shield to protect your favorite cookbooks from messy spatters. The slanted vertical design keeps cookbooks conveniently open and upright, so you can quickly refer to cooking instructions at a glance. The adjustable shield easily accommodates everything from hefty cooking encyclopedias to small church cookbooks. Rounded corners add a pleasant touch and soften the overall appearance. To keep the easel from sliding around on the countertop, we added self-adhesive rubber feet to the bottom.

OVERALL SIZE:
11½" HIGH
21" WIDE
5½" LONG

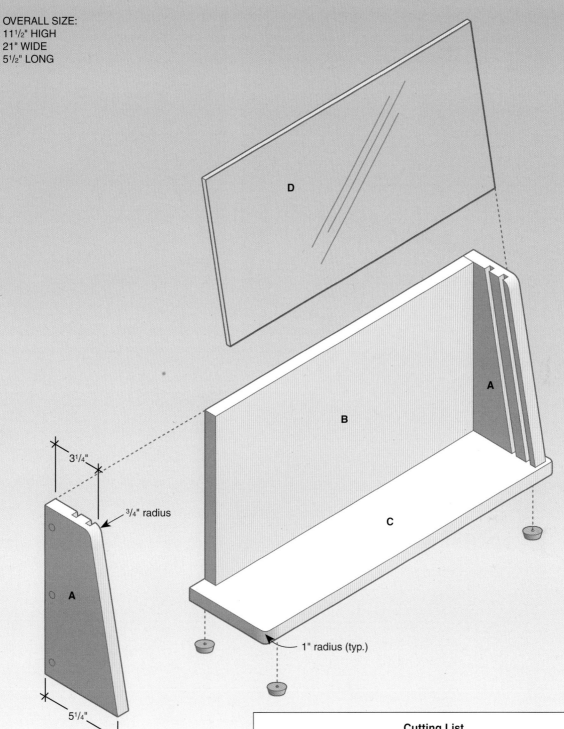

3¼"

¾" radius

5¼"

A

B

A

C

1" radius (typ.)

D

Cutting List				
Key	**Part**	**Dimension**	**Pcs.**	**Material**
A	Side	¾ × 5¼ × 10¼"	2	Basswood
B	Back	¾ × 18¾ × 10¼"	1	Basswood
C	Base	¾ × 5½ × 21"	1	Basswood
D	Shield	¼ × 19¼ × 10¼"	1	Acrylic

Materials: Wood glue, wood screws (#6 × 1½"), self-adhesive rubber feet (4), ⅜"-dia. birch plugs, finishing materials.

Note: Measurements reflect the actual thickness of dimension lumber.

To make the jig, trace an outline of a side on a piece of plywood and cut with a jig saw.

Draw lines to mark the placement and width of the dadoes.

Directions:
Cookbook Easel

MAKE THE SIDES.
1. Cut the sides (A) from ¾" basswood panel, using a circular saw. Each side is 5¼" wide at the bottom and 3¼" wide at the top.
2. Sand the cuts smooth with medium-grit sandpaper.

CUT THE DADOES.
Use a plywood jig to keep the small sides stationary.
1. Place a side on the center of a piece of ¾" scrap plywood and trace its outline.
2. Drill an access hole in the plywood and use a jig saw to make the cut **(photo A).**
3. Draw parallel lines ⅝", ⅞", 1¾" and 2" from the angled edge on the inside face of each side to mark the dado locations **(photo B).**

TIP

A shooting board is nothing more than a piece of hardboard with a straightedge guide attached. The distance between the straightedge and the edge of the hardboard exactly equals the distance between the edge of the router base and the bit.

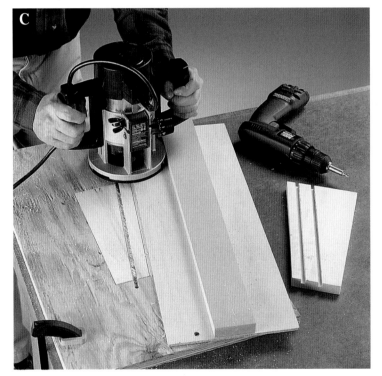

Using a shooting board as a guide, begin and end the dadoes in the plywood jig to avoid any tearouts.

4. Position one side in the plywood jig. Align a shooting board on the plywood so the edge of the shooting board aligns with the marked lines on the side, and temporarily screw it in place.
5. Cut the dadoes using a ¼" bit set ⅝" deep (to allow for a ⅜"-deep dado and the ¼" shooting

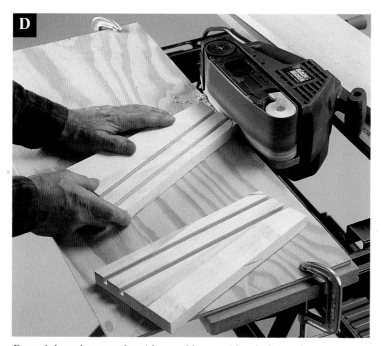
Round the edges on the sides and base with a belt sander.

Find the center of the assembly and mark on the base and back to properly place the screw holes.

board). Begin the router cut in the plywood, proceed smoothly across the side piece and continue into the plywood **(photo C).** Reposition the shooting board to make the second cut.
6. Turn the jig over, insert the other side piece, and repeat the cutting process.

ROUND THE CORNERS.
1. Cut the back (B) and base (C) to size, and sand smooth.
2. Draw ¾"-rad. roundovers on the top front corners of the sides and 1"-rad. roundovers on the two front corners of the base, using a compass.
3. Clamp a belt sander to your worksurface at a 90° angle and round the corners on each part **(photo D).**

ASSEMBLE THE EASEL.
1. Position the back between the sides so the edges are flush, and drill three counterbored pilot holes evenly spaced in the sides.

2. Apply glue to the edges and drive 1½" wood screws through pilot holes into the back. Mark centerpoints on the base and back to help you align the parts correctly **(photo E).**
3. Drill pilot holes in the base and counterbore from the underside. Position the base and back so the centerpoints are aligned and join the base to the assembly with glue and wood screws. Make sure the screws don't interfere with the dadoes.
4. Cut the acrylic shield (D) to size with a circular saw, sand the short edges, and insert. Leave the protective covering on the acrylic while sawing.

APPLY FINISHING TOUCHES.
1. Pound glued ⅜" birch plugs into the counterbored holes **(photo F).**
2. Sand the plugs flush with a power sander, and finish-sand the easel.

Use a wood mallet to drive in glued ⅜" birch plugs without damaging the surface of the wood.

3. Apply the finish of your choice.
4. Attach self-adhesive feet to the base after the finish dries.

Spice Holder

A light, open design keeps all your spices in plain sight and within easy reach.

PROJECT
POWER TOOLS

CONSTRUCTION MATERIALS

Quantity	Lumber
1	1 × 6" × 8' pine
1	1 × 10" × 8' pine

So often, spices for your favorite dishes are hidden away in the back corners of kitchen cabinets—used, and then stuffed behind other cooking supplies without a moment's thought. Until, that is, the next time you are fumbling in a dark cabinet for the oregano while a sauce burns on the stove. Experienced chefs always have a spice holder within reach. Ours has four shelves, with room for a variety of ingredients. You can take an instant inventory of your supplies and have favorite herbs handy for sudden culinary inspirations.

The series of arcs cut into the spice holder form gentle waves that gives the pine construction a soft, flowing appeal, and a small scallop in the back echoes this pattern. The front of the shelves are rounded, so you can reach for spices without worrying about sharp edges. Though it's designed to rest on a countertop, this spice holder can also be fitted with another shelf and mounted on the wall.

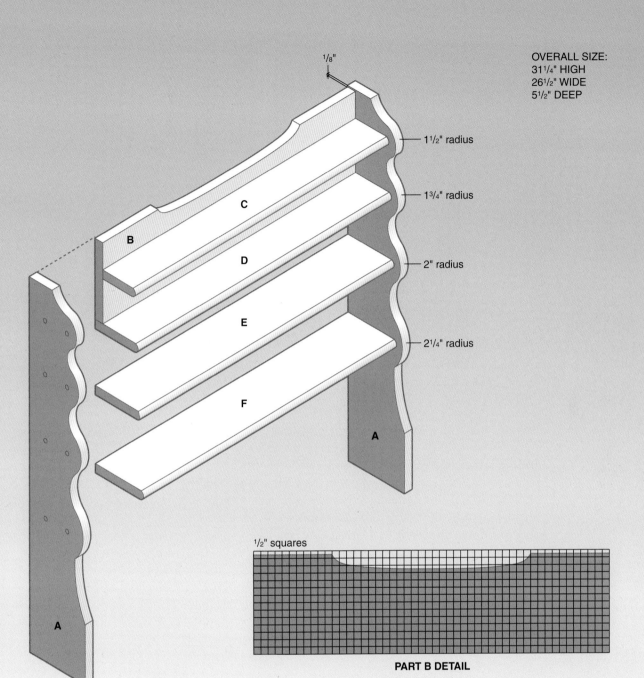

1/8"

OVERALL SIZE:
31¼" HIGH
26½" WIDE
5½" DEEP

1½" radius

1¾" radius

2" radius

2¼" radius

A

B

C

D

E

F

A

½" squares

PART B DETAIL

Cutting List				
Key	**Part**	**Dimension**	**Pcs.**	**Material**
A	Side	¾ × 5½ × 31¼"	2	Pine
B	Back	¾ × 6¾ × 25"	1	Pine
C	Shelf	¾ × 3¼ × 25"	1	Pine
D	Shelf	¾ × 4¼ × 25"	1	Pine
E	Shelf	¾ × 4½ × 25"	1	Pine
F	Shelf	¾ × 4¾ × 25"	1	Pine

Materials: Wood glue, #8 screws (1⅝"), ⅜" birch plugs, finishing materials.

Note: Measurements reflect the actual thickness of dimension lumber.

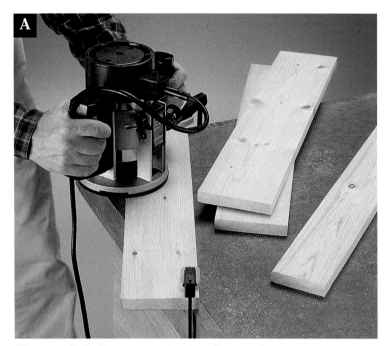

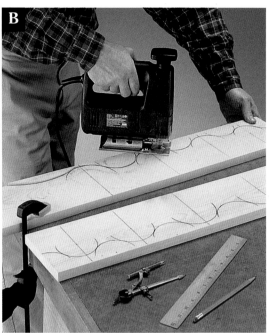

Clamp each shelf to your worksurface for smooth, even router cuts. Flip the shelves to complete each roundover.

Make the side curves with a jig saw. Use clamps to keep parts steady while cutting.

Directions: Spice Holder

MAKE THE SHELVES.

The shelves all differ in depth and are cut from dimension lumber.

1. Measure and rip shelves C, D, and E from 1 × 10 pine, and shelf F from 1 × 6 pine, using

Sand the curves with a drum sanding attachment and a drill.

your circular saw.
2. Clamp each shelf to your worksurface, and round the front using a router with a ⅜" roundover bit and bearing guide **(photo A)**. Sand all edges smooth.

MAKE THE SIDES.

A series of arcs and reference lines indicate cutting lines and shelf positions.
1. Cut the sides (A) to size from 1 × 6 pine, and sand all cuts smooth.
2. Draw reference lines across the sides for the curves and shelves, starting from the bottom of each side, at points 12",

18½", 24", and 28½" along a long edge. The arcs you draw from the template (see *Part A Detail*) will be centered on these lines.
3. Transfer the template arcs to each side, and blend all of the arcs together with graceful curves.
4. Clamp each side to your worksurface, and use a jig saw to cut along the arcs **(photo B).**

MAKE THE BACK ASSEMBLY.

1. Cut the back (B) to size from 1 × 10 stock.
2. Draw a curve 1" deep and 14" long, centered on one long

TIPS

If you do not own a router, you can complete the roundovers on the front edges of each shelf by planing down the edges with a block plane. Planing goes more smoothly if you plane so the wood grain runs "uphill" ahead of the plane. Don't try to remove too much wood at one time; smooth, easy strokes will achieve the best results. Sand to smooth the plane cuts.

Attach the top shelf to the back assembly from behind with glue and countersunk screws.

Be sure to counterbore all the pilot holes on the sides before driving screws.

edge of the back, and cut with a jig saw (see *Part B Detail*).

3. Attach a 1"-dia. drum sander to your drill, and sand the curves of each piece smooth **(photo C).**

4. Clamp the bottom edge of the back against shelf D, keeping the back flush with the square edge of the shelf. Attach with glue and countersunk 1⅝" screws driven through the bottom of the shelf and into the edge of the back.

5. Align the top shelf (C) on the back so the top edge is 2¼" down from the top edge of the back. Glue and clamp in place, and secure with countersunk screws driven through the back and into the shelf **(photo D).**

ATTACH THE REMAINING PARTS.

1. Place the back assembly and remaining shelves in position between the sides. Center the shelves on the reference lines

and keep the back edges flush.

2. Use pipe clamps to hold the spice rack together, and counterbore ⅜" pilot holes through the sides and into the ends of each shelf. Keep the counterbores lined up horizontally for an even look.

3. Remove the clamps, apply glue, and then reclamp, continually checking to make sure the assembly is square. Secure the shelves with 1⅝" screws driven through the counterbored pilot holes **(photo E).**

APPLY FINISHING TOUCHES.

1. Insert glued birch button plugs into each counterbored hole and let dry.

2. Finish-sand the entire project, and apply a light oil or stain and a polyurethane topcoat.

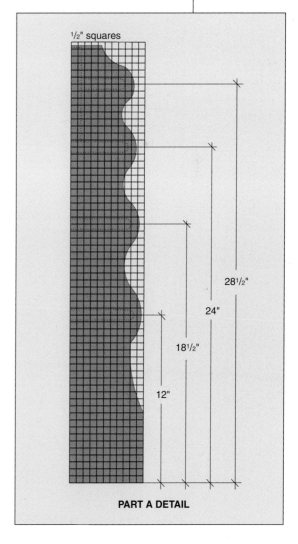

½" squares

28½"

24"

18½"

12"

PART A DETAIL

Mug Rack

Your everyday coffee mugs become decorative kitchen items when displayed on this original mug rack.

CONSTRUCTION MATERIALS

Quantity	Lumber
1	1 × 4" × 10' pine
1	1 × 8" × 8' beaded siding board

A mug rack gives you a great way to combine storage and decoration. Just put your mugs in this simple, convenient frame to display them on your kitchen countertop or hang them on a wall. The mugs are always there when you need them, and instead of taking up valuable shelf space, they become decorative kitchen items for all to see. Colorful mug designs look great against the beaded siding board backing on the rack. Paint the project to match your kitchen, or cover it with a clear finish to preserve the natural look of the wood. You can hang your mugs on Shaker pegs, which are easy to install. Fit the bottom and back of the mug rack with rubber bumpers for increased stability. With a minimum investment of work and expense, you can create this mug rack as a decorative home accent.

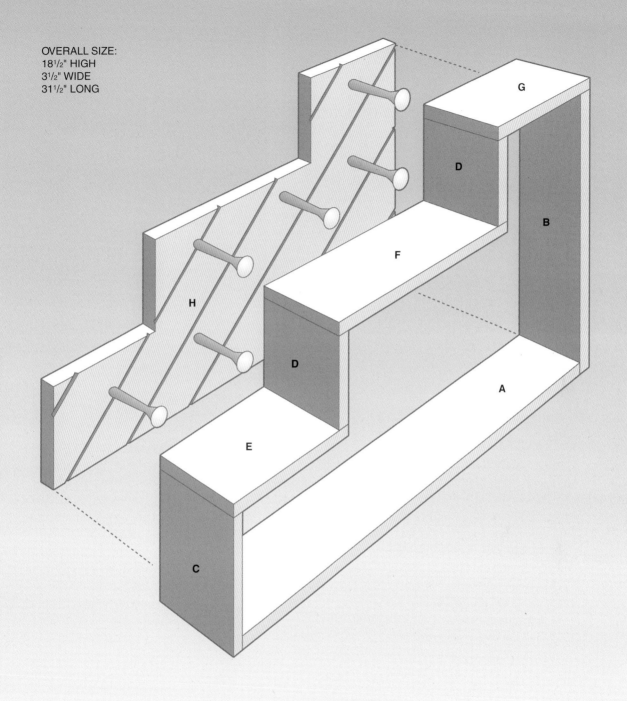

OVERALL SIZE:
18½" HIGH
3½" WIDE
31½" LONG

		Cutting List		
Key	**Part**	**Dimension**	**Pcs.**	**Material**
A	Frame bottom	¾ × 3½ × 29½"	1	Pine
B	Tall end	¾ × 3½ × 17¾"	1	Pine
C	Short end	¾ × 3½ × 9¾"	1	Pine
D	Divider	¾ × 3½ × 3¼"	2	Pine

		Cutting List		
Key	**Part**	**Dimension**	**Pcs.**	**Material**
E	Lower shelf	¾ × 3½ × 7½"	1	Pine
F	Middle shelf	1½ × 3½ × 15"	1	Pine
G	Top shelf	¾ × 3½ × 10½"	1	Pine
H	Backing	18½ × 31½"*	1	Siding

Materials: Wood glue, 4d finish nails, Shaker pegs (8), rubber feet (4), finishing materials.

Note: Measurements reflect the actual thickness of dimension lumber.

*Cut to fit

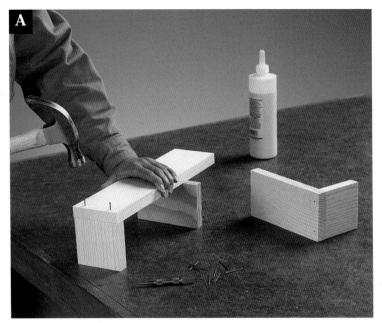

Attach the dividers to the tops of the lower and middle shelves using glue and finish nails.

Fasten the top shelf to the middle shelf divider.

Directions:
Mug Rack

ASSEMBLE THE FRAME.

1. Cut the frame bottom (A), tall end (B), short end (C), lower shelf (E), middle shelf (F), top shelf (G) and dividers (D) to size from 1 × 4 pine.

2. Sand out any rough edges with medium (100- or 120-grit) sandpaper, then finish-sand with fine (150- or 180-grit) sandpaper.

3. Fasten the ends to the bottom with glue and 4d finish nails driven through the ends into the frame bottom edges. Make sure the edges are flush.

4. Attach the dividers to the tops of the lower and middle shelves with glue and finish nails **(photo A).** Make sure the end of each shelf is flush with the end of each divider. Use support blocks to help you keep the pieces stationary on the worksurface.

5. Glue and nail the middle shelf to the top of the lower shelf divider. Make sure the divider edges and middle shelf edges are flush. Fasten the top shelf to the middle shelf divider, once again keeping the edges flush **(photo B).**

6. Glue and finish nail the shelves flush with the tall and short ends to complete the mug rack frame.

> **TIP**
>
> *Siding is available in many different patterns, such as tongue-and-groove, shiplap or channel groove. Each pattern has a different joint pattern and appearance. These siding styles all cut easily with a circular saw or jig saw, but be careful of kickback, which can cause the material to jump off the table with dangerous force.*

BUILD AND ATTACH
THE BACKING.

The backing (H) fits into the frame and holds the Shaker pegs. Make the backing from pieces of beaded siding.

1. Cut and join backing pieces as necessary to create an 18½ × 31½" panel.

2. Place the mug rack frame on the backing pieces so their grooves run diagonally at about a 60° angle. The backing should completely fill the space inside the frame.

3. Remove the frame, then glue the backing pieces together and let them dry.

4. Place the frame on the backing pieces and trace the cutting lines onto the back panel, following the inside of the frames **(photo C).** Remove the frame and use a straight-edge or square to retrace or straighten the lines.

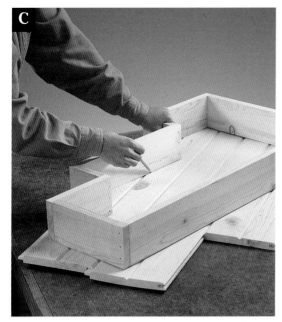

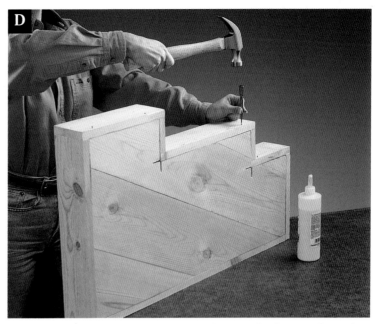

Trace the shape of the frame onto beaded siding and cut it to fit.

Fasten the backing into the frame with finish nails, then set the nails.

5. Cut the backing to shape with a straightedge guide and a jig saw. Test-fit the backing in the mug rack frame. If necessary, trim it to fit the frame.
6. Fasten the backing with glue and 4d finish nails driven through the frame and into the edges of the backing panel **(photo D)**.
7. Set the nails and fill all the nail holes.

ATTACH THE MUG PEGS.
1. Measure and mark a vertical line 4½" from the tall end. Then draw three more vertical lines spaced 7¼" apart, marking the peg centerpoints along these lines at 5½", 11" and 16½" from the bottom shelf.
2. Drill ½ × ⅝"-deep holes for the mug pegs at these centerpoints **(photo E)**.
3. Glue and insert pegs into the holes. Remove any excess glue.

APPLY THE FINISHING TOUCHES.
1. Sand all the surfaces smooth.
2. Apply paint or finish. We used a linseed oil finish on our mug rack. Use a finish that will

withstand kitchen moisture levels.
3. Hang the mug rack on the wall, or install rubber bumpers on the bottom for stable countertop placement after the finish has dried.

Measure and mark peg locations on the backing, then drill peg holes with a spade bit. Do not drill all the way through the backing.

PROJECT
POWER TOOLS

Stepstool

*Make every step a step in the right direction
with our oak stepstool.*

CONSTRUCTION MATERIALS

Quantity	Lumber
1	1 × 10" × 3' oak
1	¾" × 2 × 4' oak plywood

The next time you need to retrieve an out-of-reach item in your kitchen, don't stand on a dining-room chair. Instead, make use of our handy stepstool—it's wide, stable, and reinforced with stretchers underneath each step. The stepstool brings you to the right height for dusting hard-to-reach areas, like valances and windowtops, and for reaching what you need from that topmost shelf. You'll find the stepstool is also a great place for small children to sit safely out of your way and still feel part of the kitchen action. The steps are cut from solid oak to guarantee a flat, stable surface. We cut shallow arcs into the bottom of each side panel to create four "feet," and repeated the curves on the front stretchers. A roundover router bit softens the front edge of each step.

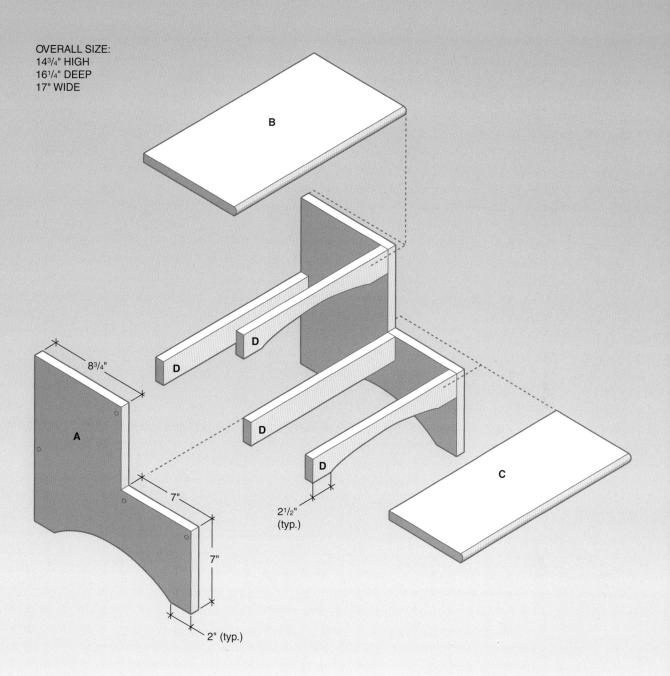

OVERALL SIZE:
14¾" HIGH
16¼" DEEP
17" WIDE

B

D

D

8¾"

A

D

7"

7"

D

2½"
(typ.)

C

2" (typ.)

Cutting List				
Key	**Part**	**Dimension**	**Pcs.**	**Material**
A	Side	¾ × 15¾ × 14"	2	Plywood
B	Top step	¾ × 9¼ × 17"	1	Oak
C	Bottom step	¾ × 7½ × 17"	1	Oak
D	Stretcher	¾ × 2 × 14"	4	Plywood

Materials: Wood glue, wood screws (#8 × 1⅝"), ⅜"-dia. oak wood plugs, oak-veneer edge tape (5'), finishing materials.

Note: Measurements reflect the actual thickness of dimension lumber.

Use a makeshift bar compass to achieve smooth, uniform arcs on the front stretchers.

Shorten the compass to draw the arcs on each side piece.

Directions: Stepstool

CUT THE SIDES
AND STRETCHERS.

1. Cut the side pieces (A) and stretchers (D) to size from oak plywood.

2. Cut a 7 × 7" notch out of one corner on each side piece using a jig saw.

3. Sand the cut smooth.

4. Clamp a stretcher and a ¾"-thick piece of scrap wood at least 2 ft. long to your worksurface. Mark the center of the stretcher, and extend the line down the scrap. Mark 2½" in from each end along the bottom edge of the stretcher to indicate the ends of the arc.

5. Cut a narrow strip of wood 21½" long for the arm of the bar compass. Drill a small hole ½" in from both ends, one for the pencil tip, one for the brad.

With the pencil on one of the reference marks, nail the brad to the centerline. Then draw arcs on two of the stretchers **(photo A).**

6. Cut the compass to 10½", and drill a new pencil hole ½" from the end. Clamp the side pieces to your worksurface and make reference marks 2" in from each corner on the bottom edge of the sides. Position the compass as for the stretchers, nail in place, and draw arcs on each side piece **(photo B).**

7. Cut all arcs with a jig saw. Clamp the stretchers together and gang-sand the cuts smooth with a drum sander attached to your drill **(photo C).** Do the same for the arcs on the side pieces.

8. Cut iron-on veneer tape to length, and apply it to the ex-

posed front and back edges of the side pieces with an iron **(photo D).** To ensure a strong adhesive bond, press a clean block of scrap wood against the strip to flatten the tape as you go. Let the tape cool, and trim the edges with a utility knife.

ASSEMBLE THE FRAME.

1. Position the arched stretchers between the side pieces so the edges and corners are flush (see *Diagram*), and drill counterbored pilot holes. Attach the side pieces to the stretchers with glue and screws.

2. Position the non-arched stretchers at the same height as the lower arched stretcher. Drill counterbored pilot holes for the remaining stretchers, and attach with wood glue and screws.

Clamp the stretchers together and sand the arcs smooth, using a drum sander attached to a drill.

Apply veneer tape to the front and back edges of the side pieces to give them a solid wood appearance.

CUT AND ATTACH THE STEPS.

1. Cut the top step (B) and bottom step (C) to length from 1 × 10 oak. Rip the bottom step to width.

2. Clamp each step to your worksurface, and round the front edges with a router and a ⅜" roundover bit. Sand the edges smooth.

3. Position the top step on the assembly so the rear edges are flush and the front overhangs the stretcher by ½". Center the top step from side to side.

4. Drill counterbored pilot holes to connect the step to the side pieces and the arched stretcher. Apply glue, and drive screws through the holes.

5. Repeat this process for the bottom step.

APPLY FINISHING TOUCHES.

1. Fill all counterbored holes with glued oak plugs.

2. Finish-sand the project. We used two stains for a two-tone look, applying a light cherry stain for the steps and a dark mahogany stain for the side pieces and stretchers. When staining, mask off the edges of the steps where they contact the side pieces and stretchers **(photo E).** If you wish, you can stencil a decorative design on the sides of the stool. Complete the finish with several coats of water-based polyurethane.

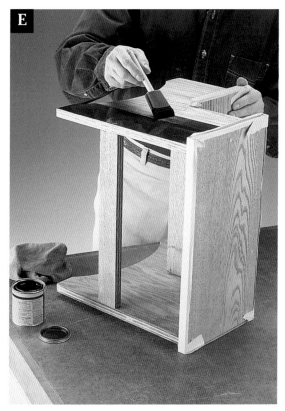

Use masking tape to mask off borders where different stains meet.

Silverware Caddy

*This decorative display rack brings convenience
to dinnertime chores.*

CONSTRUCTION MATERIALS

Quantity	Lumber
1	½ × 8" × 4' oak

Silverware caddies used to be common accessories when large family gatherings were regular occurrences. A caddy eliminated lugging handfuls of silverware to and from the table, made setting the table a speedy chore and kept utensils ready at attention for the next meal. Our silverware caddy is crafted from traditional, sturdy oak and features a decorative cloverleaf carrying grip. The rounded handle and divider interlock,

creating four sections to keep knives, spoons and dinner and salad forks separate and upright for easy access. This is an easy afternoon project that will give long-lasting "service" to any dinner table. If you will be painting the caddy, choose ½" birch plywood rather than oak.

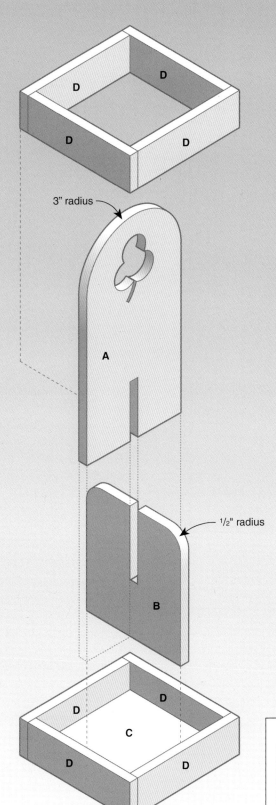

OVERALL SIZE:
12½" HIGH
7" WIDE
7" LONG

3" radius

A

½" radius

B

D D D D

D D D D

C

½" squares

PART A DETAIL

Cutting List

Key	Part	Dimension	Pcs.	Material
A	Handle	½ × 6 × 12"	1	Oak
B	Divider	½ × 6 × 6"	1	Oak
C	Base	½ × 6 × 6"	1	Oak
D	Side	½ × 2 × 6½"	8	Oak

Materials: Wood glue, 16-ga. 1" finish nails, finishing materials.

Note: Measurements reflect the actual thickness of dimension lumber.

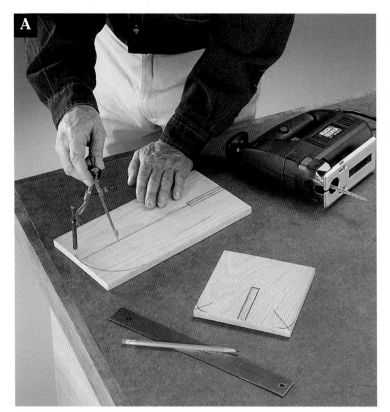

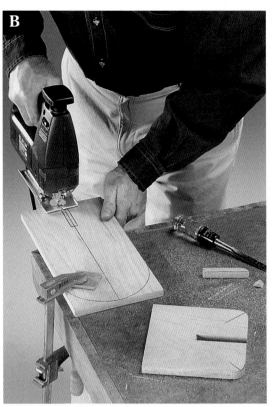

Mark curves and notch locations on reference lines using a compass.

Clamp pieces to your worksurface to ensure steady cuts.

Directions: Silverware Caddy

MAKE THE HANDLE AND DIVIDER.

Corners on the handle and divider are curved, and the pieces are notched to fit together.

1. Cut the handle (A) and divider (B) to size.

2. Mark a centerline down the length of each piece, and draw a $\frac{1}{2} \times 3$" notch at one end centered along each line. At the other end of the handle, place a compass point on the centerline, 3" from the edge, and draw a 3"-rad. curve. At the notched end of the divider, bisect each corner with a 45° line. Place a compass point on the 45° line $1\frac{1}{16}$" from the corner, and draw $\frac{1}{2}$"-rad. curves on each corner **(photo A).**

3. Clamp each piece to your worksurface, and cut the curves and notches with a jig saw **(photo B).**

4. Slide the notched ends together to test-fit, then use a chisel to clean out the notches and make adjustments.

CUT THE HANDHOLD.

1. Transfer the clover template to paper, and trace the pattern onto the handle surface, using the centerline for correct alignment (see *Diagram*).

2. Cut out each leaf of the clover with a $1\frac{1}{2}$"-dia. hole saw **(photo C).** Keep a scrap piece of wood underneath to prevent the hole saw tearing through the other side of the handle.

3. Cut out the clover stem with a jig saw and chisel.

4. Sand all cuts to remove splinters, and sand the inside of

the clover leaf with a 1"-dia. or smaller drum sander attached to your drill **(photo D).**

ASSEMBLE THE BASE AND SIDES.

1. Cut the sides (D) and base (C) to size, and sand smooth.

2. Butt each side end against the face of another side to make the side frames square (see *Diagram*). Drill pilot holes at the side joints to ease assembly. Glue and nail four sides together with finish nails and repeat to make two square frames. Check for square when nailing, then recess all nail heads with a nail set.

3. Place the base inside one of the frames, drill pilot holes and attach the base with glue and nails.

4. Set the handle and divider inside to test-fit, then apply

Use a hole saw to cut quickly and cleanly. Place a backer board underneath to prevent tearouts on the other side of handle.

Use a drum sander or sandpaper wrapped around a dowel to smooth the inside of the cutout.

glue to the joint. Attach the handle and divider to the base assembly with glue and finish nails.

5. Slide the remaining frame over the handle and divider. Keep a 1¼" gap between frames, and attach the frame to the handle and divider with glue and finish nails **(photo E).**

APPLY FINISHING TOUCHES.

1. Fill all nail holes with wood putty.

2. Sand smooth, and apply the finish of your choice. We used a light cherry stain. If you choose paint, use a nontoxic interior-rated latex enamel.

Maintain a 1¼" gap between frames when assembling.

Plate Rack

This compact plate rack is a handsome display case for your favorite dinnerware.

CONSTRUCTION MATERIALS

Quantity	Lumber
1	1 × 2" × 4' oak
1	1 × 6" × 2' oak
1	1 × 10" × 3' oak
3	¾ × ¾" × 2' oak stop molding
7	⅜"-dia. × 3' oak dowels

The holding capacity and clean vertical lines of this plate rack could easily make it a beloved fixture in your kitchen. An open design lets air circulate to dry mugs, bowls and plates efficiently. The rack is handsome enough to double as a display rack to showcase your dinnerware. Even though it has a small 9¼ × 21½" footprint, the rack lets you dry or store up to 20 full-size dinner plates plus cups or glasses. The tall dowels in the back of the rack are removable so you can rearrange them to accommodate large or unusually shaped dishes.

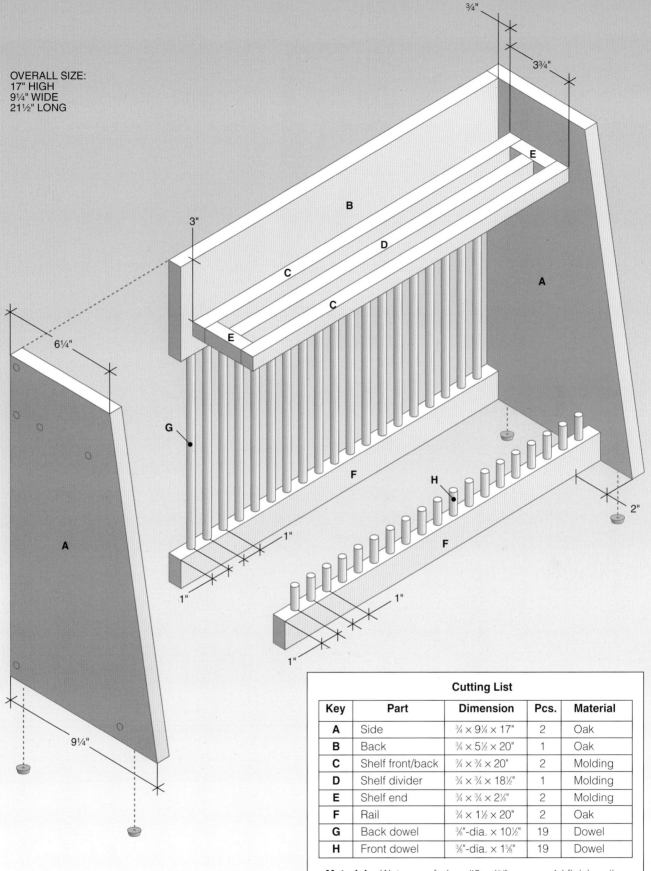

OVERALL SIZE:
17" HIGH
9¼" WIDE
21½" LONG

¾"

3¾"

E

B

D

C

C

3"

E

A

6¼"

G

F

H

2"

A

1"

1"

F

1"

9¼"

1"

Cutting List

Key	Part	Dimension	Pcs.	Material
A	Side	¾ × 9¼ × 17"	2	Oak
B	Back	¾ × 5½ × 20"	1	Oak
C	Shelf front/back	¾ × ¾ × 20"	2	Molding
D	Shelf divider	¾ × ¾ × 18½"	1	Molding
E	Shelf end	¾ × ¾ × 2¼"	2	Molding
F	Rail	¾ × 1½ × 20"	2	Oak
G	Back dowel	⅜"-dia. × 10½"	19	Dowel
H	Front dowel	⅜"-dia. × 1⅝"	19	Dowel

Materials: Waterproof glue, #8 × 1⅝" screws, 4d finish nails, ⅜"-dia. flat oak plugs, rubber feet (4), finishing materials.

Note: Measurements reflect the actual thickness of dimension lumber.

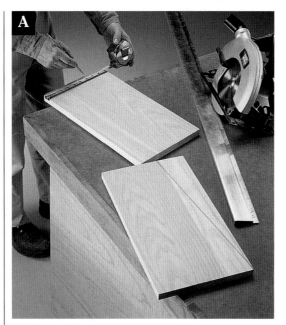

Lay out the sides so they are 9¼" long at the bottom and 6¼" wide at the top.

Clamp the rails and back together and mark the dowel holes.

Directions:
Plate Rack

CUT THE SIDES.
1. Lay out and mark the sides (A) so they are 9¼" long at the bottom and 6¼" wide at the top.
2. Connect these marks, and cut along the diagonal line with a circular saw **(photo A).**

CUT AND DRILL BACK AND RAILS.
1. Cut the back (B) and rails (F) to length, and clamp them together.
2. Measure and mark the dowel holes (see *Diagram*) on the edge of each part **(photo B).** Mark the bit with tape, and drill the ¼"-deep dowel holes in

the two rails. Move the tape to ½" and drill the deeper dowel holes in the back.

ASSEMBLE SIDES, BACK AND RAILS.
1. Drill ⅜"-dia. counterbored pilot holes through the sides where the back and back rail will be attached.
2. Apply waterproof glue, and attach the pieces with wood screws.

BUILD THE SHELF.
1. Cut the shelf front and back pieces (C), divider (D) and ends (E) to length.
2. Position the shelf front, back and ends together, and drill pilot holes for 4d finish nails.

Glue and nail divider in place.

Apply glue, and nail together.
3. Glue and nail the divider in place **(photo C).**

TIP

To make installing the longer 10½" back dowels easier, drill the dowel holes in the back a full ½" deep. When assembling, slide the dowels into the ½" holes in the back piece and let them drop down into the ¼" holes in the back rail. This lets you easily remove specific dowels to accommodate larger dishes or bowls. Dowel sizes tend to vary so test your dowel sizes by drilling a hole in scrap wood first, using a brad-point bit slightly larger than the ⅜" dowel.

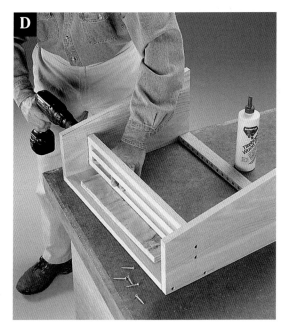

Use a ¾" spacer to position shelf while you drill counterbored pilot holes.

Insert dowels into the holes under the back first, then drop them down into the holes in the rail.

4. Carefully drill counterbored pilot holes through the sides where the shelf attaches. To properly position the shelf, lay the entire unit on its back. Position the shelf 3" down from the top of the rack, using a ¾"- thick piece of scrap material as a spacer between the shelf and the back **(photo D).** Drill the pilot holes into the long shelf pieces and not through the dividers. Apply glue, and secure the shelf with wood screws.

CUT AND INSERT DOWELS.

1. Cut the back dowels (G) to length. Position these longer dowels by inserting them into the holes in the back, then dropping them down into the back rail **(photo E).**

2. Cut the front dowels (H) to length. Sand the edges of one end of each dowel. Using waterproof glue, secure the unsanded ends of the front dowels into the front rail holes.

ATTACH THE FRONT RAIL.

1. Position the front rail 2" back from the front edge of the rack, and drill counterbored pilot holes through the sides.

2. Apply waterproof glue, and screw the front rail in place **(photo F).**

APPLY FINISHING TOUCHES.

1. Fill all counterbored screw holes with oak plugs. Sand the entire rack and all dowels with 150-grit sandpaper.

2. Apply a water-based polyurethane finish.

3. Attach rubber feet to the bottom of the rack.

Clamp the front rail, predrill the sides, counterbore, glue and screw in place.

TIP

If you plan on consistently using dishes of unusual size, you may choose to change the location of the front rail. The location specified will work well for plates as small as 7" and as large as 11".

Bread Box

*This easy-to-build bread box creates a safe,
crush-proof haven for a loaf of bread or other
tasty bakery goods.*

The old guessing game "20 Questions" would often start with the query, "Is it bigger than a bread box?" Though bread boxes aren't as common as they once were, they're still useful items that add a decorative touch to any kitchen. Our classic design emphasizes simplicity, featuring a compact footprint so it easily fits between other appliances or on a countertop, kitchen table or pantry shelf. The sturdy, oak construction has rounded edges and an angled lid that shows off the rich oak grain and warm color. The solid oak lid is mounted with a 12"-wide piano hinge. We stained our bread box and then applied a stenciled label to add a personal touch. Choose a stain or style that matches your kitchen decor, or try adding decorative painting effects like borders, antique letters or rosemaling to add the finishing touch to your own bread box.

CONSTRUCTION MATERIALS

Quantity	Lumber
2	½ × 7¼ × 36" oak
1	¾ × 7¼ × 24" oak

We found ½ × 7¼"-wide oak available in 24", 36" and 48" lengths.

OVERALL SIZE:
8" HIGH
13⅝" WIDE
6" DEEP

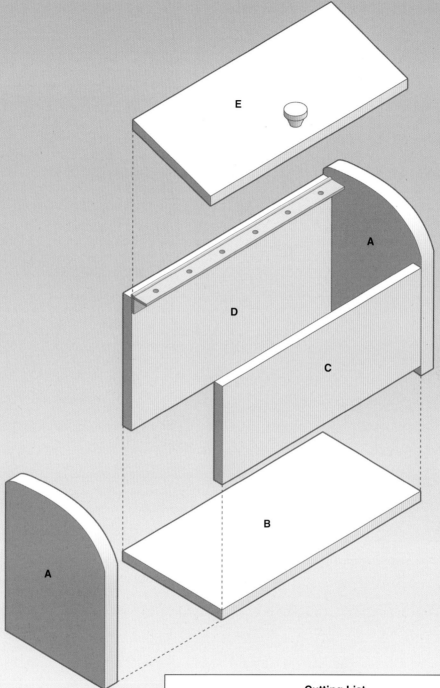

Cutting List

Key	Part	Dimension	Pcs.	Material
A	Side	¾ × 6 × 8"	2	Oak
B	Bottom	½ × 6 × 12⅛"	1	Oak
C	Front	½ × 5 × 12⅛"	1	Oak
D	Back	½ × 6¾ × 12⅛"	1	Oak
E	Lid	½ × 5⅝ × 12"	1	Oak

Materials: Wood glue, 12" piano hinge, porcelain knob (1"-dia. × ¾" length), 4d finish nails, finishing materials.

Note: Measurements reflect the actual thickness of dimension lumber.

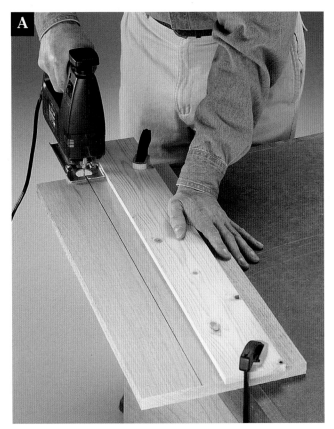

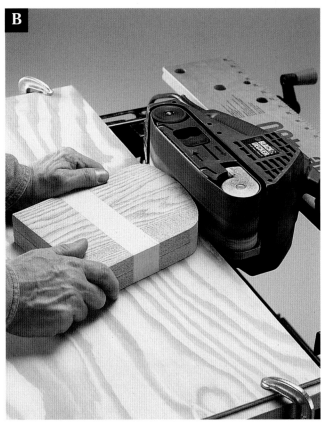

Rip the sides from one piece of wood then cut them to length.

Tape sides together and sand the corners to create identical profiles.

Directions: Bread Box

RIP-CUT THE SIDES.
The sides are narrower than common lumber width, so it is necessary to rip the lumber lengthwise.
1. Rip the sides (A) to width from ¾" oak lumber. Rip both sides at the same time, using a straightedge to guide your jig saw or circular saw **(photo A).**
2. Cut the sides to length.

PROFILE THE SIDES.
The sides are curved to soften the overall profile of the bread box.
1. Transfer the curve outline (see *Part A Detail*) onto each

side, and cut the rough profile with a jig saw.
2. Tape the sides together, and use a belt sander clamped to your worksurface to sand matching profiles on each side **(photo B).** Take care when sanding not to remove too much material from the sides.

> **TIP**
>
> *When ripping lumber to obtain the correct width, use a straightedge to guide your saw. Make sure you use a new, sharp blade to minimize rip marks and rough edges. Then belt-sand or block-plane the pieces smooth.*

CUT THE
REMAINING PIECES.
1. Cut the bottom (B), front (C), back (D) and lid (E) to length from ½" stock.
2. Cut each piece to its appropriate width, then sand all the pieces smooth. The bottom, front and back pieces are ⅛" longer than the lid to allow it to swing freely up and down on the piano hinge.

ASSEMBLE THE
BREAD BOX.
1. Drill ¹⁄₁₆"-dia. pilot holes through the bottom. Glue the front and back pieces to the bottom, clamp them in place, and nail with 4d finish nails.
2. Position the sides against the

Lay the assembly on its back, position the lid and install the piano hinge.

Use a stencil to transfer a pattern onto the bread box lid.

assembly, and drill pilot holes through the sides. Apply glue, clamp and nail.

ATTACH THE HINGE.
1. Center the hinge on the lid, drill pilot holes, and fasten with hinge screws. Be careful not to drill too far into the ½" wood.
2. Lay the box on its back with the lid in the open position. Open the hinge and fasten the hinge to the back **(photo C).**

APPLY FINISHING TOUCHES.
1. Sand all surfaces smooth.
2. Finish the bread box. We used a classic walnut stain and a non-toxic, water-based polyurethane topcoat. Finish the inside as well as the outside of the box and lid to prevent warping from moisture and to make cleaning the entire box easier. If you decide to add your own graphic element to the lid or to other areas of the box, do so before applying a topcoat. You can personalize your bread box by stenciling words, distressing surfaces to create special antiquing effects, transferring unique designs, or rosemaling. We created a stencil out of a sheet of acetate and painted a simple graphic on the lid **(photo D).**
3. Locate and drill a pilot hole and attach a knob to the lid after the finish cures.

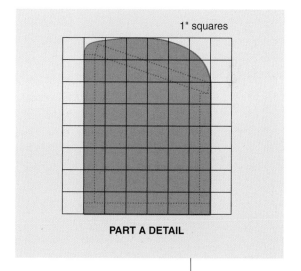

1" squares

PART A DETAIL

Vegetable Bin

Whether your vegetables come from the garden or the grocer, our oak bin keeps them organized and out of the way.

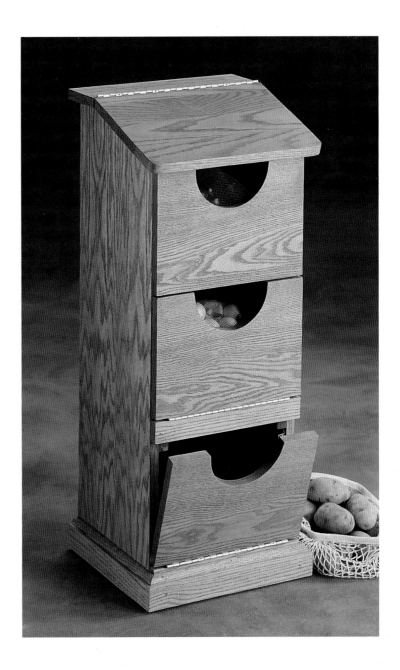

N ot all foods require immediate refrigeration. Onions, potatoes, garlic, shallots and avocados are just some of the foods that don't need to take up precious refrigerator space. But when countertop real estate is at a premium, veggies clutter up needed table space or remain in paper bags. Our vegetable bin provides an attractive, spacious alternative for storing fresh vegetables and fruits. Three separate sections, with hinged bin faces on the sides and top, keep vegetables apart and in place and make access easy. The sturdy oak construction also provides protection for more fragile items, so your prize tomatoes can stay safely in the shade. The bin's compact vertical design takes up just over a square foot, and the rich oak finish trim makes it a handsome addition to any kitchen.

CONSTRUCTION MATERIALS

Quantity	Lumber
1	¾" × 4 × 4' oak plywood
1	¾ × 1½" × 4' oak
1	¾ × 11¼" × 6' oak
1	½ × ½" × 4' quarter-round molding

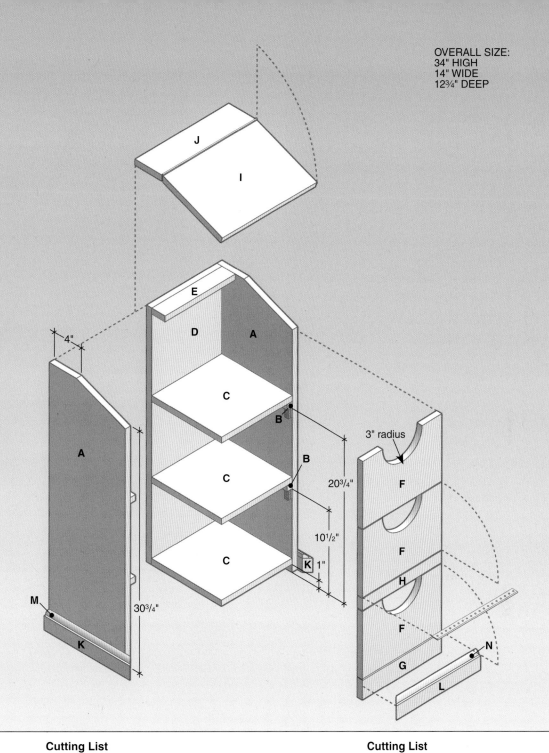

OVERALL SIZE:
34" HIGH
14" WIDE
12¾" DEEP

Cutting List

Key	Part	Dimension	Pcs.	Material
A	Side panel	¾ × 11¼ × 33¼"	2	Plywood
B	Shelf cleat	¾ × ¾ × 10½"	4	Oak
C	Shelf	¾ × 10½ × 10½"	3	Plywood
D	Back	¾ × 10½ × 32¼"	1	Plywood
E	Top cleat	¾ × 2 × 10½"	1	Plywood
F	Bin face	¾ × 8½ × 12"	3	Oak
G	Lower rail	¾ × 2½ × 12"	1	Oak

Cutting List

Key	Part	Dimension	Pcs.	Material
H	Upper rail	¾ × 1½ × 12"	1	Oak
I	Lid	¾ × 9½ × 14"	1	Oak
J	Fixed top	¾ × 4 × 14"	1	Oak
K	Base trim side	¾ × 1½ × 12¾"	2	Oak
L	Base trim front	¾ × 1½ × 13½"	1	Oak
M	Quarter-round side	½ × ½ × 12½"	2	Molding
N	Quarter-round front	½ × ½ × 13"	1	Molding

Materials: Wood glue, oak-veneer edge tape (20'), #6 × 1¼" wood screws, wire brads (1¼", 1½"), 1½" × 36" piano hinge, magnetic door catches (2), chain stops (2), finishing materials.

Note: Measurements reflect the actual thickness of dimension lumber.

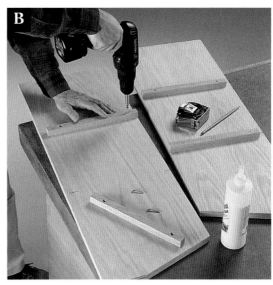

Apply oak-veneer edge tape with a household iron, and trim with a utility knife when cool.

Align cleats on the reference lines, and fasten with glue and screws.

Directions: Vegetable Bin

MAKE THE SIDES.

1. Cut the side panels (A), shelves (C), back (D) and top cleat (E) to size from plywood, and rip the shelf cleats (B) to size from 1 × 12 oak. Sand all edges smooth.

2. Draw a cutting line for the front corners on each side panel (see *Diagram*), and cut along the line with a jig saw to shape the side panels.

3. Clamp each side panel in an upright position, and apply oak-veneer edge tape to all edges, using a household iron **(photo A).** Let cool, and trim the edges with a utility knife.

4. Measure and mark cleat and shelf locations across the inner face of each panel 1", 10½" and 20¾" from the bottom. Drill countersunk pilot holes, then use glue and screws to attach the cleats to the side panels **(photo B).** The bottom of the cleats should be flush with the marked lines, and the front of the cleats should be flush with the front edges of the side panels.

Use a nail set to recess nail heads flush with the shelves.

ATTACH THE SIDES AND BACK.

1. Position the bottom shelf between the side panels so the bottom edge of the shelf rests on the 1" reference line. Keep the front edge flush with the side panels, and fasten with glue and screws. Attach the remaining shelves to the cleats with glue and 1¼" brads, using a nail set to recess the nail heads **(photo C).**

2. Use glue and screws to attach the back to the shelves.

Place the top cleat flush against the top of the assembly, and fasten with screws driven through the back and into the cleat **(photo D).**

3. Drive 1½" brads through each side panel into the ends of the top cleat and the edges of the back piece.

MAKE THE BIN FACES AND LID.

The lower bin faces are hinged for easy access. The upper bin face is permanently fixed, and

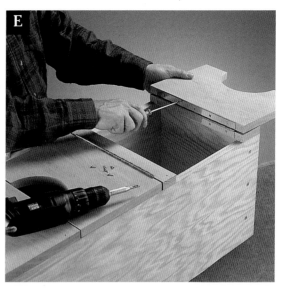

Attach the top cleat from behind with glue and screws, and set in place with two brads at each end.

Attach the rails, and then adjust and fasten the bin lids to the hinges.

access is gained through a hinged lid.

1. Rip-cut the bin faces (F) lower rail (G), upper rail (H), lid (I) and fixed top (J) to size.

2. Use a circular saw to cut a 10° bevel into the back edge of the lid.

3. Mark the lengthwise center-point of each bin face. Draw a 3"-rad. arc centered on each point. Cut each arc with a jig saw and sand smooth.

4. Cut the piano hinge into two 11" sections and one 13" section, using a hacksaw. Center the 11" piano hinges on the lower and upper rails. Drill pilot holes and attach the hinges with the enclosed screws.

5. Position the hinged rails on the bin. The lower rail should be flush with the bottom of the bin. The bottom edge of the upper rail should be flush with the middle shelf, 11¼" from the bottom of the bin. Drill pilot holes and attach the rails to the front of the bin with glue and 1½" brads. Secure the bin faces to the hinges using the enclosed mounting hardware **(photo E).**

6. Lay the upper bin face in position, flush with the bottom of the top shelf. Drill pilot holes and attach the upper bin face with glue and 1½" brads.

7. Center and attach the 13" piano hinge onto the fixed top, drill pilot holes, and fasten with screws.

8. Center the fixed top (hinge up) on top of the assembly, flush with the back edge, then drill pilot holes. Fasten with glue and 1¼" screws driven up through the top cleat into the fixed top. Attach the beveled edge of the lid to the hinge so it folds down correctly over the side panels.

MAKE THE BASE TRIM.

1. Cut base trim sides (K) and base trim front (L) from 1 × 2 oak, and cut the quarter-round sides (M) and quarter-round front (N) to length, mitering the butting ends at 45° angles.

2. Drill pilot holes and attach the base trim pieces with glue and 1¼" brads, and add the quarter-round pieces above the base trim.

APPLY FINISHING TOUCHES.

1. Fill any exposed nail holes, and finish-sand the entire project, using caution around veneered edges. Use a non-toxic finish, such as water-based polyurethane, and let dry.

2. Install magnetic catches in the two lower bins, and fasten stop-chains to support the lids when open **(photo F).**

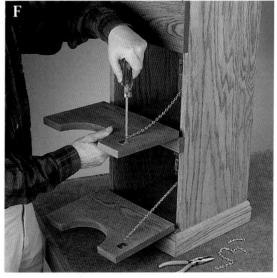

Attach stop-chains to hold bin lids in place when open and magnetic catches to secure the lids when closed.

Pantry Cabinet

This adjustable cabinet provides the versatility needed to organize your pantry.

PROJECT
POWER TOOLS

CONSTRUCTION MATERIALS	
Quantity	**Lumber**
14	1 × 4" × 8' pine
2	¾ × ¾" × 6' pine stop molding

Most pantries are great for storing kitchen supplies or appliances that you don't use every day but like to have nearby. However, if your pantry itself is poorly organized and inconvenient to use, it winds up as wasted space in your home. To get the most from your pantry, we devised our cabinet for maximum vertical storage capacity. Standing 84" high, the cabinet features three solid shelves for storing heavy goods and two adjustable shelves to fit large or awkward items. You can use this pantry cabinet as a freestanding unit against a wall or as a divider in a larger pantry. The open construction also means you can identify what you have on hand at a glance. Included in the instructions is a simple option for converting an adjustable shelf into a rack that is perfect for stable storage of wine, soda or other bottled liquids.

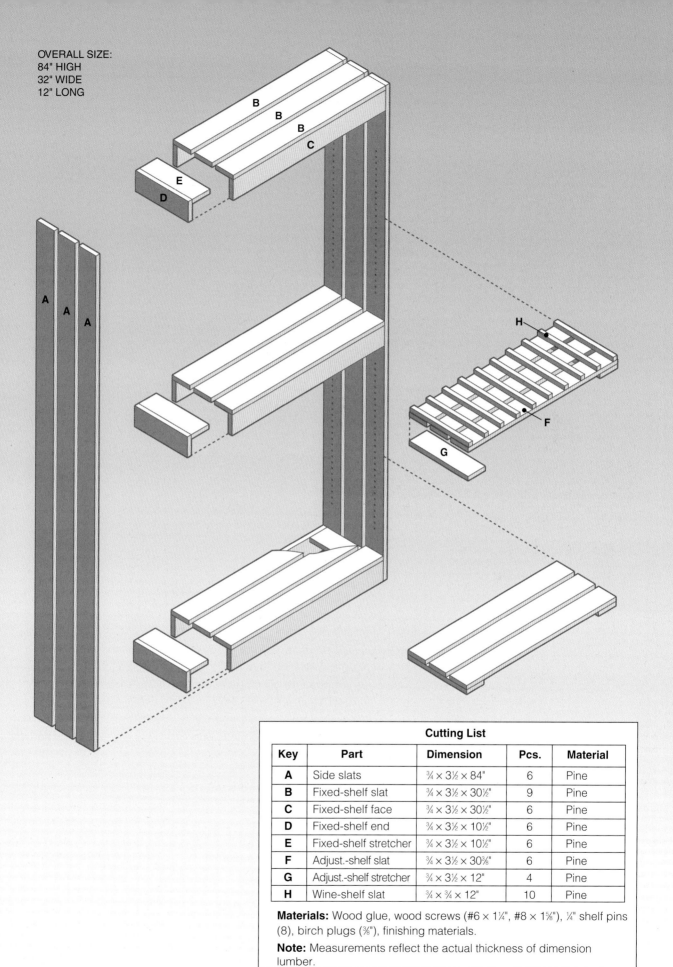

OVERALL SIZE:
84" HIGH
32" WIDE
12" LONG

Cutting List

Key	Part	Dimension	Pcs.	Material
A	Side slats	¾ × 3½ × 84"	6	Pine
B	Fixed-shelf slat	¾ × 3½ × 30½"	9	Pine
C	Fixed-shelf face	¾ × 3½ × 30½"	6	Pine
D	Fixed-shelf end	¾ × 3½ × 10½"	6	Pine
E	Fixed-shelf stretcher	¾ × 3½ × 10½"	6	Pine
F	Adjust.-shelf slat	¾ × 3½ × 30⅜"	6	Pine
G	Adjust.-shelf stretcher	¾ × 3½ × 12"	4	Pine
H	Wine-shelf slat	¾ × ¾ × 12"	10	Pine

Materials: Wood glue, wood screws (#6 × 1¼", #8 × 1⅝"), ¼" shelf pins (8), birch plugs (⅜"), finishing materials.

Note: Measurements reflect the actual thickness of dimension lumber.

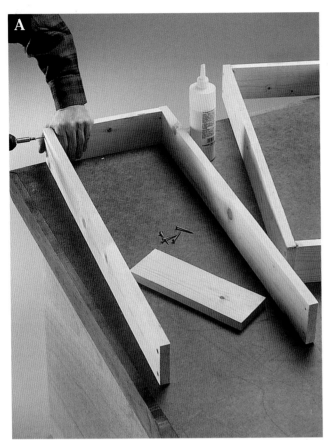

Join the shelf faces to the ends by driving 1⅝" screws through counterbored pilot holes.

Apply glue and drive counterbored screws into the shelf faces and shelf ends to connect the stretchers.

Directions: Pantry Cabinet

MAKE THE FIXED SHELVES.
The fixed shelves comprise the bottom, middle and top of the pantry cabinet.
1. Cut the shelf faces (C), shelf ends (D), and shelf stretchers (E) to size from 1 × 4" pine. Sand the cuts smooth with medium-grit sandpaper.
2. Position the shelf ends between the shelf faces so the corners are flush.
3. Drill ⅜" counterbored pilot holes through the shelf faces into each shelf end. (Keep all counterbores aligned throughout the project to ensure a professional look.) Join the shelf faces and the shelf ends together with wood glue and 1⅝" wood screws driven through the pilot holes **(photo A).** Repeat for the other two fixed-shelf frames.
4. Place a stretcher inside the corner of a shelf frame so the stretcher face is flush with the top edges of the frame. Counterbore pilot holes on the shelf faces and ends, and attach the stretcher with glue and 1⅝" screws driven through the pilot holes. Repeat for the other side of the shelf frame and for the other two shelves **(photo B).**
5. Cut the shelf slats (B) to size and sand the edges smooth.
6. Place three slats on your worksurface. Turn one shelf frame over so the stretchers are on the bottom, and place the shelf frame on top of the slats. Move the slats so the corners and edges are flush with the shelf frame. Space the slats ¾" apart and then attach the slats with glue and 1¼" screws countersunk through the bottom of the stretchers into each of the shelf slats **(photo C).** Repeat for the remaining two fixed shelves.

ASSEMBLE THE CABINET.
The fixed shelves are connected directly to the side slats

*Join the fixed-shelf slats to the stretchers with glue and 1¼"
screws driven through the undersides of the stretchers.*

*When attaching the side slats, position the outer side slats
so the edge is flush with the edges of the fixed shelves.*

to provide stability. The base of
the pantry cabinet is wide
enough to allow the cabinet to
stand alone so long as the cabinet is square. Make sure all
joints are square and the
edges are flush during this final
assembly.

1. Cut the side slats (A) to size,
and sand to smooth out rough
edges.

2. On each side slat, draw a reference line 40" from the
bottom end. These lines mark
the location of the bottom edge
of the middle fixed shelf. To attach the side slats, align all
three shelves on end roughly
40" apart, and lay a side slat
over them. Adjust the top and
bottom shelves so they are
flush with the side slat ends
and corners. Adjust the lower
edge of the middle shelf so it

rests on the reference line.
3. Make sure the fixed shelves
are correctly aligned and that
the corners are square. Counterbore pilot holes through the
side slats into the fixed-shelf
ends and attach with glue and
1¼" screws. Position the next
side slat flush with the other
edge of the fixed shelves, and
attach with glue and screws
driven through counterbored
pilot holes. Center the middle
side slat by spacing the slat ¾"
between the outer slats and attach with glue and screws.
4. With a helper, carefully turn
the assembly over so it rests on
the attached side slats. Position
a side slat over the fixed-shelf
ends as before, check to make
sure the corners and edges are
flush, and attach the side slat to
the fixed shelves **(photo D).**

Attach the remaining side slats
to the fixed shelves, checking
for square as you go.

DRILL THE PEG HOLES.
The rows of holes on the inner
faces of the side slats are used
to hold the pegs for adjustable
shelving. Using a drilling template ensures that the holes are

TIP

*You may find it helpful to clamp workpiece parts
during the assembly process. Clamping will hold
glued and squared parts securely in place until
you permanently fasten them with screws. Large,
awkward assemblies are more manageable with
the help of a few clamps.*

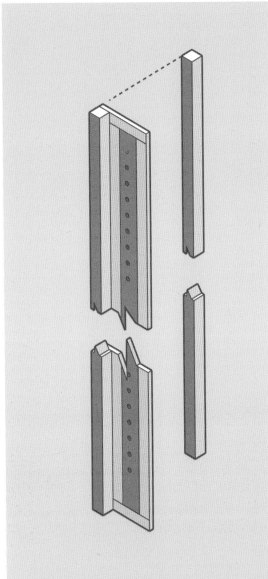

Use a pegboard template for uniform placement of peg holes.

TIP

MAKE A DRILLING TEMPLATE.

Drilling the holes for shelf pegs is simplified by using a template made from a 4 × 34" strip of ⅛ or ¼" pegboard and two 34"-long strips of ¾ × ¾" scrap wood (you can also use stop molding).

First, use masking tape to outline a row of holes on the pegboard. Position one of the ¾" strips against the pegboard so the edge is about 1¾" from the outlined holes. Fasten this guide strip with glue. When the glue dries, turn the template over and attach the second ¾" guide strip, aligning it with the first strip.

perfectly aligned, and the shelves are level when installed (see *Tip*).

1. Wrap masking tape around the tip of a ¼" drill bit at a depth of ½" to mark drilling depth.

2. Position the drilling template against the inside face of a side slat with the ¾" guide strip resting against the edge of the slat. Drill a row of peg holes along the inner face of the side slat, using the pegboard holes as a guide. Make sure not to drill beyond the masking tape depth guide attached to your bit.

3. Rotate the template and position it against the other side slat so the other guide strip is resting against the edge of the slat and the opposite face of the template is facing out. Drill another row of holes exactly parallel to the first **(photo E).**

After drilling all the holes, sand the slats to remove any roughness.

MAKE THE ADJUSTABLE SHELVES.

Our project includes two adjustable shelves, but you can choose to build more. The adjustable shelves are similar in design to the fixed shelves, but without shelf faces or ends.

1. Cut two stretchers (G) and three slats (F) for each shelf, and sand smooth.

2. Lay three slats on your worksurface. Arrange the stretchers over the ends of the slats so the edges and corners are flush, and the slats are spaced ¾" apart.

3. Drill pilot holes through the stretchers into the slats, and fasten with glue and countersunk 1¼" wood screws.

4. Cut the wine shelving slats (H) to size from ¾" pine, using a circular saw and straightedge guide. (Or, you can use pine stop molding.) Sand the cuts smooth.

5. Place the first slat on the adjustable shelf, ⅛" from one end. Keep the ends of the wine slats even with the edges of the shelf slats, and attach with glue and 4d finish nails. Use a 2½"-wide spacer to guide placement for the rest of the slats, and nail in place. Recess all the nail heads on the wine slats with a nail set as you go **(photo F).**

APPLY FINISHING TOUCHES.

1. Pound glued ⅜"-dia. birch plugs into all counterbored holes using a wood or rubber mallet **(photo G).**

2. Carefully sand the plugs flush with a belt sander, then finish-sand the pantry with fine-grit sandpaper.

3. Apply your choice of finish. We brushed a light coat of linseed oil onto the pantry to preserve the natural appearance. If you prefer paint, use a primer and a good-quality enamel.

4. Insert ¼" shelf pins at the desired heights and rest the adjustable shelves on top of the pins after the finish dries.

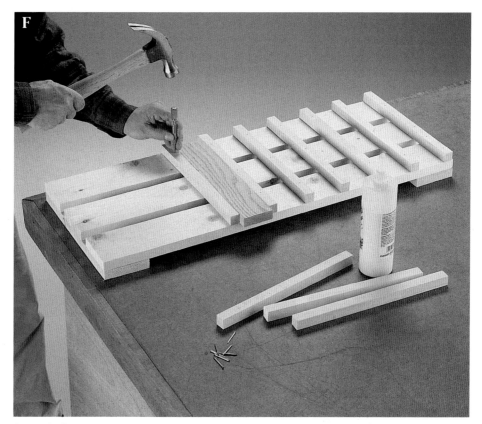

Use a 2½"-wide spacer to ensure uniform placement of the wine shelf cleats.

Pound glued ⅜" birch plugs into counterbored screw holes.

PROJECT
POWER TOOLS

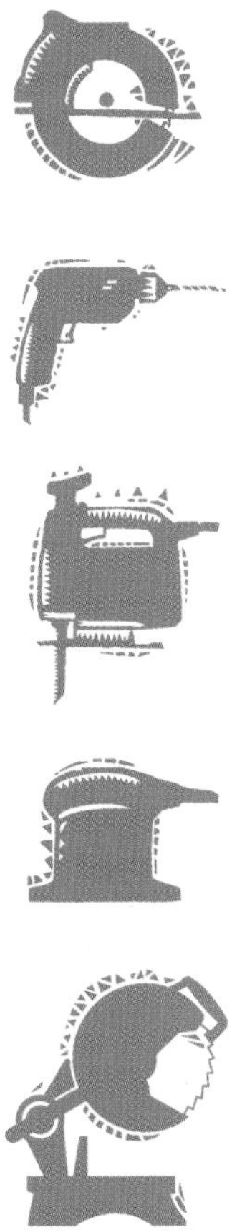

Kitchen Island

Our stand-alone cabinet and countertop island expands the versatility of any kitchen.

CONSTRUCTION MATERIALS

Quantity	Lumber
7	⅝" × 2' × 4' pine panel
4	1 × 2" × 8' pine
1	1 × 4" × 4' pine
1	2 × 8" × 2' pine
4	¾ × ¾" × 8' pine stop molding
1	¾" × 4' × 4' particleboard
1	¼" × 4' × 4' tileboard

This project is a great looking alternative to more expensive custom cabinetry. The kitchen island gives you additional space for preparing food, as well as a convenient spot to enjoy a light snack or a quick meal. The ends, back panels and shelves are constructed from edge-glued pine, a convenient building material with an appealing pattern. The front of the island has a finished face frame and adjustable shelving for storage. The countertop has an 8" overhang and provides room for two to sit comfortably. We used tileboard as the countertop, but laminate or ceramic tile are also good choices.

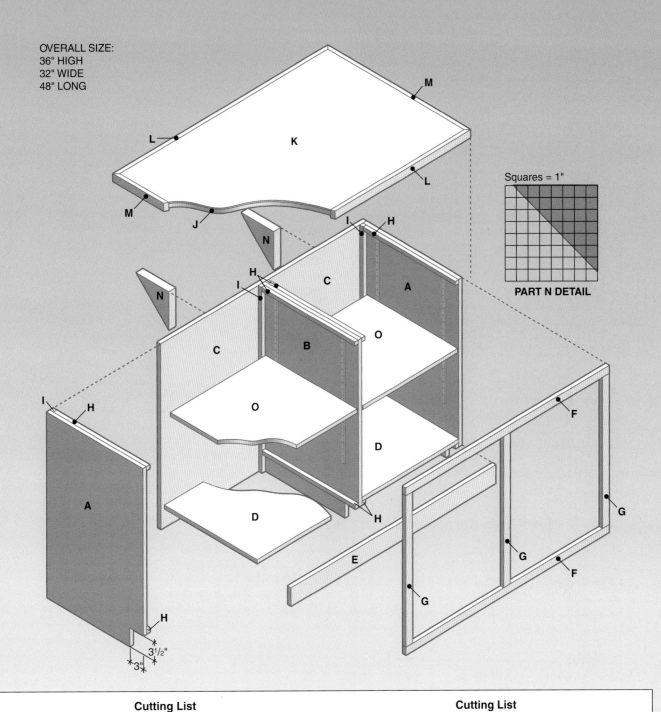

OVERALL SIZE:
36" HIGH
32" WIDE
48" LONG

Squares = 1"

PART N DETAIL

3½"

3"

Key	Part	Dimension	Pcs.	Material
A	End	⅝ × 21½ × 35"	2	Pine panel
B	Divider	⅝ × 21½ × 35"	1	Pine panel
C	Back	⅝ × 22⅛ × 35"	2	Pine panel
D	Bottom	⅝ × 21⅛ × 21½"	2	Pine panel
E	Toe board	¾ × 3½ × 44¼"	1	Pine
F	Rail	¾ × 1½ × 44¼"	2	Pine
G	Stile	¾ × 1½ × 28½"	3	Pine
H	Horiz. cleat	¾ × ¾ × 20¾"	8	Molding

Cutting List

Key	Part	Dimension	Pcs.	Material
I	Vert. cleat	¾ × ¾ × 35"	4	Molding
J	Substrate	¾ × 30½ × 46½"	1	Particleboard
K	Top	¼ × 30½ × 46½"	1	Tileboard
L	Long edge	¾ × 1½ × 48"	2	Pine
M	Short edge	¾ × 1½ × 32"	2	Pine
N	Support	1½ × 7¼ × 7¼"	2	Pine
O	Shelf	⅝ × 20½ × 20½"	2	Pine panel

Materials: Wood glue, #6 wood screws (1", 1¼", 1½"), ½" tacks, 4d finish nails, 24" shelf standards (8), shelf standard supports, contact cement, finishing materials.

Note: Measurements reflect the actual thickness of dimension lumber.

Cut the toe board notches into the ends and divider using a jig saw.

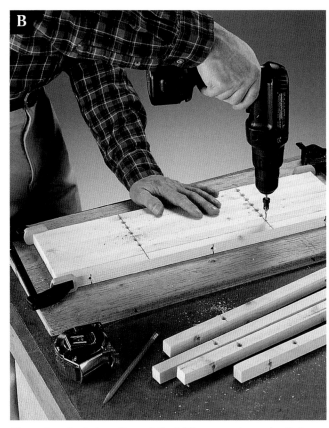

Gang the cleats together while drilling countersunk pilot holes.

Directions: Kitchen Island

CUT THE ENDS AND DIVIDER.

1. Cut the ends (A) and divider (B) to size from pine panels, using a circular saw.

2. Measure and mark the 3"-wide × 3½"-tall toe board notches on the lower front corners of all three pieces using a combination square (see *Diagram*). This notch allows you to approach the cabinet without stubbing your toes against the bottom.

3. Clamp each piece to your worksurface, and cut out the toe board notches using a jig saw **(photo A)**.

PREPARE THE CLEATS.

The cleats reinforce the internal joints of the cabinet. Countersunk pilot holes are drilled through each cleat in two directions, and are offset so the screws won't hit one another.

1. Cut the horizontal cleats (H) and the vertical cleats (I) to length from ¾ × ¾" stop molding.

2. Clamp the vertical cleats together so the ends are flush, and mark four pilot hole locations along the length of each cleat (see *Detail* for pilot hole locations). Drill countersunk pilot holes at each marked location.

3. Remove the clamps and give each cleat a quarter turn. Reclamp the cleats, then mark and drill the second set of offset pilot holes. Repeat the process for the horizontal cleats, drilling three holes through one edge of each cleat and two offset holes through an adjacent edge **(photo B)**.

PARTS H AND I DETAIL

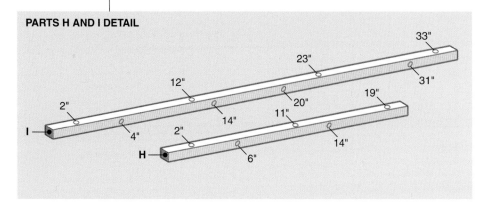

Center a marked template between the cleats to uniformly attach the shelf standards.

Clamp the back to the divider along the centerline, and adjust when attaching to the end.

ASSEMBLE THE ENDS AND DIVIDER.

1. Align a vertical cleat along the inside back edge of one of the ends. Align the pilot holes so the back can be attached through the offset holes.

2. Apply glue and fasten the cleat to the end with countersunk 1" screws. Attach vertical cleats to the inside face of the other end, and to both back edges of the divider. Attach the horizontal cleats to the ends and divider, using glue and 1" screws.

ATTACH THE SHELF STANDARDS.

1. Cut a 15 × 30" template from scrap particleboard or heavy-stock cardboard. Make sure the standards are properly aligned in the same direction so the holes for the supports line up.

2. Place the template on the lower horizontal cleat, and center the template between the vertical cleat and the front edge. Measure 2" up from the bottom edge along each side of the template and make a reference mark.

3. Place a standard against each edge of the template and adjust so the bottom of the standard is on the 2" mark. Nail the standards in place with the provided nails.

4. Repeat for the other end, and on both faces of the divider **(photo C).**

ASSEMBLE THE CABINET.

1. Cut the backs (C), bottoms (D) and toe board (E) to size, and sand the edges smooth.

2. Cut ¾ × ¾" notches in the back corners of each bottom to

Arrange the toe board so the corners and edges are flush, and attach to the divider and ends with glue and 4d finish nails.

Sand the rails after the stiles to avoid cross-sanding marks on the rails.

accommodate the vertical cleats.

3. Stand one end and the divider upright on their front edges. Position a bottom piece against the lower horizontal cleats. Use bar clamps to hold the assembly in place, and attach the bottom with glue and 1" screws driven through the pilot holes in each cleat. Position the remaining bottom and end in place, and attach the bottom to the cleats.

4. Attach the back pieces one at a time, using glue and 1" screws driven through the vertical cleats inside the cabinet. Make sure each back piece is aligned with its inside edge flush against a marked reference centerline on the divider. Check frequently for square,

and use pipe clamps to hold the pieces in position as you attach them **(photo D).**

5. Carefully turn the assembly over, and fasten the toe board in place with glue and 4d finish nails.

ASSEMBLE THE FACE FRAME.

1. Cut the rails (F) and stiles (G) to size, and sand them smooth. Position the top rail so the top edges and corners are flush, and attach with glue and finish nails. Attach the stiles so the outside edges are flush with the end faces and centered on the divider. Finally, attach the bottom rail **(photo E).**

2. Reinforce the joints by drilling pilot holes through the rails into the ends of each stile

and securing with 4d finish nails.

3. Use an orbital sander to smooth the face frame and the joints between stiles and rails. By sanding the stiles before the rails, you can avoid cross-sanding marks at the joints **(photo F).**

BUILD THE COUNTERTOP.

1. Cut the particleboard substrate (J), tileboard top (K), long edges (L) and short edges (M) to size. Make sure the top fits perfectly over the substrate, and trim if necessary.

2. Miter-cut the ends of the long edges and short edges at 45° angles to fit around the countertop.

3. Apply contact cement to the substrate, and clamp the tile-

Clamp scrap boards to the tileboard to distribute pressure and establish good contact.

Attach the supports to the back from inside the cabinet using glue and screws.

board top in place, using scrap wood under the clamps to distribute pressure and ensure even contact with the cement **(photo G).**

4. Unclamp and flip the assembly on its top when dry. Arrange the long and short edges around the countertop, so the top surface will be flush with the tops of the edge pieces. Glue and clamp the edges in place. Drill pilot holes and drive 4d finish nails through the edges into the substrate.

ATTACH THE COUNTERTOP AND SHELVES.

1. Cut the shelves (O) from pine panels and the supports (N) from 2 × 8 dimensional pine. Round the cut corners at the long ends of each diagonal,

using a jig saw or a sander to soften the profile of the supports.

2. Mark a line on the top edge of the back, 11" in from each end. Position the supports so they are centered on the lines. Drill pilot holes through the back and attach the supports with glue and 1½" countersunk screws driven from the inside of the cabinet **(photo H).**

3. Center the countertop from side to side on the cabinet with a 1" overhang on the front. Attach with glue and 1¼" screws driven up through the top horizontal cleats. Insert supports into the shelf standards at the desired height, and install the shelves inside the cabinet with the grain running left to right.

APPLY FINISHING TOUCHES.

1. Recess all visible nail heads with a nail set, and fill the holes with putty. Sand all surfaces, outer edges and corners smooth.

2. Finish the kitchen island with a light stain and apply a nontoxic topcoat. We used a traditional American pine finish.

Pine Pantry

*Turn a remote corner or closet into a kitchen pantry
with this charming pine cabinet.*

CONSTRUCTION MATERIALS

Quantity	Lumber
2	1 × 10" × 10' pine
3	1 × 8" × 8' pine
1	1 × 8" × 10' pine
1	1 × 6" × 8' pine
1	1 × 4" × 8' pine
5	1 × 3" × 8' pine
1	1 × 2" × 10' pine
1	¾" × 4 × 8' plywood
1	¼" × 4 × 8' plywood

This compact pantry cabi-
net is ideal for keeping
your kitchen organized
and efficient. It features a convenient turntable shelf, or "Lazy
Susan," on the inside of the
cabinet for easy access to
canned foods. A swing-out
shelf assembly lets you get the
most from the pantry's space.
Its roominess allows you to
store most of your non-

refrigerated food items.
 But the best feature of the
pantry is its appearance. The
rugged beauty of the cabinet
hides its simplicity. For such an
impressive-looking project, it is
remarkably easy to build. Even
if you don't have a traditional
pantry in your home, you can
have a convenient,
attractive storage center.

OVERALL SIZE:
42" HIGH
30" WIDE
25¾" DEEP

Cove molding

TURNTABLE DETAILS

TOP VIEW

SIDE VIEW

Cove molding

Pine stop molding

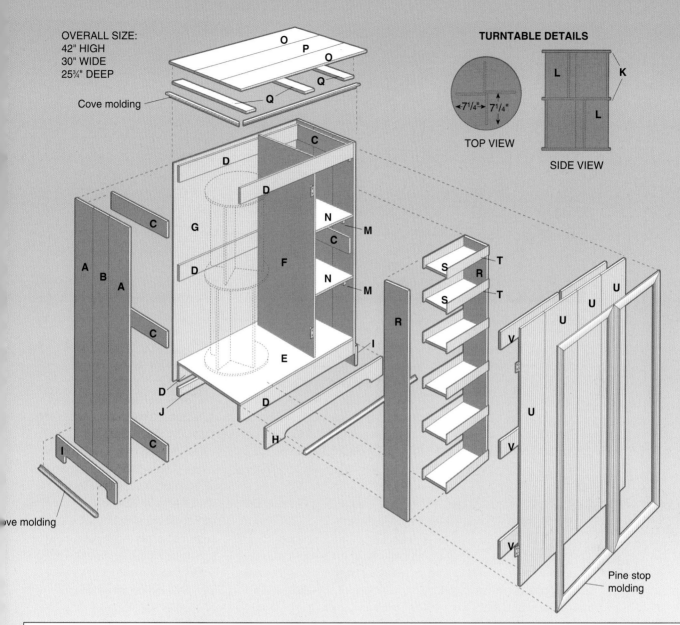

Cutting List

Key	Part	Dimension	Pcs.	Material
A	Side board	¾ × 9¼ × 39¼"	4	Pine
B	Middle board	¾ × 5½ × 39¼"	2	Pine
C	Panel cleat	¾ × 2½ × 22½"	6	Pine
D	Stretcher	¾ × 2½ × 26½"	5	Pine
E	Floor	¾ × 24 × 26½"	1	Plywood
F	Divider	¾ × 22½ × 36"	1	Plywood
G	Back	¼ × 28 × 39¼"	1	Plywood
H	Base front	¾ × 3½ × 29½"	1	Pine
I	Base side	¾ × 3½ × 24¼"	2	Pine
J	Base back	¾ × 1½ × 28"	1	Pine
K	Turntable shelf	¾ × 16"-dia.	3	Plywood

Cutting List

Key	Part	Dimension	Pcs.	Material
L	Supports	¾ × 7¼ × 12"	8	Pine
M	Shelf cleat	¾ × 1½ × 22"	4	Pine
N	Fixed shelf	¾ × 9 × 23"	2	Plywood
O	Top board	¾ × 9¼ × 30"	2	Pine
P	Middle board	¾ × 7¼ × 30"	1	Pine
Q	Top cleat	¾ × 2½ × 22¼"	3	Pine
R	Swing-out end	¾ × 6 × 32"	2	Pine
S	Swing-out shelf	¾ × 6 × 10"	6	Pine
T	Swing-out side	¼ × 2 × 11½"	12	Plywood
U	Door board	¾ × 6⅝ × 35"	4	Pine
V	Door cleat	¾ × 2½ × 11"	6	Pine

Materials: #6 × 1¼", 1½" and 2" wood screws, 2d, 4d and 6d finish nails, 16-ga. × 1" wire nails, turntable hardware, cabinet handles, 3 × 3" brass hinges (2), cabinet door hinges (4), ¾" cove molding, ⅜ × 1¼" stop molding, glue, finishing materials.

Note: Measurements reflect the actual size of dimension lumber.

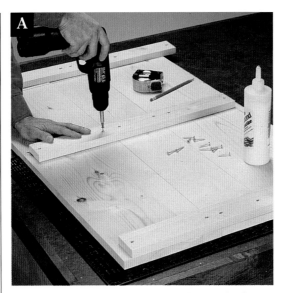

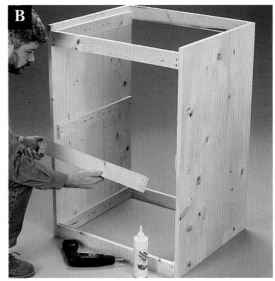

Fasten cleats to the side and middle boards, forming the cabinet sides.

Attach front and back stretchers at the top and bottom, and a middle stretcher at the back.

Directions: Pine Pantry

For all screws used in this project, drill ⁵⁄₆₄" pilot holes. Counterbore the holes ⅛" deep, using a ⅜" counterbore bit.

MAKE THE CABINET SIDES.
1. Cut the side boards (A), middle boards (B) and panel cleats (C) to length. Sand all of the parts smooth.
2. Position a middle board between two side boards with the ends flush. Butt the boards against a framing square to keep them in line. Position a panel cleat flat across the boards so the bottom edge of the cleat is flush with the bottom edges of the boards. The ends of the cleat should be ¾" from the outside edges of the side boards. Fasten the cleat to the boards with glue, and drive 1¼" wood screws through the cleat and into the side and middle boards.
3. Attach the next panel cleat to the boards so its top edge is 21½" up from the bottom edge of the first cleat **(photo A).** Maintain a ¾" distance from the

cleat ends to the board edges.
4. Install the top panel cleat with its top edge 1" down from the board tops.
5. Repeat these steps to make the other cabinet side.

ATTACH THE SIDES.
1. Cut the side stretchers (D) to length.
2. Connect the cabinet sides by attaching the stretchers to the ends of the panel cleats. Position bottom stretchers at the front and back of the cabinet, keeping their top and bottom edges flush with the top and bottom edges of the panel cleats. The top two stretchers are each positioned a little differently—the back stretcher is flush with the tops and bottoms of the panel cleats, and the front stretcher is flush with the top edges of the cabinet sides. Apply glue and drive 1½" wood screws through the stretcher faces and into the ends of the cleats.
3. Attach the remaining stretcher at the back of the cabinet, flush with the panel cleats on the middle of the cabinet

sides **(photo B).**

ATTACH THE FLOOR.
1. Cut the floor (E) to size. Sand the top face smooth, and fill any voids in the front edge of the floor with wood putty.
2. Position the floor on top of the bottom stretchers and panel cleats, with the floor's front edge flush with the face of the front stretcher. Glue the parts. Drive 1½" wood screws through the floor and into the stretchers and panel cleats.

ATTACH THE DIVIDER.
1. Cut the divider (F) and shelf cleats (M) to size.
2. Draw a reference line across the floor from front to back, 9" from the right cabinet side. This line marks the position of the divider's shelf-side face. Measure and mark shelf cleat position lines on the right cabinet side, 10" and 20¾" up from the cabinet floor. Draw corresponding lines on the divider. These lines mark the top edges of the shelf cleats.
3. Use glue and 1¼" wood screws to fasten the shelf cleats

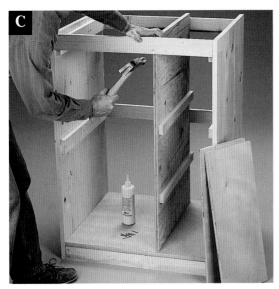

Install the divider 9" in from the right side of the cabinet.

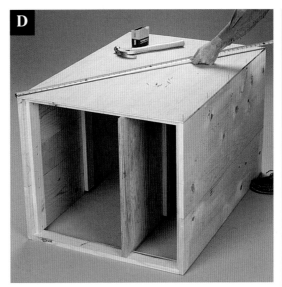

Check for square by measuring diagonally between the corners to make sure the distances are equal.

to the divider and side with their top edges at the lines. Keeping all back edges flush, drive the screws through the cleats and into the divider and side panel.

4. Apply glue to the bottom edge of the divider. Insert the divider into the cabinet with its cleated face toward the cleated cabinet side. Drive 1½" wood screws up through the cabinet floor and into the divider edge. Drill ¹⁄₁₆" pilot holes through the top stretchers and drive 6d finish nails through the top stretchers and into the divider edges **(photo C).**

ATTACH THE BACK.

1. Cut the back (G) to size, and position it on the cabinet.

2. Drive evenly spaced 1" wire nails through the back and into the edge of one side panel.

3. Measure diagonally across the opposite corners to check if the cabinet is square **(photo D).** Square the cabinet, if needed, by applying pressure to opposite corners. When the diagonal measurements are equal, complete the nailing of

the back to the stretchers and the remaining side panel.

ATTACH THE FIXED SHELVES.

1. Cut the fixed shelves (N) to size. Sand them smooth.

2. Position the shelves on the shelf cleats, with their ends butted against the cabinet back. Attach the shelves with glue, and drive 1½" wood screws through the shelves and into the cleats.

MAKE THE BASE.

Three of the four base boards have cutouts that create a foot at each corner.

1. Cut the base front (H), base sides (I) and base back (J) to length. Sand the parts smooth.

2. Use a compass to draw 1¾"-radius semicircles, centered 7¼" from each end of the base front. Hold the point of the compass as close as possible to the bottom edge. Using a straightedge, draw a straight line connecting the tops of the semicircles. Repeat these steps on the base sides, but center the semicircles 4¾" from the

front end and 5½" from the back end. Cut along the lines with a jig saw.

3. Mark lines on the rear edges of the base sides, ½" from the bottom edge. These lines mark the position of the bottom edge of the base back.

4. Attach the base sides to the base front with glue, and drive 4d finish nails through the base front and into the ends of base sides.

5. Attach the base back between the base sides at the reference lines, using glue and 4d finish nails.

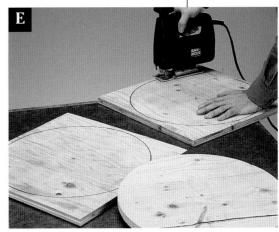

Cut the round turntable shelves with a jig saw. Each turntable shelf has an 8" radius.

Assemble the turntable supports in three pairs, joined at right angles.

Using glue and 4d finish nails, attach the swing-out shelf sides.

ATTACH THE CABINET AND BASE.

1. Turn the cabinet on its back, slide the base over its bottom end until the base back meets the bottom cleats. The base should extend 2" beyond the cabinet's bottom edges. Drive 2" wood screws through the bottom cleats and side boards and into the base sides.

2. Drive 1¼" wood screws through the front stretcher and into the base front.

BUILD THE TURNTABLE SHELVES.

1. Cut the turntable shelves (K) to size. To cut the circular shape, mark the center of the turntable shelves, and use a compass to draw a 16"-dia. circle. Cut the shelves to shape with a jig saw, and sand the cuts smooth **(photo E).**

2. Cut the turntable supports (L) to length.

3. Attach pairs of turntable supports at right angles by applying glue and driving 1½" wood screws through one support's face and into the other support's edge, forming simple butt joints **(photo F).**

4. Use a straightedge to draw a line across the turntable shelves, directly through their centerpoints. Place one pair of turntable supports along the line with the joint at the centerpoint (see *Diagram*). Make sure the support pair forms a right angle. Then, draw the outline of the supports on the shelf. Position another support pair on the other side of the line and draw the outline. Drill pilot holes through the shelves, centered within the outlines, and fasten the turntable shelves to the turntable supports with glue and 1½" wood screws. The supports should have their spines meeting at the centerpoint of the turntable. Offset the upper and lower sets of supports on the opposite sides of the middle shelf to allow room for driving the screws.

5. Attach the turntable hardware to the bottom face of the bottom turntable shelf, following manufacturer's directions. The turntable must be centered on the shelf, or the assembly will not rotate smoothly. Install

the turntable assembly after you apply the finish to the pantry.

BUILD THE SWING-OUT RACK.

1. Cut the swing-out shelves (S), swing-out ends (R) and swing-out sides (T) to size. Sand the parts smooth.

2. Draw lines 6" apart starting from the bottom of the swing-out ends. These lines mark the positions of the bottom faces of the swing-out shelves. Apply glue to the shelf edges. Then, attach them to the swing-out ends by driving 1½" wood screws through the ends and into the shelf edges. The bottom shelf should be flush with the bottom of the end edges.

3. Attach the swing-out shelf sides (T) on the edges of the shelves with glue and 4d finish nails **(photo G).**

MAKE THE TOP.

1. Cut the top boards (O), middle board (P) and top cleats (Q) to length. Sand them smooth.

2. Attach a top cleat across the inside faces of the boards, 1¾" from each end. Make sure that

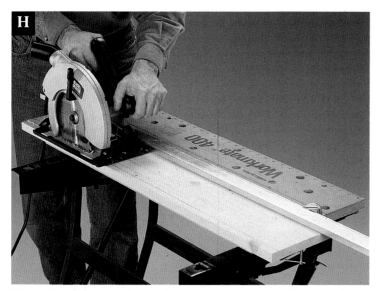

Use a circular saw with a straightedge as a guide to rip-cut the door boards to size.

Attach pine stop molding to create a frame around the edges of the door boards.

the ends of the boards are flush and that the cleats are centered from front to back. Apply glue and drive 1¼" wood screws through the cleats and into the top and middle boards. Fasten the middle cleat so its right edge is 11½" from the right end of the top.

3. Position the top on the cabinet so it overhangs the front and sides of the cabinet by 1". Fasten the top by driving 4d finish nails into the cabinet sides and toenailing through the middle cleat and into the divider.

BUILD THE DOORS.

1. Cut the door boards (U) and door cleats (V) to size **(photo H).** Sand them smooth.
2. Lay the boards in pairs, with their ends flush. Center the top and bottom cleats, keeping them 2" in from the top and bottom ends. Apply glue and drive 1¼" wood screws through the cleats and into the door boards. Attach the middle cleat, centered between the top and bottom cleats.
3. Miter-cut ⅜" stop molding to frame the front faces of the

doors. Fasten the molding with glue and 2d finish nails **(photo I).**

APPLY FINISHING TOUCHES.

1. Miter-cut ¾" cove molding to fit around the base and top (see *Diagram*). Attach the molding with glue and 2d finish nails.
2. Set all nails with a nail set, and fill the nail and screw holes with wood putty. Finish-sand the pantry, and apply the finish of your choice.
3. Attach two evenly spaced 3 × 3" butt hinges to the edge of

the swing-out rack. Mount the rack to the divider, using ¼"-thick spacers between the rack and divider **(photo J).**
4. Install the turntable assembly on the floor of the pantry.
5. Attach hinges and handles to the doors. Mount the doors to the cabinet sides.

With spacers in place to help align the parts, attach the swing-out rack to the divider with 3 × 3" butt hinges.

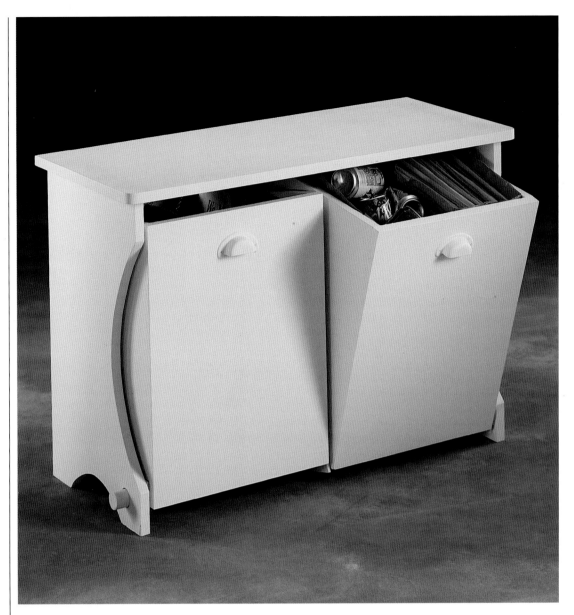

Recycling Center

Recycling is no longer a chore when this convenient recycling center is a fixture in your kitchen.

CONSTRUCTION MATERIALS

Quantity	Lumber
1	¾" × 4 × 8' birch plywood
1	1¼"-dia. × 36" birch dowel
3	¼ × 3 × 3" hardboard or scrap wood

Finding adequate storage for recyclables in a kitchen or pantry can be a challenge. Gaping paper bags of discarded aluminum, newspaper, glass and plastic are an unsightly nuisance. Our recycling center eliminates the nuisance and makes recycling easy. The recycling center holds up to four bags of recy-clables, keeping the materials in one place and out of sight. Arches create four feet on the bottom of the cabinet and a bold detail on the front edges. The two spacious bins pivot forward on a dowel for easy deposit and removal of recy-clables, and the broad top of the cabinet serves as a handy low shelf.

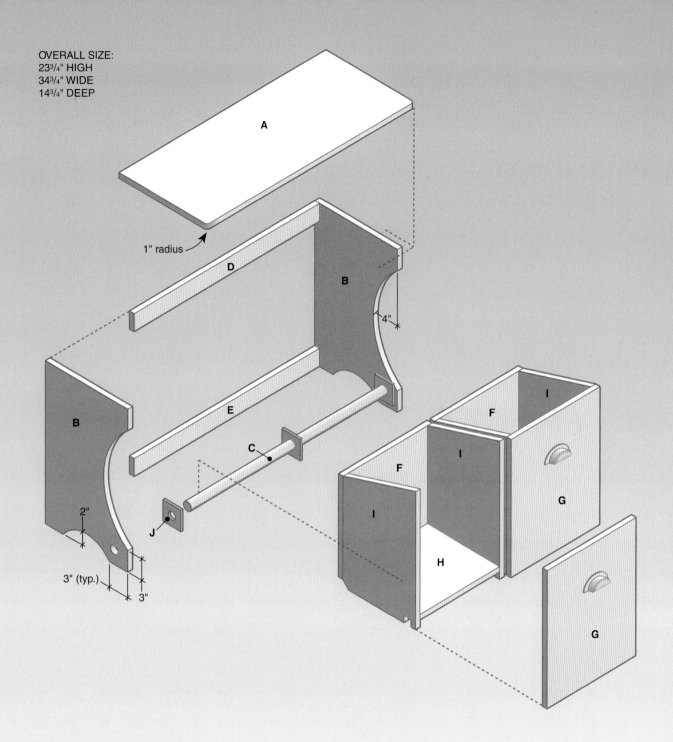

OVERALL SIZE:
23¾" HIGH
34¾" WIDE
14¾" DEEP

1" radius

4"

2"

3" (typ.)

3"

A

D

B

B

E

C

J

F

I

F

I

I

H

G

G

Cutting List				
Key	Part	Dimension	Pcs.	Material
A	Top	¾ × 14¾ × 34¾"	1	Plywood
B	End	¾ × 13¾ × 23"	2	Plywood
C	Dowel	1¼"-dia. × 34"	1	Birch dowel
D	Top stretcher	¾ × 2½ × 31"	1	Plywood
E	Bottom stretcher	¾ × 2½ × 31"	1	Plywood

Cutting List				
Key	Part	Dimension	Pcs.	Material
F	Bin back	¾ × 15 × 16½"	2	Plywood
G	Bin front	¾ × 15 × 19½"	2	Plywood
H	Bin bottom	¾ × 12¼ × 13½"	2	Plywood
I	Bin side	¾ × 12¼ × 19½"	4	Plywood
J	Spacer	¼ × 3 × 3"	3	Masonite

Materials: #4 × ⅜", #6 × 1½" and #8 × 2" wood screws, 4d finish nails, 10" metal chains (2), screw hooks (2), drawer pulls (2), paste wax, wood glue, finishing materials.
Note: Measurements reflect the actual size of dimension lumber.

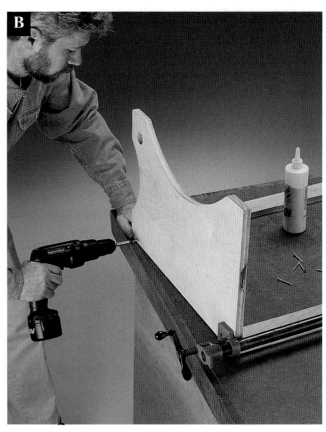

Drill pilot holes for the anchor screws through the bottom edges and into the dowel holes.

Apply glue and drive screws through the ends and into the stretchers. Use pipe clamps to ensure square joints.

Directions: Recycling Center

For all #6 wood screws used in this project, drill $\frac{5}{64}$" pilot holes. Counterbore the holes $\frac{1}{8}$" deep, using a $\frac{3}{8}$" counterbore bit.

MAKE THE TOP AND ENDS.
1. Cut the top (A) and ends (B) to size. Sand the edges smooth with medium-grit sandpaper.
2. Create rounded front corners on the top by marking reference points 1" in from the side and front edges at each front corner. Set a compass to 1", and draw the roundovers, holding the compass point on the reference marks. Sand the corners down to the curved lines with a belt sander.
3. Draw the arches on the end pieces by using a thin, flexible piece of metal, plastic or wood as a tracing guide. Along the front edge of each piece, make marks 3" in from each corner. Make a mark on the side face of each piece, 4" in from the center point of the front edge. Tack small finish nails at these three points. Hook the flexible guide behind the center nail, then flex each end and set them in front of the edge nails so the guide bows in to create a smooth curve. Trace the arches with a pencil, and remove the guide and nails.
4. Draw the curves for the bottom edges using the same technique. Along the bottom edges, measure 3" in from the bottom corners and 2" up from the center point of the bottom edge. Tack finish nails at the marks, set the guide and trace the arches.
5. Make the cuts for the bottom and front arches with a jig saw. Sand the cuts smooth with medium-grit sandpaper.
6. Mark the location for the dowel hole on each end piece, 2¼" in and 2" up from the bottom front corner. Set the end pieces with their inside faces

TIP

When checking a cabinet for square, measure diagonally from corner to corner. If the measurements are equal, the cabinet is square. If not, apply pressure to one side or the other with your hand or clamps until the cabinet is square.

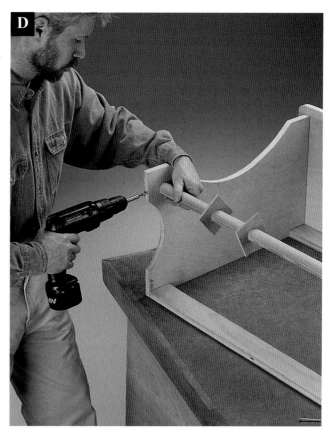

Draw reference lines on the top to use for positioning when attaching it to the sides.

Anchor the dowel by driving screws through the pilot holes and into the dowel.

down onto a backer board to prevent splintering during drilling. Drill the dowel holes, using a 1¼" spade bit.

7. Drill pilot holes for the dowel anchor screws, using a ³⁄₃₂" bit **(photo A).** Align the drill bit with the center of the dowel hole, and drill through the bottom edge of the end piece and into the dowel hole.

ASSEMBLE THE CABINET FRAME.

Attach the stretchers between the ends to form the back of the cabinet frame.

1. Cut the dowel (C), the top stretcher (D) and the bottom stretcher (E) to size. Sand all of the parts smooth.

2. Apply glue to the ends of the stretchers and position them

between the ends so they are flush at the back edges and corners. Clamp the parts together and measure diagonally between opposite corners to make sure the assembly is square (see *Tip*). Then, drive

1½" wood screws through the end pieces and into the ends of the stretchers **(photo B).**

3. Set the cabinet on its back. Lay the top piece flat on your worksurface, bottom-side-up. Butt the back edge of the top

---

TIP

Careful planning can prevent valuable wood from being wasted. With the exception of the dowel and the spacers, all of the parts for this project can be cut from a 4 × 8' piece of birch plywood (see pattern below):

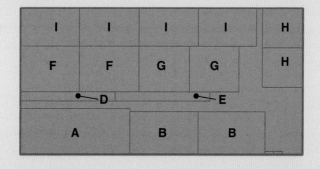

Clamp the bin sides to your worksurface, and use a jig saw to cut the notches and bevels.

Position the bin bottom flush with the dowel notch, and attach it with glue and screws.

against the top stretcher so the ends overhang the cabinet equally on both sides. Mark the bottom face of the top piece to indicate where it will rest on the cabinet ends **(photo C).**

4. Set the cabinet upright and position the top, aligning the reference lines with the outside faces of the ends. The back edge of the top should be flush with the back face of the top stretcher. Attach the top with glue, and drive 1½" wood screws through the top and into the edges of the ends and top stretcher.

INSERT THE DOWEL.

Place spacers along the dowel to separate the bins and ensure smooth operation.

1. Make the three spacers (J) by cutting 3" squares from

hardboard or scrap ¼" material. Hardboard is a good choice because its hard, smooth surfaces create little friction.

2. Mark the center points of the spacers, and drill holes with a 1¼" spade bit to accommodate the dowel.

3. Apply paste wax to the dowel for lubrication. Slide dowel through one end piece. Install the spacers, and slide the dowel end through the hole in the other end. Position the dowel so it protrudes an equal distance from both ends. Anchor the dowel in position by driving #8 × 2" wood screws through the pilot holes on the bottom edges of the ends and into the dowel **(photo D).**

MAKE THE BIN SIDES.

The bin sides have a notch near

the bottom front edge so they can rock safely on the dowel. There are bevels on the top edges and at the bottom rear corners to provide clearance.

1. Cut the bin sides (I) to size. Sand the pieces smooth.

2. Use a jig saw to cut a 1¼"-wide, 1"-high notch, ¾" from the bottom front corner of each bin side (see *Part I Detail*).

3. Make the short bevel on the bottom by measuring and drawing marks along the bottom and back edges, 1" from the bottom rear corner. Draw a diagonal cut line between these two marks, and cut off the corner with a jig saw.

4. Make the long bevel on the top edge by measuring down 2" from the top back corner, and drawing a mark. With a straightedge, draw a diagonal cut line from the mark to the upper front corner, and make the cut with a jig saw **(photo E)**. Sand all of the cuts smooth.

ASSEMBLE THE BINS.

1. Cut the bin backs (F), bin fronts (G) and bin bottoms (H) to size. Sand the pieces smooth.

2. Position a front over the ends of two sides so their tops and outside edges are flush. Attach the bin front to the bin sides with glue, and drive 1½" wood screws through the bin front and into the edges of the bin sides.

3. Position a bin bottom between the sides so it is recessed 1" and is flush with the top of the dowel notches. Attach the sides to the bottom with glue and 1½" wood screws **(photo F)**.

4. Set the bin back over the edges of the bin sides, keeping the top edges flush. Attach the back with glue, and drive 1½" wood screws through the back and into the edges of the bin sides and bottom.

5. Repeat this process to assemble the other bin.

ATTACH THE CHAIN.

To prevent the bins from falling forward when adding or removing recyclables, our design uses chain and screw hooks to attach the bins to the top. The chains can easily be detached when the recycling center needs cleaning.

1. Center and attach the screw hooks on the top edge of the bin backs. Attach 10" chains with #4 × ⅜" wood screws to the underside of the top, 8" from the front edge and 8" from the inside faces of the ends.

2. Place the bins in the cabinet, with spacers in between and

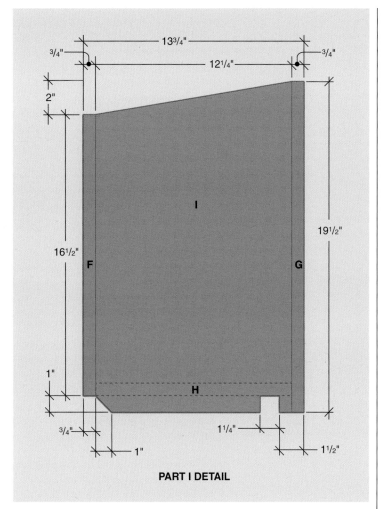

PART I DETAIL

on both sides. For smoother movement, sand the notches as necessary.

APPLY FINISHING TOUCHES.

1. Fill all screw holes with wood putty. Finish-sand the cabinet and bins with fine-grit sandpaper. Paint with an enamel with a medium gloss or eggshell finish to make clean up easy.

2. Install a metal drawer pull on the front of each bin when the finish is dry.

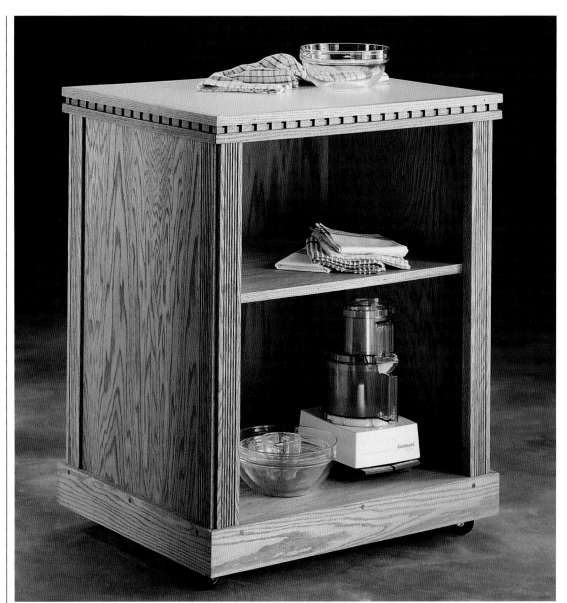

Utility Cart

Form and function combine in this richly detailed rolling cart.

CONSTRUCTION MATERIALS

Quantity	Lumber
2	1 × 2" × 6' oak
2	1 × 4" × 6' oak
1	2 × 4" × 4' pine
1	1 × 4" × 6' pine
1	¾" × 4 × 8' oak plywood
2	⅜ × ⅝" × 6' dentil molding
4	¾ × ¾" × 6' stop molding
8	⅜ × 2¼" × 3' beaded casing
4	¾" × 2 × 3' melamine-coated particleboard

You'll appreciate the extra space, and your guests will admire the classic style of this rolling cabinet. The cart features decorative dentil molding around a scratch-resistant 22½ × 28½" countertop that provides additional work-surface for preparing special dishes. Two storage or display areas, framed by beaded cor-ner molding, can hold food, beverages, dinnerware and appliances. Underneath, the cart has casters, so it easily rolls across floors to the preparing or serving area. Time and again, you'll find this versatile cart a great help in the kitchen, dining room or other entertainment areas of your home.

OVERALL SIZE:
36" HIGH
30" WIDE
24" DEEP

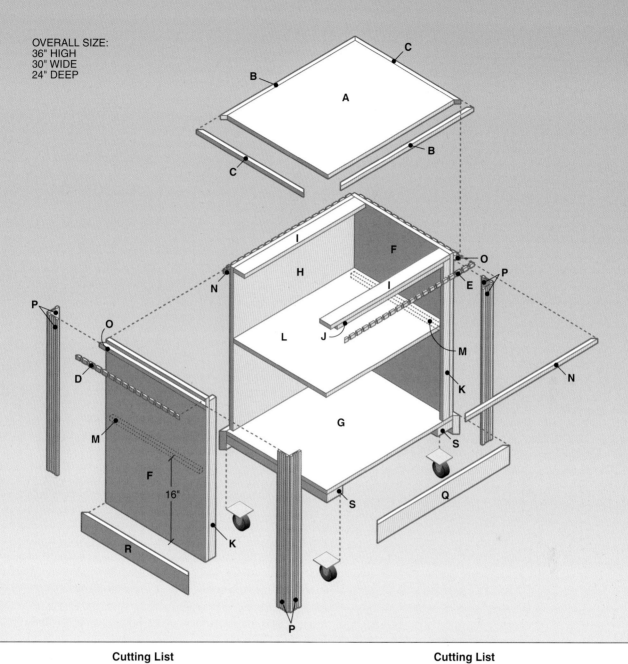

Cutting List

Key	Part	Dimension	Pcs.	Material
A	Top	¾ × 22½ × 28½"	1	Particleboard
B	Long upper trim	¾ × ¾ × 30"	2	Stop mld.
C	Short upper trim	¾ × ¾ × 24"	2	Stop mld.
D	Short dentil	⅜ × ⅝ × 23¼"	2	Dentil mld.
E	Long dentil	⅜ × ⅝ × 29¼"	2	Dentil mld.
F	Side panel	¾ × 22½ × 30⅞"	2	Plywood
G	Bottom	¾ × 22½ × 28½"	1	Plywood
H	Back	¾ × 27 × 30⅞"	1	Plywood
I	Stretcher	¾ × 3½ × 27"	2	Pine
J	Brace	¾ × 1½ × 24"	1	Oak

Cutting List

Key	Part	Dimension	Pcs.	Material
K	Post	¾ × 1½ × 30⅛"	2	Oak
L	Shelf	¾ × 20¾ × 27"	1	Plywood
M	Cleat	¾ × ¾ × 20¼"	2	Stop mld.
N	Long lower trim	¾ × ¾ × 30"	2	Stop mld.
O	Short lower trim	¾ × ¾ × 24"	2	Stop mld.
P	Corner trim	⅜ × 2¼ × 29½"	8	Bead. csg.
Q	Long base	¾ × 3½ × 30"	2	Oak
R	Short base	¾ × 3½ × 24"	2	Oak
S	Caster mount	1½ × 3½ × 22½"	2	Pine

Materials: #6 × 1", 1¼", 1⅝" and 2" wood screws, 16-ga. × 1" brads, 3d finish nails, 2" casters (4), ¾" shelf nosing or oak veneer edge tape (30"), ⅜"-dia. oak plugs, wood glue, finishing materials.

Note: Measurements reflect the actual size of dimension lumber.

A

Use a ¾" piece of scrap wood as a spacer to inset the cleats ¾" from the back edges of the side panels.

B

Drive screws through the top of the stretcher to secure the oak brace.

Directions: Utility Cart

For all screws used in this project, drill ³⁄₃₂" pilot holes. Counterbore the holes ¼" deep, using a ⅜" counterbore bit.

PREPARE THE SIDES AND BOTTOM.

1. Cut the side panels (F), bottom (G), back (H) and cleats (M) to size. Sand them smooth.
2. Drill four evenly spaced pilot holes along the long edges of each side panel, ⅜" in from each edge.
3. Flip each side over and, on the inside face, place a cleat so the bottom edge is 16" from the bottom of the side panel. Attach the cleats with glue, and

drive 1" wood screws through the cleats and into the side panels. Make sure the ends of the cleats are inset ¾" from the back edges of the side panels **(photo A)**.
4. Drill pilot holes along the side and back edges of the bottom, keeping the holes ⅜" in from the edges.

ASSEMBLE THE CABINET.

1. Position the back between the side panels. Attach it with glue, and drive 1⅝" wood screws through the pilot holes in the side panels and into the edges of the back.
2. Apply glue to the bottom edges of the side panels and back. Attach the bottom by

driving 1⅝" wood screws through the bottom and into the edges of the sides and back. The side and back edges of the bottom piece should be flush with the outside faces of the side panels and back.
3. Cut the stretchers (I), brace (J), posts (K) and shelf (L) to size. Sand the parts smooth.
4. Position the front stretcher between the side panels, flush with the top and front edges of the side panels. Attach the stretcher with glue, and drive 1⅝" wood screws through the side panels and into the ends of the stretcher. Apply glue to the back edge and ends of the rear stretcher, and butt it against the back, flush with the

Use glue and brads to attach shelf nosing to the front edge of the shelf.

Fasten the dentil molding around the top edge of the cabinet with glue and brads.

top edge. Drive screws through the side panels and back and into the stretcher.

5. Set the posts in place, faces flush with the front side edges. Attach them with glue, and drive 1⅝" wood screws through the pilot holes in the sides and into the edges of the posts.

6. Apply glue to the brace, and clamp it to the front stretcher so their front edges are flush. Drive 1" wood screws through the stretcher and into the brace **(photo B).**

7. Clamp the shelf vertically to your worksurface. Cut a strip of shelf nosing to match the length of the front edge. Apply glue, and attach the nosing to the shelf with 1" brads **(photo C).**

8. Apply glue to the tops of the cleats, and set the shelf into place, butting the back edge against the back. Drive 3d finish nails through the shelf and into the cleats.

ATTACH THE UPPER MOLDING.

1. Cut the short dentils (D), long dentils (E), long lower trim (N) and short lower trim

(O) to length.

2. Make 45° miter cuts on the ends of each piece of molding, always angling the cuts inward. When cutting the miters for the dentil molding, make sure to cut through the blocks, or "teeth," so the return piece will match at the corners (see *Tip*).

3. Fit the dentil pieces, with the gap edge up, flush to the top edge of the cabinet. Drill ¹⁄₁₆"

TIP

Instead of fastening shelf nosing to the shelf edge, an option is to apply self-adhesive oak veneer edge tape. Cut the tape to length, and press it onto the wood, using a household iron to activate the adhesive. When cool, trim away excess tape with a sharp utility knife.

pilot holes through the molding, and attach it with glue and 1" brads **(photo D)**.

4. Attach the lower trim pieces snug against the bottom of the dentil molding, using glue and 3d finish nails. Set the nails with a nail set **(photo E)**.

ATTACH THE BASE MOLDING.

1. Cut the caster mounts (S) to length.

2. Lay the cart on its back, and attach the caster mounts to the bottom of the cart, flush with the edges of the bottom. Apply glue and drive 2" wood screws through the mounts and into the bottom. Angle the screws slightly to avoid breaking through the top face of the bottom with the tip of the screw.

3. Miter-cut the long bases (Q) and short bases (R) to length.

4. Attach the trim to the cabinet, keeping the top edges flush with the top face of the bottom. Apply glue to all mating surfaces, and drive 1¼" wood screws through the trim pieces and into the edges of the bottom.

5. Cut the corner trim (P) pieces to length.

6. Apply glue to a corner trim piece, and clamp it in place over a post so the inside edges are flush **(photo F)**. Drill ¹⁄₁₆" pilot holes through the corner piece, and nail it to the post and side panel with 1" brads.

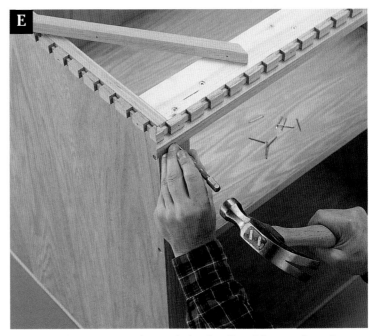

Attach the lower trim underneath the dentil molding, and set the nails with a nail set.

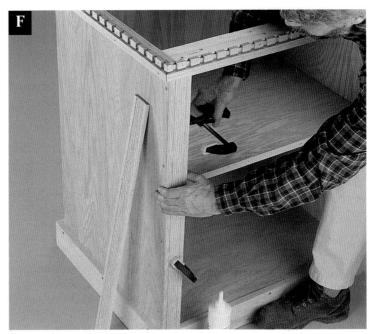

Clamp the corner molding in place to ensure a tight bond with the posts as the glue dries.

7. When the glue is dry, complete the corner by attaching another trim piece with glue and brads. The edges of the trim pieces should touch but should not overlap. Attach the corner trim to the remaining corners.

MAKE THE TOP.

1. Mark the dimensions for the top (A) on a piece of melamine-coated particleboard. Apply masking tape over the cut lines, and mark new cut lines onto the tape. Use a sharp utility knife and a

Score the cutting lines on the melamine with a sharp utility knife to prevent chipping.

TIP

The size of the "teeth" in dentil molding can vary, as can the gaps between the teeth. You might want to purchase extra molding to allow for cutting adjustments that may be necessary to form the corners properly.

Apply glue and clamp the top in place. Then, secure it by driving screws through the stretchers.

straightedge to score the board along the cut lines. This will help prevent chipping and splintering from the saw blade **(photo G).** To minimize chipping when making the cut, use a sharp blade on your circular saw. Cut the top to size, using the straightedge clamped in place as a guide. Then, remove the masking tape.

2. Cut the long upper trim (B) pieces and short upper trim (C) pieces to length, mitering the ends at 45°.

3. Drill pilot holes through the trim pieces, and attach them to the edges of the top with glue and 1" brads. Make sure the tops of the trim pieces are flush with the top face of the top.

4. Center the top over the cabinet, and attach it with glue. Drive 1" wood screws up through the stretchers and into the underside of the top **(photo H).**

APPLY FINISHING TOUCHES.

1. Lay the utility cart on its back, and attach the casters to the caster mounts.

2. Set all nails with a nail set, and fill the nail holes with wood putty. Fill the screw holes on the base trim with glued oak plugs. Finish-sand the utility cart.

3. Finish the cart with the stain or sealer of your choice. We used a rustic oak stain to enhance the grain of the wood.

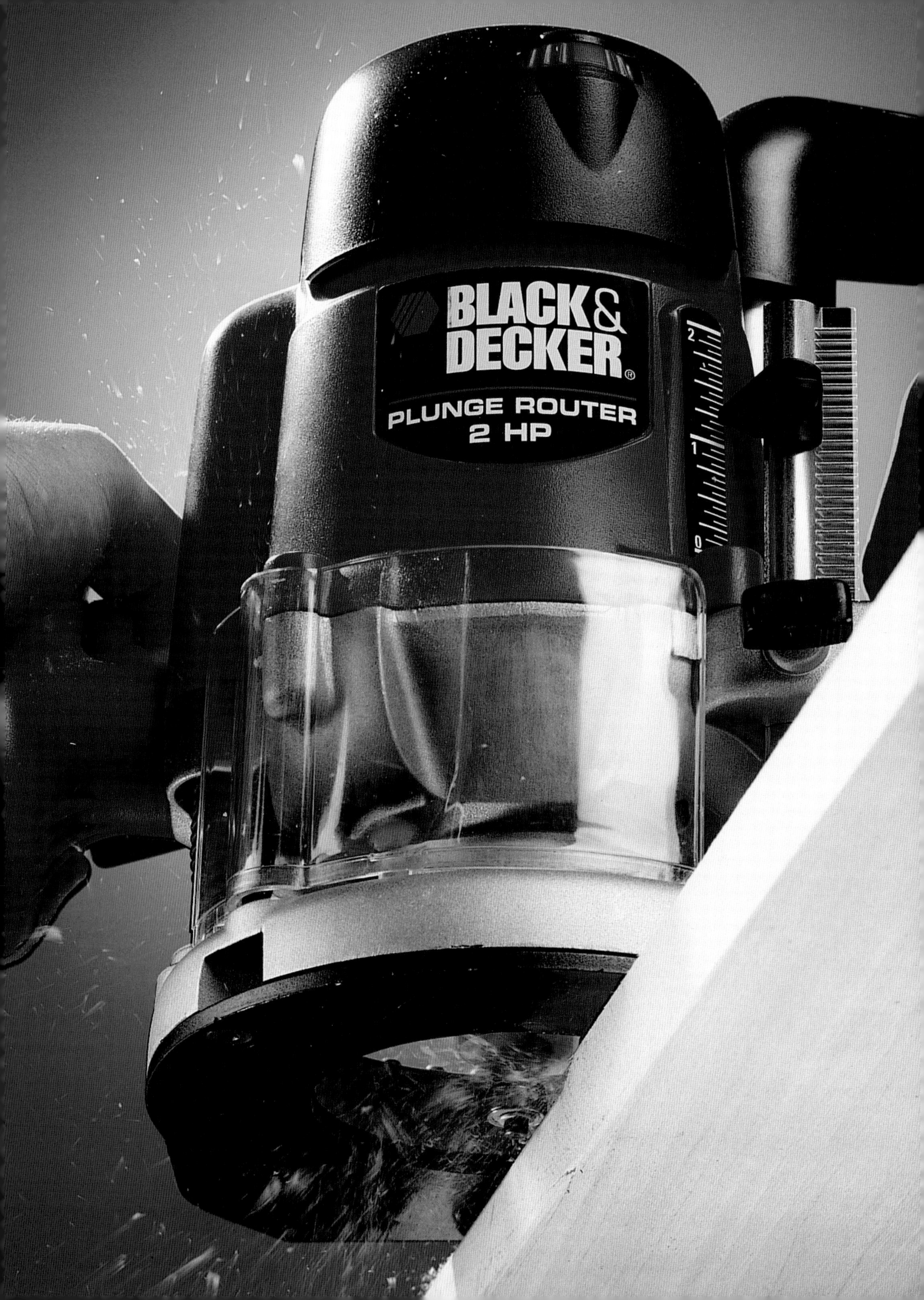
BLACK&DECKER
PLUNGE ROUTER
2 HP

Ornaments & Decorations

Outdoor ornaments and decorations provide the special touches that make your outdoor home a reflection of your personal style. Whether it's an arbor that leads to your perennial garden, a planter that displays showy flowers, or an accent piece for your yard, the simple projects shown here will help you distinguish your landscape with eye-catching wood structures.

Freestanding Arbor

Create a shady retreat on a sunny patio or deck with this striking arbor.

This freestanding arbor combines the beauty and durability of natural cedar with an Oriental-inspired design. Set it up on your patio or deck, or in a quiet corner of your backyard—it adds just the right finishing touch to turn your outdoor living space into a showplace geared for relaxation and quiet contemplation. The arbor has a long history as a focal point in gardens and other outdoor areas throughout the world. And if privacy and shade are concerns, you can enhance the sheltering quality by adding climbing vines that weave their way in and out of the trellis. Or simply set a few potted plants around the base to help the arbor blend in with the outdoor environment. Another way to integrate plant life into your arbor is to hang decorative potted plants from the top beams.

This arbor is freestanding, so it easily can be moved to a new site whenever you desire. Or, you can anchor it permanently to a deck or to the ground and equip it with a built-in seat.

Sturdy posts made from 2×4 cedar serve as the base of the arbor, forming a framework for a 1×2 trellis system that scales the sides and top. The curved cutouts that give the arbor its Oriental appeal are made with a jig saw, then smoothed out with a drill and drum sander for a more finished appearance.

CONSTRUCTION MATERIALS

Quantity	Lumber
9	$1 \times 2" \times 8'$ cedar
9	$2 \times 4" \times 8'$ cedar
3	$2 \times 6" \times 8'$ cedar

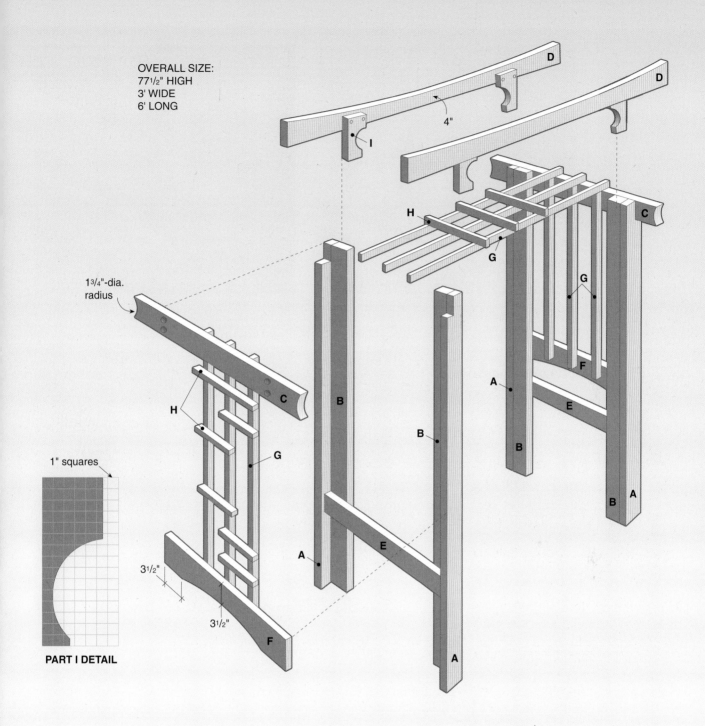

OVERALL SIZE:
77½" HIGH
3' WIDE
6' LONG

4"

1¾"-dia.
radius

1" squares

3½"

3½"

PART I DETAIL

		Cutting List		
Key	**Part**	**Dimension**	**Pcs.**	**Material**
A	Leg front	1½ × 3½ × 72"	4	Cedar
B	Leg side	1½ × 3½ × 72"	4	Cedar
C	Cross beam	1½ × 3½ × 36"	2	Cedar
D	Top beam	1½ × 5½ × 72"	2	Cedar
E	Side rail	1½ × 3½ × 21"	2	Cedar

		Cutting List		
Key	**Part**	**Dimension**	**Pcs.**	**Material**
F	Side spreader	1½ × 5½ × 21"	2	Cedar
G	Trellis strip	⅞ × 1½ × 48"	9	Cedar
H	Cross strip	⅞ × 1½ × *	15	Cedar
I	Brace	1½ × 5½ × 15"	4	Cedar

Materials: Wood glue, wood sealer or stain, #10 × 2½" wood screws, ⅜"-dia. × 2½" lag screws (8), 6" lag screws (4), 2½" and 3" deck screws, finishing materials.

Note: Measurements reflect the actual size of dimension lumber.

*Cut to fit

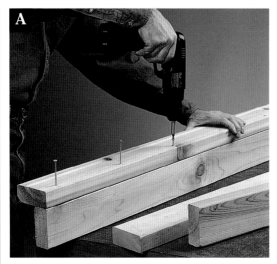

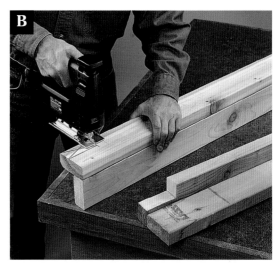

Create four legs by fastening leg sides to leg fronts at right angles.

Cut a notch in the top of each of the four legs to hold the cross beams.

Directions:
Freestanding Arbor

MAKE THE LEGS.

Each of the four arbor legs is made from two 6'-long pieces of 2 × 4 cedar, fastened at right angles with 3" deck screws.

1. Cut the leg fronts (A) and leg sides (B) to length. Position the leg sides at right angles to the leg fronts, with top and bottom edges flush. Apply moisture-resistant glue to the joint. Attach the leg fronts to the leg sides by driving evenly spaced screws through the faces of the fronts and into the edges of the sides **(photo A).**

2. Use a jig saw to cut a 3½"-long × 2"-wide notch at the top outside corner of each leg front **(photo B).** These notches cradle the cross beams when the arbor is assembled.

MAKE THE CROSS BEAMS, RAILS & SPREADERS.

1. Cut cross beams (C) to

A piece of cardboard acts as a template when you trace the outline for the arc on the cross beams.

length. Cut a small arc at both ends of each cross beam. Start by using a compass to draw a 3½"-diameter semicircle at the edge of a strip of cardboard. Cut out the semicircle, and use the strip as a template for marking the arcs **(photo C).** Cut out the arcs with a jig saw. Sand the cuts smooth with a drill and drum sander.

2. Cut two spreaders (F) to length. The spreaders fit just above the rails on each side. Mark a curved cutting line on the bottom of each spreader

(see *Diagram,* page 23). To mark the cutting lines, draw starting points 3½" in from each end of a spreader. Make a reference line 2" up from the bottom of the spreader board. Tack a casing nail on the reference line, centered between the ends of the spreader. With the spreader clamped to the work surface, also tack nails into the work surface next to the starting lines on the spreader. Slip a thin strip of metal or plastic between the casing nails so the strip bows

Lag-screw the cross beams to the legs, and fasten the spreaders and rails with deck screws to assemble the side frames.

Attach trellis strips to the cross brace and spreader with deck screws.

out to create a smooth arc. Trace the arc onto the spreader, then cut along the line with a jig saw. Smooth with a drum sander. Use the first spreader as a template for marking and cutting the second spreader.

3. Cut the rails (E) to length. They are fitted between pairs of legs on each side of the arbor, near the bottom, to keep the arbor square.

ASSEMBLE THE SIDE FRAMES.

Each side frame consists of a front and back leg, joined together by a rail, spreader and cross beam.

1. Lay two leg assemblies parallel on a work surface, with the notched board in each leg facing up. Space the legs so the inside faces of the notched boards are 21" apart. Set a cross beam into the notches, overhanging each leg by 6".

Also set a spreader and a rail between the legs for spacing.
2. Drill ⅜" pilot holes in the cross beam. Counterbore the holes to a ¼" depth, using a counterbore bit. Attach the cross beam to each leg with glue. Drive two ⅜"-dia. × 2½" lag screws through the cross beam and into the legs **(photo D)**.
3. Position the spreader between the legs so the top is 29½" up from the bottoms of the legs. Position the rail 18" up from the leg bottoms. Drill ⅛" pilot holes in the spreader and rail. Counterbore the holes. Keeping the legs parallel, attach the pieces with glue and drive 3" deck screws through the outside faces of the legs and into the rail and spreader.

ATTACH THE SIDE TRELLIS PIECES.

Each side trellis is made from vertical strips of cedar 2 × 2 that are fastened to the side frames. Horizontal cross strips will be added later to create a decorative cross-hatching effect.
1. Cut three vertical trellis strips (G) to length for each side frame. Space them so they are 2⅜" apart, with the ends flush with the top of the cross beam **(photo E)**.
2. Drill pilot holes to attach the trellis strips to the cross beam and spreader. Counterbore the holes and drive 2½" deck screws. Repeat the procedure for the other side frame.

> **TIP**
>
> *Drill counterbores for lag screws in two stages: first, drill a pilot hole for the shank of the screw; then, use the pilot hole as a center to drill a counterbore for the washer and screw head.*

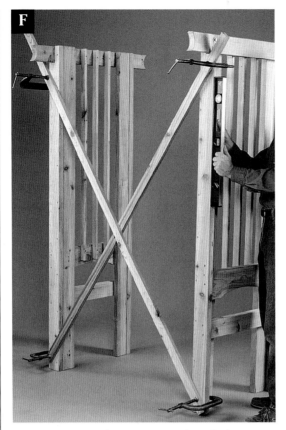

Use long pieces of 1×4 to brace the side frames in an upright, level position while you attach the top beams.

Lock the legs in a square position after assembling the arbor by tacking strips of wood between the front legs and between the back legs.

CUT AND SHAPE TOP BEAMS.

1. Cut two top beams (D) to length. Draw 1½"-deep arcs at the top edges of the top beams, starting at the ends of each of the boards.

2. Cut the arcs into the top beams with a jig saw. Sand smooth with a drum sander.

ASSEMBLE TOP AND SIDES.

1. Because the side frames are fairly heavy and bulky, you will need to brace them in an upright position to fasten the top beams between them. A simple way to do this is to use a pair of 1 × 4 braces to connect the tops and bottoms of the side frames **(photo F).** Clamp the ends of the braces to the side frames so the side frames are 4' apart, and use a level to make sure the side frames are plumb.

2. Mark a centerpoint for a lag bolt 12¾" from each end of each top beam. Drill a ¼" pilot hole through the top edge at the centerpoint. Set the top beams on top of the cross braces of the side frames. Mark the pilot hole locations onto the cross beams. Remove the top beams and drill pilot holes into the cross beams. Secure the top beams to the cross beams with 6" lag screws.

3. Cut four braces (I) to length, and transfer the brace cutout pattern from the *Diagram* on page 23 to each board. Cut the patterns with a jig saw. Attach the braces at the joints where the leg fronts meet the top beams, using 2½" deck screws. To make sure the arbor assembly stays in position while you complete the project, attach 1 × 2 scraps between the front legs and between the back legs **(photo G).**

4. Cut and attach three trellis strips (G) between the top beams.

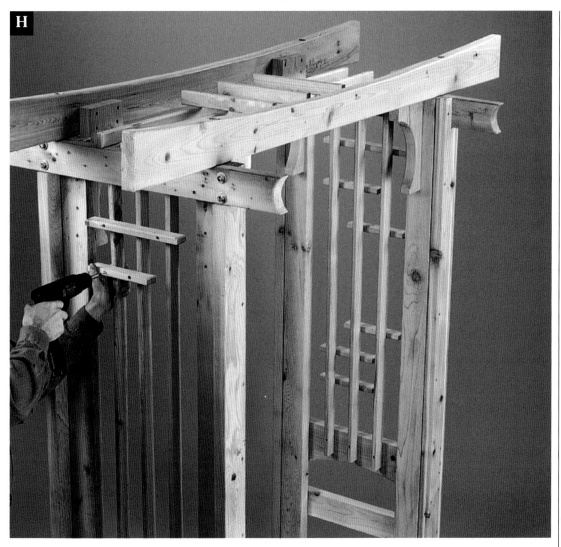

Attach the trellis cross strips to spice up the design and assist climbing plants.

ADD TRELLIS CROSS STRIPS.

1. Cut the cross strips (H) to 7" and 10" lengths. Use wood screws to attach them at 3" intervals in a staggered pattern on the side trellis pieces **(photo H).** You can adjust the sizes and placement of the cross strips but, for best appearance, retain some symmetry of placement.

2. Fasten cross strips to the top trellis in the same manner. Make sure the cross strips that fit across the top trellis are arranged in similar fashion to the side strips.

APPLY FINISHING TOUCHES.

1. To protect the arbor, coat the cedar wood with clear wood sealer. After the finish dries, the arbor is ready to be placed onto your deck or patio or in a quiet corner of your yard.

2. Because of its sturdy construction, the arbor can simply be set onto a hard, flat surface. If you plan to install a permanent seat in the arbor, you should anchor it to the ground. For decks, try to position the arbor so you can screw the legs to the rim of the deck or toenail the legs into the deck

boards. You can buy fabricated metal post stakes, available at most building centers, to use when anchoring the arbor to the ground.

> **TIP**
>
> *Create an arbor seat by resting two 2 × 10 cedar boards on the rails in each side frame. Overhang the rails by 6" or so, and drive a few 3" deck screws through the boards and into the rails to secure the seat.*

Trellis Planter

Two traditional yard furnishings are combined into one compact package.

The decorative trellis and the cedar planter are two staples found in many yards and gardens. By integrating the appealing shape and pattern of the trellis with the rustic, functional design of the cedar planter, this project showcases the best qualities of both furnishings.

Because the 2 × 2 lattice trellis is attached to the planter, not permanently fastened to a wall or railing, the trellis planter can be moved easily to follow changing sunlight patterns, or to occupy featured areas of your yard. It is also easy to move into storage during non-growing seasons. You may even want to consider installing wheels or casters on the base for greater mobility.

Building the trellis planter is a very simple job. The trellis portion is made entirely of strips of 2 × 2 cedar, fashioned together in a crosshatch pattern. The planter bin is a basic wood box, with panel sides and a two-board bottom with drainage holes, that rests on a scalloped base. The trellis is screwed permanently to the back of the planter bin.

Stocking the trellis planter with plantings is a matter of personal taste and growing conditions. In most areas, ivy, clematis and grapevines are good examples of climbing plants that can be trained up the trellis. Ask at your local gardening center for advice on plantings. Plants can be set into the bin in containers, or you can fill the bin with potting soil and plant directly in the bin.

CONSTRUCTION MATERIALS

Quantity	Lumber
1	2 × 6" × 8' cedar
1	2 × 4" × 6' cedar
4	2 × 2" × 8' cedar
3	1 × 6" × 8' cedar
1	1 × 2" × 6' cedar

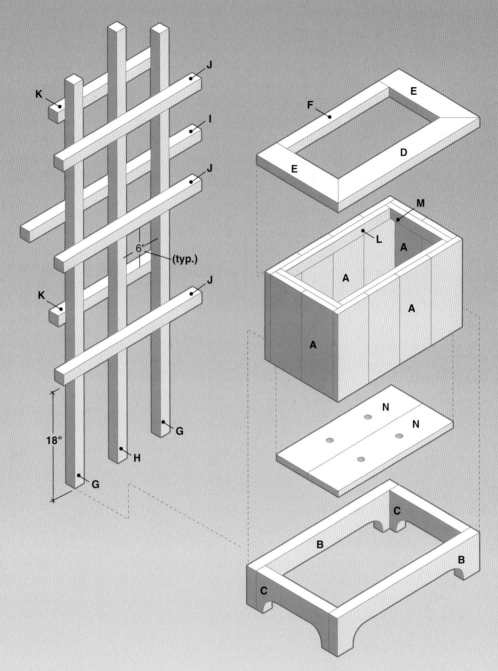

OVERALL SIZE:
69" HIGH
17¼" DEEP
30" LONG

6" (typ.)

18"

Cutting List				
Key	**Part**	**Dimension**	**Pcs.**	**Material**
A	Box slat	⅞ × 5½ × 13"	12	Cedar
B	Base front/back	1½ × 5½ × 25"	2	Cedar
C	Base end	1½ × 5½ × 12¾"	2	Cedar
D	Cap front	1½ × 3½ × 25"	1	Cedar
E	Cap end	1½ × 3½ × 14¼"	2	Cedar
F	Cap back	1½ × 1½ × 18"	1	Cedar
G	End post	1½ × 1½ × 59½"	2	Cedar

Cutting List				
Key	**Part**	**Dimension**	**Pcs.**	**Material**
H	Center post	1½ × 1½ × 63½"	1	Cedar
I	Long rail	1½ × 1½ × 30"	1	Cedar
J	Medium rail	1½ × 1½ × 24"	3	Cedar
K	Short rail	1½ × 1½ × 18"	2	Cedar
L	Long cleat	⅞ × 1½ × 18½"	2	Cedar
M	Short cleat	⅞ × 1½ × 11"	2	Cedar
N	Bottom board	⅞ × 5½ × 20¼"	2	Cedar

Materials: Moisture-resistant glue, #8 2" wood screws, 1⅝" and 2½" deck screws, finishing materials.

Note: Measurements reflect the actual size of dimension lumber.

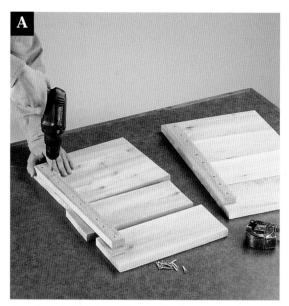

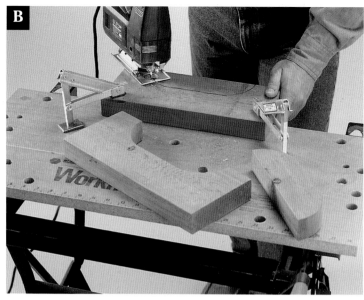

Attach the side cleats flush with the tops of the side boards.

Use a jig saw to make scalloped cutouts in all four base pieces— make sure the cutouts in matching pieces are the same.

Directions: Trellis Planter

BUILD THE PLANTER BIN.
1. Cut the box slats (A) and cleats (L, M) to length. Arrange the slats edge to edge in two groups of four and two groups of two, with tops and bottoms flush.
2. Center a long cleat (L) at the top of each set of four slats, so the distance from each end of the cleat to the end of the panel is the same. Attach the cleats to the four-slat panels by driving 1⅝" deck screws **(photo A)** through the cleats and into the slats.
3. Lay the short cleats (M) at the tops of the two-slat panels. Attach them to the slats the same way.
4. Arrange all four panels into a box shape and apply moisture-resistant wood glue to the joints. Attach the panels by driving 1⅝" deck screws through the four-slat panels and into the ends of the two-slat panels.

INSTALL THE BIN BOTTOM.
1. Cut the bottom boards (N) to length. Set the bin upside down on your work surface, and mark reference lines on the inside faces of the panels, ⅞" in from the bottom of the bin. Insert the bottom boards into the bin, aligned with the reference lines to create a ⅞" recess. Scraps of 1× cedar can be slipped beneath the bottom boards as spacers.
2. Drill ⅛" pilot holes through the panels. Counterbore the holes slightly with a counterbore bit. Fasten the bottom boards by driving 1⅝" deck screws through the panels, and into the edges and ends of the bottom boards.

BUILD THE PLANTER BASE.
The planter base is scalloped to create feet at the corners.
1. Cut the base front and back (B) and the base ends (C) to length. To draw the contours for the scallops on the front and back boards, set the point of a compass at the bottom edge of the base front, 5" in from one end. Set the compass to a 2½" radius, and draw a curve to mark the curved end of the cutout (see *Diagram,* page 295). Draw a straight line to connect the tops of the curves, 2½" up from the bottom of the board, to complete the scalloped cutout.
2. Make the cutout with a jig saw, then sand any rough spots in the cut. Use the board as a template for marking a matching cutout on the base back.
3. Draw a similar cutout on one base end, except with the point of the compass 3½" in from the ends. Cut out both end pieces with a jig saw **(photo B).**
4. Draw reference lines for wood screws, ¾" from the ends of the base front and back. Drill three evenly spaced pilot holes through the lines. Counterbore the holes. Fasten the base ends between the base front and back by driving three evenly spaced deck screws at each joint.

ATTACH THE BIN TO THE BASE.
1. Set the base frame and planter bin on their backs. Position the planter bin inside

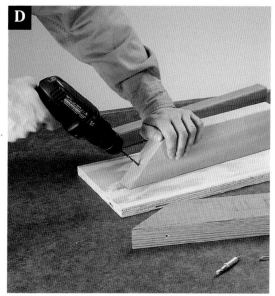

The recess beneath the bottom boards in the planter bin provides access for driving screws.

Before attaching the cap ends, drill pilot holes through the mitered ends of the cap front ends.

the base so it extends ⅞" past the top of the base.

2. Drive 1⅝" deck screws through the planter bin and into the base to secure the parts **(photo C).**

MAKE THE CAP FRAME.

1. Cut the cap front (D), cap ends (E) and cap back (F) to length. Cut 45° miters at one end of each cap end, and at both ends of the cap front.

2. Join the mitered corners by drilling pilot holes through the joints **(photo D).** Counterbore the holes. Fasten the pieces with glue and 2½" deck screws. Clamp the cap front and cap ends to the front of your worktable to hold them while you drive the screws.

3. Fasten the cap back between the cap ends with wood screws, making sure the back edges are flush. Set the cap frame on the planter bin so the back edges are flush. Drill pilot holes. Counterbore them. Drive 2½" deck screws through the cap frame and into the side and end cleats.

MAKE THE TRELLIS.

The trellis is made from pieces in a crosshatch pattern. The exact number and placement of the pieces is up to you—use the same spacing we used (see *Diagram),* or create your own.

1. Cut the end posts (G), center post (H) and rails (I, J, K) to length. Lay the end posts and center post together side by side with their bottom edges flush, so you can gang-mark the rail positions.

2. Use a square as a guide for drawing lines across all three posts, 18" up from the bottom. Draw the next line 7½" up from the first. Draw additional lines across the posts, spaced 7½" apart.

3. Cut two 7"-wide scrap blocks, and use them to separate the posts as you assemble the trellis. Attach the rails to the posts in the sequence shown in the *Diagram,* using 2½" screws **(photo E).** Alternate from the fronts to the backs of the posts when installing the rails.

APPLY FINISHING TOUCHES.

Fasten the trellis to the back of the planter bin so the bottoms of the posts rest on the top edge of the base. Drill pilot holes in the posts. Counterbore the holes. Drive 2½" deck screws through the posts and into the cap frame. With a 1"-dia. spade bit, drill a pair of drainage holes in each bottom board. Stain the project with an exterior wood stain.

Temporary spacers hold the posts in position while the trellis crossrails are attached.

Planters

These cedar planters are simple projects that can transform a plain plant container into an attractive outdoor accessory.

CONSTRUCTION MATERIALS

Quantity	Lumber
1	1 × 10" × 6' cedar
1	¼ × 20 × 20" hardboard or plywood

Add a decorative touch to your deck, porch or patio with these stylish cedar planters. Created using square pieces of cedar fashioned together in different design patterns, the styles shown above feature circular cutouts that are sized to hold a standard 24-ounce coffee can. To build them, simply cut 1 × 10 cedar to 9¼" lengths, then make 7¼"-diameter cutouts in the components as necessary. We used a router and template to make the cutouts with production speed. Follow the assembly instructions to create the three designs above. Or, you can create your own designs by rearranging the components or altering the cutout size.

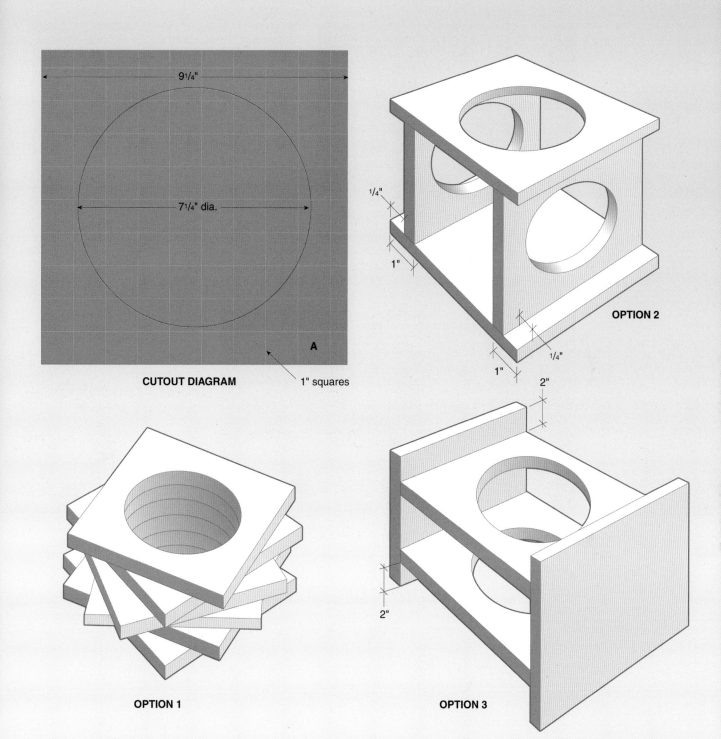

9¼"

7¼" dia.

A

CUTOUT DIAGRAM

1" squares

¼"

1"

¼"

1"

2"

OPTION 2

OPTION 1

2"

2"

OPTION 3

Cutting List				
Key	**Part**	**Dimension**	**Pcs.**	**Material**
A	Component	¾ × 9¼ × 9¼"	*	Cedar

Materials: Moisture-resistant glue, 2" deck screws, 24-ounce coffee can, finishing materials.

* Number of pieces varies according to planter style.

Note: Measurements reflect the actual size of dimension lumber.

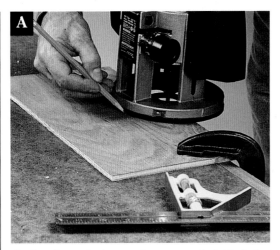

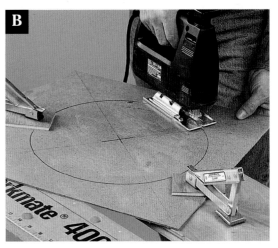

Outline the router base onto scrap material to help determine the router-base radius.

Cut out the router template using a jig saw.

Drill a starter hole for the router bit in the centers of the components.

Directions:
Planters

MAKE THE ROUTER TEMPLATE.

Using a router and a router template is an excellent method for doing production-style work with uniform results. To create the cutout components for the planters, make a circular template to use as a cutting guide for the router. To determine the size of the template circle, add the radius of your router base to the radius of your finished cutout (3⅝" in the project as shown).

1. Begin by finding the radius of your router base. First, install a 1"-long straight bit in your router. (For fast cutting, use a ¾"-diameter bit, but make sure you use the same bit for making the template and cutting the components.) Make a shallow cut into the edge of a piece of scrap wood. With the router bit stopped, trace around the outside edge of the router base with a pencil **(photo A).**

2. Measure from the perimeter of the router cut to the router-base outline to find the radius.

Add 3⅝" for the radius of a 24-ounce coffee can. Using a compass, draw a circle with this measurement onto the template material. Cut out the template with a jig saw **(photo B).**

MAKE THE PARTS.

The planters are built from identical components (A).

1. Cut the number of components required for your design. Make circular cutouts on those components that require them. To do that, draw diagonal lines connecting the corners of the component. The point of intersection is the center of the square board. Center the template on the component and clamp it in place.

2. Use a drill to bore a 1"-diameter starter hole for the router bit (unless you are using a plunge router—see *Tip,* left) at the center **(photo C).** Position the router bit inside the hole.

3. Turn the router on and move it away from the starter hole until the router base contacts the template. Pull the router in a counterclockwise direction around the inside of the template to make the cutout. Sand sharp edges with sandpaper.

Assembly Options

Option 1. *Attach the pieces on the stacked planter from top to bottom, ending with a solid base. To make this stacked planter, you need six pieces of 1 × 10 cedar. Cut them to length, and rout circular shapes in five of them. The solid piece will be the base. Stack the pieces on top of the base component. Place a painted coffee can in the center and arrange the sections to achieve a spiraling effect (see* Diagram, *page 299). Use a pencil to mark the locations of the pieces. Remove the can and fasten the pieces together using glue and deck screws. Attach the pieces by driving the deck screws through the lower pieces into the upper pieces, fastening the base last.*

Option 2. *Use four components on this option to create a planter with three cutout components and a solid base. Measure and mark lines 1" from each side edge on the solid component and one of the cutout components. Attach the inner components with their inside faces flush with these lines. Fasten the solid component to the sides with moisture-resistant glue and deck screws. Attach the remaining cutout component to finish the planter. Insert a painted coffee can.*

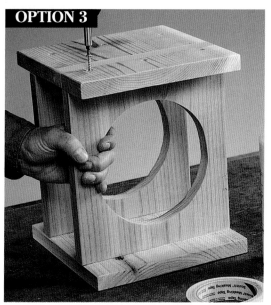

Option 3. *Attach two components with circular cutouts to the inside faces of two solid components to make this planter. Measure and mark guidelines 2" from the top and bottom edges on the two solid components. Fasten the two cutout components between the others with moisture-resistant glue and deck screws, making sure their outside edges are flush with the drawn guidelines. Insert a painted coffee can.*

Sundial

This throwback to ancient times casts a shadow of classical elegance in your yard or garden— and it tells time, too.

Sundials have been popular garden accessories for just about as long as there have been formal gardens. While their time-telling function is not as critical as it was around the time of the Roman Empire, sundials today continue to dot formal gardens, and even suburban flower beds, throughout the world.

The design for the cedar sundial shown here contains a few elements that harken back to ancient times. The fluted pillar suggests the famous architectural columns of Old World cathedrals and amphitheaters. The plates at the top and base are trimmed with a Roman Ogee router bit for a Classical touch. Making these cuts requires a router and several different types of router bits. If you don't mind a little plainer look, you can bypass the router work and simply round over the parts with a power sander.

This sundial is not just another stylish accent for your yard or garden. You can actually use it to tell time. Simply mount the triangular shadow-caster (called a "gnomon") to the face of the sundial, and orient it so it points north. Then calibrate the face at twelve hourly intervals. That way you know that the positioning of the numbers is accurate.

This sundial is secured to the ground with a post anchor that fits around a mounting block on the underside of the sundial. The anchor is driven into the ground, making it easy to move the sundial (you'll appreciate this the first time Daylight Saving Time comes around).

CONSTRUCTION MATERIALS

Quantity	Lumber
1	1 × 12" × 4' cedar
1	6 × 6" × 4' cedar
1	4 × 4" × 4' cedar

OVERALL SIZE:
40⅛" HIGH
11¼" WIDE
11¼" LONG

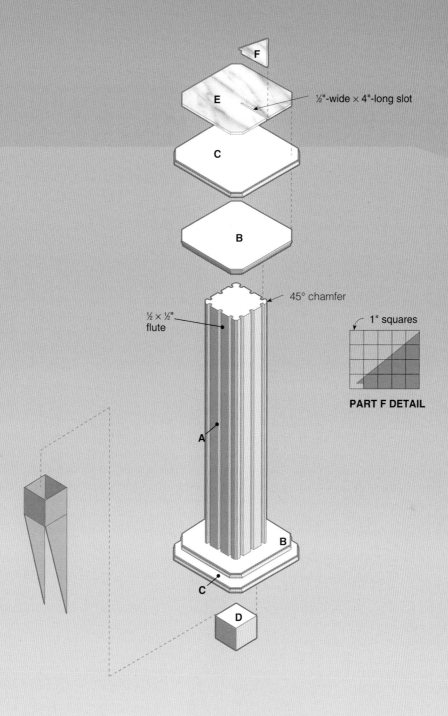

½"-wide × 4"-long slot

45° chamfer

½ × ½"
flute

1" squares

PART F DETAIL

Cutting List				
Key	**Part**	**Dimension**	**Pcs.**	**Material**
A	Column	5½ × 5½ × 32¾"	1	Cedar
B	Inner plate	⅞ × 10 × 10"	2	Cedar
C	Outer plate	⅞ × 11¼ × 11¼"	2	Cedar

Cutting List				
Key	**Part**	**Dimension**	**Pcs.**	**Material**
D	Mounting block	3½ × 3½ × 3"	1	Cedar
E	Dial face	⅜ × 10 × 10"	1	Ceramic tile
F	Gnomon	¼ × 3½ × 16½"	1	Plexiglass

Materials: 1¼" and 2" galvanized deck screws, construction adhesive, silicone caulk, clock-face numbers, 4 × 4 metal post anchor.

Note: Measurements reflect the actual size of dimension lumber.

Directions: Sundial

MAKE THE COLUMN.
1. Cut the column (A) to length from a 4'-long 6 × 6" cedar post.
2. Use a combination square as a marking gauge to lay out three pairs of parallel lines lengthwise on each face of the column—the lines in each pair should be ½" apart **(photo A)**. These lines form the outlines for the fluted grooves that will be cut into the post. The two outer-flute outlines should start ¾" from the edge, and the middle flute should be 1¼" from each outer outline. Install a ½" core box bit in your router—a core box bit is a straight bit with a rounded bottom.

3. Hook the edge guide on the foot of your router over the edge of the post (or, use a straightedge cutting guide to guide the router), and cut each ½"-deep flute in two passes.
4. After all 12 flutes are cut, install a 45° chamfering bit in your router and trim off all four edges of the column **(photo B)**.

CUT THE FLAT PARTS.
Two flat, square boards are sandwiched together and attached at the top and bottom of the column.
1. Cut the inner plates (B) and outer plates (C) to size from 1 × 12 cedar.
2. After the plates are cut to final size, trim off a corner with 1" legs from all four corners of each plate, using a jig saw **(photo C)**.
3. Install a piloted bit in your router to cut edge contours (we used a double ogee fillet bit), then cut the roundovers on all edges of the plates **(photo D)**.

MAKE THE SUNDIAL FACE.
We used a piece of octagonal marble floor tile for the face (E) of our sundial. If you prefer, you can use inexpensive ceramic floor tile instead of marble, but either way you should purchase a piece of tile that is already cut to the correct size and shape for the project (cutting floor tile is very difficult).
1. Lay out the ¼"-wide, 4"-long slot for the gnomon, centered on one edge of the sundial face. Have the slot cut at a tile shop (if this is a problem, you are probably better off eliminating the slot than trying to cut it yourself).
2. Next, mark a 1"-square grid pattern on a small piece of ¼"-thick white plexiglass.
3. Lay out the shape and dimensions of the gnomon, following the *Grid Pattern* (F) on page 303.
4. Mount a wood-cutting blade with medium-sized teeth in your jig saw, and cut the gnomon shape.
5. Sand the edges with 100-grit sandpaper, then finish-sand with fine paper, up to 180-or 220-grit.

Lay out three ½"-wide flutes on each column face using a combination square as a marking gauge.

Trim off the corners of the column with a router and a 45° chamfering bit.

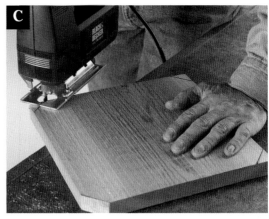
Cut triangular cutoffs with 1" legs at each corner of each plate.

Cut decorative profiles along the edges of the inner and outer plates.

Make sure screws driven through the outer plate are at least 2" in from the edges.

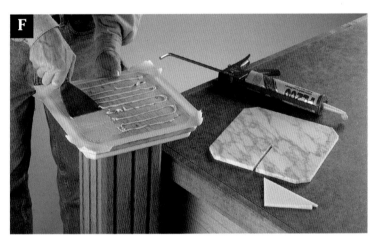

Frame the top of the top outer plate with masking tape, then apply a layer of construction adhesive to attach the sundial face.

6. Fit the gnomon into the slot on the sundial face.

ASSEMBLE THE SUNDIAL.

1. Attach an inner plate, centered, to each end of the column, using 2½" deck screws.
2. Cut the mounting block (D) to length from 4 × 4 cedar (or two pieces of cedar 2 × 4).
3. Attach the block to one face of the bottom outer plate, centered, using deck screws driven through the plate and into the block. Do not attach the base plate to the column assembly yet.
4. Attach the top outer plate to the top inner plate, making sure

the overhang is equal on all four sides and the corners align **(photo E).**
5. Set the post on its base, and attach the sundial face (E) to the top outer plate, using construction adhesive **(photo F).** Make sure the face is centered and in alignment.
6. Place construction adhesive into the gnomon slot, then insert the gnomon (F) into the slot and press firmly. Seal all joints around the edges of the gnomon and the edges of the face, using clear silicone caulk.
7. Attach the bottom outer plate by laying the column on its side and driving 1¼" deck

screws up through the outer plate and into the inner plate.
8. Coat wood parts with exterior wood stain.

INSTALL & CALIBRATE THE SUNDIAL.

1. Choose a sunny spot to install your sundial. Lay a piece of scrap wood on the spot, pointing directly north (use a magnetic compass for reference).
2. Purchase a metal post anchor for a 4 × 4 post (most have an attached metal stake about 18" long).
3. Drive the post anchor (G) into the ground at the desired location, making sure one side of the box part of the anchor is perpendicular to the scrap piece facing north.
4. Insert the mounting block on the base of the post into the anchor, making sure the gnomon is facing north.
5. Calibrate the sundial by marking a point at the edge of the shadow from the gnomon at the top of every hour. Apply hour markers at those points. We used metal Roman numerals from a craft store, attached with clear silicone caulk.

Driveway Marker

Build an inviting yard ornament that graces the entrance to your driveway or front walk and directs foot traffic where you want it to go.

CONSTRUCTION MATERIALS

Quantity	Lumber
1	2 × 4" × 8' cedar
1	1 × 6" × 6' cedar
1	1 × 6" × 8' cedar
4	1 × 2" × 8' cedar

Bestow a sense of order on your front yard by building this handsome cedar driveway marker. Position it on your lawn at the entry to your driveway to keep cars from wandering off the paved surface. Or, set a driveway marker on each side of your front walk to create a formal entry to your home.

This freestanding driveway marker has many benefits you'll appreciate. The fence-style slats slope away from the corner post to create a sense of flow. The broad corner post can be used to mount address numbers, making your home easier to find for visitors and in emergencies. And behind the front slats you'll find a spacious planter.

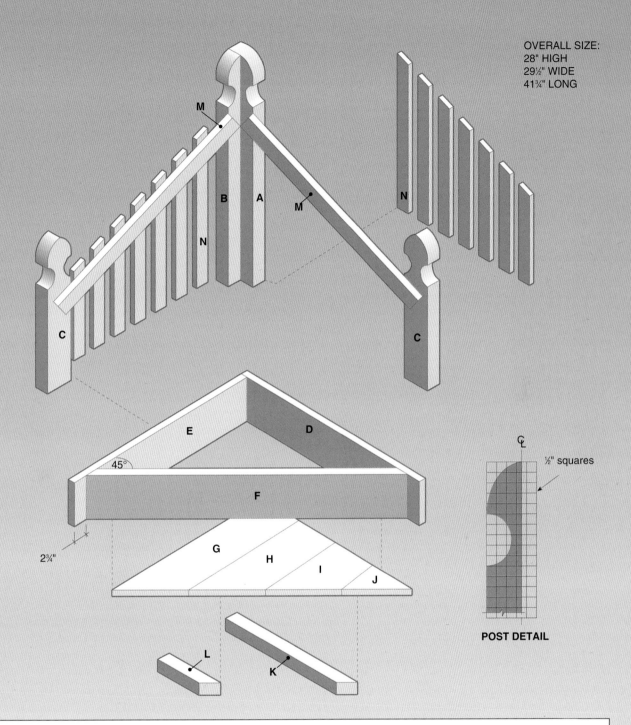

½" squares

2¾"

45°

POST DETAIL

Cutting List				
Key	Part	Dimension	Pcs.	Material
A	Corner post	1½ × 3½ × 28"	1	Cedar
B	Corner post	1½ × 1½ × 28"	1	Cedar
C	End post	1½ × 3½ × 18½"	2	Cedar
D	Planter side	⅞ × 5½ × 26½"	1	Cedar
E	Planter side	⅞ × 5½ × 25⅝"	1	Cedar
F	Planter back	⅞ × 5½ × 33"	1	Cedar
G	Bottom board	⅞ × 5½ × 23"	1	Cedar

Cutting List				
Key	Part	Dimension	Pcs.	Material
H	Bottom board	⅞ × 5½ × 17"	1	Cedar
I	Bottom board	⅞ × 5½ × 11"	1	Cedar
J	Bottom board	⅞ × 5½ × 6"	1	Cedar
K	Long cleat	1½ × 1½ × 19"	1	Cedar
L	Short cleat	1½ × 1½ × 9"	1	Cedar
M	Stringer	⅞ × 1½ × 27"	2	Cedar
N	Slat	⅞ × 1½ × 20"	14	Cedar

Materials: Moisture-resistant glue, 1¼", 1½", 2" and 2½" deck screws, 2" brass numbers (optional), finishing materials.

Note: Measurements reflect the actual size of dimension lumber.

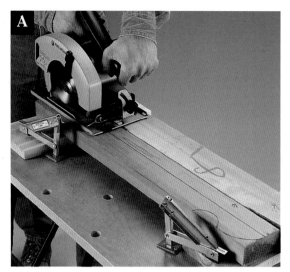

Rip the thin corner post to width with a circular saw.

Sand the top of the corner post assembly so the joint is smooth.

Lay the bin frame on the bottom boards and trace along the back inside edge to mark cutting lines.

Directions: Driveway Marker

CUT THE POSTS.

This driveway marker is a free-standing yard ornament supported by single 2 × 4 posts at each end and a doubled 2 × 4 post at the corner.

1. Cut the corner posts (A, B) and end posts (C) to length. Draw a ½"-square grid pattern at the top of one of the end posts, using the grid pattern on page 307 as a reference. Mark a centerpoint at the top of the post and draw the pattern as shown on one side. Reverse the pattern on the other side to create the finished shape. Use a jig saw to cut the end post to shape. Mount a drum sander attachment in your electric drill and use it to smooth out the cut.

2. Use the shaped end post as a template to mark the other end post. Cut and sand it.

3. To make the corner posts, mark centerpoints at the top of each corner post. Trace the contour of one end post on one side of the centerline.

4. On one corner post, draw a line down the length of the post, 2" in from the side with no contour cutout. This will be the narrower post (B). To rip this post to width, attach two pieces of scrap wood to your work surfaces. Screw the post, facedown, to the wood scrap (making sure to drive screws in the waste area of the post).

5. Butt a scrap of the same thickness as the post next to the post, to use as a guide for the circular saw. Attach the guide board to the wood scraps. Set the edge guide on the saw so it follows the outside edge of the scrap. Make the rip cut along the cutting line **(photo A).** Cut the contours at the tops of the corner posts and sand smooth.

BUILD THE CORNER POST.

1. Apply glue to the ripped edge of the narrower post board (B). Lay it on the face of the wider post board (A), so the joint at the corner is flush and the tops of the contours come together in a smooth line.

2. Drill ⅛" pilot holes in the wider board at 4" intervals. Counterbore the holes ¼" deep, using a counterbore bit. Drive 2½" deck screws through the wider board and into the edge of the narrower board. After the glue sets, sand the tops smooth **(photo B).**

MAKE THE PLANTER FRAME.

The triangular planter fits in the back of the driveway marker.

1. Cut the planter sides (D, E) to length, making square cuts at the ends. The ends of the planter back (F) are mitered so they fit flush against the sides when the bin is formed. Set your circular saw to make a 45° cut. Cut the planter back to length, making sure the bevels

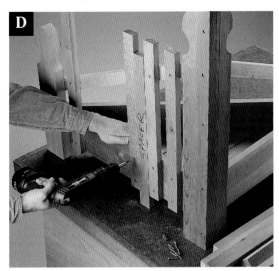

Use one slat as a spacer to set the correct gap as you fasten the slats to the bin and the stringers.

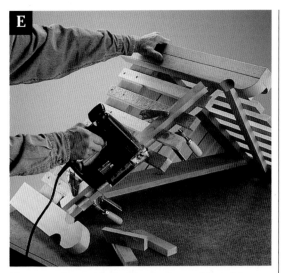

Use a cutting guide to trim the tops of the slats so they extend beyond the tops of the stringers.

both go inward from the same side (see *Diagram,* page 307).
2. Apply glue to the ends of the planter back. Assemble the back and the sides by drilling pilot holes in the outside faces of the sides. Counterbore the holes. Drive 2" deck screws through the sides and into the ends of the back. This will create a setback of about 2¾" from the joints to the ends of the sides.

ATTACH THE BIN BOTTOM.
1. Cut the bottom boards (G, H, I, J) to length. Lay the boards on your work surfaces, arranged from shortest to longest, and butted together edge to edge. Set the bin frame on top of the boards so the inside edges of the frame sides are flush with the outer edges of the boards, and the boards extend past the back edge of the frame. Trace along the inside of the frame back to mark cutting lines on the bottom boards **(photo C).** Cut them with a circular saw.
2. Cut the long cleat (K) and short cleat (L) to length, making a 45° miter cut at one end of each cleat. Turn the planter

bin upside down. Attach the reinforcing cleats so one is 2½"-3" from Side D and the other is about 12" from the same side. Attach them by driving two 2" deck screws through each plant side and back into the end of each cleat.
3. Right the frame. Position the bottom boards flush with the bottom of the frame and attach them with glue and 2" deck screws, driven through the frame and into the ends of the bottom boards.

ATTACH THE
BIN AND POSTS.
1. Set the bin on 2"-tall spacers. Fit the corner post assembly over the front corner of the bin and attach with glue and 1½" deck screws.
2. Attach the end posts so each is 29½" away from the corner post assembly.

ATTACH THE
STRINGERS AND SLATS.
The stringers (M) are attached between the tops of the posts to support the tops of the slats.
1. Cut the stringers to length. Attach them to the insides of

the posts so the top edges are 1½" below the bottom of the post contour at the point where the stringer meets each post.
2. Cut all slats (N) to length. (The tops will be trimmed after the slats are installed.) Attach them to the bin and the stringers, spaced at 1½" intervals, using 1¼" deck screws. Use a slat as a spacer **(photo D).** Install all 14 slats, making sure the bottoms are flush with the bin bottom.
3. Clamp a piece of 1 × 2 scrap against the outside faces of the slats for a cutting guide—the scrap should be directly opposite the stringer on the back side of the slats. Cut along the guide with a jig saw to trim the slats so the tops are slightly above the top of the stringer **(photo E).**

APPLY FINISHING TOUCHES.
Sand all exposed surfaces and apply two or more coats of exterior wood stain. If your marker will be visible from the curb, you may want to attach 2"-high brass numbers to the corner post to indicate your street address.

PROJECT
POWER TOOLS

Plant Boxes

*Build these simple plant boxes in whichever
size or number best meets your needs.*

CONSTRUCTION MATERIALS*

Quantity	Lumber
3	1 × 2" × 8' cedar
6	1 × 4" × 8' cedar
1	⅜" × 4 × 8' fir siding
1	¾" × 2 × 4' CDX plywood

*To build all three plant boxes as shown

Planters and plant boxes come in a vast array of sizes and styles, and there is a good reason for that. Everyone's needs are different. Rather than build just one planter that may or may not work for you, try this handy planter design. It can easily be changed to fit your space and planting demands.

This project provides measurements for planters in three sizes and shapes: short and broad for flowers or container plants; medium for spices and herbs or small trees and shrubs; and tall and narrow for vegetables or flowering vines that will cascade over the cedar surfaces. The three boxes are proportional to one another— build all three and arrange them in a variety of patterns, including the tiered effect shown above.

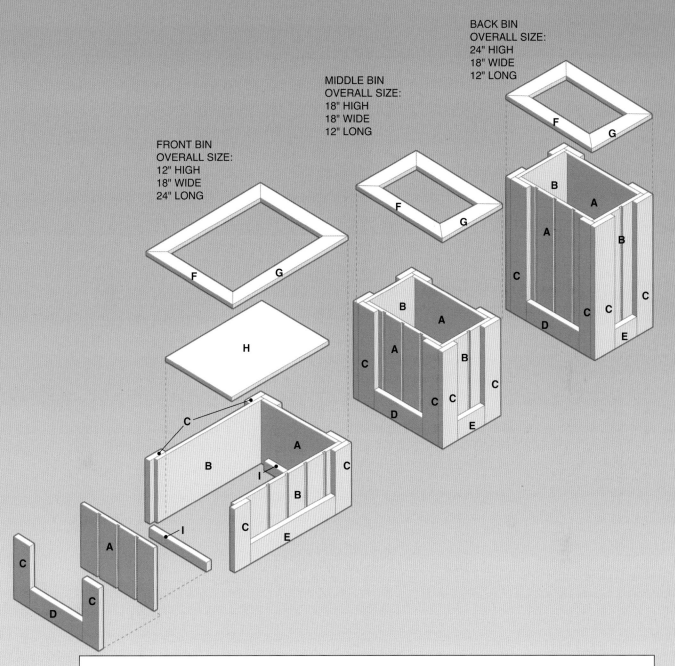

FRONT BIN
OVERALL SIZE:
12" HIGH
18" WIDE
24" LONG

MIDDLE BIN
OVERALL SIZE:
18" HIGH
18" WIDE
12" LONG

BACK BIN
OVERALL SIZE:
24" HIGH
18" WIDE
12" LONG

		Cutting List						
Key	**Part**	**Front Bin Dimension**	**Pcs.**	**Middle Bin Dimension**	**Pcs.**	**Back Bin Dimension**	**Pcs.**	**Material**
A	End panel	⅝ × 15 × 11⅛"	2	⅝ × 15 × 17⅛"	2	⅝ × 15 × 23⅛"	2	Siding
B	Side panel	⅝ × 22¼ × 11⅛"	2	⅝ × 10¼ × 17⅛"	2	⅝ × 10¼ × 23⅛"	2	Siding
C	Corner trim	⅞ × 3½ × 11⅛"	8	⅞ × 3½ × 17⅛"	8	⅞ × 3½ × 23⅛"	8	Cedar
D	Bottom trim	⅞ × 3½ × 9¼"	2	⅞ × 3½ × 9¼"	2	⅞ × 3½ × 9¼"	2	Cedar
E	Bottom trim	⅞ × 3½ × 17"	2	⅞ × 3½ × 5"	2	⅞ × 3½ × 5"	2	Cedar
F	Top cap	⅞ × 1½ × 18"	2	⅞ × 1½ × 18"	2	⅞ × 1½ × 18"	2	Cedar
G	Top cap	⅞ × 1½ × 24"	2	⅞ × 1½ × 12"	2	⅞ × 1½ × 12"	2	Cedar
H	Bottom panel	¾ × 14½ × 19½"	1	¾ × 14½ × 8½"	1	¾ × 14½ × 8½"	1	Plywood
I	Cleat	⅞ × 1½ × 12"	2	⅞ × 1½ × 12"	2	⅞ × 1½ × 12"	2	Cedar

Materials: 1¼", 1½" and 3" deck screws, 6d galvanized finish nails, finishing materials.

Note: Measurements reflect the actual size of dimension lumber.

Directions:
Plant Boxes

Whatever the size of the plant box or boxes you are building, you'll use the same basic steps for construction. The only difference between the three boxes is the size of some components. If you need larger, smaller, broader or taller plant boxes than those shown, it's easy to create your own cutting list based on the *Diagram* and dimensions shown on page 311. If you are building several planters, do some planning and sketching to make efficient use of your wood and to save time by gang-cutting parts that are the same size and shape.

MAKE AND ASSEMBLE THE BOX PANELS.

The end and side panels are rectangular pieces of sheet siding fastened together with deck screws. You can use fir sheet siding with 4"-on-center grooves for a decorative look. Or, you can substitute any exterior-rated sheet goods (or even dimension lumber) to match the rest of your yard or home.
1. Cut the end panels (A) and side panels (B) to size, using a circular saw and straightedge cutting guide **(photo A).**
2. Lay an end panel facedown

Cut the end panels and side panels to size using a circular saw and a straightedge cutting guide.

on a flat work surface and butt the side panel, face-side-out, up to the end of the end panel. Mark positions for pilot holes in the side panel. Drill ⅛" pilot holes. Counterbore the holes slightly so the heads are beneath the surface of the wood. Fasten the side panel to the end panel with 1½" deck screws.
3. Position the second side panel at the other end of the end panel and repeat the procedure.
4. Lay the remaining end panel facedown on the work surface. Position the side panel assembly over the end panel, placing the end panel between the side panels and keeping the edges of the side panels flush with the edges of the end panel. Drill pilot holes in the side panels. Counterbore the holes. Fasten the side panels to the end panel with deck screws.

ATTACH THE TRIM.

The cedar trim serves not only as a decorative element, but also as a structural reinforcement to the side panels. Most

cedar has a rough texture on one side. For a rustic look, install your trim pieces with the rough side facing out. For a more finished appearance, install the pieces with the smooth side facing out.
1. Cut the corner trim (C) to length. Overlap the edges of the corner trim pieces at the corners to create a square butt joint. Fasten the corner trim pieces directly to the panels by driving 1¼" deck screws through the inside faces of the panels and into the corner trim pieces **(photo B).** For additional support, drive screws or galvanized finish nails through the overlapping corner trim pieces and into the edges of the adjacent trim piece (this is called "lock-nailing").
2. Cut the bottom trim pieces (D, E) to length. Fasten the pieces to the end and side panels, between the corner trim pieces. Drive 1¼" deck screws through the side and end panels and into the bottom trim pieces.

TIP

Make plant boxes portable by adding wheels or casters. If your yard or garden is partially shaded, attaching locking casters to the base of the plant boxes lets you move your plants to follow the sun, and can even be used to bring the plants indoors during colder weather. Use locking wheels or casters with brass or plastic housings.

Fasten the corner trim to the panels by driving deck screws through the panels into the trim.

TIP

Line plant boxes with landscape fabric before filling them with soil. This helps keep the boxes from discoloring, and also keeps the soil in the box, where it belongs. Simply cut a piece of fabric large enough to wrap the box (as if you were gift-wrapping it), then fold it so it fits inside the box. Staple it at the top, and trim off the excess. For better soil drainage, drill a few 1"-dia. holes in the bottom of the box and add a layer of small stones at the bottom of the box.

INSTALL THE TOP CAPS.

The top caps fit around the top of the plant box to create a thin ledge that keeps water from seeping into the end grain of the panels and trim pieces.

1. Cut the top caps (F, G) to length. Cut 45° miters at both ends of one cap piece, using a power miter saw or a miter box and backsaw. Tack the mitered cap piece to the top edge of the planter, keeping the outside edges flush with the outer edges of the corner trim pieces. For a proper fit, use this cap piece as a guide for marking and cutting the miters on the rest of the cap pieces.

2. Miter both ends of each piece and tack it to the box so it makes a square corner with the previously installed piece. If the corners do not work out exactly right, loosen the pieces and adjust the arrangement until everything is square. Permanently fasten all the cap pieces to the box with 6d galvanized finish nails.

INSTALL THE BOX BOTTOM.

The bottom of the planter box is supported by cleats (I) that are fastened inside the box, flush with the bottoms of the side and end panels.

1. Cut the cleats to length. Screw them to the end panels with 1½" deck screws **(photo C).** On the taller bins you may want to mount the cleats higher on the panels so the box won't need as much soil when filled. If you choose to do this, add cleats on the side panels for extra support.

2. Cut the bottom panel (H) to size from ¾"-thick exterior-rated plywood, such as CDX plywood. Set the bottom panel onto the cleats. You do not need to fasten it in place.

APPLY FINISHING TOUCHES.

After you've built all the boxes, sand all the edges and surfaces to remove rough spots and splinters. Apply two or three coats of exterior wood stain to all the surfaces to protect the wood. When the finish has dried, fill the boxes with potting soil. If you are using shorter boxes, you can simply place potted plants inside the planter box.

Attach 1 × 2 cleats to the inside faces of the box ends to support the bottom panel.

Prairie Windmill

With a mill section that turns and spins in the wind, this lively little windmill becomes the focal point of any garden.

Modeled loosely after the old turn-of-the-century windmills that dotted the prairie landscape, this fun, active garden accent may be just the thing to put some spice into your yard. With a solid, staked base firmly planted on the ground, this windmill spins and turns with the passing breezes.

We used cedar siding for the blades and tail of the mill section. The beveled cedar is the perfect shape and weight for catching the wind, and, because it's cedar, it will withstand the elements. The moving parts spin on lag screws and nylon washers, which perform better with moving parts than metal washers.

Overall, the most impressive part of this prairie windmill may be the geometrically strik-ing tower section, which rises from the base to anchor the spinning mill above. Despite its size, the tower section is very easy to make. You can set the completed windmill in the heart of your garden, or position it in a corner of your yard to create a unique accent. Either way, you won't be disappointed. This is a fun project, and you'll get a glowing sense of satisfaction when you see it spinning and turning in the wind like a real windmill—just the way you built it.

CONSTRUCTION MATERIALS

Quantity	Lumber
2	4 × 4" × 6' cedar
1	2 × 10" × 6' cedar
1	2×6" × 6' cedar
1	2×4" × 6' cedar
5	2×2"× 8' cedar
1	⅝ × 7" × 6' cedar siding
2	¾-dia. × 3' hardwood dowel

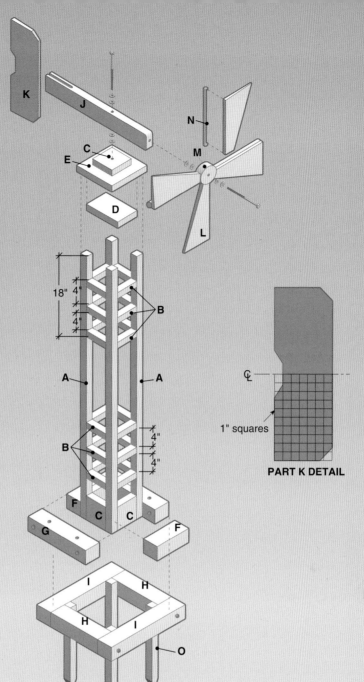

OVERALL SIZE:
80½" HIGH
19¼" WIDE
28" LONG

PART K DETAIL

1" squares

18" 4" 4"

4" 4"

		Cutting List					Cutting List		
Key	**Part**	**Dimension**	**Pcs.**	**Material**	**Key**	**Part**	**Dimension**	**Pcs.**	**Material**
A	Post	1½ × 1½ × 60"	4	Cedar	**I**	Foot side	3½ × 3½ × 19"	2	Cedar
B	Rail	1½ × 1½ × 5"	24	Cedar	**J**	Shaft	1½ × 3½ × 26½"	1	Cedar
C	Spacer	1½ × 5 × 5"	5	Cedar	**K**	Tail	⅝ × 7 × 24	1	Cedar siding
D	Top insert	1½ × 5 × 8"	1	Cedar	**L**	Blade	⅝ × 7 × 12"	4	Cedar siding
E	Top	1½ × 9¼ × 9¼"	1	Cedar	**M**	Hub	1½ × 4 × 4"	1	Cedar
F	Base end	3½ × 3½ × 8"	2	Cedar	**N**	Backer rod	¾ × ¾ × 13"	4	Dowel
G	Base side	3½ × 3½ × 15"	2	Cedar	**O**	Stake	1½ × 1½ × 18"	4	Cedar
H	Foot end	3½ × 3½ × 12"	2	Cedar					

Materials: Moisture-resistant glue, epoxy glue, ⅜ × 6" and ⅜ × 8" lag screws, 1¼", 2½" and 3" deck screws, #4 × 1" panhead screws, 1"-dia. nylon washers, finishing materials.

Note: Measurements reflect the actual size of dimension lumber.

Directions:
Prairie Windmill

BUILD THE TOWER FRAME.

The main frame for the windmill tower is made up of four posts connected by a series of short rails.

1. Cut the posts (A) and rails (B).

2. Clamp all four posts in a row, and mark the rail locations on all the posts, starting 9" up from one end of the posts and following the spacing shown in the *Diagram* on page 315.

3. Unclamp the posts, and arrange them in pairs. Attach the rails between the posts at the location marks to create two ladderlike assemblies. Use moisture-resistant glue and a single countersunk 2½" deck screw, driven through each post and into each rail.

4. Once the two assemblies are completed, join them together with rails to create the tower frame.

ADD THE TOWER BOTTOM & TOP.

1. Cut the spacers (C), top insert (D), and tower top (E) to size.

2. Fit four of the spacers between the posts at the bottom of the tower, and attach them with glue and 2½" deck screws driven through countersunk pilot holes.

3. Draw diagonal lines between opposite corners on the fifth spacer—the point where the lines intersect is the center of the board. Center the spacer on the tower top (E), and attach it with glue and 1¼" deck screws. Do not drive screws within 1" of the centerpoint.

4. Drill a ¼"-dia. pilot hole for a ⅜"-dia. lag screw through the center, making sure to keep

your drill perpendicular—the lag screw is driven later to secure the windmill to the tower.

5. Slip the top insert between the posts at the top of the tower, and fasten the insert with glue and screws.

6. Center the spacer and tower top over the top insert and fasten with glue and screws. After assembly is complete, use a power sander to smooth out all sharp edges **(photo A).**

The tower for the windmill is basically two ladder frames joined by rails. Sand sharp edges smooth.

ATTACH THE TOWER BASE.

The base of the tower is a heavy frame made from 4 × 4 cedar. When the windmill is installed in your yard, the base is attached to a 4 × 4 frame that is staked into the ground.

1. Cut the base ends (F) and base sides (G) to size.

2. Attach the base ends to the tower with 3" deck screws. To attach the base sides, drill ¼"-dia. pilot holes for ⅜"-dia. lag screws in the base sides, then counterbore the pilot holes with a 1" spade bit. Drive ⅜ × 8" lag screws with metal washers through the base sides and into the base ends.

3. Cut the foot ends (H) and foot sides (I) to size.

4. Drill pilot holes for counterbored lag screws through the the foot sides, and secure each foot side to the foot ends with a ⅜ × 8" lag screw.

MAKE THE TAIL.

1. Cut the tail (K) to length from beveled cedar lap siding.

2. Draw a 1" grid pattern onto the board, then draw the shape shown in the *Part K Detail*, page 315. Make sure the notch is on the thick edge. Cut with a jig saw.

MAKE THE SHAFT.

1. Cut the shaft (J) to size from a cedar 2 × 4.

2. Draw a centerline on one long edge of the shaft.

3. Measure the thickness of the beveled siding at several points, including the thin edge and the thick edge. Using drill bits with the same diameters as the thicknesses of the siding, drill holes along the centerline at points that correspond with the width of the tail (make sure that you drill holes at each end of the slot outline).

4. Connect the holes with a pair of straight lines to create an outline for the tail notch. Cut along the outlines with a handsaw **(photo B).**

5. Next, drill a centered, ⁷⁄₁₆"-dia. guide hole (for the lag screw that secures the shaft to the tower) through the top edge of the shaft, 9" from the front end. Also drill a ¼"-dia. pilot hole in the center of the front end of the shaft.

B

Drill holes of varying diameter to create an outline, then cut a slot for the tail into the shaft.

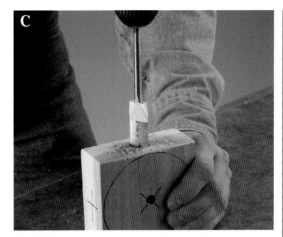

C

Drill ¾"-dia. × 1"-deep guide holes into the four sides of the hub to hold the backer rods.

MAKE THE BLADES & HUB.

1. Cut the propeller blades (L) and hub (M) to the full sizes indicated in the *Cutting List*.
2. On the thin edge of each blade board, draw a cutting line so the blade tapers from 7" in width at one end to 2" in width at the other end. Cut the blades to shape with a circular saw.
3. To make the circular hub, first draw diagonal lines between opposite corners on the face of the hub board. Set the point of a compass at the intersection point of the diagonal lines, and draw a circle with a 2" radius. Drill a ⁷⁄₁₆"-dia. hole through the centerpoint. Then mark drilling points on all four edges of the hub board, centered end to end and side to side, for drilling the holes that will hold the backer rods. Install a ¾"-dia. spade bit in your drill, then wrap a piece of masking tape 1" up from the bottom of the cutting part of the bit. Use the masking tape as a guide for stopping the holes when they reach 1" in depth. Drill ¾"-dia. × 1"-deep holes at the centerpoints in each edge of the hub board **(photo C).** Cut out the hub with a jig saw, following the round cutting line.

4. Cut the backer rods (N) from ¾" doweling, then sand a flat edge onto each rod, using a belt sander. Stop the flat edges 1" from the end of each dowel (this creates a flat mounting surface).

ASSEMBLE THE PROPELLER.

1. Attach the thick edge of each blade to the flat surface of a backer rod with three #4 × 1" panhead screws and epoxy glue **(photo D).**
2. Apply epoxy glue to the tail where it meets the shaft, and fasten it in the slot with 1¼" deck screws.
3. Before proceeding, apply exterior wood stain to all the wood parts, and apply paste wax in the guide holes in the hub and shaft.
4. Attach the blade assembly to the shaft with a ⅜ × 6" lag screw and pairs of 1"-dia. nylon washers inserted on each side of the hub.
5. Fasten the shaft to the tower with a ⅜ × 6" lag screw and pairs of nylon washers at the top and bottom edges of the shaft. Do not over-tighten the screws.

SET UP THE WINDMILL.

Position the 4 × 4" frame in the desired location in your yard or garden.
1. Cut the stakes (O), sharpening one end of each stake. Attach the stakes at the inside corners of the foot frame with screws, then drive the stakes into the ground. Attach the base frame to the foot frame with counterbored lag screws. Drive counterbored lag screws through the base sides and into the foot ends.

D

Glue the propeller blades into the holes to mount them on the hubs.

Luminary

Dress up your yard or garden with these warm, decorative accents that look even better in bunches.

CONSTRUCTION MATERIALS*

Quantity	Lumber
1	2 × 8 × *" cedar
1	1 × 2" × 8' cedar
1	1"-wide × 5' copper strip

*The shortest length available at most lumber yards is 6'. Since this is much more than you need for a single luminary, ask a yardworker if they have any scraps that are at least 6" long.

Luminaries are decorative outdoor accents that hold and protect candles or glass lamp chimneys. Traditionally, they are arranged in groups around an entrance or along a garden pathway. The simple slat-built luminary design shown here is easy and inexpensive to make. All you need are a few pieces of 1 × 2"

cedar, some 1"-thick strips of copper and a 6"-dia. cedar base. The copper trim, glass chimneys, and candles can be purchased at most craft stores. We used 22-gauge copper strips, which are thin enough to cut with scissors and will form easily around the luminary. Make sure to use copper nails to attach the strips.

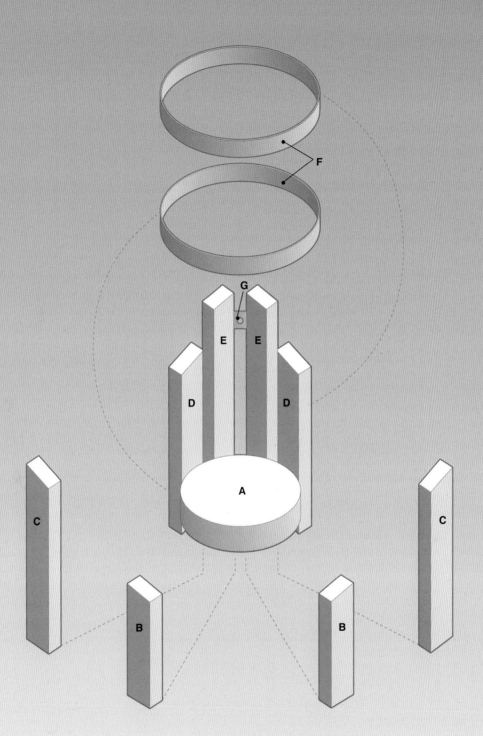

OVERALL SIZE:
14" HIGH
7¾" DIA.

Cutting List				
Key	Part	Dimension	Pcs.	Material
A	Base	1½ × 6 × 6"	1	Cedar
B	Front slat	⅞ × 1½ × 8"	2	Cedar
C	Short slat	⅞ × 1½ × 10"	2	Cedar
D	Middle slat	⅞ × 1½ × 12"	2	Cedar

Cutting List				
Key	Part	Dimension	Pcs.	Material
E	Back slat	⅞ × 1½ × 14"	2	Cedar
F	Strap	1 × 25"	2	Copper
G	Hanger	1 × 3½"	1	Copper

Materials: 1⅝" deck screws, ¾" copper nails, candle and glass candle chimney.

Note: Measurements reflect the actual size of dimension lumber.

Directions: Luminary

MAKE THE BASE.

The base for the luminary is a round piece of cedar cut with a jig saw. Because the luminary slats are attached to the sides of the base, it is important that the base be as symmetrical and smooth as you can get it.

1. Start by cutting the base (A) to 7¼" in length from a piece of 2 × 8 cedar (this will result in a square workpiece).

2. Draw diagonal lines between opposite corners. The point where the lines intersect is the center of the board. Set the point of a compass at the centerpoint, and draw a 6"-dia., circular cutting line with the compass. Cut the base to shape along the cutting line, using a jig saw with a coarse-wood cutting blade (thicker blades are less likely to "wander" than thinner blades).

3. Clamp a belt sander to your worksurface on its side, making sure the sanding belt is perpendicular to the worksurface. Sand the edges of the base to smooth out any rough spots, using the belt sander as a stationary grinder **(photo A).** If you are making more than one luminary, cut and sand all the bases at once for greater efficiency.

MAKE THE SLATS.

The sides of each luminary are formed by four pairs of 1 × 2 cedar, cut to different lengths. All the slats are mitered on their top ends for a decorative effect that moves upward from front to back.

1. Cut the front slats (B), short slats (C), middle slats (D) and back slats (E) to length.

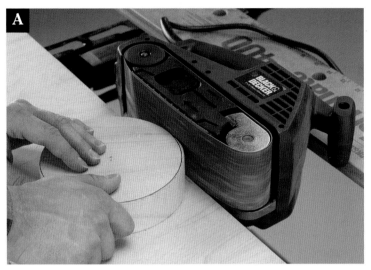

Smooth out the edges of the luminary base with a belt sander clamped to your worksurface.

Make a miter cut at the top of one slat, then use that slat as a guide for marking miter cuts on the rest of the slats.

2. On one slat, mark a point on one long edge, ½" in from an end. Draw a straight line from the point to the corner at the opposite edge. Cut along the line with a saw and miter box or with a power miter box. Using this slat as a guide, trace mitered cutting lines onto the tops of all the slats **(photo B).** Miter-cut the rest of the slats along the cutting lines.

ATTACH THE SLATS TO THE BASE.

1. Drill a pair of ⅛"-dia. pilot holes at the bottom of each slat. The pilot holes should be staggered to avoid splitting the base; drill one pilot hole ½" from the side and 1" up from the bottom; drill the other pilot hole ½" from the other side and 1½" up from the bottom. Countersink the pilot holes enough so the screw heads will be recessed.

2. Use four ¾"-wide spacers to align the slats to form a gradual upward slope (see *Diagram*, page 319). Set the base on a ½"-thick block to create a recess.

Use ¾"-wide spacers to maintain the gaps between the slats as you attach them to the base.

Then, arrange the four spacers in a stack so they form a hub over the center of the base (from above, the spacers should look like a pie cut into eight equal-sized pieces). Set the slats between the spacers so the bottoms are resting on the worksurface and they are flush against the base. Adjust the positions of the slats and spacers until each slat is opposite a slat across the base. Once you get the layout set, wrap a piece of masking tape around the slats, near the bottom, to hold them in place while you fasten them to the base.

3. Drive a 1⅝" deck screw through each pilot hole in each slat, and into the base **(photo C).** Do not overtighten the screws. Remove the spacers.

ATTACH THE STRAPS.
We wrapped two 1"-wide straps made of 22-gauge (fairly lightweight) copper around the luminary to brace the slats. Purchase copper strips that are 25" long or longer at your local craft store. If you cannot find strips that long, buy shorter ones and splice them together with a 1" overlapping seam.

1. Cut two 1"-wide copper strips to 25" in length to make the straps (F). Ordinary scissors will cut thin copper easily.

2. Test-fit the straps by taping them in place around the slats.

3. Mark drilling points for guide holes on the copper straps—one hole per slat, centered between the top and bottom of the strap.

4. Drill 1/16"-dia. pilot holes through the drilling points, then reposition the straps around the luminary. The bottom strap should conceal the screw heads at the bottoms of the slats. The second strap should be about 6¼" up from the bottom of the luminary.

5. Insert a 6"-long block of wood between two slats that are opposite one another, then drive a ¾" copper nail through the pilot holes in those straps to secure them to the slats **(photo D).** Move the block, and drive copper nails through the rest of the pilot holes.

APPLY FINISHING TOUCHES.
1. Cut a 1 × 3½"-long strip of copper to make a hanger (G).

2. Drill a ⅜"-dia. hole through the center, then nail the hanger to the outsides of the back slats, about 1" down from the tops.

3. Make a centering pin to hold a candle to the base by driving a 1¾" screw or a 6d nail up through the center of the base.

4. Apply a coat of exterior wood stain if you plan to keep the luminary outdoors.

Brace the slats with a spacer as you tack on the copper strips.

PROJECT
POWER TOOLS

Garden Bridge

*Whether it's positioned over a small ravine or a swirl of stones,
this handsome bridge will add romance and charm to your yard.*

CONSTRUCTION MATERIALS

Quantity	Lumber
4	4 × 4" × 8' cedar
2	2 × 10" × 8' cedar
10	2 × 4" × 8' cedar
2	1 × 8" × 8' cedar
2	1 × 3" × 8' cedar
8	1 × 2" × 8' cedar
2	½" × 2" × 8' cedar lattice

A bridge can be more than simply a way to get from point A to point B without getting your feet wet. This striking cedar footbridge will be a design centerpiece in any backyard or garden. Even if the nearest trickle of water is miles from your home, this garden bridge will give the impression that your property is graced with a tranquil brook, and you'll spend many pleasurable hours absorbing the peaceful images it inspires. You can fortify the illusion of flowing water by laying a "stream" of landscaping stones beneath this garden bridge. If you happen to have a small ravine or waterway through your yard, this sturdy bridge will take you across it neatly and in high style.

OVERALL SIZE:
46½" HIGH
38½" WIDE
97" LONG

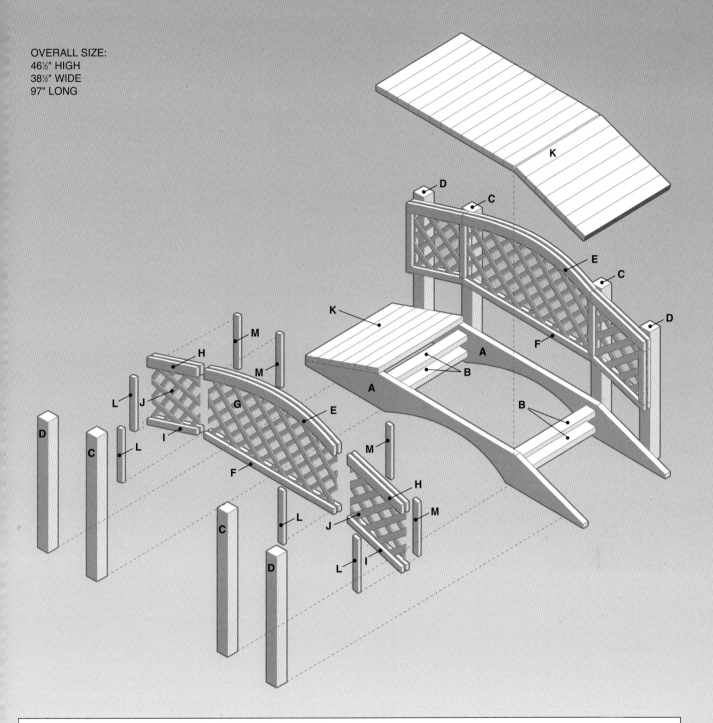

Cutting List

Key	Part	Dimension	Pcs.	Material
A	Stringer	1½ × 9¼ × 96"	2	Cedar
B	Stretcher	1½ × 3½ × 27"	4	Cedar
C	Middle post	3½ × 3½ × 42"	4	Cedar
D	End post	3½ × 3½ × 38"	4	Cedar
E	Center handrail	1½ × 7¼ × 44½"	4	Cedar
F	Center rail	⅞ × 1½ × 44½"	4	Cedar
G	Center panel	½ × 23½ × 44½"	2	Cedar lattice

Cutting List

Key	Part	Dimension	Pcs.	Material
H	End handrail	⅞ × 2¼ × 19½"	8	Cedar
I	End rail	⅞ × 1½ × 24"	8	Cedar
J	End panel	½ × 19 × 24"	4	Cedar lattice
K	Tread	1½ × 3½ × 30"	26	Cedar
L	Filler strip	⅞ × 1½ × 19"	8	Cedar
M	Trim strip	⅞ × 1½ × 21"	8	Cedar

Materials: ⅜ × 4" lag screws, 2" and 3" deck screws, finishing materials.

Note: Measurements reflect the actual size of dimension lumber.

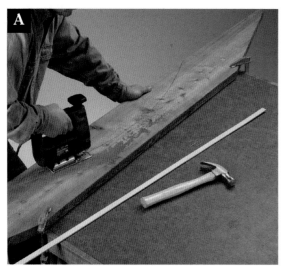

Use a jig saw to make the arched cutouts in the bottoms of the 2 × 10 stringers.

Attach pairs of stretchers between the stringers with 3" deck screws.

Directions: Garden Bridge

MAKE THE STRINGERS.

The stringers are the main structural members of this bridge. Both stringers have arcs cut into their bottom edges, and the ends are cut at a slant to create the gradual tread incline of the garden bridge.

1. Draw several guidelines on the stringers (A) before cutting. First, draw a centerline across the width of each stringer; then mark two more lines across the width of each stringer, 24" to the left and right of the centerline; finally, mark the ends of each stringer, 1" up from one long edge, and draw diagonal lines from these points to the top of each line to the left and right of the center.

2. Use a circular saw to cut the ends of the stringers along the diagonal lines.

3. Tack a nail on the centerline, 5¼" up from the same long edge. Also tack nails along the bottom edge, 20½" to the left and right of the centerline.

4. Lay out the arc at the bottom of each stringer with a marking

Cut the 4 × 4 posts to their finished height, then use lag screws to attach them to the outsides of the stringers.

guide made from a thin, flexible strip of scrap wood or plastic.

5. Hook the middle of the marking guide over the center nail and slide the ends under the outside nails to form a smooth curve. Trace along the guide with a pencil to make the cutting line for the arc (you can mark both stringers this way, or

mark and cut one, then use it as a template for marking the other).

6. Remove the nails and marking guide, and cut the arcs on the bottom edge of each stringer with a jig saw **(photo A).**

ASSEMBLE THE BASE.

Once the two stringers are cut

Attach the treads to the stringers with deck screws.

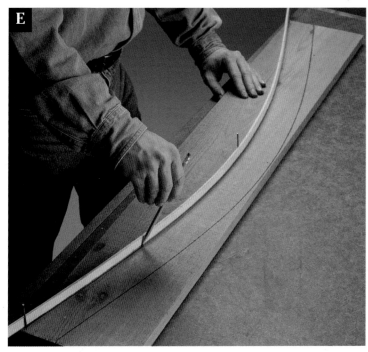

Use a flexible piece of plastic or wood as a marking guide when drawing the cutting lines for the center handrails.

stringers with countersunk 3" deck screws, driven through the stringers and into the ends of the stretchers.

4. Turn the stringer assembly upside down, and attach the top stretchers **(photo B).** The foot-bridge will get quite heavy at this stage: you may want to build the rest of the project on-site.

5. Clamp the middle posts to the outsides of the stringers so their outside edges are 24" from the center of the stringers. Make sure the middle posts are perpendicular to the stringers.

6. Drill ¼"-dia. pilot holes through the stringers and into the middle posts. Attach the middle posts with ⅜"-dia. × 4"-long lag screws, driven through the stringers and into the posts **(photo C).**

7. Clamp the end posts to the stringers, starting 7" from the stringer ends. Drill pilot holes and secure the end posts to the stringers with lag screws.

ATTACH THE TREADS.

1. Cut the treads (K) to size.

2. Position the treads on the stringers, making sure to space them evenly. The treads should be separated by gaps of about ¼".

3. Test-fit all the treads before you begin installing them. Then, secure the treads with 3"-long countersunk deck screws **(photo D).**

to shape, they are connected with four straight boards, called stretchers (B), to form the base of the bridge.

1. Cut the stretchers (B), middle posts (C) and end posts (D) to size.

2. Mark the stretcher locations on the insides of the stringers, 1½" from the top and bottom of the stringers. The outside edges of the stretchers should be 24" from the centers of the stringers (see *Diagram*, page 323), leaving the inside edges flush with the bottoms of the arcs.

3. Stand the stringers upright and position the stretchers between them. Support the bottom stretchers with 1½"-thick spacer blocks for correct spacing. Fasten the stretchers between the

TIP

Lattice panels must be handled carefully, or they may fall apart. This is especially true when you are cutting the lattice panels. Before making any cuts, clamp two boards around the panel, close to the cutting line, to stabilize the lattice and protect it from the vibration of the saw. Always use a long, fine blade on your saw when cutting lattice.

Use a jig saw to cut the panels and center handrails to shape.

Fasten 1 × 2 filler strips to the posts to close the gaps at the sides of the lattice panels.

ATTACH THE CENTER HANDRAIL PANELS.

The center panels are made by sandwiching lattice sections between 1 × 2 cedar frames. Each center panel has an arc along its top edge. This arc can be laid out with a flexible marking guide, using the same procedure used for the stringers.

1. Cut the center handrails (E), center rails (F) and center panels (G) to size.

2. Using a flexible marking guide, trace an arc that begins 2½" up from one long edge of one center handrail. The top of this arc should touch the top edge of the workpiece.

3. Lower the flexible marking guide 2½" down on the center handrails. Trace this lower arc, starting at the corners, to mark the finished center handrail shape **(photo E).**

4. Cut along the bottom arc with a jig saw.

5. Trace the finished center handrail shapes onto the other workpieces, and cut along the bottom arc lines.

6. Cut the center panels (G) to size from ½"-thick cedar lattice.

7. Sandwich each center panel between a pair of center handrails so the top and side edges are flush. Clamp the parts, and gang-cut through the panel and center handrails along the top arc line with a jig saw **(photo F).**

8. Unfasten the boards, and sand the curves smooth.

9. Refasten the center panels between the arcs, ½" down from the tops of the arcs. Drive 2" deck screws through the inside center handrail and into the center panel and outside center handrail. Drive one screw every 4 to 6"—be sure to use pilot holes and make an effort to drive screws through areas where the lattice strips cross, so the screws won't be visible from above.

10. Fasten the center rails to the bottom of the center panels, flush with the bottom edges.

11. Center the panels between the middle posts, and fasten them to the posts so the tops of the handrails are flush with the

inside corner of the middle posts at each end. The ends of the handrails are positioned at the center of the posts. Drive 3" deck screws through the center handrails and center rails to secure the panel to the center posts.

12. Cut the filler strips (L) to size. The filler strips fit between the center handrails and center rails, bracing the panel and providing solid support for the loose ends of the lattice.

13. Position the filler strips in the gaps between the center panels and the middle posts, and fasten them to the middle posts with 2" deck screws **(photo G).**

ATTACH THE END HANDRAIL PANELS.

Like the center panels, the end panels are made by sandwiching cedar lattice sections between board frames and fastening them to posts. The ends of the end panels and the joints between the end and center panels are covered by trim strips (M), which are

Clamp the rough end panels to the posts at the ends of the bridge, and draw alignment markers so you can trim them to fit exactly.

attached with deck screws.

1. Cut the end handrails (H), end rails (I), and end panels (J) to size.

2. Position an end handrail and an end rail on your worksurface, then place an end panel over the pieces. Adjust the end handrail and end rail so the top of the panel is ½" down from the top edge of the end handrail.

3. Sandwich the end panels between another set of end handrails and end rails, and attach the parts with 2" deck screws.

4. Repeat steps 2 and 3 for each end panel.

5. Clamp or hold the panels against the end posts and middle posts, and adjust the end panels so they are aligned with the center panel and the top inside corner of the end posts.

6. Draw alignment marks near the end of the panels along the outside of the end posts **(photo H)**, and cut the end panels to size.

7. Unclamp the panels, and draw cutting lines connecting the alignment marks. Cut along the lines with a jig saw.

8. Sand the end panels, and attach them to the posts with countersunk 3" deck screws, driven through the end handrails and end rails.

9. Slide filler strips between the end panels and the posts. Fasten the filler strips with 2" deck screws.

10. Cut the trim strips (M) to size.

11. Attach the trim strips over each joint between the end and center panels, and at the outside end of each end panel, with countersunk 3" deck screws **(photo I)**.

APPLY FINISHING TOUCHES.

1. Sand all the surfaces to smooth out any rough spots.

2. Apply an exterior wood stain to protect the wood, if desired. You may want to consider leaving the cedar untreated, since that will cause the wood to turn gray—this aging effect may help the bridge blend better with other yard elements.

3. Get some help, and position the bridge in your yard.

4. For a dramatic effect, dig a narrow, meandering trench between two distinct points in your yard, line the trench with landscape fabric, then fill the trench with landscaping stones to simulate a brook.

Use deck screws to attach a trim strip over each joint between the end panels and center panels.

Benches & Seats

Let's face it. Sometimes it's nice to just sit and admire the hard work you've put into your yard and garden. What better place to do that than on a custom-made bench or seat? No matter what style you prefer, you'll find plans here to create a beautiful seating option for your porch, patio, or garden. From ceramic-tiled benches to dreamy porch swings, there's bound to be a seat that beckons you.

Tiled Garden Bench

Ornamental, weather-resistant tiles take your garden bench to a whole new level of beauty.

CONSTRUCTION MATERIALS

Quantity	Lumber
2	2 × 4" × 8' cedar
1	2 × 6" × 8' cedar
1	4 × 4" × 8' cedar
1	¾" × 4' × 4' exterior plywood
1	½" × 4' × 4' cementboard

Here's a splendid example of the term "return on investment." Four decorative tiles and a handful of accent tiles produce quite an impact. In fact, those accents and a few dozen 4 × 4" tiles transform a plain cedar bench into a special garden ornament. And you can accomplish the whole thing over one weekend. In addition to the standard *Outdoor Wood Projects* tools, you'll need some specialized, but inexpensive tile setting tools. A notched trowel, grout float and sponge are necessary for setting the tiles. A tile cutter is a more expensive tool, but typically can be rented at most tile retailers and home centers. These stores often have free tile setting classes, if you feel unsure of your skills or want to hone your technique.

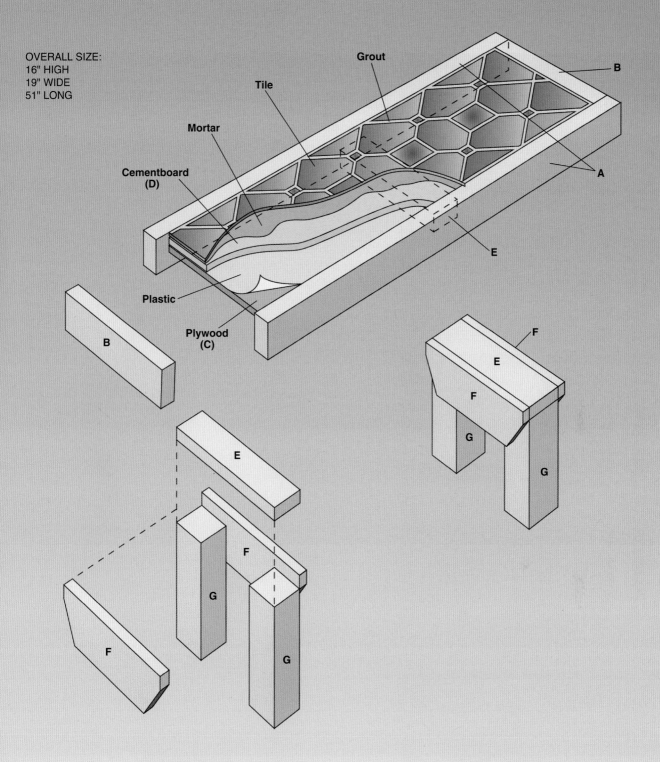

OVERALL SIZE:
16" HIGH
19" WIDE
51" LONG

Grout

Tile

Mortar

Cementboard
(D)

B

A

E

Plastic

Plywood
(C)

B

E

F

E

F

G

G

F

G

G

F

G

		Cutting List					Cutting List		
Key	Part	Dimension	Pcs.	Material	Key	Part	Dimension	Pcs.	Material
A	Sides	1½ × 3½ × 51"	2	Cedar	E	Stretchers	1½ × 3½ × 16"	3	Cedar
B	Ends	1½ × 3½ × 16"	2	Cedar	F	Braces	1½ × 5½ × 16"	4	Cedar
C	Core	15 × 48"	1	Ext. Plywood	G	Legs	3½ × 3½ × 13"	4	Cedar
D	Core	15 × 48"	1	Cementboard					

Materials: plastic sheeting, 2" and 3" coated or galvanized deck screws, 1¼" cementboard screws, clear wood sealer, field and accent tiles, thin-set mortar, tile spacers, grout, grout sealer.

Note: Measurements reflect the actual size of dimension lumber.

Use 1½" blocks to support the stretchers. Drill pilot holes and fasten the stretchers to the sides with 3" screws.

Position the frame over the plywood/cementboard core. Drill pilot holes and then drive 2" galvanized deck screws through the stretchers and into the plywood.

Position each leg between a set of braces and against the sides of the bench frame. Drill pilot holes through each brace and attach the leg to the braces.

Directions: Tiled Garden Bench

BUILD THE FRAME.

1. Cut two sides and two ends, then position the ends between the sides so the edges are flush. Make sure the frame is square. Drill ⅛" pilot holes through the sides and into the ends. Drive 3" screws through the pilot holes.
2. Cut three stretchers. Mark the sides, 4½" from the inside of each end. Using 1½" blocks beneath them as spacers, position the stretchers and make sure they're level. Drill pilot holes and fasten the stretchers to the sides with 3" screws **(photo A).**

MAKE THE TILE BASE.

Cementboard is the typical substrate for tile setting. It has no structural strength, so it must be supported with a layer of exterior plywood.

1. Cut one core (C) from ¾" exterior-grade plywood. Cut the other (D) from cementboard. To cut the cementboard, use a utility knife or cementboard knife and a straightedge to score through the mesh on one side. Snap the panel back and cut through the mesh on the back side.
2. Staple plastic sheeting over the plywood, draping it over the edges. Lay the cementboard rough-side up on the plywood and attach it with 1¼" cementboard screws driven every 6". Make sure the screw heads are flush with the surface.
3. Turn the plywood/cementboard core so the cementboard is on the bottom. Position the bench frame upside down and over the plywood/cementboard core. Drill pilot holes and then drive 2" galvanized deck screws through the stretchers and into

the plywood **(photo B).**

BUILD THE LEGS.

The legs are made of cedar 4 × 4s braced between two cedar 2 × 6s. The braces are angled to be more asthetically pleasing.

1. Cut four braces from a cedar 2 × 6. Mark the angle on each end of each brace by measuring down 1½" from the top edge and 1½" along the bottom edge. Draw a line between the two points and cut along that line, using a circular saw.
2. On each brace, measure down ¾" from the top edge and draw a reference line across the stretcher for the screw positions. Drill ⅛" pilot holes along the reference line. Position a brace on each side of the end stretchers and fasten them with 3" galvanized deck screws driven through the braces and into the stretchers.
3. Cut four 13" legs from a 4 × 4. Position each leg between a set of braces and against the sides of the bench frame. Drill pilot holes through each brace and attach the leg to the braces by driving 3" screws through the braces and into the leg **(photo C).** Repeat the process for each leg.
4. Sand all surfaces with 150-grit sandpaper, then seal all wood surfaces with clear wood sealer.

LAY OUT THE TILE.

Field tiles are the main tiles in a design. In this project, square field tiles are cut to fit around four decorative picture tiles and bright blue accent tiles.

1. Snap perpendicular reference lines to mark the center of the length and width of the bench. Beginning at the center of the bench, dry-fit the field tiles; using spacers. Set the ac-

Dry-fit the field tiles, using spacers. Set the accent tile in place and mark the field tile for cutting.

Apply thin-set mortar over the cementboard, using a notched trowel.

cent tile in place and mark the field tile for cutting **(photo D).**
2. Cut the field tile and continue dry-fitting the bench top, including the accent and border tiles.

SET THE TILE.
Tile is set into a cement product called thin-set mortar.
1. Mix the mortar, starting with the dry powder and gradually adding water. Stir the mixture to achieve a creamy consistency. The mortar should be wet enough to stick to the tiles and the cementboard, but stiff enough to hold the ridges made when applied with the notched trowel.

2. Remove the tiles from the bench and apply thin-set mortar over the cementboard, using a notched trowel **(photo E).** Apply only as much mortar as you can use in 10 minutes. (If the mortar begins to dry before you have set the tile, throw it away and spread new mortar.)
3. Set the tile into the thin-set mortar, using a slight twisting motion. Continue adding thin-set and setting the tile until the bench top is covered **(photo F).** Remove the spacers, using a needlenose pliers. Let the

mortar dry according to manufacturer's directions.

GROUT THE TILE.
Grout fills the gaps between the tiles. A latex additive makes the grout more resistant to stains.
1. Apply masking tape around the wood frame to prevent the grout from staining the wood. Mix the grout and latex grout additive according to package instructions. Use a grout float to force the grout into the joints surrounding the tile, holding the float at an angle **(photo G).** Do not apply grout to the joint between the tile and the wood frame.
2. Wipe the excess grout from the tiles with a damp sponge. Rinse the sponge between each wipe. When the grout has dried slightly, polish the tiles with a clean, dry cloth to remove the slight haze of grout.
3. After the grout has dried (2-3 days) apply grout sealer to the grout lines, using a small foam brush or paintbrush. Take care to keep the sealer off the tiles. Caulk the gap between the tiles and the wood frame, using caulk that matches the grout color.

Set the tile into the thin-set mortar, using a slight twisting motion.

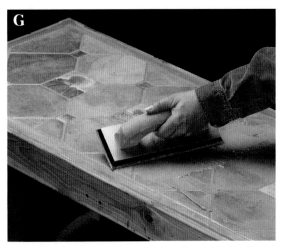

Mix grout and use a grout float to force it into the joints surrounding the tile.

Adirondack Chair

You will find dozens of patterns and plans for building popular Adirondack chairs in just about any bookstore, but few are simpler to make or more attractive than this clever project.

Adirondack furniture has become a standard on decks, porches and patios throughout the world. It's no mystery that this distinctive furniture style has become so popular. Attractive—but rugged—design and unmatched stability are just two of the reasons, and our Adirondack chair offers all of these benefits, and more.

But unlike most of the Adirondack chair designs available, this one is also very easy to build. There are no complex compound angles to cut, no intricate details on the back and seat slats, and no mortise-and-tenon joints. Like all of the projects in this book, our Adirondack chair can be built by any do-it-yourselfer, using basic tools and simple techniques. And because this design features all the elements of the classic Adirondack chair, your guests and neighbors may never guess that you built it yourself.

We made our Adirondack chair out of cedar and finished it with clear wood sealer. But you may prefer to build your version from pine (a traditional wood for Adirondack furniture), especially if you plan to paint the chair. White, battleship gray and forest green are popular color choices for Adirondack furniture. Be sure to use quality exterior paint with a glossy or enamel finish.

CONSTRUCTION MATERIALS

Quantity	Lumber
1	2 × 6" × 8' cedar
1	2 × 4" × 10' cedar
1	1 × 6" × 14' cedar
1	1 × 4" × 8' cedar
1	1 × 2" × 10' cedar

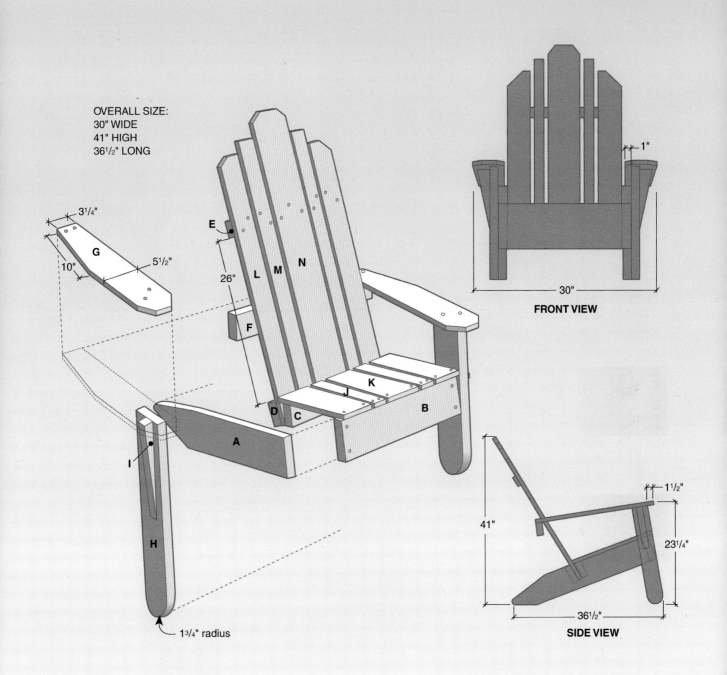

OVERALL SIZE:
30" WIDE
41" HIGH
36½" LONG

FRONT VIEW

SIDE VIEW

1¾" radius

Key	Part	Dimension	Pcs.	Material
A	Leg	1½ × 5½ × 34½"	2	Cedar
B	Apron	1½ × 5½ × 21"	1	Cedar
C	Seat support	1½ × 3½ × 18"	1	Cedar
D	Low back brace	1½ × 3½ × 18"	1	Cedar
E	High back brace	¾ × 1½ × 18"	1	Cedar
F	Arm cleat	1½ × 3½ × 24"	1	Cedar
G	Arm	¾ × 5½ × 28"	2	Cedar
H	Post	1½ × 3½ × 22"	2	Cedar

Key	Part	Dimension	Pcs.	Material
I	Arm brace	1½ × 2¼ × 10"	2	Cedar
J	Narrow seat slat	¾ × 1½ × 20¼"	2	Cedar
K	Wide seat slat	¾ × 5½ × 20¼"	3	Cedar
L	End back slat	¾ × 3½ × 36"	2	CedaM
M	Narrow back slat	¾ × 1½ × 38"	2	Cedar
N	Center back slat	¾ × 5½ × 40"	1	Cedar

Cutting List (both tables titled)

Materials: Moisture-resistant glue, 1¼", 1½", 2" and 3" deck screws, ⅜ × 2½" lag screws with washers, finishing materials.

Note: Measurements reflect the actual size of dimension lumber.

Cut tapers into the back edges of the legs.

Round the sharp slat edges with a router or a power sander.

Directions: Adirondack Chair

CUT THE LEGS.

Sprawling back legs that support the seat slats and stretch to the ground on a near-horizontal plane are signature features of the Adirondack style.

1. Cut the legs (A) to length.

2. To make the tapers, mark a point on one end of the board, 2" from the edge. Then, mark another point on the adjacent edge, 6" from the end. Connect the points with a straightedge.

3. Mark a point on the same end, 2¼" in from the other edge. Then, mark a point on that edge, 10" from the end. Connect these points to make a cutting line for the other taper.

4. Cut the two taper cuts with a circular saw.

5. Use the tapered leg as a template to mark and cut identical tapers on the other leg of the chair **(photo A).**

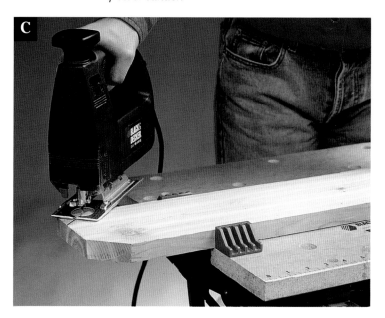

Make decorative cuts on the fronts of the arms (shown) and the tops of the back slats, using a jig saw.

BUILD THE SEAT.

The legs form the sides of the box frame that supports the seat slats. Where counterbores for deck screws are called for, drill holes ¼" deep with a counterbore bit.

1. Cut the apron (B) and seat support (C) to size.

2. Attach the apron to the front ends of the legs with glue and 3" deck screws, in the manner described above.

3. Position the seat support so the inside face is 16½" from the inside edge of the apron. Attach the seat support between the legs, making sure the tops of the parts are flush.

4. Cut the seat slats (J) and (K) to length, and sand the ends smooth. Arrange the slats on

D

Attach the square ends of the posts to the undersides of the arms, being careful to position the part correctly.

top of the seat box, and use wood scraps to set ⅜" spaces between the slats. The slats should overhang the front of the seat box by ¾".

5. Fasten the seat slats by drilling counterbored pilot holes and driving 2" deck screws through the holes and into the tops of the apron and seat support. Keep the counterbores aligned so the cedar plugs form straight lines across the front and back of the seat.

6. Once all the slats are installed, use a router with a ¼" roundover bit (or a power sander) to smooth the edges and ends of the slats **(photo B).**

MAKE THE BACK SLATS.
The back slats are made from three sizes of dimension lumber.

1. Cut the back slats (L), (M) and (N), to size.

2. Trim the corners on the wider slats. On the 1 × 6 slat (N), mark points 1" in from the outside, top corners. Then, mark points on the outside edges, 1" down from the corners. Connect the

points and trim along the lines with a jig saw. Mark the 1 × 4 slats 2" from one top corner, in both directions. Draw cutting lines and trim.

ATTACH BACK SLATS.
1. Cut the low back brace (D) and high back brace (E) and set them on a flat surface.

2. Slip ¾"-thick spacers under the high brace so the tops of the braces are level. Then, arrange the back slats on top of the braces with ⅝" spacing between slats. The untrimmed ends of the slats should be flush with the bottom edge of the low back brace. The bottom of the high back brace should be 26" above the top of the low brace. The braces must be perpendicular to the slats.

3. Drill pilot holes in the low brace and counterbore the holes. Then, attach the slats to the low brace by driving 2" deck screws through the holes. Follow the same steps for the high brace and attach the slats with 1¼" deck screws.

CUT THE ARMS.
The broad arms of the chair are supported by posts in front, and a cleat attached to the backs of the chair slats.

1. Cut the arms (G) to size.

2. To create decorative angles at the outer end of each arm, mark points 1" from each corner along both edges. Use the points to draw a pair of 1½" cutting lines on each arm. Cut along the lines using a jig saw or circular saw **(photo C).**

3. As an option, mark points for cutting a tapered cut on the inside, back edge of each arm (see *Diagram*). First, mark points on the back of each arm, 3¼" in from each inside edge. Next, mark the outside edges 10" from the back. Then, connect the points and cut the tapers with a circular saw or jig saw. Sand the edges smooth.

Drive screws through each post and into an arm brace to stabilize the arm/post joint.

Clamp wood braces to the parts of the chair to hold them in position while you fasten the parts together.

ASSEMBLE THE ARMS, CLEATS AND POSTS.

1. Cut the arm cleat (F) and make a mark 2½" in from each end of the cleat.

2. Set the cleat on edge on your work surface. Position the arms on the top edge of the cleat so the back ends of the arms are flush with the back of the cleat and the untapered edge of each arm is aligned with the 2½" mark. Fasten the arms to the cleats with glue.

3. Drill pilot holes in the arms and counterbore the holes. Drive 3" deck screws through the holes and into the cleat.

4. Cut the posts (H) to size. Then, use a compass to mark a 1¾"-radius roundover cut on each bottom post corner (the roundovers improve stability).

5. Position the arms on top of the square ends of the posts. The posts should be set back 1½" from the front ends of the arm, and 1" from the inside edge of the arm. Fasten the arms to the posts with glue.

6. Drill pilot holes in the arms and counterbore the holes. Then, drive 3" deck screws through the arms and into the posts **(photo D).**

7. Cut tapered arm braces (I) from wood scraps, making sure the grain of the wood runs lengthwise. Position an arm brace at the outside of each arm/post joint, centered side to side on the post. Attach each brace with glue.

8. Drill pilot holes in the inside face of the post near the top and counterbore the holes. Then, drive deck screws through the holes and into the brace **(photo E).** Drive a 2" deck screw down through each arm and into the top of the brace.

ASSEMBLE THE CHAIR.

All that remains is to join the back, seat/leg assembly and arm/post assembly to complete construction. Before you start, gather scrap wood to brace the parts while you fasten them.

1. Set the seat/leg assembly on your work surface, clamping a piece of scrap wood to the front apron to raise the front of the assembly until the bottoms of the legs are flush on the surface (about 10").

2. Use a similar technique to

> **TIP**
>
> *Making tapered cuts with a circular saw is not difficult if the alignment marks on your saw base are accurate. Before attempting to make a tapered cut where you enter the wood at an angle, always make test cuts on scrap wood to be sure the blade starts cutting in alignment with the alignment marks on your saw. If not, either re-set your alignment marks, or compensate for the difference when you cut the tapers.*

brace the arm/post assembly so the bottom of the back cleat is 20" above the work surface. Arrange the assembly so the posts fit around the front of the seat/leg assembly, and the bottom edge of the apron is flush with the front edges of the posts.

3. Drill a ¼"-dia. pilot hole through the inside of each leg and partway into the post. Drive a ⅜ × 2½" lag screw and washer through each hole, but do not tighten completely **(photo F).** Remove the braces.

4. Position the back so the low back brace is between the legs, and the slats are resting against the front of the arm cleat. Clamp the back to the seat support with a C-clamp, making sure the top edge of the low brace is flush with the tops of the legs.

5. Tighten the lag screws at the post/leg joints. Then, add a second lag screw at each joint.

6. Drill three evenly spaced pilot holes near the top edge of the arm cleat and drive 1½" deck screws through the holes and into the back slats **(photo G).** Drive 3" deck screws through the legs and into the ends of the low back brace.

APPLY FINISHING TOUCHES.

1. Glue ¼"-thick, ⅜"-dia. cedar wood plugs into visible counterbores **(photo H).**

2. After the glue dries, sand the plugs even with the surrounding surface. Finish-sand all exposed surfaces with 120-grit sandpaper.

3. Finish the chair as desired— we simply applied a coat of clear wood sealer.

Drive screws through the arm cleat, near the top, and into the slats.

Glue cedar plugs into the counterbores to conceal the screw holes.

Porch Swing

*You'll cherish the pleasant memories created
by this porch swing built for two.*

CONSTRUCTION MATERIALS

Quantity	Lumber
9	1 × 2" × 8' pine
1	1 × 4" × 4' pine
2	2 × 4" × 10' pine
1	2 × 6" × 10' pine

Nothing conjures up pleasant images of a cool summer evening like a porch swing. When the porch swing is one that you've built yourself, those evenings will be all the more pleasant. This porch swing is made from sturdy pine to provide years and years of memory making. The gentle curve of the slatted seat and the relaxed angle of the swing back are designed for your comfort. When you build your porch swing, pay close attention to the spacing of the rope holes drilled in the back, arms and seat of the swing. They are arranged to create perfect balance when you hang your swing from your porch ceiling.

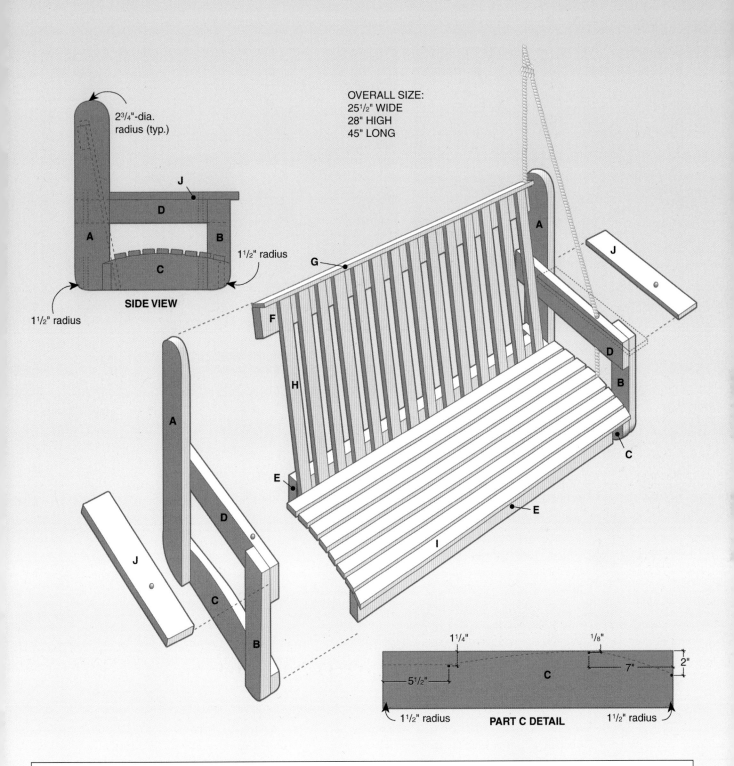

2³/₄"-dia.
radius (typ.)

OVERALL SIZE:
25½" WIDE
28" HIGH
45" LONG

J

D

A   B

C

1½" radius

SIDE VIEW

1½" radius

A

J

D

B

C

A

F

G

H

E

D

B

C

E

I

J

1¼"   1/8"

5½"   7"   2"

C

1½" radius   **PART C DETAIL**   1½" radius

Cutting List				
Key	**Part**	**Dimension**	**Pcs.**	**Material**
A	Back upright	1½ × 5½ × 28"	2	Pine
B	Front upright	1½ × 3½ × 13½"	2	Pine
C	Seat support	1½ × 5½ × 24"	2	Pine
D	Arm rail	1½ × 3½ × 24"	2	Pine
E	Stretcher	1½ × 3½ × 39"	2	Pine

Cutting List				
Key	**Part**	**Dimension**	**Pcs.**	**Material**
F	Back cleat	1½ × 3½ × 42"	1	Pine
G	Top rail	¾ × 1½ × 42"	1	Pine
H	Back slat	¾ × 1½ × 25"	14	Pine
I	Seat slat	¾ × 1½ × 42"	8	Pine
J	Arm rest	¾ × 3½ × 20"	2	Pine

Materials: Moisture-resistant glue, ½"-dia. nylon rope (20'), #8 x 2", #10 x 2½" and #10 x 3" wood screws.

Note: Measurements reflect the actual size of dimension lumber.

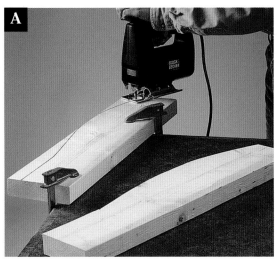

Use a jig saw to cut the contours into the tops of the seat supports.

Use a ⅝" spade bit and a right-angle drilling guide when drilling rope holes through the seat supports.

Directions: Porch Swing

MAKE THE SEAT SUPPORTS.
1. Cut the seat supports (C) to length. Using the pattern on page 341 as a guide, lay out the contour on one of the seat supports. Use a flexible ruler, bent to follow the contour, to ensure a smooth cutting line.
2. Cut along the cutting line with a jig saw **(photo A).** Sand the contour and round the bottom front edge with a belt sander. Use the contoured seat support as a template to mark, cut and sand a matching contour on the other seat support.

BUILD THE SEAT FRAME.
1. Cut the arm rails (D) and stretchers (E) to length. Attach one stretcher between the seat supports, ¾" from the front edges and ½" from the bottom edges, using glue and 2½" wood screws. Fasten the other stretcher between the supports so the front face of the stretcher is 6" from the backs of the supports, and all bottom edges are flush.
2. Use a ⅝" spade bit and drill guide holes for the ropes through the seat supports and

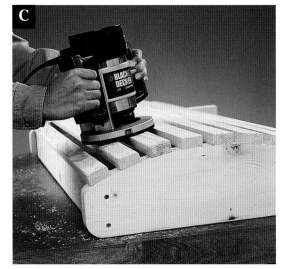

Smooth out the top exposed edges of the seat slats with a router and ¼" roundover bit (or use a power sander).

the arm rails. Drill a hole 1½" from the back end of each piece. Also drill a hole 4½" from the front end of each piece. Use a right-angle drill guide to make sure holes stay centered all the way through **(photo B).**

INSTALL THE SEAT SLATS.
1. Cut the seat slats (I) to length. (Make sure you buy full-sized 1 × 2s, not 1 × 2 furring strips.) Arrange the slats across the seat supports, using ½"-thick spacers to make sure the gaps are even. The front slat should overhang the front stretcher by about ¼", and the back slat

should be flush with the front of the back stretcher.
2. Fasten the slats to the seat support with glue and #8 × 2" wood screws (one screw at each slat end). Smooth the top edges of the slats with a router and ¼" roundover bit, or a power sander **(photo C).**

BUILD THE BACK.
1. Cut the back cleat (F) and the back slats (H) to length.
2. Fasten the slats to the back cleat, leaving a 1½" gap at each end, and spacing the slats at 1⅜" intervals **(photo D).** The tops of the slats should be flush

Use 1 × 2 spacers to align the back slats, then fasten the slats to the back cleat.

Fasten the top rail to the back cleat, so the front edge of the rail is flush with the fronts of the slats.

Slide the back assembly against the seat assembly and attach.

rails between the uprights, flush with the tops and with rope holes aligned.

4. Slide the back slat assembly behind the seat assembly **(photo F).** Attach the back cleat to the back uprights with 3" screws, so the upper rear corners of the cleat are flush with the back edges of the uprights.

5. Cut and sand the arm rests (J) and set them on the arm rail, centered side to side and flush with the back uprights.

6. Mark the locations of the rope holes in the arm rails onto the arm rests. Drill matching holes into the arm rests. Attach the arm rests to the rails with glue and 2" screws.

APPLY FINISHING TOUCHES.
Sand and paint swing. Thread ½"-dia. nylon rope through all four sets of rope holes. Tie them to hang the swing.

TIP
Use heavy screw eyes driven into ceiling joists to hang porch swings. If the ropes don't line up with the ceiling joists, lag-screw a 2 × 4 cleat to the ceiling joists and attach screw eyes to the cleat.

with the top of the cleat.
3. Cut the top rail (G) to length. Fasten it to the cleat so the front edge of the rail is flush with the fronts of the slats **(photo E).** Drill a ⅝"-dia. rope hole at each end of the top cleat, directly over the back holes in the arm rails.

ATTACH THE UPRIGHTS AND ARM REST.
1. Cut the back uprights (A) and front uprights (B). Make a round profile cut at the tops of the back uprights (see pattern, page 341), using a jig saw. Attach the uprights to the outside faces of the seat supports, flush with the ends of the supports, using glue and 3" wood screws.
2. Round the bottom front edges of the front uprights with a sander so they are flush with the seat supports.
3. Use 2½" screws to attach arm

PROJECT
POWER TOOLS

Garden Bench

*Graceful lines and trestle construction make this bench a charming
complement to porches, patios and decks—as well as gardens.*

CONSTRUCTION MATERIALS

Quantity	Lumber
1	2 × 8" × 6' cedar
4	2 × 2" × 10' cedar
1	2 × 4" × 6' cedar
1	2 × 6" × 10' cedar
1	2 × 2" × 6' cedar
1	1 × 4" × 12' cedar

Casual seating is a welcome addition to any outdoor setting. This lovely garden bench sits neatly at the borders of any porch, patio or deck. It creates a pleasant resting spot for up to three adults without taking up a lot of space. Station it near your home's rear entry and you'll have convenient seating for removing shoes or setting down grocery bags while you unlock the door.

The straightforward design of this bench lends itself to accessorizing. Station a rustic cedar planter next to the bench for a lovely effect. Or, add a framed lattice trellis to one side of the bench to cut down on wind and direct sun.

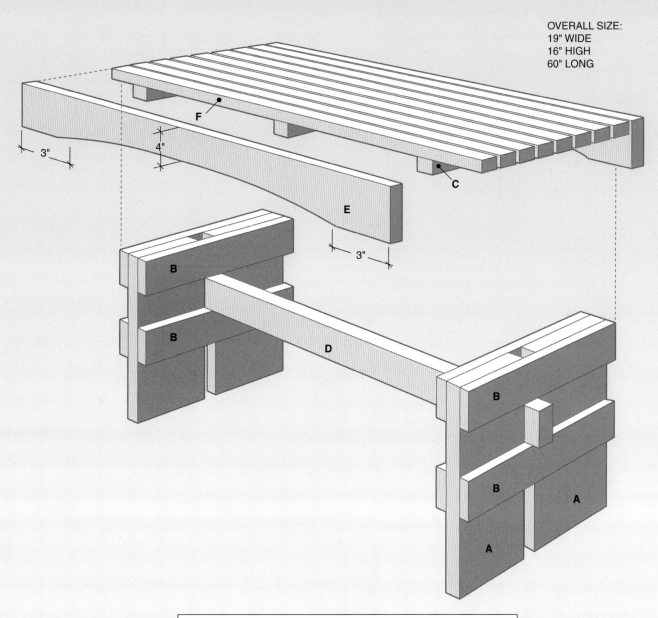

OVERALL SIZE:
19" WIDE
16" HIGH
60" LONG

3"

4"

F

C

E

3"

B

B

D

B

B

A

A

Cutting List

Key	Part	Dimension	Pcs.	Material
A	Leg half	1½ × 7¼ × 14½"	4	Cedar
B	Cleat	¾ × 3½ × 16"	8	Cedar
C	Brace	1½ × 1½ × 16"	3	Cedar
D	Trestle	1½ × 3½ × 60"	1	Cedar
E	Apron	1½ × 5½ × 60"	2	Cedar
F	Slat	1½ × 1½ × 60"	8	Cedar

Materials: Moisture-resistant glue, wood sealer or stain, 1½" and 2½" deck screws.

Note: Measurements reflect the actual size of dimension lumber.

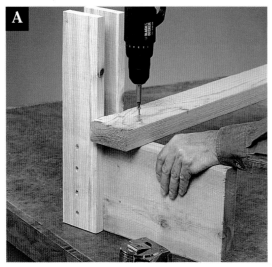

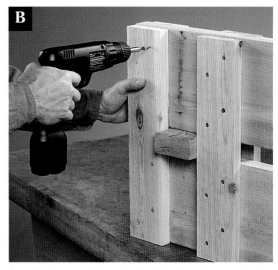

Make sure the trestle is positioned correctly against the cleats, and attach it to the leg.

Attach the remaining leg half to the cleats on both ends to complete the leg assembly.

Directions:
Garden Bench

BUILD THE BASE.

1. Cut the leg halves (A), cleats (B) and trestle (D) to length. Sandwich one leg half between two cleats so the cleats are flush with the top and the outside edge of the leg half. Then, join the parts by driving four 1½" deck screws through each cleat and into the leg half. Assemble two more cleats with a leg half in the same fashion.

2. Stand the two assemblies on their sides, with the open ends of the cleats pointing upward. Arrange the assemblies so they are roughly 4' apart. Set the trestle onto the inner edges of the leg halves, pressed flush against the bottoms of the cleats. Adjust the position of the assemblies so the trestle overhangs the leg half by 1½" at each end. Fasten the trestle to each leg half with glue and 2½" deck screws **(photo A).**

TIP

Take extra care to countersink screw heads completely whenever you are building furnishings that will be used as seating. When sinking galvanized deck screws, use a counterbore bit or a standard ⅜"-dia. bit to drill ¼"-deep counterbores, centered around ⅛"-dia. pilot holes.

Attach the outer brace for the seat slats directly to the inside faces of the cleats.

3. Attach another pair of cleats to each leg half directly below the first pair, positioned so each cleat is snug against the bottom of the trestle.

4. Slide the other leg half between the cleats, keeping the top edge flush with the upper cleats. Join the leg halves with the cleats using glue and 2½" deck screws **(photo B).**

5. Cut the braces (C) to length. Fasten one brace to the inner top cleat on each leg assembly, so the tops are flush **(photo C).**

MAKE THE APRONS.

1. Cut the aprons (E) to length.

2. Lay out the arch onto one apron, starting 3" from each end. The peak of the arch, located over the midpoint of the apron, should be 1½" up from the bottom edge.

3. Draw a smooth, even arch by driving a casing nail at the peak of the arch and one at each of the starting points. Slip a flexible ruler behind the nails at the starting points and in front of the nail at the peak to create a smooth arch. Then, trace along the inside of the ruler to make a cutting line **(photo D).**

4. Cut along the line with a jig saw and sand the cut smooth.

5. Trace the profile of the arch onto the other apron and make and sand the cut.

6. Cut the slats (F) to length. Attach a slat to the top, inside edge of each apron with glue and deck screws **(photo E).**

INSTALL THE APRONS AND SLATS.

1. Apply glue at each end on the bottom sides of the attached slats. Flip the leg and trestle assembly and position it flush with the aprons so that it rests on the glue on the bottoms of the two slats. The aprons should extend 1½" beyond the legs at each end of the bench. Drive 2½" deck screws through the braces and into both slats.

2. Position the middle brace (C) between the aprons, centered end to end on the project. Fasten it to the two side slats with deck screws.

3. Position the six remaining slats on the braces, using ½"-thick spacers to create equal gaps between them. Attach the slats with glue and drive 2½" deck screws up through the braces and into each slat **(photo F).**

APPLY FINISHING TOUCHES.

Sand the slats smooth with progressively finer sandpaper. Wipe away the sanding residue with a rag dipped in mineral spirits. Let the bench dry. Apply a finish of your choice—a clear wood sealer protects the cedar without altering the color.

TIP

Sometimes our best efforts produce furniture that wobbles because it is not quite level. One old trick for leveling furniture is to set a plastic wading pool on a flat plywood surface that is set to an exact level position with shims. Fill the pool with about ¼" of water. Set the furniture in the pool, then remove it quickly. Mark the tops of the waterlines on the legs, and use them as cutting lines for trimming the legs to level.

Use a flexible ruler pinned between casing nails to trace a smooth arch onto the aprons.

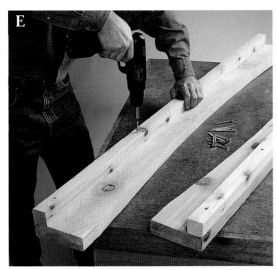

Attach a 2 × 2 slat to the top, inside edge of each apron, using 2½" deck screws and glue.

Attach the seat slats with glue and 2½" deck screws. Insert ½"-thick spacers to set gaps between the slats.

Patio Chair

You won't believe how comfortable plastic tubes can be until you sit in this unique patio chair. It's attractive, reliable and very inexpensive to build.

For solid support, you can't go wrong with this patio chair. Crashing painfully to the ground just when you're trying to sit and relax outdoors is nobody's idea of fun. This patio chair is designed for durability and comfort. It uses rigid plastic tubing for cool, comfortable support that's sure to last through many fun-filled seasons. Say good-bye to expensive or highly-specialized patio furniture with this outdoor workhorse.

This inventive seating project features CPVC plastic tubing that functions like slats for the back and seat assemblies. The ½"-dia. tubes have just the right amount of flex and support, and can be purchased at any local hardware store. Even though the tubing is light, there is no danger of this chair blowing away in the wind. It has a heavy, solid frame that will withstand strong gusts of wind and fearsome summer showers. For even greater comfort, you can throw a favorite pillow, pad or blanket over the tubing and arms and relax in the sun.

The materials for this project are inexpensive. All the parts except the seat support are made from 2 × 4 cedar. The seat support is made from 1 × 3 cedar. For a companion project to this patio chair, see *Gate-Leg Picnic Tray,* pages 396-399.

CONSTRUCTION MATERIALS

Quantity	Lumber
3	2 × 4" × 10' cedar
1	1 × 3" × 2' cedar
7	½" × 10' CPVC tubing

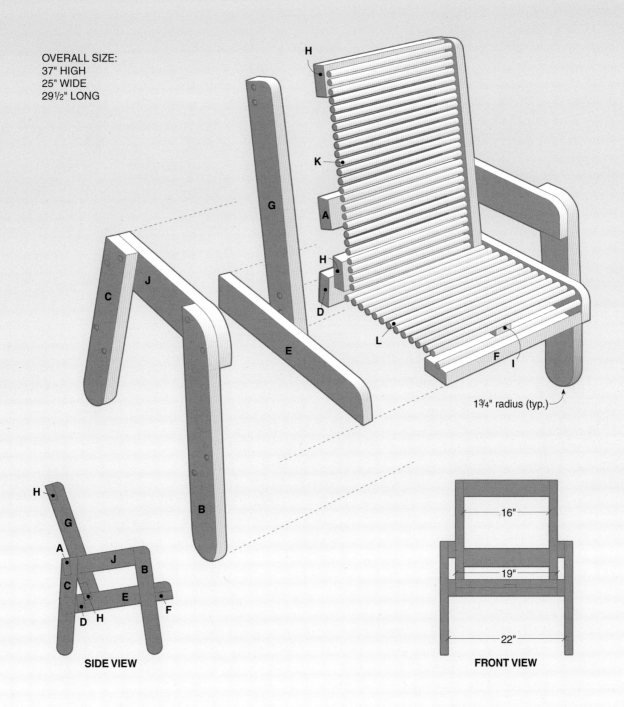

OVERALL SIZE:
37" HIGH
25" WIDE
29½" LONG

1¾" radius (typ.)

SIDE VIEW

16"

19"

22"

FRONT VIEW

	Cutting List			
Key	**Part**	**Dimension**	**Pcs.**	**Material**
A	Back support	1½ × 3½ × 19"	1	Cedar
B	Front leg	1½ × 3½ × 22½"	2	Cedar
C	Rear leg	1½ × 3½ × 21"	2	Cedar
D	Seat stop	1½ × 3½ × 19"	1	Cedar
E	Seat side	1½" × 3½ × 24½"	2	Cedar
F	Seat front	1½ × 3½ × 19"	1	Cedar

	Cutting List			
Key	**Part**	**Dimension**	**Pcs.**	**Material**
G	Back side	1½ × 3½ × 28"	2	Cedar
H	Back rail	1½ × 3½ × 16"	2	Cedar
I	Seat support	¾ × 2½ × 17¾"	1	Cedar
J	Arm rail	1½ × 3½ × 19½"	2	Cedar
K	Back tube	½-dia. × 17½"	25	CPVC
L	Seat tube	½-dia. × 20½"	14	CPVC

Materials: Moisture-resistant glue, 1¼", 2½" and 3" deck screws, ⅜"-dia. cedar plugs, finishing materials.

Note: Measurements reflect the actual size of dimension lumber.

Use a portable drilling guide when drilling the holes for the tubes in the seat sides.

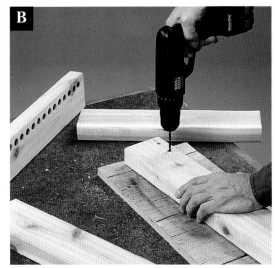

Drill pilot holes before attaching the back rails and sides.

Directions:
Patio Chair

MAKE THE BACK SIDES.
The back sides of the patio chair provide the frame for the CPVC tubing. Make sure all your cuts are accurate and smooth to achieve good, snug-fitting joints.

1. Cut the back sides (G) to length, using a circular saw.

2. Drill the stopped holes for the plastic tubes on the inside faces of the back sides. These holes must be accurately positioned and drilled. Use a pencil with either a combination square or a straightedge to draw a centering line to mark the locations for the holes. Make the centering line ⅝" from the front edge of each back side.

3. Drill ⅝-dia. × ¾"-deep holes and center them exactly 1" apart along the centerline. Start the first hole 3" from the bottom end of each back side. Use a

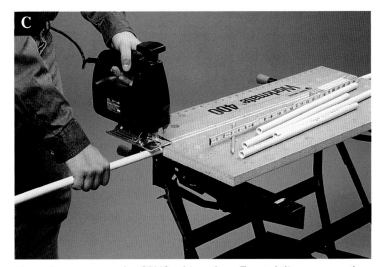

Use a jig saw to cut the CPVC tubing slats. For stability, arrange the tubing so the saw blade is very close to the work surface.

portable drilling guide and a square to make sure the holes are straight and perfectly aligned **(photo A).** A portable drilling guide fits easily onto your power drill to ensure quick and accurate drilling. Some portable drilling guides are equipped with depth stops, making them the next best thing to a standard drill press.

4. Cut 1"-radius roundovers on the top front corner of each back side.

BUILD THE BACK FRAME.

1. Use a circular saw to cut the back rails (H) to length. These pieces will be attached to the inside faces of the back sides.

2. To eliminate the sharp edges, clamp the pieces to a stable work surface and use a sander or a router to soften the edges on the top and bottom of the back rails, and the top edges of the back sides.

3. Dry-fit the back rails and back sides and mark their positions with a pencil.

Attach the remaining side to complete the back assembly.

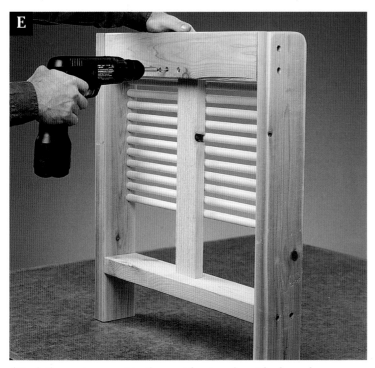

Attach the seat support to the seat front and seat lock as shown.

4. Drill ⅛" pilot holes in the back side and counterbore the holes to a ¼" depth, using a counterbore bit. **(photo B).**

5. Apply moisture-resistant glue to one end of each rail and fasten the rails to a single back side with 3" deck screws

COMPLETE THE BACK ASSEMBLY.

Before assembling the back, you need to prepare the CPVC tubing for the frame holes. Make sure the tubing is ½"-dia. CPVC, which is rated for hot water. This plastic tubing is usually available in 10' lengths. (Standard PVC tubing is not usually sold in small diameters

that will fit the ⅝"-dia. holes you have drilled.)

1. Use a jig saw to cut 25 pieces of the ½"-dia. CPVC tubing. Remember, these pieces will be used for the back seat assembly only. The seat assembly requires additional pieces. Cut the back tubes to 17½" lengths **(photo C).**

2. Wash the grade stamps off the tubing with lacquer thinner. (Wear gloves and work in a well-ventilated area when using lacquer thinner.) Rinse the tubing with clean water.

3. Once the pipes are clean and dry, insert them into the holes on one of the back sides. Slide the remaining back side into place, positioning the plastic tubes into the holes.

4. Attach the rails to the back side by driving 3" deck screws through the pilot holes **(photo D).**

BUILD THE SEAT FRAME.

One important difference between the seat frame and the back frame is the positioning of the CPVC tubing. On the seat frame, one tube is inserted into the sides slightly out of line at the front to make the chair more comfortable for your legs.

1. Cut the seat sides (E), seat front (F), seat stop (D) and seat support (I) to length. Use the

TIP

The easiest way to cut CPVC tubing is with a power miter box, but no matter what kind of saw you are using, remember to work in a well-ventilated room. Although plastic tubing generally cuts easily without melting or burning, it can release some toxic fumes as it is cut. When you're finished, you might consider treating the tubes with some automotive plastic polish to help preserve them.

same methods as with the back frame to draw the centering line for the plastic tubing on the seat sides. Drill the tube holes into each seat side. Start the holes 2" from the front end of the seat sides.

2. Position a single tube hole on the seat frame ⅞" below the top edge and 1" from the front end of each seat side. This front tube provides a gradual downward seat profile for increased leg comfort.

3. To eliminate the sharp edges on the seat assembly, round the seat sides, seat support edges and seat front edges with a sander or router. Cut 1"-radius roundovers on the top front corners of the seat sides.

4. Use a combination square to mark a line across the width of the inside of the seat sides, 3½" from the back edges. This is where the back face of the seat stop is positioned. Test-fit the pieces to make sure their positions are correct. Lay out and mark the position of the seat stop and seat front on each seat side.

5. Drill pilot holes to fasten one of the seat sides to the seat stop and seat front, as you did with the back assembly. Counterbore the holes. Connect the parts with moisture-resistant glue and deck screws.

COMPLETE THE SEAT FRAME.

1. Cut 14 pieces of ½"-dia. CPVC pipe. Each piece should be 20½" long. Once again, clean the grade stamps off the tubes with lacquer thinner and rinse them with clean water. Let them dry and insert them into the holes on one seat side.

2. Carefully slide the remaining seat side into place and fasten

Make identical radius cuts on the bottoms of the legs.

Use a square to make sure the seat is perpendicular to the leg.

the pieces with moisture-resistant glue and deck screws.

3. Position the seat support (I) under the tubing in the center of the seat. Attach the seat support to the middle of the seat front and seat stop with moisture-resistant glue and 1¼" deck screws **(photo E).**

BUILD THE ARMS AND LEGS.

The arms and legs are all that remain for the patio chair assembly. When you make the radius cuts on the bottom edges of the front and back legs, make sure the cuts are exactly the same on each leg (see *Diagram,* page 349). Otherwise, the legs may be uneven and rock

Slide the back frame into the seat frame so the back sides rest against the seat stop and seat support.

attach the back support between the rails with glue and drive 2½" deck screws through the arm rails and into the back support. The back support should be flush with the ends of the arm rails.

7. Round and sand all rough edges smooth.

ATTACH THE BACK FRAME.

1. Slide the back frame into the seat frame **(photo H)** so that the back sides rest against the seat stop and the back rail rests on the seat support.

2. Drill pilot holes in the seat stop and counterbore the holes. Apply glue, and attach the back frame by driving deck screws through the seat stop and into the back rail.

APPLY FINISHING TOUCHES.

1. For a refined look, apply glue to the bottoms of ⅜"-dia. cedar wood plugs, and insert the plugs into the screw counterbores. Sand the tops of the plugs until they are flush with the surrounding surface.

2. Wipe the chair with mineral spirits and finish the chair with a clear wood sealer.

---

back and forth when you sit.

1. Cut the back support (A), front legs (B), rear legs (C) and arm rails (J) to length.

2. Use a jig saw to cut a full-radius roundover on the bottoms of the legs **(photo F).** Cut a 1"-radius roundover on the top front corners of the arms and the front legs.

3. To attach the front legs to the outsides of the arm rails, drill pilot holes in the front legs and counterbore the holes. Then, attach the parts at a 90° angle, using 2½" deck screws. The legs should be flush with the front ends of the rails.

4. Attach the leg/arm rail assembly to the seat frame so that the top edge of the seat frame is 15" from the bottom of the

leg. The front of the seat should extend exactly 3½" past the leg. Use a square to make sure the seat is perpendicular to the legs **(photo G).**

5. To attach the rear legs, drill pilot holes in the rear legs and counterbore the holes. Attach the rear legs to the arm rails and seat sides with glue. Then, drive 2½" deck screws through the rear legs and into the arm rails and seat sides. The back edge of the legs should be flush with the ends of the arm rails and seat sides. Trim the excess material from the tops of the legs so they are flush with the tops of the arm rails.

6. To attach the back support, drill pilot holes in the arm rails. Counterbore the holes. Then,

> **TIP**
>
> *When using a jig saw, it is tempting to speed up a cut by pushing the tool with too much force. When cutting curves or roundovers, this is likely to cause the saw blade to bend. This often causes irregular cuts and burns, especially when working with cedar. You can achieve smoother curves and roundovers with multiple gentle passes with the saw, until the proper curve is achieved. Finish the job by sanding the curves smooth.*

Trellis Seat

Spice up your patio or deck with this sheltered seating structure. Set it in a secluded corner to create a warm, inviting outdoor living space.

CONSTRUCTION MATERIALS

Quantity	Lumber
1	4 × 4" × 6' cedar
2	2 × 8" × 8' cedar
5	2 × 4" × 12' cedar
1	1 × 6" × 10' cedar
11	1 × 2" × 8' cedar
2	½" × 4 × 4' cedar lattice

Made of lattice and cedar boards, our trellis seat is ideal for conversation or quiet moments of reading. The lattice creates just the right amount of privacy for a small garden or patio. It's an unobtrusive structure that is sure to add some warmth to your patio or deck. Position some outdoor plants along the top cap or around the frame sides to dress up the project and bring nature a little closer to home. For a cleaner appearance, conceal visible screw heads on the seat by counterboring the pilot holes for the screws and inserting cedar plugs (available at most woodworking stores) into the counterbores.

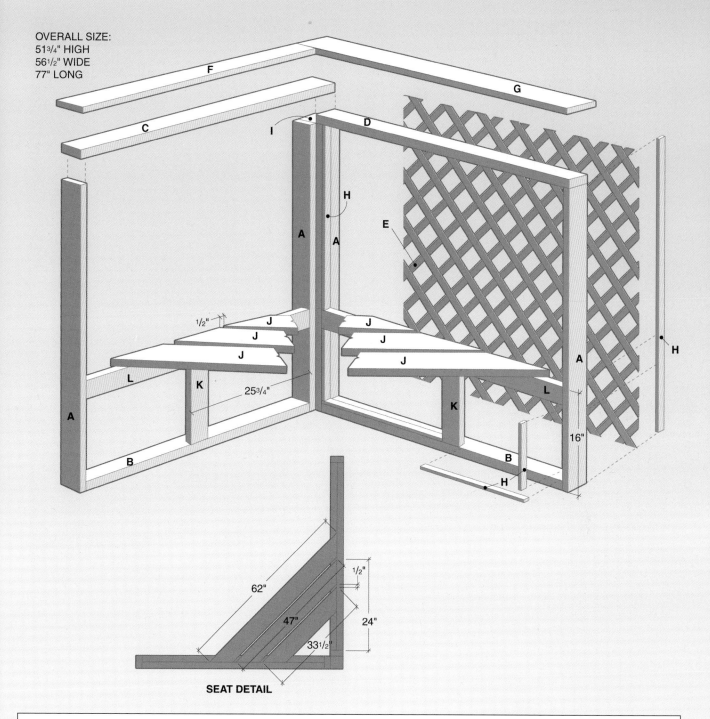

OVERALL SIZE:
51¾" HIGH
56½" WIDE
77" LONG

SEAT DETAIL

Cutting List				
Key	Part	Dimension	Pcs.	Material
A	Frame side	1½ × 3½ × 49½"	4	Cedar
B	Frame bottom	1½ × 3½ × 48"	2	Cedar
C	Long rail	1½ × 3½ × 56½"	1	Cedar
D	Short rail	1½ × 3½ × 51"	1	Cedar
E	Lattice	½ × 4 × 4'	2	Cedar
F	Short cap	¾ × 5½ × 51"	1	Cedar

Cutting List				
Key	Part	Dimension	Pcs.	Material
G	Long cap	¾ × 5½ × 56½"	1	Cedar
H	Retaining strip	¾ × 1½" cut to fit	22	Cedar
I	Post	3½ × 3½ × 49½"	1	Cedar
J	Seat board	1½ × 7¼ × *	3	Cedar
K	Brace	1½ × 3½ × 11"	2	Cedar
L	Seat support	1½ × 3½ × 48"	2	Cedar

Materials: Moisture-resistant glue, 1¼", 2", 2½" and 3" deck screws, 4d galvanized casing nails, finishing materials.

Note: Measurements reflect the actual size of dimension lumber.   *Cut one each: 32", 49", 63"

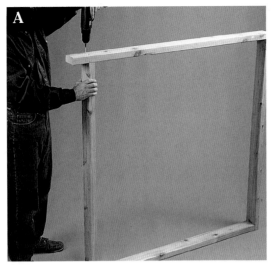

Attach the long rail at the top of one trellis frame
with a 3½" overhang at one end to cover the post.

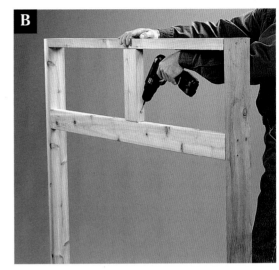

Drive deck screws toenail-style through the braces
and into the seat supports.

Directions:
Trellis Seat

MAKE THE TRELLIS FRAME.
1. Cut the frame sides (A),
frame bottoms (B), long rail
(C), short rail (D), braces (K)
and seat supports (L) to length.
To attach the frame sides and
frame bottoms, drill two evenly
spaced ³⁄₁₆" pilot holes in the
frame sides. Counterbore the
holes ¼" deep, using a counterbore bit. Fasten with glue and
drive 2½" deck screws through
the frame sides and into the
bottoms.
2. Drill pilot holes in the top
faces of the long and short
rails. Counterbore the holes. Attach the long and short rails to
the tops of the frame sides with
glue. Drive deck screws
through the rails and into the
ends of the frame sides. The

long rail should
extend 3½" past
one end of
the frame
(photo A).
3. Mark points
22¼" from each
end on the
frame bottoms
to indicate posi-
tion for the
braces. Turn the
frame upside-
down. Drill pilot
holes in the
frame bottoms
where the
braces will be attached. Counterbore the holes. Position the
braces flush with the inside
frame bottom edges. Attach the
pieces by driving 3" deck
screws through the frame bottoms and into the ends of the
braces.
4. Position the seat supports
16" up from the bottoms of the
frame bottoms, resting on the
braces. Make sure the supports
are flush with the inside edges
of the braces. Attach with glue
and 3" deck screws driven
through the frame sides and into
the ends of the seat supports.

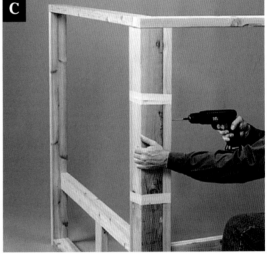

Fasten the trellis frames to the post at right angles.

5. Attach the braces to the seat
supports by drilling angled ³⁄₁₆"
pilot holes through each brace
edge. Drive 3" deck screws toenail style through the braces
and into the top edges of the
seat supports **(photo B).**

JOIN THE TRELLIS FRAMES
TO THE POST.
1. Cut the post (I) to length.
2. Attach the two frame sections to the post. First, drill pilot
holes in the frame sides. Counterbore the holes. Drive evenly
spaced 3" deck screws through
the frame sides and into the

TIP

*Fabricated lattice panels are sold at any building
center in standard ¾" thickness. For our trellis
seat project, we found and used ½"-thick lattice
panels. If you cannot locate any of the thinner
panels, use ¾"-thick lattice, and substitute ½"-thick
retaining strips at the backs of the trellis frames.*

Nail 1 × 2 retaining strips for the lattice panels to the inside faces of the trellis frames.

Fasten the lattice panels to the seat supports with 1¼" deck screws, then attach outer retaining strips.

post **(photo C).** Make sure the overhang of the long rail fits snugly over the top of the post.

ATTACH THE LATTICE RETAINING STRIPS.

1. Cut the lattice retaining strips (H) to fit along the inside faces of the trellis frames (but not the seat supports or braces).
2. Nail the strips to the frames, flush with the inside frame edges, using 4d galvanized casing nails **(photo D).**

CUT AND INSTALL THE LATTICE PANELS.

1. Since you will probably be cutting through some metal fasteners in the lattice, fit your circular saw with a remodeler's blade. Sandwich the lattice panel between two boards near the cutting line to prevent the lattice from separating. Clamp the boards and the panel together, and cut the lattice panels to size. Always wear protective eyewear when operating power tools.
2. Position the panels into the frames against the retaining strips, and attach them to the seat supports with 1¼" deck

screws **(photo E).** Secure the panels by cutting retaining strips to fit along the outer edges of the inside faces of the trellis frame. Nail strips in place.

BUILD THE SEAT.

1. Cut the seat boards (J) to length. On a flat work surface, lay the seat boards together, edge to edge. Insert ½"-wide spacers between the boards.
2. Draw cutting lines to lay out the seat shape onto the boards as if they were one board (see *Seat Detail,* page 355, for seat board dimensions). Gang-cut the seat boards to their finished size and shape with a circular saw.
3. Attach the seat boards to the seat supports with evenly spaced deck screws, maintaining the ½"-wide gap. Smooth the seat board edges with a sander or router.

INSTALL THE TOP CAPS.

1. Cut the short cap (F) and long cap (G).
2. Attach the caps to the tops of the long and short rails with deck screws **(photo F).**

APPLY FINISHING TOUCHES.

Brush on a coat of clear wood sealer to help preserve the trellis seat.

Attach the long and short caps to the tops of the trellis frames. The long cap overlaps the long rail and the post.

PROJECT
POWER TOOLS

Fire Pit Bench

With seating for three and storage room below,
this versatile bench will be at home anywhere in your yard.

CONSTRUCTION MATERIALS

Quantity	Lumber
2	2 × 2" × 8' cedar
4	1 × 4" × 8' cedar
4	2 × 4" × 8' cedar
1	1 × 2" × 8' cedar

Summer cookouts, moon-lit bonfires or even a mid-winter warm-up are all perfect occasions to use this cedar fire pit bench. If you are extremely ambitious, you can build four benches to surround your fire pit on all sides. If you don't need that much seating, build only two and arrange them to form a cozy conversation area around the fire. Even without a fire pit, you can build a single bench as a stand-alone furnishing for your favorite spot in the yard or garden.

This solid cedar bench will seat up to three adults comfortably. The slats below give the bench strength, while providing a convenient spot for storing and drying firewood.

OVERALL SIZE:
18" HIGH
18½" WIDE
48" LONG

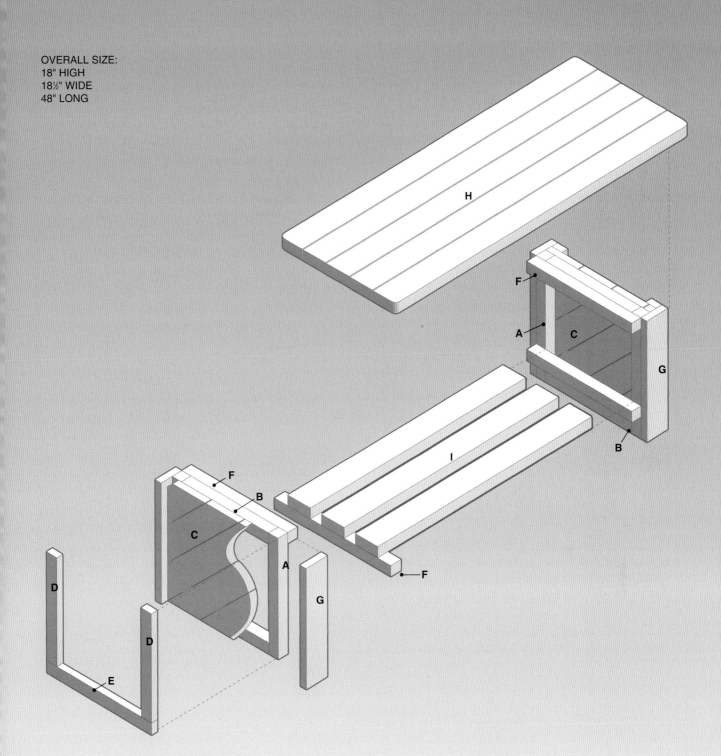

Cutting List

Key	Part	Dimension	Pcs.	Material
A	Frame side	1½ × 1½ × 16½"	4	Cedar
B	Frame end	1½ × 1½ × 14"	4	Cedar
C	End slat	⅞ × 3½ × *	12	Cedar
D	End trim	⅞ × 1½ × 15"	4	Cedar
E	Bottom trim	⅞ × 1½ × 17"	2	Cedar

Cutting List

Key	Part	Dimension	Pcs.	Material
F	Cleat	1½ × 1½ × 17"	4	Cedar
G	Side trim	⅞ × 3½ × 16½"	4	Cedar
H	Seat slat	1½ × 3½ × 48"	5	Cedar
I	Shelf slat	1½ × 3½ × 35"	3	Cedar

Materials: 1½" and 2½" deck screws, finishing materials.

Note: Measurements reflect the actual size of dimension lumber.

* Cut to fit

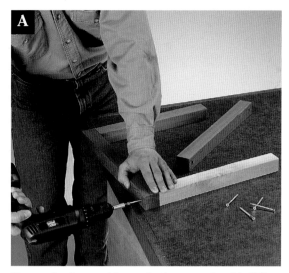

Fasten the frame sides to the frame ends with 2½" galvanized deck screws.

Trim off the ends of the slats so the ends are flush with the outside edges of the end frames.

Directions:
Fire Pit Bench

BUILD THE END FRAMES.

1. Cut the frame sides (A) and frame ends (B) to length. Place a frame end between two frame sides. Drill ⅛" pilot holes in the frame sides. Counterbore the holes ¼" deep, using a counterbore bit. Drive 2½" deck screws through the frame sides and into the ends of the frame end **(photo A).** Attach another frame end between the free ends of the frame sides.

2. Follow the same procedure to build the second end frame.

ATTACH THE END SLATS.

The end slats are mounted at 45° angles to the end frames.

1. Lay the frames on a flat surface. Use a combination square as a guide for drawing a reference line at a 45° angle to one corner on each frame, starting 3½" in from the corner.

2. To measure and cut the end slats (C), lay the end of a full-length 1 × 4 cedar board across one frame so one edge meets the corner and the other edge

Use shelf slats to set the correct distance between the end-frame assemblies, then attach the end frames to the bottoms of the seat slats.

follows the reference line. Position the board so the end overhangs the frame by an inch or two. Mark a point with an equal overhang on the other side of the frame.

3. Cut the 1 × 4, then fasten the cut-off piece to the frame by driving pairs of 1½" deck screws into the end frame. Lay a 1 × 4 back across the frame, butted up against the attached

slat, and mark and cut another slat the same way. Attach the slat. Continue cutting and attaching the rest of the slats to cover the frame. Attach slats to the other end frame.

4. Draw straight cutting lines on the tops of the slats, aligned with the outside edges of the end frames. Using a straightedge and circular saw, trim off the ends of the slats along the cutting lines **(photo B).**

Fasten the bottom cleats to the shelf slats, keeping the ends of the slats flush with the outside edges of the cleats.

Attach the bottom cleats to the end frames with deck screws. Use a spacer to keep the cleat 1½" up from the bottom of the bench.

COMPLETE THE END FRAMES.

1. Cut the end trim (D) and bottom trim (E) to length. Fasten them to the outside faces of the end slats to create a frame the same length and width as the end frame. Cut the side trim (G) pieces to length and fasten to the frame assembly with 1½" deck screws, making sure the edges of the side trim are flush with the outside edges of the

end frames and trim frames.
2. Cut the cleats (F). Fasten a top cleat to the inside of each frame with 2½" deck screws. The top cleats should be flush with the tops of the end frames. (The bottom cleats will be attached later.)

ATTACH THE SEAT SLATS.

1. Cut the seat slats (H) to length. Lay them on a flat surface with the ends flush and ⅛"

spaces between slats. Cut the shelf slats (I). Set the end frame assemblies on top of the seat slats. Slip two of the shelf slats between the ends to set the correct distance.
2. Fasten the end-frame assemblies to the seat slats by driving 1½" deck screws through the cleats on the end frames **(photo C).**

ATTACH THE SHELF SLATS.

1. Arrange the shelf slats on your work surface so the ends are flush, with 1½" gaps between the slats. Lay the remaining two cleats across the ends of the slats. Fasten the cleats to the slats with 2½" deck screws **(photo D).**
2. Set the shelf assembly between the ends of the bench, resting on a 1½" spacer. Attach the shelf by driving 2½" screws through the cleats and into the end frames **(photo E).**

APPLY FINISHING TOUCHES.

1. With a compass, draw a 1½"-radius roundover at the corners of the seat. Cut the roundovers with a jig saw. Sand the entire fire pit bench—especially the edges of the seat slats—to eliminate any possibility of slivers. Or, use a router with a roundover bit to trim off the sharp edges.
2. Apply exterior wood stain to all exposed surfaces.

TIP

When storing firewood, it is tempting to cover the wood with plastic tarps to keep it dry. But more often than not, tarps will only trap moisture and keep the firewood permanently damp. With good ventilation wood dries out quickly, so your best bet is to store it uncovered or in an open shelter.

Fold-up Lawn Seat

*With this fold-up seat built for two, you won't have to
sacrifice comfort and style for portability.*

CONSTRUCTION MATERIALS

Quantity	Lumber
1	2 × 8" × 6' cedar
4	2 × 4" × 8' cedar
2	1 × 6" × 8' cedar

Even though this cedar lawn seat folds up for easy transport and storage, it is sturdier and more attractive than just about any outdoor seating you are likely to make or buy. The backrest and legs lock into place when the seat is in use. To move or store this two-person seat, simply fold the backrest down and tuck the legs into the seat frame to convert the seat into a compact package.

Because it is portable and stores in a small space, you can keep the fold-up lawn seat tucked away in a garage or basement and set it up for extra seating when you are entertaining. Or, if security around your home is an issue, you can bring it inside easily during times when you're not home.

OVERALL SIZE:
34⅛" HIGH
22" DEEP
42" LONG

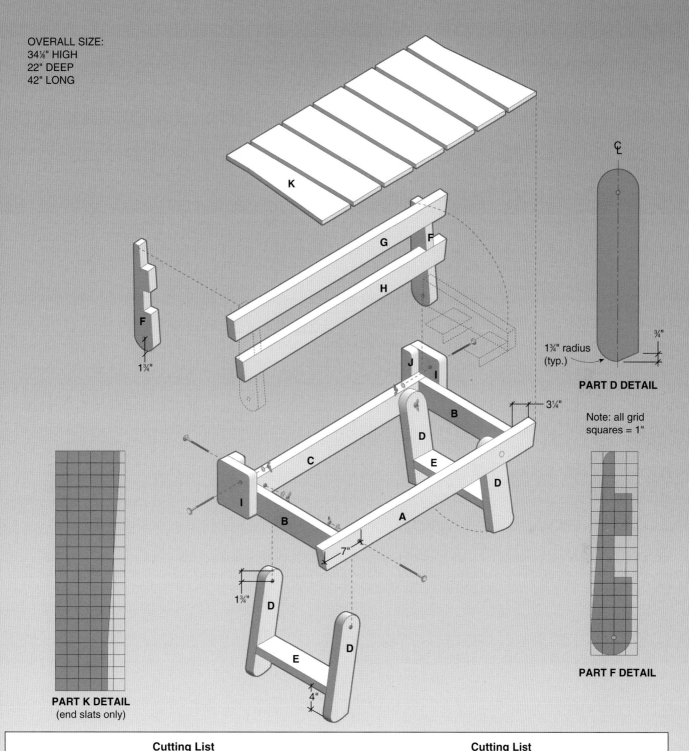

PART D DETAIL

1¾" radius
(typ.)

¾"

Note: all grid
squares = 1"

3¼"

PART F DETAIL

PART K DETAIL
(end slats only)

Cutting List				
Key	**Part**	**Dimension**	**Pcs.**	**Material**
A	Front seat rail	1½ × 3½ × 42"	1	Cedar
B	Side seat rail	1½ × 3½ × 17"	2	Cedar
C	Back seat rail	1½ × 3½ × 35½"	1	Cedar
D	Leg	1½ × 3½ × 16¼"	4	Cedar
E	Stretcher	1½ × 3½ × 13⅞"	2	Cedar
F	Backrest post	1½ × 3½ × 17"	2	Cedar

Cutting List				
Key	**Part**	**Dimension**	**Pcs.**	**Material**
G	Top rest	1½ × 3½ × 42"	1	Cedar
H	Bottom rest	1½ × 3½ × 40"	1	Cedar
I	Cleat	1½ × 7¼ × 6"	2	Cedar
J	Stop	1½ × 7¼ × 2"	2	Cedar
K	Slat	⅞ × 5½ × 20"	7	Cedar

Materials: Moisture-resistant glue, ⅜ × 4" carriage bolts (6) with washers and wing nuts, 1¼", 2" and 2½" deck screws.

Note: Measurements reflect the actual size of dimension lumber.

Directions:
Fold-up Lawn Seat

MAKE THE LEGS.

The lawn seat is supported by two H-shaped legs that fold up inside the seat.

1. Cut the legs (D) to length. Mark a point 1¾" in from one end of each leg. Make sure the point is centered on the leg.

2. Set the point of a compass on each point and draw a 1¾"-radius semicircle to make a cutting line for a roundover at the top of each leg. Cut the roundovers with a jig saw. Then, drill a ⅜"-dia. pilot hole through each point.

3. At the other end of each leg, mark a centerpoint measured from side to side. Measure in ¾" from the end along one edge, and mark another point. Connect the points with a

Fasten the stretchers between the legs with glue and deck screws.

Smooth out the post notches with a wood file.

straight line, and cut along the line with a jig saw to create the flat leg bottoms.

4. Mark 1¾"-radius roundovers at the opposite edges of the leg bottoms, using the approach from Steps 1 and 2. Cut the roundovers with a jig saw.

5. Measure 5½" from the flat end of each leg and drill two pilot holes, 1" from the edge. Counterbore the holes to ¼" depth, using a counterbore bit.

6. Cut the stretchers (E) to length. Attach one stretcher between each pair of legs so the bottoms of the stretchers are 4" from the bottoms of the legs **(photo A)**. Attach the legs with glue and drive 2½" deck screws through the pilot holes. Check that the flat ends of the legs are at the same end.

MAKE THE BACKREST POSTS.

Two posts are notched to hold the two boards that form the backrest.

1. Cut the backrest posts (F) to size. On one edge of each post, mark points 6½", 10" and 13½" from the end of the post. Draw a line lengthwise on each post, 1½" in from the edge with the marks. Extend lines from each point across the lengthwise line. These are the outlines for the notches in the posts (see *Diagram*, page 363). Use a jig saw to cut the notches, then file or sand the cuts smooth **(photo B).**

2. Use a compass to draw a semicircle with a 1¾" radius at the bottom of each post. Measure 1¾" from the bottoms, and mark drilling points centered side to side. Drill a ⅜"-dia. pilot hole at each point.

3. Mark 1" tapers on the back edges of the posts (see *Part F Detail*, page 363). Cut the tapers with a jig saw. Then, sand the posts smooth. Make sure to sand away any sharp edges.

ASSEMBLE THE BACKREST.

1. Cut the top rest (G) and bottom rest (H). Mark trim lines at the ends, starting ½" in from the ends on one edge and tapering to the opposite corner. Check that the trim lines on each end are symmetrical. Trim the ends with a jig saw.

2. Position the posts on their back (tapered) edges, and insert the top and bottom rests into their notches. Position the posts 32½" apart. Center the rests on the posts. The overhang should be equal on each rest. Then, attach the rests to the posts with glue and 2" deck screws **(photo C).**

BUILD THE SEAT FRAME.

The seat frame is made by attaching two side rails between a front rail and back rail. The front rail is tapered to match the backrest.

1. Cut the front seat rail (A), side seat rails (B) and back seat rail (C) to length. Sand the parts smooth.

2. Drill three evenly spaced ⅛" pilot holes, 4" in from each end of the front rail to attach the side rails. Counterbore the holes, using a ¼" drill bit. Make a ½" taper cut at each end of the front rail.

3. Drill centered, ⅜"-dia. holes, 7" in from each end for the leg assemblies. Also drill ⅜"-dia. pilot holes for carriage bolts through the back rail, centered 3¾" in from each end.

4. Apply moisture-resistant glue to one end of each side rail, and position the side rails against the front rails. Fasten the side rails to the back of the front rail by driving deck screws through the pilot holes in the front rail and into the ends of the side rails.

5. Fasten the back rail to the free ends of the side rails with glue and screws. Check that the ends are flush. Then, sand

Center the top and bottom rests in the post notches, and fasten them with glue and deck screws.

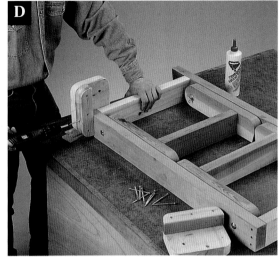

Attach the cleats and stops to the rear edges of the seat frame.

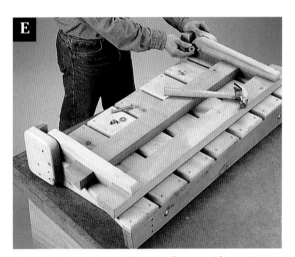

Attach the backrest to the seat frame with carriage bolts and wing nuts.

the frame to round the bottom outside edges.

JOIN THE LEGS AND SEAT FRAME.

1. Position the leg assemblies inside the seat frame. Make certain the rounded corners face the ends of the frame.
2. Apply paste wax to four carriage bolts. Align the pilot holes in the legs and seat frame, and attach the parts with the carriage bolts (see *Diagram*).

ATTACH THE CLEATS AND STOP.

The cleats (I) and stops (J) are attached to each other on the back corner of the seat frame to provide an anchor for the backrest. Once the cleats and stops are attached, carriage bolts are driven through the cleats and into the posts on the backrest. The stops fit flush with the back edges of the cleats to prevent the backrest from folding all the way over.
1. Cut the cleats and stops to size. Then, position a stop against a cleat face, flush with one long edge. The top and bottom edges must be flush. Attach the stop to the cleat with glue and 2½" deck screws.

2. Drill a ⅜"-dia. hole through each cleat, centered 1¾" in from the front and top edges.
3. Smooth the edges of the cleats and stops with a sander. Attach them to the rear corners of the seat frame with glue and 2½" deck screws **(photo D).** Make certain the bottom edges of the cleats and stops are ½" above the bottom of the frame.

ATTACH THE SEAT SLATS.

The seat slats are all the same length, but the end slats are tapered from front to back.
1. Cut the slats (K). Then, plot a 1"-grid on two of the slats (see *Part K Detail,* page 363).
2. Draw cutting lines at the edges of the two slats (see *Part K Detail*). NOTE: The taper straightens 4" from the back of the slat. Cut the tapers with a circular saw or jig saw. Smooth the edges with a router and roundover bit, or a sander.
3. Attach the slats to the seat frame, using glue and 1¼" screws. Make sure the wide ends of the end slats are flush with the ends of the frame, and the back ends of all slats are flush with the back edge of the frame. The gaps between slats should be equal.

ASSEMBLE THE LAWN SEAT.

1. Finish all of the parts with an exterior wood stain.
2. Fit the backrest assembly between the cleats. Align the holes in the posts and cleats, and insert the bolts.
3. Place washers and wing nuts on the ends of the bolts to secure the backrest to the seat frame **(photo E).** Hand-tighten the wing nuts to lock the backrest and legs in position. Loosen the wing nuts when you want to fold the lawn seat for transport or storage.

Sun Lounger

*Designed for the dedicated sun worshipper, this sun lounger has a
backrest that can be set in either a flat or an upright position.*

CONSTRUCTION MATERIALS

Quantity	Lumber
3	2 × 2" × 8' pine
1	2 × 4" × 8' pine
5	2 × 4" × 10' pine
2	2 × 6" × 10' pine

L eave your thin beach
towel and flimsy plastic
chaise lounge behind, as
you relax and soak up the sun
in this solid wood sun lounger.
Set the adjustable backrest in
an upright position while you
make your way through your
summer reading list. Then, for
a change of pace, set the backrest in the flat position and drift
off in a pleasant reverie. If
you're an ambitious suntanner,
take comfort in the fact that
this sun lounger is lightweight
enough that it can be moved
easily to follow the path of direct sunlight. Made almost entirely from inexpensive pine or
cedar, this sun lounger can be
built for only a few dollars—
plus a little sweat equity.

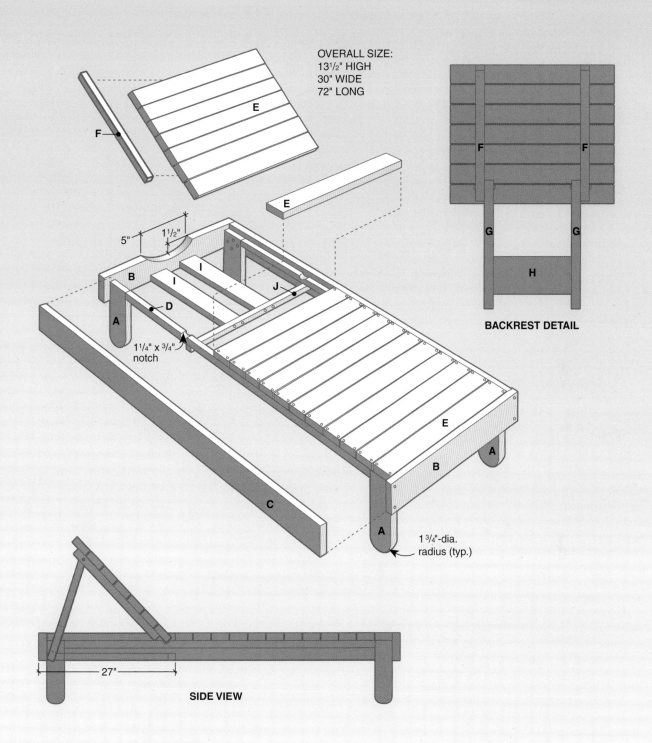

OVERALL SIZE:
13½" HIGH
30" WIDE
72" LONG

BACKREST DETAIL

5"   1½"

1¼" × ¾"
notch

1 ¾"-dia.
radius (typ.)

27"

SIDE VIEW

Cutting List				
Key	**Part**	**Dimension**	**Pcs.**	**Material**
A	Leg	1½ × 3½ × 12"	4	Pine
B	Frame end	1½ × 5½ × 30"	2	Pine
C	Frame side	1½ × 5½ × 69"	2	Pine
D	Ledger	1½ × 1½ × 62"	2	Pine
E	Slat	1½ × 3½ × 27"	19	Pine

Cutting List				
Key	**Part**	**Dimension**	**Pcs.**	**Material**
F	Back brace	1½ × 1½ × 22"	2	Pine
G	Back support	1½ × 1½ × 20"	2	Pine
H	Cross brace	1½ × 5½ × 13"	1	Pine
I	Slide support	1½ × 3½ × 24"	2	Pine
J	Slide brace	1½ × 1½ × 27"	1	Pine

Materials: Moisture-resistant wood glue, 2½" deck screws, ¼"-dia. × 3½" carriage bolts (2) with washers and nuts.

Note: Measurements reflect the actual size of dimension lumber.

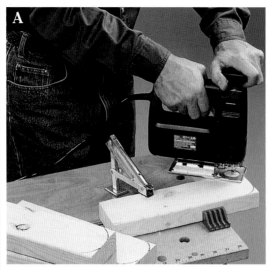

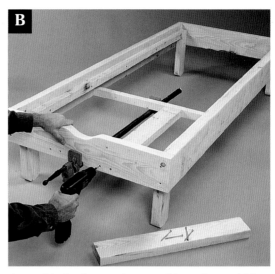

Use a jig saw to cut roundovers on the bottoms of the legs.

Assemble the frame pieces and legs, then add the support boards for the slats and backrest.

Use ⅛"-thick spacers to keep an even gap between slats as you fasten them to the back braces and the ledgers in the bed frame.

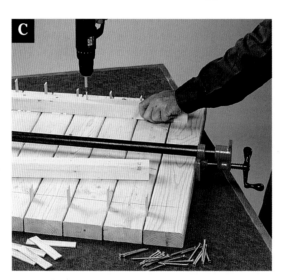

Directions: Sun Lounger

MAKE THE LEGS.
The rounded leg bottoms help the sun lounger rest firmly on uneven surfaces.

1. Cut the legs (A) to length. To ensure uniform length, cut four 2 × 4s to about 13" in length.

TIP

For a better appearance, always keep the screws aligned. In some cases, you may want to add some screws for purely decorative purposes: in this project, we drove 1" deck screws into the backrest slats to continue the lines created by the screw heads in the lower lounge slats.

Clamp them together edge to edge and gang-cut them to final length (12") with a circular saw.

2. Use a compass to scribe a 3½"-radius roundoff cut at the bottom corners of each leg. Make the roundoff cuts with a jig saw **(photo A).** Sand smooth.

CUT THE FRAME PIECES AND LEDGERS.
1. Cut the frame ends (B) and frame sides (C) to length. Use a jig saw to cut a 5"-wide, 1½"-deep notch into the top edge of one frame end, centered end to end, to create a handgrip.

2. Cut the ledgers (D) to length. Measure 24" from one end of each ledger. Place a mark, then cut a 1¼"-wide, ¾"-deep notch into the top edge of each ledger, centered on the 24" mark. Smooth out the notch with a 1½"-radius drum sander mounted on a power drill. (This mark will serve as a pivot for the back support.) Sand all parts and smooth out all sharp edges.

ASSEMBLE THE FRAME.
1. Attach the frame sides and frame ends to form a box around the legs, with the tops of the frame pieces 1½" above the tops of the legs to leave space for the 2 × 4 slats. Fasten with glue and drive 2½" deck screws through the legs and into the frame sides. Also drive screws through the frame ends and into the legs.

2. Attach the ledgers to the frame sides, fitted between the legs, using glue and 2½" deck screws. Make sure the ledger tops are flush with the tops of the legs and the notches are at the same end as the notch in the frame.

CUT AND INSTALL THE BACKREST SUPPORTS.

1. Cut the slide brace (J) to length. Position the slide brace between the frame sides, 24" from the notched frame end, fitted against the bottom edges of the ledgers. Glue and screw the slide brace to the bottom edges of the ledgers.

2. Cut the slide supports (I) to length. Position the supports so they are about 3" apart, centered below the notch in the frame end. The ends of the supports should fit neatly against the frame end and the slide brace. Attach with glue and drive screws through the frame end and the slide brace, and into the ends of the slide supports **(photo B).**

FASTEN THE SLATS.

1. Cut all the slats (E) to length. Use a straightedge guide to ensure straight cuts (the ends will be highly visible). Or, simply hold a speed square against the edges of the boards and run your circular saw along the edge of the speed square.

2. Cut the back braces (F) to length. Lay seven of the slats on a flat work surface, and slip ⅛"-wide spacers between the slats. With the ends of the slats flush, set the back braces onto the faces of the slats, 4" in from the ends. Drive a 2½" deck screw through the brace and into each slat **(photo C).**

3. Install the remaining slats in the lounge frame, spaced ⅛" apart, by driving two screws through each slat end and into the tops of the ledgers. One end slat should be ⅛" from the inside of the uncut frame end, and the other 27" from the outside of the notched frame end.

ASSEMBLE THE BACKREST SUPPORT FRAMEWORK.

The adjustable backrest is held in place by a small framework attached to the back braces. The framework can either be laid flat so the backrest lies flat, or raised up and fitted against the inside of the notched frame end to support the upright backrest.

1. Cut the back supports (G) to length. Clamp the pieces together face to face, with the ends flush. Clamp a belt sander to your work surface, and use it as a grinder to round off the supports on one end.

2. Cut the cross brace (H) to length. Position the cross brace between the back supports, 2" from the non-rounded ends. Attach with glue and drive 2½" deck screws through the supports and into the cross brace.

3. Position the rounded ends of the supports so they fit between the ends of the back braces, overlapping by 2½" when laid flat. Drill a ¼" guide hole through the braces and the supports at each overlap joint.

4. Thread ¼"-dia. × 3½"-long carriage bolts through the guide holes, with a flat washer between each support and brace. Hand-tighten a washer and nylon locking nut onto each bolt end (see **photo D).**

INSTALL THE BACKREST.

1. Set the backrest onto the ledger boards near the notched end of the frame.

2. With the backrest raised, tighten the locking nut on the backrest support framework until it holds the framework together securely while still allowing the joint to pivot **(photo D).**

APPLY FINISHING TOUCHES.

Sand all surfaces and edges **(photo E)** to eliminate slivers. Apply two coats of water-based, exterior polyurethane for a smooth, protective finish. Or, use a primer and a light-colored exterior paint.

Use a washer and nylon locking nut to fasten the back braces to the back supports.

Sand all surfaces carefully to eliminate splinters, and check to make sure all screw heads are set below the wood surface.

Tree Surround
*Turn wasted space beneath a mature tree
into a shady seating area.*

CONSTRUCTION MATERIALS

Quantity	Lumber
11	2 × 4" × 8' cedar
2	1 × 6" × 8' cedar
24	1 × 4" × 8' cedar

This tree surround with built-in benches provides ample seating in your yard, while protecting the base of the tree trunk. Situated in a naturally shady area, the surround/bench creates an ideal spot to relax with a good book or spend a quiet moment alone.

The tree surround can be built in four pieces in your garage or basement, then assembled on-site to wrap around the tree. As shown, the tree surround will fit a tree trunk up to 25" in diameter. But with some basic math, it's easy to adjust the sizes of the pieces so the surround fits just about any tree in your yard.

Unlike most tree bench designs, this project is essentially freestanding and does not require you to set posts (digging holes at the base of a tree can be next to impossible in some cases). And because it is cedar, it will blend right into most landscapes.

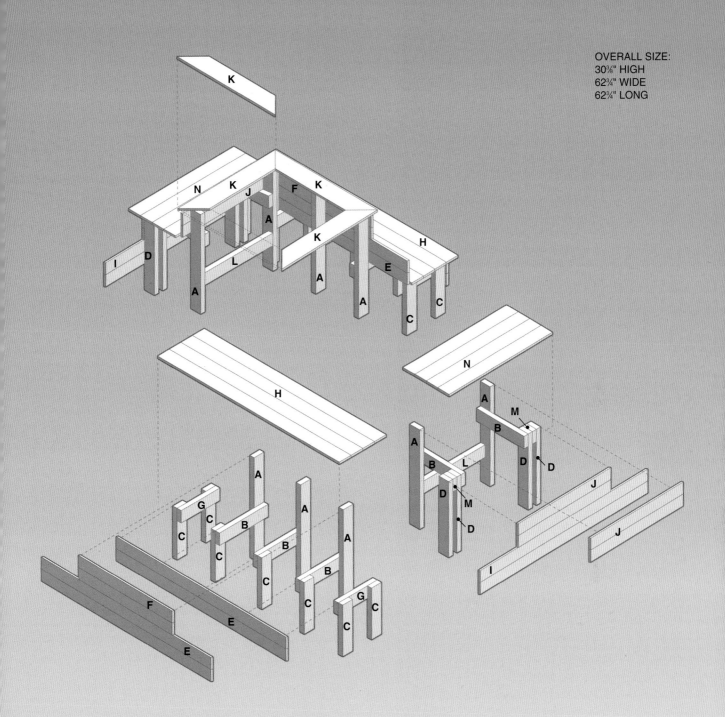

OVERALL SIZE:
30⅜" HIGH
62¾" WIDE
62¾" LONG

Cutting List

Key	Part	Dimension	Pcs.	Material
A	Inside post	1½ × 3½ × 29½"	10	Cedar
B	Seat rail	1½ × 3½ × 16¾"	10	Cedar
C	Short post	1½ × 3½ × 15"	14	Cedar
D	Long post	1½ × 3½ × 22¼"	8	Cedar
E	Face board	⅞ × 3½ × 60½"	8	Cedar
F	Face board	⅞ × 3½ × 34"	4	Cedar
G	Side seat rail	1½ × 3½ × 13¼"	4	Cedar

Cutting List

Key	Part	Dimension	Pcs.	Material
H	Bench slat	⅞ × 3½ × 62¾"	8	Cedar
I	Face board	⅞ × 3½ × 58¾"	4	Cedar
J	Face board	⅞ × 3½ × 32¼"	8	Cedar
K	End cap	⅞ × 5½ × 36"	4	Cedar
L	Stringer	1½ × 3½ × 22¼"	2	Cedar
M	Nailer	1½ × 3½ × 3½"	4	Cedar
N	Bench slat	⅞ × 3½ × 36¼"	8	Cedar

Materials: Moisture-resistant glue, 1½" and 2½" deck screws, finishing materials.

Note: Measurements reflect the actual size of dimension lumber.

Directions: Tree Surround

BUILD THE SHORT BENCH FRAMES.

The tree surround is built as two short benches on the sides, and two taller benches on the ends. The benches are joined together to wrap around the tree. Drill a ⅛" pilot hole for every screw used in this project. Counterbore the holes to a ¼" depth, using a counterbore bit.

1. To build the support frames for the short benches, cut the inside posts (A), seat rails (B) and short posts (C) to length. Lay a short post on top of an inside post, with the bottom ends flush. Trace a reference line onto the face of the inside post, following the top of the short post.

2. Separate the posts. Lay a seat rail across the faces of the two posts so it is flush with the outside edge and top of the short post, and just below the reference line on the inside post.

Use a square to make sure the seat rails are perpendicular to the posts and their ends are flush with the post edges. Join the pieces with moisture-resistant glue. Drive 2½" deck screws through the seat rails and into the short posts and inside posts. Make six of these assemblies **(photo A).**

3. Cut the four side seat rails (G) to length. Attach them to pairs of short posts so the tops and ends are flush.

TIP

Leave room for the tree to grow in trunk diameter when you build and install a tree surround. Allow at least 3" between the tree and the surround on all sides. Adjust the dimensions of your tree surround, if needed, to create the additional space.

Seat rails are attached to the short posts and inside posts to make the bench frames.

The face boards attached at the fronts of the short posts on the short benches should extend ⅞" past the edges of the posts.

ATTACH THE SHORT BENCH FACE BOARDS.

1. Cut the face boards (E) to length for the fronts of the short benches. Draw lines on the inside faces of these face boards, ⅞" and 14⅞" from each end, and at their centers. These reference lines will serve as guides when you attach the face boards to the short bench frames.

2. Lay the two frames made with two short posts on your work surface, with the back edges of the back posts down. Attach a face board to the front edges of the front posts, with 1½" deck screws, so the ends of the face board extend ⅞" be-

Attach face boards to the inside posts to create the backrest. The lowest board should be ⅛" above the seat rails.

TIP

Cover the ground at the base of a tree with a layer of landscaping stone or wood bark before you install a tree surround. To prevent weeds from growing up through the ground cover, lay landscaping fabric in the area first. Add a border of landscape edging to keep everything contained. If the ground at the base of the tree is not level, you can make installation of the tree surround easier by laying a base of landscaping rock, then raking it and tamping it until it is level.

yond the outside edges of the frames (the seat rail should be on the inside of the frame). Attach another face board ⅛" below the top face board, making sure the reference lines are aligned **(photo B).**

ASSEMBLE THE SHORT BENCHES.

1. Stand the frame and face board assemblies on their feet. Fit the short bench frames made with the inside posts against the inside faces of the face boards. Center the short posts of the frames on the reference lines drawn on the face boards. Attach these frames to the face boards with 1½" deck screws.

2. Set another face board at the backs of the seat rails, against the inside posts. Slip a 10d finish nail under the face board where it crosses each seat rail to create a ⅛" gap. Make sure the ends of the face board extend ⅞" beyond the edges of the end frames. Attach the face board to the inside posts with 1½" deck screws **(photo C).** Attach another face board ⅛" up

on the inside posts.

3. Cut the face boards (F) to length. Fasten two of these shorter face boards to each bench assembly so the ends overhang the inside posts by ⅞". Maintain a ⅛" gap between the face boards. The top edge of the highest face board on each bench assembly should be flush with the tops of the inside posts.

4. Cut the bench slats (H) to length. Position the front bench slat so it overhangs the front of the face board below it by 1⅛" and both ends of the face board by 1⅛" **(photo D).** Attach the front slat by driving two 1½" deck screws through the slat and into each seat rail. Fasten the back seat slat so it butts against the inside posts. Attach the remaining bench slats so the spaces between the slats are even.

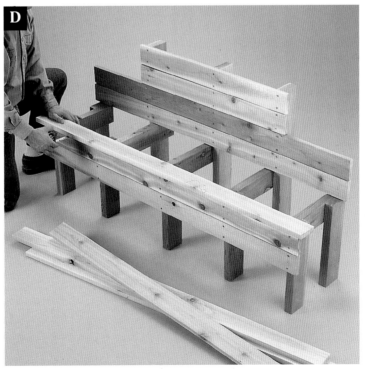

Measure to make sure the front bench slat overhangs the face board below it by 1⅛".

MAKE THE TALL BENCHES.

The two tall benches are built much like the short benches, but with doubled posts at the front, for extra strength, and a stringer to support the frames.

1. Cut the long posts (D) and four nailers (M) to length. Arrange the long posts in pairs, with nailers in between at the tops. Fasten the doubled posts and nailers together with glue and 2½" deck screws, making sure the nailers are aligned with the fronts and tops of the posts.

2. Attach a seat rail to the doubled posts **(photo E).** Then, attach the free end of each seat rail to an inside post, as you did for the short benches.

3. Cut the stringers (L) to length. Position a stringer between each pair of inside posts, flush with the back edges and 8" up from the bottoms of the posts. Attach them with glue and 2½" deck screws driven through the inside posts and into the ends of the stringers.

4. Cut the face boards for the tall benches (I, J) to length. Use 10d finish nails to leave ⅛" gaps between the face boards, as before, including the gap above the back ends of the seat rails. Use 1½" deck screws to attach two of the shorter boards (J) to the long posts so the top board is flush with the tops of the posts and seat rails, and the ends overhang the outside edges of the doubled posts by ½" **(photo F).**

5. Attach the longer face boards (I) below the shorter face boards, so they overhang the doubled posts by the same amount on each end **(photo G).** The overhang portions will cover the sides of the short

After making doubled posts for the tall benches, attach the seat rails.

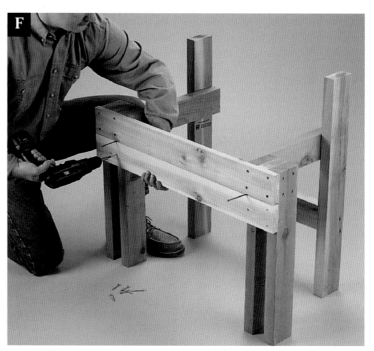

The shorter face boards for the tall benches are attached so the ends are flush with the outsides of the doubled posts.

bench frames after assembly. Attach two of the shorter face boards (J) to the front edges of the inside posts so their ends overhang the outside faces of the posts by 3½".

6. Cut the bench slats for the tall benches (N) to length. Position the slats on the seat rails. Fasten the front slat so it overhangs the front of the face board below it by 1⅛" and the ends of the face board by 2". Fasten a slat flush with the

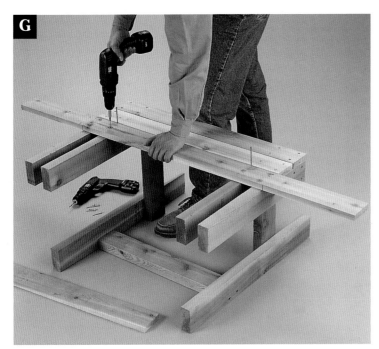

The longer face boards attached to the tall benches overhang the doubled posts so they cover the sides of the short bench frames when the tree surround is assembled.

back of the bench. Attach the remaining slats on each tall bench so the spaces between the slats are even.

APPLY THE FINISH.

Now is a good time to apply a finish to the benches. Sand all the surfaces smooth and wipe the wood clean. Apply at least two coats of exterior wood stain to protect the wood.

ASSEMBLE THE TREE SURROUND.

1. If necessary, prepare the ground around the tree where the tree surround will stand (see *Tip Box,* page 373). When the ground is roughly level, you can assemble the tree surround and shim beneath the posts to level it.

2. Set all four benches around the tree so the overhang on the tall bench face boards covers the end frames of the short benches. The ends of the face boards should butt against the backs of the face boards on the short benches. Clamp or tack the benches together. Don't fasten the pieces together until you've made adjustments to level the tree surround.

3. Use a carpenter's level to check the tree surround. Set the level on each of the benches to determine whether adjustments are needed. For shims, use flat stones, such as flagstone, or prefabricated concrete pavers. If you don't want to use shims, mark the spots on the ground that need raising or lowering, and separate the benches to make the required adjustments.

4. When the tree surround is level and the benches fit together squarely, attach the tall benches to the short benches by driving 2½" deck screws through the face boards on the tall benches and into the posts on the short benches.

ATTACH THE CAP.

1. Cut the end caps (K) to length. Draw 45° miter lines at each end of one cap, with both miter lines pointing inward. Make the miter cuts with a circular saw **(photo H)** or—even better—a power miter box.

2. Tack or clamp the end cap in place. Mark and cut the three remaining end caps one at a time to ensure even joints. Attach the caps with 1½" deck screws driven through the caps and into the ends of the inside posts. Sand the parts smooth and apply the same finish to the caps that you applied to the tree surround benches.

The 1 × 6 caps are mitered to make a square frame around the top of the tree surround after it is assembled around your tree.

Park Bench

This attention-grabbing park bench is a real showpiece that can transform even a plain yard into a formal garden.

CONSTRUCTION MATERIALS

Quantity	Lumber
5	2 × 4" × 8' pine
1	2 × 2" × 4' pine
4	1 × 6" × 8' pine

Add color and style to your backyard or garden with this bright, elegant park bench. Some careful jig saw work is all it takes to make the numerous curves and contours that give this bench a sophisticated look. But don't worry if your cuts aren't all perfect—the shapes are decorative, so the bench will still work just fine. In fact, if you prefer a simpler appearance, you can build the park bench with all straight parts, except the roundovers at the bottoms of the legs. But if you are willing to do the extra work, you're sure to be pleased with the final result. You may even want to finish it with bright red paint so no one will miss it.

OVERALL SIZE:
38" HIGH
23" DEEP
52" LONG

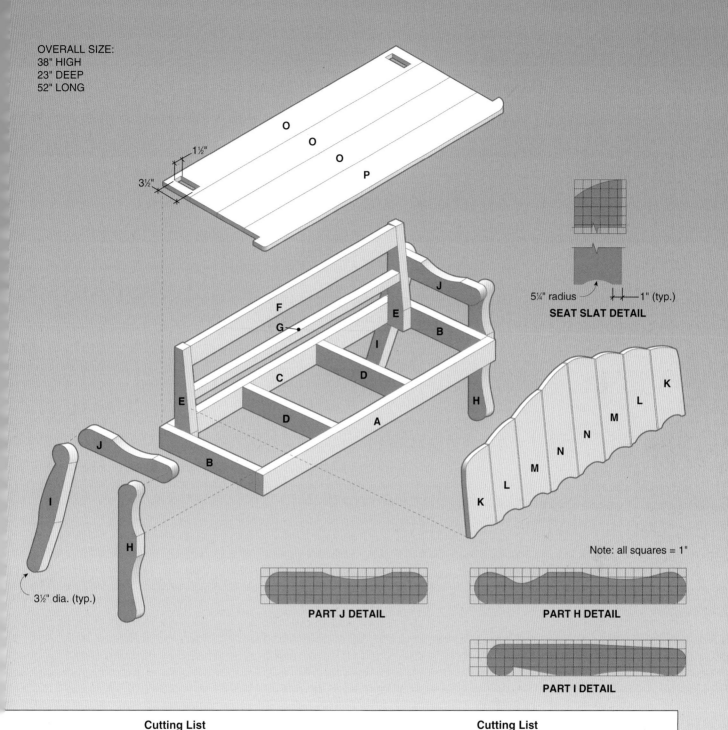

SEAT SLAT DETAIL

5¼" radius   1" (typ.)

Note: all squares = 1"

PART J DETAIL

PART H DETAIL

PART I DETAIL

3½" dia. (typ.)

Cutting List				
Key	Part	Dimension	Pcs.	Material
A	Front rail	1½ × 3½ × 49"	1	Pine
B	Side rail	1½ × 3½ × 20¼"	2	Pine
C	Back rail	1½ × 3½ × 46"	1	Pine
D	Cross rail	1½ × 3½ × 18¾"	2	Pine
E	Post	1½ × 3½ × 18"	2	Pine
F	Top rail	1½ × 3½ × 43"	1	Pine
G	Bottom rail	1½ × 1½ × 43"	1	Pine
H	Front leg	1½ × 3½ × 24½"	2	Pine

Cutting List				
Key	Part	Dimension	Pcs.	Material
I	Rear leg	1½ × 3½ × 23"	2	Pine
J	Armrest	1½ × 3½ × 18½"	2	Pine
K	End slat	¾ × 5½ × 14"	2	Pine
L	Outside slat	¾ × 5½ × 16"	2	Pine
M	Inside slat	¾ × 5½ × 18"	2	Pine
N	Center slat	¾ × 5½ × 20"	2	Pine
O	Seat slat	¾ × 5½ × 49"	3	Pine
P	Seat nose slat	¾ × 5½ × 52"	1	Pine

Materials: Moisture-resistant glue, 1¼", 2½" deck screws, finishing materials.

Note: All measurements reflect the actual size of dimension lumber.

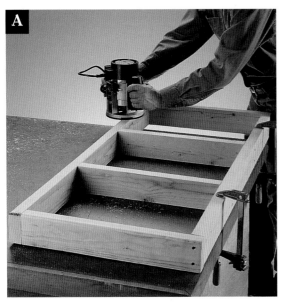

Use a router or sander to round over the sharp bottom edges and corners of the completed seat frame.

Attach the seat slats and nose slat to the top of the seat frame with glue and deck screws.

Directions: Park Bench

BUILD THE SEAT FRAME.

The seat frame is made by assembling rails and cross rails to form a rectangular unit.

1. Cut the front rail (A), side rails (B), back rail (C) and cross rails (D) to length. Sand rough spots with medium-grit sandpaper.

2. Fasten the side rails to the front rail with moisture-resistant glue. Drill ⅛" pilot holes in the front rail. Counterbore the holes to accept ⅜"-dia. wood plugs. Drive 2½" deck screws through the front rail and into the side rail ends. Make sure the top and bottom edges of the side rails are flush with the top and bottom edges of the front rail.

3. Attach the back rail between the side rails. Drill pilot holes in the side rails. Counterbore the holes. Fasten with glue and drive screws through the side rails and into the ends of the back rail. Keep the back

rail flush with the ends of the side rails.

4. Use glue and deck screws to fasten the two cross rails between the front and back rails, 14½" in from the inside face of each side rail.

5. Complete the seat frame by rounding the bottom edges and corners with a router and a ⅜"-dia. roundover bit **(photo A)** or a hand sander.

MAKE THE SEAT SLATS.

The seat nose slat has side cutouts to accept the front legs. The back seat slat has cutouts, called mortises, to accept the posts that support the backrest.

1. Cut the seat nose slat (P) and one seat slat (O) to length. To mark the 2 × 4 cutouts, use

the end of a 2 × 4 as a template.

2. Position the 2 × 4 on the seat slat at each end, 1½" in from the back edge and 1½" in from the end. The long sides of the 2 × 4 should be parallel to the ends of the back seat slat. Trace the outline of the 2 × 4 onto the slat. Drill a starter hole within the outline on the back seat slat. Make the cutout with a jig saw.

3. Use a jig saw to cut a 3"-long × 1½"-wide notch at each end of the nose slat, starting at the back edge (see *Diagram*, page 377). Sand the notches and mortises with a file or a thin sanding block. Use a router with roundover bit to shape the front edge of the nose slat.

ATTACH THE SEAT SLATS.

1. Cut the rest of the seat slats (O) to length. Lay the slats on the seat frame so the ends of the slats are flush with the frame, and the nose slat overhangs equally

---

TIP

Making smooth contour cuts with a jig saw can be a little tricky. To make it easier, install fairly thick saw blades, because they are less likely to "wander" with the grain of the wood. Using a scrolling jig saw will also help, since they are easier to turn than standard jig saws.

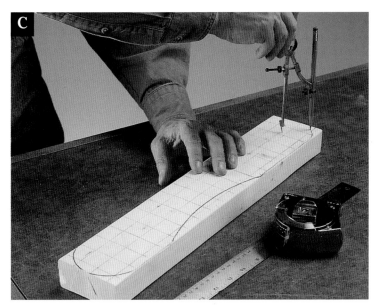

After drawing a 1" grid on the legs and armrests, draw the finished shape of the parts, following the Grid Patterns on page 377.

at the sides of the frame.

2. Draw reference lines onto the tops of the seat slats and nose slat, directly over the top of each rail in the frame. Mark two drilling points on each slat on each line—on all but the front of the nose slat. Points should be ¾" in from the front and back of the slats. On the nose slat, mark drilling points 1½" in from the front of the slat. Drill pilot holes and counterbore the holes.

3. Sand the seat slats and nose slat. Attach them to the seat frame with glue. Drive 1¼" deck screws through the slats and into the frame and cross rails **(photo B).** Start with the front and back slats, and space the inner slats evenly.

MAKE THE LEGS AND ARMRESTS.

The front legs (H), rear legs (I) and armrests (J) are shaped using the grid patterns on page 377.

1. Cut workpieces for the parts to the full sizes shown in the *Cutting List.* Use a pencil to draw a 1"-square grid pattern on each workpiece.

2. Using the grid patterns as a reference, draw the shapes onto the workpieces **(photo C).** (It will help if you enlarge the patterns on a photocopier or draw them to a larger scale on a piece of graph paper first.)

3. Cut out the shapes with a jig saw. Sand the contour cuts smooth. Use a drum sander mounted in your electric drill for best results.

ATTACH THE LEGS.

The front and rear legs are attached to the armrests, flush with the front and rear ends.

1. Fasten the front legs to the outside faces of the armrests. Drill pilot holes in the legs. Counterbore the

holes. Drive deck screws through the holes and into the armrests. Use a framing square to make sure the legs are perpendicular to the armrests.

2. Temporarily fasten the rear legs to the outside faces of the armrests by drilling centered pilot holes and driving a screw through each rear leg and into the armrest. The rear leg must, for now, remain adjustable.

3. Clamp the seat to the legs. The front of the edge of the seat should be 16¾" up from the bottoms of the front legs. The back of the seat should be 14¼" up from the bottoms of the rear legs. Position square wood spacers between the seat and each armrest to keep the armrest parallel to the frame.

4. Adjust the rear legs so their back edges are flush with the top corners of the side rails. The rear legs extend slightly beyond the back of the seat frame.

5. Drill pilot holes in the front and rear legs. Counterbore the holes. Drive deck screws through the front and rear legs and into the side. Drive an ad-

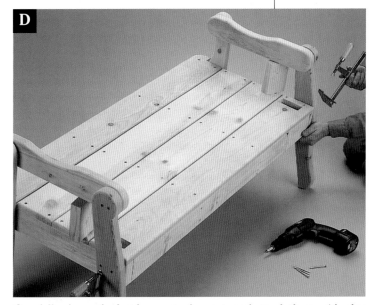

Carefully clamp the leg frames to the seat, and attach them with glue and screws, driven through centered, counterbored pilot holes.

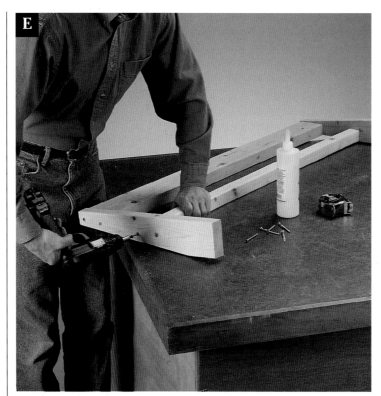

E

Glue the ends of the top and bottom rails, then drive deck screws through the posts to attach them to the rails.

rear leg into the armrests to secure the rear legs in position.
6. Unclamp the leg assemblies, and remove them from the frame **(photo D).** Apply glue to the leg assemblies where they join the frame and reattach the legs and armrests using the same screw holes.

BUILD THE BACK FRAME.
The back frame is made by attaching a top rail (F) and bottom rail (G) between two posts (E). Once the back frame has

been built, it is inserted into the mortises in the rear seat slats. Tapers cut on the front edges of the posts will create a backward slope so the back slats make a more comfortable backrest. When you attach the rails between the posts, make sure they are flush with the front edges of the posts.
1. Cut the posts, top rail and bottom rail to length. Mark a tapered cutting line on each post, starting 1½" in from the back edge, at the top. Extend the line so it meets the front edge 3½" up from the bottom. Cut the taper in each post, using a circular saw or jig saw.
2. Use glue and deck screws to fasten the top rail between the posts so the front face of the top rail is flush with the front (tapered) edge of each post. The top front corner of the top rail should be flush with the top of the posts.

3. Position the bottom rail between the posts so its bottom edge is 9" up from the bottoms of the posts. Make sure the front face of the bottom rail is flush with the front edges of the posts. Drill pilot holes in the posts. Counterbore the holes. Attach the parts with glue and 2½" deck screws **(photo E).** Use a router with a ⅜"-dia. roundover bit or a hand sander to round over the back edges of the back frame.

MAKE THE BACK SLATS.
The back slats are shaped on their tops and bottoms to create a scalloped effect. If you'd rather not spend the time cutting these contours, you can simply cut the slats to length and round over the top edges.
1. Cut the end slats (K), outside slats (L), inside slats (M) and center slats (N) to length. Draw a 1"-square grid pattern on one slat. Then, draw the shape shown in the back slat detail on page 111 onto the slat. Use a compass to mark a 5¼"-radius scalloped cutout at the bottom of the slat.
2. Cut the slat to shape with a jig saw and sand smooth.
3. Use the completed slat as a template to trace the same profile on the tops and bottoms of the remaining slats **(photo F).** Cut them to shape with a jig saw and sand the cuts smooth.

ATTACH THE BACK SLATS.
1. Before attaching the back slats to the back frame, clamp a straight board across the fronts of the posts with its top edge 8½" up from the bottoms of the posts **(photo G).** Use this board as a guide to keep the slats aligned as you attach them.
2. Fasten the end slats to the

TIP

Depending on the location of your yard and garden furnishings, you may encounter some uneven terrain. If the ground is hard, you can install adjustable leveler glides to the bottoms of the legs to keep your projects level. If the project is resting on softer ground, the easiest solution is to use flat stones to shim under the lower sides or legs. Or, you can throw down a loose-stone base under the project, and tamp it until it is level.

Use the first completed back slat as a template for tracing cutting lines on the rest of the back slats.

Clamp a straight board to the back frame to help keep the back slats aligned along their bottom edges as you install them.

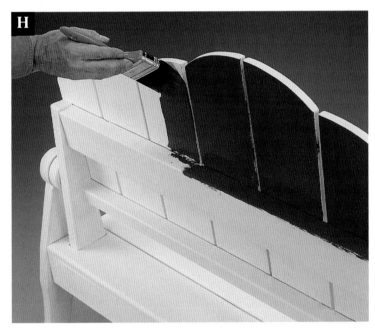

Apply two thin coats of exterior primer to seal the pine, then paint the park bench with two coats of enamel house trim paint.

back frame with glue and deck screws, making sure the bottoms are resting flat against the clamped guide board. (For more information on back slat positioning, see the *Diagram.*) Make sure the outside edges of the end slats are flush with the outside edges of the posts.

3. Attach the remaining slats between the end slats, spaced so the gaps are even.

ASSEMBLE THE BENCH.

1. Attach the rear frame by sliding the back into place inside the notches in the rear seat slat. The posts should rest against the back rail and side rails.

Keep the bottoms of the posts flush with the bottom edges of the side rails.

2. Drill pilot holes in the posts and the back rail. Counterbore the holes. Drive 2½" screws through the posts and into the side rails, and through the back rail and into the posts.

APPLY FINISHING TOUCHES.

1. Apply moisture-resistant glue to ⅜"-dia. wood plugs, and insert them into each counterbored screw hole. Sand the plugs flush with the wood.

2. Sand all surfaces smooth with medium (100- or 120-grit) sandpaper. Finish-sand with fine (150- or 180-grit) sandpaper.

3. Finish as desired—try two thin coats of primer and two coats of exterior house trim paint **(photo H)**. Whenever you use untreated pine for an outdoor project, be sure to use an exterior-rated finish to protect the wood.

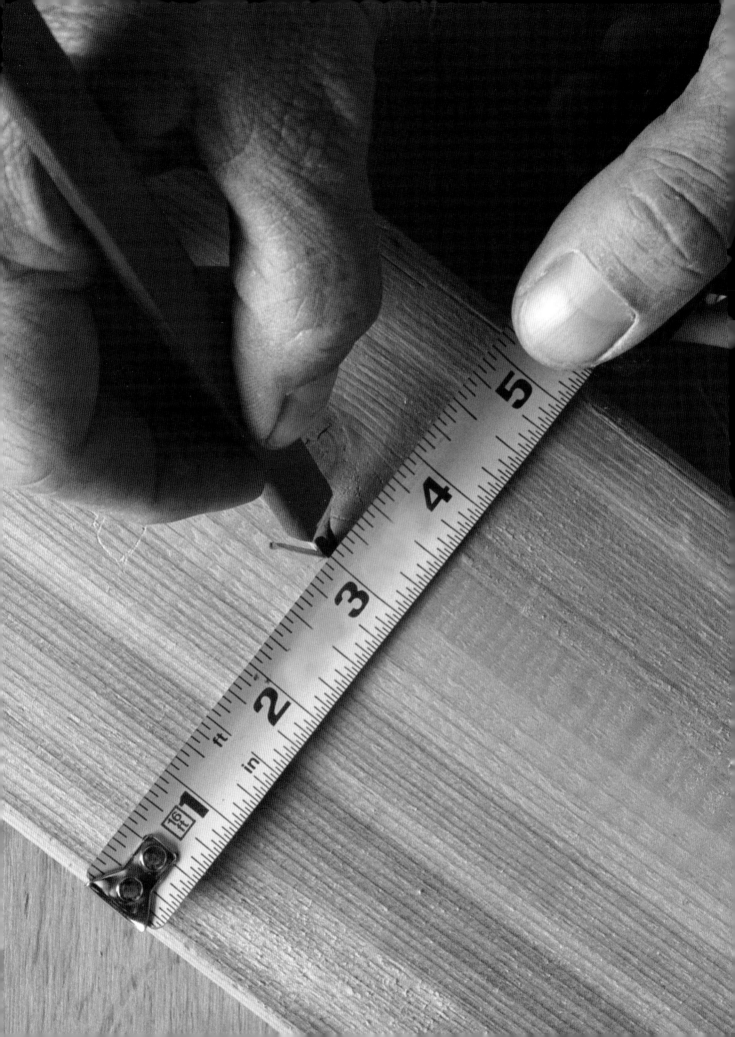

Tables

Tables are the backbone of the outdoor entertainment scene. They hold food and beverages, display collections, and provide places for family and friends to gather. A structure that plays such a varied role should be given some thoughtful design consideration. Create a table that fills your needs—whether it be entertaining, intimate dining, or design—and you'll find your outdoor home is instantly transformed into a place of comfort and convenience.

Outdoor Occasional Table

The traditional design of this deck table provides a stylishly simple addition to any porch, deck or patio.

CONSTRUCTION MATERIALS

Quantity	Lumber
2	1 × 3" × 8' cedar
6	1 × 4" × 8' cedar

Create a functional yet stylish accent for your porch, deck or patio with this cedar deck table. This table makes an ideal surface for serving cold lemonade on hot summer days, a handy place to set your plate during a family cookout, or simply a comfortable place to rest your feet after a long day. Don't be fooled by its lightweight design and streamlined features—the little table is extremely sturdy. Structural features such as middle and end stringers tie the aprons and legs together and transfer weight from the table slats to the legs. This attractive little table is easy to build and will provide many years of durable service.

OVERALL SIZE:
26½" WIDE
18" HIGH
42" LONG

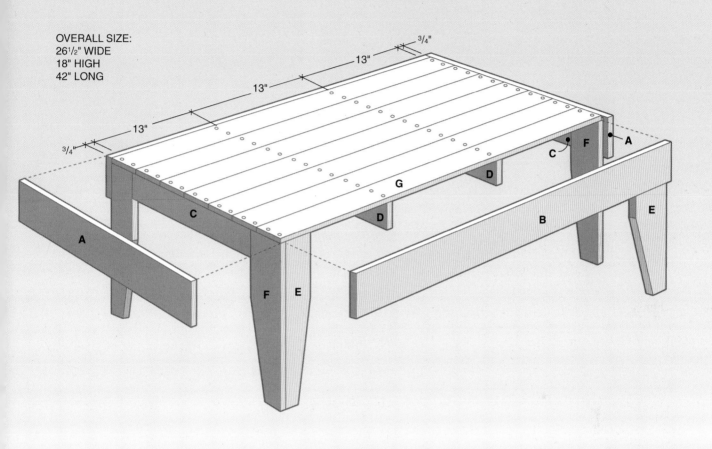

Cutting List				
Key	**Part**	**Dimension**	**Pcs.**	**Material**
A	End apron	¾ × 3½ × 26½"	2	Cedar
B	Side apron	¾ × 3½ × 40½"	2	Cedar
C	End stringer	¾ × 2½ × 18"	2	Cedar
D	Middle stringer	¾ × 2½ × 25"	2	Cedar

Cutting List				
Key	**Part**	**Dimension**	**Pcs.**	**Material**
E	Narrow leg side	¾ × 2½ × 17¼"	4	Cedar
F	Wide leg side	¾ × 3½ × 17¼"	4	Cedar
G	Slat	¾ × 3½ × 40½"	7	Cedar

Materials: Moisture-resistant glue, 1¼" deck screws.

Note: Measurements reflect the actual size of dimension lumber.

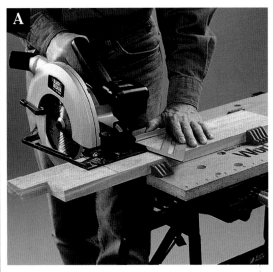

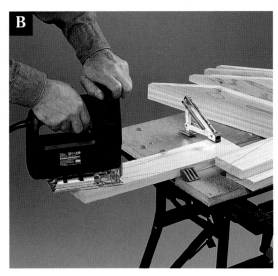

Use a speed square as a cutting guide and gang-cut the table parts when possible for uniform results.

Mark the ends of the tapers on the leg sides, then connect the marks to make taper cutting lines.

Directions: Outdoor Occasional Table

MAKE THE STRINGERS AND APRONS.

1. The stringers and aprons form a frame for the tabletop slats. To make them, cut the end aprons (A) and side aprons (B) to length **(photo A).** For fast, straight cutting, use a speed square as a saw guide—the flange on the speed square hooks over the edge of the boards to hold it securely in place while you cut.

2. Cut the end stringers (C) and middle stringers (D) to length.

MAKE THE LEG PARTS.

1. Cut the narrow leg sides (E) and wide leg sides (F) to length.

2. On one wide leg side piece, measure 8¾" along one edge of the leg side and place a mark. Measure across the bottom end of the leg side 1½" and place a

TIP

Rip-cut cedar 1 × 4s to 2½" in width if you are unable to find good clear cedar 1 × 3s (nominal). When rip-cutting, always use a straightedge guide for your circular saw. A straight piece of lumber clamped to your workpiece makes an adequate guide, or buy a metal straightedge guide with built-in clamps.

Use a jig saw or circular saw to cut the leg tapers.

mark. Connect the two marks to create a cutting line for the leg taper. Mark cutting lines for the tapers on all four wide leg sides **(photo B).**

3. On the thin leg sides, measure 8¾" along an edge and ¾" across the bottom end to make endpoints for the taper cutting lines.

4. Clamp each leg side to your work surface. Cut along the taper cutoff line, using a jig saw or circular saw, to create the tapered leg sides **(photo C).** Sand all leg parts smooth.

ASSEMBLE THE LEG PAIRS.

1. Apply a ½"-wide layer of moisture-resistant glue on the face of a wide leg side, next to the untapered edge. Then apply a thin layer of glue to the untapered edge of a narrow leg side. Join the leg sides together at a right angle to form a leg pair. Reinforce the joint with 1¼" deck screws.

2. Glue and screw the rest of the leg pairs in the same manner **(photo D).** Be careful not to use too much glue. Excess glue can get messy and could

Fasten the leg pairs by driving deck screws through the face of the wide side and into the narrow edge.

Test the layout of the slats before you fasten them, adjusting as necessary to make sure gaps are even.

cause problems later if you plan to stain or clear-coat the finish.

MAKE THE TABLETOP FRAME.

1. Fasten the side aprons (B) to the leg pairs with glue and screws. Be sure to screw from the back side of the leg pair and into the side aprons so the screw heads will be concealed. The narrow leg side of each pair should be facing in toward the center of the side apron, with the outside faces of the wide leg sides flush with the ends of the side apron. The tops of the leg pairs should be ¾" down from the tops of the side aprons to create recesses for the tabletop slats.

2. Attach the end aprons (A) to the leg assemblies with glue. Drive screws from the back side of the leg pairs. Make sure the end aprons are positioned so the ends are flush with the outside faces of the side aprons.

3. Attach the end stringers (C) to the end aprons between the leg pairs with glue. Drive the screws from the back sides of the end stringers and into the end aprons.

4. Cut the middle stringers (D) to length. Measure 13" in from the inside face of each end stringer and mark reference lines on the side aprons for positioning the middle stringers.

5. Use glue to attach the middle stringers to the side aprons—centered on the reference lines. Drive deck screws through the side aprons and into the ends of the middle stringers. Make sure the middle stringers are positioned ¾" down from the tops of the side aprons.

CUT AND INSTALL THE SLATS.

1. Before you cut the slats (G), measure the inside dimension between the end aprons to be sure that the slat length is correct. Then cut the slats to length, using a circular saw and a speed square to keep the cuts square. It is extremely important to make square cuts on the ends of the slats since they're going to be the most visible cuts on the entire table.

2. Run a bead of glue along the top faces of the middle and end stringers. Screw the slats to

the stringers leaving a gap of approximately ¹⁄₁₆" between each of the individual slats **(photo E).**

APPLY FINISHING TOUCHES.

1. Smooth all sharp edges by using a router with a roundover bit or a power sander with medium-grit (#100 to 120) sandpaper. Finish-sand the entire table and clean off the sanding residue.

2. Apply a finish, such as clear wood sealer. If you want, fill any screw counterbores with tinted wood putty.

PROJECT
POWER TOOLS

Picnic Table for Two

*Turn a quiet corner of your yard into an intimate setting for dining
alfresco with this compact picnic table.*

CONSTRUCTION MATERIALS

Quantity	Lumber
1	2 × 8" × 6' cedar
1	2 × 6" × 8' cedar
4	2 × 4" × 8' cedar
3	1 × 6" × 8' cedar
4	1 × 2" × 8' cedar

A picnic table doesn't have to be a clumsy, uncomfortable family feeding trough. In this project, you'll create a unique picnic table that's just the right size for two people to enjoy. Portable and lightweight, it can be set in a corner of your garden, beneath a shade tree or on your deck or patio to enhance your outdoor dining experiences.

The generously proportioned tabletop can be set with full table settings for a formal meal in the garden. But it's intimate enough for sharing a cool beverage with a special person as you watch the sun set. Made with plain dimensional cedar, this picnic table for two is both sturdy and long-lasting.

OVERALL SIZE:
28⅛" HIGH
30" WIDE
68" LONG

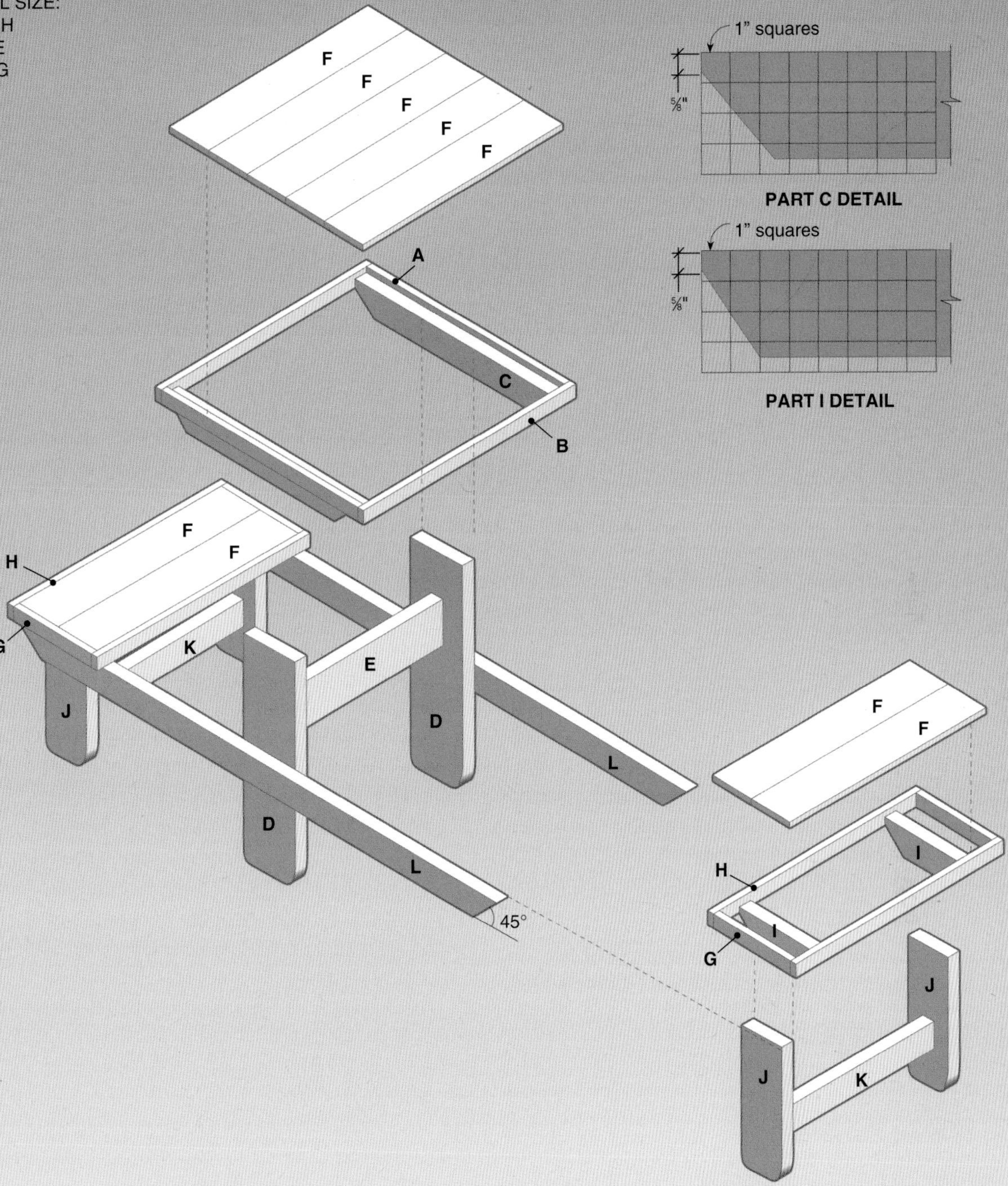
F
F
F
F
F
A
C
B
F
F
H
G
K
E
J
D
L
D
L
45°
F
F
H
I
I
G
J
J
K
1" squares
⅝"
PART C DETAIL
1" squares
⅝"
PART I DETAIL

Cutting List

Key	Part	Dimension	Pcs.	Material
A	Tabletop frame	⅞ × 1½ × 27¾"	2	Cedar
B	Tabletop frame	⅞ × 1½ × 30"	2	Cedar
C	Table stringer	1½ × 3½ × 27¾"	2	Cedar
D	Table leg	1½ × 7¼ × 27¼"	2	Cedar
E	Table stretcher	1½ × 5½ × 22¼"	1	Cedar
F	Slat	⅞ × 5½ × 28¼"	9	Cedar

Cutting List

Key	Part	Dimension	Pcs.	Material
G	Bench frame	⅞ × 1½ × 11¼"	4	Cedar
H	Bench frame	⅞ × 1½ × 30"	4	Cedar
I	Bench stringer	1½ × 3½ × 11¼"	4	Cedar
J	Bench leg	1½ × 5½ × 15¼"	4	Cedar
K	Bench stretcher	1½ × 3½ × 22¼"	2	Cedar
L	Cross rail	1½ × 3½ × 68"	2	Cedar

Materials: Moisture-resistant glue, 1⅝" and 2½" brass or galvanized deck screws, finishing materials.

Note: Measurements reflect the actual size of dimension lumber.

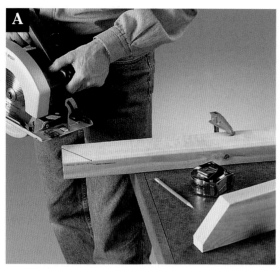

Make triangular cutoffs at the ends on the table stringers, using a circular saw.

Install the tabletop slats by driving screws through the tabletop frame and into the ends of the slats.

Directions:
Picnic Table for Two

BUILD THE TABLETOP.
1. Cut the tabletop frame pieces (A, B), the table stringers (C) and the table slats (F) to length. Sand the parts.
2. Draw cutting lines that start 2½" from one end of each stringer and connect with a point at the same end, ⅝" in from the opposite edge of the board (see *Diagram,* page 389). Cut along the lines with a circular saw to make the cutoffs **(photo A)**.
3. Fasten the shorter tabletop frame pieces (A) to the sides of the stringers. The tops of the frame pieces should extend ⅛" above the tops of the stringers, and the ends should be flush. First, drill ⅛" pilot holes in the frame pieces. Counterbore the holes ¼" deep, using a counterbore bit. Attach the pieces with glue and drive 1⅝" deck screws through the frame pieces and into the stringers.
4. Position the longer tabletop frame pieces (B) so they overlay the ends of the shorter frame pieces. Fasten them to-

gether with glue and 1⅝" deck screws to complete the frames.
5. Set the slats inside the frame so the ends of the slats rest on the stringers. Space the slats evenly. Drill two pilot holes through the tabletop frame by the ends of each slat. Counterbore the holes. Drive 1⅝" deck screws through the frame and into the end of each slat, starting with the two end slats **(photo B)**.

MAKE AND ATTACH THE
TABLE-LEG ASSEMBLY.
1. Cut the table legs (D) and table stretcher (E) to length. Use a compass to draw a 1½"-radius roundover curve on the corners of one end of each leg. Cut the curves with a jig saw.
2. Hold an end of the stretcher against the inside face of one of the table legs, 16" up from the bottom of the leg and centered side to side. Trace the outline of the stretcher onto the leg. Repeat the procedure on the other leg.
3. Drill two evenly spaced pilot holes through the stretcher outlines on the legs. Counterbore

the holes on the outside faces of the legs. Attach the stretcher with glue and drive 2½" deck screws through the legs and into the ends of the stretcher.
4. Turn the tabletop upside down. Apply glue to the table stringers where they will contact the legs. Position the legs in place within the tabletop frame. Attach them by driving 2½" deck screws through the legs and into the table stringers **(photo C)**.

BUILD THE BENCH TOPS.
1. Cut the bench slats (F), bench frame pieces (G, H) and bench stringers (I). Cut the ends of the bench stringers in the same way you cut the table stringers, starting ⅝" from the top edge and 2" from the ends on the bottom edges.
2. Assemble the frame pieces into two rectangular frames by driving 1⅝" deck screws through the longer frame pieces and into the ends of the shorter pieces.
3. Turn the bench frames upside down. Center the bench slats inside them so the outer edges of the slats are flush

Position the table legs inside the tabletop frame, and attach them to the table stringers.

Set the bench legs against the outer faces of the stringers. Attach the legs to the stringers, then attach the stretcher between the legs.

against the frame. Attach the slats by driving 1⅝" deck screws through the frames and into the ends of the slats.

4. Fasten the stringers inside the frame so the tops of the stringers are flat against the undersides of the slats, 3" from the inside of each frame end. Attach with glue and drive 1⅝" deck screws through the angled ends of the stringers and into the undersides of the slats. Locate the screws far enough away from the ends of the stringers so they don't stick out through the tops of the slats. The stringers are not attached directly to the bench frames.

BUILD THE BENCH LEGS.

1. Cut the bench legs (J) and bench stretchers (K) to length. With a compass, draw a roundover curve with a 1½" radius on the corners of one end of each leg. Cut the roundovers with a jig saw.

2. Center the tops of the bench legs against the outside faces of the bench stringers. Drill pilot holes in the stringers. Counterbore the holes. Attach the legs to the stringers with glue, and

drive 2½" deck screws through the stringers and into the legs.

3. Drill pilot holes in the bench legs and counterbore the holes in similar fashion to the approach described in "Make and Attach the Table-Leg Assembly," above. Glue the bench stretchers and attach them between the legs with 2½" deck screws **(photo D)**.

JOIN THE TABLE AND BENCHES.

1. Cut the cross rails (L) to length, miter-cutting the ends at a 45° angle (see *Diagram*). Position the benches so the ends of the cross rails are flush with the outside ends of the bench frames. Drill pilot holes in the cross rails. Counterbore the holes. Apply glue and attach the cross rails to the bench legs with 2½" deck screws.

2. Stand the benches up and center the table legs between the cross rails. Apply glue to the joints between the cross rails and legs. Clamp the table legs to the cross rails, making sure the parts are perpendicular **(photo E)**. Secure the parts by driving several 2½" deck screws through the cross rails and into the outside face of each leg.

APPLY FINISHING TOUCHES.

Sand all the sharp edges and flat surfaces of the table. Apply a nontoxic wood sealant.

Center the table within the cross rails, and clamp it in place.

Patio Table

*This patio table blends sturdy construction with rugged style
to offer many years of steady service.*

CONSTRUCTION MATERIALS

Quantity	Lumber
2	4 × 4" × 10' cedar
3	2 × 2" × 8' cedar
2	1 × 4" × 8' cedar
4	1 × 6" × 8' cedar

Everyone knows that a shaky, unstable patio table is a real headache. But you won't be concerned about wobbly legs with this patio table. It's designed for sturdiness and style. As a result, it's a welcome addition to any backyard patio or deck.

This all-cedar patio table is roomy enough to seat six, and strong enough to support a large patio umbrella—even in high wind. The legs and cross braces are cut from solid 4 × 4 cedar posts, then lag-bolted together. If you can find it at your local building center, buy heartwood cedar posts. Heartwood, cut from the center of the tree, is valued for its density, straightness and resistance to decay. Because it's used for an eating surface, you'll want to apply a natural, clear linseed-oil finish.

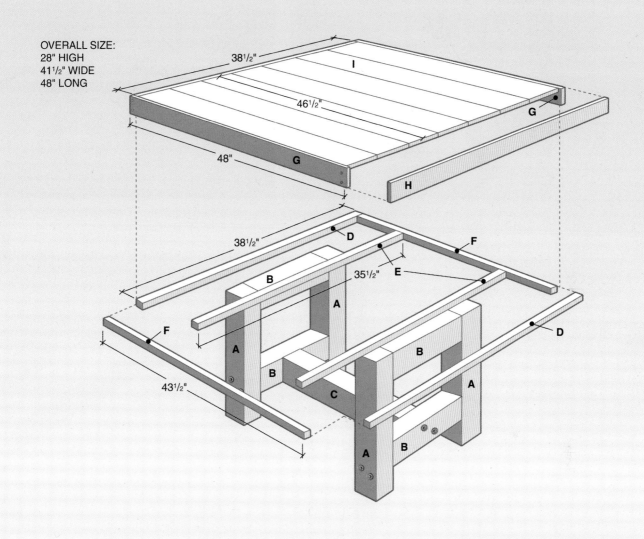

OVERALL SIZE:
28" HIGH
41½" WIDE
48" LONG

Cutting List						Cutting List				
Key	**Part**	**Dimension**	**Pcs.**	**Material**		**Key**	**Part**	**Dimension**	**Pcs.**	**Material**
A	Leg	3½ × 3½ × 27¼"	4	Cedar		**F**	Side cleat	1½ × 1½ × 43½"	2	Cedar
B	Stretcher	3½ × 3½ × 20"	4	Cedar		**G**	Side rail	¾ × 3½ × 48"	2	Cedar
C	Spreader	3½ × 3½ × 28"	1	Cedar		**H**	End rail	¾ × 3½ × 40"	2	Cedar
D	End cleat	1½ × 1½ × 40"	2	Cedar		**I**	Top slat	¾ × 5½ × 46½"	7	Cedar
E	Cross cleat	1½ × 1½ × 37"	2	Cedar						

Materials: Moisture-resistant glue, 2" and 3" deck screws, ⅜ × 6" lag screws with washers (20), finishing materials.

Note: Measurements reflect the actual size of dimension lumber.

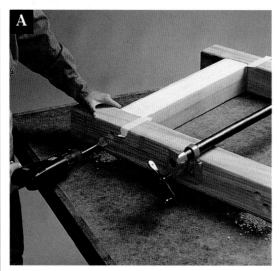

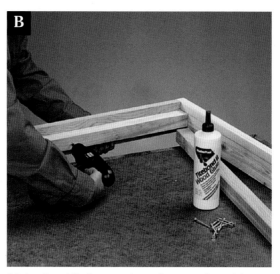

Counterbore two sets of holes on each leg to recess the lag bolts when you attach the legs to the stretchers.

Maintain a ¾" distance from the top edge of the rails to the top edge of the cleats.

Directions:
Patio Table

PREPARE THE LEG ASSEMBLY.

1. Cut the legs (A), stretchers (B) and spreader (C) to length. Measure and mark 4" up from the bottom edge of each leg to mark the positions of the bottom edges of the lower stretchers.
2. Test-fit the legs and stretchers to make sure they are square. The top stretchers should be flush with the top leg ends.
3. Carefully position the pieces and clamp them together with pipe clamps. The metal jaws on the pipe clamps can damage the wood, so use protective clamping pads.

Use pencils or dowels to set even gaps between top slats. Tape slats in position with masking tape.

> ### TIP
> Buy or make wood plugs to fill screw holes and conceal screw heads. Building centers and woodworker's stores usually carry a variety of plug types in several sizes and styles. To cut your own wood plug, you can either use a special-purpose plug-cutting tool (sold at woodworker's stores), or a small hole saw that mounts to your power drill (sold at building centers). The diameter of the plug must match the counterbore drilled into the wood.

BUILD THE LEG ASSEMBLY.

1. Drill ⅞"-× ⅜"-deep counterbores positioned diagonally across the bottom end of each leg and opposite the lower stretchers **(photo A).** Drill ¼" pilot holes through the counterbores and into the stretchers.
2. Unclamp the pieces and drill ⅜" holes for lag screws through the legs, using the pilot holes as center marks.
3. Apply moisture-resistant glue to the ends of the stretchers. Attach the legs to the stretchers

by driving lag screws with washers through the legs and into the stretchers. Use the same procedure to attach the spreader to the stretchers.

ATTACH CLEATS AND RAILS.

1. Cut the side rails (G) and end rails (H) to length. Drill two evenly spaced, ⅛" pilot holes through the ends of the side rails. Counterbore the holes ¼" deep, using a counterbore bit. Apply glue and fasten the side rails to the end rails

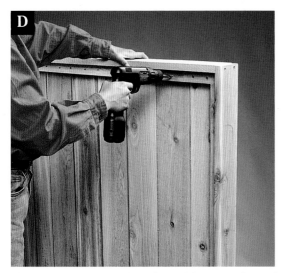

Fasten cross cleats to the tabletop for strength, and to provide an anchor for the leg assembly.

Keep a firm grip on the tabletop slats when drilling deck screws through the cleats.

Before you stain or treat the patio table, sand the surfaces smooth.

CONNECT THE LEGS AND TOP.

1. Turn the tabletop over and center the legs on the underside. Make sure the legs are the same distance apart at the top as they are at the bottom.

2. Lay the cross cleats along the insides of the table legs. Fasten the cross cleats to the tabletop with 2" deck screws **(photo E)**. Fasten the cross cleats to the legs with 3" deck screws.

APPLY FINISHING TOUCHES.

1. For a more finished appearance, fill exposed screw holes with cedar plugs or buttons (see *Tip,* page 394). Smooth the edges of the table and legs with a sander or router **(photo F)**.

2. If you want to fit the table with a patio umbrella, use a 1½"-dia. hole saw to cut a hole into the center of the tabletop. Use a drill and spade bit to cut the 1½"-dia. hole through the spreader.

3. Finish the table as desired— use clear linseed oil for a natural, nontoxic, protective finish.

with 2" deck screws.

2. Cut the end cleats (D), cross cleats (E) and side cleats (F) to length. Fasten the end cleats to the end rails ¾" below the top edges of the rails with glue and 2" deck screws **(photo B)**. Repeat this procedure with the side cleats and side rails.

CUT AND ATTACH THE TOP SLATS.

1. Cut the top slats (I) to length. Lay the slats into the tabletop frame so they rest on the cleats.

Carefully spread the slats apart so they are evenly spaced. Use masking tape to hold the slats in place once you achieve the correct spacing **(photo C)**.

2. Stand the tabletop frame on one end and fasten the top slats in place by driving two 2" deck screws through the end cleats and into each slat **(photo D)**. Hold or clamp each slat firmly while fastening to prevent the screws from pushing the slats away from the frame.

Gate-leg Picnic Tray

Make outdoor dining on your porch, patio or deck a trouble-free activity with our picnic tray. Built with gate legs, it provides a stable surface for plates or glasses, yet folds up easily for convenient storage.

PROJECT
POWER TOOLS

Outdoor dining doesn't need to be a messy, shaky experience. Whether you're on the lawn or patio, you can depend on our gate-leg picnic tray. A hinged leg assembly allows you to fold the tray for easy carrying and storage. Two of the legs are fastened directly to supports beneath the main tray surface with hinges, while the third is attached only to the other legs, allowing it to swing back and forth like a gate and aid compact storage. A small wedge fits under the tray to prevent the swinging leg from moving once the tray is set up.

Our picnic tray also features a hinged bottom shelf that swings down and locks in place with a hook-and-eye clasp to keep the legs in place. Of course, the most conspicuous feature of the project is the tray surface. Plastic tubing is a durable material, and it makes cleaning the tray top easy. The tubing also gives the project an interesting look—it's a companion piece to the patio chair on pages 348-353. Use a portable drill and drill stand to make the holes in the tray sides and insert the plastic tubing. CPVC tubing is a relatively light-weight material, but the strong cedar frame gives our project more stability than you'll get in conventional folding trays.

Even on grass, our gate-leg picnic tray will serve you well, allowing you to enjoy your meal without fear of a messy, dinnertime disaster.

CONSTRUCTION MATERIALS

Quantity	Lumber
1	1 × 2" × 12' cedar
1	1 × 3" × 6' cedar
1	1 × 4" × 8' cedar
1	1 × 12" × 2' cedar
4	½" × 10' CPVC tubing

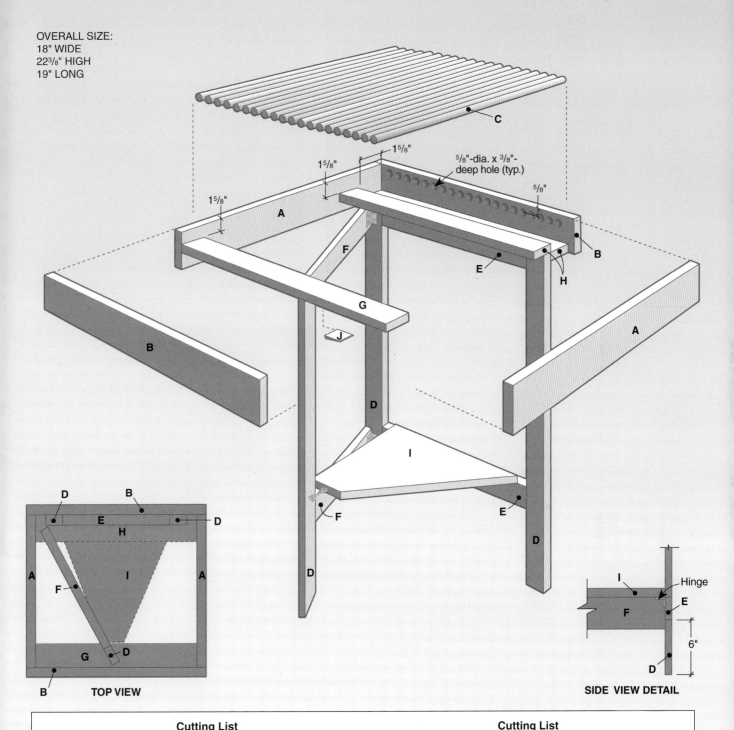

OVERALL SIZE:
18" WIDE
22³/₈" HIGH
19" LONG

⁵/₈"-dia. x ³/₈"-deep hole (typ.)

1⁵/₈"

1⁵/₈"

1⁵/₈"

⁵/₈"

A

B

C

F

E

H

G

J

D

A

B

I

E

D

D

F

TOP VIEW

D   B
E   D
H
A   I   A
F
G   D
B

SIDE VIEW DETAIL

I   Hinge
F   E
D   6"

Cutting List				
Key	**Part**	**Dimension**	**Pcs.**	**Material**
A	Side	³/₄ × 3½ × 16½"	2	Cedar
B	Cap	³/₄ × 3½ × 19"	2	Cedar
C	Tube	⁵/₈"-dia. × 17¼"	20	CPVC
D	Leg	³/₄ × 1½ × 20"	3	Cedar
E	Short rail	³/₄ × 2½ × 13"	2	Cedar

Cutting List				
Key	**Part**	**Dimension**	**Pcs.**	**Material**
F	Long rail	³/₄ × 1½ × 13½"	2	Cedar
G	Gate support	³/₄ × 2½ × 17½"	1	Cedar
H	Hinge support	³/₄ × 1½ × 17½"	2	Cedar
I	Shelf	1 × 10 × 12¾"	1	Cedar
J	Wedge	¼ × 2 × 2"	1	Cedar

Materials: Moisture-resistant glue, deck screws (1¼", 1½", 2", 3"), wire brads, exterior wood putty, hinges, finishing materials.

Note: Measurements reflect the actual size of dimension lumber.

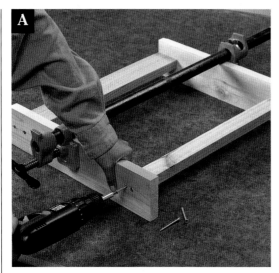

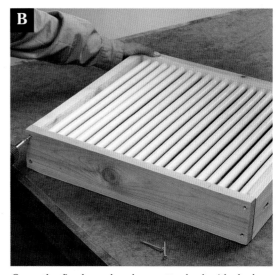

Clamp the pieces to hold them in place, and attach the hinge support 1⅝" from the top side edge.

Once the final cap has been attached with deck screws and glue, the basic tray frame is complete.

Directions:
Gate-leg Picnic Tray

MAKE THE TRAY FRAME.
1. Cut the sides (A) and caps (B) to length from 1 × 4 cedar.
2. Use a power drill to make ⅝ × ⅜"-deep holes for CPVC tubing, 1" apart on the inside faces of the caps. We recommend using a portable drill stand for this step (see *Tip,* below). Start the holes 1½" from one end and center the holes ⅝" from the top cap edges.
3. Cut the gate support (G) from 1 × 3 cedar and cut the hinge supports (H) from 1 × 2 cedar.
4. Drill two evenly spaced ¼ × ⅜"-dia. counterbored holes into

Attach the rails to the legs with counterbored deck screws and glue.

TIP

Mount your electric hand drill on a portable drill stand for accurate vertical or angled drilling. Drill guides can keep bits centered on the workpiece. Make sure these tools are securely attached to the worksurface when you use them. Always protect the worksurface with a piece of scrap wood to avoid damaging tearout on the other side of the workpiece. To prevent drilling too far into a piece of wood, some portable drill stands are equipped with depth stops.

the outside face of the front end of each of the sides, where the gate support will be attached. Drill the holes 1⅝" down from the top edges of the sides.
5. Apply moisture-resistant glue to the joints and clamp the piece with a bar clamp. Drill ³⁄₁₆"-dia. pilot holes through each center, then fasten the gate support to the sides with 2" deck screws.
6. On the opposite side of the frame, fasten one hinge support between the sides **(photo A)**. Make sure the hinge support is fastened 1⅝" from the

ends of the sides, and 1⅝" from the top side edges.
7. Fasten one of the caps to the side assembly with deck screws.

CUT & INSTALL THE TUBES.
1. Use a jig saw or compound miter saw to cut 24 pieces of ½"-dia. CPVC tubing (C) to 17¼" in length. For more information on working with plastic tubing, see *Patio Chair,* pages 348-353.
2. Wash the grade stamps from the tubing with lacquer thinner and rinse them with clean water.
3. When the tubes are dry, insert them into their holes in the frame.

Attach the leg frames with high-quality hinges.

Fasten the stationary leg frame to the lower hinge support on the underside of the tray frame.

Use wire brads and glue to attach the lock wedge, which holds the gate leg assembly in place.

4. Fasten the remaining cap to the frame with glue and deck screws **(photo B).**

5. Attach the remaining hinge support to the sides, starting ⅞" from the end on the outside edge. This hinge support should be flush with the bottom edges of the sides. Use glue and countersunk deck screws to attach the pieces.

BUILD THE LEG ASSEMBLY.
The leg assembly consists of two leg frames and a series of rails. One leg frame is stationary and attached to the bottom hinge support with hinges. The

other frame has one leg, which swings like a gate and is attached only to the first frame. These braces are attached to the other leg frame.

1. Cut the legs (D), short rails (E), and long rails (F) from 1 × 2 cedar.

2. Fasten the rails to the legs (see *Diagram,* page 397) with counterbored deck screws and glue to form two leg frames **(photo C).** The bottom edge of the rails should be 4" from the bottom of the legs. The top rails should be flush with the top leg edges.

3. Attach the gate leg frame to

the stationary frame with hinges **(photo D).**

4. Fasten the stationary legs to the bottom hinge support **(photo E).**

5. To prevent the gate leg from swinging back and collapsing the picnic tray, cut a lock wedge (J) from 1 × 3 cedar.

6. Open the gate leg to the normal standing position, which should be roughly the center of the gate support. Draw a line on the gate support along the edge of the gate leg to locate the wedge position. Use wire brads and glue to attach the lock wedge so that its thin end is against the gate leg **(photo F).** The leg will slide over this wedge slightly and be held fast.

7. Cut the shelf (I) to size and shape.

8. Attach it to the short rails with hinges.

9. Install a hook-and-eye clasp on the gate leg and shelf to secure the open assembly.

10. Sand all sharp edges and finish the project with clear wood sealer.

TIP

Use cedar plugs to fill the counterbores for the screws in the tray frame.

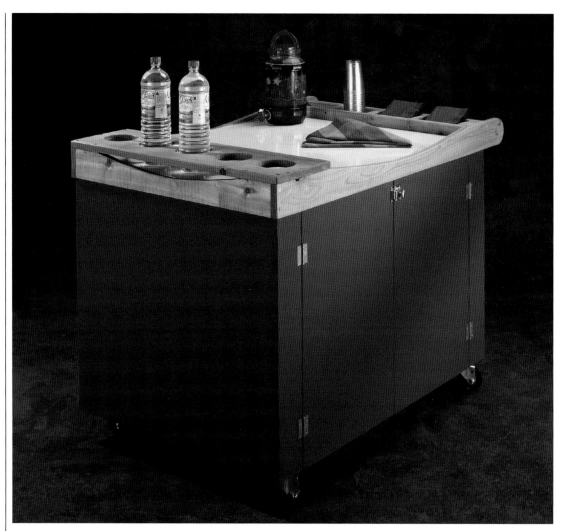

Party Cart

A fully insulated cooler on wheels, our party cart has some clever bells and whistles, as well as distinctive design elements, so it will fit in even at the most formal outdoor gatherings.

CONSTRUCTION MATERIALS

Quantity	Lumber
4	2 × 4" × 8' cedar
2	1 × 4" × 8' cedar
1	1 × 10" × 4' cedar
3	1 × 3" × 8' cedar
1	1 × 2" × 6' cedar
2	4 × 8' × ½"-thick BCX plywood
1	4 × 8' sheet tileboard
1	1"-dia. × 3' oak dowel
1	1½" × 4 × 8' foam insulation

Outdoor entertaining events often turn into an endless parade between the patio and the refrigerator, or a loose huddle around an old foam cooler. With this portable party cart, you can keep your guests refreshed on site and in style. The tileboard top is generously proportioned and easy to clean. With a capacity of 15 cubic feet, the insulated cooler compartment has plenty of room

for cans, bottles, even kegs, as well as ice and snacks. You can add accessories to help the cart meet your needs. A few suggestions: attach a bottle opener, paper towel holder, or plastic cup dispenser to the cabinet side; drill a 1"-diameter hole through the side to create a passage for a keg hose, then cover the hole with a plastic grommet; mount a flagpole holder on the back of the cart to hold a beach umbrella.

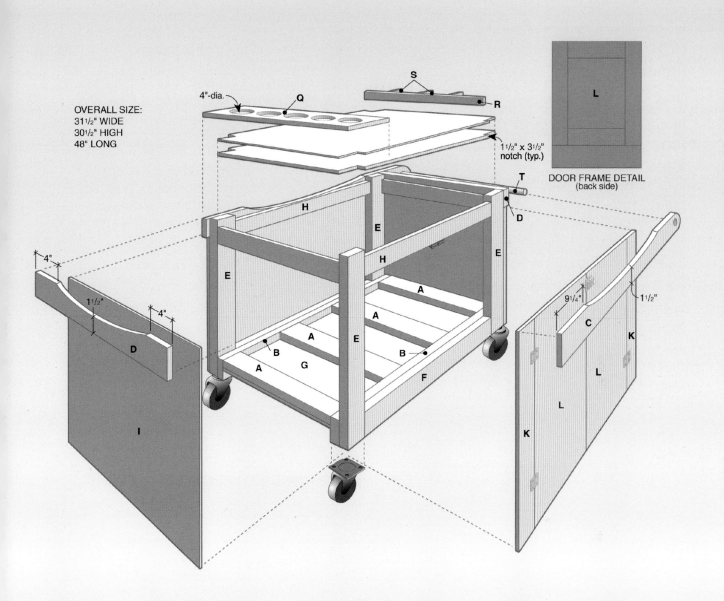

OVERALL SIZE:
31½" WIDE
30½" HIGH
48" LONG

4"-dia.

1½" × 3½" notch (typ.)

DOOR FRAME DETAIL
(back side)

9¼"

1½"

4"

1½"

4"

Cutting List

Key	Part	Dimension	Pcs.	Material
A	Bottom stretcher	1½ × 3½ × 24"	4	Cedar
B	Bottom side rail	1½ × 3½ × 42"	2	Cedar
C	Top side rail	⅞ × 3½ × 48"	2	Cedar
D	Top end rail	⅞ × 3½ × 30"	2	Cedar
E	Post	1½ × 3½ × 30"	4	Cedar
F	Rail filler	1½ × 3½ × 35"	2	Cedar
G	Bottom	½ × 24 × 42"	1	BCX plywood
H	Tabletop cleat	⅞ × 2½ × 35"	2	Cedar
I	End panel	½ × 30 × 27"	2	BCX plywood
J	Side panel	½ × 43 × 27"	1	BCX plywood
K	Post cover	½ × 4 × 27"	2	BCX plywood

Cutting List

Key	Part	Dimension	Pcs.	Material
L	Door	½ × 17⅜ × 27"	2	BCX plywood
M	Door stile	⅞ × 2½ × 21⅞"	4	Cedar
N	Door rail	⅞ × 2½ × 10¼"	4	Cedar
O	Tabletop	½ × 30 × 42"	1	BCX plywood
P	Waterproof panel	⅛ × 30 × 42"	2	Tileboard
Q	Bottle caddy	⅞ × 9¼ × 31½"	1	Cedar
R	Bin side	⅞ × 1½ × 30"	1	Cedar
S	Bin divider	⅞ × 1½ × 8¼"	3	Cedar
T	Handle	1"-dia. × 31½"	1	Oak dowel
U	Tabletop end cleat	¾ × 2½ × 27"	2	Cedar

Materials: 1", 1½", 2", 2½" and 3" deck screws, 6d casing nails, 2" brass butt hinges (4), brass clasp, magnetic door catches (2), brass window sash handles (2), heavy-duty locking casters (4), moisture-resistant glue, tileboard adhesive, panel adhesive, ⅜"-dia. cedar plugs.

Note: Measurements reflect the actual size of dimension lumber.

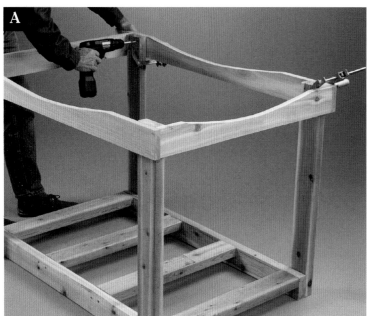

A

Attach the scooped top frame pieces to the posts with 2" deck screws. Posts are attached to the base frame with 3" deck screws.

Directions: Party Cart

BUILD THE CABINET FRAME.

The main structural element of our party cart is a cabinet frame made from 2 × 4 and 1 × 4 cedar.

1. Cut the bottom stretchers (A) and bottom side rails (B) from 2 × 4s.

2. Lay the rails on edge on a worksurface, then set the stretchers facedown between the rails. One stretcher should be set flush at each end, with the other two spaced evenly between the ends (the assembly should look like a ladder).

3. Drill pilot holes, then fasten the side rails to the stretchers with 3" deck screws.

4. Cut the top side rails (C) and top end rails (D) from 1 × 4s.

5. Cut a gentle, 1½"-deep scoop into each top rail, using a jig saw. The scoops should start 4" from each end of the top end rails. In the top side rails, cut the scoops 9¼" from the front ends, and 11¼" from the back ends.

6. Assemble the top side and top end rails into a square frame. The back end rail should be recessed 6" from the back ends of the side rails.

7. Drill pilot holes with ⅜"-dia. × ¼"-deep counterbores through the side rails and into the end rails.

8. Fasten the rails together with glue and 2" deck screws, then plug the counterbores with ⅜"-dia. cedar plugs.

9. Cut the 2 × 4 posts (E), and arrange them so they fit at the outside corners of the 2 × 4 frame base and the inside corners of the 1 × 4 frame top. Make sure the frame base is positioned with the recesses beneath the stretchers, facing down.

10. Attach the top and bottom frames to the posts with 3" deck screws and glue at the bottom, and 2" deck screws and glue at the top **(photo A)**.

ATTACH SIDE PANELS TO CABINET FRAME.

1. Cut and attach a 2 × 4 rail filler (F) to the outer face of each bottom side rail in the frame base with 2½" deck screws. The rail fillers eliminate gaps between the side rails and the sides of the cabinet.

2. Cut the bottom panel (G) from ½"-thick plywood and attach it to the underside of the

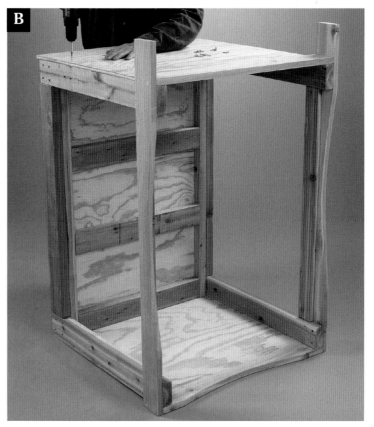

B

Attach the plywood cabinet sides and the cabinet base to the cabinet frame with 1¼" deck screws

Attach the 1 × 3 door rails and stiles by driving 1" screws through the front faces of the plywood door panels.

Bond tileboard to the plywood tabletop with tileboard adhesive.

frame base with 1½" deck screws.

3. Measure down 2¼" from the tops of the frame pieces and draw reference lines for the cleats that support the top panel.

4. Cut the 1 × 3 tabletop cleats (H) and attach them just below the reference lines, using 1½" deck screws.

5. Cut the end panels (I) and the side panel (J) from plywood, and position them against the cabinet frame so all panels overhang the frame base by ½". Attach the panels to the frame with 1" deck screws **(photo B).**

6. Cut post covers (K) from ½" plywood and attach them to the 2 × 4 posts at the open side.

BUILD THE DOORS.

The cooler compartment doors are made from ½" plywood, with 1 × 3 rails and stiles attached to the back side to stiffen the plywood.

1. Cut the door panels (L), door stiles (M), and door rails (N).

2. Attach the door rails and stiles with glue and 1" screws driven through the fronts of the door panels **(photo C);** attach the upper door rail to the inside (unsanded) edge of each door panel, 1⅝" down from the top edge and centered side to side; attach the lower rail 4⅛" up from the bottom of the panel; attach vertical stiles so they are flush with the outer edges of the rails to complete the doors.

BUILD AND INSTALL THE CART TOP.

The cart top is cut from ½" plywood, then covered with tileboard to create a smooth, water-resistant surface that is easy to clean.

1. Cut the plywood tabletop panel (O).

2. Cut a piece of ¼"-thick tileboard (P) to the same size as the tabletop panel (O). Tileboard is usually sold in 4 × 8' sheets that resemble interior paneling. It is available in a wide variety of textures and finishes. We chose a fairly neutral, biscuit-colored style. If you are willing to spend the extra money, you can substitute fiberglass shower liner panels for a more long-lasting tabletop surface.

3. Attach the tileboard to the sanded side of the top panel with exterior-rated tileboard adhesive **(photo D),** according to the recommended application methods and drying times.

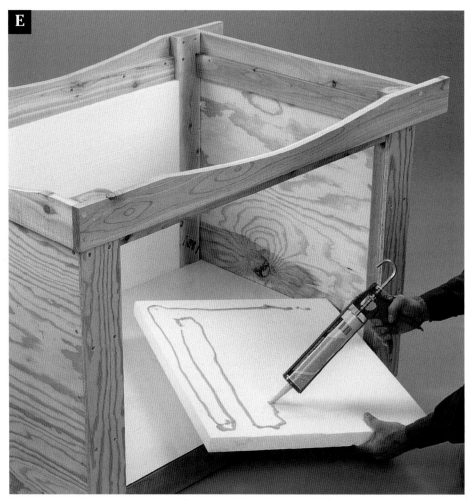

E

Use panel adhesive to install rigid foam insulation on the interior walls of the cooler compartment.

4. After the adhesive has set, use a jig saw to cut out 1½ × 3½" notches from the corners of the cart top to fit around the cabinet-frame posts. Make sure the cutouts are oriented correctly.

5. Apply a thick bead of panel adhesive to the tops of the 1 × 3 cleats mounted on the inside faces of the frame top, then set the cart top onto the cleats and press down firmly. Do not nail or screw the top in place. Set some heavy weights on the surface while the adhesive dries.

TIP

Read the usage recommendations before purchasing panel adhesive. Some products may dissolve foam or plastic.

LINE THE COOLER COMPARTMENT.

We used 1½"-thick open-cell foam insulation boards to insulate the cooler compartment. For greater durability and better insulation performance, you can substitute closed-cell insulation boards with a puncture-resistant facing.

1. Use a sharp utility knife to cut insulation boards to fit into the gaps between the stretchers on the floor of the cabinet, to fit between the rails and stiles on the doors, and to fit the walls and top of the compartment. Cut insulation slightly over-sized, so compression will help

hold it in place. Attach all the insulation boards with a panel adhesive **(photo E).**

2. Cut a second piece of tile-board (P) the same size as the top panel.

3. Apply tileboard adhesive to the tops of the exposed stretchers in the frame bottom, and install the tileboard to make a bottom for the compartment.

4. To protect the inside walls and top of the compartment, cut tileboard to fit, and attach it to the insulation boards with panel adhesive (optional).

HANG THE DOORS.

1. Center the doors over the door opening, with the top edges aligned, and hang them from the plywood post covers (K) with 2" brass butt hinges. Leave a gap of about ⅛" between the doors.

ACCESSORIZE THE TOP.

The bottle caddy and napkin/condiment bin are optional features that give the party cart greater versatility.

1. Cut the bottle caddy (Q) from 1 × 10 cedar.

2. Cut evenly spaced 4"-dia. holes in the board, then smooth out the cuts with a drum sander mounted on your electric drill.

3. Set the bottle caddy over the frame top at the front end of the cart, and attach it to the frame with 1" screws.

4. Cut the bin side (R) and the bin dividers (S) from 1 × 2 cedar.

5. Space the dividers evenly along the divider side, and attach with 1" deck screws.

6. Apply panel adhesive to the bottoms of the dividers and divider side, then set the assembly on the tabletop, with the free ends of the dividers flush against the back rail. Secure the rail to the dividers with 1" screws.

INSTALL THE HANDLE.

We used a 1"-dia. oak dowel to make the handle that is mounted between the top frame rails at the back of the cart.

1. Cut the handle (T) to length.
2. Measure in 1" from the back ends of the top frame rails, and mark a point that is centered top-to-bottom. Use this point as a centerpoint to drill 1"-dia. holes through the rails, using a spade bit, to accommodate the handle. For added visual appeal, we used a jig saw to round off the ends of the rails once our handle position was established.
3. Insert the handle through both 1" holes, so the ends are flush with the outside faces of the rails. Secure the handle by drilling ⅛" pilot holes through the rails and into the ends of the handle, then driving a 6d casing nail into each pilot end of the handle.

FINISH THE CART.

1. Fill exposed plywood edges and nail hole with wood putty, then sand smooth with at least 120-grit sandpaper.
2. Apply a clear finish to exposed cedar trim, and paint plywood surfaces with an exterior grade enamel.
3. To keep the doors closed securely, install a brass clasp and magnetic door catches.
4. Attach door pulls. We used brass window sash handles.
5. Because the cart is designed to carry a load in excess of 100 pounds, install heavy-duty, locking casters to the bottom of each post.

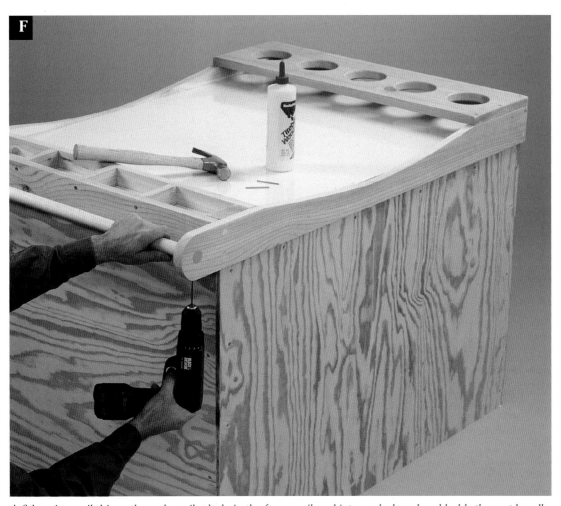

A 6d casing nail driven through a pilot hole in the frame rail and into each dowel end holds the cart handle in position.

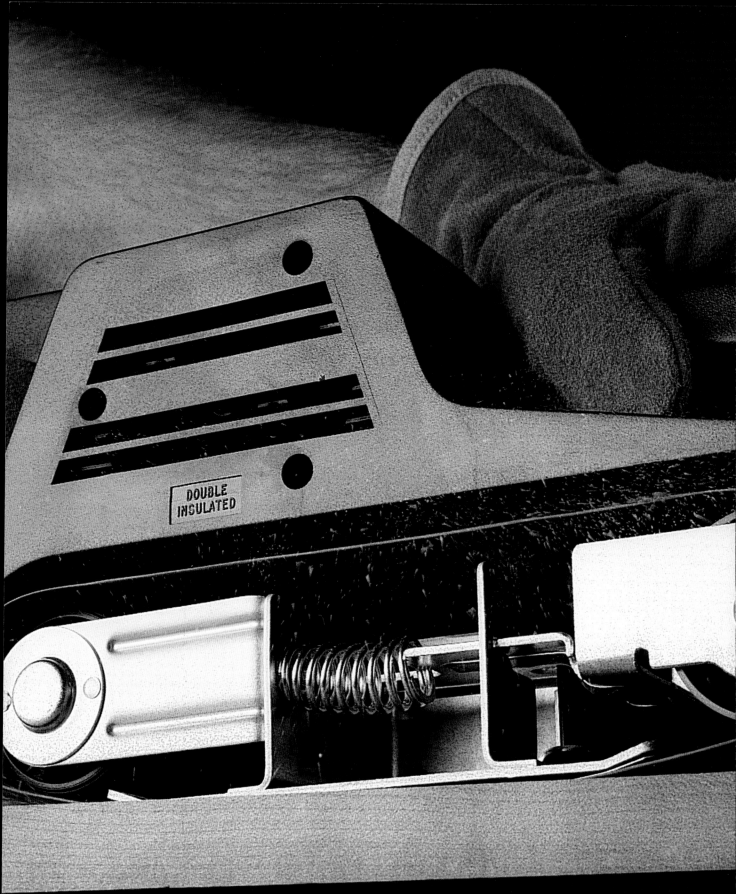

DOUBLE
INSULATED

Children's Play Projects

Children are naturally drawn to the outdoors. It's a great big, wonderful playground filled with bugs, dirt, and challenges. Inspire your youngsters to cultivate their curiosity and expend their energy with kid-sized projects that make bug collecting, gardening, and playing easier for them. The projects shown here bring the big, beautiful world down to kid size. Your little ones thank you with hours of outdoor play.

Observation Station

Create a temporary viewing station for bugs and small animals.

CONSTRUCTION MATERIALS

Quantity	Lumber
3	2 × 2" × 12' cedar
1	½" × 4' × 4' exterior plywood
6	¼" × 1⅛" × 8' molding

An observation station allows children to safely observe bugs, insects, and wildlife in their own backyard. If the station will be used primarily for caterpillars, fireflies, grasshoppers, and butterflies, use a dense screen so they won't escape. For snakes, turtles, and frogs, a stronger screen with larger holes is appropriate.

Remember that wild animals don't make good pets, so open the lid and tip the observation station on its side to release critters after watching them. Also, don't place the station in direct sun, as many animals can be injured by the heat.

OVERALL SIZE:
24" HIGH
24" DEEP
24" LONG

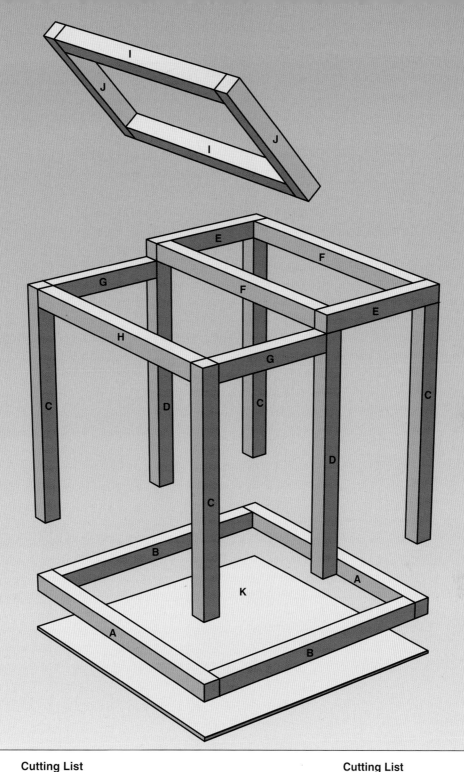

Cutting List

Key	Part	Dimension	Pcs.	Material
A	Base side	1½ × 1½ × 24"	2	Cedar
B	Base rail	1½ × 1½ × 21"	2	Cedar
C	Corner post	1½ × 1½ × 20½"	4	Cedar
D	Center post	1½ × 1½ × 20½"	2	Cedar
E	Top side	1½ × 1½ × 12"	2	Cedar
F	Top rail	1½ × 1½ × 21"	2	Cedar

Cutting List

Key	Part	Dimension	Pcs.	Material
G	Lid support	1½ × 1½ × 10½"	2	Cedar
H	Lid support rail	1½ × 1½ × 21"	1	Cedar
I	Lid rail	1½ × 1½ × 21"	2	Cedar
J	Lid side	1½ × 1½ × 12"	2	Cedar
K	Base	½ × 24 × 24"	1	Plywood
L	Trim	¼ × 1⅛ × *	24	Molding

Materials: 2½" and 1¼" deck screws, brad nails, aluminum screen, staples, butt hinges (2), handle, sandpaper.

Note: Measurements reflect actual size of dimension lumber.

* cut to fit.

Directions: Observation Station

ASSEMBLE THE FRAME.

1. Cut the base sides (A) and base rails (B) to length.

2. Butt the end of a base rail against the inside edge of a side rail. With the top and the ends of the rails flush and square, drill two ³⁄₃₂" pilot holes through the side and into the end of the rail. Attach the rails using 2½" deck screws. Fasten the second base side on the outside of the opposite end of the base rail by drilling pilot holes and using deck screws. Fasten the second base rail between the base sides at the open end to complete the base.

3. Cut the corner posts (C) and side posts (D) to length. Place the base assembly on its side and fasten a corner post at each corner, making sure the edges are flush. Drill pilot holes and use deck screws to fasten the corners in place.

4. Measure 9" from the inside

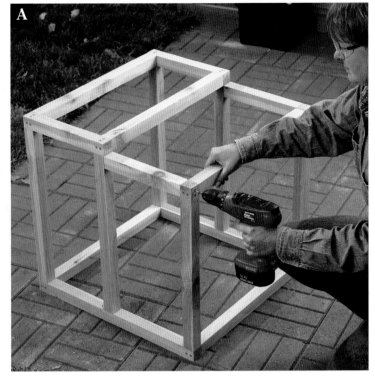

Fasten the rails together by drilling pilot holes and inserting 2½" deck screws.

of a corner on the base and mark the base side. Attach a side post outside the mark, making sure the outside edges are flush. Attach the other side post on the opposite side of the frame at the same location.

5. Cut the top sides (E), top rails (F), lid supports (G), and lid support rail (H) to length. Return the frame to an upright position. Place a top side piece over a side and corner post, making sure it's flush on the outside and end. Drill pilot

holes and insert 2½" deck screws through the top of the top side piece into the ends of the corner and side posts. Repeat with the other top side piece.

6. Place a top side rail between the ends of the side pieces. Align the rail with the top and outside corners of the sides, drill pilot holes, and insert deck screws. Repeat with second rail at the other end of the top sides.

7. Place the lid rail between the remaining corner support posts, flush with the top of the posts. Drill pilot holes, and fasten with 2½" deck screws.

8. Place a lid support between a corner and side support post, flush with the top of the posts. Drill pilot holes, and fasten with 2½" deck screws. Repeat with the other lid support **(photo A).** Note: the lid supports are 1½" lower than the top sides and rails.

Attach the hinges to the lid and the frame.

Place the screen flat over the framework, then staple it every 2".

ATTACH THE LID AND THE BASE.

1. Cut the lid rails (I) and sides (J) to length. Butt the lid sides against the ends of the lid rails. Align the edges. Drill pilot holes and fasten with 2½" deck screws.
2. Attach two hinges to the back of the lid using the screws that came with the hinges.
3. Place the lid on the observation station. Attach the other end of the hinges to the adjacent rail **(photo B).** When closed, the lid should sit securely on the lid supports.
4. Cut the base (K) to size. Turn the station on its side and fasten the plywood to the base rails using 1¼" deck screws. The plywood should be flush with all four corners of the station. If it isn't, adjust the box so it's square before fastening the screws.
5. Lightly sand any rough areas using 220-grit sandpaper. Wipe away any dust, then stain or paint the wood. Wait until the stain or paint is completely dry before continuing. Fasten the screen to the box.

1. Cut the aluminum screen to size using wire cutters. Cut four screens at 22½ × 22½" for the sides and two screens at 10½ × 22½" for the top and lid.
2. Place each section of screen on the outside of the rails, overlapping each rail by ¾". Make sure the screen is flat against the rails. Staple

the screen to the rails every 2" **(photo C).**

ATTACH THE HANDLE AND TRIM.

1. Center a handle on the face of the front rail of the lid and attach it using the screws that came with the handle.
2. Cut a piece of ¼" × 1⅛" molding at 24" and place it along a rail on one side of the observation station. Align the molding with the end and outside edge of the rail, covering the screen, and fasten it to the rail using brad nails.
3. Measure the distance between the inside edge of the molding and the opposite corner. Cut a piece of trim to that size, then nail it in place. Do the same for the remaining two sides **(photo D).** Repeat to fasten trim to all sides of the observation station.
4. Paint or stain the molding to match the box.

Cut pieces of trim to size, then nail them over the edges of the screen.

PROJECT
POWER TOOLS

Rolling Garden

Why not take the garden with you? This rolling garden allows children to have their own garden spot and still be close to mom or dad at all times.

CONSTRUCTION MATERIALS

Quantity	Lumber
1	1 × 10" × 4' cedar
1	1 × 8" × 6' cedar
3	1 × 2" × 8' cedar

This garden on wheels is sure to be a favorite with your children. The unique design features dividers in the cart so kids can plant different flowers and vegetables or leave one section empty for carrying their watering can or other treasures. The back of the cart contains a tool caddy so children can take their gardening tools with them wherever they go. The 3" caster wheels make the cart easy to pull, and the swivel wheels in the front allow the cart to turn smoothly without tipping over.

OVERALL SIZE:
13" HIGH
14" WIDE
28¾" LONG

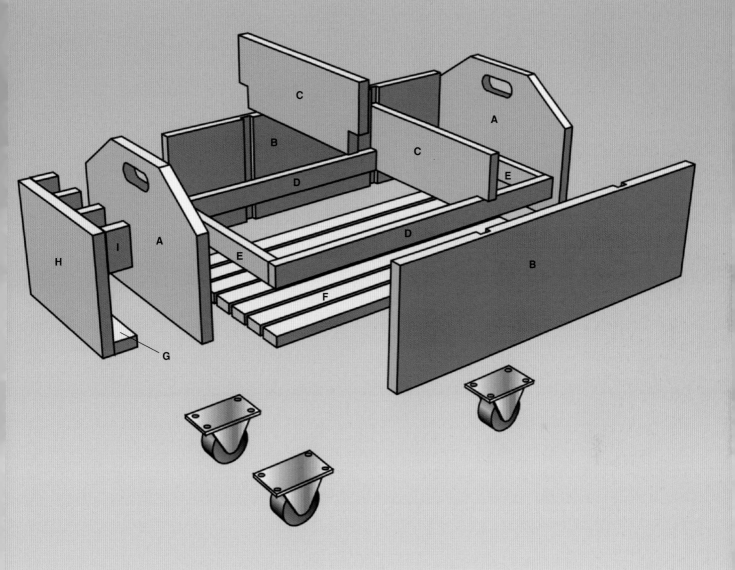

Cutting List				
Key	**Part**	**Dimension**	**Pcs.**	**Material**
A	End panel	¾ × 9½ × 14"	2	Cedar
B	Side panel	¾ × 7½ × 24"	2	Cedar
C	Divider	¾ × 4½ × 12½"	2	Cedar
D	Side cleats	¾ × 1½ × 24"	2	Cedar
E	End cleats	¾ × 1½ × 10½"	2	Cedar

Cutting List				
Key	**Part**	**Dimension**	**Pcs.**	**Material**
F	Floor slats	¾ × 1½ × 24"	7	Cedar
G	Caddy floor	¾ × 1½ × 10"	1	Cedar
H	Caddy wall	¾ × 7½ × 10"	1	Cedar
I	Caddy dividers	¾ × 1½ × 2½"	4	Cedar

Materials: 1½" galvanized screws, 3" swivel caster wheels (2), 3" rigid caster wheels (2), ¼ × 1" lag screws, landscape fabric, rope, exterior wood glue, sandpaper.

Note: Measurements reflect actual size of dimension lumber.

Mark the angled cut-offs. Drill holes for the handles, then cut away the remaining material.

Cut dado grooves in the side panels for the removable divider walls.

Directions: Rolling Garden

PREPARE THE END PANELS.

1. Cut the end panels (A) using a circular saw.

2. Make a mark 2¾" from the top along an edge of an end panel for the corner angle. Make another mark 4" from that edge along the top of the panel. Connect the two points using a straightedge. Repeat for the other corner.

3. Mark a horizontal line across the panel 1½" from the top edge. Measure 6" from each side and mark cross points on the horizontal line.

4. Set the two end panels together, making sure the edges are flush, and clamp them to your work surface. Drill holes for the handles using a 1⅛" spade bit centered on the cross points **(photo A)**. Cut away the remaining material from the handle using a jig saw. Cut the corner angles using a jig saw. Sand all edges smooth using 220-grit sandpaper.

BUILD THE CART FRAME AND DIVIDERS.

1. Cut the side panels (B) to size.

2. To make grooves for the removable dividers, clamp the two side panels side by side on your work surface. Cut two ¾"-wide × ⅜"-deep dadoes in the side panels, 6" from each end, using a router and a straight-edge guide **(photo B)**.

3. Butt the panels together with the end panels over the side panels. Drill ⅛" pilot holes through the end into the side panels. Attach the side and end panels using glue and 1½" galvanized screws.

4. Cut the dividers (C) by cutting a 1 × 10 to length and use a circular saw to rip this piece in half to form two dividers. Use a jig saw to cut a 1"-wide × 1½"-long notch in the bottom corners of each divider to fit around the support cleats.

BUILD THE CART FLOOR.

1. Cut the side cleats (D), end cleats (E) and floor slats (F).

2. Make two marks on the inside of each side panel 1½" from the bottom edge. Align the bottom edge of a side cleat along the marks and attach one to each side panel using 1½" galvanized screws spaced every 6-8".

3. Position the end cleats between the side cleats, making sure the edges are flush. Attach the cleats to the end panels with 1½" galvanized screws.

4. Turn the cart upside down and install the floor slats, leaving about ¼" of space between each slat to allow for drainage. Drill pilot holes through the

Attach the floor slats to the support cleats with galvanized screws.

Assemble the tool caddy and attach it to the back end panel.

ends of the slats and attach them to the end cleats using 1½" galvanized screws **(photo C).**

INSTALL THE TOOL CADDY.

1. Cut the tool caddy floor (G), wall (H) and dividers (I) to size.
2. Assemble the pieces of the tool caddy, then fasten the pieces together by drilling pilot holes and inserting 1½" screws **(photo D).**
3. Position the caddy on the back end panel so the base is flush with the bottom edge of the cart. From inside the cart, drill pilot holes and insert screws into the two outer caddy dividers. Insert two additional screws from the underside of the cart into the caddy base.

FINISH THE CART.

1. Attach caster wheels to the floor slats, using ¼ × 1" lag screws **(photo E).** The wheels should be recessed inside the frame. For easy maneuvering, install the swivel casters at the front of the cart.
2. Drill two ½" holes for the pull rope in the front panel, 3" from the side and 2" from the top. Thread a 36" piece of rope through the holes and knot the ends.
3. Line the bottom of the cart with landscape fabric and staple it along the panels. Insert dividers into the grooves to make separate growing or storage areas. Fill the cart with 6" of potting soil, then add seeds or plants.

Attach caster wheels so they are recessed inside the frame.

PROJECT
POWER TOOLS

Children's Picnic Table

*Grown-ups get a picnic table their size, why not build a sturdy,
beautiful table sized just for kids?*

CONSTRUCTION MATERIALS

Quantity	Lumber
2	2 × 4" × 6' cedar
5	2 × 6" × 6' cedar
3	2 × 8" × 8' cedar

A picnic table is a wonderful addition to any backyard. Like other projects in this section, the children's picnic table is built at the right size for kids. Its light weight allows you to move the table around the yard for impromptu tea parties on the deck or dinner under the trees.

OVERALL SIZE:
30" HIGH
46" WIDE
48" LONG

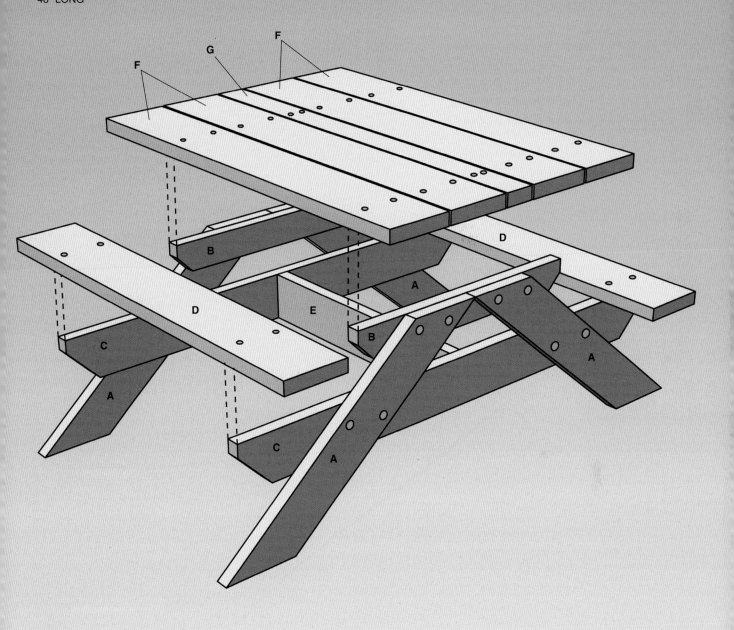

Cutting List						Cutting List				
Key	**Part**	**Dimension**	**Pcs.**	**Material**		**Key**	**Part**	**Dimension**	**Pcs.**	**Material**
A	Leg	1½ × 5½ × 32"	4	Cedar		**E**	Brace	1½ × 5½ × 30"	1	Cedar
B	Table support	1½ × 3½ × 29¾"	2	Cedar		**F**	Table top	1½ × 7½ × 48"	4	Cedar
C	Seat support	1½ × 5½ × 60"	2	Cedar		**G**	Table top	1½ × 3½ × 48"	1	Cedar
D	Seat	1½ × 7½ × 48"	2	Cedar						

Materials: 2½" deck screws, ⅜ × 3" carriage bolts with nuts (16) and washers (32).

Note: Measurements reflect the actual size of dimension lumber.

Directions: Children's Picnic Table

CUT THE ANGLED LEGS AND SUPPORTS.

1. To make the angled legs (A), use a saw protractor to mark a 50° angle on one end of a 2 × 6 **(photo A).** Cut the angle using a circular saw. Measure 32" from the tip of the angle, then mark and cut another 50° angle parallel to the first. Do this for all four legs, cutting two legs from one piece of lumber.

3. Cut the tabletop supports (B) to length. Measure 1½" in from each end of both supports and make a mark. Make a 45° angle starting at the mark and going in the direction of the board end. This relieves the sharp end of the board to prevent injuries and also looks more pleasing.

4. Cut the seat supports (C) to length. Measure 2½" from the ends of both supports, make a mark, and cut a 45° angle to relieve the sharp ends.

ASSEMBLE THE A-FRAMES.

1. Place one of the legs against the tabletop support so the inside edge of the leg is at the centerpoint of the support. Align the top of the leg with the top of the support. Clamp the pieces together.

2. Drill two ⅜" holes through the leg and support. Stagger the holes. To keep the bolts from causing scrapes, recess both the bolt head and the nut. Countersink 1" holes about ¼" deep into the leg and the tabletop support using the ⅜" holes

Use a saw protractor to mark a 50° angle on the end of the table leg, then cut the angle using a circular saw.

as a guide. Insert a ⅜ × 3" carriage bolt and washer into each hole. Tighten a washer and nut on the end of the bolt using a ratchet wrench. Repeat these steps to fasten the second leg in place. NOTE: If your washers are larger than 1", you'll need a larger recess.

3. Measure along the inside edge of each leg and make a mark 12½" from the bottom. Center the seat support over the leg assembly, on the same side of the legs as the tabletop support, with the 45° cuts facing down and the bottom flush with the 12½" marks. Drill ⅜" holes, countersink 1" holes,

and fasten the seat support to the legs using carriage bolts, nuts and washers **(photo B).**

4. Repeat this step to assemble the second A-frame.

ATTACH THE TABLE TOP AND SEATS.

1. Cut the seats (D) to length.

2. Stand one of the A-frames upright. Place a seat on the seat support so the seat overhangs the outside of the support by 7½". Align the back edge of the seat with the end of the support. Drill two 3⁄32" pilot holes through the seat into the support, then insert 2½" deck screws. Attach the seat to the second A-frame the same way. Fasten the seat on the other side of the table using the same method.

2. Cut the brace. Center the brace between the seat supports, making sure they're flush at the bottom. Drill two ³⁄₃₂" pilot holes through the supports on each side, then fasten the brace to the supports using 2½" deck screws.

3. Cut the table top boards (F & G) to length. Place the 2 × 4 table top across the center of the table top supports, overhanging the supports by 7½". Drill two ³⁄₃₂" pilot holes on both ends of the top board where it crosses the supports. Attach it to the supports with 2½" deck screws.

4. Place a 2 × 8 table top board across the supports, keeping a ¼" gap from the 2 × 4. Drill pilot holes in the end of the board, then insert 2½" deck screws **(photo C)**. Install the remaining top boards the same way, spacing them evenly with a ¼" gap. Allow the outside boards to overhang the end of the tabletop supports.

5. Sand any rough surfaces and splinters, and round over edges on the seat and tabletop, using 220-grit sandpaper.

6. Apply a stain, sealer, or paint following the manufacturer's instructions.

Fasten the table top and seat supports to the legs with carriage bolts. The nuts are recessed to prevent injury.

Install the table top boards by drilling pilot holes and inserting deck screws.

Children's Balance Beam & Portable Putting Green

These two easy-to-build projects will provide hours of fun for your children.

CONSTRUCTION MATERIALS

BALANCE BEAM

Quantity	Lumber
1	4 × 4" × 8' cedar
2	2 × 6" × 4' cedar

PORTABLE PUTTING GREEN

Quantity	Lumber
1	1 × 2" × 10' cedar
1	1 × 4" × 8' cedar
1	½" × 4 × 4' plywood

Large play structures are great for building children's strength, but children also need practice building balance and hand-eye coordination. This two projects are fun to play with and develop both of these skills.
The safe balance beam has rounded corners and sturdy supports to keep it stable. Just because it sits on the ground doesn't mean it won't challenge your child's sense of balance. Try it yourself!

The portable putting green is a great toy for developing the next generation of golfers. Use it with plastic putters for young kids, then graduate to the real thing as they grow. You can practice your technique right alongside them.
Both of these durable projects will continue to challenge your children as they grow.

OVERALL SIZE:
5" HIGH
24" WIDE
96" LONG

OVERALL SIZE:
3½" HIGH
31½" WIDE
72" LONG

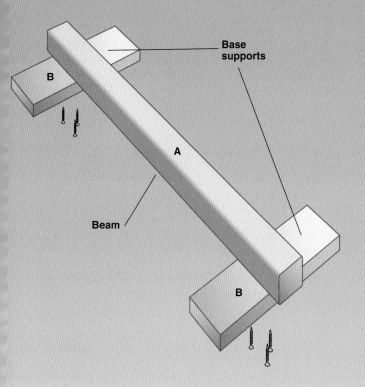

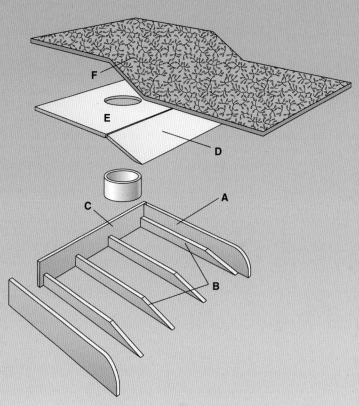

Cutting List–Balance Beam				
Key	**Part**	**Dimension**	**Pcs.**	**Material**
A	Beam	3½ × 3½ × 96"	1	Cedar
B	Base	1½ × 5½ × 24"	2	Cedar

Materials: 2½" galvanized screws, sandpaper, finishing materials.

Note: Measurements reflect the actual size of dimension lumber.

Cutting List–Portable Putting Green				
Key	**Part**	**Dimension**	**Pcs.**	**Material**
A	Side panel	¾ × 3½ × 30½"	2	Cedar
B	Base support	¾ × 1½ × 29"	4	Cedar
C	Back panel	¾ × 3½ × 31½"	1	Cedar
D	Ramp	½ × 11 × 30"	1	½" plywood
E	Base	½ × 20 × 30"	1	½" plywood
F	Green	30 × 72"	1	Carpet

Materials: 1¼" galvanized screws, sandpaper, 4" pvc end cap, staples, indoor/outdoor carpet, doublestick carpet tape.

Note: Measurements reflect actual size of dimension lumber.

Round the top edges and ends of the balance beam with a router.

Directions: Balance Beam

ROUND THE BEAM AND SUPPORTS.

1. Round the top edges of the beam (A), using a router with a ⅜" rounding bit, and round both ends of the beam, using a router.

2. Lightly sand the rounded edges using a finish sander and 220-grit sandpaper.

3. Sand the beam to remove any splinters.

4. Cut the base supports (B) using a circular saw.

5. Round the edges and ends of the two base supports, using a router.

6. Lightly sand the base supports.

ASSEMBLE THE BEAM.

1. Position the beam on your work surface so the bottom is facing up.

2. Center the base supports on the beam. Keep the edge of the supports 2" from the end of the beam. Use a framing square to make sure the supports are perpendicular to the beam. Clamp the supports to the beam.

3. Drill three ³⁄₃₂" pilot holes in each base support. Stagger the holes to prevent splitting.

4. Fasten the supports to the beam using 2½" galvanized screws.

5. Sand out any rough spots using 220-grit sandpaper. Stain or paint the balance beam.

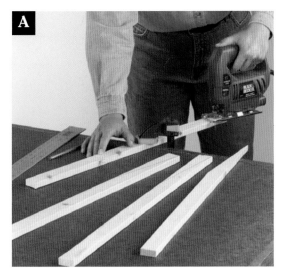

Cut the slope on the first base support, then use it as a template for the others.

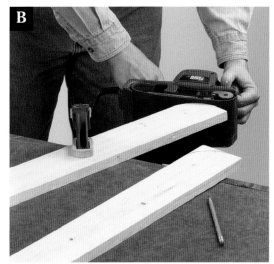

Round one corner at each side panel, using a belt sander.

Directions: Putting Green

CUT THE SLOPED BASE SUPPORTS

1. Cut four 1 × 2 base supports (B) at 29".

2. Cut the slope on the first base support by first marking a point 9" from one end. Then draw a line from that point to the opposite corner at the end of the board. Cut the line using a jig saw. Use this board as a template to cut the other supports.

BUILD THE PLYWOOD BASE.

1. Cut the base (E) at 20 × 30" and the ramp (D) at 11 × 30" from ½" plywood, using a circular saw.

2. Position the supports (B) across the bottom of the base. Align the two outside supports with the outside and back edges of the base, and evenly space the other two supports about 9" apart. Drill countersunk pilot holes in the base, then attach the base to the supports, using glue and 1¼" galvanized screws.

3. Sand one long edge of the ramp (D) to a gentle bevel

(approximately 15°), using a belt sander. Apply glue to the beveled edge of the ramp and the sloped edge of the supports. Butt the ramp against the edge of the base, then attach it to the supports using 1¼" screws driven through countersunk pilot holes. Don't worry if there is a slight gap between the base and ramp since the carpet will cover it.

4. Use a belt sander to bevel the leading edge of the ramp until it lies flat.

5. Cut two 1 × 4 side panels (A) at 30½" and one back panel (C) at 31½". Round one corner of each side panel using a belt sander. Attach the back and side panels to the base, using 1¼" screws driven through pilot holes.

INSTALL CUP & CARPET.

1. Center the cup hole about 8" from the back wall. Trace the PVC end cap onto the plywood base (E) at the hole location. Drill a starter hole to insert the blade of a jig saw, then cut out the hole. Attach the cup using hot glue.

2. Cut a 30" wide piece of indoor/outdoor carpeting (F) using a utility knife. Attach the carpet to the base using double stick carpet tape and staples. Cut away the carpet over the hole.

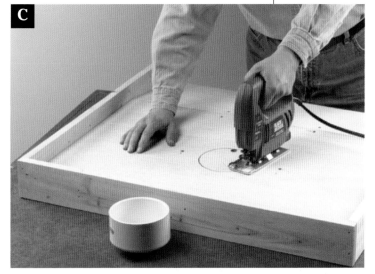

Drill a starter hole to insert the blade of a jig saw, then cut out the cup hole.

Timberframe Sandbox

A playground just isn't complete without a sandbox, and this version gives an old favorite a new look.

CONSTRUCTION MATERIALS

Quantity	Lumber
14	4 × 4" × 8' cedar
1	1 × 8" × 12' cedar
2	1 × 6" × 8' cedar
2	2 × 2" × 6' cedar

This sandbox is much more refined than nailing four boards together and hoping for the best. The timber construction is not only charming, it's solid. A storage box at one end gives kids a convenient place to keep their toys. The other end has built-in seats, allowing children to sit above the sand as they play. The gravel bed and plastic sheathing provide a nice base for the sandbox, allowing water to drain while keeping weeds from sprouting in the sand. The structure is set into the ground for stability, and to keep the top of the pavers at ground level so you can easily mow around them. When your children outgrow the sandbox, turn it into a garden bed.

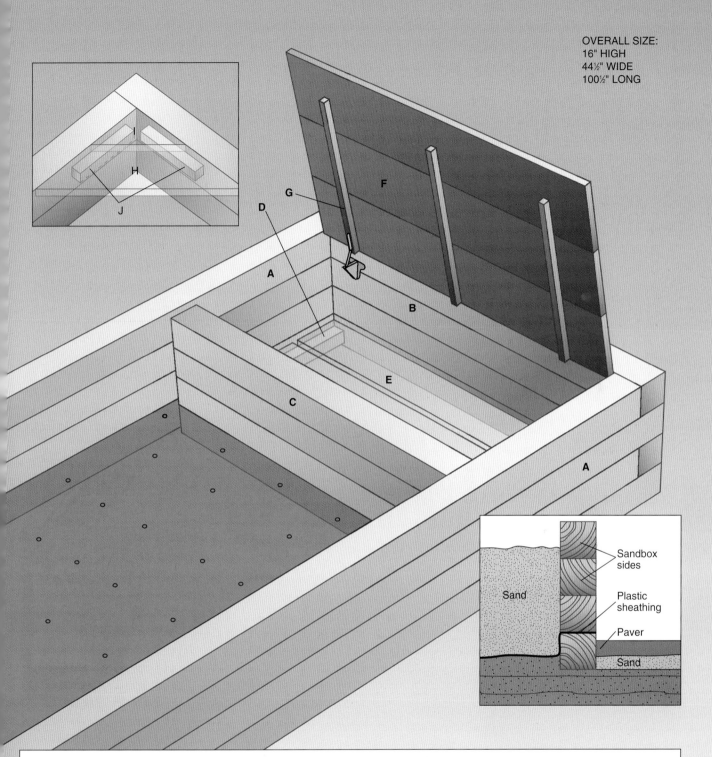

OVERALL SIZE:
16" HIGH
44½" WIDE
100½" LONG

Sandbox sides

Plastic sheathing

Paver

Sand

Sand

Cutting List				
Key	**Part**	**Dimension**	**Pcs.**	**Material**
A	Sandbox sides	3½ × 3½ × 92½"	8	Cedar
B	Sandbox ends	3½ × 3½ × 44½"	8	Cedar
C	Storage box wall	3½ × 3½ × 41"	4	Cedar
D	Floor cleats	1½ × 1½ × 18"	2	Cedar
E	Floor boards	¾ × 5½ × 43"	3	Cedar

Cutting List				
Key	**Part**	**Dimension**	**Pcs.**	**Material**
F	Lid boards	¾ × 7½ × 43½"	3	Cedar
G	Lid cleats	1½ × 1½ × 18"	3	Cedar
H	Bench boards	¾ × 5½ × 18"	2	Cedar
I	Corner bench boards	¾ × 5½ × 7"	2	Cedar
J	Bench cleats	1½ × 1½ × 10"	4	Cedar

Materials: Coarse gravel, sand, wood sealer/protectant, heavy duty plastic sheathing, 2" galvanized screws, 6" barn nails, pavers, hinges.

Note: Measurements reflect the actual size of dimension lumber.

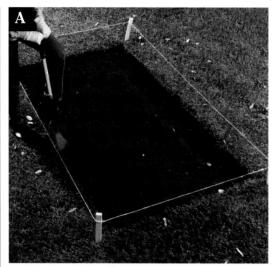

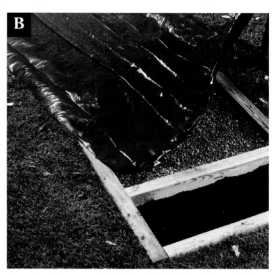

Use a shovel to remove the grass in the sandbox location, then dig a trench for the first row of timbers.

Lay the first row of timbers, including the wall for the storage box. Fill the sandbox area with a 2" layer of gravel and cover with plastic sheathing.

Directions: Timberframe Sandbox

PREPARE THE SITE.

1. Outline a 48 × 96" area using stakes and strings.

2. Use a shovel to remove all of the grass inside the area. Dig a flat trench 2" deep by 4" wide around the perimeter of the area, just inside the stakes and string **(photo A).**

LAY THE FIRST ROW OF TIMBERS.

1. Cut the side (A), end (B) and storage box wall timbers, using a reciprocating saw. Coat the timbers with a wood sealer and let dry completely.

2. Place the first tier of sides and ends in the trench so the corners alternate (see opening photo). Place a level across a corner, then add or remove soil to level it. Level the other three corners the same way. Drill two ³⁄₁₆" pilot holes through the timbers at the corners, then drive 6" barn nails through the pilot holes.

4. Measuring from the inside of one end, mark for the inside edge of the storage box at 18" on both sides. Align the storage box wall with the marks, making sure the corners are square, then score the soil on either side of it. Remove the timber and dig a 3" deep trench at the score marks.

5. Replace the storage box timber in the trench. Its top edge must be ³⁄₄" lower than the top edge of the first tier of the sandbox wall. Add or remove dirt until the storage box timber is at the proper height.

6. Drill ³⁄₁₆" pilot holes through the sandbox sides into the ends of the storage box timber, then drive 6" barn nails through the pilot holes.

7. Pour 2" of coarse gravel into the sandbox section. Rake the gravel smooth.

8. Cover the gravel bed section with heavy duty plastic sheathing **(photo B).** Pierce the plastic with an awl or screwdriver at 12" intervals for drainage.

BUILD THE SANDBOX FRAME.

1. Set the second tier of timbers in place over the first tier and over the plastic sheathing, staggering the joints with the joint pattern in the first tier.

2. Starting at the ends of the timbers, drill ³⁄₁₆" pilot holes every 24", then drive 6" galvanized barn nails through the pilot holes. Repeat for the remaining tiers of timbers, staggering the joints.

3. Stack the remaining storage box timbers over the first one. Drill ³⁄₁₆" pilot holes through the sandbox sides into the ends of the storage box timbers, then drive 6" barn nails into the pilot holes **(photo C).**

4. Cut the excess plastic from

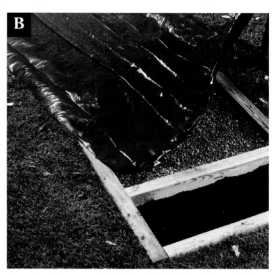

Build the rest of the sandbox frame, staggering the corner joints. Drill holes and drive barn nails through the holes.

Attach the bench lid using heavy-duty hinges. Install a child-safe lid support to prevent the lid from falling shut.

Install 2 × 2 support cleats ¾" from the top of the sandbox. Attach the corner bench boards using galvanized screws.

around the outside of the sandbox timbers, using a utility knife.

BUILD THE STORAGE BOX FLOOR AND LID.

1. Cut the floor cleats (D) and position one against each side wall along the bottom of the storage box and attach them using 2" galvanized screws.
2. Cut the floor boards (E) and place over the cleats with a ½" gap between each board to allow for drainage. Fasten the floor boards to the cleats using 2" screws.
3. Cut the lid boards (F) and lay out side by side with the ends flush. Cut the lid cleats (G) and place across the lid, one at each end and one in the middle, making sure the end of each cleat is flush with the back edge of the lid. Drill pilot holes and attach the cleats using 2" galvanized screws.
4. Attach the lid to the sandbox frame using heavy-duty child safe friction hinges **(photo D).**

BUILD CORNER BENCHES.

1. Cut the bench cleats (J).

Mark ¾" down from the top edge of the sandbox at two corners. Align the top edge of the bench cleats with the mark and fasten using 2" galvanized screws.
2. Cut the corner bench board (I) to length with a 45° angle at each end. Place it in the corner and attach it to the cleats using 2" screws **(photo E).** Cut the bench board (H) to length with a 45° angle at each end. Butt it against the corner bench board, then attach it to the cleats. Repeat this step to install the second corner bench.

FILL SANDBOX AND INSTALL BORDER.

1. Fill the sandbox section with sand.
2. Mark an area the width of your pavers around the perimeter of the sand box. Remove the grass and soil in the paver area to the depth of your pavers plus another 2", using a spade.
3. Spread a 2" layer of sand into the paver trench. Smooth the sand level using a flat board.
4. Place the pavers on top of the sand base, beginning at a

corner of the sandbox **(photo F).** Use a level or a straightedge to make sure the pavers are even and flush with the surrounding soil. If necessary, add or remove sand to level the pavers. Set the pavers in the sand by tapping them with a rubber mallet.
5. Fill the gaps between the pavers with sand. Wet the sand lightly to help it settle. Add new sand as necessary until the gaps are filled.

Place the pavers into the sand base. Use a rubber mallet to set them in place.

PROJECT
POWER TOOLS

Kid-sized Porch Swing

Your children will cherish the memories of spending pleasant summer days on their very own porch swing.

CONSTRUCTION MATERIALS

Quantity	Lumber
1	2 × 4" × 8' cedar (1)
1	2 × 6" × 8' cedar (1)
10	1 × 2" × 10' cedar (10)

This swing is about three-quarters of the size of a full-sized porch swing and is designed specifically for children. The gentle curves of the slatted seat and back are built for their comfort.

You can hang the swing from your porch, a tree branch, or under a deck. Be sure to balance the swing by properly adjusting the links on the chain. This particular swing was built with cedar lumber, which is long-lasting and attractive.

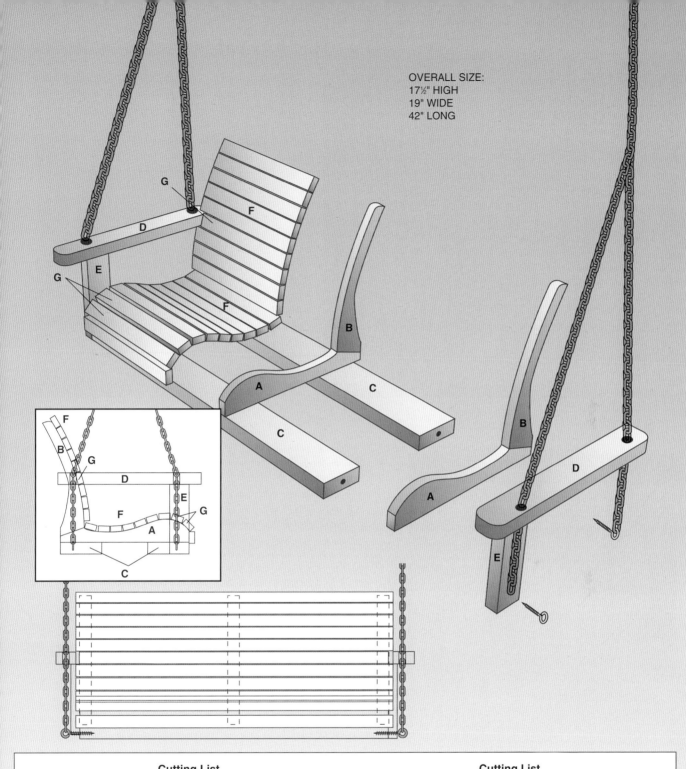

OVERALL SIZE:
17½" HIGH
19" WIDE
42" LONG

Cutting List				
Key	**Part**	**Dimension**	**Pcs.**	**Material**
A	Seat Support	1½ × * × 17½"	3	Cedar
B	Back Support	1½ × * × 14½"	3	Cedar
C	Support Rail	1½ × 3½ × 39"	2	Cedar
D	Arm	1½ × 2⅝ × 19"	2	Cedar

Cutting List				
Key	**Part**	**Dimension**	**Pcs.**	**Material**
E	Arm Upright	1½ × 2⅝" × 8¾	2	Cedar
F	Long Slats	¾ × 1½ × 40"	16	Cedar
G	Short Slats	¾ × 1½ × 39"	3	Cedar

Materials: Exterior wood glue, 2½" galvanized screws, ¼ × 3" lag screws (2), ⁵⁄₁₆ × 6" lag eye screw (4), heavy chains (2), 2" chain connectors (6)

Note: Measurements reflect the actual size of dimension lumber.

* cut to size using template

Make sure the inside corner is flush, then attach each seat support to a back support with glue and galvanized screws.

Attach support rails to the seat supports using galvanized screws.

Drill a hole through the back support into the arm and attach it with a lag screw.

Directions: Kid-sized Porch Swing

BUILD THE SEAT AND BACK SUPPORTS.

1. Enlarge the seat support and back support templates on page 431 using the grid system or a photocopier.

2. Trace the patterns for three sets of seat (A) and back supports (B) onto a 2 × 6, then cut out the pieces using a jig saw. Sand the edges smooth using a belt sander.

3. Apply wood glue to the flat section on the top of the seat support. Position the back support on top of the seat support, making sure the two pieces are flush at the inside corner, and clamp. Drill two ³⁄₁₆" pilot holes, then attach the two pieces using 2½" galvanized screws **(photo A).** Repeat this process for each seat-back support set.

ATTACH THE SUPPORT RAILS.

1. Cut the support rails (C) to size.

2. Set the joined seat and back supports face down on the edge of your work surface so the back support sections hang off the edge. Place a support rail across the seat supports. Align the end of the rail with the outside and back edges of a side seat support. Drill two pilot holes in the support rail, then attach it using 2½" galvanized screws. Attach the rail to the other side seat support the same way.

3. Align the second support rail along the front edge of the seat supports, making sure the edges are flush. Drill pilot holes and attach the rail to the two outside seat supports using 2½" galvanized screws **(photo B).**

4. Center the third seat support between the side seat supports and attach it to the front and rear rails using two 2½" galvanized screws through each rail.

BUILD AND ATTACH ARMS.

1. Cut the arms (D) and arm uprights (E) by ripping a 2 × 6 down the middle, then cutting the pieces to length to create two sets of arms and uprights about 2⅝" wide. Round the corners of the arms using a jig saw or a belt sander. Sand all the edges smooth.

2. Align the edge of an arm upright with the front edge of the

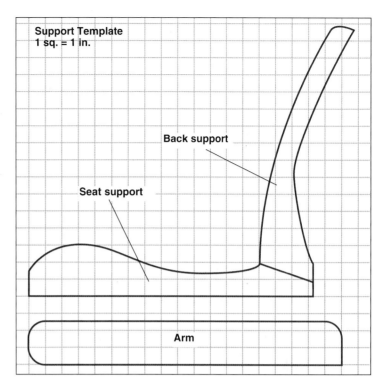

Support Template
1 sq. = 1 in.

Back support

Seat support

Arm

Install the finished slats, started at the crook and covering the seat and back. Space the slats evenly.

front support rail. Make sure the upright is plumb, then drill two pilot holes and attach it to the support rail using 2½" galvanized screws.

3. Position the arm on top of the upright so it is flush with the inside of the upright and overhangs the front by 1½". Drill two pilot holes, then attach the arm to the upright using 2½" galvanized screws.

4. Make sure the arm is level, then drill a ⅛" pilot hole through the back support into the arm. Attach the arm to the back support using a ¼ × 3" lag screw **(photo C)**. Repeat steps 2 through 4 for the other arm and upright.

CUT AND ATTACH SLATS.

1. Cut the long slats (F) and short slats.

2. Paint or stain the swing and the slats as desired. Allow the paint 24 hours to dry before continuing.

3. Install the long slats, beginning at the crook of the seat,

spacing them evenly. Drill pilot holes, then attach each slat using a 1¼" galvanized screw driven into each seat support.

4. Install the short slats between the arms by driving a 1¼" galvanized screw into each seat support.

HANG THE SWING.

1. Measure and make a mark on top of the arm 3" from the front edge and ¾" from the outside edge for the front chain hole. Make a mark for the rear chain hole at 1½" from the back edge and centered from side to side. Drill holes through the marked points using a ¾" spade bit.

2. Drill pilot holes and insert screw eyes into the ends of the rear support rail and ¾" from the bottom of the arm uprights.

3. Insert the chain through the arm holes and hook the chain to the screw eyes using chain connectors. Suspend the swing and adjust the length of the chain and the position of the connectors until the swing bal-

ances properly.

4. Hang the swing using heavy screw eyes inserted into ceiling joists or into a 2 × 4 lag-screwed across the ceiling joists.

Suspend the swing and adjust the chain length and the position of the connectors until the swing balances.

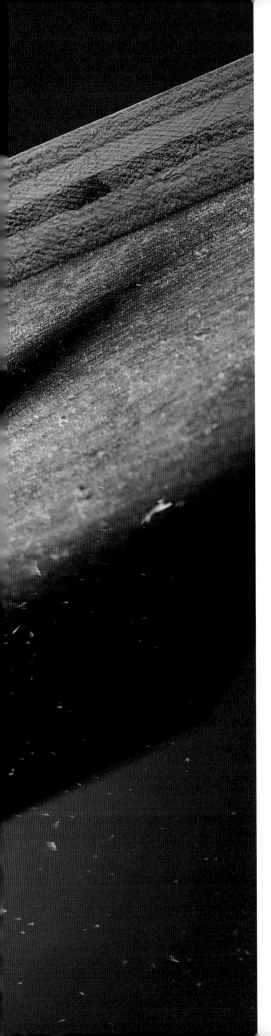

Bird & Pet Projects

Birds bring motion and sound to the yard and garden. Invite them to linger a while longer by creating a stationary or hanging feeder designed just for them. For those animals that hold a permanent place in your yard and heart, we've included plans for cozy homes that provide security for them and style for your outdoor home.

Birdhouse

Give your local birds a dry, clean shelter with these easy-to-build birdhouses.

CONSTRUCTION MATERIALS

Quantity	Lumber
1	1 × 6" × 4' cedar

Birds are always looking for nesting areas. Why not help out with this simple house? It's also a great project for children.

Our version is constructed with a swing-out door to make annual fall cleaning easy. There is no perch because it is not necessary.

You can embellish this basic birdhouse many ways, as in the examples below. There are,

however, a few important things to keep in mind: don't paint or apply preservatives to the inside of the house, the inside edge of the entrance hole, or within ¼" of the face of the entrance hole or it will keep away the birds. The birdhouse can be hung with simple eye-screws and a chain, mounted on a post, or vertically mounted to a tree or other structure.

OVERALL SIZE:
9½" HIGH
5½" WIDE
5½" LONG

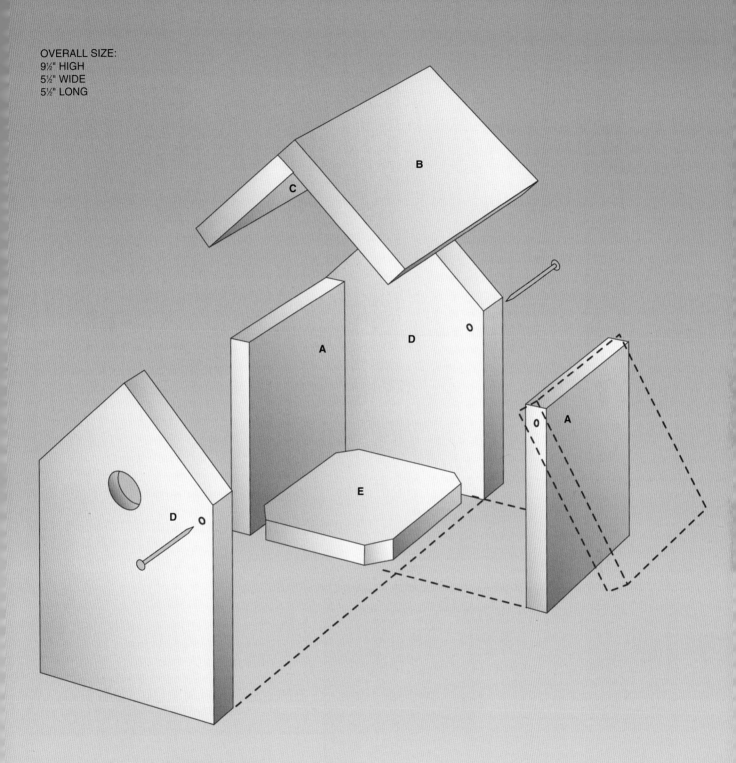

Cutting List

Key	Part	Dimension	Pcs.	Material
A	Side	¾ × 4 × 5½"	2	Cedar
B	Roof	¾ × 5½ × 6½"	1	Cedar
C	Roof	¾ × 4¾ × 6½"	1	Cedar

Cutting List

Key	Part	Dimension	Pcs.	Material
D	Front/Back	¾ × 5½ × 8¾"	2	Cedar
E	Bottom	¾ × 4 × 4"	1	Cedar

Materials: 4d galvanized finish nails, exterior wood glue, shoulder hook.

Note: Measurements reflect the actual size of dimension lumber.

Directions: Birdhouse

PREPARE THE PARTS.

1. Cut the sides (A) and bottom (E) by first ripping a 15¼" piece of 1 × 6 to a width of 4". Cut the pieces to length. On the bottom piece, make a diagonal cut across each corner, ½" from the end, to allow for drainage.

2. Cut the front and back (D) to length. To make the peaks, make a mark on each side of these pieces, 2¾" from the top. Mark the center point at the top. Mark lines from the center point to each side, then cut along them **(photo A).**

3. Mark a point on the front piece 6¾" from the base, centering the mark from side to side. Use an appropriately-sized spade bit to drill an entrance hole, usually 1¼ to 1½" (see Tip).

4. Use a wood screw or awl to make several deep horizontal scratches on the inside of the front piece, starting 1" below the entrance hole. (These grip lines help young birds hold on

Use a speed square as a cutting guide and gang-cut the table parts when possible for uniform results.

as they climb up to the entrance hole.)

ASSEMBLE THE BASE AND SIDES.

1. Apply wood glue to one edge of the bottom piece. Butt a side piece against the bottom

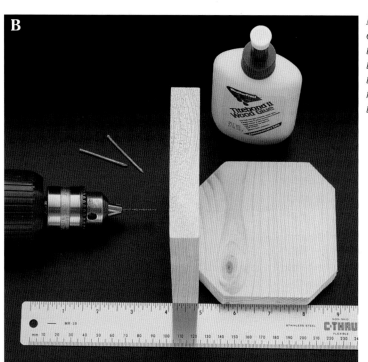

Mark the ends of the tapers on the leg sides, then connect the marks to make taper cutting lines.

piece so the bottoms of the two pieces are flush.

2. Drill ¹⁄₁₆" pilot holes and attach the pieces using 4d galvanized finish nails. Repeat this process for the front and back pieces, aligning the edges with the side piece **(photo B).**

3. Set the remaining side piece in place, but do not glue it. To attach the side to the front and back pieces, drill ¹⁄₁₆" pilot holes and drive a 4d nail through the front wall and another through the back wall, each positioned about ⅝" from the top edge. This arrangement allows the piece to pivot.

ADD THE ROOF AND FINISH.

1. Cut the roof (B & C) pieces to size.

2. Apply glue to the top edges of one side of the front and back pieces. Set the smaller roof piece on the house so its upper edge is aligned with the peak of the house.

3. Apply glue to the top edges

Use a jig saw or circular saw to cut the leg tapers.

on the opposite side of the front and back pieces. Place the larger roof piece in position. Drill pilot holes and drive 4d nails through the roof into the front piece and then the back **(photo C).**

4. Drill a pilot hole in the edge of the front piece on the pivot wall side, placed about 1" from the bottom edge of the house. Screw in a shoulder hook, positioning it to hold the side piece closed.

5. Sand the birdhouse smooth, then paint or decorate it as desired. We hot-glued sticks and straw to the bird houses on the opposite page to create a "Three Little Pigs" theme. The brick exterior on the third bird house is contact paper and the roof is hot-glued into place. These items can be purchased at craft stores.

TIP

Different bird species prefer different sized nesting boxes. Some species, like robins, will not nest in boxes, but prefer platforms on which to build their nests. Many publications give even more specific information on how to attract nesting birds to your yard.

Keeping predators and invasives species like sparrows from invading nesting boxes is important. Drilling the proper size entrance hole protects your house from becoming a home to sparrows or squirrels. Do not use perches, as these allow predatory birds to sit and wait for adults and nestlings to emerge.

The following chart shows nesting box dimensions for common bird species.

NEST BOX DIMENSIONS

Species	Box floor	Box height	Hole height	Hole diameter	Box placement
Eastern Bluebird	5 × 5"	8 to 12"	6 to 10"	1½"	4 to 6 ft.
Chickadees	4 × 4"	8 to 10"	6 to 8"	1⅛"	4 to 15 ft.
Titmice	4 × 4"	10 to 12"	6 to 10"	1¼"	5 to 15 ft.
Red-breasted Nuthatch	4 × 4"	8 to 10"	6 to 8"	1¼"	5 to 15 ft.
White-breasted Nuthatch	4 × 4"	8 to 10"	6 to 8"	1⅜"	5 to 15 ft.
Northern Flicker	7 × 7"	16 to 18"	14 to 16"	2½"	6 to 20 ft.
Yellow-bellied Sapsucker	5 × 5"	12 to 15"	9 to 12"	1½"	10 to 20 ft.
House wrens	4 × 4"	6 to 8"	4 to 6"	1¼"	5 to 10 ft.
Carolina Wren	4 × 4"	6 to 8"	4 to 6"	1½"	5 to 10 ft.
Wood Ducks	10 × 18"	10 to 24"	12 to 16"	4"	10 to 20 ft.

Bird Feeder

*A leftover piece of cedar lap siding is put to good use
in this rustic bird feeder.*

CONSTRUCTION MATERIALS

Quantity	Lumber
1	¾ × 16 × 16" plywood scrap
1	¾" × 6' cedar stop molding
1	8" × 10' cedar lap siding
1	1 × 2" × 8' cedar
1	1"-dia. × 3' dowel

Watching birds feeding in your backyard can be a very relaxing pastime. In this bird feeder project, you will use a piece of 8"-wide cedar lap siding to build a decorative feeder box and then mount it on a piece of scrap plywood. The birds won't mind the leftover building materials. And you'll like the bird feeder because it costs almost nothing to build. Even the plastic viewing window covers that you place inside the feeder box can be made with clear acrylic scrap left over from another project. To fill this cleverly designed bird feeder with seed, turn the threaded rod that serves as a hook so it is aligned with the slot in the roof. Then, simply lift up the roof and add the bird food.

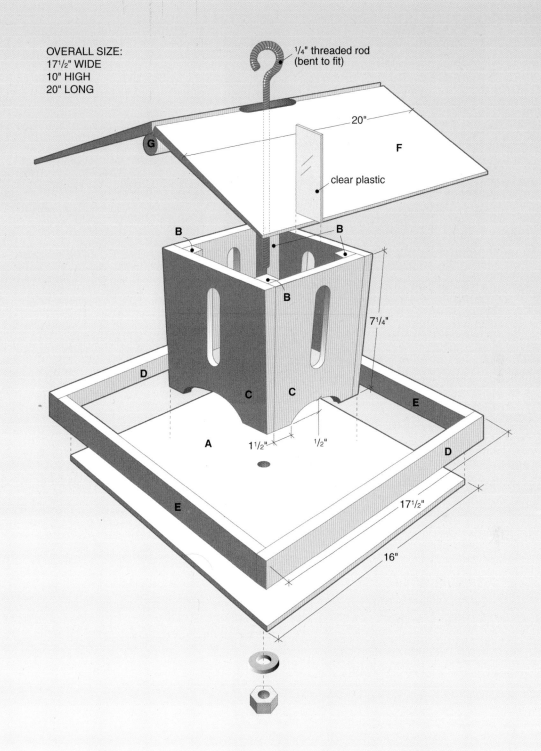

OVERALL SIZE:
17½" WIDE
10" HIGH
20" LONG

¼" threaded rod
(bent to fit)

20"

F

clear plastic

G

B

B

B

7¼"

D

C

C

E

A

1½"

½"

D

E

17½"

16"

Cutting List				
Key	**Part**	**Dimension**	**Pcs.**	**Material**
A	Base	¾ × 16 × 16"	1	Plywood
B	Post	¾ × ¾ × 7¼"	4	Cedar
C	Box side	⁵⁄₁₆ × 6 × 7¼"	4	Cedar siding
D	Ledge side	¾ × 1½ × 17½"	2	Cedar

Cutting List				
Key	**Part**	**Dimension**	**Pcs.**	**Material**
E	Ledge end	¾ × 1½ × 16"	2	Cedar
F	Roof panel	⁵⁄₁₆ × 7¼ × 20"	2	Cedar siding
G	Ridge pole	1"-dia. × 20"	1	Dowel

Materials: ¼"-dia. threaded rod with matching nut and washer, hot glue, 4d common nails, rigid acrylic or plastic.

Note: Measurements reflect the actual size of dimension lumber.

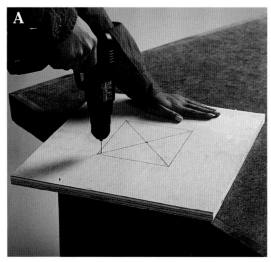

Drill pilot holes in the corners of the feeder box location that is laid out on the plywood base.

Cover the viewing slots by hot-gluing clear plastic or acrylic pieces to the inside face of each panel.

Directions: Bird Feeder

CUT AND PREPARE THE BASE.

The base provides room for several feeding birds and seed.
1. Cut the base (A) from ¾" plywood. Draw straight diagonal lines from corner to corner to locate the center of the base.
2. Measure and mark a 6" square in the middle of the base, making sure the lines are parallel to the edges of the base. This square marks the location for the feeder box.
3. Drill a ¼"-dia. hole through the center of the base where the lines cross.
4. Measure in toward the center ⅜" from each corner of the 6" square and mark points. Drill ¹⁄₁₆" pilot holes all the way through at these points **(photo A).**

PREPARE THE FEEDER BOX PARTS.

The posts and box sides form the walls of the feeder box. Vertical grooves in the box

Mark the profile of the bevel of the siding onto two of the box sides for trimming.

sides let you check seed levels. Seed flows through small arcs cut in the bottoms of the box sides.

1. Cut the posts (B) to length from ¾"-square cedar stop molding. (Or, rip a 3'-long piece of ¾"-thick cedar to ¾" in width to make the posts.)
2. From 8" cedar lap siding (actual dimension is 7¼") cut two 6"-wide box sides (C). Then, cut two more panels to about 7" in width to be trimmed later to follow the lap-siding bevels.
3. Cut viewing slots. First, drill two ½" starter holes for a jig saw blade along the center of each box side—one hole 2" from the

top, and the other 2" from the bottom. Connect the starter holes by cutting with a jig saw to form the slots.
4. Cut a ½"-deep arc into the bottom of each box side, using the jig saw. Start the cuts 1½" from each end. Smooth out the arcs with a drum sander on a power drill.
5. Cut strips of clear acrylic or plastic slightly larger than the viewing slots. Hot-glue them over the slots on the inside of the box sides **(photo B).**
6. To mark cutting lines for trimming two of the box sides to follow the siding bevel, tape the box sides together into a

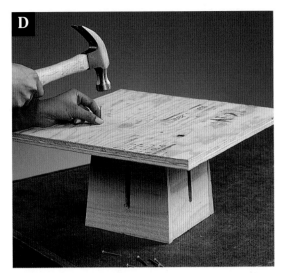

Drive 4d common nails through pilot holes to fasten the feeder box to the base.

Insert spacers 2" in from the "eaves" of the roof to set the pitch before applying glue to the seam.

box shape. The wide ends of the beveled siding should all be flush. Trace the siding profile onto the inside faces of the two box ends **(photo C).** Disassemble the box. Cut along the profile lines with a jig saw.

ASSEMBLE THE FEEDER BOX.

1. Hot-glue the posts flush with the inside edges on the box sides that were trimmed in Step 6 (above).

2. Hot-glue the untrimmed box sides to the posts.

ATTACH THE BASE.

1. Align the assembled feeder box with the 6" square outline on the base. Hot-glue the box to the base on these lines. Turn the assembly upside down.

2. Attach the base to the feeder box by driving 4d galvanized common nails through the predrilled pilot holes in the base, and into the posts on the feeder box **(photo D).**

3. Cut the ledge sides (D) and ledge ends (E) to length. Next, build a frame around the base that prevents seed spills. Using hot glue, attach the ledge

pieces so the bottoms are flush with the bottom of the base. Reinforce the joint with 4d common nails.

MAKE THE ROOF.

1. Cut the ridge pole (G) from a 1"-dia. dowel. Cut the roof panels (F) from 8" siding.

2. To create the roof pitch, lay the panels on your work surface so the wide ends butt together. Place a 1"-thick spacer under each of the narrow ends, 2" in from each end.

3. Apply a heavy bead of hot glue into the seam between the panels **(photo E).** Quickly press the ridge pole into the seam. Let the glue harden for at least 15 minutes.

4. Set the roof right-side-up, and rest each end of the ridge pole on a 2 × 4 block. Drill ⅜" starter holes down through the roof and the ridge pole, 1" to either side of the ridge's midpoint. Connect the starter holes by cutting a slot between them, using a jig saw. Widen the slot until the ¼"-dia. threaded rod passes through with minimal resistance.

5. Cut the threaded rod to 16"

in length. Use pliers to bend a 1½"-dia. loop in one end of the rod. Place the roof on the feeder box. Then, thread the unbent end of the rod through the roof and the hole in the base **(photo F).** Spin the rod loop so it is perpendicular to the roof ridge.

6. Tighten a washer and nut onto the end of the rod, loosely enough so the loop can be spun with moderate effort. For a rustic look, don't apply a finish to your bird feeder.

The bird feeder is held together by a looped, threaded rod that runs through the roof and is secured with a washer and nut on the underside of the base.

Bird Feeder Stand

Send an invitation to flocks of colorful backyard guests by hanging bird feeders from this sturdy cedar stand.

Create a hub of avian activity in your backyard by building this clever bird feeder stand. Bird feeders vary widely in size and style—from small and plain to large and fanciful. This stand can support more than one kind of bird feeder at a time, letting you show off your favorite types. If you want to attract different species of birds to your feeding area, hang feeders that contain different foods. Then sit and enjoy the sight of a variety of birds fluttering and roosting in one central area.

One important benefit of this cedar bird feeder stand is that it has a freestanding, open design. Birds are always in full view as they eat.

The heavy stand base, made from cedar frames, provides ample support for the post and hanging arms. To simplify cleanup of any spilled food (and to make it accessible to hungry birds), you can attach a layer of window screening over the slats in the top of the base. Cleaning the bird feeder stand is easy—just remove the feeders, tip the stand on its side and spray it down with a hose.

CONSTRUCTION MATERIALS

Quantity	Lumber
1	1 × 4" × 8' cedar
1	1 × 4" × 10' cedar
2	1 × 4" × 12' cedar
2	1 × 6" × 12' cedar
2	2 × 4" × 12' cedar
1	2 × 6" × 6' cedar

OVERALL SIZE:
72" HIGH
35¼" WIDE
35¼" LONG

1" squares

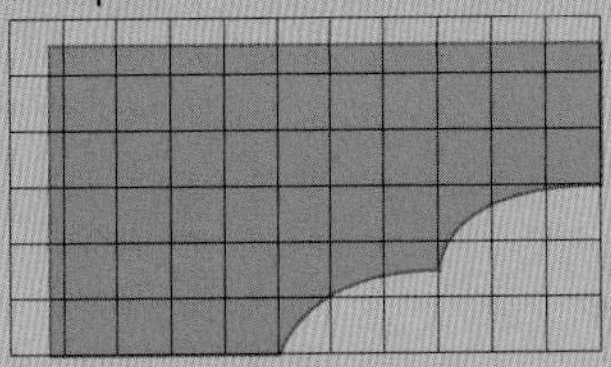

PART H DETAIL

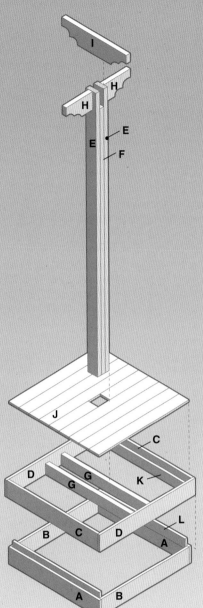

	Cutting List			
Key	**Part**	**Dimension**	**Pcs.**	**Material**
A	Bottom end	⅞ × 5½ × 33½"	2	Cedar
B	Bottom side	⅞ × 5½ × 31¾"	2	Cedar
C	Top end	⅞ × 5½ × 33½"	2	Cedar
D	Top side	⅞ × 5½ × 35¼"	2	Cedar
E	Post board	1½ × 3½ × 72"	2	Cedar
F	Center board	1½ × 3½ × 66½"	1	Cedar

	Cutting List			
Key	**Part**	**Dimension**	**Pcs.**	**Material**
G	Post support	1½ × 3½ × 33½"	2	Cedar
H	Outside arm	1½ × 5½ × 10¼"	2	Cedar
I	Inside arm	1½ × 5½ × 36"	1	Cedar
J	Floor board	⅞ × 3½ × 33½"	9	Cedar
K	Floor support	⅞ × 3½ × 33½"	2	Cedar
L	Bottom cleat	⅞ × 3½ × 31¾"	2	Cedar

Materials: 1½" and 2½" deck screws, 18 × 36" window screening (2), eye hooks, finishing materials.

Note: Measurements reflect the actual size of dimension lumber.

| A | B |

Join the top base frame to the bottom base frame by driving screws through the frame cleats.

Use a square to make sure the inside arm is perpendicular to the post before you secure it into the gap at the top of the post.

Directions:
Bird Feeder Stand

BUILD THE BASE FRAMES.
1. Cut the bottom ends (A), bottom sides (B), top ends (C) and top sides (D) to length. Sand the parts smooth. Drill ⅛" pilot holes near the ends of the bottom ends and counterbore the holes to a ¼" depth with a counterbore bit. Fasten the bottom sides between the bottom ends by driving 1½" deck screws through the pilot holes. Repeat this procedure with the top sides and top ends to complete the second base frame.
2. Cut the floor supports (K) to length. Fasten them to the inside faces of the top ends so the bottoms of the supports are flush with the bottoms of the ends. Cut the bottom cleats (L) to length. Attach them

with 1½" deck screws to the inside faces of the bottom ends. Make sure the top edge of each bottom cleat is 1½" above the top edge of each bottom end.
3. Set the top frame over the bottom frame. Fasten the top and bottom frames together by driving deck screws through the bottom cleats and into the top frame **(photo A).**

INSTALL POST SUPPORTS.
1. Mark the centerpoints of the top sides on their inside faces. Draw reference lines, 2¼" to each side of the centerpoints. These lines mark the locations for the post supports (G).
2. Cut the post supports to length. Place them in the top frame so their bottom edges rest on the tops of the bottom sides. Position the post supports with their inside faces just outside the reference lines. Drill pilot holes through the frame and counterbore the holes. Fasten the post supports to the top frame by driving 2½" deck screws through the frame and into the supports.

BUILD THE ARMS.
1. Cut the two outside arms (H) and the inside arm (I) to length. Use a pencil to draw a 1"-square grid pattern on one of the arms. Using the grid patterns as a reference (see *Diagram,* page 443), lay out the decorative scallops at the end of the arm.
2. Cut along the layout lines with a jig saw. With a 1"-dia. drum sander mounted in an electric drill, smooth the insides of the curves. Use the arm as a template to draw identical scallops on the other arms. Then, cut and sand the other arms to match.

MAKE THE POST.
The post is constructed by sandwiching the center board (F) between two post boards (E). It's easiest to attach the outside arms before you assemble the post.
1. Cut the post boards (E) to length and draw 5½"-long center lines on one face of each post board, starting at the top. Then, draw a 5½"-long line, ¾"

TIP

There is a real art to making and stocking bird feeders, identifying species and enjoying bird watching. If you are just a budding ornithologist, make a visit to your local library—the more knowledge you acquire, the more enjoyment you will experience.

to each side of the center line, to mark the outlines for the outside arms on the post. On the center line, drill pilot holes for the deck screws, 1½" and 4½" down from the top edge. Counterbore the holes.

2. Attach the outside arms to the side posts by driving 2½" deck screws through the posts and into the straight ends of the outside arms. Sandwich the center board between the side post boards, with the bottom and side edges flush.

3. Drive pairs of 2½" deck screws at 8" to 12" intervals, screwing through the face of one post board. Then, flip the assembly over and drive screws through the other post board. Make sure to stagger them so you don't hit screws driven from the other side.

4. Center the inside arm in the gap at the top of the post **(photo B).** Then, drive 2½" deck screws through the post boards and into the inside arm.

5. Install the post assembly by standing the post up between the post supports in the base frame. Be sure the post is centered between the top frame sides and is perpendicular to the post supports. Drive 2½" deck screws through the post supports and into the post to secure the parts.

MAKE THE FEEDING FLOOR.

Floor boards are attached to the floor supports within the top base frame.

1. Cut the floor boards (J) to length. One floor board should be cut into two 14½"-long pieces to fit between the post and frame.

2. Arrange the floor boards across the post supports and

Attach the floor boards by driving deck screws through the floor boards and into the post and floor supports.

floor supports, using ¼"-wide scraps to set ¼"-wide gaps between the boards.

3. To fasten the floor boards to the floor supports and post supports, first drill pilot holes in the floor boards and counterbore the holes. Then, drive 1½" deck screws through the pilot holes and into the floor supports **(photo C).**

APPLY FINISHING TOUCHES.

1. Apply exterior wood stain to the bird feeder stand. After it dries, staple two 18 × 36" strips of window screening to the floor to keep food from falling through the gaps **(photo D).**

2. Insert brass screw eyes or other hardware at the ends of the arms to hang your bird feeders. Set the stand in a semi-sheltered area in clear view of your favorite window or deck.

Staple window screening over the tops of the floor boards to keep bird food from falling through the gaps.

Doghouse

Add a contemporary twist to a traditional backyard project with this cedar-trimmed, arched-entry doghouse.

CONSTRUCTION MATERIALS

Quantity	Lumber
2	1 × 2" × 8' cedar
3	2 × 2" × 8' pine
2	2 × 4" × 8' cedar
2	⅜" × 4 × 8' siding
1	¾" × 4 × 8' ABX plywood

Close your eyes and picture the first image that comes to mind when you think of a doghouse. More than likely it's a boxy, boring little structure. Now consider this updated doghouse, with its sheltered breezeway and contemporary styling. What dog wouldn't want to call this distinctive dwelling home? The

sturdy 2 × 4 frame provides a stable foundation for the wall panels and roof. The main area has plenty of room to house an average-sized dog comfortably, and the porch area shelters the entry, while providing an open, shady area for your pet to relax. The rounded feet keep the inside of the house dry by raising the base up off the ground.

OVERALL SIZE:
30" HIGH
27¼" WIDE
48" LONG

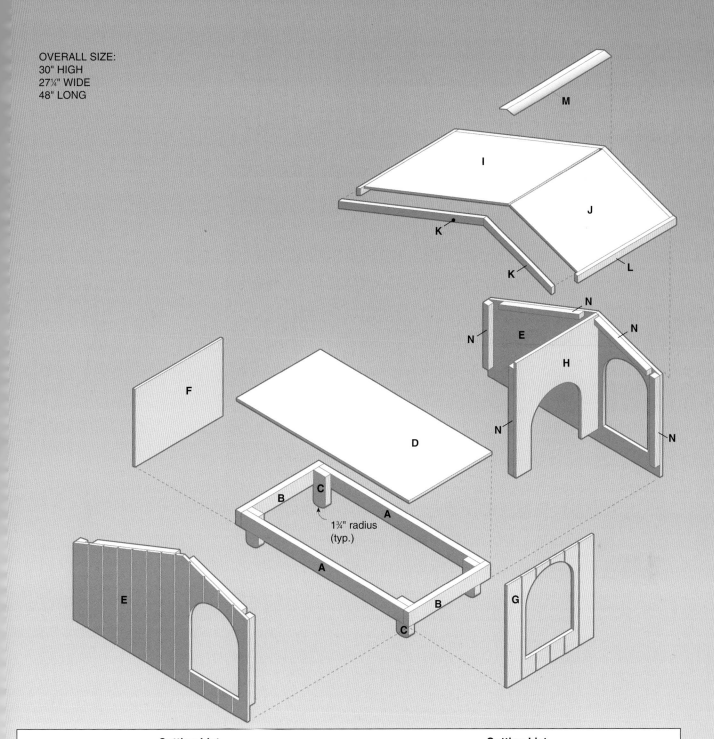

1¾" radius
(typ.)

Cutting List

Key	Part	Dimension	Pcs.	Material
A	Frame side	1½ × 3½ × 45"	2	Cedar
B	Frame end	1½ × 3½ × 22⅞"	2	Cedar
C	Feet	1½ × 3½ × 7½"	4	Cedar
D	Floor	¾ × 22⅞ × 48"	1	ABX Plywood
E	Side panel	⅝ × 30 × 48"	2	Siding
F	House end panel	⅝ × 18 × 24"	1	Siding
G	Porch end panel	⅝ × 24 × 24"	1	Siding

Cutting List

Key	Part	Dimension	Pcs.	Material
H	Center panel	⅝ × 22⅞ × 29¾"	1	Siding
I	House roof	¾ × 25½ × 35"	1	ABX Plywood
J	Porch roof	¾ × 25½ × 23"	1	ABX Plywood
K	Side roof trim	⅞ × 1½ × *	4	Cedar
L	End roof trim	⅞ × 1½ × 27¼"	2	Cedar
M	Flashing	1⁄16 × 4 × 27¼"	1	Galv. flashing
N	Cleat	1½ × 1½ × *"	10	Pine

Materials: 2" and 3" deck screws, 6d galvanized finish nails, 2d galvanized common nails, silicone caulk, roofing nails with rubber washers, finishing materials.

*Cut to fit   **Note:** Measurements reflect the actual size of dimension lumber.

Directions: Doghouse

BUILD THE FRAME & FLOOR.

The frame of the doghouse is the foundation for the floor, sides and roof. It is built from 2 × 4 cedar lumber.

1. Cut the frame sides (A) and frame ends (B) to length. Place the frame sides between the frame ends to form a rectangle, then fasten together with 3" deck screws. Make sure to keep the outside edges flush.

2. Cut the feet (C) to length. Use a compass to lay out a 1¾"-radius roundover curve on one end of each foot, then cut with a jig saw to form the roundover. Smooth out the jig-saw cuts with a power sander.

3. Fasten a foot in each corner of the frame with 3" deck screws **(photo A).** Be sure to keep the top edges of the feet flush with the top edges of the frame.

4. Cut the floor (D) to size from ¾"-thick exterior plywood, and fasten it to the top of the frame with 2" deck screws. The edges of the floor should be flush with the outside edges of the frame.

MAKE THE WALLS.

The walls for the doghouse are cut from ⅝"-thick siding

Fasten the 2 × 4 cedar feet to the inside frame corners with 3" galvanized deck screws.

Lay out the roof angle on the side panels using a straightedge.

panels—we chose panels with grooves cut every 4" for a more decorative effect.

1. Cut the side panels (E) to the full size listed in the *Cutting List* on page 447.

2. Create the roof line by cutting peaks on the top of the panels. To make the cuts, first mark points 18" up from the bottom on one end, and 24" up from the bottom on the other end. Measure in along the top edge 30" out from the end with the 24" mark, and mark a point to indicate the peak of the roof. Connect the peak mark to the marks on the ends with straight lines to create the cutting lines **(photo B).** Lay the side panels on top of one another, fastening them with a screw or two in the waste area. Then cut both panels at the same time, using a circular saw or jig saw and straight-edge cutting guide.

3. Make the arched cutouts in the front (taller) sections of the side panels, by first measuring and marking a point 2" and 16" in from the 24"-tall end of one panel, then drawing lines from the bottom to the top of the panel, through the points. Measure up 4¼" and 15¾" from the bottom edge and draw horizontal lines to complete the square. Find the centerpoint between the sides of the square cutout outline, and measure down 7" from the top of the cutout at that point. Press down on the end of a ruler so it pivots at that point, and use the ruler and a pencil like a compass to draw a curve with a 7" radius across the top of the cutout **(photo C).** Drill a starter hole at a corner of the cutout outline, then cut the opening with a jig saw **(photo D).** Trace the cutout onto the other side panel, then make that cutout.

4. Cut the center panel (H) and porch end panel (G) to full size. Use one of the side panel cutouts to trace an arched

Lay out the opening archway on the side panels using a ruler and pencil.

Cut out the openings in the panels with a jig saw.

Fasten the center panel by driving screws through the side panels into the cleats. Use a combination square to keep the panel even.

TIP

If plan dimensions do not meet your needs, you can recalculate them to a different scale. The doghouse shown here is designed for an average dog (about 15" tall). If you own a larger dog, add 1" to the size of the entry cutouts and panels for every inch that your dog is taller than 15".

cutout outline onto the porch end panel so the sides are 4½" from each side edge and the top is 15¾" up from the bottom. Mark an arched cutout outline on the center panel, 3⅞" from each side edge and 15¾" up from the bottom.
5. Make the cutouts with a jig saw, then sand all cut edges smooth.

ATTACH THE WALLS & FRAME.
1. Cut the house end panel (F).
2. Fasten the side panels (E) to the frame with 2" deck screws, so the bottoms of the panels are flush with the bottoms of the frame, and the ends of the panels are flush with the

frame ends.
3. Fasten the house end panel (F) and the porch end panel (G) to the frame so the bottoms of the panels are flush with the bottom of the frame (the sides of the end panels will overlap the side panels by ⅝" on each side).
4. Cut the 10 cleats (N) long enough to fit in the positions shown in the *Diagram* on page 447—there should be a little space between the ends of the cleats, so exact cutting is not important. Just make sure the edges are flush with the edges of the panel they are attached to.
5. Fasten four cleats along the perimeter of each side panel (E), using 2" deck screws.
6. Fasten the remaining two cleats at the edges of the back side of the center panel (H).
7. Set the center panel be-

tween the side panels so the front is aligned with the peak in the roof. Make sure the center panel is perpendicular, then attach it with 2" deck screws driven through the side panels and into the cleats at the edges of the center panel **(photo E).**

ATTACH THE ROOF & TRIM.
The roof and trim are the final structural elements to be fastened to the doghouse.
1. Cut the house roof (I) and porch roof (J) to size from ¾"-thick exterior plywood.
2. Fasten the roof panels to the cleats at the tops of the side walls, making sure the edges of the panels butt together to form the roof peak.
3. Cut the trim pieces to frame the roof (K, L) from 1 × 2 cedar. The end roof trim pieces are square-cut at the ends, but

the ends of the side roof trim pieces (K) need to be miter-cut to form clean joints at the peak and at the ends, where they meet the end trim. To mark the side trim pieces for cutting, first cut the side trim pieces so they are an inch or two longer than the space between the end of the roof panel and the roof peak. Lay each rough trim piece in position, flush with the top of the roof panel. On each trim piece, mark a vertical cut-off line that is aligned with the end of the roof panel. Then, mark a cutoff line at the peak, making sure the line is perpendicular to the peak. Cut the trim pieces with a power miter saw or miter box and backsaw.
4. Attach the trim pieces to the side panels with 6d galvanized finish nails **(photo F).**

Cut each side roof trim piece to fit between the peak and the end of the roof panel, mitering the ends so they will be perpendicular when installed. Attach all the roof trim pieces with galvanized finish nails.

APPLY FINISHING TOUCHES.

1. Sand all the wood surfaces smooth, paying special attention to any sharp edges, then prime and paint the doghouse. Use a good-quality exterior primer and at least two coats of paint, or you can do as we did and simply apply two or three coats of nontoxic sealant to preserve the natural wood tones. We used linseed oil.
2. Cut a strip of galvanized steel flashing (M) to cover the roof peak (or you can use aluminum flashing, if you prefer). Use tin snips or aviator snips to cut the flashing, and buff the edges with emery paper to help smooth out any sharp points.
3. Lay the flashing lengthwise on a wood scrap, so the flashing overhangs by 2". Bend the flashing over the edge of the board to create a nice, crisp peak, then attach the flashing with roofing nails with neoprene (rubber) washers driven at 4" intervals **(photo G).**

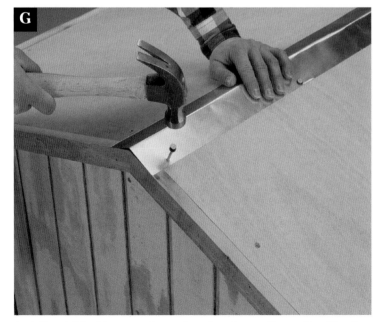

Install metal flashing over the roof peak, using roofing nails with rubber washers.

Rabbit Hutch

With its two compartments, this rabbit hutch provides both a breezy and cozy home for your bunny.

CONSTRUCTION MATERIALS

Quantity	Lumber
7	2 × 2 × 6' cedar
7	2 × 4" × 6' cedar
1	⅝" × 4 × 8' grooved cedar plywood siding

This rabbit hutch is an easy to build outdoor shelter for your bunny. The floor is made of hardware cloth which allows droppings to fall through but is easy on the rabbit's feet. A large airy compartment is enclosed with hardware cloth and a cozy smaller compartment is sided. Each compart-ment has a door to make feeding and cage cleaning an easier task.

Place straw or wood shavings in the compartment to make comfortable bedding for bunny.

Finish the rabbit hutch with an animal safe exterior stain. Place the hutch in a protected area out of direct sun.

OVERALL SIZE:
54" HIGH
32" WIDE
48" LONG

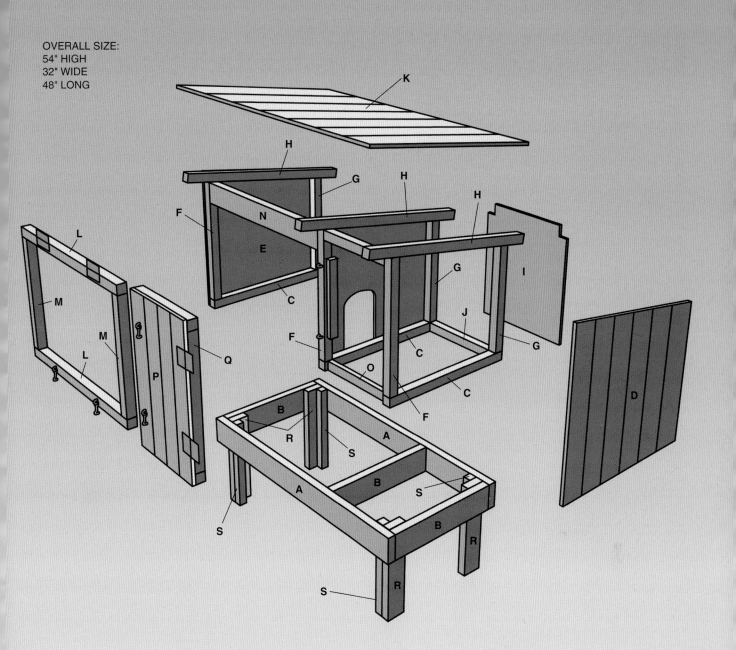

Cutting List				
Key	Part	Dimension	Pcs.	Material
A	Floor side	1½ × 3½ × 47½"	2	Cedar
B	Floor crosspiece	1½ × 3½ × 21"	3	Cedar
C	Frame base	1½ × 1½ × 24"	3	Cedar
D	Right side wall	½ × 24 × 24"	1	Siding
E	Left side wall	½ × 24 × 24"	1	Siding
F	Frame front	1½ × 1½ × 21"*	3	Cedar
G	Frame back	1½ × 1½ × 17½"*	3	Cedar
H	Frame top	1½ × 1½ × 32"	3	Cedar
I	Back wall	½ × 17¼ × 20"	1	Siding
J	Back wall stop	1½ × 1½ × 13¼"	1	Siding

Cutting List				
Key	Part	Dimension	Pcs.	Material
K	Roof	½ × 32 × 48"	1	Siding
L	Door crosspiece	1½ × 1½ × 29½"*	2	Cedar
M	Door side	1½ × 1½ × 17¾"*	2	Cedar
N	Hinge support	1½ × 3½ × 29½"*	1	Cedar
O	Door jamb	1½ × 1½ × 13¼"*	1	Cedar
P	Compartment door	½ × 13 × 22½"*	1	Siding
Q	Door supports	1½ × 1½ × *	4	Cedar
R	Legs	1½ × 3½ × *	4	Cedar
S	Legs	1½ × 1½ × *	4	Cedar

Materials: ½" × 4' × 8' hardware cloth, ¾" fence staples, 1¼" and 2½" deck screws, 3 × 3" hinges (4), hook and eye fasteners (4).
Note: Measurements reflect the actual size of dimension lumber.
*cut to fit.

Attach the crosspieces between the sides to make the floor.

Center the frame top and mark the ends so they are parallel to the wall sides.

Attach the frame top to the frame back, sides, and base to create the cage side.

Directions: Rabbit Hutch

BUILD THE FLOOR.

For all screws in this project, drill a ⁹⁄₆₄" pilot hole and a ⅛" deep counterbore.

1. Cut the floor sides (A) and crosspieces (B). Mark a point 15¾" from the right ends of the side pieces.

2. Set the pieces on edge and apply exterior glue to the crosspiece ends. Drive 2½" deck screws through the sides into the ends. Center the third crosspiece at the mark and attach **(photo A).**

3. Cut a six foot section of hardware cloth. Align one corner of the cloth with the right front

corner of the floor. Attach it with ¾" fence staples every 4".

BUILD THE COMPARTMENT SIDES.

1. Cut the frame bases (C) and side walls (D and E). Place the walls together with the smooth sides facing in. Make a mark at 20" on a lengthwise side. Draw a line from the mark to the nearest opposite corner. Cut on the line to create the left and right peaked walls.

2. Make the door cutout on the inside wall by marking a 5 × 5" square 1½" up from the bottom and 4" from the front (longer) edge. Use a compass to draw an arch on top of the square. Drill a starter hole and use a jig saw to cut along the lines.

3. Align a frame base with the inside bottom of a wall. Attach the wall to the frame with 1¼" deck screws. Repeat with the second wall and base.

4. Draw a line across the inside of the walls, 1½" down from the peaked edge. Cut three sets of frame fronts (F) and backs (G) to fit between the frame base and the angled line. Attach using 1¼" deck screws through the siding into the frames.

5. Cut the frame tops (H). Center a top against each wall.

Mark the ends so they are parallel with the sides and cut **(photo B).** Using one of these frame tops, cut the third frame top to match.

BUILD THE CAGE SIDE.

1. Assemble the third set of frame pieces cut in the previous step. Drive 2½" deck screws through the frame base into the square ends of the frame front and frame back.

2. Center the frame top across the front and back. Make sure it matches the extension of the two compartment sides. Use 2½" deck screws to attach the top to the mitered ends of the front and back **(photo C).**

ATTACH THE FRAMES.

1. Place the cage frame over the left floor crosspiece and attach using 2½" deck screws.

2. Place the sided frames on the middle and right end crosspiece, and attach using 2½" deck screws **(photo D).**

MAKE THE CAGE.

1. Fold the hardware cloth against the back of the frames. Attach it to the left side frame and middle frame, using ¾" fencing staples every 4". Cut the hardware cloth along the

Attach the frames to the floor crosspieces.

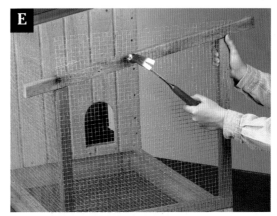

After folding and attaching the hardware cloth to the back, cut off excess cloth.

edges of the middle and left end frame. Cut along the floor by the enclosed compartment and discard this piece.

2. Fold the hardware cloth up against the left frame and attach using ¾" fencing staples every 4" **(photo E).** Cut off the excess hardware cloth.

MAKE THE ROOF AND BACK WALL.

1. Cut the back wall (I) and back wall stop (J). Notch the wall upper corners to fit around the top frames.

2. Attach the stop to the floor between the side walls using 2½" deck screws. Attach the back to the back frames and stop with 1¼" deck screws.

3. Cut the roof (K), with the siding grooves oriented vertically. Attach the roof to the top frames with 1¼" deck screws **(photo F).**

MAKE THE DOORS.

1. Measure the openings for the doors to make sure sizing is correct, then cut the door crosspieces (L), sides (M) hinge support (N) and door jamb (O).

2. Place the sides between the crosspieces, apply exterior glue and attach with 2½" deck screws. Cut hardware cloth to fit the frame and attach with ¾" fencing staples.

3. Position the door jamb between the compartment sides and attach with 2½" deck screws. Position the hinge sup-

port between the cage sides and attach with 2½" deck screws.

4. Cut the compartment door (P) and door supports (Q). Attach the door supports to the back of the door, using 1¼" deck screws.

5. Mount the doors with two 3" hinges each **(photo G).** Attach two hook and eye fasteners to secure each door.

ATTACH THE LEGS.

Cut the legs (R and S) to the desired length. Align a 2 × 2 against the wide side of a 2 × 4 to make an L. Use 2½" deck screws to attach. Attach the legs to the inside corners of the base with 2½" deck screws.

Attach the roof to the frames using 1¼" deck screws.

Mount the doors with 3" hinges.

BLACK&DECKER ™

Finishing Sander

1/4 Sheet   All Ball Bearing

Orbital Action

Garden Accessories

O utdoor living comes with its own list of accessories. For gardeners, it's tools, supplies, and compost bins. For boaters, it's life vests, swimsuits, and sporting equipment. For those who like to get away from it all at the cabin, it's food, beverages, and weekend supplies. Hauling all that stuff around is back-breaking work. The projects on the following pages will make moving and organizing your outdoor life quicker and easier, so there'll be more time for enjoying your outdoor activity.

Gardener's Tote

*Organize and transport your essential gardening supplies
with this handy cedar tote box.*

CONSTRUCTION MATERIALS

Quantity	Lumber
1	1 × 10" × 6' cedar
1	1 × 6" × 6' cedar
1	1 × 4" × 6' cedar
1	1 × 2" × 6' cedar

This compact carrying tote has plenty of room and is ideal for gardeners. With special compartments sized for seed packages, spray cans and hand tools, it is a quick and easy way to keep your most needed supplies organized and ready to go. The bottom shelf is well suited to storing kneeling pads or towels.

The gentle curves cut into the sides of the storage compartment make for easy access and provide a decorative touch. The sturdy cedar handle has a comfortable hand-grip cutout. You'll find this tote to be an indispensable gardening companion, whether you're tending a small flower patch or a sprawling vegetable garden.

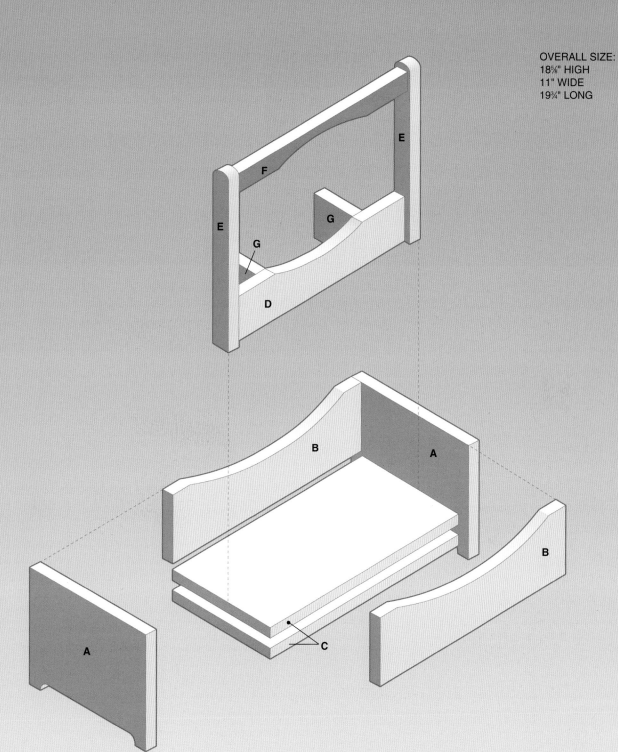

OVERALL SIZE:
18⅝" HIGH
11" WIDE
19¾" LONG

Cutting List				
Key	Part	Dimension	Pcs.	Material
A	End	⅞ × 9¼ × 11"	2	Cedar
B	Side	⅞ × 5½ × 18"	2	Cedar
C	Shelf	⅞ × 9¼ × 18"	2	Cedar
D	Divider	⅞ × 3½ × 16¼"	1	Cedar

Cutting List				
Key	Part	Dimension	Pcs.	Material
E	Post	⅞ × 1½ × 14"	2	Cedar
F	Handle	⅞ × 1½ × 16¼"	1	Cedar
G	Partition	⅞ × 3½ × 3⅞"	2	Cedar

Materials: Moisture-resistant glue, 1¼" and 2" deck screws, finishing materials.

Note: Measurements reflect the actual size of dimension lumber.

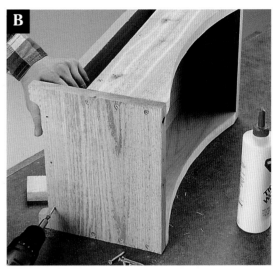

Use a jig saw to cut the curves on the bottom edge of each end, forming feet for the box.

Attach the shelves by driving deck screws through the end pieces and into the ends of the shelves.

Directions: Gardener's Tote

BUILD THE BOX.

The gardener's tote has curved cutouts to improve access and scalloped ends to create feet. All screws are counterbored to ¼" depth for a smooth appearance. A counterbore bit will help you avoid drilling too deep.

1. Cut the ends (A), sides (B) and shelves (C) to size. Sand all parts smooth with medium-grit sandpaper.

2. On one side, mark points on one long edge, 1½" in and 1½" down. Draw a graceful curve between the points to form the cutting line for the curve. Cut the curve with a jig saw and sand it smooth.

3. Position the sides so the edges and ends are flush. Then, trace the curve onto the uncut side and cut it to match. Clamp the sides together, and gang-sand both curves until smooth.

4. Use a compass to draw ¾"-radius semicircles on the bottom edge of the end pieces, with centerpoints 1¾" from each end.

5. Using a straightedge, draw a line connecting the tops of the semicircles to complete the cutout shape. Cut the curves with a jig saw **(photo A),** and sand the ends smooth.

6. To attach the end and side pieces, drill ⅛" pilot holes at each end, ⁷⁄₁₆" in from the edges. Position the pilot holes 1", 3" and 5" down from the tops of the ends. Counterbore the holes.

7. Apply glue to the ends of the side pieces—making sure the top and outside edges are flush—and fasten them to the end pieces with 2" deck screws, driven through the end pieces and into the side pieces.

8. Mark the shelf locations on the inside faces of the ends. The bottom of the lower shelf is ¾" up from the bottoms of the ends, and the bottom of the upper shelf is 3¾" up from the bottoms of the ends.

9. Drill pilot holes ⁷⁄₁₆" up from the lines. Apply glue to the shelf ends, and position the shelves flush with the lines marked on the end pieces. Drive 2" deck screws through the pilot holes in the end pieces and into the shelves **(photo B).**

BUILD THE DIVIDER ASSEMBLY.

The divider and partitions are assembled first, and then inserted into the box.

1. Cut the divider (D), posts (E), handle (F) and partitions (G) to size.

2. Draw a ⅜"-radius semicircle, using a compass, to mark the cutting line for a roundover at one end of each post. Use a sander to make the roundover.

3. The divider and handle have shallow arcs cut on one long edge. To draw the arcs, mark points 4" in from each end. Then, mark a centered point, ⅝" in from one long edge on the handle. On the divider, mark a centered point, ⅝" in from one long edge.

4. Draw a graceful curve to connect the points, and cut along the lines with a jig saw. Sand the parts smooth.

5. Drill two pilot holes on each end of the divider, ⁷⁄₁₆" out from the start of the curve. Counterbore the holes. Attach the divider to the partitions, using glue and 2" deck screws, driven through the divider and

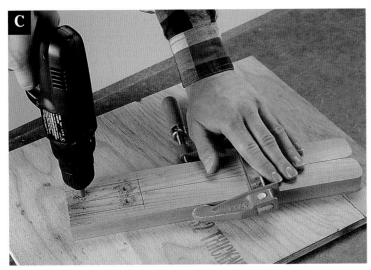

Drill and counterbore pilot holes in the posts before you attach them to the handle and divider.

TIP

Many seed types, soil additives and other common gardening supplies should not be stored outdoors in subfreezing temperatures. If you live in a colder climate, load up your tote with these items in the fall, and store the tote in a warm spot for the winter.

into the edges of the partitions.
6. To mark the positions of the divider ends, clamp the posts together with their edges flush, and mark a 3½"-long reference line on each post, ⅞" from the meeting point between the two posts **(photo C).** Start the reference lines at the square post ends. Connect the lines at the tops to indicate the position of the divider ends.
7. Drill two pilot holes through the posts, centered between each reference line and the inside edge **(photo C).** Counterbore the holes. Drill and counterbore two more pilot holes in each post, centered ½" and 1" down from the tops.
8. Position the handle and divider between the posts, aligned with the pilot holes. One face of the divider should be flush with a post edge. Fasten the handle and divider between the posts with moisture-resistant glue and 2" deck screws, driven through the post holes. Set the assembly in the box. Make sure the partitions fit square with the side.

INSTALL THE DIVIDER ASSEMBLY.
1. Trace position lines for the posts on the end pieces **(photo D).** Apply glue where the posts will be fastened. Drill pilot holes through the posts and counterbore the holes. Then, attach the posts with 1¼" deck screws, driven through the pilot holes and into the ends.
2. Drill two evenly spaced pilot

holes in the side adjacent to the partitions. Counterbore the holes. Then, drive 2" deck screws through the holes and into the edges of the partitions.

APPLY THE FINISHING TOUCHES.
Sand all surfaces smooth with medium (100- or 120-grit) sandpaper. Then finish-sand with fine (150- or 180-grit) sandpaper. If you want to preserve the cedar tones, apply exterior wood stain to all surfaces. Or, you can leave the wood uncoated for a more rustic appearance. As you use the tote, it will slowly turn gray.

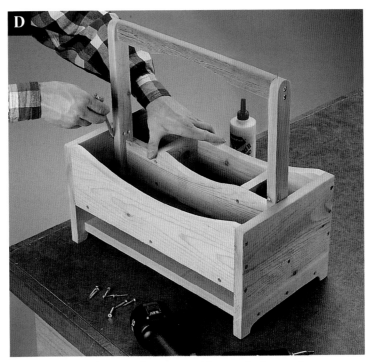

Draw reference lines for the post position on the box ends.

Yard & Garden Cart

With a 4-cubic-foot bin and a built-in rack for long-handled tools, this sleek utility cart is hardworking and versatile.

CONSTRUCTION MATERIALS

Quantity	Lumber
1	2 × 6" × 8' cedar
4	2 × 4" × 8' cedar
2	1 × 6" × 8' cedar
2	1 × 4" × 8' cedar
1	1"-dia. × 3' dowel

This sturdy yard-and-garden cart picks up where a plain wheelbarrow leaves off. It includes many clever features that help make doing yard work more efficient, without sacrificing hauling capacity. And because it's made of wood, this cart will never dent or rust. The notches in the handle frame keep long-handled tools from being jostled about as the cart rolls across your yard. The handle itself folds down and locks in place like a kickstand when the cart is parked. When you're pushing the cart, the handle flips up to form an extra-long handle that takes advantage of simple physics to make the cart easier to push and steer.

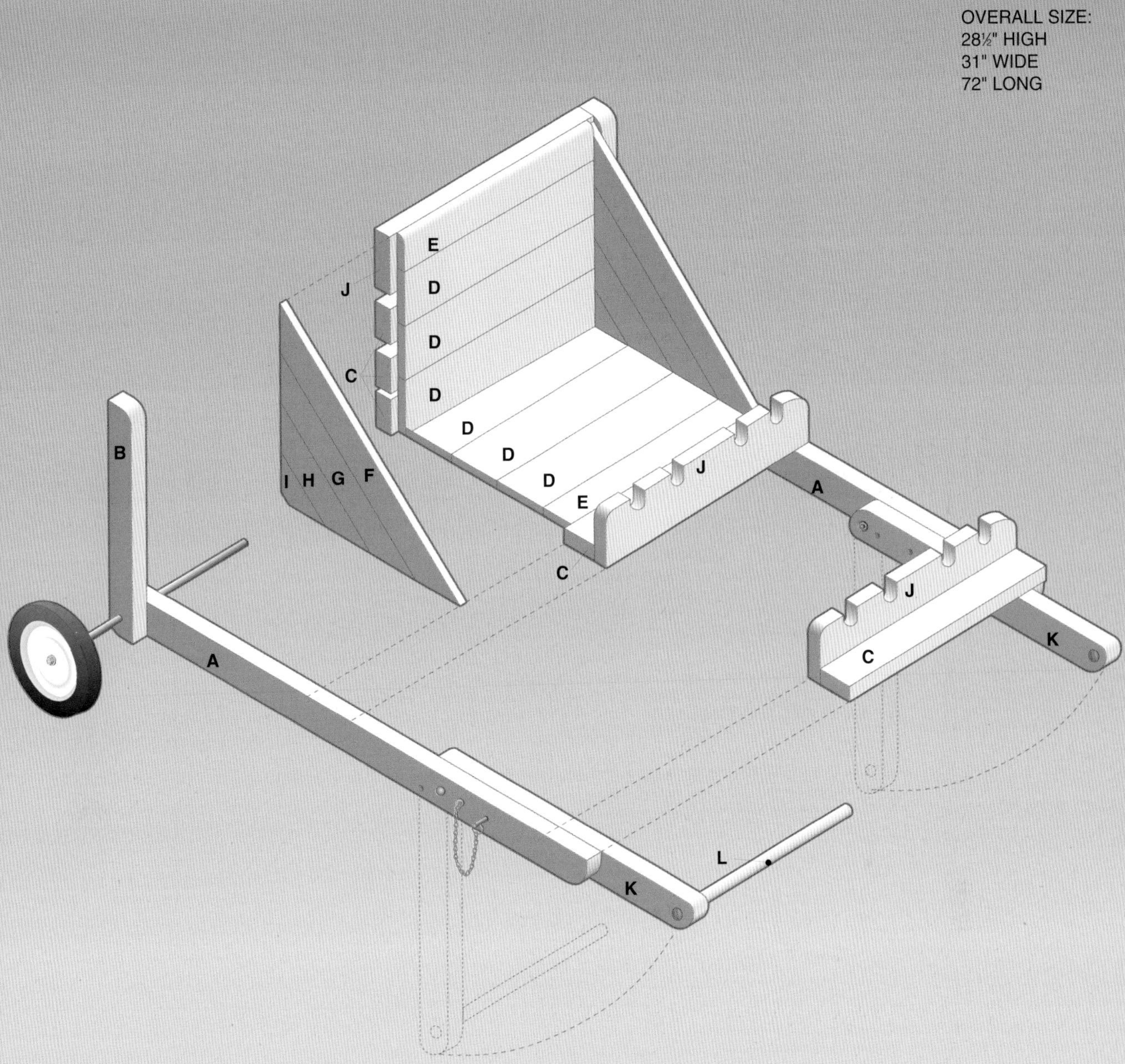

Cutting List

Key	Part	Dimension	Pcs.	Material
A	Back support	1½ × 3½ × 57"	2	Cedar
B	Front support	1½ × 3½ × 23½"	2	Cedar
C	Cross rail	1½ × 3½ × 24"	5	Cedar
D	Bin slat	⅞ × 5½ × 22¼"	6	Cedar
E	End slat	⅞ × 3½ × 22¼"	2	Cedar
F	Bin side	⅞ × 3½ × 28"	2	Cedar

Cutting List

Key	Part	Dimension	Pcs.	Material
G	Bin side	⅞ × 3½ × 21"	2	Cedar
H	Bin side	⅞ × 3½ × 14"	2	Cedar
I	Bin side	⅞ × 3½ × 7"	2	Cedar
J	Top rail	1½ × 5½ × 24"	3	Cedar
K	Arm	1½ × 3½ × 32"	2	Cedar
L	Handle	1"-dia. × 20⅞"	1	Dowel

Materials: 2" and 2½" deck screws, 4d finish nails (2), 10" utility wheels (2), 30" steel axle rod, ³⁄₁₆"-dia. cotter pins, ⅜"-dia. hitch pins and chain (2), ⅜ × 4" carriage bolts (2) with lock nuts (2) and washers (4), finishing materials.

Note: Measurements reflect the actual size of dimension lumber.

Test with a square to make sure the front supports and back supports are joined at right angles.

Make straight cuts from the edge of each rail to the sides of the holes to make the tool notches.

Directions:
Yard & Garden Cart

BUILD THE CART FRAME.
Counterbore all pilot holes in this project, using a counterbore bit, so the screw heads are recessed for improved safety and visual appeal.

1. Cut the back supports (A), front supports (B), three cross rails (C) and one of the top rails (J) to length.

2. Use a compass to draw a curve with a 3½" radius on each end of the back supports on the same side, and on each end of the front supports on opposite sides. When the curves are cut, the ends of these parts will have one rounded corner and one square corner. Cut the curves

with a jig saw and sand out any rough spots or saw marks.

3. Position a top rail between the ends of the front supports, flush with the square corners of the front supports. Drill ⅛" pilot holes in the supports. Counterbore the holes ¼" deep, using a counterbore bit. Fasten the rail between the supports with glue and drive 2½" deck screws through the supports and into the rail.

4. Position two cross rails between the front supports, 7½" and 13" down from the top ends of the front supports. Make sure the cross rails are aligned with the top rail. Attach them with glue and 2½" deck screws. Fasten another cross rail between the bottom ends of the front supports. The bottom edge of this cross rail should be 3½" up from the bottoms of the front supports and aligned with the other rails.

5. Attach the front supports to the back supports with glue and 2½" deck screws, using a square to make sure the parts are joined at right angles

(photo A). The unshaped ends of the back supports should be flush with the front and bottom edges of the front supports, and the back supports should be attached to the inside faces of the front supports.

6. Drill centered, ½"-dia. holes for the wheel axles through the bottoms of the front supports and back supports. Position the holes 1¾" from both the bottom ends and the sides of the front supports.

CUT THE NOTCHED
TOP RAILS.

1. Cut the two remaining top rails (J) to length. These rails contain notches that are aligned to create a tool rack. Before cutting the notches, use a compass to draw 1½"-radius roundover curves at each end along one side of each rail. Cut the roundovers with a jig saw.

2. To make the tool notches in the top rails, first draw a reference line 1½" in from the rail edge between the roundovers. Mark four drilling points on the line, 3¾" and 8¼" in from each

TIP

If you need to round over the end of a board, one easy solution that gets good results is to use your belt sander like a bench grinder. Simply mount the belt sander to a work surface sideways, so the belt is perpendicular to the work surface and has room to spin. Turn on the sander, lay your workpiece on the work surface, and grind away.

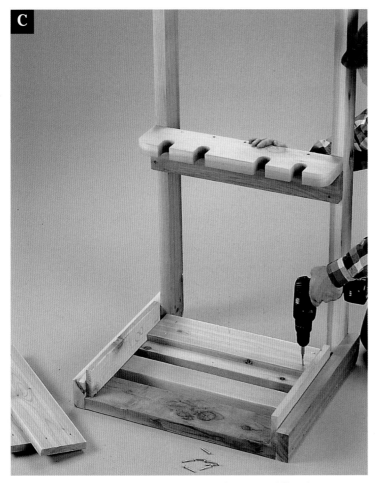

C

Attach the bin slats to the front supports, leaving a ⅞"-wide gap at both ends of each slat.

end. Use a drill and a spade bit to drill 1½"-dia. holes through the drilling points on each rail.

3. Use a square to draw cutting lines from the sides of the holes to the near edge of each rail. Cut along the lines with a jig saw to complete the tool notches **(photo B).**

ATTACH RAILS BETWEEN THE BACK SUPPORTS.

1. Cut two cross rails (C) to length and lay them flat on your work surface. Attach a top rail to one edge of each cross rail, so the ends are flush and the notched edges of the top rails are facing up. Drive 2½" deck screws at 4" intervals through the top rails and into the edges of the cross rails.

2. Set one of the assemblies on the free ends of the back supports, flush with the edges. The free edge of the cross rail should be flush with the ends of the back supports. Attach the cross rail with 2½" deck screws driven down into the back support.

3. Attach the other rail assembly to the top edges of the back supports so the top rail faces the other rail assembly, and the free edge of the cross rail is 22⅜" from the front ends of the back supports.

ATTACH THE BIN SLATS.

1. Cut the bin slats (D) and end slats (E) to length. Position one end slat and three bin slats be-

tween the front supports, with the edge of the end slat flush with the edge of the top rail and the last bin slat butted against the back supports. There should be a ⅞" gap between the ends of each slat and the front supports. Attach the slats with glue and 2" deck screws driven down through the slats and into the cross rails and top rail **(photo C).**

2. Fasten the rest of the bin slats to the top edges of the back supports, with a ⅞" recess at each end. Start at the bottom of the bin, and work your way up, driving 2½" deck screws through the slats and into the tops of the back supports. Fasten the end slat between the last bin slat and the lower cross rail on the back supports.

3. Use a grinder or belt sander with a coarse belt to round the front edges of the front end slat **(photo D).**

ATTACH THE BIN SIDES.

1. Square-cut the bin sides (F, G, H, I) to the lengths shown in the *Cutting List,* page 463. Draw a 45° miter-cutting line at each end of each bin side. Make the miter cuts with a circular saw and straightedge, or with a power miter saw.

2. Fit the short, V-shaped sides into the recesses at the sides of the bin, and attach them to the front supports with glue and 2"

TIP

Cut pieces of sheet aluminum or galvanized metal to line the cart bin for easy cleaning after hauling. Simply cut the pieces to fit inside the bin, then attach them with special roofing nails that have rubber gaskets under the nail heads. Make sure that no sharp metal edges are sticking out from the bin.

Round the tips of the front supports and the front edge of the end slat, using a belt sander.

Fasten the bin sides in a V-shape with glue and deck screws.

Drill a pilot hole through each arm and into the ends of the handle, then drive 4d finish nails into the holes to secure the handle.

deck screws. Install the rest of the bin sides **(photo E).**

MAKE THE ARMS.

The arms serve a dual purpose. First, they support the handles when you wheel the cart. Second, they drop down and lock in place to support the cart in an upright position.

1. Cut the arms (K) to length. Mark the center of each end of each arm, measured from side to side. Measure down 3½"

from each end, and mark a point. Set the point of a compass at each of these points, and draw a 1¾"-radius semicircle at each end on both arms. Cut the curves with a jig saw.

2. Drill a 1"-dia. hole for the handle dowel at one of the centerpoints at the end of each arm. At the other centerpoint, drill a ⅜"-dia. guide hole for a carriage bolt.

ATTACH THE ARMS.

1. Drill ⅜"-dia. holes for carriage bolts through each back support, 19" from the handle end, and centered between the top and bottom edges of the supports.

2. Insert a ⅜"-dia. × 4"-long carriage bolt through the outside of each ⅜"-dia. hole in the back supports. Slip a washer over each bolt, then slip the arms over the carriage bolts. Slip another washer over the end of each bolt, then secure the arms to the supports by tightening a lock nut onto each bolt. Do not overtighten the lock nut—the arms need to be loose enough to pivot freely.

3. Cut the handle (L) to length from a 1"-dia. dowel (preferably hardwood). Slide it into the 1"-dia. holes in the ends of the arms. Secure the handle by drilling pilot holes for 4d finish nails through each arm and into the dowel **(photo F).** Then, drive a finish nail into the dowel at each end.

Secure the wheels by inserting a cotter pin into a hole at the end of each axle, then bending the ends of the pin down with pliers.

the way through the arms **(photo H).** Insert a ⅜"-dia. hitch pin (or hinge pin) into each hole to secure the arms.
2. To avoid losing the pins when you remove them, attach them to the back supports with a chain or a piece of cord. Now, remove the pins and lift the arms so they are level with the tops of the back supports. Drill ⅜"-dia. holes through the arms and back supports, about 12" behind the first pin holes, for locking the arms in the cart-pushing position.

APPLY FINISHING TOUCHES.
Smooth out all the sharp edges on the cart with a sander. Also sand the surfaces slightly. Apply two coats of exterior wood stain to the wood for protection. Squirt some penetrating/lubricating oil or synthetic lubricant on the axle on each side of the wheels to reduce friction.

ATTACH THE WHEELS.
Make sure to buy a steel axle rod that fits the holes in the hubs of the 10" wheels.
1. Cut the axle rod to 30" in length with a hacksaw. Remove any burrs with a file or bench grinder. (Rough-grit sandpaper also works, but it takes longer and is harder on the hands.) Secure the axle rod in a vise, or clamp it to your work surface, and use a steel twist bit to drill a ³⁄₁₆"-dia. hole through the rod ⅛" in from each end of the axle.
2. Slip the axle through the ½"-dia. holes drilled at the joints between the front and back supports. Slide two washers over each end of the axle.
3. Slip a wheel over each axle end, add two washers and insert ³⁄₁₆"-dia. cotter pins into the holes drilled at the ends of the axle. Secure the wheels by bending down the ends of the cotter pins with a pair of pliers **(photo G).**

LOCK THE ARMS IN PLACE.
1. On a flat surface, fold down the arm/handle assembly so the arms are perpendicular to the ground. Drill a ⅜"-dia. guide hole through each back support, 1" below the carriage bolt that attaches the arms to the supports. Extend the holes all

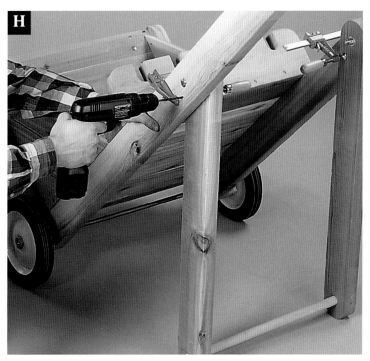

Drill ⅜"-dia. holes through the back supports and into the arms for inserting the hitch pins that lock the arms in position.

Cabin Porter

*Shuttle heavy supplies from car to cabin or down to your dock
with this smooth-riding cedar cart.*

CONSTRUCTION MATERIALS

Quantity	Lumber
3	2 × 4" × 8' cedar
11	1 × 4" × 8' cedar

Transporting luggage and supplies doesn't need to be an awkward, back-breaking exercise. Simply roll this cabin porter to your car when you arrive, load it up and wheel your gear to your cabin door or down to the dock. The porter is spacious enough to hold coolers, laundry baskets or grocery bags, all in one easy, convenient trip. Both end gates are removable, so you can transport longer items like skis, ladders or lumber for improvement projects. The cabin porter is also handy for moving heavy objects around your yard. The 10" wheels ensure a stable ride, and the porter is designed to minimize the chances of tipping. The wheels, axle and mounting hardware generally can be purchased as a set from a well-stocked hardware store. For winter use, you might try adding short skis or sled runners, allowing the cabin porter to glide over deep snow and decreasing your chances of dropping an armful of supplies over slippery ice.

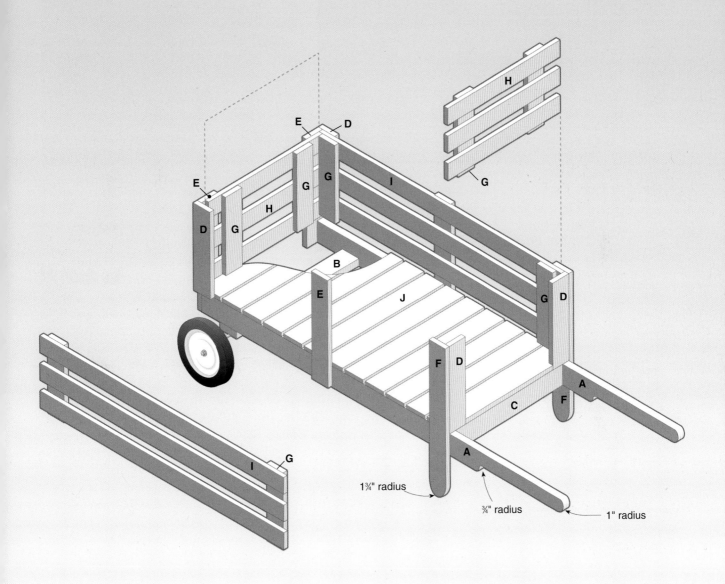

OVERALL SIZE:
24½" HIGH
28½" WIDE
73¾" LONG

1¾" radius

¾" radius

1" radius

Cutting List

Key	Part	Dimension	Pcs.	Material
A	Handle	1½ × 3½ × 72⅞"	2	Cedar
B	Front stringer	1½ × 3½ × 24"	1	Cedar
C	Rear stringer	1½ × 3½ × 21"	1	Cedar
D	Short stile	⅞ × 3½ × 14⅜"	4	Cedar
E	Long stile	⅞ × 3½ × 17⅞"	4	Cedar

Cutting List

Key	Part	Dimension	Pcs.	Material
F	Rear stile	⅞ × 3½ × 24½"	2	Cedar
G	Gate stile	⅞ × 3½ × 13½"	8	Cedar
H	Gate rail	⅞ × 3½ × 22"	6	Cedar
I	Side rail	⅞ × 3½ × 46⅝"	6	Cedar
J	Slat	⅞ × 3½ × 24"	12	Cedar

Materials: 1½", 2", and 2½" deck screws, wood glue, 10"-dia. wheels (2), axle, ¾ × 4" metal straps (3), ¼ × 1" lag screws, washers, crimp caps, finishing materials.
Note: Measurements reflect the actual size of dimension lumber.

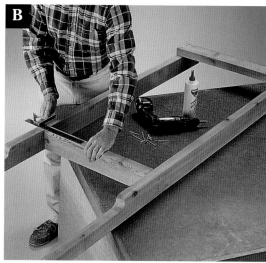

Clamp the handles together and draw reference lines at the stringer locations.

When installing the stringers, make sure they are square with the handles.

Directions:
Cabin Porter

ASSEMBLE THE HANDLES AND FRAMEWORK.

The framework for the cabin porter consists of handles connected by stringers at each end.

1. Cut the handles (A), front stringer (B) and rear stringer (C) to length. Sand the edges smooth.

2. Trim the back ends of the handles to create gripping surfaces. Draw a 16"-long cutting line on the face of each handle,

Apply glue and drive screws through the rails and into the corner pieces.

starting at one end, 1½" up from the bottom edge. Set the point of a compass at the bottom edge, 14½" in from the end, and draw a 1½"-radius arc, creating a smooth curve leading up to the cut line. To round the ends of each handle, use a compass to draw a 1"-radius semicircle centered 1" below the top edge and 1" in from the end (see *Diagram,* page 469). Shape the handles by cutting with a jig saw, then sand the edges smooth.

3. Stringers and slats fit across the handles, creating the bottom frame of the porter. Clamp the handles together, edge to edge, so the ends are flush, and draw reference lines 25¾" from the grip ends and 3½" from the square ends to locate the stringers **(photo A).** Place the front stringer flat across the bottom edges of the handles so the front edge of the stringer is flush with the 3½" reference lines. Attach it with glue and 2½" deck screws. Position the rear stringer between the handles so the back face of the stringer is flush with the 25¾" reference lines. Attach it

with glue and 2½" deck screws **(photo B).**

4. Cut the slats (J) to length, and round over their top edges with a sander.

5. Position the handle assembly so the shaped grip edges face down. Lay one slat over the handles at the front end so the corners of the slat are flush with the ends of the handles. Drill ⅛" pilot holes through the slat, and counterbore the holes to a ¼" depth. Fasten the slat with glue and 2" deck screws.

6. Notch the rear end slat to receive the rear short stiles. Draw lines at both ends of the slat ⅞" from a common long edge and 3½" from the ends. Cut the notches with a jig saw. Position the slat flush with the rear face of the rear stringer, and fasten it with glue and 2" screws.

7. Space the remaining slats evenly between the end slats with gaps of about ½". Fasten them with glue and 2" screws.

MAKE THE CORNERS.

Join the stiles to make the corners, which will support the side rails and end gates.

1. Cut the short stiles (D), long

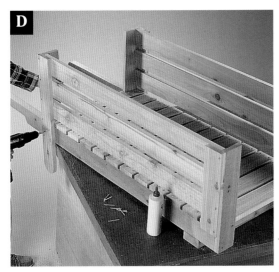

Anchor the sides to the framework with glue and screws driven through the stiles into the handles.

Attach the axles to the bottom of the front stringer with metal straps fastened with lag screws.

stiles (E) and rear stiles (F) to length. Use a compass to draw a 1¾"-radius semicircle at the bottom of each rear stile (see *Diagram*). Shape the ends with a jig saw, and sand the edges smooth.

2. Butt the edge of a short stile against the face of a rear stile so the pieces form a right angle. With the square ends flush, drill pilot holes every 2" through the rear stile and into the edge of the short stile. Counterbore the holes. Join the stiles with glue and 2" deck screws. Assemble the other rear corner.

3. Repeat this procedure to assemble the front corners, butting the edge of a long stile against the face of a short stile so the edges and tops are flush.

MAKE THE SIDES.

1. Cut the side rails (I) to length. Place three side rails tight between one front corner and one rear corner so the top of the upper rail is flush with the tops of the corners. Leave a 1" gap between rails. Fasten the rails to the corners with glue and 1½" deck screws **(photo C).**

2. Fasten the side assemblies to the handles with glue and 2" deck screws **(photo D).** Drive an additional screw through each stile and into the edge of an adjacent slat. Position the remaining stiles (E) on the outer sides of the rails, midway between the front and rear corners. Fasten the stiles to the rails with glue and 1½" deck screws.

MAKE THE GATES.

1. Cut the gate stiles (G) and gate rails (H) to length. Sand the short edges of the rails.

2. Lay the rails facedown together in groups of three with the ends flush. Draw reference lines across the rails 2" in from each end to locate the stiles.

3. Place two stiles on one rail with the tops flush and the outer stile edges on the reference lines. Fasten them with glue and 1½" deck screws driven through the stiles and into the rails.

4. Attach two more rails below the first one, leaving a 1" gap between the rails.

5. Follow the same procedure to make the other gate.

6. Set the gates in place be-

tween the porter sides to locate the four remaining gate stiles (G). These form the slots that keep the gates in place. Position the stiles flush with the tops of the top side rails and almost flush with the faces of the gate rails. Attach them with glue and 1½" deck screws driven through the stiles and into the rails. Slide the gates in and out of the slots to test for smooth operation.

7. Sand any rough areas, and apply the finish of your choice.

ATTACH THE WHEELS.

1. Cut the axle to length (24" plus the width of the two wheels plus 1½"). Attach the axle to the bottom of the front stringer with lag screws and metal straps bent in the center **(photo E).** Place one strap at each end of the stringer and one in the middle.

2. Slide three washers followed by a wheel over each end of the axle. Secure the wheels with crimp caps or by drilling a small hole in each end of the axle and installing an additional washer and a cotter pin.

Compost Bin

*Convert yard waste to garden fertilizer inside this
simple and stylish cedar compost bin.*

CONSTRUCTION MATERIALS

Quantity	Lumber
4	4 × 4" × 4' cedar posts
5	2 × 2" × 8' cedar
8	1 × 6" × 8' cedar fence boards

Composting yard debris is an increasingly popular practice that makes good environmental sense. Composting is the process of converting organic waste into rich fertilizer for the soil, usually in a compost bin. A well-designed compost bin has a few key features. It's big enough to contain the organic material as it decomposes. It allows cross-flow of air to speed the process. And the bin area is easy to reach whether you're adding waste, turning the compost or removing the composted material. This compost bin has all these features, plus one additional benefit not shared by most compost bins: it's very attractive.

OVERALL SIZE:
30" HIGH
40½" WIDE
48" LONG

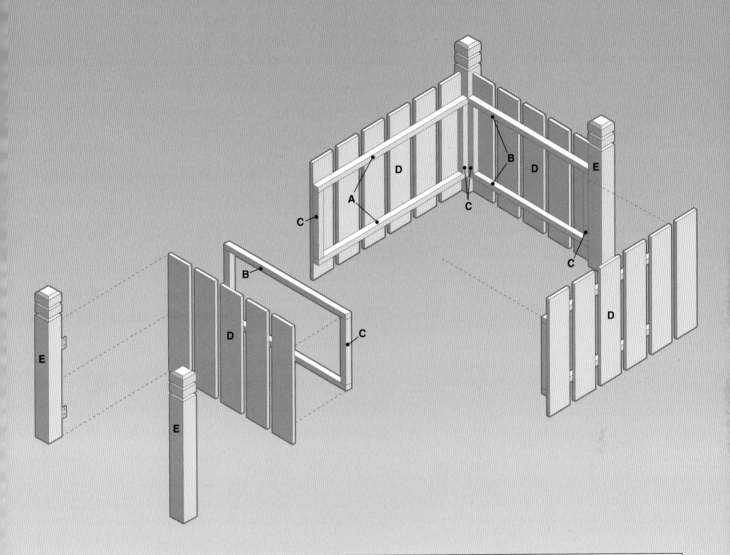

Cutting List

Key	Part	Dimension	Pcs.	Material
A	Side rail	1½ × 1½ × 40½"	4	Cedar
B	End rail	1½ × 1½ × 33½"	4	Cedar
C	Cleat	1½ × 1½ × 15"	8	Cedar
D	Slat	¾ × 5½ × 27"	22	Cedar
E	Post	3½ × 3½ × 30"	4	Cedar

Materials: 1½" and 3" galvanized deck screws, hook-and-eye latch mechanism, 3 × 3" brass butt hinges (one pair) and screws.

Note: Measurements reflect the actual size of dimension lumber.

Fasten the cleats between the rails to construct the panel frames.

Attach a slat at each end of the panel frame so the outer edges of the slats are flush with the outer edges of the frame.

Directions: Compost Bin

BUILD THE PANELS.

The four fence-type panels that make up the sides of this compost bin are cedar slats that attach to panel frames. The panel frames for the front and back of the bin are longer than the frames for the sides.

1. Cut the side rails (A), end rails (B) and cleats (C) to length. Group pairs of matching rails with a pair of cleats. Assemble each group into a frame—the cleats should be between the rails, flush with the ends. Drill ⅛" pilot holes into the rails. Counterbore the holes ¼" deep, using a counterbore bit. Fasten all four panel frames together by driving 3" deck screws through the rails and into each end of each cleat **(photo A)**.

2. Cut all of the slats (D) to length. Lay the frames on a flat surface and place a slat at each end of each frame. Keep the edges of these outer slats flush with the outside edges of the frame and let the bottoms of the slats overhang the bottom frame rail by 4". Drill pilot holes in the slats. Counterbore the holes slightly. Fasten the outer slats to the frames with 1½" deck screws **(photo B)**.

3. When you have fastened the outer slats to all of the frames, add slats between each pair of outer slats to fill out the panels. Insert a 1½" spacing block between the slats to set the correct gap. (This will allow air to flow into the bin.) Be sure to keep the ends of the slats aligned. Check with a tape measure to make sure the bottoms of all the slats are 4" below the bottom of the panel frame **(photo C)**.

ATTACH THE PANELS AND POSTS.

The four slatted panels are joined with corner posts to make the bin. Three of the panels are attached permanently to the posts, while one of the end panels is installed with hinges and a latch so it can swing open like a gate. You can use plain 4 × 4 cedar posts for the corner posts. For a more decorative look, you can buy prefabricated fence posts or deck rail posts with carving or contours at the top.

1. Cut the posts (E) to length. If you're using plain posts, you may want to do some decorative contouring at one end or attach post caps.

2. Stand a post upright on a flat work surface. Set one of the longer slatted panels next to the post, resting on the bottoms of the slats. Hold or clamp the panel to the post, with the back of the panel frame flush with

The inner slats should be 1½" apart, with the ends 4" below the bottom of the frame.

Stand the posts and panels upright, and fasten the panels to the posts by driving screws through the cleats.

one of the faces of the post. Fasten the panel to the post by driving 3" deck screws through the frame cleats and into the posts. Space screws at roughly 8" intervals.

3. Stand another post on end, and fasten the other end of the panel frame to it, making sure the posts are aligned.

4. Fasten one of the shorter panels to the adjoining face of one of the posts. The back faces of the frames should just meet in a properly formed corner **(photo D).** Fasten another post at the free end of the shorter panel.

5. Fasten the other longer panel to the posts so it is opposite the first longer panel, forming a U-shaped structure.

ATTACH THE GATE.

The unattached shorter panel is attached at the open end of the bin with hinges to create a swinging gate for loading and unloading material. Exterior wood stain will keep the cedar from turning gray. If you are planning to apply a finish, you'll find it easier to apply it before you hang the gate. Make sure all hardware is rated for exterior use.

1. Set the last panel between the posts at the open end of the bin. Move the sides of the bin slightly, if needed, so there is about ¼" of clearance between each end of the panel and the posts. Remove this panel gate and attach a pair of 3" butt hinges to a cleat, making sure the barrels of the hinges extend past the face of the outer slats.

2. Set the panel into the opening, and mark the location of the hinge plates onto the post. Open the hinge so it is flat, and attach it to the post **(photo E).**

3. Attach a hook-and-eye latch to the unhinged end of the panel to hold the gate closed.

Attach the hinges to the end panel frame, then fasten to the post.

Dock Box

This spacious dockside hold protects all your boating supplies, with room to spare.

CONSTRUCTION MATERIALS

Quantity	Lumber
2	⅝" × 4 × 8' plywood siding
7	1 × 2" × 8' cedar
4	1 × 4" × 8' cedar
1	1 × 6" × 8' cedar
3	2 × 2" × 8' cedar

With its spacious storage compartment and appealing nautical design, this box is a perfect place for stowing water sports equipment. You won't have to haul gear inside anymore after offshore excursions. Life preservers, beach toys, ropes and even small coolers conveniently fit inside this attractive chest, which has ventilation holes to discourage mildew. Sturdy enough for seating, the large top can hold charts, fishing gear or a light snack while you await your next voyage. With a dock box to hold your gear, you can spend your energy carrying more important items—like the fresh catch of the day—up to your cabin.

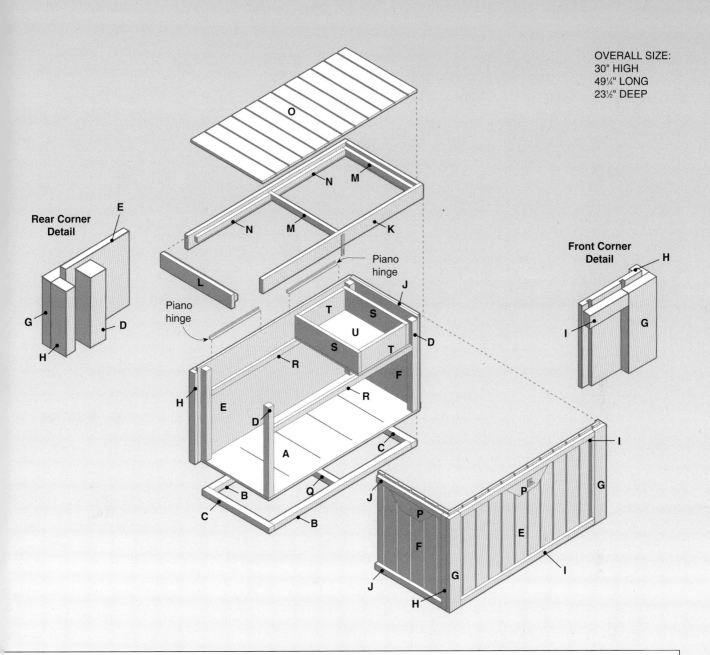

OVERALL SIZE:
30" HIGH
49¼" LONG
23½" DEEP

Rear Corner Detail

Front Corner Detail

Piano hinge

Piano hinge

Cutting List

Key	Part	Dimension	Pcs.	Material
A	Bottom	⅝ × 46¼ × 20½"	1	Plywood siding
B	Bottom brace	1½ × 1½ × 43¼"	2	Cedar
C	End brace	1½ × 1½ × 20½"	2	Cedar
D	Corner brace	1½ × 1½ × 24⅜"	4	Cedar
E	Large panel	⅝ × 47½ × 27"	2	Plywood siding
F	Small panel	⅝ × 20½ × 27"	2	Plywood siding
G	Corner trim	⅞ × 3½ × 26½"	4	Cedar
H	Corner batten	⅞ × 1½ × 26½"	4	Cedar
I	Long trim	⅞ × 1½ × 42¼"	4	Cedar
J	End trim	⅞ × 1½ × 18¾"	4	Cedar
K	Lid side	⅞ × 3½ × 49¼"	2	Cedar

Cutting List

Key	Part	Dimension	Pcs.	Material
L	Lid end	⅞ × 3½ × 21¾"	2	Cedar
M	Top support	⅞ × 1½ × 21¾"	3	Cedar
N	Ledger	⅞ × 1½ × 22⅜"	4	Cedar
O	Top panel	⅝ × 47½ × 21¾"	1	Plywood siding
P	Handle	⅞ × 3½ × 13½"	4	Cedar
Q	Cross brace	1½ × 1½ × 17½	1	Cedar
R	Tray slide	⅞ × 1½ × 43¼"	2	Cedar
S	Tray side	⅞ × 5½ × 20¼"	2	Cedar
T	Tray end	⅞ × 5½ × 14"	2	Cedar
U	Tray bottom	⅝ × 15¾ × 20¼"	1	Plywood siding

Materials: 1¼" and 1⅝" deck screws, 6d finish nails, 1" wire brads, construction adhesive, 1½ × 30" or 36" piano hinge, hasp, lid support chains (2), finishing materials.

Note: Measurements reflect the actual size of dimension lumber.

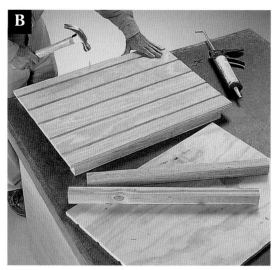

For ventilation, cut slots into the bottom panel, using a straightedge as a stop block for the foot of your circular saw.

Position the corner braces beneath the small panels, and fasten them with adhesive and finish nails.

Directions:
Dock Box

MAKE THE BOX BOTTOM.
The box bottom is made of grooved plywood siding attached to a rectangular 2 × 2 box frame.

1. Cut the bottom (A), bottom braces (B), end braces (C) and cross brace (Q) to size. Apply construction adhesive or moisture-resistant wood glue to the ends of the bottom braces. Clamp them between the end braces so the edges are flush. Drill ⅛" pilot holes through each end brace into the bottom braces. Counterbore the holes ¼" deep, using a counterbore bit. Drive 1⅝" deck screws through the pilot holes to reinforce the joints.

2. Center the cross brace in the frame and attach it with adhesive and 1⅝" deck screws.

3. Attach the box bottom to the box frame with 1⅝" deck screws.

4. Cut six ventilation slots in the bottom panel. First, clamp a straightedge near one edge of the bottom panel. Then, set the cutting depth on your circular saw to about 1" and press the foot of the saw up against the straightedge. Turn on the saw, and press down with the blade in a rocking motion until

you've cut through the bottom panel **(photo A).** The slots should be spaced evenly, 8" to 9" apart.

ATTACH THE BOX SIDES.
1. Cut the corner braces (D), large panels (E) and small panels (F) to size. Align two corner braces under a small panel (grooved side up). Make sure the edges are flush, with a ½"-wide gap at one end of the panel and a 2⅛"-wide gap at the other end. Fasten the braces with construction adhesive and 6d finish nails **(photo B).**

2. Repeat the procedure for the other small panel.

3. Attach the small panels, with the 2" space facing downward, to the end braces, using 6d nails and construction adhesive.

4. Place the large panels in position and drive nails through the panels into the bottom braces and corner braces.

MAKE THE TRIM PIECES.
1. Cut the corner trim (G) and corner battens (H) to length. Set the project on its side. Use construction adhesive and nails to attach the corner bat-

Attach the corner trim pieces flush with the edges of the corner battens to cover the plywood joints.

A handle block is attached to each face of the box, up against the bottom of the top trim piece.

Counterbore the screw heads so they don't obstruct the movement of the tray on the tray slides.

tens flush with the bottom, covering the seam between panels. There should be a ½"-wide gap between the tops of the corner pieces and the top of the box. Then, attach the corner trim **(photo C).**

2. Cut the long trim (I) and the end trim (J) to length. Attach the lower trim flush with the bottom, using construction adhesive and finish nails.

3. Attach the upper trim pieces flush with the corner pieces, using adhesive. Drive 1¼" deck screws from inside the box into the trim pieces.

ATTACH THE HANDLES.

The handles (P) are trapezoid-shaped blocks cut from cedar.

1. Cut four handles to length. Mark each piece 3¾" in from each end along one long edge. Connect the marks diagonally to the adjacent corners to form cutting lines. Cut with a circular saw or a power miter box.

2. Center a handle against the bottom edge of the top trim piece on each face. Attach each handle with adhesive and 1¼" deck screws **(photo D).**

MAKE THE TRAY.

The tray rests inside the dock box on slides.

1. Cut the tray slides (R) to length. Mount the slides inside the box, 7" down from the top edge, using adhesive and 1¼" deck screws.

2. Cut the tray sides (S), tray ends (T) and tray bottom (U) to size. Drill pilot holes in the tray ends and counterbore the holes. Then, fasten the tray ends between the tray sides with adhesive and 1⅝" deck screws **(photo E).** Attach the tray bottom with adhesive and 1" wire brads.

MAKE THE LID.

1. Cut the lid sides (K) and lid ends (L) to length. Fasten them together with adhesive and drive 6d nails through the lid sides and into the ends.

2. Cut the top panel (O), top supports (M) and ledgers (N) to length. Attach two top supports to the inside edges of the frame, ⅝" down from the top edge, using adhesive and 1¼" screws **(photo F).** Attach the ledgers to the long sides of the lid—one at each corner—with

adhesive and 1¼" deck screws. Place the remaining top support into the gap in the middle. Fasten it by driving 6d nails into the ends of the support.

3. Fit the top panel into the lid. Fasten with 6d nails and adhesive. Sand all exposed edges.

4. Attach the lid to the box with a piano hinge cut in two. Attach a pair of chains between the bottom of the lid and the front of the box to hold the lid upright when open. To lock the box, attach a hasp to the handle and lid at the front of the box.

5. Apply exterior stain or water sealer for protection. Caulk the gap around the top panel and lid frame with exterior caulk.

Top supports in the lid frame support the top panel.

Storage & Utility Projects

There just never seems to be enough space to store everything. Instead, we put up with messy woodpiles, scattered garbage cans, and jumbled boots in the back entryway. See how much easier everyday life can be by adding a few simple outdoor storage and utility solutions to your home. You'll also find stylish solutions to mailboxes and address markers, as well as grills and trash collection areas.

Outdoor Storage Center

Create additional storage space for backyard games and equipment with this efficient outdoor storage center.

CONSTRUCTION MATERIALS

Quantity	Lumber
2	⅜" × 4 × 8' textured cedar plywood siding
2	¾" × 2 × 4' BC fir plywood handy panels
2	1 × 2" × 8' cedar
6	1 × 3" × 8' rough-sawn cedar
2	1 × 4" × 8' rough-sawn cedar
1	2 × 2" × 8' pine
1	1 × 2" × 8' pine

Sturdy cedar construction and a rustic appearance make this storage center an excellent addition to any backyard or outdoor setting. The top lid flips up for quick and easy access to the upper shelf storage area, while the bottom doors swing open for access to the lower storage compartments. The raised bottom shelf keeps all stored items up off the ground, where they stay safe and dry. Lawn chairs, yard games, grilling supplies, fishing and boating equipment, and much more can be kept out of sight and protected from the weather. If security is a concern, simply add a locking hasp and padlock to the top lid to keep your property safe and secure. If you have a lot of traffic in and out of the top compartment, add lid support hardware to prop the lid open.

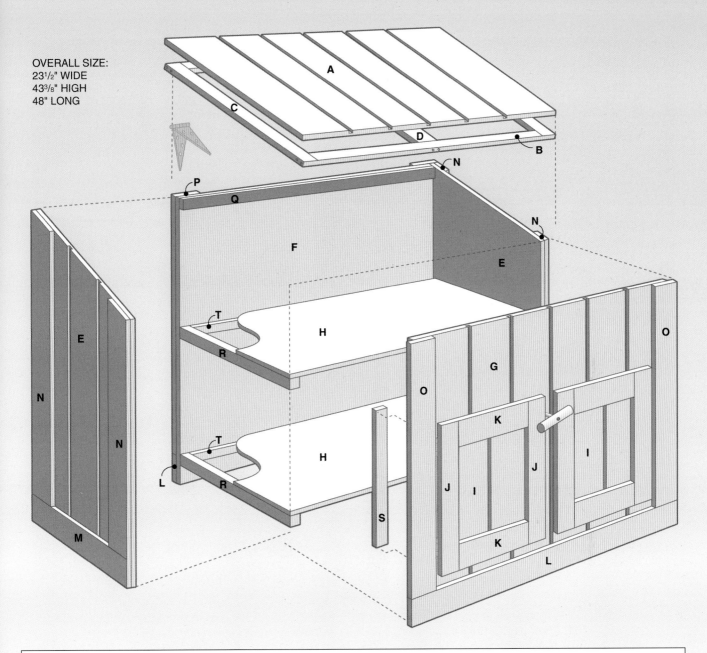

OVERALL SIZE:
23½" WIDE
43⅜" HIGH
48" LONG

Cutting List

Key	Part	Dimension	Pcs.	Material
A	Lid	⅝ × 24 × 48"	1	Plywood siding
B	Lid edge	¾ × 1½ × 45"	2	Cedar
C	Lid end	¾ × 1½ × 24"	2	Cedar
D	Lid stringer	¾ × 2½ × 21"	1	Cedar
E	End panel	⅝ × 22 × 42"	2	Plywood siding
F	Back panel	⅝ × 44¾ × 42"	1	Plywood siding
G	Front panel	⅝ × 44¾ × 37½"	1	Plywood siding
H	Shelf	¾ × 20¾ × 44¾"	2	Fir plywood
I	Door panel	⅝ × 15¾ × 17¾"	2	Plywood siding
J	Door stile	¾ × 3½ × 21¼"	4	Cedar

Cutting List

Key	Part	Dimension	Pcs.	Material
K	Door rail	¾ × 3½ × 12¼"	4	Cedar
L	Kickboard	¾ × 2½ × 47½"	2	Cedar
M	End plate	¾ × 2½ × 22"	2	Cedar
N	End trim	¾ × 2½ × 39½"	4	Cedar
O	Front trim	¾ × 2½ × 35"	2	Cedar
P	Back trim	¾ × 2½ × 39½"	2	Cedar
Q	Hinge cleat	¾ × 1½ × 44¾"	1	Pine
R	Shelf cleat	1½ × 1½ × 20¾"	4	Pine
S	Back cleat	1½ × 1½ × 41¾"	2	Pine
T	Door cleat	¾ × 1½ × 18"	2	Pine

Materials: Moisture-resistant glue, butt hinges (4), 4" strap hinges (2), 1¼" and 2½" deck screws, door catches (2) or a 1"-dia. × 12" dowel and a ¼"-dia. × 4" carriage bolt, finishing materials.

Note: Measurements reflect actual size of dimension lumber.

Cut and fasten the lid to the lid framework with the grooves in the panel running back to front.

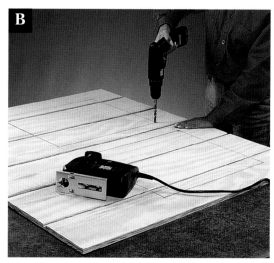

Drill a ⅜"-dia. starter hole at a corner of each door opening and cut out the openings with a jig saw.

Directions:
Outdoor Storage Center

MAKE THE LID ASSEMBLY.
1. Use a circular saw and a straightedge to cut the lid (A).
2. Cut the lid edges (B), lid ends (C) and lid stringer (D).
3. Lay the lid ends and edges on their faces, smooth side up. Attach the lid ends flush with the outsides of the lid edges, using glue and 2½" deck screws. Attach the lid stringer midway between the lid ends in the same manner.
4. Apply glue to the top faces of the lid ends, stringer and lid edges. Set the lid on the frame assembly **(photo A)** and screw it in place with 1¼" deck screws.

MAKE THE PANELS.
1. Cut the back panel (F) and front panel (G) to size. On the inside face of the front panel, measure up from the bottom and draw straight lines at 5" and 23". Measure in 4" and 20" from each side and draw lines. These lines mark the cutout lines for the door openings.
2. Drill a ⅜"-dia. starter hole at one corner in each door open-

Attach the end panels to the back panel, keeping the back panel flush with the back edges of the end panels.

ing **(photo B).** Cut out the door openings with a jig saw and sand the edges smooth.
3. Cut the end panels (E) to size. On the front edge of each panel, measure down 4½" and place a mark. Draw a line connecting each mark with the top corner on the back edge of the panel, creating cross-cutting lines for the back-to-front tapers. Cross-cut along the lines with a circular saw.

ASSEMBLE THE PANELS.
1. Stand the back panel on its bottom edge and butt it up between the end panels, flush with the back edges.
2. Fasten the back panel between the side panels with glue and 1¼" deck screws **(photo C).**

ATTACH THE SHELVES.
1. Cut the shelves (H) to size. Measure up 25" from the bottoms of the end panels and draw reference marks for positioning the top shelf. Cut the shelf cleats (R) and back cleats (S) to length. Attach the cleats just below the reference lines

Place the shelf on top of the cleats and fasten with glue and screws.

with glue. Drive 1¼" deck screws through the end panels and back panels and into the cleats.

2. Fasten the shelf to the cleats with 1¼" deck screws **(photo D).** Drive 1¼" deck screws through the back panel and into the shelf.

3. Mark reference lines for the bottom shelf, 4" from the bottoms of the side panels. Install the bottom shelves in the same manner as the top shelves.

4. Fasten the front panel (G) between the end panels with glue and 2½" deck screws.

CUT AND INSTALL TRIM.

1. Cut the kickboards (L), the end plates (M), the end trim (N), the front trim (O) and the back trim (P) to length. Sand the ends smooth. Attach the end plates at the bases of the side panels. Drill ⅛" pilot holes in the end plates. Counterbore the holes ¼" deep, using a counterbore bit. Drive 1¼" deck screws through the end plate and into the side panels.

2. Attach the front and back kickboards to the bases of the front and back panels.

3. Hold the end trim pieces against the side panels at both the front and back edges. Trace the profile of the tapered side panels onto the trim pieces to make cutting lines. The trim pieces at the fronts should be flush with the front panel. Cut at the lines with a circular saw.

4. Attach the end trim pieces to the side panels with 1¼" deck screws **(photo E).** Attach front and back trim to the front and back panels, covering the edges of the end trim.

ATTACH THE DOORS AND LID.

1. Cut the door stiles (J) and door rails (K) to length. Attach them to the cutout door panels (I), forming a frame that extends 1¾" past the edges of the door panels on all sides.

2. Cut door cleats (T) to length. Screw them to the inside faces of the front panel directly behind the hinge locations at the outside edges of the openings. Mount two butt hinges on the outside edge of each door, using 1¼" deck screws.

3. Install a door catch for each door or use a 1" dowel bolted to the front panel as a turnbuckle.

4. Cut the hinge cleat (Q) to length and attach it to the inside face of the back panel, flush with the top edge.

5. Put the lid and strap hinges in place, with the upper hinge plates positioned between the back trim and lid ends. Drill pilot holes on the back trim for the lower hinge plate and mark the hinge pin location on the back edge of the lid end. Remove the lid and use the location marks to attach the upper hinge plate with 1¼" deck screws. Put the lid in place and attach the lower hinge plates in the same manner.

APPLY FINISHING TOUCHES.

Sand edges smooth. Apply a clear wood sealer or any other finish of your choice.

Attach the end trim to the end panel, keeping the front edge of the trim flush with the front edge of the front panel.

Grill Garage

*Eliminate mess and clutter, and shelter grilling appliances
from the elements with this spacious grill garage.*

CONSTRUCTION MATERIALS

Quantity	Lumber
2	½" × 4 × 8' textured cedar sheet siding
1	¾" × 2 × 2' plywood
10	1 × 2" × 8' cedar

Summer cookouts will be more enjoyable with this handy grill garage and storage unit. Unlike most pre-fabricated grill garages, this project is sized to store today's popular gas grills, as well as traditional charcoal grills. And while you're using your grill, the spacious top platforms of the grill garage can be used as convenient staging and serving areas. The walls of this grill garage are made from inexpensive, attractive rough cedar siding panels. Fitted with a cabinet-style door, the storage compartment can accommodate two large bags of charcoal, plus all your grilling accessories.

OVERALL SIZE:
25½" WIDE
49³/₁₆" HIGH
62⁷/₈" LONG

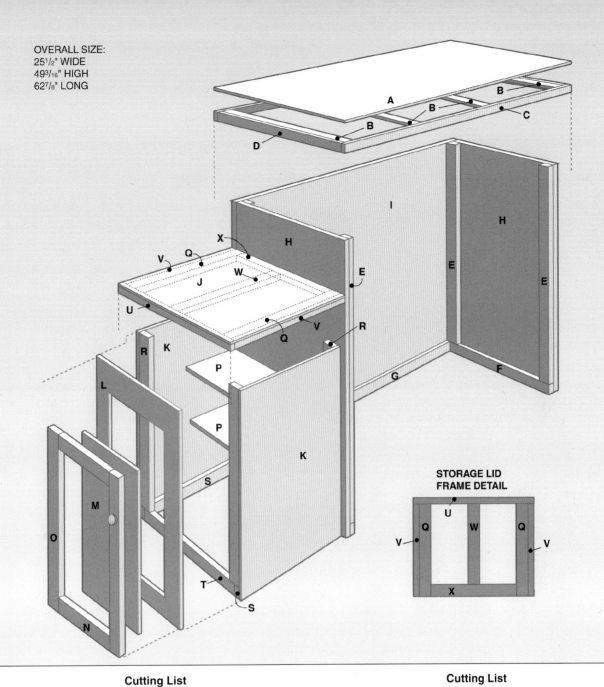

STORAGE LID FRAME DETAIL

Cutting List

Key	Part	Dimension	Pcs.	Material
A	Garage lid	⁷/₁₆ × 25½ × 43⁵/₈"	1	Cedar siding
B	Lid stringer	¾ × 1½ × 24"	4	Cedar
C	Lid-frame side	¾ × 1½ × 43⁵/₈"	2	Cedar
D	Lid-frame end	¾ × 1½ × 24"	2	Cedar
E	Posts	¾ × 1½ × 46½"	4	Cedar
F	End plate	¾ × 1½ × 22¹³/₁₆"	2	Cedar
G	Back plate	¾ × 1½ × 41¼"	1	Cedar
H	End panel	⁷/₁₆ × 23⁹/₁₆ × 48"	2	Cedar siding
I	Back panel	⁷/₁₆ × 42⅛ × 48"	1	Cedar siding
J	Storage lid	⁷/₁₆ × 20 × 24"	1	Cedar siding
K	Side panel	⁷/₁₆ × 19¼ × 29¼"	2	Cedar siding
L	Face panel	⁷/₁₆ × 22½ × 29¼"	1	Cedar siding

Cutting List

Key	Part	Dimension	Pcs.	Material
M	Door panel	⁷/₁₆ × 18½ × 23¼"	1	Cedar siding
N	Door rail	¾ × 1½ × 17"	2	Cedar
O	Door stile	¾ × 1½ × 24¾"	2	Cedar
P	Shelf	¾ × 10 × 21⅜"	2	Plywood
Q	End stringer	¾ × 1½ × 19¼"	2	Cedar
R	Short post	¾ × 1½ × 27¾"	4	Cedar
S	Side plate	¾ × 1½ × 19¼"	2	Cedar
T	Front plate	¾ × 1½ × 20⅛"	1	Cedar
U	Front lid edge	¾ × 1½ × 24"	1	Cedar
V	Storage lid end	¾ × 1½ × 19¼"	2	Cedar
W	Center stringer	¾ × 1½ × 17¾"	1	Cedar
X	Rear lid edge	¾ × 1½ × 19½"	1	Cedar

Materials: Moisture-resistant glue, 1", 1½", 2" and 3" deck screws, hinges, door pull, finishing materials.

Note: Measurements reflect actual size of dimension lumber.

Install stringers inside the garage-lid frame to strengthen the garage lid.

Use 1 × 2 posts to create the framework for the main garage compartment.

Directions: Grill Garage

MAKE THE GARAGE LID PANEL.

1. Cut the garage lid (A) to size. (Use a straightedge cutting guide whenever cutting sheet goods.) Cut the lid stringers (B), lid-frame sides (C) and lid-frame ends (D) to length. On a flat work surface, arrange the frame ends and sides on edge to form the lid frame. Fasten the lid sides and lid ends together with glue. Drive 1½" deck screws through the sides and into the ends of the lid-frame ends.

2. Position the lid stringers facedown in the frame, with one on each end and two spaced evenly in between. Attach the stringers and frame with glue and 1½" deck screws **(photo A).**

3. Turn the frame over so the side where the stringers are flush with the top edges of the frame is facing up. Lay the garage lid on top of the frame assembly and test the fit—the edges of the lid should be flush with the edges of the frame.

4. Remove the garage lid and run a bead of glue on the top edges of the frame. Drill ⅛" pilot holes in the lid. Counterbore the holes ¼" deep, using a counterbore bit. Reposition the lid on the frame assembly. Drive 1" deck screws through the lid and into the tops of the frame components.

BUILD THE GARAGE WALLS.

1. Cut the posts (E) and end plates (F) to length. Cut the end panels (H) to size. Assemble an end plate and two posts into an open-end frame on your work surface. Fasten the parts together with glue. Drive 1½" deck screws through

the end plate and into the ends of the posts **(photo B).**

2. Test the fit. Drill pilot holes in the end panel. Counterbore the holes. Attach an end panel to the frame with glue. Drive 1" deck screws through the panel and into the frame **(photo C).**

3. Build the other end panel the same way.

ASSEMBLE THE GARAGE PANELS.

1. Cut the back plate (G) to length. Cut the back panel (I) to size.

2. Stand one end-panel assembly up so it rests on the plate. Place a bead of glue along the edge of the post that will join the back panel. Position one end of the back panel flush against the post, making sure the rough side of the cedar siding is facing out. Attach the back panel to the end-panel assembly with 1½" screws. Attach the other end-panel assembly to the other side of the back

Attach the end panel to the open-ended frame assembly, making sure that the rough side of the cedar siding is facing outward.

panel the same way **(photo D).**

3. Place a bead of glue along the outside face of the back plate. Position the plate at the bottom of the back panel, so the ends of the plate form butt joints with the end-panel assemblies. Secure by driving 1" deck screws through the back panel and into the back plate.

4. Fit the garage lid panel around the tops of the end and back panels, shifting the panels slightly to create a tight fit. Drill pilot holes in the lid frame. Counterbore the holes. Attach the lid panel with glue. Drive 2" deck screws through the lid frame and into the tops of the end and back panels and frame posts.

BUILD THE CABINET LID.

1. Cut the storage lid (J) to size. Cut the end stringers (Q), center stringer (W), front lid edge (U), rear lid edge (X) and storage lid ends (V) to length.

2. Lay the two storage lid ends and the front lid edge on edge on a flat surface. Position the storage lid ends so that they butt into the back face of the front lid edge. Fasten the ends and edge together with glue and 1½" deck screws.

3. Lay the rear lid edge on its face between the end stringers, which are facedown, flush with the ends of the stringers. Mounting the rear lid edge in this way provides a flush fit at the rear of the storage unit assembly while maintaining an overhang on the sides and front. Fasten the rear lid edge and end stringers together with glue and 3" deck screws.

4. Fasten the storage-lid end/edge assembly to the end

stringer/rear-lid edge assembly with glue and 3" deck screws to form a frame. Position the center stringer midway between the end stringers and attach with glue and 3" deck screws.

5. Turn the storage lid frame over so the side with the stringers flush with the tops of the frame faces up. Lay the storage lid panel on top of the frame so the edges are flush. Drill pilot holes in the lid and counterbore the holes. Attach the lid panel with glue and drive 1" deck screws through the panel and into the frame.

BUILD THE CABINET WALLS.

1. Cut the short posts (R) and side plates (S) to length. Cut the side panels (K) to size.

2. Attach a side plate to the bottom, inside edge of a side panel, so the plate is flush with the front edge of the panel **(photo E).** Attach the short

Attach the back panel to the posts of the end panels to assemble the walls of the main grill garage compartment.

Attach the side plate, with the face against the panel, to the bottom edge of the side panel.

Drill a ⅜"-dia. hole on the inside of one of the corners of the door layout, then cut out the door opening with a jig saw.

posts upright, flush with the ends of the side plates and the the side panels, by driving 2½" deck screws through each plate and into the end of the corresponding post. Drive a 1" deck screw through each side panel and into the corresponding post. Build the second cabinet side panel the same way.

MAKE THE CABINET DOOR FACE FRAME.

1. Cut the face panel (L) to size. On the inside of the panel, mark a cutout for the cabinet door opening. First, measure down from the top 4", and draw a line across the panel. Then, measure in from both sides 2" and draw straight lines across the panel. Finally, draw a line 2" up from the bottom. The layout lines should form an 18½" × 23¼" rectangle.
2. Drill a ⅜"-dia. starter hole for a jig saw blade at one corner of the cutout area **(photo F).** Cut out the door opening with a jig saw. Sand the edges smooth.

Save the cutout piece for use as the door panel (M).

ASSEMBLE THE CABINET.

1. Arrange the cabinet walls so they are 22½" apart. Attach the face frame to a short post on each wall, using glue and 1" deck screws. Make sure the face frame is flush with the outside faces of the cabinet walls, and that the wide "rail" of the face frame is at the top of the cabinet, where there are no plates **(photo G).**
2. Cut the front plate (T) and fasten it to the bottom, inside edge of the face frame, butted against the short posts.
3. Place the cabinet lid assembly onto the cabinet walls and face frame. Attach the cabinet lid with glue. Drive 1" deck screws through the insides of the cabinet walls and into the frame of the lid **(photo H).**

MAKE AND INSTALL THE SHELVES.

1. Cut the shelves (P) to size. Lay out ¾ × 1½" notches in the back corners of the shelves so they fit around the cabinet posts that attach the cabinet to the garage wall. Cut out the notches in the shelves, using a jig saw.
2. On the inside of each cabinet wall, draw lines 8" down from the top and 11" up from the bottom to mark shelf locations. Fit the shelf notches around the back posts, then attach the shelves by driving 1½" deck screws through the cabinet sides and into the edges of the shelves. Drive at least two screws into each shelf edge.

ATTACH THE CABINET TO THE GARAGE.

1. Push the cabinet flush against the left wall of the garage.
2. Fasten the cabinet to the garage by driving 3" deck screws through the garage

Fasten the cutout face frame to the cabinet sides.

Set the cabinet-lid assembly over the cabinet walls and face frame. Fasten them with glue and screws.

Fasten the door rails and door stiles to the door panel using glue and screws, leaving a ¾" overlap on all sides of the door panel.

2. Attach door hinges 3" from the top and bottom of one door stile. Mount the door to the face frame. Install the door pull.

APPLY THE FINISHING TOUCHES.

Sand and smooth the edges of the grill garage and prepare it for the finish of your choice. Since it is constructed with cedar, you can chose a clear wood sealer that leaves the rich wood grain and color visible. If you prefer a painted finish, use a quality primer and durable exterior enamel paint.

posts and into the short posts of the cabinet. Three screws into each post will provide sufficient holding power.

BUILD AND ATTACH THE DOORS.

1. Cut the door rails (N) and stiles (O) to length. Using the cutout from the face frame panel for the door panel (M), fasten the rails and stiles to the door panel using glue and 1½" deck screws. Leave a ¾" overlap on all sides **(photo I).** Be sure to mount the rails between the stiles, but flush with the stile ends.

> **TIP**
>
> *The grill garage is designed as a handy storage center for your grill and such supplies as charcoal and cooking utensils. Do not store heavy items on top of the garage lid, and never light your grill while it is still in the grill garage. Do not store lighter fluid in the grill garage— always keep lighter fluid out of reach of children, in a cool, sheltered area, such as a basement.*

Firewood Shelter

Those stacks of firewood won't be an eyesore anymore once you build this ranch-style firewood shelter for your yard.

CONSTRUCTION MATERIALS

Quantity	Lumber
10	2 × 4" × 8' cedar
5	2 × 6" × 8' cedar
10	⅝ × 8" × 8' cedar lap siding

This handsome firewood shelter combines rustic ranch styling with ample sheltered storage that keeps firewood off the ground and obscured from sight. Clad on the sides and roof with beveled cedar lap siding, the shelter has the look and feel of a permanent structure. But because it's freestanding, you can move it around as needed. It requires no time-consuming foundation work.

This firewood shelter is large enough to hold an entire face cord of firewood. And since the storage area is sheltered and raised to avoid ground contact and allow air flow, wood dries quickly and is ready to use when you need it.

OVERALL SIZE:
62" HIGH
32" DEEP
8' LONG

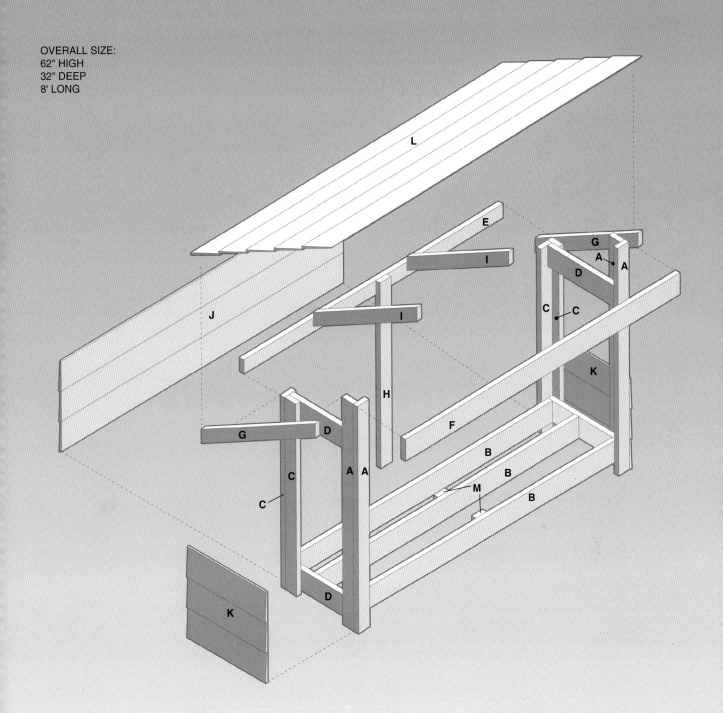

Cutting List

Key	Part	Dimension	Pcs.	Material
A	Front post	1½ × 3½ × 59"	4	Cedar
B	Bottom rail	1½ × 5½ × 82½"	3	Cedar
C	Rear post	1½ × 3½ × 50"	4	Cedar
D	End rail	1½ × 5½ × 21"	4	Cedar
E	Back rail	1½ × 3½ × 88½"	1	Cedar
F	Front rail	1½ × 5½ × 88½"	1	Cedar
G	Roof support	1½ × 3½ × 33¾"	2	Cedar

Cutting List

Key	Part	Dimension	Pcs.	Material
H	Middle post	1½ × 3½ × 50"	1	Cedar
I	Middle support	1½ × 3½ × 28"	2	Cedar
J	Back siding	⅝ × 8 × 88½"	3	Cedar siding
K	End siding	⅝ × 8 × 24"	6	Cedar siding
L	Roof strip	⅝ × 8 × 96"	5	Cedar siding
M	Prop	1½ × 3½ × 7½"	2	Cedar

Materials: ⅜ × 3½" lag screws (24), ⅜ × 4" lag screws (8), 1½" spiral siding nails, 2½" and 3" deck screws, finishing materials.

Note: Measurements reflect the actual size of dimension lumber.

Directions: Firewood Shelter

BUILD THE FRAME.

1. Cut the front posts (A) and rear posts (C) to length. Butt the edges of the front posts together in pairs to form the corner posts. Drill ⅛" pilot holes at 8" intervals. Counterbore the holes ¼" deep, using a counterbore bit. Join the post pairs with 2½" deck screws. Follow the same procedure to join the rear posts in pairs.

2. Cut the bottom rails (B) and end rails (D). Assemble two bottom rails and two end rails into a rectangular frame, with the end rails covering the ends of the bottom rails. Set the third bottom rail between the end rails, centered between the other bottom rails. Mark the ends of the bottom rails on the outside faces of the end rails. Drill two ⅜" pilot holes for lag screws through the end rails at each bottom rail position—do not drill into the bottom rails. Drill a ¾" counterbore for each pilot hole, deep enough to recess the screw heads. Drill a smaller, ¼" pilot hole through each pilot hole in the end rails, into the ends of the bottom rails **(photo A)**. Drive a ⅜ × 3½" lag screw fitted with a washer at each pilot hole, using a socket wrench.

3. Draw reference lines across the inside faces of the corner posts, 2" up from the bottoms. With the corner posts upright and about 82" apart, set 2"-high spacers next to each corner post to support the frame. Position the bottom rail frame between the corner posts, and attach the frame to the corner posts by driving two 2½" deck screws through the corner posts and into the outer faces of the bottom rails. Drill pilot holes in the sides of the corner posts. Counterbore the holes. Drive a pair of ⅜ × 4" lag screws, fitted with washers, through the sides of the corner posts and into the bottom rails. The lag screws must go through the post and end rail, and into the end of the bottom rail. Avoid hitting the lag screws that have already been driven through the end rails.

4. Complete the frame by installing end rails at the tops of the corner posts. Drill pilot holes in the end rails. Counterbore the holes. Drive 2½" deck screws through the end rails and into the posts. Make sure the tops of the end rails are flush with the tops of the rear posts **(photo B)**.

MAKE THE ROOF FRAME.

1. Cut the back rail (E), front rail (F), roof supports (G), middle post (H) and middle supports (I) to length. The roof supports and middle supports are mitered at the ends. To make the miter cutting lines, mark a point 1½" in from each end, along the edge of the board. Draw diagonal lines from each point to the opposing corner. Cut along the lines

A

Use a smaller bit to extend the pilot holes for the lag screws into the ends of the bottom rails.

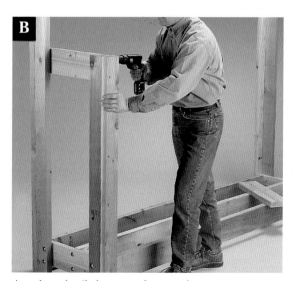

B

Attach end rails between front and rear corner posts.

C

Miter-cut the middle supports and roof supports with a circular saw.

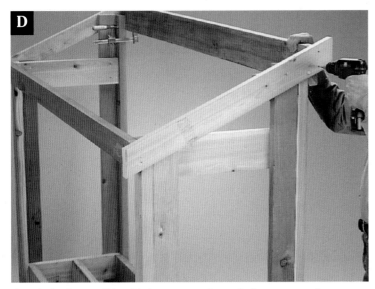

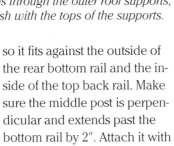

Attach the front rail by driving screws through the outer roof supports, making sure the top of the rail is flush with the tops of the supports.

Attach the middle roof supports by driving screws through the front and back rails.

Attach the roof strips with siding nails, starting at the back edge and working your way forward.

with a circular saw **(photo C).**
2. Drill pilot holes in the back rail. Counterbore the holes. Use 3" deck screws to fasten the back rail to the backs of the rear corner posts, flush with their tops and sides. Use the same procedure to fasten a roof support to the outsides of the corner posts. Make sure the top of each support is flush with the high point of each post end. The supports should overhang the posts equally in the front and rear.
3. Drill pilot holes in the roof supports. Counterbore the holes. Drive deck screws to attach the front rail between the roof supports **(photo D),** with the top flush with the tops of the roof supports. Attach the middle supports between the front rail and back rail, 30" in from each rail end. Drive 3" deck screws through the front and back rails into the ends of the middle supports **(photo E).** Use a pipe clamp to hold the supports in place as you attach them.
4. Drill pilot holes in the middle post (H). Counterbore the holes. Position the middle post

so it fits against the outside of the rear bottom rail and the inside of the top back rail. Make sure the middle post is perpendicular and extends past the bottom rail by 2". Attach it with 2½" deck screws.
5. Cut a pair of props (M) to length. Attach them to the front two bottom rails, aligned with the middle post. Make sure the tops of the props are flush with the tops of the bottom rails.

ATTACH SIDING AND ROOF.
1. Cut pieces of 8"-wide beveled cedar lap siding to length to make the siding strips (J, K) and the roof strips (L). Starting 2" up from the bottoms of the rear posts, fasten the back siding strips (J) with two 1½" siding nails driven through each strip and into the posts, near the top and bottom edge of the strip. Work your way up, overlapping each piece of siding by ½", making sure the thicker edges of the siding face down. Attach the end siding (K) to the corner posts, with the seams aligned with the seams in the back siding.

2. Attach the roof strips (L) to the roof supports, starting at the back edge. Drive two nails into each roof support. Make sure the wide edge of the siding faces down. Attach the rest of the roof strips, overlapping the strip below by about ½" **(photo F),** until you reach the front edges of the roof supports. You can leave the cedar wood untreated or apply an exterior wood stain to keep it from turning gray as it weathers.

Cabin Marker

Hidden driveways and remote roads won't escape first-time visitors if they are marked with a striking, personalized cabin marker.

Trips to a friend's cabin or vacation home, though usually enjoyable, often start on a confusing note. "Do you have the address written down?" is a common refrain after the fourth left into a dead end in the woods. You can save your friends confusion and wasted time by displaying your name, address and mailbox at the head of your driveway. And on a safety note, emergency vehicles can spot your home more quickly with a well-marked name and address on it.

The simple design of this cabin marker and mailbox stand makes it suitable for almost any yard. Its height ensures a certain level of prominence, but the cedar material and basic construction allow it to fit right in with its natural surroundings.

One of the best features of the cabin marker may be the least noticed—the base section. The base is a multi-tiered pyramid of 4×4 cedar timbers. It provides ample weight and stability, so you won't need to go to the trouble of digging a hole or pouring concrete. Just position the marker wherever you want it, and stake it in place. Much more attractive than a simple mailbox stand, this project will provide just the touch of originality that your cabin or vacation home deserves.

CONSTRUCTION MATERIALS

Quantity	Lumber
1	$1 \times 6" \times 8'$ cedar
1	$2 \times 2" \times 6'$ cedar
4	$2 \times 4" \times 8'$ cedar
3	$4 \times 4" \times 8'$ cedar

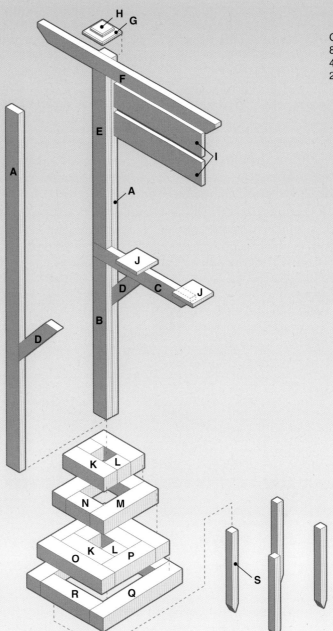

OVERALL SIZE:
85¾" HIGH
48½" WIDE
22" DEEP

Cutting List

Key	Part	Dimension	Pcs.	Material
A	Post side	1½ × 3½ × 84"	2	Cedar
B	Post section	1½ × 3½ × 36½"	1	Cedar
C	Mailbox arm	1½ × 3½ × 23½"	1	Cedar
D	Mailbox brace	1½ × 3½ × 17½"	2	Cedar
E	Post section	1½ × 3½ × 40½"	1	Cedar
F	Sign arm	1½ × 3½ × 48½"	1	Cedar
G	Top plate	⅞ × 5½ × 5½"	1	Cedar
H	Cap	⅞ × 3½ × 3½"	1	Cedar
I	Sign board	⅞ × 5½ × 24"	2	Cedar
J	Mailbox cleat	⅞ × 5½ × 5⅞"	2	Cedar

Cutting List

Key	Part	Dimension	Pcs.	Material
K	Base piece	3½ × 3½ × 10½"	4	Cedar
L	Base piece	3½ × 3½ × 4½"	4	Cedar
M	Base piece	3½ × 3½ × 15"	2	Cedar
N	Base piece	3½ × 3½ × 7"	2	Cedar
O	Base piece	3½ × 3½ × 17½"	2	Cedar
P	Base piece	3½ × 3½ × 11½"	2	Cedar
Q	Base piece	3½ × 3½ × 22"	2	Cedar
R	Base piece	3½ × 3½ × 14"	2	Cedar
S	Stake	1½ × 1½ × 18"	4	Cedar

Materials: Moisture-resistant glue, epoxy glue, 2", 2½" and 4" deck screws, #10 screw eyes (8), S-hooks (4), ⅜"-dia. × 5" galvanized lag screws with 1" washers (8), finishing materials.

Note: Measurements reflect the actual size of dimension lumber.

Directions: Cabin Marker

MAKE THE POST.

The post is made in three layers. Two post sections and two arms form the central layer, which is sandwiched between two post sides. The arms extend out from the post to support a mailbox and an address sign.

1. Cut the mailbox arm (C) and sign arm (F) to length. One end of the mailbox arm and both ends of the sign arm are cut with decorative slants on their bottom edges. To cut the ends of the arms to shape, mark a point on the three ends, 1" down from a long edge. On the opposite long edge, mark a point on the face 2½" in from the end. Draw a straight line connecting the points, and cut along it.

2. Cut the post sides (A) and post sections (B, E) to length. To assemble the post, you will sandwich the sections and the arms between the sides. Set one of the post sides on a flat work surface, and position the lower post section (B) on top of it, face to face, with the ends flush. Attach the lower post section to the side with wood glue and 2½" deck screws.

3. Position the mailbox arm on the side, making sure the square end is flush with the edge of the side. Use a square to make sure the mailbox arm is perpendicular to the side. Attach the mailbox arm, using glue and 2½" deck screws.

4. Butt the end of the upper post section (E) against the top edge of the mailbox arm, and attach it to the side in the same manner **(photo A).**

5. Position the sign arm at the top of the assembly so it extends 30" past the post on the side with the mailbox arm. Attach the sign arm to the post side with glue and deck screws.

6. Apply glue to the remaining side. Attach it to the post sections with glue and 4" deck screws, making sure all the ends are flush.

ATTACH THE MAILBOX CLEATS AND BRACES.

The cleats on the mailbox arm

Butt an end of the upper section against the top edge of the mailbox arm, and fasten it to the side.

Position a mailbox brace on each side of the mailbox arm, and fasten them to the post and arm.

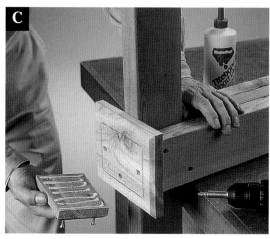

Apply glue to the bottom face of the cap, and center it on the top of the post.

provide a stable nailing surface for a "rural-style" mailbox. The mailbox braces fasten to the post and mailbox arm to provide support.

1. Cut the mailbox cleats (J) to length and sand smooth. Center the cleats on the top of the mailbox arm. The frontmost cleat should overhang the front of the mailbox arm by 1". Center the remaining cleat 12½" in from the front of the mailbox arm. Attach the cleats with glue and 2½" deck screws.

2. Cut the mailbox braces (D) to length. Their ends must be cut at an angle. Use a power miter box, or a backsaw and miter box, to miter-cut each end of each mailbox brace at a 45° angle. Make sure the cuts at either end slant toward each other (see *Diagram*, page 497).

3. Position a mailbox brace against the side of the mailbox arm so one end is flush with the top edge of the mailbox arm and the other rests squarely against the post. Drill ⅛" pilot holes. Counterbore the holes ¼" deep, using a counterbore bit. Attach the mailbox braces with glue and 2½" deck screws **(photo B)**.

COMPLETE THE POST TOP.
The post assembly is capped with a post top and cap made of 1" dimension lumber.

1. Cut the top plate (G) and cap (H) to size. Using a power sander, make ¼"-wide × ¼"-deep bevels along the top edges of the top and cap.

2. Center the top on the post, and attach it with glue and 2" deck screws. Center the cap on the top and attach it **(photo C).**

MAKE THE BASE.
The base for the cabin marker is made from cedar frames that increase in size from top to bottom. The frames are stacked to create a four-level pyramid. A fifth frame fits inside one of the frames to make a stabilizer for the post. The bottom frame is fastened to stakes driven into the ground to provide a secure anchor that does not require digging holes and pouring concrete footings.

1. Cut the 4 × 4 base pieces (K, L, M, N, O, P, Q, R) to length for all five frames. Assemble them into five frames according to the *Diagram*. To join the pieces, use 4" deck screws driven into pilot holes that have been counterbored 1½" deep.

2. After all five frames are built, join one of the small frames and the two next-smallest frames together in a pyramid, using glue and 4" deck screws **(photo D)**. Insert the other small frame into the opening in the third-smallest frame. Secure with deck screws.

3. Set the base assembly on top of the large frame; do not attach them. Insert the post into the opening, and secure it with lag screws, driven through the top frame and into the post. (NOTE: The bottom frame is anchored to the ground on site before being attached to the pyramid.)

MAKE THE SIGN BOARDS.
1. Cut the sign boards (I) to size. Sand them smooth.

2. Stencil your name and address onto the signs. Or, you can use adhesive letters, free-hand painting, a router with a veining bit or a woodburner. Be sure to test the technique on a sanded scrap of cedar before working on the signs.

Attach the base tiers to each other, working from top to bottom.

APPLY FINISHING TOUCHES.
1. Join the two signs together with #10 screw eyes and S-hooks. Drill pilot holes for the screw eyes in the sign arm and signs. Apply epoxy glue to the threads of the screws before inserting them. Apply your finish of choice.

2. Position the bottom frame of the base in the desired location. The area should be flat and level so the post is plumb. Check the frame with a level. Add or remove dirt around the base to achieve a level base before installing.

3. Cut the stakes (S) to length, and sharpen one end of each stake. Set the stakes in the inside corners of the frame. Drive them into the ground until the tops are lower than the tops of the frame. Attach the stakes to the frames with 4" deck screws.

4. Center the cabin marker on the bottom frame. Complete the base by driving 5" lag screws through the tops of the base into the bottom frame.

Front-porch Mailbox

This cedar mailbox is a practical, good-looking project that is very easy to build. The simple design is created using basic joinery and mostly straight cuts.

If you want to build a useful, long-lasting item in just a few hours, this mailbox is the project for you. Replace that impersonal metal mailbox you bought at the hardware store with a distinctive cedar mailbox that's a lot of fun to build. The lines and design are so simple on this project that it suits nearly any home entrance. The mailbox features a hinged lid and a convenient lower shelf that is sized to hold magazines and newspapers.

We used select cedar to build our mailbox, then applied a clear, protective finish. Plain brass house numbers dress up the flat surface of the lid, which also features a decorative scallop that doubles as a handgrip.

If you are ambitious and economy-minded, you can build this entire mailbox using just one 8'-long piece of 1 × 10 cedar. That means, however, that you'll have to do quite a bit of rip-cutting to make the parts. If you have a good straightedge and some patience, rip-cutting is not difficult. But you may prefer to simply purchase dimensional lumber that matches the widths of the pieces (see the *Construction Materials* list to the left).

If your house is sided with wood siding, you can hang the mailbox by screwing the back directly to the siding. If you have vinyl or metal siding, be sure that the screws make it all the way through the siding and into wood sheathing or wood wall studs. If you have masonry siding, like brick or stucco, use masonry anchors to hang the mailbox.

CONSTRUCTION MATERIALS

Quantity	Lumber
1	1 × 10" × 4' cedar
1	1 × 8" × 3' cedar
1	1 × 4" × 3' cedar
1	1 × 3" × 3' cedar
1	1 × 2" × 3' cedar

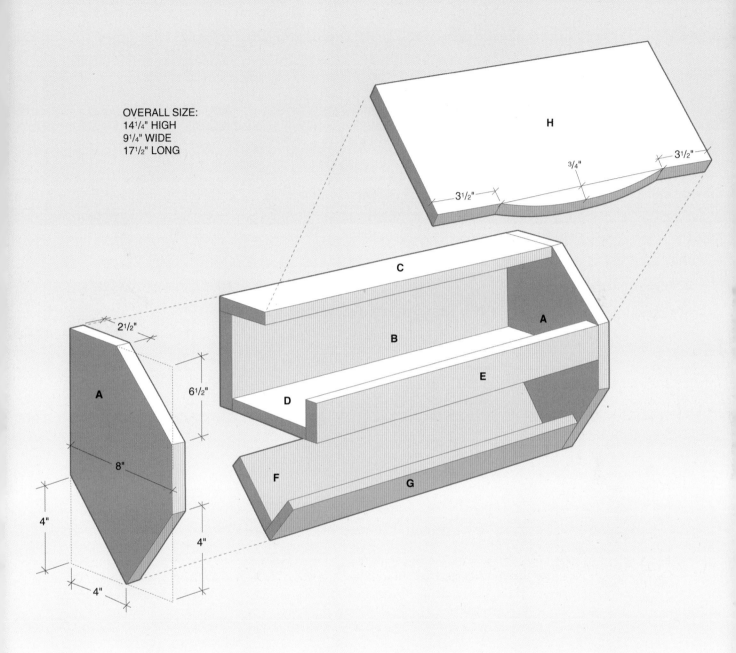

OVERALL SIZE:
14¼" HIGH
9¼" WIDE
17½" LONG

2½"

6½"

8"

4"

4"

4"

3½"

¾"

3½"

A

A

B

C

D

E

F

G

H

Cutting List				
Key	**Part**	**Dimension**	**Pcs.**	**Material**
A	Side	¾ × 8 × 14¼"	2	Cedar
B	Back	¾ × 7¼ × 16"	1	Cedar
C	Top	¾ × 2½ × 16"	1	Cedar
D	Box bottom	¾ × 6½ × 16"	1	Cedar

Cutting List				
Key	**Part**	**Dimension**	**Pcs.**	**Material**
E	Box front	¾ × 1½ × 16"	1	Cedar
F	Shelf bottom	¾ × 3½ × 16"	1	Cedar
G	Shelf lip	¾ × 2½ × 16"	1	Cedar
H	Lid	¾ × 9¼ × 17½"	1	Cedar

Materials: Moisture-resistant wood glue, 2" deck screws, masking tape, piano hinge with screws, finishing materials.

Note: Measurements reflect the actual size of dimension lumber.

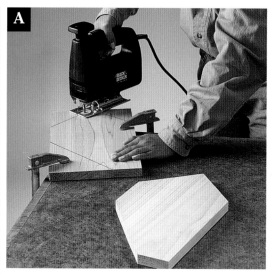

Cutlines are drawn on the sides, and the parts are cut to shape with a jig saw.

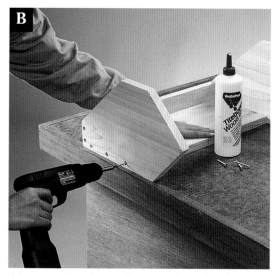

After fastening the top between the sides, fasten the back with deck screws.

Directions:
Front-porch Mailbox

BUILD THE SIDES.

The sides are the trickiest parts to build in this mailbox design. But if you can use a ruler and cut a straight line, you should have no problems.

1. Cut two 8 × 14¼" pieces to make the sides (A).

2. Pieces of wood that will be shaped into parts are called "blanks" in the wood-workers' language. Lay out the cutting pattern onto one side blank, using the measurements shown on page 501. Mark all of the cutting lines, then double-check the dimensions to make sure the piece will be the right size when it is cut to shape. Make the cuts in the blank, using a jig saw, to create one side. Sand edges smooth.

3. Use this side as a template to mark the second blank.

Attach the box bottom to the back with glue and screws driven through the back and sides.

Arrange the template so the grain direction is the same in the blank and the template. Cut out and sand the second side **(photo A).**

ATTACH THE BACK AND TOP.

Fasten all the pieces on the mailbox with exterior wood glue and 2" deck screws. Although cedar is a fine outdoor wood, it can be quite brittle. To prevent splitting, drill ⅛" pilot holes and counterbore the holes ¼" deep, using a counter-bore bit. Space the screws evenly when driving them.

1. Cut the back (B) and top (C) to length. Fasten the top be-tween the 2½"-wide faces on the two sides with glue and 2" deck screws. Position the top so that the rear face is flush with the rear side edges, and the top face is flush with the top side edges.

2. Use glue and deck screws to fasten the back between the sides, flush with the 10¼"-long edges **(photo B),** and butted against the top.

Keep the lip edges flush with the side edges to form the newspaper shelf.

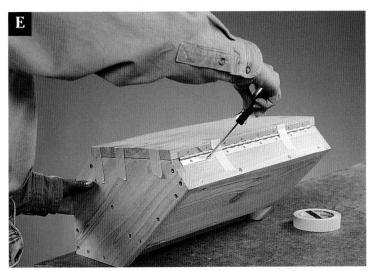

Once the pieces are taped in place, the continuous hinge is attached to join the lid to the top.

ATTACH THE BOX BOTTOM AND FRONT.

The bottom and front pieces form the letter compartment inside the mailbox.

1. Cut the bottom (D) and front (E) to length. Fasten the bottom to the back and sides, making sure the bottom edges are flush **(photo C).**

2. Once the bottom is attached, fasten the front to the sides and bottom, keeping the bottom edges flush.

ATTACH THE NEWSPAPER SHELF.

The lower shelf on the underside of the mailbox is designed for overflow mail.

1. To make the lower shelf, cut the shelf bottom (F) and shelf lip (G) to size. Fasten the shelf lip to the leg of the "V" formed by the sides that are closer to the front.

2. Fasten the shelf bottom to the sides along the back edges to complete the shelf assembly **(photo D).**

CUT AND ATTACH THE LID.

1. Cut the lid (H) to length (9¼" is the actual width of a 1 × 10). Draw a reference line parallel to and ¾" away from one of the long edges.

2. With a jig saw, make a 3½"-long cut at each end of the line. Mark the midpoint of the edge (8¾"), then cut a shallow scallop to connect the cuts with the midpoint. Smooth out the cut with a sander.

3. Attach a brass, 15"-long continuous hinge known as a piano hinge to the top edge of the lid. Then position the lid so the other wing of the hinge fits squarely onto the top of the mailbox. Secure the lid to the mailbox with masking tape. Attach the hinge to the mailbox **(photo E).**

APPLY FINISHING TOUCHES.

1. Sand all surfaces smooth with 150-grit sandpaper.

2. Finish the mailbox with a clear wood sealer or other finish of your choice. Add 3" brass house numbers on the lid. Or, stencil an address or name onto it (see *Tips*, page 502). Once the finish has dried, hang the mailbox on the wall by driving screws through the back.

TIP

Clear wood sealer can be refreshed if it starts to yellow or peel. Wash the wood with a strong detergent, then sand the surface lightly to remove flaking or peeling sealer. Wash the surface again, then simply brush a fresh coat of sealer onto the wood.

PROJECT
POWER TOOLS

Trash Can Corral

*This two-sided structure keeps trash cans out of sight
but accessible from the curb or alley.*

CONSTRUCTION MATERIALS

Quantity	Lumber
3	2 × 4" × 6' cedar
2	2 × 2" × 10' cedar
1	1 × 8" × 2' cedar
7	1 × 6" × 10' cedar
8	1 × 4" × 8' cedar

Nothing ruins a view from a favorite window like the sight of trash cans—especially as garbage-collection day draws near. With this trash can corral, you'll see an attractive, freestanding cedar fence instead of unsightly trash cans.

The two fence-style panels support one another, so you don't need to set fence posts in the ground or in concrete. And because the collars at the bases of the posts can be adjusted, you can position the can corral on uneven or slightly sloping ground. The staggered panel slats hide the cans completely, but still allow air to pass through to ensure adequate ventilation.

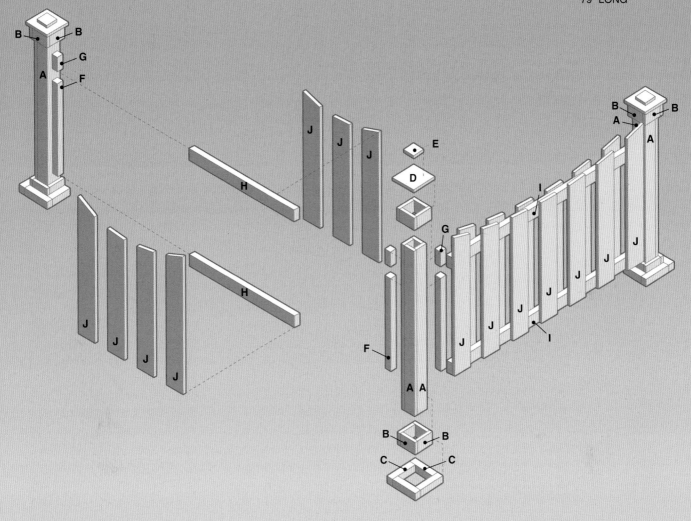

OVERALL SIZE:
49¾" HIGH
49" WIDE
79" LONG

Cutting List

Key	Part	Dimension	Pcs.	Material
A	Post board	⅞ × 3½ × 48"	12	Cedar
B	Collar strip	⅞ × 3½ × 5¼"	24	Cedar
C	Foot strip	1½ × 1½ × 7⅝"	12	Cedar
D	Collar top	⅞ × 7¼ × 7¼"	3	Cedar
E	Collar cap	⅞ × 3½ × 3½"	3	Cedar

Cutting List

Key	Part	Dimension	Pcs.	Material
F	Long post cleat	1½ × 1½ × 26⅞"	4	Cedar
G	Short post cleat	1½ × 1½ × 4"	4	Cedar
H	Short stringer	1½ × 3½ × 35½"	2	Cedar
I	Long stringer	1½ × 3½ × 65½"	2	Cedar
J	Slat	⅞ × 5½ × 39½"	20	Cedar

Materials: 1½" and 2" deck screws, finishing materials.

Note: Measurements reflect the actual size of dimension lumber.

The post is made from four edge-joined boards.

Fit the top collar assemblies onto each post and attach them.

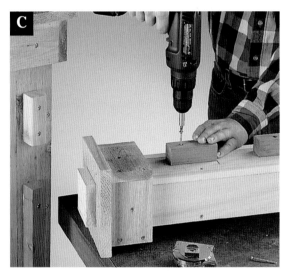

Attach the short post cleats 3⅝" up from the tops of the long post cleats. The top stringers on the panels fit between the cleats when installed.

Directions:
Trash Can Corral

BUILD THE POSTS.

Each post is made of four boards butted together to form a square.

1. Cut the post boards (A) to length and sand them smooth.

2. Clamp one post board to your work surface. Then, butt another post board against it at a right angle. With the ends flush, drill ⅛" pilot holes at 8" intervals and counterbore the holes to a ¼" depth. Connect the boards by driving 2" deck

screws through the pilot holes **(photo A).** Repeat the step until the post boards are fastened together in pairs. Then, fasten the pairs together to form the three posts.

MAKE AND ATTACH THE COLLARS.

Each post is wrapped at the top and bottom by a four-piece collar. The top collars have two-piece flat caps, and the base collars are wrapped with 2 × 2 strips for stability.

1. Cut the collar strips (B), collar tops (D) and collar caps (E) to size.

2. Join the collar strips together to form square frames, using 1½" deck screws.

3. Center each collar cap on top of a collar top, and attach the caps to the tops with 1½" deck screws.

4. To center the tops on the frames, mark lines on the bottoms of the top pieces, 1⅛" in from the edges. Then, drill pilot holes ½" in from the lines, and counterbore the holes.

5. Use the lines to center a frame under each top. Then, drive 1½" deck screws through the holes and into the frames.

6. Slip a top collar assembly over one end of each post **(photo B),** and drill centered pilot holes on each side of the collar. Counterbore the holes and drive 1½" deck screws into the posts.

7. Attach the remaining frames to the other ends of the posts, with the bottom edges flush.

8. Cut the foot strips (C) to length. Lay them around the bottoms of the base collars, and screw them together with 2" deck screws. Make sure the bottoms of the frames are flush with the bottoms of the collars. Then, attach the frames to the collars with 2" deck screws.

ATTACH THE CLEATS AND SUPPORTS.

The long and short post cleats (F, G) attach to the posts between and above the stringers.

1. Cut the post cleats to length. Center a long post cleat on one face of each post and attach it with 2" deck screws so the bottom is 4" above the top of the base collar on each post.

2. For the corner post, fasten a second long post cleat on an adjacent post face, 4" up from the bottom collar.

Use 4½"-wide spacers to set the gaps between panel slats.

Use a flexible guide to mark the top contours.

3. Center the short post cleats on the same post faces, 3⅝" up from the tops of the long post cleats. Attach the short post cleats to the posts, with 2" deck screws, making sure the short cleats are aligned with the long cleats **(photo C).**

BUILD THE FENCE PANELS.

1. Cut the short stringers (H), long stringers (I) and slats (J).
2. Position the short stringers on your work surface so they are parallel and separated by a 26⅞" gap. Attach a slat at each end of the stringers, so the ends of the stringers are flush with the outside edges of the slats. Drive a 1½" deck screw through each slat and into the face of each stringer.
3. Measure diagonally from corner to corner to make sure the fence panel is square. If the measurements are equal, the fence is square. If not, apply pressure to one side of the assembly until it is square. Drive another screw through each slat and into each stringer.
4. Cut 4½" spacers to set the gaps between panel slats, and attach the remaining slats on the same side of the stringers

by driving two 1½" deck screws at each end. Check that the bottoms of the slats are flush with the stringer **(photo D).**
5. Turn the panel over and attach slats to the other side, starting 4½" from the ends so slats on opposite sides are staggered—there will only be three slats on this side. Build the long panel the same way.

CONTOUR THE PANEL TOPS.

To lay out the curve at the top of each fence panel, you will need to make a marking guide.
1. Cut a thin, flexible strip of wood at least 6" longer than the long fence panel. On each panel, tack nails at the top outside corner of each end slat, and another nail midway across each panel, ½" above the top stringer.
2. Form a smooth curve by positioning the guide with the ends above the outside nails, and the midpoint below the nail in the center. Trace the contour onto the slats **(photo E),** and cut along the line with a jig saw. Use a short blade to avoid striking the slats on the other side. Use the same procedure on the other side of each

Set the completed fence panels between the cleats on the faces of the posts.

panel. Sand the cuts smooth.
3. Position the fence panels between the posts so the top stringer in each panel fits in the gap between the long and short post cleats **(photo F).** Drive 2" deck screws through the slats and into the cleats.

APPLY FINISHING TOUCHES.

Apply exterior wood stain to protect the cedar. You can increase the height of any of the posts slightly by detaching the base collar, lifting the post and reattaching the collar.

Glossary

Belt sander — a tool used to resurface rough wood.

Breezeway — an open passageway, featuring a roof, that connects two structures.

Carpenter's level — a tool that features a bubble within a liquid that centers to indicate when a surface is properly aligned.

Carriage bolts — a bolt featuring a domed head and a square neck to securely fasten wood.

Casing nail — similar to a finishing nail, but with a slightly larger dimpled head for better holding power.

Caster wheels — wheels that swivel for easy positioning.

Caulk — a mastic substance, usually containing silicone, used to seal joints. Caulk is waterproof and flexible when dry and adheres to most dry surfaces.

Cedar — a lightweight, aromatic softwood with a natural resistance to moisture and insects.

Cedar lap siding — cedar boards cut with a bevel.

Cementboard — a rigid material with a fiberglass facing and a cement core that is undamaged by water.

Ceramic floor tile — sturdy tile suitable where durability is required.

Ceramic tile adhesive — multipurpose thin-set mortar applied with a V-notch trowel.

Circular saw — a type of saw used to make straight cuts.

Combination square — a measuring tool that combines a straight edge with a sliding head to measure both 45 ° and 90° angles.

Common nails — nails that have wide, flat heads.

Concrete — a mixture of Portland cement, sand, coarse gravel, and water.

Core box bit — a straight bit with a rounded bottom.

Cotter pin — a split pin whose shaft is inserted through a hole, then bent to fasten separate pieces together.

Counterboring — a technique for drilling holes that allows nail heads to be set below the surface of the wood when finished.

CPVC — chlorinated polyvinyl chloride; rigid plastic material used for high-quality water-supply pipe products.

Deck screws — screws with a light shank and coarse threads that are ideal for fastening soft woods.

Dimension lumber — the nominal size by which lumber is sold—usually larger than the actual size.

Dowels — round wooden rods.

Drill — a tool used to drill holes and drive screws.

Epoxy — a two-part glue that bonds powerfully and quickly.

Exterior plywood — plywood made with 100% waterproof glue.

Fencing staples — barbed staples that grab tightly onto wood.

Finish nails — nails with a thin shank and a cup-shaped head that are driven below the surface with a nail set.

Flagstone — large slabs of quarried stone cut into pieces up to 3" thick.

Flashing — aluminum or galvanized steel sheeting cut and bent into various sizes and shapes; used to keep water from entering joints between roof elements and to direct water away from structural elements.

Gang-sanding — a technique whereby matching pieces are clamped together before sanding to ensure identical shaping.

GFCI receptacle — a receptacle outfitted with a ground-fault circuit-interrupter. Also used on some extension cords to reduce the possibility of electric shock when operating an appliance or power tool.

Gnomon — the triangular part of a sundial face that casts a shadow to tell time.

Grommet — a metal ring used to line a hole cut into wood.

Grout — a fluid cement product used to fill spaces between ceramic tiles or other crevices.

Hardware cloth — galvanized, welded, and woven screening in a variety of mesh sizes; also called welded wire fabric.

Hasp — a two-part, hinged metal fastener featuring a loop, through which a lock is placed for security.

Heartwood — wood cut from the center of the tree; valued for its density, straightness, and resistance to decay.

Hot glue — a glue that is melted for application, then hardens as it cools to create a strong, durable bond; typically used for crafts, but very effective for lightweight exterior projects and indoor patching jobs.

Jig saw — a type of saw used to make contours, internal cuts, and short, straight cuts.

Lag screw — a heavy screw with a square or hexagonal head.

Lattice — panels woven from ¼" or ⅜" strips of cedar or treated lumber.

Linseed oil — a nontoxic drying oil obtained from the flax plant that is used to obtain a natural, protective finish on wood projects.

Locking nut — a nut that holds two pieces together securely, while still allowing the joint to pivot.

Miter — a 45° angled end-cut for fitting two pieces together at a corner.

Moisture-resistant glue — any exterior wood glue, such as plastic resin glue.

Mortar — a mixture of Portland cement, lime, and sand used to bond the bricks or blocks of a masonry wall.

Pine — a basic softwood used for interior projects.

Pipe clamp — a clamp that slides on a pipe to adjust to various sizes.

Plunge router — a router with a bit chuck that can be raised or lowered to start internal cuts.

Plywood — a wood product made of layers of thin veneer glued together.

Plywood siding — decorative exterior plywood, faced with either Douglas fir, cedar, or redwood, in a variety of textures, such as smooth, rough sawn, and grooved patterns.

Power miter saw — a type of saw used to make angled cuts in narrow stock.

Power sander — a tool used to prepare wood for a finish and to smooth sharp edges.

Prefabricated concrete pavers — decorative concrete blocks, available in a variety of shapes and sizes, that can be used to make walkways, patios, and walls.

Primer — a sealer that keeps wood resins from bleeding through the paint layer.

Redwood — a lightweight, moisture-resistant, rot-resistant, and insect-resistant wood.

Rip-cut — to cut a piece of wood parallel to the grain.

Router — a tool used to cut structural grooves, decorative edges, and roundover cuts in wood.

Sheet acrylic — clear plastic product available in thicknesses from ⁄16" to 1".

Sheet goods — manufactured products generally sold in 4 ft. x 8 ft. sheets of various thicknesses.

Shim — a thin wedge of wood used to make a slight adjustment to achieve square alignment.

Squaring — a technique that ensures straight assembly by measuring diagonally from corner to corner in a frame.

Stain — a product that seals and adds color to wood.

Treated lumber — construction-grade pine that has been treated with chemical preservatives and insecticides.

Wood moldings — decorative trims for finishing projects.

Wood plugs — ⅜"-dia. x ¼"-thick disks with a slightly conical shape used to plug screw holes.

Wood sealer — a product that partially or totally blocks the wood's pores, preventing water penetration.

Conversion Charts

Drill Bit Guide

Twist Bit  **Self-piloting**  **Spade Bit** 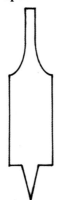 **Adjustable Counterbore** 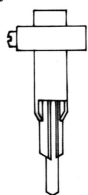 **Hole Saw**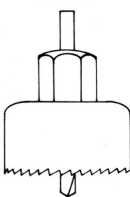

Counterbore, Shank & Pilot Hole Diameters

Screw Size	Counterbore Diameter for Screw Head	Clearance Hole for Screw Shank	Pilot Hole Diameter	
			Hard Wood	Soft Wood
#1	.146 (9/64)	5/64	3/64	1/32
#2	1/4	3/32	3/64	1/32
#3	1/4	7/64	1/16	3/64
#4	1/4	1/8	1/16	3/64
#5	1/4	1/8	5/64	1/16
#6	5/16	9/64	3/32	5/64
#7	5/16	5/32	3/32	5/64
#8	3/8	11/64	1/8	3/32
#9	3/8	11/64	1/8	3/32
#10	3/8	3/16	1/8	7/64
#11	1/2	3/16	5/32	9/64
#12	1/2	7/32	9/64	1/8

Abrasive Paper Grits - (Aluminum Oxide)

Very Coarse	Coarse	Medium	Fine	Very Fine
12 - 36	40 - 60	80 - 120	150 - 180	220 - 600

Saw Blades

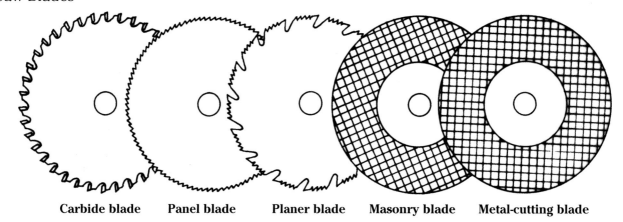

| Carbide blade | Panel blade | Planer blade | Masonry blade | Metal-cutting blade |

Adhesives

Type	Characteristics	Uses
White glue	**Strength:** moderate; rigid bond **Drying time:** several hours **Resistance to heat:** poor **Resistance to moisture:** poor **Hazards:** none **Cleanup/solvent:** soap and water	**Porous surfaces:** Wood (indoors) Paper Cloth
Yellow glue (carpenter's glue)	**Strength:** moderate to good; rigid bond **Drying time:** several hours; faster than white glue **Resistance to heat:** moderate **Resistance to moisture:** moderate **Hazards:** none **Cleanup/solvent:** soap and water	**Porous surfaces:** Wood (indoors) Paper Cloth
Two-part epoxy	**Strength:** excellent; strongest of all adhesives **Drying time:** varies, depending on manufacturer **Resistance to heat:** excellent **Resistance to moisture:** excellent **Hazards:** fumes are toxic and flammable **Cleanup/solvent:** acetone will dissolve some types	**Smooth & porous surfaces:** Wood (indoors & outdoors) Metal Masonry Glass Fiberglass
Hot glue	**Strength:** depends on type **Drying time:** less than 60 seconds **Resistance to heat:** fair **Resistance to moisture:** good **Hazards:** hot glue can cause burns **Cleanup/solvent:** heat will loosen bond	**Smooth & porous surfaces:** Glass Plastics Wood
Cyanoacrylate (instant glue)	**Strength:** excellent, but with little flexibility **Drying time:** a few seconds **Resistance to heat:** excellent **Resistance to moisture:** excellent **Hazards:** can bond skin instantly; toxic, flammable **Cleanup/solvent:** acetone	**Smooth surfaces:** Glass Ceramics Plastics Metal
Construction adhesive	**Strength:** good to excellent; very durable **Drying time:** 24 hours **Resistance to heat:** good **Resistance to moisture:** excellent **Hazards:** may irritate skin and eyes **Cleanup/solvent:** soap and water (while still wet)	**Porous surfaces:** Framing lumber Plywood and paneling Wallboard Foam panels Masonry
Water-base contact cement	**Strength:** good **Drying time:** bonds instantly; dries fully in 30 minutes **Resistance to heat:** excellent **Resistance to moisture:** good **Hazards:** may irritate skin and eyes **Cleanup/solvent:** soap and water (while still wet)	**Porous surfaces:** Plastic laminates Plywood Flooring Cloth
Silicone sealant (caulk)	**Strength:** fair to good; very flexible bond **Drying time:** 24 hours **Resistance to heat:** good **Resistance to moisture:** excellent **Hazards:** may irritate skin and eyes **Cleanup/solvent:** acetone	**Smooth & porous surfaces:** Wood Ceramics Fiberglass Plastics Glass

Index